The Spanish Revolution

The Spanish Revolution

The Left and the Struggle for Power during the Civil War

by Burnett Bolloten

The University of North Carolina Press
Chapel Hill

Library of Congress Cataloging in Publication Data

Bolloten, Burnett, 1909–
    The Spanish revolution.

    Editions of 1961 and 1968 published under title:
The grand camouflage.
    Bibliography: p.
    Includes index.
    1. Spain—History—Civil War, 1936–1939.
    2. Communism—Spain—History.   I. Title.
DP269.B656 1978   946.081   78-5011
ISBN 0-8078-1297-8

To Betty and Gregory

Contents

Maps

Foreword

In 1961 Burnett Bolloten published *The Grand Camouflage*. Perhaps the title was unfortunate, in itself a camouflage which hid the fact that this was the work of a dedicated scholar who had combed every available source in order to reconstruct the confused politics of republican Spain in the Civil War. Already in 1961 it was a major contribution.

This new expanded edition carries on the same standards and exhibits the same qualities while incorporating much new material—for instance on the fate of the Russians who served in Spain and who later were liquidated at home. The treatment of the May events of 1937 in Barcelona is likewise a new and valuable contribution.

Burnett Bolloten was the first historian to establish the depth and extent of the "spontaneous revolution" that swept over much of Spain —especially Catalonia and the Levante—in the first weeks of the Civil War as a proletarian response to the military rising. In its most violent form this social revolution was the work of the CNT-FAI and its bulwark was the militia. Therefore the whole question of creating an "orthodox" Popular Army implied the destruction of the militia system. Mr. Bolloten again brings new material and new insights.

To Left Republicans and Communists the reversal of the achievements of the spontaneous revolution was a necessity: partly in order to organize a war effort, partly to encourage the West to help a "respectable" democracy. The militant anarchists argued that both aims were misguided. To dismantle the spontaneous revolution (which, as Mr. Bolloten demonstrates, was done with brutality) if it consoled the middle classes would alienate the working class, the ultimate defense of the republic. As to help from the West, this was "hypothetical."

The second great contribution of this book is its investigation of the rise of the Communist party—small in 1936—into a dominating force in the army, the police, and the political apparatus. The dramatic center is the ousting of Largo Caballero; the epilogue the dismissal of Indalecio Prieto, treated by Mr. Bolloten in his new epilogue.

How do we explain the rise of the party to influence? Certainly one could argue that the party's military policies were "objectively" correct—hence its appeal to some army officers. Certainly its manipulation of Soviet supplies to a republic left without arms supplies by the West gave it a unique leverage. Certainly the excesses of collectivization in the spontaneous revolution gave the Communists a handle in their offensive against collectivization.

All these factors were specific to the Civil War. Mr. Bolloten, it seems to me, makes a point of much more general importance, a point reinforced by the history of Eastern Europe after the Second World War. It is the political naivete of other parties combined with their fissiparous proclivities that allows the Communist party to neutralize, utilize and even absorb them. Short-term tactical alliances with a party whose monolithic character and hierarchical command structure makes these temporary allies look like dupes and allows the Communists to play on and exacerbate their divisions.

There are two quotations in this book that carry home this point. "'What did the others have,'" writes the ex-Communist minister Jesús Hernández, "'in face of this granite monolith [the Communist party]? A broken, divided Socialist party working in three different directions. . . . We managed to exploit their suicidal antagonisms. . . . Thus, to destroy Largo Caballero we relied principally on Negrín and, to a certain extent, on Prieto. To get rid of Prieto we utilized Negrín. . . . Among the anarchosyndicalists the panorama was no better. . . . Although their ranks were tighter . . . we managed nevertheless to create a breach. We helped to deepen the schism—a product of evolution—that was developing in the CNT by drawing into governmental collaboration a large part of the anarchist movement, which thereafter experienced a process of internal strife'" (pp. 464–65).

The other repentant Communist was the "peasant" military commander El Campesino. "'The Communist parties [of the world] are strong in proportion as the other parties and trade-union organizations are weak and vacillating and play their game. That was the lesson of Spain and that, today, is the lesson of Europe and the world. If they understand this lesson, they will save themselves, but if they do not, then they are lost'" (p. 448).

During the Civil War the Communists' tactics of infiltration and their police methods—the murder of Nin, for instance—left a visceral distrust of the party on sectors of the Spanish Left, which long blocked the emergence of a unified opposition in Spain. Now that the party has accepted democratic pluralism and rejected Leninism it will be interesting to observe its leaders' reactions to Mr. Bolloten's book.

It is Mr. Bolloten's extensive quotation from primary sources which will make his book a mine that will be worked over by subsequent historians. They may not accept all his judgments, but they will remain in his debt.

Raymond Carr

Oxford
May 1978

Preface

This volume, which is a vast revision and expansion of *The Grand Camouflage*, published in 1961, is the product of many years of exhaustive research. Forty years ago I set to work to reconstruct from limited materials and a limited knowledge of the subject, acquired as a United Press correspondent in Republican Spain from 1936 to 1938, some of the principal political events of the Spanish Civil War and Revolution; but no sooner had I begun than I realized that the information at my disposal was not in keeping with the complexity and magnitude of the subject, so I undertook the work of investigation on a scale commensurate with the need. From that time on, I consulted and re-consulted more than one hundred thousand issues of newspapers and periodicals published during the Civil War and the years of exile, over three thousand books and pamphlets, and a large number of published and unpublished documents. This massive documentation was not available in any one institution or in any one country, but had to be obtained from Spain, Great Britain, France, Germany, Italy, and the United States, as well as from Mexico and other Latin American republics, where thousands of Spaniards took refuge after the Civil War. In the course of forty years of research and inquiry I corresponded with or interviewed a large number of refugees, and combed and recombed essential institutions and libraries for fresh material. From these sources alone I obtained one hundred and twenty thousand microfilm frames, and years went by in an effort to bring order and meaning into this chaotic welter of material, much of which had to be consulted several times.

In preparing this volume I have allowed myself to be guided solely by a desire to reveal the truth. I have endeavored by the most diligent research and by the most conscientious selection of materials to maintain the highest possible standard of objectivity, and regret that in so doing I have had to ignore the political susceptibilities of friends and acquaintances who provided me so generously with personal testimony and documentary material.

Readers of *The Grand Camouflage*, in its English, Spanish, or Mexican editions, will find in the present vastly expanded volume a wealth of new materials. These illuminate more clearly the origins of the Spanish Revolution, the machinations of the Great Powers, the obscure events of May 1937, and the internecine struggles that determined the fate of the revolution and the eventual defeat by General Franco of the left-wing forces.

Because of the highly controversial nature of the subject, I have substantiated every important point in my exposition. Hence the large number of direct quotations in the text from conscientiously selected sources and the even larger number of footnote references. These should be helpful to scholars and students in furthering their own research on the Spanish Civil War and Revolution.

I should like to express my gratitude to all those persons, institutions, and publishers listed alphabetically on pp. 611–14. Considerations of space do not permit a detailed account of the manner in which each made a contribution, such as furnishing me with testimony; searching for, or collecting, giving, loaning, or microfilming materials, helping me to make valuable contacts; authorizing me, when permission was necessary, to quote from books, articles, and documents; giving me the benefit of their knowledge and experience; and rendering many other services, such as translating, typing, and proofreading, for which I am sincerely grateful.

But special mention must be made of those persons to whom I am particularly thankful:

I am deeply indebted to Professors Raymond Carr and Hugh Trevor-Roper of Oxford University as well as to Professor Noam Chomsky of the Massachusetts Institute of Technology for defending *The Grand Camouflage* at a time when the unorthodox conclusions expressed or implied therein were unacceptable and even shocking to a large segment of the academic world. I am likewise grateful to Professor Joan Connolly Ullman of the University of Washington, Professor Juan J. Linz of Yale University, Professor Edward E. Malefakis of Columbia University, and to Professor Stanley G. Payne of the University of Wisconsin for their support of *The Grand Camouflage* at a time when I most needed their encouragement.

I owe a special debt of gratitude to Professor Ronald Hilton, now Executive Director of the California Institute of International Studies, who invited me in 1962 to direct research and lecture on the Spanish Civil War at Stanford University, where he was director of the Institute of Hispanic American and Luso-Brazilian Studies, and who constantly encouraged me and prodded me, with his contagious drive and vitality, to continue the project I had begun so many years before.

To Professor Hilton I owe the enthusiastic backing of Dr. Milorad M. Drachkovitch, Senior Fellow and Director of Archives of the Hoover Institution on War, Revolution and Peace, Stanford, where a large part of my collection is now deposited. He read the finished manuscript and gave me invaluable advice and help in matters of publication, for which I am truly grateful.

I must also express deep gratitude to the late Bertram D. Wolfe and to his wife, Ella, for reading the manuscript, for providing me with material, and for their generous support. To Ella, I owe the assistance of Midge Decter, Senior Editor of Basic Books, who read the manuscript with "enthusiasm and even passion" and whose knowledge of the publishing world led indirectly to the publication of this work by the University of North Carolina Press, to whose administrative and editorial staffs I am most grateful.

To Hilja Kukk of the Hoover Institution, I express special gratitude for her assistance and advice, always unstintingly given, for ferreting out materials from Soviet and other sources, and for painstakingly reading the manuscript.

To Dr. David Wingeate Pike of the American College in Paris I render thanks for his support and help; to Jordi Arquer, a veteran of the Spanish Civil War, for furnishing me with information and material over a period of twenty-five years; and to Mark Sharron for reading the manuscript and making useful critical comments. I also wish to express appreciation to Melody Phillips for her contribution and patience over a number of years in typing, retyping and again retyping the manuscript and for performing many other tasks essential to the completion of this work, and also to Rosemary Kurpuis and Naida Glick for their secretarial help at a time of special need.

To my wife, Betty, I express deep appreciation for her patience and tolerance, and for providing the ambience that made this book possible.

None of these persons, however, bears the slightest responsibility for any conclusions expressed or implied in this volume.

But to more than anyone else I owe special gratitude to Gladys Evie Bolloten. Her devoted assistance, enthusiasm, suggestions, and hard work from 1938 to 1952 in connection with *The Grand Camouflage* helped to provide the foundation for this new book.

Burnett Bolloten
California, 1978

Author's Note

All data used in the preparation of this volume can be found in newspapers, periodicals, books, pamphlets, documents, and clippings held by one or more of the following United States and European libraries or institutions unless otherwise stated in the Bibliography:

Biblioteca Nacional, Madrid.
Biblioteca Universitaria de Barcelona, Barcelona.
Bibliothèque Nationale, Paris.
British Museum Newspaper Library, London.
Harvard College Library, Cambridge, Massachusetts.
Hemeroteca Municipal de Madrid, Madrid.
Hemeroteca Nacional, Madrid.
Hoover Institution on War, Revolution and Peace, Stanford
    University, California (Bolloten Collection).
Instituto Municipal de Historia de Barcelona, Barcelona.
Library of Congress, Washington, D.C.
New York Public Library, New York.
Servicio Histórico Militar, Madrid.
Stanford University Library, Stanford.
University of California Library, Berkeley.
University of California Library, San Diego (Southworth Collection).
University of Michigan Library, Ann Arbor, Michigan (Labadie
    Collection).

FOOTNOTE REFERENCES

As a general rule, when no more than one book or pamphlet by an author is listed in the Bibliography only the name of the author is given after the first mention in each chapter. When more than one work by the same author is included in the Bibliography the full title or an abbreviated one is given in the notes to ensure proper identification.

The place of publication of all newspapers and periodicals cited in the text or notes is given in the Bibliography. In the case of newspapers

Author's Note

having identical titles, those references relating to the Civil War years are Spanish newspapers while those published in Mexico and South America relate to the postwar years of exile.

The precise location of all documents cited, whether originals or copies, is given in the Bibliography.

PLACE NAMES

The following anglicized forms have been used:

Andalusia	(Andalucía)	Estremadura	(Extremadura)
Castile	(Castilla)	Navarre	(Navarra)
Catalonia	(Cataluña)	Saragossa	(Zaragoza)
Cordova	(Córdoba)	Seville	(Sevilla)

Accents on Spanish place names have been omitted in most instances to conform with English usage, for example, Aragon: Aragón; Cadiz: Cádiz; Malaga: Málaga.

PROPER NAMES

The names of all Spaniards have been arranged in the index on the basis of the paternal name in accordance with Spanish usage. For example, references to Francisco Largo Caballero will be found under Largo, the paternal name, and not under Caballero, the maternal name. However, he is frequently referred to by me and in quotations from Spanish sources as Caballero, which is the name both friends and opponents often used.

CATALAN NAMES

In most cases the Spanish equivalent of Catalan proper names has been used: for example, Juan Comorera: Joan Comorera; Luis Companys: Lluis Companys; Federico Escofet: Frederic Escofet; Carlos Pi Sunyer: Carles P. Sunyer; José Tarradellas: Josep Terradellas. One notable exception is the Catalan name, Generalitat, which has been used throughout the text.

Acronyms and Other Abbreviations

AIT — Asociación Internacional de Trabajadores (anarchosyndicalist labor international)

CADCI — Centre Autonomista de Dependents del Comcerç i de la Industria (office workers' and retail clerks' labor union in Catalonia)

CEDA — Confederación Española de Derechas Autónomas (federation of right-wing Catholic parties)

CLUEA — Consejo Levantino Unificado de la Exportación Agrícola (agricultural export organization in the Valencia region controlled by the CNT)

CNT — Confederación Nacional del Trabajo (anarchosyndicalist labor federation)

Comintern — Communist International or Third International, controlled by Moscow, uniting the Communist organizations in various countries

FAI — Federación Anarquista Ibérica (anarchist federation)

FOUS — Federación Obrera de Unidad Sindical (POUM-controlled labor federation)

GEPCI — Federación Catalana de Gremios y Entidades de Pequeños Comerciantes e Industriales (Catalan federation of small businessmen, manufacturers, and handicraftsmen controlled by the PSUC)

GPU — Gosudarstvennoe Politicheskoe Upravelenie (State Political Administration—See Chapter 14, n. 26 on Soviet secret police)

JAP — Juventudes de Acción Popular (Catholic youth organization controlled by José María Gil Robles)

Acronyms

JCI	Juventud Comunista Ibérica (POUM youth organization)
JSU	Federación de Juventudes Socialistas Unificadas (Communist-controlled merger of the Socialist and Communist youth organizations)
NKVD	Narodnyi Komissariat Vnytrennikh Del (People's Commissariat of Internal Affairs—See Chapter 14, n. 26 on Soviet secret police)
OGPU	Ob''edinennoe Gosudarstvennoe Politicheskoe Upravelenie (Unified State Political Administration attached to the Sovnarkom, the Council of People's Commissars—See Chapter 14, n. 26 on Soviet secret police)
PCE	Partido Comunista de España (Spanish Communist party)
Politburo	Political Buro or Political Bureau (the inner executive committee or controlling body of the Communist party)
POUM	Partido Obrero de Unificación Marxista (anti-Communist Marxist party)
PSOE	Partido Socialista Obrero Español (Socialist party)
PSUC	Partit Socialista Unificat de Catalunya (Communist-controlled merger of the Socialist and Communist parties of Catalonia)
SIM	Servicio de Investigación Militar (military intelligence service)
UGT	Unión General de Trabajadores (Socialist trade-union federation)
UME	Unión Militar Española (right-wing military organization)
UMRA	Unión Militar Republicana Antifascista (left-wing military organization)

Some Leading Participants

Abad de Santillán, Diego, prominent leader of the CNT and FAI in Catalonia

Aguirre, José Antonio, premier of the autonomous Basque government

Alcalá-Zamora, Niceto, President of the Republic until May 1936

Alvarez del Vayo, Julio, left-wing Socialist and ally of the Communists

Azaña, Manuel, liberal republican, premier until May 1936, President of the Republic from May 1936 until February 1939

Berzin, Ian K., principal Soviet military adviser in 1936–1937

Calvo Sotelo, José, monarchist leader

Carrillo, Santiago, secretary of the JSU, member of the Communist party from November 1936

Casado, Segismundo, republican army officer, operations chief of the general staff in the war ministry, commander of the Central Army, formed National Council of Defense against Negrín government and the Communists in March 1939

Casares Quiroga, Santiago, liberal republican, premier and war minister from May 1936 until outbreak of Civil War

Castro, Enrique, member of the central committee of the Communist party, first commander of the Fifth Regiment

Codovila, Vittorio, Comintern delegate

Comorera, Juan, leader of the PSUC, member of the Catalan government

Companys, Luis, liberal republican, President of the Generalitat, the autonomous government of Catalonia

Díaz, José, secretary of the Communist party

Durruti, Buenaventura, anarchist leader

Franco, Francisco, chief of central general staff in February 1936, commander in the Canary Islands at the outbreak of the Civil War, leader of the military rebellion in Morocco in July 1936, Nationalist Generalissimo and Head of State from October 1936

García Oliver, Juan, anarchist leader and minister of justice from November 1936 to May 1937

Gerö, Ernö, Comintern delegate in Catalonia

Gil Robles, José María, leader of the CEDA

Giral, José, liberal republican, premier from the outbreak of the Civil War in July 1936 to September 1936

Hernández, Jesús, Communist member of the politburo, minister of education

Some Leading Participants

from September 1936 to April 1938, chief political commissar of the central army from April 1938 to the end of the Civil War

Ibárruri, Dolores, Communist leader and member of the politburo

Kléber, Emilio, Soviet general, commander in November 1936 of the 11th International Brigade

Koltzov, Mikhail, Pravda's representative and Stalin's personal agent in Spain

Lamoneda, Ramón, moderate socialist, secretary of the Socialist party, later supporter of Negrín

Largo Caballero, Francisco, left-wing Socialist leader, secretary of the UGT, premier and war minister from September 1936 to May 1937

Líster, Enrique, Communist military leader

Martínez Barrio, Diego, leader of the moderate republican Unión Republicana party, vice-president of the Republic, premier of the stillborn government of 18–19 July 1936

Marty, André, leading French Communist and Comintern delegate

Mera, Cipriano, anarchist military leader

Miaja, José, republican general, war minister in Martínez Barrio's ill-fated government of 18–19 July 1936, entrusted with Madrid's defense in November 1936, joined Communist party in November 1936, and entered National Council of Defence against the Negrín government and the Communists in March 1939

Mola, Emilio, Nationalist general, organizer of the military rebellion on the peninsula

Montseny, Federica, anarchist leader, minister of health from November 1936 to May 1937

Negrín, Juan, moderate Socialist, later pro-communist, finance minister in September 1936, premier in May 1937, and premier and defense minister from April 1938 until the end of the Civil War

Nin, Andrés, POUM leader assassinated in 1937

Orlov, Alexander, NKVD chief in Spain from September 1936 until his defection to the United States in August 1938

Prieto, Horacio M., secretary of the CNT until November 1936

Prieto, Indalecio, moderate Socialist, navy and air minister in September 1936, defense minister from May 1937 until ousted by Negrín and the Communists in April 1938

Rojo, Vicente, republican chief of staff during the defense of Madrid from November 1936 to May 1937, chief of the central general staff from May 1937 to February 1939, pro-Communist

Rosenberg, Marcel, Soviet Ambassador in September 1936 until mid 1937

Sánchez Román, Felipe, leader of the conservative National Republican party, to the right of the Popular Front

Stefanov, Boris, leading Bulgarian Communist and Comintern delegate

Tarradellas, José, liberal republican, premier of the Generalitat (Catalan) government

Some Leading Participants

Togliatti, Palmiro, leading Italian Communist and Comintern delegate

Vázquez, Mariano, secretary of the national committee of the CNT from November 1936 to the end of the Civil War

Vidali, Vittorio, prominent Italian Communist, chief political commissar of the Fifth Regiment

Zugazagoitia, Julián, moderate Socialist, director of *El Socialista* until May 1937, minister of the interior from May 1937 to April 1938

"The deepest tragedy for the intelligentsia involved in the Spanish struggle was that truths and lies were inextricably entangled, that the deceivers were also deceived."

"It has been said that those who fought and died in Spain, with the bloom of their illusions untouched, were the lucky ones."

Julian Symons,
The Thirties: A Dream Revolved

Part I
The Spanish Revolution

1. The Brewing Upheaval

The enmities that gave rise to the Spanish Civil War and Revolution in July 1936 were not of sudden growth. They had been steadily developing since the fall of the Monarchy and the proclamation of the Republic in April 1931 and, with increasing intensity, since the victory of the Popular Front—the left coalition—in the February 1936 elections.

In the months between the elections and the Civil War, the Republic had experienced, both in town and country, a series of labor disturbances without precedent in its history, disturbances that were partly a reaction to the policies of the governments of the center-right that had ruled Spain from December 1933. In that two-year period—named *el bienio negro*, the black biennium, by the Spanish left—not only had the laws fixing wages and conditions of employment been revoked, modified, or allowed to lapse,[1] but much of the other work of the Republic had been undone. The labor courts, writes Salvador de Madariaga, a moderate republican and onetime minister of justice, who, according to his own testimony, remained equidistant from both sides during the Civil War, assumed a different political complexion, and their awards were as injurious to the workers as they had previously been to the employers. "Simultaneously, the Institute of Agrarian Reform was deprived of funds. Viewed from the standpoint of the countryside and in terms of practical experience, of the bread on the peasant's table, these changes were disastrous. There were many, too many, landowners who had learned nothing and forgotten nothing and who behaved themselves in such an inhuman and outrageous fashion toward their working folk—perhaps out of revenge for the insults and injuries suffered during the period of left rule—that the situation became worse not only in a material but also in a moral sense. The wages of the land workers again fell to a starvation level; the guarantee of employment vanished, and the hope of receiving land disappeared altogether."[2]

Speaking in the Cortes, the Spanish parliament, on 23 July 1935, José Antonio Primo de Rivera, the leader of the Falange Española, the fascist party, described life in the countryside as "absolutely intolerable." "Yesterday," he declared, "I was in the province of Seville. In that province there is a village called Vadolatosa, where the women leave their homes at three in the morning to gather chick-peas. They end their work at noon, after a nine-hour day, which cannot be prolonged for technical reasons. And for this labor these women receive one peseta."[3]

Especially illuminating was the moderate republican newspaper *El Sol.* "Since the advent of the Republic," it stated on 9 June 1936, "we have been oscillating dangerously between two extremes, particularly in the countryside. During the first biennium [1931–33] agriculture was burdened with a ridiculous working day, and the wave of idleness and indiscipline through which it passed ended by ruining it. The farm laborers received high wages and worked as little as possible.[4] . . . During the second biennium [1933–35] we fell into the other extreme. Within a few months wages declined sharply from ten and twelve pesetas a day to four, three, and even two. Property took revenge on labor, and did not realize that it was piling up fuel for the social bonfire of the near future. At the same time many landlords who had been forced on government orders to reduce rents devoted themselves to evicting tenant farmers. . . . These errors prepared the triumph of the Popular Front, a triumph that was due less to the real strength of the left, considerable though it was, than to the lack of political understanding of the right."[5]

José María Gil Robles, leader of the Catholic Confederación Española de Derechas Autónomas—a loose federation of right-wing parties, known by its initials as the CEDA—who became war minister in May 1935, avowed after his term of office had ended: "There are many, very many [employers and landowners] who know how to fulfill their obligations with justice and charity, but there are also many who, with suicidal egotism, as soon as the right entered the government, lowered wages, raised rents, tried to carry out unjust evictions, and forgot the sad experience of the years 1931–33. As a result, in many provinces the left increased its votes among the small cultivators and agricultural workers, who would have remained with us had a just social policy been followed."[6]

It was largely for the above-mentioned reasons that the victory of the Popular Front in February 1936 was followed by a grave crisis in the countryside that found expression in the strikes of land workers for higher wages and shorter hours; employers often replied by allowing the grain to burn or rot in the field. Two versions of this aspect of the agrarian crisis that complement rather than contradict each other were given by the republican press: "Every day," said *El Sol* on 14 June 1936, "we receive letters telling us the same thing. The harvest is less than the average, but the laborers, without worrying about it, demand ridiculous conditions for reaping and threshing. In some villages, these conditions are such that the tenant farmers, landowners, small peasant proprietors, and *colonos* [peasants settled on the land under the Agrarian Reform Law] . . . affirm that they will have to let the grain rot or burn, because if they were to accede to the imperious and menacing demands of the unions they would have to sell every bushel at a price that would scandalize the purchasers. . . . Not only powerful landowners and comfortable absentee landlords cultivate the Spanish soil. There are hundreds of thousands of small proprietors and *colonos* for whom an equitable solution of the present agricultural strikes is a question of life and death."[7]

On the other hand, the left-wing republican *La Libertad* stated on 26 June 1936: "In the countryside . . . there clearly exists a definite aim on the part of reactionary elements to boycott the regime, to drive the peasant masses to desperation, and place the government in a very difficult position. Otherwise, how can it be explained that there are entire provinces where employers intend leaving the harvest in the fields . . . , using it exclusively as fodder, whereas it would be far more profitable to pay the wages they should pay and gather the crop? How, too, can cases like that of Almendralejo be explained, where the employers swore not to offer a single day's work, threatening to kill any proprietor who did?"

The agrarian crisis also expressed itself in the rebellious mood of landless peasants, who had grown impatient of the Agrarian Reform Law of the Republic and of what they regarded as dilatoriness by government officials in the matter of land distribution. "Time is passing and the land remains in the hands of the political bosses," wrote a local peasant leader on 30 May in *El Obrero de la Tierra*, the organ of the left-wing Socialist Federación Nacional de los Trabajadores de la Tierra, the National Federation of Land Workers. "Disappointment is once again setting in, and we are on the same road as that of 1931. Is the Popular Front government going to destroy the illusions of the peasants? Are the peasants ready to see their hopes evaporate yet again? No. They want land, and those whose job it is to let them have it must not be surprised, should they fail to quicken their pace, if the peasants seize what the government does not give them and what they need so badly."[8]

On 11 April, José Díaz, secretary of the small but rapidly expanding

Communist party, had demanded that the government accelerate the distribution of land. The number of settlements was insufficient. The big landowners should be expropriated and their lands distributed among the peasants without delay. The government, he continued, was not treating the matter seriously enough. "This is one of the fundamental conquests of the democratic revolution, and we should put forth every effort to achieve it."[9]

But in many villages patience had already evaporated, the peasants refusing to wait until the government—which was composed entirely of liberal and moderate republicans—might satisfy their needs. On 7 March, *El Obrero de la Tierra* reported:

The peasants of Cenicientos in the province of Madrid have occupied in a body the pasture land called "Encinar de la Parra," covering an area of 1,317 hectares, and have begun to work it. When the occupation was completed, they sent the following letter to the minister of agriculture:

"In our village there is an extensive pasture land susceptible of cultivation, which in the past was actually cultivated, but which today is used for shooting and grazing. Our repeated requests to lease the land from the owner, who, together with two or three other landowners, possesses almost the entire municipal area—at one time communal property—have been in vain. As our hands and ploughs were idle and our children hungry, we had no course but to occupy the land. This we have done. With our labor it will yield what it did not yield before; our misery will end and the national wealth will increase. In doing this, we do not believe that we have prejudiced anyone, and the only thing we ask of Your Excellency is that you legalize this situation and grant us credits so that we can perform our labors in peace."

On 17 March, *La Libertad* reported from Manasalbas in Toledo province: "Two thousand hungry peasants of this locality have just seized the estate 'El Robledo' which [Count] Romanones appropriated to himself twenty years ago without giving anything to the people."

And an article in a Communist organ stated: "The agricultural workers of a small village near Madrid showed the way by taking over the land for themselves. Two weeks later the farm laborers of ninety villages in the province of Salamanca did the same thing.[10] A few days afterward this example was followed by the peasants of several villages in Toledo province; and at daybreak on 25 March, eighty thousand peasants of the provinces of Cáceres and Badajoz occupied the land and began to cultivate it. The revolutionary action of [these] peasants caused absolute panic in government circles. . . . [But] instead of using force, the government was obliged to send a large contingent of experts and officials from the Institute of Agrarian Reform to give an appearance of legality to the seizure of the land."[11]

A Spanish Communist wrote that the peasant leaders "calculate that the agrarian law plans fifty thousand settlements a year, which means that it will take twenty years to settle a million peasants and more than a century to give land to all. Realizing this, the peasants just occupy the land."[12]

The full extent of the social tension that gripped the Spanish countryside in the spring and early summer of 1936, writes Edward E. Malefakis, a leading authority on the agrarian situation before the Civil War, cannot be understood solely from a discussion of organized land seizures and strikes. "Just as the electoral victory of the center-right in 1933 had permitted the established classes to revenge themselves upon the workers in hundreds of small ways, most of them in defiance of the law, so, too, the victory of the Popular Front gave the workers license to impose their will with impunity. . . . Intimidation of all those who did not belong to the labor unions seems to have become the order of the day. Perhaps the most constant source of trouble was the gangs of workers who entered farms to force their managers to grant work. The stealing of animals and crops, and the cutting of trees for firewood or for lumber also became common." Referring to the province of Badajoz, Malefakis says: "Thousands of peasants wandered around the province in a futile search for jobs; farm managers of any importance continued to be subjected to repeated *alojamientos* [the forced hiring of extra workers], and small owners lived in constant fear that they, too, would become victims of the workers' aggression as the definition of the words 'bourgeois' and 'fascist' expanded to include property of every size." Malefakis observes that *El Sol*—"as objective a source as we have for these troubled times"—was deeply preoccupied by the fate of the small owners and tenants, whom it considered to have been more severely injured by the social and economic crisis than were the large holders.[13]

If the unrest in the countryside was a source of acute disquietude to the government, no less so were the labor disputes in the urban centers. From the end of May until the outbreak of the Civil War, the Republic had been convulsed by strikes affecting almost every trade and every province. Despite the censorship, the columns of the press abounded with reports of strikes in progress, of old strikes settled, of new strikes declared, and of others threatened, of partial strikes and general strikes, of sit-down strikes, and sympathetic strikes.[14] There were strikes not only for higher wages, shorter hours, and paid holidays, but for the enforcement of the decree of 29 February, compelling employers to reinstate and indemnify all workmen who had been discharged on political grounds after 1 January 1934.[15] This measure was promised in Section I of the Popular Front program and was particularly resented by employers.[16] "We have had men pushed back on to our payroll for whom we have no economic work," reported Sir Auckland Geddes, chairman of the British-owned Rio Tinto Company, in April 1936, "and within the last few days we have had an irritating stoppage, the result of demands for compensation for what amount to accusations of wrongful dismissals of men who were in fact in prison for taking part in the revolutionary movement in October 1934 and to whom naturally we did not pay wages while they were in jail."[17]

The most serious of the stoppages that plagued the urban centers was the paralyzing strike of the Madrid construction workers. Although the Socialist trade-union federation, the UGT—the Unión General de Trabajadores—accepted a settlement proposed by the government's arbitration board, the more radical anarchosyndicalist CNT, the anarchist-oriented labor union—the Confederación Nacional del Trabajo—seeking to transform the strike into a revolutionary confrontation with the employers and the state rejected the award. In a sterile attempt to end the stoppage that was punctuated by bloody and even lethal confrontations between members of the contending unions, the government arrested some of the anarchosyndicalist leaders and closed their headquarters. Adding to the turmoil were the efforts of Falangist gunmen to crush the strike and the intransigence of the building contractors themselves, whose "rebelliousness," to quote from a statement issued by their national association after the outbreak of the Civil War, "contributed so much to the preparation of a favorable atmosphere for the crusade to reconquer immortal Spain. . . . It was we who gave the order on 10 June to close down all our workshops and buildings with a view to initiating this epic."[18] The building contractors accepted the government's award on 3 July, but the CNT continued the strike in spite of the UGT's efforts to end it.[19]

A powerful psychological factor contributing to the prevailing turbulence was the memory of the repression that followed the left-wing rebellion in Asturias in October 1934. The rebellion had been triggered by President Niceto Alcalá-Zamora's decision to allow three members of the Catholic CEDA led by José María Gil Robles to join the cabinet formed on 4 October by Alejandro Lerroux, the leader of the Radical party. Since the victory of the center-right in the November 1933 elections, the Radical party had governed with the parliamentary support of the CEDA, but without its participation in the cabinet. The Socialists, who were the strongest opposition force, regarded the CEDA, whose avowed aim was the establishment of an authoritarian Catholic state, as the principal "fascist" threat and decided that if it were allowed to enter the government they would fight.

Because he distrusted Gil Robles and feared that the Socialists might revolt, President Alcalá-Zamora had avoided bringing the CEDA into the first government formed by Lerroux after the November elections, but since it was the largest parliamentary group and political organization, its democratic right to representation could not be forever denied. Although Gil Robles had never formally accepted the Republic because of its assault upon the church, he had nevertheless proclaimed his intention to respect the democratic method of attaining power and denounced fascism as a heresy. Still, his inconsistent and ambiguous statements alarmed the Socialists.[20]

"Clearly, the CEDA leadership did not regard itself as Fascist," writes Richard Robinson in his admirably dispassionate and meticulously documented study of the Spanish right, "but for Socialists the internal doctrinal niceties of the Right were unimportant. The negative critique of pure Fascism was for them irrevelant; the real question was, what were the positive intentions of Gil Robles? He had, in practice, accepted the Republic and constantly advocated the legal, democratic method of attaining power, the path of evolution; but in power, what would he do? . . . The ultimate goal of the CEDA was a State based on Catholic corporative principles. This State would be the result of a process of gradual transformation of the liberal-democratic structure by constitutional and democratic means. . . . The socialists, however, were not inclined to draw a distinction between fascism and evolutionary Catholic corporativism, which, if it were attained would mean the end of Socialism just as the attainment of Socialism would mean suppression of political Catholicism."[21]

Although Gil Robles had ruled out violence and dissociated himself from fascism, he nevertheless alarmed the opposition when he declared in the heat of the 1933 election campaign: "We must proceed to a new State. . . . What does it matter if it costs us bloodshed! We need complete power. . . . Democracy is for us not an end, but a means for proceeding to the conquest of a new State. When the time comes Parliament either agrees or we make it disappear."[22]

"While it was inherent in [Gil Robles's] declared aims," writes Robinson, "that liberal-parliamentarism would be abolished some time, the bald manner in which he had now stated this conveyed the impression that it might be sooner rather than later. . . . Whether or not

The Spanish Revolution

Gil Robles was clear in his mind about his intentions, his socialist opponents were clear in theirs. . . . Largo Caballero [the left Socialist leader] told socialists [in November 1933]: '. . . The enemies have already begun the war, and say through the mouth of Gil Robles that if Parliament does not serve their purpose they will go against it. All right. We reply: 'We are proceeding legally towards the evolution of society. But if you do not want this, we shall make the revolution violently. . . . If legality is of no use to us, if it hinders our advance, we shall bypass bourgeois democracy and proceed to the revolutionary conquest of power.' "[23]

When, on 4 October 1934, President Alcalá-Zamora yielded to the CEDA's demands for representation in the government, the Socialists declared a general strike. The strike failed everywhere except in the mining region of Asturias, where, supported by the anarchists and Communists, it quickly developed into a struggle for power. After almost two weeks of fighting this dress rehearsal in proletarian revolution and prelude to the Civil War was crushed with the aid of Moorish troops and Foreign Legionaries.[24]

The repression, writes a conservative republican, a onetime Radical party deputy and an uncompromising opponent of the left, was savage and pitiless in its methods: "The accused were tortured in the jails; prisoners were executed without trial in the courtyards of the barracks, and eyes were closed to the persecutions and atrocities committed by the police during those sixteen months. Officially, there were only three executions. What clemency! But there were thousands of prisoners and hundreds of dead, tortured, and mutilated. Execrable cruelty! There we have the tragic balance-sheet of a repression that, had it been severe yet legal, clean and just in its methods, would have caused far less harm to the country."[25] And a liberal historian writes: "Every form of fanaticism and cruelty that was to characterize the Civil War [of 1936] occurred during the October [1934] revolution and its aftermath: utopian revolution marred by sporadic red terror; systematically bloody repression by the 'forces of order.' "[26]

As a result of the revengeful feelings that the repression engendered,[27] the animosity between workers and employers in the towns and rural areas, and, finally, the rooted antagonism between the forces of the left and right, the spring and early summer following the victory of the Popular Front in the February 1936 elections passed in a continual commotion heightened by provocations and retaliations on both sides. When, on 12 March, gunmen of José Antonio Primo de Rivera's Falange Española, which contributed its share to the swell of violence, attempted—in retaliation for the slaying on 6 March of several party members—to assassinate the famous jurist and moderate Socialist deputy, Luis Jiménez de Asúa,[28] the government proscribed the party and imprisoned its leaders.[29] But this measure was to no avail, for the Falange survived and even grew in clandestinity and, according to one right-wing historian, "served as a catalyst unifying the will to resist of certain segments in the country that were growing constantly."[30]

In fact, none of the measures adopted by the beleaguered government of Premier Manuel Azaña, the leader of the liberal Izquierda Republicana, the Republican Left party, to calm the situation achieved their purpose and the State of Alarm—a milder form of security alert than martial law—that had been proclaimed on the morrow of the elections was prolonged month after month at the expense of civil liberties. Day after day and week after week there occurred fresh scenes of violence and effervescence: mass meetings and demonstrations, arson and destruction, including the burning of churches and Catholic schools, the closing of party and trade-union headquarters, seizures and attempted seizures of property, rioting and bloody clashes with the police, and assassinations and counterassassinations.[31] "Government censorship tried to suppress the news of strikes and assassinations because the ministers feared the contagion of violence," attests Frank E. Manuel. "Copy for daily newspapers had to be rushed to the official press bureau for examination; the deleted sections appeared as blank space or with broken type. The Paris *Temps*, arriving a few days late in Madrid, was often more informative than the newspapers of the Spanish capital. Only when one gathered a batch of provincial papers and turned to the pages entitled *Social Conflicts* could one fully realize the scope of labor discontent for which there were no official statistics."[32]

"Everyone in his senses knew," writes a republican army officer, "that Spain, far from being a happy and blissful country, was living on a volcano."[33]

In this turmoil, the military revolt—supported by a large section of the police, by monarchists and Falangists, by the powers of finance and business, by the majority of the Catholic clergy, by large landowners, by those medium and small holders, tenant farmers, sharecroppers, and *colonos* who chafed at the aggressive demands of their farm workers, and by the more prosperous segment of the urban middle class—broke out in Spanish Morocco on 17 July 1936, initiating the Civil War. Because of the extraordinary diversity of property relations among the small peasantry in the various regions in which they lived, the people of the countryside saw the Civil War not simply as a conflict between the landed aristocracy and landless peasants, as has been commonly supposed. As Edward Malefakis observes, "What is unusual about the Spanish case is that the peasantry instead of lending the bulk of its support to one side or the other remained so divided within itself that it is impossible to determine which side a majority of its members favored in the conflict. . . . [Other] civil wars . . . can be interpreted essentially as struggles by the peasantry against other social groups. In Spain, although this type of struggle was not lacking, the civil war was also to a very significant degree a fratricidal conflict of peasant against peasant."[34]

It must be stressed that the advocates of military rebellion did not wait for the psychic temperature to reach its peak before planning a coup d'etat. According to the testimony of one right-wing historian, directives for an insurrection were prepared at the end of February 1936, shortly after the elections, "should circumstances make it necessary as was easily imagined at the time."[35] The same historian reveals that the idea of a coup had been stirring in the minds of monarchist and army leaders ever since General José Sanjurjo's abortive revolt against the Republic in August 1932.[36] In a speech on 22 November 1937, Antonio Goicoechea, the leader of Renovación Española, the party of Alphonsine monarchists, declared that in March 1934, he and certain right-wing leaders had planned a coup d'etat backed by an insurrection of the army. He and other monarchists had visited Italy to secure the support of the Italian government in the event civil war should break out in Spain.[37] An eyewitness account of the meeting with Mussolini, attended by both Alphonsine and Carlist monarchists, and of the resultant political and military accord, is given by Antonio de Lizarza Iribarren, commander of the Carlist militia.[38] According to this version, it was understood that no copy or record of the agreement would be taken back to Spain, but Goicoechea violated his promise to Mussolini by taking his own draft to Madrid, where it was discovered during the Civil War, much to the anxiety of Lizarza, the only conspirator who had not been able to flee the republican zone. According to Lizarza, nothing came of the Rome agreement because the July 1936 rebellion was undertaken by officers not involved in the negotiations with Mussolini,[39] and the significance attached to the agreement is described by Ricardo de la Cierva, one of Spain's leading historians of the Civil War, as "grossly exaggerated."[40] But it is probably true, as Lizarza claims, that the accord helped to create in Rome "a climate favorable to the rebellion and therefore made it easier for Italy to decide to support the [Spanish] Army on 27 July 1936."[41]

Moreover, according to his biographer, General Sanjurjo, the leader of the abortive revolt of August 1932, had been urging that a coup d'etat be carried out just before the February 1936 elections.[42] Nothing came of this conspiracy, but the electoral triumph of the left coalition increased the resolve of rightist leaders to transmute their designs into practice.

Indeed, even as the results of the first-round voting were still coming in, together with reports of attempted jailbreaks, demonstrations, church burnings, and other outbursts of revolutionary exultation, *ABC*, the mouthpiece of Renovación Española, declared on 18 February that the revolution begun in 1931 would continue its violent course until it encountered an effective reaction in the form of "radical solutions without formulas for compromise and accommodation."[43]

Immediately following the first round of the elections, General Francisco Franco, the chief of the central general staff, apprehensive of the consequences of a leftist takeover, urged the interim premier and head of the recently formed Center party, Manuel Portela Valladares, to declare martial law rather than give power to the Popular Front. Having received adverse reports from various garrisons to the effect that the army lacked the "moral unity" necessary to take matters into its own hands, Franco insisted that the initiative for martial law lay with the government. Portela, pleading that he was too old and that he lacked the energy for such an undertaking, suggested that the army accept responsibility, but Franco felt that "the moment had not arrived." José Calvo Sotelo, the monarchist leader, then urged Portela to call upon General Franco "to save Spain," but to no avail. Fearing that the impatience of the left could not be controlled unless power were given to the Popular Front without delay, Portela, shunning further responsibility, resigned on 19 February. President Alcalá-Zamora, who had also recoiled from a declaration of martial law on the ground that he did not want to "provoke the revolutionaries," then appointed the liberal republican Manuel Azaña as the new prime minister. Azaña hastily put together a cabinet of liberal and moderate republicans to govern the country in the name of the Popular Front.[44]

It was not a moment too soon. Already local organizations of the Popular Front, according to José Díaz, the Communist leader, were overturning city councils, "not through legal channels, but through revolutionary channels, placing them in the hands of Communists, Socialists, and Left Republicans."[45]

To protect itself from the right, Azaña's government immediately adopted measures to secure key military posts. General Franco, who on 17 July was to head the rising in Morocco and later the entire insurrectionary movement, was relegated to the obscure post of military commander in the Canary Islands; General Emilio Mola, in charge of the vitally important Army of Africa, was posted to the provincial garrison at Pamplona in Navarre, the center of the Carlist monarchists and their zealous militia, the *requetés*, where it was thought he would be isolated, but from where in fact he was able to direct unhindered the plans for the insurrection on the mainland and to conspire with the disaffected Navarrese;[46] while General Manuel Goded, inspector general in the war ministry, was transferred to the minor post of garrison commander in the Balearic Islands.[47]

"In wholesale changes on February 22 and 28 all the top positions were given to generals considered more or less friendly to the liberal Republic," writes Stanley Payne in his imposing study of the Spanish military. "In the spring of 1936, there were but 84 generals on the active list in the Spanish Army, for most of the 425 names in the *Anuario* [*Militar de España*] belonged to generals in various stages of retirement. Of the 84 men in command positions, the majority held moderate views on politics, and after the sifting and shifting of recent years few were monarchists or outright reactionaries. Almost all the major territorial commands and posts in the ministry of war were by March in the hands of generals known either for their pro-republicanism or for their sense of duty to the constitution."[48]

The measures taken by Azaña's government were so far-reaching and well-considered, writes Vicente Palacio Atard, a right-wing historian, that only one of the eight chiefs of the organic divisions into which Spain was territorially divided supported the rebellion. Moreover, none of the three general inspectors of the army rebelled, and the top positions in the Army of Africa were placed in the hands of persons of absolute trust. "The two most dangerous chiefs, Franco and Goded, on active service and with command positions, were confined to insular posts and were practically without mobility." Generals Joaquín Fanjul, José Enrique Varela, and Luis Orgaz who, with Franco and Goded, enjoyed great ascendancy in the army, were deprived of commands, and the last two were imprisoned. Thus assured of the control of the top positions in the army, Palacio Atard continues, the government assumed that it possessed "control of the army *from above*, the most effective method, based on the operation of hierarchical discipline in the armed forces." Other steps were taken to ensure control by the government. "If the changes in the military commands by executive order from the month of March to the very day of the rising are examined, there is evidence of unusual shifts in command positions, the meaning of which is very clear. To be sure, these changes did not disrupt the entire conspiratorial process, but caused confusion and agitated those who understood their significance."[49]

By mid-March the changes in command positions caused such unrest in military circles that Azaña's war minister, General Carlos Masquelet, issued the following communiqué to reassure leftist opinion: "Certain rumors, which would appear to be circulating insistently concerning the state of mind of officers and noncommissioned officers, have come to the knowledge of the minister of war. These rumors, which, of course, can be described as false and without foundation, tend indubitably to maintain public disquiet, sow animosities against the military, and undermine, if not destroy, discipline, which is the fundamental basis of the army. The minister of war has the honor of making public that all the officers and noncommissioned officers of the Spanish Army, from the highest to the most modest posts, maintain themselves within the limits of the strictest discipline, disposed at any moment to fulfill their duties scrupulously and—needless to say—to obey the orders of the legally constituted government."[50]

But the communiqué did nothing to allay leftist fears. El Socialista, the organ of the Socialist party executive, stated that its intelligence service had furnished it with alarming news and that to disregard the "ominous and threatening tone" of leaflets circulating in the barracks was dangerous.[51]

Although the conspirators were concerned about the government's measures, they pursued their plans with undiminished vigor.[52] That they might eventually rely upon the moral and material support of a large segment of the population seemed certain in view of the prevailing climate of apprehension and inasmuch as the parties of the right and center had received at least half the votes.[53]

The landed proprietors feared that the measures adopted by the center-right since December 1933 to undo the agrarian reform of the first two years of the Republic would be repealed. In fact, the abrogation of two of these measures was promised in Section III of the Popular Front program,[54] namely, the law providing for the return of their estates to landowners implicated in the Sanjurjo rising of August 1932[55] and the Law of Leases,[56] which had resulted in the expulsion of eighty thousand tenant farmers during the first two months.[57]

The employers of labor both large and small in the towns and rural areas feared that the laws establishing the system of labor arbitration and fixing wages and conditions of work, which had been rescinded, undermined, or allowed to lapse, would once more be revived. Indeed, Section VII of the Popular Front program stated that labor legislation would be restored "in all the purity of its principles."

The church feared that the anticlerical provisions of the Constitution, which had been disregarded, would once more be enforced, for Section VIII of the Popular Front program declared that "the Republic must regard the educational system as the indefeasable function of the State." Referring to the situation after the victory of the center-right in the 1933 elections, Salvador de Madariaga writes: "The Jesuits went on teaching: Azaña's plans for the substitution of lay for religious education in new institutions were shelved, and a law was passed granting the priests two-thirds of their salaries for the year 1934 as a gracious act of the Republic, politically wise, perhaps, but of doubtful fidelity to the Constitution."[58] Azaña's government, formed after the victory of the Popular Front, at first acted cautiously on this issue, for on 28 April only the Socialist and Communist deputies voted in favor of a motion to abolish stipends, and the motion was defeated.[59] But the new government formed on 19 May, with Francisco J. Barnés, a Left Republican, as minister of public instruction, opened old wounds. "Azaña's government," writes Richard Robinson, "had on 28 February ordered inspectors to visit schools run by religious congregations. Apparently these inspectors often closed down schools on their own initiative. With the appointment of Barnés, however, it would seem that closure of schools run by the congregations and the illegal confiscation of private schools became, in effect, official policy. Cedista spokesmen [members of the CEDA] asked that no schools be closed unless there were places for their pupils in State schools. The minister replied that Catholics must now suffer for their sins of omission in failing to develop sufficiently the State system since 1933. On 4 June, the CEDA temporarily withdrew from the Cortes because the minister's insulting language as much as his policy gave 'intolerable offence to the Catholic conscience of the country.' Cedistas continued to complain of religious persecution, while the government went ahead with its laicising policies."[60]

Furthermore, right-wing and even moderate army officers, disquieted by the public displays of enmity toward the army since the victory of the Popular Front,[61] feared that their grievances against the military reforms of the Republic that had been instituted by Manuel Azaña, premier and war minister during the first biennium (1931–33), and had been partially redressed by the governments of the center-right, would now go unheeded.[62]

And, finally, all the forces of the center-right feared that although the liberal government formed by Azaña wished to remain within the framework of the Popular Front program—a program he promised to fulfill "without removing a period or a comma"[63]—broad sections of the working class and peasantry, spurred by their electoral triumph and apparently oblivious of the formidable power of the defeated, were determined to go beyond it, and that, judging from the revolutionary fervor that had gripped the country, the course of events could only be reversed by force, or, as one history favorable to the military rising expressed it, by "a surgical operation."[64]

Premier Manuel Azaña's inability to temper the revolutionary ebullience of the left soon became apparent. True, he had declared on assuming the headship of the government in February 1936 that he wished to govern "within the law and without dangerous experiments,"[65] and on 3 April in the Cortes he had condemned the acts of violence and the seizures of property that were embarrassing his government.[66] But, as *El Sol* pointed out on 28 March, his government was being subjected every day to greater pressure from the extreme left, which not only demanded, and obtained, the fulfillment of the basic points of the Popular Front program, but on many occasions hastened to carry out measures whose execution was being delayed. "This tactic," *El Sol* commented, "is in conflict with the sobriety of the prime minister. No one doubts this, but what can he do at the present time?"

It was clear from Azaña's speech in the Cortes on 15 April—three months before the Civil War—that he already discerned the approaching hecatomb: "I am fully aware that violence, rooted as it is in the Spanish character, cannot be proscribed by law, but it is my deepest wish that the hour may sound when Spaniards will cease shooting one another. Let no one take these words for incapacity or as an expression of a coward who is inhibited by or shrinks from the dangers that beset the regime that he has been entrusted to defend. No! We have not come here to preside over a civil war, but rather to avoid one."[67]

Despite this show of confidence, Azaña was in truth already an exhausted and demoralized man. His inability to cope with the situation, writes Stanley Payne, was demonstrated. "The Prime Minister lacked the will to throttle extremists, perhaps because he was not certain that the Army would prove a reliable instrument of suppression. Azaña's reluctance or incapacity to use the forces of order to maintain order aroused great discontent among the military, the Civil Guard and even the Assault Guards. Young activists in the Officer Corps more nearly agreed with the disgruntled minority of ranking generals than they did with the majority of senior republican generals who tried to smile benignly at the dissolution of civic discipline."[68]

Under the aggressive directorship of José Calvo Sotelo, parliamentary leader of Renovación Española and the Bloque Nacional, the National Front, representing both the Alphonsine and Carlist branches of the Monarchy, the monarchists made what capital they could of the prevailing turbulence. "If a state does not know how to guaranty order, peace, and the rights of all its citizens," Calvo Sotelo declared in the Cortes on 15 April 1936, "then the representatives of the state should resign." Later in his speech he warned: "We look at Russia and Hungary, we read and review the pages of their recent history, and because we know that it was a tragedy, a short one for Hungary, a permanent one still for Russia, we want Spain to avoid that tragedy. And we tell the government that this task devolves upon it and that in order to fulfill that task it will certainly not lack the votes or support of those who are present. Ah! But if the government shows weakness, if it vacillates . . . we must stand up here and shout that we are ready to resist with every means, saying that the precedent of extermination, of tragic destruction that the bourgeois and conservative classes experienced in Russia will not be repeated in Spain."[69]

The right was becoming convinced, writes Richard Robinson in his detailed chronicle of this period, that the continued disorder and prevalence of strikes were part of a plan to bring economic collapse as the precondition for revolution. "On 11 June, the Cedista Carrascal stated that the Minister of the Interior had simply lost control of the country; [provincial] governors were acting independently of the ministry, mayors independently of the governors and the masses were doing as they pleased. A statement from the government the next day [publicly appealing to governers and mayors to put an end to the usurpation of authority by armed bands] suggests that Carrascal's claims were substantially true."[70]

Gil Robles, the dynamic and ambitious leader of the CEDA, had particular reason for alarm, inasmuch as a large number of his followers, disillusioned by the results of the elections and his advocacy of nonviolence, were either openly deserting him or, according to his own testimony, "were helping other parties [of the right] that advocated solutions of force, especially the Falange Española."[71] True, during the campaign prior to the November 1933 elections, he had threatened to abolish the Cortes if he could not conquer the state by democratic means,[72] but after the electoral victory of the center-right he had defended evolutionary rather than dictatorial methods for achieving his Catholic corporative state despite monarchist criticism and increasing pressure for violent action from his youth movement, the JAP, the Juventudes de Acción Popular.[73] Ricardo de la Cierva, a supporter of the military rising, affirms: "Gil Robles is absolutely right when he described in [*Ya*, 17 Apr. 1968] the attitude of Luca de Tena [the owner of the Alphonsine monarchist newspaper *ABC*] in the following words, which are also applicable to the militant monarchists in general: 'He had no faith in legal methods; he regarded my efforts to get the right to live and govern under the Republic as causing serious damage to the Monarchy and believed in good faith that an appeal to force would better serve his ideals. . . . For this reason he always advocated insurrection, collaborated in its preparation as far as he could, gave maximum support to the [insurrectionary] movement in his newspaper.' "[74]

Even after becoming war minister in May 1935, Gil Robles had refused to seize power with the help of the military and the monarchists,[75] a refusal that in the years ahead they would not forgive. In 1936, faced by the mounting defection of his followers, particularly within his youth movement—which, according to a leader of the Falange, joined his party "almost en masse" between January and July[76]—and by the decision of the Derecha Regional Valenciana, one of the principal components of the CEDA, to prepare for violence,[77] Gil Robles declared forebodingly in the Cortes on 15 April: "Do not deceive yourselves, Señores Diputados! A substantial body of public opinion that represents at least half the nation will not resign itself to inevitable death, I assure you. If it cannot defend itself in one way, it will defend itself in another. Faced by the violence propounded by one side, the violence of the other will assert itself and the government will play the abject role of spectator in a civil strife, which will ruin the nation spiritually and materially. On the one hand, civil war is being fomented by the violence of those who wish to proceed to the conquest of power by means of revolution and, on the other, it is being nourished, supported, and encouraged by the apathy of a government that does not dare turn against its supporters who are making it pay such a heavy price for their help."[78]

Although aware, according to his own admission, that "fascism was sweeping ahead largely at the expense of the CEDA,"[79] Gil Robles nevertheless stuck to his nonviolent stand and declared in the Cortes on 19 May 1936: "Those of us who comprise the party, in whose name I speak, can feel neither enthusiasm for nor affinity with fascist ideology. You must understand that I do not say this in order to gain goodwill, which I know will by no means be granted to me; I say it because it conforms to a profound conviction both of myself and my party. Viewed from a purely national standpoint, a movement that carries a foreign label and is not in keeping with the characteristics and traditions of the Spanish people can have little appeal to us; if we look at the philosophical content of certain totalitarian doctrines regarding the state we cannot forget that they are saturated with a philosophical and political pantheism that is deeply opposed to our doctrinal convictions . . . ; if we consider the question of tactics we cannot, on any account, as believers, accept methods whose sole and exclusive aim is the conquest of power through violence."[80]

In response to his nonviolent stand, *No Importa*, the underground bulletin of the Falange, declared on 6 June that it was "shameful to try to narcotize the people with the lure of peaceful solutions. *There are no longer any peaceful solutions.*"[81] The Falange's aggressive self-confidence can undoubtedly be attributed not only to its mounting influence among civilians, but also to what Ricardo do la Cierva describes as its "increasingly preponderant role in the army, thanks to the growing number of [Falangist] members or sympathizers among the younger army chiefs and lesser officers." This, he points out, is another demonstration of the "youthful character of the uprising."[82] "It is most important to realize," he writes elsewhere, "that the average age of the military supporters of the rising was considerably lower than that of those loyal to the government."[83]

"The panorama was distressing," recalls Gil Robles in his memoirs. "I felt certain that it was necessary to do everything possible to divert the right from the path of violence . . . , but the truth is that the conviction was becoming rooted in everybody's mind that there was no other course but dictatorship to halt the anarchy that was draining our blood. Nobody sincerely believed any longer in the possibility of democratic normalcy."[84] And, on 15 July, after the assassination of the monarchist leader Calvo Sotelo,[85] he declared before the Permanent Deputation of the Cortes, in what proved to be his last speech in Spain: "When the lives of our citizens are at the mercy of the first gunman, when the government is incapable of putting an end to this state of affairs, do not imagine that people can have faith either in legality or democracy. Rest assured that they will proceed further and further down the paths of violence and that those among us who are incapable of preaching violence or of profiting from it will be slowly displaced by others, more audacious and more violent, who will exploit this deep national feeling."[86]

Although Gil Robles argues in his memoirs that he wished to remain within the framework of legality, that he had never been a supporter of military coups, that, because of his opposition to violence, he was not kept apprised by the organizers of the insurrection of their preparations, that he did everything possible to avoid civil war, that neither the CEDA nor he personally participated "in any concrete way in the preparation of the rebellion, though some members collaborated in the initial work," that he rejected a proposal by General Mola, who was in charge of the rebel plans on the peninsula, for all rightist deputies to gather in Burgos on 17 July to declare the government and parliament unlawful, and that only after the insurrection occurred did the majority of his followers support it,[87] he himself offers ample evidence to suggest that he did more than straddle the fence, but was at times an active, if not enthusiastic, participant in the military conspiracy.

Rarely a day passed, he records in his memoirs, that some friend or provincial delegate of the party did not come to him for advice. "To all of them I gave the same instructions: to act individually according to their consciences without implicating the party; to establish direct contact with the military forces, not to form autonomous militias, but to wait for concrete orders when the rising occurred."[88] He acknowledges furthermore that at the beginning of July 1936 several party members requested him to turn over to General Mola part of what remained of the party's electoral fund and that he authorized the transfer of 500,000 pesetas to the general. "I was faced by a grave moral crisis," he confesses. "The donations to the party had been made solely for electoral purposes because at that time the struggle was confined to legal grounds. I am absolutely sure that, under the new circumstances, had the donors been consulted as to the employment of the funds, nearly all of them would have demanded that they be applied to what, unfortunately, was now the only way to prevent the triumph of anarchy."[89]

Moreover, in a document signed on 27 February 1942, while he was in exile in Portugal, but revealed many years later, Gil Robles stated that after the 1936 elections the use of force for the restoration of public order was legally justified. "No solution other than a military one could be envisaged, and the CEDA was prepared to give it all possible support. I cooperated with advice, with moral support, with secret orders for collaboration, and with financial aid in not insignificant amounts taken from the party's electoral funds."[90]

Nevertheless, he seems to have given this support only halfheartedly, in the knowledge that the CEDA was disintegrating, and his refusal to comply with General Mola's suggestion that all rightist deputies convene in Burgos on 17 July to declare the government and parliament unlawful contributed to the "contempt," as one leading historian favorable to the uprising put it, in which he was held by the conspirators.[91] "My refusal obviously placed me in a very difficult position in relation to the insurgent military," Gil Robles affirms. "I deliberately attempted until the last moment to remain aloof from anything that would signify an incitement to violence. In view of the fact that I had advocated legal action for five years as the only form of public conduct, it would have been improper to attempt to ensure my political survival by any action that betrayed my clearly defined trajectory."[92]

Because of his indecisive stand and because after the outbreak of the Civil War the military preferred to dissociate themselves from the policies of the "old-time politicians,"[93] Gil Robles—whose organization in February 1936 held more seats in the Cortes than any other party—sank into oblivion only five months later. To be sure, his political eclipse appeared inevitable from the moment his policy of nonviolence resulted in mass defections to the Falange and in the growth of middle-class sentiment for violent and fascist solutions. The mounting support for fascist ideology and the spectacular change in the political panorama that had occurred since the February elections were noted on 12 June by "Gaziel," the pen name of Agustín Calvet, director of *La Vanguardia*, who was regarded as politically sympathetic to Manuel Azaña. Charging that the Popular Front had itself created the fascist menace, he asked:

How many votes were cast for the fascists in the last elections? Nothing to speak of: a ridiculous figure. If, after the victory of the Popular Front, we had had a good government in Spain concerned with the general interests of the country and capable of imposing its will on everyone, starting with its own supporters, that handful of fascists would have disappeared, pulverized by the force of reality. Today, on the contrary, travelers arrive from Spain saying, "Everyone there is becoming fascist." What has changed? What has happened? Is it perhaps possible that people have suddenly undertaken a profound study of political science and after extensive reading and numerous comparisons have come to the theoretical conclusion that the fascist regime is the best of all? No, man, no! . . . What is happening is simply that one cannot live there, that there is no government. Owing to the strikes and the conflicts, the state of uneasiness and the damage, and the thousand and one daily annoyances—not to mention the crimes and the attempted assassinations— many citizens are fed up and disgusted. In this situation they instinctively seek some relief and a way out, and since they cannot find them they begin little by little to hanker for a regime where these things at least appear possible. What is the type of political regime that radically suppresses these intolerable excesses? Dictatorship, fascism. Hence, without wanting it, almost without realizing it, the people "feel" themselves fascist. Of the inconveniences of a dictatorship they know nothing, as is natural. Of these they will learn later, when they have to put up with them, and then they will worry about them. But meanwhile they see in that form of strong government nothing more than an infallible means of shaking off the insufferable vexations of the existing lawlessness.[94]

Viewed from this angle of social and political antagonisms, the Civil War was strictly Spanish in its origin. No foreign intervention was necessary to ignite the tinder of civic strife, although it is true that foreign powers used the war for their own purposes. Weeks before the outbreak of the military revolt, weeks before the first foreign airplane or tank reached Spain, the country was ripe for a conflagration. Only the failure of the revolt in the main cities of Madrid, Barcelona, Valencia, Malaga, and Bilbao, a failure that ruined all possibility of the decisive initial victory planned by the insurgents,[95] was necessary to precipitate a far-reaching social revolution that was more profound in some respects than the Bolshevik Revolution in its early stages. Instead of protecting the propertied classes from the incursions of the left, the military revolt—to use the phrase of Federica Montseny, a leading member of the FAI, the Federación Anarquista Ibérica, the formidable Iberian Anarchist Federation, whose goal was the establishment of anarchist or libertarian communism—"hastened the revolution we all desired, but no one had expected so soon."[96]

She was addressing herself, of course, to the powerful anarchosyndicalist or anarchist-oriented labor federation, the CNT, over which the FAI exercised a guiding influence and which had condemned the Popular Front program as a "profoundly conservative document"[97] out of harmony with the "revolutionary fever that Spain was sweating through her pores."[98]

But she in no way expressed the feelings of the substantial body of moderate opinion represented in the Popular Front coalition. Certainly a revolution was not desired by Premier Manuel Azaña, the leader of the Republican Left party, who became president of the Republic on 10 May. Nor was it desired by his party colleague and intimate associate, Santiago Casares Quiroga, who succeeded him in the premiership on 13 May and at the same time assumed control of the war ministry.[99]

Nor was a revolution desired by other leading politicians of the party, whose membership was mainly recruited from the civil service, liberal professions, small landowners and tenant farmers, and small traders and manufacturers. Nor was it desired by Diego Martínez Barrio, speaker of the Cortes, vice-president of the Republic, and grand master of the Spanish Grand Orient, whose party, the Unión Republicana, the Republican Union party—a split-off from Alejandro Lerroux's Radical party—formed the most moderate section of the Popular Front coalition, and had, together with Azaña's party, declared its opposition, in the Popular Front program itself, to working-class control of production as well as to the nationalization and free distribution of the land to the peasants.[100]

Nor, indeed, was a revolution desired by Julián Besteiro, the leader of the small right-wing faction of the Socialist party, or by Indalecio Prieto, the leader of the moderate or center faction, who, in distinction from the numerically stronger left-wing Socialists led by Francisco Largo Caballero, the secretary of the powerful labor federation, the UGT, had pursued a policy of restraint in the months preceding the rebellion and had denounced the strikes and disorders that had racked the country.[101]

"Two positions, equally disinterested and honest," writes Julián Zugazagoitia, a moderate Socialist and director before the Civil War of *El Socialista*, "confronted each other in the Socialist party: the majority, led by Largo Caballero, that regarded the coalition with the republicans as a thing of the past and advocated the formation of a united working-class front with a view to the total exercise of power . . . : the minority personified by Prieto, that took into account the realities of the Spanish scene, and considered, inasmuch as the conservative parties were fighting resolutely, that any dissociation from the Republic and the republicans would be extremely dangerous. . . . Largo Caballero and his principal collaborators, Araquistáin and Alvarez del Vayo, believed that a military coup would be condemned to inevitable defeat both by the opposition of the state and the action of the workers through a general strike. . . . [The] social symptoms of the period . . . , far from causing them the slightest anxiety, aroused in them a secret sense of satisfaction in view of the fact that the strikes, disputes, and bloody encounters represented the governmental failure of the republicans."[102]

Although Largo Caballero had signed the Popular Front program, he did not regard the alliance with the liberal republicans as more than a temporary coalition to achieve victory at the polls. On 12 January 1936, a few days before the publication of the program, he had made his future position sufficiently clear:

[Our] duty is to establish socialism. And when I speak of socialism . . . I speak of Marxist socialism. And when I speak of Marxist socialism I speak of revolutionary socialism. . . . Our aspiration is the conquest of political power. By what means? Those we are able to use! . . . [Let] it be well understood that by going with the left republicans we are mortgaging absolutely nothing of our ideology and action. Nor do I believe that they demand this of us, because to do so would be the same as asking us to betray our ideas. It is an alliance, a circumstantial coalition, for which a program is being prepared that is certainly not going to satisfy us, but that I say here and now to all those present and to all those who can hear and read that . . . everyone, everyone united, must fight to defend. . . . Do not be dismayed, do not be disheartened, if you do not see things in the program that are absolutely basic to our ideology. No! That must never be a reason for ceasing to work with complete faith and enthusiasm for victory. We must do so in spite of everything. That way, comrades, after victory, and freed of every kind of commitment, we shall be able to say to everyone, absolutely everyone, that we shall pursue our course without interruption, if possible, until the triumph of our ideals.[103]

A former stucco worker by trade, a reformist for more than forty years, except for an occasional spurt of revolutionary activity, a counselor in General Primo de Rivera's cabinet during the dictatorship, Caballero, after two years of disillusionment as minister of labor during the Republican-Socialist coalition, had been fired in 1933 by revolutionary ideas and had become metamorphosed—at the age of sixty-four—into the exponent of the left wing of Spanish socialism.

This radical transformation had been brought about to a large extent by the apathy or indifference of the liberal republicans led by Manuel Azaña toward the implementation of the Agrarian Reform Law enacted in September 1932. The republican parties, writes Malefakis, had been nurtured on anticlericalism, antimilitarism, and antimonarchism. "The deepest emotions of these heirs to the French Revolution were awakened by the antiaristocratic implications of the agrarian reform rather than by the reform itself. Azaña perfectly typified these attitudes. . . . On agrarian matters he eloquently pleaded for reform in a number of speeches during the first enthusiastic months of the Republic but thereafter remained silent. Except in two instances, one searches in vain in the three volumes of his collected speeches for more than a passing reference to what was, after all, probably the most urgent question of the day."[104] In a subsequent passage, Male-fakis affirms: "The Left Republicans were led to espouse agrarian reform partly to gain the support of the Socialists for their political and cultural reforms, partly because they considered it necessary for the maintenance of social order, and partly because the humanitarian instincts of their liberal philosophy dictated the freeing of the peasantry. None of these reasons were sufficient to sustain them once the tremendous cost of the reform, as well as its inevitable violation of the respect of the property rights and for individual economic opportunity which have constituted the core of the liberal philosophy, became apparent. As a result they began to hedge upon their commitment almost as soon as the Agrarian Reform Law was enacted."[105]

The refusal of the republican parties to treat agrarian reform seriously, writes Gerald Brenan, in his classic work, *The Spanish Labyrinth*, lay at the root of the Socialists' disillusion with the Republic. "It was a feeling that welled up from below, affecting the young more than the old, the recently joined rather than the confirmed party men. . . . This feeling found a leader in Largo Caballero. As [secretary] of the UGT he was especially alive to the danger of losing ground to the Anarcho-Syndicalists. And he had also a personal grievance. First of all he had quarrelled with Azaña. Then as Minister of Labour he had been especially disgusted at the way in which much of the legislation drawn up by him had been sabotaged. . . . Thus it came about that already in February 1934 he was saying that 'the only hope of the masses is now in social revolution. It alone can save Spain from Fascism.'"[106]

Around him had gathered the mass of Socialist workers who, dissatisfied with the results of collaboration with the liberal republicans, wished to bring about the radicalization or "Bolshevization" of the Socialist party.[107] In March 1936, four months before the Civil War, the influential Madrid Socialist organization, the Agrupación Socialista Madrileña, over which Largo Caballero presided, had drafted a new program for the Socialist Party to be submitted to its next national congress, affirming that its "immediate aim" was "the conquest of political power by the working class by whatever means possible" and "the dictatorship of the proletariat organized as a working-class democracy." "The illusion that the proletarian Socialist revolution . . . can be achieved by reforming the existing state must be eliminated," ran the preamble. "There is no course but to destroy its roots. . . . Imperceptibly, the dictatorship of the proletariat or workers' democracy will be converted into a full democracy, without classes, from which the coercive state will gradually disappear. The instrument of the dictatorship will be the Socialist party, which will exercise this dictatorship during the period of transition from one society to another and as long as the surrounding capitalist states make a strong proletarian state necessary."[108]

Clearly, some of the language of the new program was borrowed from the standard works of Lenin and Stalin, whose teachings the aging Caballero had studied and embraced only in recent years. In the succeeding months, aglow with his new-found faith, Caballero toured the provincial capitals, proclaiming before rapt audiences that the Popular Front program could not solve the problems of Spain and that a working-class dictatorship was necessary.[109]

Caballero's revolutionary stance deepened the already irreconcilable divisions within the Socialist party. Julián Besteiro, the dignified and once influential "academic" Marxist, representing the right wing of the party, who had urged his Socialist colleagues in 1933 to accept democracy and had declared himself an enemy of the dictatorship of the proletariat,[110] had retired into the background,[111] and the struggle for control of the Socialist movement between the revolutionary Caballero and the evolutionary Prieto—at once political and highly personal—had moved to center stage. To Prieto, Caballero was irresponsible: "He is a fool who wants to appear clever: He is a frigid bureaucrat who plays the role of a mad fanatic."[112] Prieto held that the Socialists were not strong enough to carry out a successful revolution and should solidify their alliance with the republicans. To Caballero, Prieto's reformism was anathema, and he regarded his opponent as a "republicanoid" rather than a Socialist. "For me," he wrote some years later, "Prieto was never a Socialist . . . either in his ideas or his actions." "[He] was envious, arrogant, and disdainful; he believed he was superior to everyone; he would tolerate no one who cast the slightest shadow in his path."[113]

Although Largo Caballero's adherents greatly outnumbered those of Prieto, the latter derived his strength from his control of the party's executive committee and its organ, *El Socialista*, as well as from his control of some of the local sections. Largo Caballero's strength, on the other hand, came from the UGT, from the vigorous Socialist youth movement, from most of the local sections of the party, particularly the Agrupación Socialista Madrileña, and from his mouthpiece *Claridad*. So bitter was the feuding between the two factions on the crucial issue of revolution or evolution that on one occasion, when Prieto and two famous Asturian miners' leaders, Ramón González Peña and Belarmino Tomás, were scheduled to speak at a mass meeting in Ecija, they were forced to flee under a hail of bullets.[114]

This infighting led Salvador de Madariaga, independent republican and historian, to assert: *"What made the Spanish Civil War inevitable was the Civil War within the Socialist Party. . . .* No wonder Fascism grew. Let no one argue that it was Fascist violence that developed Socialist violence . . . ; it was not at the Fascists that Largo Caballero's gunmen shot but at their brother Socialists. . . . It was [Largo Caballero's] avowed, nay, his proclaimed policy to rush Spain on to the dictatorship of the proletariat. Thus pushed on the road to violence, the nation, always prone to it, became more violent than ever. This suited the Fascists admirably, for they are nothing if not lovers and adepts of violence."[115]

In the months before the Civil War, the official relations between Largo Caballero and the Communists, a small if rapidly growing force,[116] were on such a friendly footing that the left Socialist leader had encouraged the fusion of the Socialist and Communist trade-union federations[117] as well as the merging of the parties' youth organizations.[118] Moreover, in March 1936, the Caballero-controlled Madrid section of the Socialist party had decided to propose at the next national congress the fusion of the Socialist and Communist parties,[119] a merger the Communists themselves also strongly advocated.[120] As Stanley Payne points out: the left-wing Socialists had "extraordinarily naïve and uncritical notions about affiliating with the Comintern and cooperating with the Communist party, and when they spoke of union with the latter they conceived of it as the eventual absorption of the Communists by the Socialist party."[121]

Largo Caballero had personally recommended this amalgamation in several public statements[122] and had replied favorably to a Communist proposal that a liason committee representing both parties be formed with a program designed "to facilitate the development of the democratic revolution and to carry it to its final consequences."[123] This stand, in strident contrast to that of Indalecio Prieto, who was hostile through and through to the Communists, was warmly praised by José Díaz, the Communist party secretary: "The masses of the Socialist party . . . see in the line of Largo Caballero the one that approaches most the revolutionary path, the path of the Communist party and the Communist International."[124]

But in spite of the smooth course of their official relations with Caballero, the Communists were disturbed by the left Socialist leader's agitation for an immediate social overturn, for they were then endeavoring to strengthen the Popular Front by reinforcing their contacts with the liberal republicans in accordance with the Kremlin's foreign policy.[125] In fact, José Díaz, while publicly urging the creation of workers' and peasants' alliances "as future organs of power"[126] and frankly acknowledging that the dictatorship of the proletariat was the party's ultimate goal,[127] declared in an oblique reference to Largo Caballero's ultrarevolutionary posture: "We must oppose every manifestation of exaggerated impatience and every attempt to break up the Popular Front prematurely. The Popular Front must continue. We have still a long way to travel with the Left Republicans."[128] In private, Communists used such phrases as "infantile leftist"[129] and "senile leftist sickness"[130] to characterize Caballero's tendencies.[131] But they could not afford to press their differences with the left Socialist leader, for his popularity had reached its peak, and they valued his utility as a link between themselves and the masses that followed him.[132] Moreover, the idea of working-class unity had laid hold of his imagination, and this promised to facilitate the fusion of the Socialist and Communist parties as it had already facilitated the merging of their respective trade-union organizations and youth movements. "The important point for the unity movement," affirmed José Díaz, "and for the whole advance of the revolution in Spain is that the line represented by Largo Caballero should gain the victory in the Socialist party."[133] Writing shortly after the fusion of the Union of Young Communists and the Socialist Youth Federation in April 1936, Santiago Carrillo, the leader of the united organization, the Federación de Juventudes Socialistas Unificadas, known as the JSU, stated in reference to conversations he and other representatives of the two youth movements had previously held in Moscow: "As Manuilski, the old Bolshevik, told us . . . , the important thing now for the movement of unity and for the whole course of the Spanish Revolution is that the tendency represented by Largo Caballero should triumph in the Socialist party. If this victory does not occur, unity and the very future of the Revolution—I continue to quote Manuilski—would be compromised."[134]

The center faction of the Socialist party led by Indalecio Prieto viewed the growing threat of Communist influence in the Socialist movement with unconcealed animosity. It condemned their campaign for the merging of the two parties as the "fraud of unification"[135] and the fusion of the two youth movements as the "absorption of the Socialist youth by the Communist party."[136] Indeed, with such distrust and revulsion did the center faction regard the Communists that it refused even to answer their proposal to establish a liaison or coordinating committee between the two parties. "The Communist party," wrote José Díaz, "has proposed to the Socialist party the formation of a liason committee with a program designed to facilitate the development of the democratic revolution and to carry it to its final consequences. This proposal has been left unanswered by the present reformist and centrist leadership. On the other hand, it has been welcomed by the left wing. The masses of the Socialist party repudiate the attitude of the present reformist executive and see in the line of Largo Caballero one that approaches most the revolutionary path, the path of the Communist party and the Communist International."[137]

Indalecio Prieto, the leading light and dominant force of the center faction, found Largo Caballero's collaboration with the Communists extremely dangerous. A masterful character of humble origins, now the owner of *El Liberal* of Bilbao, an influential newspaper in the industrial North, he enjoyed immense prestige among liberal and even conservative republicans, with whom he had infinitely more in common than with the left-wing Socialists. In fact, the differences between the two factions in the spring of 1936 were so pronounced that he declared they would result in a schism at the next party congress.[138] An expert parliamentarian, an eloquent but sometimes frenzied speaker, he would pound his chest with such force that, as one Cortes deputy expressed it, "no one knows what to admire more: the strength of his fist or the resistance of his thorax."[139] "He beats his chest so violently," writes another witness, "shouts at the top of his lungs, and frequently injures himself, causing himself to bleed."[140] Skilled in maneuvers in governing circles and his own party—maneuvers that had been instrumental not only in dislodging Alcalá-Zamora from the presidency of the Republic and raising Manuel Azaña on 10 May to that high office,[141] but in ousting Caballero from the executive committee of the Socialist party[142]—Prieto was often cited as the most astute politician in the republican regime. His ability was acknowledged by opponents as well as friends.[143]

In contrast to Caballero, before the Civil War he had thrown all his influence on the side of moderation. "[What] no country can stand," he contended in his 1936 May Day speech, "is the constant bloodletting of public disorder without any immediate revolutionary goal; what no country can stand is the waste of its public authority and economic strength through continued disquiet, anxiety, and agitation. Some simple souls may argue that this disquiet, this anxiety, and this agitation can only harm the dominant classes. This is an error. . . . [The] working class itself will not be long in feeling the pernicious effects as a result of the damage to and possible collapse of our economy. . . . What we should do is to proceed intelligently to the destruction of privileges, to demolish the foundations on which these privileges rest; but this is not done through isolated, sporadic excesses, which leave in their wake as a sign of the people's efforts some scorched images, burnt altars, or church doors blackened by flames. That, I tell you, is not revolution . . . [If] a truly revolutionary organization, intelligently revolutionary, does not capture this wasted energy, if it does not control it, guide it into fruitful channels, then listen to me when I declare: this is collaborating with fascism." In this atmosphere, he continued, fascism would flourish because a terrified middle class, unable to discern on the horizon a solution for its salvation, would turn to fascism. "[Let] it not be said, to the discredit of democracy, that barren disorder is possible only when a democratic government is in power, because then the facts will cry out that only democracy permits disorders and that only the whip of dictatorship is capable of preventing them. . . . [Should] abuse and disorder become a permanent system, that will not be the way to socialism or to the consolidation of the democratic Republic, which I believe is our concern. . . . That way does not lead to socialism or to communism; it leads to a completely hopeless anarchy that is not even in keeping with libertarian [anarchist] ideology; it leads to economic chaos that may finish off the country."[144]

On 4 May, Largo Caballero's organ, *Claridad*, issued a rebuke. "The working class wants the democratic Republic . . . not for its intrinsic virtues, not as an ideal form of government, but because within that regime the class struggle, which is stifled under despotic regimes, encounters greater freedom of action to achieve its immediate and short-range goals. If it were not for this, why would the workers want the Republic and democracy? To believe that the class struggle should cease so that only democracy and the Republic may exist is to disregard the forces that move history. It is putting the cart before the horse."[145]

In the midst of the disturbances that convulsed the country in the spring of 1936, a movement was set in motion—with which Prieto was not unconnected—to place him in the premiership. "Around his person," records a right-wing historian, "an atmosphere was being created—which Miguel Maura [leader of the moderate Conservative Republican party and one of the founders of the Republic in 1931] was trying to build up and diffuse—an atmosphere favorable to placing him in a position from which he would be able to curb as far as possible the disorders that were taking place. Prieto was the hope not only of the moderates of the Popular Front . . . but of many moderates of the right."[146] According to Maura, Prieto inspired him with "greater respect and deeper esteem" than any other politician with whom he had to deal.[147]

Yet, when President Azaña offered him the premiership, he dared not accept the post, not only because of the opposition of the executive committee of the UGT, controlled by Caballero,[148] but because a caucus of the Socialist deputies, the majority of them members of the left faction, had voted overwhelmingly not to share power with the republicans,[149] thus denying Prieto any hope of a viable government based on the parliamentary support of his own party. "What would have been said of me at that time," Prieto declared some years later, "if, ignoring the resolution of the parliamentary caucus, I had accepted the power Señor Azaña offered me? I should have appeared, with a certain degree of justification, as the only person responsible for the destruction of the Socialist party. Furthermore, if in parliament I had been denied the votes of the majority of the representatives of the Socialist party, I should have been compelled, in order to govern parliamentarily, to seek support among the right, as a result of which I should have covered myself with ignominy."[150]

Behind the left Socialists' opposition to a government headed by Prieto and the support they gave a few days earlier to Premier Azaña's election to the presidency there lay, according to Luis Araquistáin, Caballero's most trusted aide, a sinister purpose. "I am inclined . . . to give considerable weight to the following statement made to me [after the war] by Luis Araquistáin shortly before his death in Paris," attests Juan Marichal, editor of Azaña's collected works. "According to Araquistáin, the extreme wing of the Socialist party—in which he was the most 'penetrating' thinker—wanted to eliminate Azaña from any executive function and at the same time prevent Prieto from becoming premier. This would place the government in hands utterly incapable of restraining the masses or of calming the right and would hasten the advent of a purely revolutionary government. The maneuver, according to Araquistáin, was very simple: Azaña was 'pushed' toward the presidency of the Republic and when, as was to be expected, he thought of Prieto as his successor in the premiership he encountered the outright veto of the Socialist party. 'In this way, we rendered both men useless,' the former Socialist leader told me, adding, 'Don't you think we went to extremes?'"[151]

Marichal's account is confirmed by Mariano Ansó, a cabinet minister during the Civil War, who, despite political differences, remained on cordial terms with Araquistáin. He claims that during a tête-à-tête with the Socialist leader several years later, he did not omit the slightest detail regarding the "large-scale maneuver conceived by him" and executed by the Largo Caballero wing. "I agree with Marichal," Ansó affirms, "that in Araquistáin's account there was a touch of horror and even remorse over the far-reaching consequences of his action."[152] In a letter written after the war, Largo Caballero, although he stood at the epicenter of the political crisis, gave no hint of Araquistáin's political machinations. Indeed, it is curious, bearing in mind his prewar revolutionary stance, that he should claim that he regarded Azaña's elevation to the presidency as a "political error," because, as he puts it, the Republican Left party was the only party—because Azaña was its leader and also head of the Popular Front coalition—that offered any guarantee that the electoral program would be fulfilled. "If Azaña were elected president of the Republic," he claims to have thought at the time, "Spanish republicanism would become a flock without a shepherd; everyone would pull his own way; the Republic would lack a basic organ for its support and development. This fear of ours was confirmed later, unfortunately."[153] I have found no corroborative evidence that this was Caballero's thinking at the time.

In a public statement made after the war, Araquistáin confessed: "Another factor that contributed to the fall of the Republic was probably the internecine struggle within our party. I believe that the fault lay with all of us. We all contributed, some in one way, some in another, to the state of internal decomposition that showed the enemy that we were weakened and that the moment for rebellion had arrived. I believe that if we had not been in that lamentable condition . . . the result would have been different." Had a Socialist been at the helm of government, he contended, he might have aborted the military conspiracy. "Some will say that all this is water under the bridge. Ah! But the future may offer similar situations, and a knowledge of history is never useless."[154]

Because the dissensions within the Socialist party precluded any possibility of a viable government under Prieto, on 13 May—two months before the Civil War—President Azaña named Santiago Casares Quiroga, his close associate and a member of his party, to head the new administration, which, like the previous cabinet, was composed entirely of liberal and moderate republicans. Although Prieto declared after the war that he would have covered himself with ignominy if, as premier, he had been compelled to seek support among the right,[155] there is evidence that in reality he may not have been opposed to this approach. Gil Robles recounts that in April and May, conversations were held between Manuel Giménez Fernández, representing the liberal wing of the CEDA, and Miguel Maura and Julián Besteiro, with the knowledge of Prieto and Azaña, to discuss the idea of a government of national concentration. After Casares Quiroga had formed his cabinet on 15 May Gil Robles received a visit from José Larraz—the president of Editorial Católica, the owner of *El Debate*, the mouthpiece of the CEDA—who had discussed with Prieto, "the central figure in these projects," the "vague possibility of including the CEDA in a government presided by Prieto in order to counter the revolutionary solutions proposed by some elements of the Socialist party." Gil Robles replied that because Casares Quiroga had just formed his government, he judged Prieto's chances of success very problematical. "How could I under the circumstances have ventured to offer the participation of the CEDA in a hypothetical government that the majority of our deputies were not ready to support . . . ? I would simply have succeeded in destroying the only well-organized force of the Spanish right." He then suggested to Larraz that a coalition government comprising moderate Socialists, republicans, and elements of the center and supported by the parliamentary votes of the CEDA would be "more reasonable," but that a government with direct participation of the CEDA would be unworkable. "Apart from the absolute discredit into which we would have fallen among our voters, it did not appear logical to suppose that the masses of the Popular Front would agree to our ministerial collaboration, in view of the fact that the entry of the CEDA in the government [in 1934] had provoked . . . the revolutionary movement of October."[156]

Nothing came of these backstage negotiations to avert the approaching cataclysm, not only because the Socialists were riven by discord, but because the CEDA, undermined by defections to parties of the right that were bent on a violent settlement, was threatened with disintegration. Hence it fell to the hapless Casares Quiroga to preside during the next few weeks, as a premier and war minister, over Spain's precipitous descent into civil war.

On 19 May he presented his new cabinet to the Cortes. In accordance with the policy of Azaña, he endeavored to maintain a balancing position between the right and left. To appease the left, he announced that he would accelerate the rhythm of the Popular Front program, that he would defend the Republic from its enemies, and that leniency no longer would be shown toward the foes of the Republic. "I tell you that wherever the enemy presents himself, whether he be open or concealed, we shall crush him." On the other hand, to appease the right he said that he would not be coerced from below, and he condemned the illegal political strikes, confiscations of property, and acts of violence. "The government cannot work in dignity under these conditions. I appeal to all of you to help me with your loyal and cordial cooperation."[157]

But, during his few short weeks in office, he did little to calm the social turbulence and, like Azaña, turned a deaf ear to every warning concerning the brewing military revolt.[158] A consumptive, who tried hard to present a tough and energetic exterior, Casares proved impetuous and ineffectual. His threats and invective against the right—rarely matched by equal vehemence against the left—angered his opponents but were little more than bluster. "The political climate required a man of greater energy," writes Zugazagoitia, director of the moderate *El Socialista*. "Persons of good judgment who had collaborated with him when he was minister of the interior [1931–33] advised me to distrust his energetic appearance. They maintained that his energy, like that of Don Manuel Azaña, was purely oral and that once the parliamentary debate had ended was without consequence."[159]

By mid-June, Casares Quiroga's government was adrift, and it was evident that his attempts to maintain the precarious social equilibrium were failing. Government authority had now declined to such a point that Miguel Maura, the liberal Catholic leader, was calling in *El Sol* for a multiparty national republican dictatorship.[160] "[The] dictatorship that Spain needs today," he wrote on 23 June, "is a national dictatorship with a broad social base extending from the nonrevolutionary Socialist working class to the conservative middle class, which is now convinced that the hour of renunciation and sacrifice in the interest of genuine social justice has sounded. . . . The dictatorship would be directed by men of the Republic, by republicans of probity, who . . . place the supreme interests of Spain and the Republic above class or party objectives."

The Spanish Revolution

On 25 June he wrote:

National indiscipline is now unbearable. The government is powerless to control it. The warring sides—and there are more than two—abandon themselves to the barbaric sport of man hunting. Illegal strikes and employer violations of government orders germinate with tropical fertility. The irreparable ruin of the economy and the collapse of government finances are terrifyingly near. To the right and to the left of the regime the aligned forces, organized and armed, pressure the state to the point of asphyxiation, and proclaim their intention to attack and overthrow it. And all this is happening because the Popular Front, which was an excellent electoral tool, is not and cannot be an instrument of government. It is an amalgam, which in addition to being hybrid, is destructive of peace and of the wealth of the country. . . .

Today, the Republic is no more than the tool—unconscious I would like to believe—of the extreme, revolutionary segment of the working class, which, shielded by the liberal democratic system and the blindness of certain representatives of the republican parties, is preparing in minute detail an assault on the government and the extermination of capitalist and middle-class society. . . .

We republicans who eagerly made the greatest personal sacrifice to collaborate in the birth of the regime . . . are called fascists and, as such, merit extermination. . . .

If the Republic is to be this, it is inexorably condemned to imminent extinction at the hands of those who claim to be its only defenders, or, what is more probable, at the hands of a reaction from the opposite direction. . . .

[Either] all republicans—and I include in this denomination those on the left and right who wish to maintain the republican regime . . . —decide to subordinate their party interests to the supreme interests of the regime . . . or they resign themselves to watching it die in the agonies of a bloody civil war, whose outcome will be either a fascist or a Red dictatorship. . . .

A regime that does not defend itself does not deserve to live. But a regime that surrenders itself passively and merrily to its declared enemies, in addition to deserving death, deserves the contempt of history. . . . The Republic knows that if, under the protection of its democratic laws . . . , either one side or the other prevails, the Republic in Spain, together with freedom and democracy, will die. The Republic knows that if this should happen Spain will be devastated by disasters heretofore unknown in its history, because none of its adversaries is equipped to establish a political and social regime that is humane and habitable.

On 27 June, Maura wrote wistfully: "I do not harbor the slightest hope that my reasoning will convince those who currently bear the weight of government responsibility in Spain."

If through their passivity Azaña and Casares Quiroga appeared supine or even impotent before the dangers closing in more menacingly every day upon the Republic from the left and right, this was partly because they were afraid to provoke the left to greater agitation and aggression and partly because they underrated the ability of the army dissidents to stage a successful insurrection.[161] As Palacio Atard, a supporter of the military rising, points out, they were confident that their control of the top command positions guaranteed the "effective subordination" of the army and overlooked "the ability of the young officers to assure the success of the rebellion in many garrisons by overpowering their superiors."[162] Furthermore, to quote Juan Marichal, the reports of the conspiratorial activities in the army "did not play in Manuel Azaña's anguished mind the same role as the attitudes and actions of the extreme left."[163] This is confirmed by Zugazagoitia, who recounts that on his commenting in his newspaper upon certain subversive military activities, Manuel Azaña, then prime minister, personally reprimanded him on the ground that such comments did more harm than good. The truth of the matter was, he adds, that Azaña was annoyed at the time, not with the military, "who were carefully concealing their designs through the exercise of a perfect discipline," but with the voters, "who had ensured the victory of the Popular Front and were provoking a fabulous number of strikes and disturbances in the sphere of public order."[164] In a private talk with Gil Robles, after becoming president of the Republic, Azaña did not conceal his fears regarding the course of events. "I don't know where we will end up," he said. "Your friends should give me a margin of confidence. They should not make difficulties for me. I have enough problems on the other side."[165]

Because Azaña and Casares Quiroga feared the social ferment more than the conspiratorial activities reported to them day by day and because, as Richard Robinson puts it, the existence of an armed antirevolutionary force was for the Left Republicans the only hope of preserving a certain independence of action vis-à-vis the workers' organizations, they took no determined action against the military.[166] They paid scant heed to the demands of the Communists, for example, that the government should remove "the fascist and monarchist chiefs in the army" and should carry out "an energetic and thorough purge of the state apparatus," cleansing the army, the secret police, the Civil Guard, the Assault Guard, and the courts of law of "all reactionary, fascist, and monarchist officers and elements who hold positions of authority."[167]

"The most that the government would do after receiving detailed reports of an intrigue in some garrison," writes Stanley Payne, "was to transfer a number of officers to another post. It hesitated to do even this much with generals such as Mola and Goded, though lesser lights in the UME [Unión Militar Española, the right-wing military organization] were rotated two or three times during the spring of 1936. . . . Azaña and Casares seem to have believed, just as the rightists did, that the main threat would come from Azaña's own allies of the revolutionary left."[168]

The occasional shifts in command positions and the continuing agitation by the extreme left against the army were nevertheless causing apprehension among rightist officers. On 23 June, from his remote garrison in the Canary Islands, General Franco wrote a warning letter to Casares Quiroga expressing the "grave state of anxiety" in the army. He protested against the substitution of officers "with a brilliant history" by men who, he claimed, were regarded by 90 percent of their comrades as "inferior in qualifications," and stressed the peril that this implied for army discipline. "Those who represent the army as disloyal to the Republic are not telling the truth," he asserted, and he urged that it be treated with "consideration, fairness, and justice."[169] This letter, affirms Manuel Aznar, a supporter of the general, was written so that he could "arm himself with every possible justification before God, history, and his own conscience" before making a final decision.[170]

Isolated in his command post far out in the Atlantic, General Franco was proceeding cautiously and did not finally commit himself to insurrection until the end of June or the beginning of July,[171] a vacillation that infuriated some of the conspirators, who threatened to act without him.[172] "Franco's sphinx-like attitude may have simply been prompted by caution," Richard Robinson speculates. "On the other hand his conduct during the Republic suggests that he had a strong respect for legality, and therefore needed to be sure in his own mind whether or not rebellion was justified in the circumstances. His letter of 23 June to Casares Quiroga can be interpreted either as an attempt to effect a change in policy to avoid a rising, or as an effort to make the conspirators' task easier."[173] He had, it seems, good reason for delaying his pledge, for the conspiracy was not going well. In a confidential report dated 1 July to those involved in the "patriotic movement," General Emilio Mola, who was directing the conspiracy from his provincial garrison in Pamplona, stated that the enthusiasm for the cause had "not yet reached the degree of exultation necessary for a decisive victory. . . . An effort has been made to provoke a violent situation between two opposing political sectors so that, based on the violence created, we may proceed; but the fact is that up to now—notwithstanding the help given by some political elements—this has not happened, because there are still fools who believe that agreement is possible with the representatives of the masses under control of the Popular Front."[174] Furthermore, plans for the uprising were being hindered by political differences between the rival Alphonsine and Carlist monarchists as well as by disagreements between the Falange and the military conspirators.

The most valuable and fascinating account of the conspiratorial activities of military and political leaders and their difficulties in reaching agreement is given by Ricardo de la Cierva in his *Historia de la guerra civil española*.[175] Cierva, a leading historian favorable to the uprising, had access during the Franco regime to unpublished primary sources in the official Archivo de la Guerra de Liberación of the Servicio Histórico Militar of Madrid as well as to other unpublished materials made available to him by important participants in the conspiracy. In his work, Cierva effectively disposes of many of the inaccuracies and half-truths regarding the conspiracy that first appeared in official and semiofficial publications, such as the *Historia de la cruzada española*, which, he asserts, deliberately obscures the role of General Mola in the preparation of the rising "in order to place in the forefront other military figures." The principal organizer and responsible figure, he affirms, was General Mola, who "on his own initiative, managed to fuse, although imperfectly, the diverse conspiracies and rebellious impulses against the Republic and the Popular Front."[176] Thus, Cierva implicitly contradicts a statement in the *Historia de la guerra de liberación, 1936–1939*, published by the Spanish Central General Staff in 1945, that credits General Franco with full responsibility and leadership of the rebellion.[177]

Although the rivalries and dissensions among the forces of the right were still simmering when Franco finally pledged himself to support the rebellion, a dramatic event soon occurred that coalesced the disputing forces.

On 13 July, José Calvo Sotelo, the monarchist parliamentary leader and one of the most important of the civilian conspirators, was slain by leftist members of the police as a reprisal for the murder of Lieutenant José Castillo, a left-wing member of the republican Guardia de Asalto, the Assault Guard. Acting on their own intitiative, Castillo's colleagues drove to Calvo Sotelo's residence in an official truck and announced that they had orders to arrest him. "Ignorant of the enormity that was about to be perpetrated against his person," writes a Socialist historian, "the prisoner descended resolutely with the republican officers. . . . As soon as they had left the city precincts Calvo

Sotelo was killed and his corpse placed in the cemetery del Este. The ultimate barrier of disorder had been passed. Nothing more was required, after this incident, for the government and the reactionaries to lose, the former, what shreds of authority remained to it, the latter, what judgment they still possessed."[178]

"The principal monarchist support for the conspiracy," writes Ricardo de la Cierva, "was, of course, the enormous personality of José Calvo Sotelo, which was magnified by the eclipse of Gil Robles after the elections and aggrandized by his titanic struggle against the Republic and against the Popular Front, which he regarded as the logical degeneration of the Republic. . . . Calvo Sotelo was the mouthpiece of resistance, the herald of rebellion. . . . [His] death was the final call to military and civilian rebellion, the violent signal for civil war."[179]

In a later passage, he writes: "Clearly the conspiracy had been under way long before 13 July. Its point of no return had already been passed, and the uprising would almost certainly have taken place even without the terrible news. But the terrible news, which spread throughout Spain from the early hours of the morning of the thirteenth, contributed decisively to erasing the difficulties and doubts of the conspirators."[180]

Fearing that the assassination would be used as a pretext to trigger the insurrection and hoping to restrain the conspirators, Prieto sounded a warning note: "If reaction dreams of a bloodless coup d'etat . . . it is utterly mistaken. If it supposes that it will find the regime defenseless, it deludes itself. To conquer, it will have to overcome the human barrier with which the proletarian masses will bar its way. There will be . . . a battle to the death, because each side knows that the adversary, if he triumphs, will give no quarter. Even if this were to happen, a decisive struggle would be preferable to this continuous bloodletting."[181]

The government of Casares Quiroga vigorously denounced the assassination. It promised not only to take immediate steps to guarantee "elementary respect for human life," but to expedite the judicial investigation of the crime and "to apply the law to all in order that the disruptive work of so many extremists may not triumph over the aims of the Republic."[182]

But the condemnation did nothing to mollify the right. As Zugazagoitia puts it: "The conservative and military forces, for a long time organized for insurrection, were deeply wounded. Calvo Sotelo was the civilian head of the movement. He had infused respect into all the men of the Monarchy because of his superior preparation and talent.

His work in the ministry of finance, as collaborator of General Primo de Rivera, had given him experience as an administrator that could not be underestimated. . . . He had gained the confidence not only of the monarchists but also of more than half the deputies of the CEDA, whose devotion [to the party] had been chilled by the tactics of Gil Robles, whom they reproached for not using his control of the war ministry [in 1935] to bring down the regime . . . and for not instituting a dictatorship fashioned after that in Portugal."[183]

On 15 July, at a meeting of the Permanent Deputation of the Cortes two days before the Civil War began, Fernando Suárez de Tangil, the count of Vallellanos, speaking for the monarchists, charged: "This crime, without precedent in our political history, has been committed by the government's own agents. And this was possible thanks to the climate created by the incitements to violence and personal attack upon the deputies of the right uttered every day in parliament. . . . We cannot coexist with the protectors and moral accomplices of this deed a moment longer. We do not want to deceive the country and international opinion by accepting a role in a farce that pretends that a civilized and normal state exists, whereas, in reality, we have lived in complete anarchy since 16 February."[184]

And at the funeral of Calvo Sotelo, Antonio Goicoechea declared on behalf of Renovación Española: "Before this flag, placed like a cross over your breast, before God who hears us and sees us, we take a solemn oath to consecrate our lives to this triple work: to imitate your example, to avenge your death, and to save Spain."[185]

If there had remained up to this time even a glimmer of hope for compromise it was at once extinguished. Positions were now being taken up for what Prieto had warned would be a battle to the death in which the adversaries would give no quarter. The Socialists and Communists, who in the past few months had been organizing their own militia,[186] were now feverishly mobilizing their forces, and the conspirators, both military and civilian, were putting the final touches to their plans for insurrection.

There can be no doubt that the moderates of the Popular Front were aghast at the assassination of the monarchist leader, but no one deplored it more than President Manuel Azaña, who was fully aware of its dire import. Essentially a man of temperate views, he had sought to hold Spain on a middle course. He had hoped for substantial reforms within the framework of the republican Constitution, but not for a deluge that would submerge that Constitution. For this reason, when the rebellion broke out in Melilla in Spanish Morocco on 17 July —with a successful coup against the republican commander, General

Manuel Romerales, by his subordinates—and was spreading to the peninsula, Azaña still hoped for a solution that would save the Republic from being ground between the upper and nether millstones of the right and left. On the evening of 18 July, in a last-minute endeavor to prevent the country from plunging into civil war and revolution, he had the government of Casares Quiroga resign[187] and entrusted Diego Martínez Barrio—whose party, the Unión Republicana, it will be remembered, constituted the most moderate segment of the Popular Front coalition—with the formation of a new, somewhat conservative, cabinet in the expectation that this might encourage the insurgent army officers to negotiate.

"I have accepted this task," Martínez Barrio declared over the radio, "for two essential reasons: to spare my country the horrors of civil war and to protect the Constitution and the institutions of the Republic."[188] There was no time to lose, for the dangers to the Republic multiplied as garrison after garrison rose in revolt and as the left-wing organizations mobilized their members and ever more insistently demanded arms to combat the insurrection. For two days, Casares Quiroga had refused to arm the workers lest the power of state pass into their hands. "[His] ministry," an eyewitness said to Zugazagoitia, "is a madhouse, and the wildest inmate is the minister himself. He neither eats nor sleeps. He shouts and screams as though possessed. His appearance frightens you, and it would not surprise me if he were to drop dead during one of his frenzied outbursts. . . . He will hear nothing of arming the people and says in the most emphatic terms that anyone who takes it upon himself to do so will be shot."[189]

Casares Quiroga's orders were disregarded, for, prior to his resignation, five thousand rifles were handed out to the workers in Madrid on the sole authority of Lieutenant Colonel Rodrigo Gil, the chief of the Artillery Park and political associate for many years of Largo Caballero. This information, which has been amply confirmed, was given to me by Margarita Nelken, left Socialist deputy, who was sent to the Artillery Park by the Casa del Pueblo, headquarters of the Socialist UGT.[190] The version given by Lázaro Somoza Silva in his biography of General José Miaja[191] to the effect that the general, who was military commander of Madrid at the time, ordered the distribution not only lacks confirmation but conflicts with his presence a few hours later in Martínez Barrio's government which, as we shall see, was committed to the withholding of arms. In fact, when Carlos Nuñez Maza, then technical secretary in the general direction of aviation, asked Miaja to give arms to the Casa del Pueblo, the general refused to do so, according to Ignacio Hidalgo de Cisneros,[192] second in command at that time of the general direction of aviation under General Miguel Nuñez de Prado.

Even as Martínez Barrio was attempting to form a new government, the revolutionary workers—thanks in part to the distribution of arms by Lieutenant Colonel Rodrigo Gil—were beginning to assume police functions. "Groups of armed workers were patrolling the streets and beginning to stop automobiles," Martínez Barrio recalled. "Not a single soldier could be seen and, what is still more surprising, not a single guardian of public order. The absence of the coercive organs of the state was manifest."[193] And a Communist testifies: "At the stroke of midnight, all the exits from the Puerta del Sol, the approaches to the barracks, the working-class headquarters, the workers' districts, and the entrances to the city are being watched. The armed workers control motor traffic. Automobiles and streetcars are carefully searched. Flying patrols race through the different suburbs, carrying orders and inspecting sentry posts."[194]

Caught between the military rebellion and the counteraction of the left, Martínez Barrio was confronted by a double peril. To parry the danger, he would first have to withhold the distribution of arms for which workers were clamoring outside the ministry of the interior, a matter his talks with prospective members of his cabinet centered on. Felipe Sánchez Román, who became a member of Martínez Barrio's government and was the leader of the small, conservative National Republican party that had refused to join the Popular Front because of his opposition to Communist participation,[195] told me, when I interviewed him after the war, that, on arriving at the Presidential Palace, where he had been called by President Azaña before the formation of the new government, he was advised of a "serious development"— the appearance of workers demanding arms outside the ministry of the interior. Martínez Barrio, he said, was already there and had been insisting that arms be withheld.[196] Asked by Martínez Barrio for his opinion, Sánchez Román replied that the distribution of arms would be "ineffective militarily and pregnant with inconceivable dangers politically." Martínez Barrio has related that at a meeting of the Casares Quiroga government at 6 P.M. on Saturday, 18 July, attended by Indalecio Prieto, the moderate Socialist, and by Largo Caballero, the left-wing Socialist, everyone except himself remained silent in response to Caballero's "resolute opinion" that arms should be distributed, his own answer being that the people should be urged "to rally round the legitimate organs of government."[197] It is noteworthy that

Indalecio Prieto, in an article written after the war commenting on Martínez Barrio's narration of the government crisis, neither confirms nor denies the assertion that he was among those who remained silent when Caballero proposed that arms be distributed.[198]

To avert the approaching cataclysm, Martínez Barrio would not only have to withhold the distribution of arms, but above all he would have to dissuade the military leaders from their drastic course. With this end in view, he held telephone conversations with various garrisons, in an attempt, according to his own testimony, to secure the adhesion of those army leaders who were still undecided and to deflect from their purpose those who had already revolted.[199] The most important of these conversations was with General Mola, commander of the Pamplona garrison in charge of the rebel plans on the peninsula. But Martínez Barrio strove in vain to obtain the general's support. "If you and I were to reach a compromise," Mola replied, "we should betray our ideals as well as our men. We should both deserve to be lynched."[200] According to Sánchez Román, who was with Martínez Barrio at the time of this conversation, the latter pleaded desperately with Mola: "At this very moment the Socialists are ready to arm the people. This will mean the end of the Republic and democracy. We should think of Spain. We must avoid civil war at all costs. I am willing to offer you, the military, the portfolios you want, on the terms you want."[201] In fact, *El Pensamiento Navarro*, published in Pamplona, Mola's headquarters, stated in its issue of 19 July 1936, which appeared a few hours after this conversation, that Martínez Barrio had offered Mola the ministry of war.[202] "We shall demand full responsibility for everything that has happened up to now," Martínez Barrio promised Mola, "and we shall redress the damage caused."[203] To this General Mola replied with finality: "What you propose is now impossible. The streets of Pamplona are filled with *requetés* [the right-wing Carlist militia]. From my balcony all I can see are their red berets. Everyone is preparing to fight. If I were to tell these men that I had reached an agreement with you my head would be the first to roll. And the same would happen to you in Madrid. Neither of us can now control our masses."[204] In his own version of this crucial dialogue, Martínez Barrio attributes to Mola the following reply: "I have a duty toward the valiant Navarrese who have placed themselves under my command. If I wanted to act differently they would kill me. Of course, it is not death that frightens me, but the ineffectiveness of this new move and my own conviction. It is late, too late."[205]

In spite of this response, Martínez Barrio proceeded with the formation of what he later called his government of conciliation.[206] If it possessed a distinctly moderate complexion, this was not so much from the presence of five members of the Unión Republicana all known for their comparatively conservative views, as from the inclusion of three members of the National Republican party—including its leader, Sánchez Román—that had declined to join the Popular Front.[107]

In his account of the government crisis, Martínez Barrio states that he invited Indalecio Prieto to join his cabinet, but that the executive committee of the Socialist party, controlled by the moderate wing, decided against participation, although it offered its "determined and loyal support."[208] This offer is inferentially confirmed by Julián Zugazagoitia, director at the time of *El Socialista*, organ of the executive committee, who states that when the director of another newspaper asked him what the attitude of his own paper would be toward the new government in view of the fact that Martínez Barrio would deny arms, as Casares Quiroga had done, he replied: "I shall confine myself to giving the news of the crisis and its solution. I do not think we should make any violent comment. We should do more harm than good. From now on, and as long as the war lasts, *El Socialista* will be an organ that adheres scrupulously to the government unless the party should decide otherwise."[209]

But the new government was ill-fated from the outset, for the control of events had already passed into the hands of men intent on a final reckoning between the left and right.

For nearly two days the plans of the insurgent army officers had been unfolding. Following their seizure of Spanish Morocco on Friday, 17 July, they had captured the Seville garrison on Saturday at 2 P.M. thanks to a daring coup by General Gonzalo Queipo de Llano. His coolheaded seizure of the Seville garrison from the republican commander, General José Fernández de la Villa Abrile, is described by his biographers and supporters, Antonio Olmedo Delgado and Lieutenant General José Cuesta Monereo.[210] Queipo de Llano was inspector-general of the *carabineros*, or carabineers, a corps composed of customs and excise officials and guards. Under the pretense of inspecting customs posts, he was able to travel thousands of miles in conspiratorial activities without arousing suspicion.[211] Because he had enthusiastically welcomed the advent of the Republic in 1931 and was related by marriage to the first president of the Republic, Alcalá-Zamora, he was distrusted by the conspirators. But the removal by the Popular Front of Alcalá-Zamora from the presidency, which Queipo deeply resented,[212] helped to remove this distrust. Nevertheless, as the conservative historian Ricardo de la Cierva points out, the rebel generals did not have much faith in Queipo's "decision-making ability," so he was sent to what "in the last analysis" was certain defeat in Seville, a defeat that was "transformed into one of the most unexpected and decisive successes of the Civil War" thanks to the "suicidal courage" of the general.[213] But despite his initial success, not until a week later, with the aid of Moorish troops and Foreign Legionaries from Spanish Morocco, was Queipo de Llano able to subdue the working-class suburbs of Seville.[214] To quell strikes, he resorted to the threat of extreme measures. According to his biographers, he signed a proclamation declaring that all the leaders of any labor union on strike would "immediately be shot" as well as "an equal number of members selected discretionally."[215]

Shortly after Queipo de Llano's capture of the Seville garrison on Saturday, 18 July, at 2 P.M., the rebels struck in other provincial capitals. They rose in Cadiz at 4 P.M., in Malaga at 5 P.M., in Cordova at 6 P.M., in Valladolid on Sunday, 19 July, at 12:30 A.M., and in Burgos at 2 A.M. In two of these provincial capitals, Burgos and Valladolid, not only the Civil Guard—the gendarmerie created by the Monarchy—but also the Assault Guard—the police force created by the Republic—had joined the rebellion.

In Burgos, according to the *Diario de Burgos* of 20 July, "the assault and civil guards adhered to the movement from the first moment."[216] In Valladolid, according to *El Norte de Castilla* of 19 July, published in that city, the assault and civil guards "joined the movement unanimously."[217] However, in Seville, Cadiz, and Malaga, likewise according to insurgent sources, the assault guards, with few exceptions, supported the Popular Front.[218] In Cordova, on the other hand, there was only slight opposition to the rising on the part of the assault guards.[219]

It should be noted that the Assault Guard, which was created by the Republic in 1931, maintained order in the cities, whereas the Civil Guard, a survival of the Monarchy, confined its law enforcement largely to the countryside. Before the creation of the Assault Guard there had been no effective force for maintaining order in the urban areas. Stanley Payne writes:

The minister of the interior in the provisional government [of the Republic], Miguel Maura, was one of the few responsible, farsighted leaders produced by the Republic. He realized that the problem of public order was fundamental to the future of the new regime. Urban violence had plagued the country intermittently for years, in part because of the absence of an effective police force. When such a disturbance became really alarming, the Army was usually called on to restore peace in the towns, while the Civil Guard kept order in the countryside. Neither institution was properly equipped or trained for urban police duties. . . . Untrained in effective methods of crowd dispersal, the guards often resorted to bloodshed, thus exciting more violence and resentment. To avoid recourse either to the Army or to the Civil Guard, Maura created a national republican police force, armed only with pistols and clubs; these "assault guards" were to be used for the suppression of demonstrations in the larger towns. As chief of the Assault Guards, the Director General of Security [Angel Galarza, the first attorney general of the Republic and Socialist minister of the interior in Largo Caballero's wartime government in 1936–37] selected Colonel Agustín Muñoz Grandes, who had won an impressive reputation as a leader and organizer for his work with the Regulares [Moorish troops in the service of the Spanish army]."[220]

Although created by the Republic, the assault guards, according to the moderate Socialist Zugazagoitia, comprised many individuals hostile to the new regime who had entered the corps when it was under the control of Muñoz Grandes.[221] These were obviously not removed after the victory of the Popular Front in the 1936 elections; for, according to the official (Franco) history of the military rebellion, *Historia de la cruzada*, adversaries of the republican regime abounded in the corps. "Lieutenant Colonel Agustín Muñoz Grandes," it continues, "who until the advent of the Popular Front had been commander of the corps, maintains contact with many of its officers, and is therefore aware of the excellent disposition of hundreds of guards to participate in a coup against the government."[222]

Even as Martínez Barrio was announcing to the press about 5 A.M. on Sunday, 19 July, the composition of his government,[223] events were moving faster than his words. In Saragossa, where assault guards had been carrying out arrests in trade-union and left-wing party headquarters shortly after midnight, the troops under General Miguel Cabanellas had just declared martial law, and, in Huesca, General Gregorio de Benito had also risen, seconded by a small garrison of assault and civil guards. In Barcelona, where General Manuel Goded would arrive later in the day from the Balearics to assume command, the insurgents were leaving their barracks to occupy strategic posts, and in the south a force of Moorish troops that would play a decisive role in securing Cadiz for the rebel cause was nearing that vital port. Moreover, General Franco, who, in return for his pledge to support the insurrection, had been promised, according to Stanley Payne, the command of the Moorish troops and Foreign Legionaries in Morocco, "that is, of all the militarily significant units in the Spanish Army"[225] —a command that was to prove an important step toward his as-

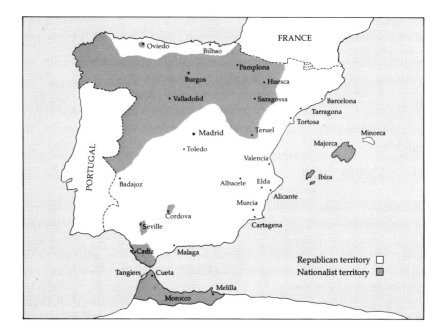

FRANCE

Oviedo
Bilbao
Pamplona
Burgos
Huesca
Valladolid
Saragossa
Barcelona
Tarragona
Tortosa
Teruel
Minorca
Madrid
Majorca
Toledo
Valencia
PORTUGAL
Ibiza
Badajoz
Albacete
Elda
Alicante
Murcia
Cordova
Cartagena
Seville
Cadiz
Malaga
Tangiers
Cueta
Melilla
Morocco

Republican territory ☐
Nationalist territory ▣

Division of Spain, 20 July 1936

sumption of supreme power on the Nationalist side two months later, when he was named generalissimo and head of state by the rebel hierarchy[226]—was flying to the protectorate from the Canary Islands to take command of the Moroccan forces and at 7 A.M. would reach his destination.

It is interesting to record that the de Havilland Dragon Rapide, piloted by Captain Cecil Bebb, that flew General Franco secretly from the Canaries to Spanish Morocco on 18–19 July, was chartered on 9 July in Croydon, England, by Luis Bolín, the London correspondent of the Madrid monarchist daily *ABC* at the request of its publisher, the Marques Juan Ignacio Luca de Tena.[227]

Before leaving the Canaries on his historic flight, General Franco declared martial law and issued the following proclamation:

Spaniards! To all those who feel the sacred love of Spain, . . . to all those who have sworn to defend it to the death against its enemies the Nation calls out for help. The situation in Spain is becoming more critical every day. Anarchy reigns in the majority of towns and villages. Officials appointed by the government preside over—if they do not actually foment—the social disorders. With revolvers and machine guns differences are settled between citizens who are cowardly and treacherously assassinated, while government authorities do nothing to impose peace and justice. Revolutionary strikes of all kinds paralyze the life of the Nation. . . . Can we cowardly and traitorously abandon Spain to the enemies of the Fatherland without resistance and without a fight? No! Traitors may do so, but we who have sworn to defend the Nation shall not! . . . We offer you justice and equality before the law; peace and love among Spaniards; liberty and fraternity free from libertinism and tyranny! . . . Viva España![228]

The liberal Republic of 1931 had now run its course and would soon be consumed by civil war, a war whose outcome for years to come could be only a dictatorship of the left or right. It was for this reason that President Azaña, fearing that Casares Quiroga could not withhold much longer the distribution of arms and that such distribution would signify the end of the democratic regime, had in a final throw appointed Martínez Barrio to form a new government to negotiate with the rebel leaders.

But if Martínez Barrio's cabinet was rejected by the right, it was also rejected by the left, which thought it purely a government of surrender. The moderate wing of the republican middle class "was confident that by breaking its ties with the working class it could reach an agreement with the rebel generals and with reaction," asseverates the official Communist history of the Civil War and Revolution. "The attitude of Martínez Barrio and those who supported him, in offering ministries to the insurgent generals and in refusing at the same time to arm the people so that they could defend the Republic, could not lead to an intermediate path between capitulation and resistance but to the surrender of the Republic by the republican leaders." And why, it asks, did Casares Quiroga and Martínez Barrio not give arms to the people? "The explanation lies in their class limitations. These republican leaders preferred to reach an understanding with the rebels rather than give arms to the people because they feared that this would result in an increase in the influence and role of the working class in the leadership of the country."[229]

In working-class circles alarm and indignation were extreme when the list of the new cabinet became known,[230] for not a little distrust was attached to some of the ministers' names.[231] *Claridad*, organ of the left Socialists, once said of Felipe Sánchez Román that, although a "republican of unquestionable sincerity," he was "one of the most reactionary figures discovered by the new [republican] regime,"[232] and of Antonio Lara, another member of the government, it said that he was a "low political trickster."[233] As for Martínez Barrio, the anarchosyndicalist *Solidaridad Obrera* stated a few months before the outbreak of the Civil War that he possessed intimate friends among the Andalusian landowners and that he had frequently been seen in the lobbies of the Cortes "conversing amicably with the fiercest enemies of the working class."[234] Some members of the middle-class Republican Left party were hostile, despite the presence of four of its leaders in the government. "In the headquarters of the Left Republicans," writes Marcelino Domingo, the president of the party, representing its right wing, and a minister in the new cabinet, "many colleagues of mine, on hearing of the formation of the government, destroyed their membership cards with shameful anger without stopping to consider that my participation at least should have been a reason for respect as well as a guarantee for them. Their understanding of duty and of the sacrifices that duty imposes was different from mine."[235] In the streets the atmosphere was explosive as members of the left-wing organizations voiced their opposition. "Large demonstrations are formed spontaneously," wrote an eyewitness. "They move toward the ministry of the interior and toward the ministry of war like an avalanche. The people shout, 'Traitors, cowards!' Impromptu speakers harangue the masses, 'They have sold us out! We must begin by shooting them first.' "[236]

Faced by this storm of popular indignation and disappointed in his hopes of a peaceful settlement with the insurgent leaders, Martínez Barrio decided to resign. "Only Prieto made a last attempt to dissuade me," he writes. "But it was a vain attempt, shattered by my attitude. Within a few minutes the political demonstration had brought about the ruin of my government. It was senseless to ask me to combat the military rebellion with mere shadows, stripped of authority, and ludicrously retaining the name of ministers."[237]

"Two Spains, ready to fight without quarter until total victory or defeat, now confront each other," writes a supporter of the military rebellion. "No other alternative is possible."[238]

2. The Revolution

Rebuffed by the left and by the right, the cabinet of Martínez Barrio passed into oblivion even before the names of its members appeared in the official *Gaceta de Madrid* on that febrile day of 19 July. All thought of compromise with the insurgent generals had to be abandoned. A new government was formed that decided that to combat the rebellion, it must accede to the demands of the working-class organizations for the distribution of arms. "When I took charge of the government of the Republic," testifies its premier, "I had to consider that the only way to combat the military rising was to hand to the people the few arms we had at our disposal."[1] Salvador Quemades, leader of the Left Republican party, attests: "Lacking the means of throttling the insurrection, the government had to yield the way to the political and trade-union organizations—the people—so that they could grapple with the rebel movement."[2] But it was a government in name only, swept along helplessly by the tide, a government that presided not over the preservation of the republican regime, but over its rapid dissolution under the double impact of military rebellion and social revolution.

Such was the government of liberal republicans formed by José Giral, confidant of Manuel Azaña, the president of the Republic. Its composition, as given in the official *Gaceta de Madrid* on 20 and 22 July, was as follows:

José Giral	Left Republican	Prime Minister
Augusto Barcia	Left Republican	Foreign Affairs
General Sebastián Pozas	Liberal Republican	Interior
General Luis Castelló	Liberal Republican	War
Plácido Alvarez Buylla	Republican Union	Industry and Commerce
Enrique Ramos y Ramos	Left Republican	Finance
Manuel Blasco Garzón	Republican Union	Justice
Bernardo Giner de los Rios	Republican Union	Communications and Merchant Marine

Mariano Ruiz Funes	Left Republican	Agriculture
Francisco Barnés	Left Republican	Education
Antonio Velao	Left Republican	Public Works
Juan Lluhí y Vallescá	Esquerra—Catalan Left Republican	Labor, Health, and Supplies

On 6 August, General Juan Hernández Sarabia, an Azañista, succeeded Luis Castelló in the ministry of war.[3] "What is admirable," President Azaña told José Giral a year later, "is the calm courage with which you took command when no one wanted to obey and when everyone, from the most important to the most obscure, was preparing to flee."[4]

In town after town and city after city the state shivered into fragments as rebellious garrisons joined the insurrectionary movement or met with defeat at the hands of armed workers and forces loyal to the government. Because the revolt collapsed in Madrid, Barcelona, Valencia, Malaga, and Bilbao, as well as in some of the smaller towns and cities, the insurgents initially captured only a third of the national territory.[5] Of the estimated 8,850 army chiefs and officers on active service—excluding Spanish Morocco, where practically the entire officer corps sided with the revolt—4,660 were located in the rebel camp on 20 July and the remainder in the left zone,[6] many of whom eventually escaped, as others had before them, into rebel territory. Although the number of regular army officers who served in the wartime Popular Army created by the left is given as two thousand by Enrique Líster, one of its Communist leaders,[7] Julio Alvarez del Vayo, its commissar general, affirms that "barely five hundred officers remained in the service of the Republic" and that "practically nothing was left of the old army that could be put to any use."[8] Inasmuch as the officer corps in general was distrusted if not execrated by the left and that officers were often pushed aside, imprisoned, or executed if their loyalty were in question, the lower figure may be closer to the mark. In fact, it is corroborated by the highly reliable republican army officer, Colonel Jesús Pérez Salas.[9] It is noteworthy that, contrary to common belief, far fewer generals on active service supported the rebellion than remained with the government. Cierva, historian and supporter of the military uprising, stated that of the eighteen divisional generals or their equivalent in Spain on 17 July, only four joined the rebellion: Cabanellas, Queipo de Llano, Franco, and Manuel Goded.[10] According to Palacio Atard, also a supporter of the military uprising, of the fifty-six brigadier generals on active service "fourteen rebelled and not less than twenty-nine remained on the side of the government."[11] Nevertheless, Madariaga, historian and independent republican, is no doubt correct when he asserts: "Of the officers who sided with the government, only a minority did so out of personal conviction. The majority would have joined their comrades had they been in a position to do so; they often tried and at times succeeded in crossing the line."[12]

The Civil Guard, the constabulary created by the Monarchy and preserved by the Republic as a rampart of the state, also crumbled.[13] Although, out of a total of 34,320 officers and men, 20,120 are estimated to have been located in the left camp on 20 July,[14] it is doubtful whether more than five to six thousand actually remained under the authority of the government, for while many discarded their uniforms and joined the proletarian militia, thousands of others deserted to the insurgents.[15] True, in November 1936, the corps numbered fifteen thousand officers and men in the left zone,[16] but this was after its reorganization as the National Republican Guard and the subsequent enlistment of thousands of new recruits.[17]

The secret police likewise dissolved, most of its agents siding with the insurrection.[18] Even the Assault Guard, the police corps created by the Republic in 1931 as a buttress for the new regime, comprising some twenty-five thousand officers and men,[19] was shattered as a result of widespread defections to the rebel cause[20] and of the assumption of police functions, in those places where the revolt had foundered, by vigilance committees and militia units improvised by the labor unions and the parties of the left.[21]

"The state collapsed and the Republic was left without an army, without a police force, and with its administrative machinery decimated by desertions and sabotage," writes Alvarez del Vayo, who became foreign minister a few weeks later.[22] "From the army leaders and the magistrates on the Supreme Tribunal down to the customs officials, we were obliged to replace the majority of the personnel who, until 18 July 1936, had been in charge of the machinery of the republican state. In the foreign ministry alone ninety per cent of the former diplomatic corps had deserted."[23] In the words of a Communist leader, "the whole state apparatus was destroyed and state power lay in the street,"[24] and the moderate Socialist, Zugazagoitia, wrote: "The power of state lay in the street, pulverized, and a fragment of it lay in the hands and at the disposal of every antifascist citizen, who used it in the manner that best suited his temperament."[25] Indeed, so complete was the collapse that, to quote a republican jurist, only "the dust of the state, the ashes of the state" remained.[26]

The control of ports and frontiers, a vital element of state power, formerly exercised by the *carabineros*, was undertaken by workmen's committees or by local bodies under the authority of the labor unions and left-wing parties. "The government could do absolutely nothing," recalled Juan Negrín when premier in a later cabinet, "because neither our frontiers nor our ports were in its hands. They were in the hands of individuals, of local, district, or provincial bodies, and naturally the government could not make its authority felt."[27] "The control of the frontier [at Ripoll]," reported a Communist daily, "is strictly maintained by workers and customs officials, who take their orders only from the working-class organizations."[28] "In the customs room at Port-Bou," wrote an eyewitness, "there is no sign of the revolution that agitated all of us in Paris. The customs officials are still in their old uniforms and they go about their tasks listlessly as though something has shorn them even of this power. A door opens into the passport room. Here is the explanation for everything. At various points in the room, members of the antifascist militia stand guard. They wear blue overalls over which an ammunition belt is thrown. They are armed to the teeth with pistols and rifles. Behind a long table sit three workers with pistols at their sides. They are examining passports and credentials."[29]

In the navy, according to its commissar general during the Civil War, 70 percent of the officers were killed by their men, and authority was exercised by sailors' committees.[30] "The group of officers that survived the acts of violence," wrote Zugazagoitia, "was dependent on committees elected by the sailors, who did exactly as they pleased."[31]

The functions of municipalities and other local governing bodies in the left camp were also assumed by committees in which the Socialist and anarchist-oriented labor unions were the ruling force.[32] "These organs of the Revolution," declared an anarchosyndicalist leader a few weeks after the outbreak of the Civil War, "have resulted in the disappearance of government delegates in all the provinces we control, because they had no option but to obey the decisions of the committees. . . . The local organs of administration of the old bourgeois regime have become mere skeletons, because their life force has been replaced by the revolutionary vitality of the workers' unions."[33] "The committees," ran an article in a left Socialist review, "were the germ of proletarian power. All revolutionary segments were represented in them. . . . In the villages they assumed control of political and economic life. In the towns . . . they took into their hands the direction of all activities."[34] "In the atmosphere charged with electricity and powder . . . that followed immediately on 19 July," wrote Rafael Tasis i Marca, director general of prisons in the region of Catalonia, "the municipalities [in the Catalan Provinces] became lifeless, colorless. . . . The rubber stamps of the committees replaced . . . the signatures of the mayors."[35] "There is not a single place," said an anarcho-syndicalist paper, with reference to the province of Tarragona, "where a local antifascist militia committee has not been set up. These committees control the entire life of the community."[36] "The center of gravity of the war and of politics," writes Antonio Ramos Oliveira, a Socialist historian, "was the street. Power was in the hands of the people, the parties, the committees."[37]

The courts of law were supplanted by revolutionary tribunals, which dispensed justice in their own way. "Everybody created his own justice and administered it himself," declared Juan García Oliver, a leading anarchist who became minister of justice in November 1936. "Some used to call this 'taking a person for a ride' [*paseo*] but I maintain that it was justice administered directly by the people in the complete absence of the regular judicial bodies."[38] In Madrid, according to Arturo Barea, a Socialist, each of the branches and groups of the trade unions and political parties set up "its own police, its own prison, its own executioners, and a special place for its executions."[39] Judges, magistrates, and district attorneys were relieved of office, some imprisoned and others executed,[40] while in many places judicial records were burned.[41]

In an attempt to curb the revolutionary terror, the government of José Giral set up "popular tribunals." These courts gave a semblance of constitutionality to the executions, but did little to bring the terror under control. In fact, Indalecio Prieto, the moderate Socialist, recounts that when in September 1936 the Popular Tribunal of Madrid—comprising three professional judges and fourteen jurors belonging to the principal parties and labor organizations of the left[42]—notified the government of its verdict to condemn to death the former Radical minister Rafael Salazar Alonso, the cabinet's decision to commute the sentence to life imprisonment could not be implemented. Prieto, a minister at the time, had cast the deciding vote in favor of commutation on the ground that Salazar Alonso's participation in the military rebellion had not been proved, but shortly afterward Mariano Gómez, the president of the tribunal, a former magistrate in Valencia and later president of the Supreme Court, told him that he was sure that the government's decision would cause a "terrible mutiny" within the Popular Tribunal and that the prisoner would be shot anyway. "The government," he added, "lacking adequate means to enforce its decisions, will not be able to save his life and . . . its authority will crumble. But this will not be the worst: The Popular Tribunal, I am very sure, will refuse to continue functioning and, after Salazar Alonso, all the political prisoners—perhaps this very evening—will be riddled with bullets." On being told that more than one hundred prisoners might be shot, Prieto reversed his decision and cast his vote in favor of the death penalty.[43]

Penitentiaries and jails were invaded, their records destroyed, their inmates liberated. "The jails were opened to release friendly political prisoners," writes a supporter of the Republic, "and the common-law criminals who came out with them acted on their own account."[44] There were, of course, singular episodes. "The judge of the Criminal Court," writes Madariaga, "suddenly found in his private apartment the thief and criminal whom he had recently sentenced to thirty years' hard labor transmogrified into a militiaman who, after demanding all the silver and gold objects of the household and tying them into a linen sheet, shot him dead in the presence of his wife and daughter."[45]

Hundreds of churches and convents were burned or put to secular uses.[46] "Catholic dens no longer exist," declared the anarchosyndicalist organ, *Solidaridad Obrera*. "The torches of the people have reduced them to ashes."[47] "The oppressed people," said an article in an anarchist youth journal, "put to the torch whatever dens of obscurantism and deception they found in their path. Churches, convents, centers of reaction, whatever smacked of incense and darkness, have been set ablaze."[48] "For the Revolution to be a fact," ran an anarchist youth manifesto, "we must demolish the three pillars of reaction: the church, the army, and capitalism. The church has already been brought to account. The temples have been destroyed by fire and the ecclesiastical crows who were unable to escape have been taken care of by the people."[49] In the province of Tarragona, reported *Solidaridad Obrera*, "the churches in all the villages have been set ablaze. Only those buildings that could be used for the benefit of the people have been kept, but not those that were a serious danger after burning. Many churches have been converted into communal warehouses as well as into garages for the antifascist militia."[50] And so it was in countless towns and villages. Nevertheless, the Reverent Hewlett Johnson, known as the "Red" dean of Canterbury, asserted, when interviewed by me in the spring of 1937 in Valencia, that "not a single church" had been destroyed or desecrated. On the other hand, the "Collective Letter of the Spanish Bishops," dated 1 July 1937, claimed that the number of churches and chapels "destroyed or completely sacked" was as high as twenty thousand.[51]

Thousands of members of the clergy and religious orders as well as of the propertied classes were killed,[52] but others, fearing arrest or execution, fled abroad, including many prominent liberal and moderate republicans. In a conversation in June 1937 with the republican jurist Angel Ossorio y Gallardo regarding the large number of "outstanding and even eminent republicans" who had left Spain, President Azaña complained: "All of them left without my consent and without my advice. And some (I gave him their names) deceived me. Those who wanted to stay, here they are, and nothing has happened to them! Of the ministers who formed my government in February [1936] do you know how many remained in Spain? Two: Casares and Giral. If anyone at all was in danger, it was Casares. He is in Madrid. Of the 'political' ambassadors I appointed, only one, on leaving his post, came to Valencia to greet [me] and to offer his services to the government: Díez-Canedo. The others remained in France. . . . I raised many of them from nothing. I saved all of them from the wreck of 1933 and made them deputies, ministers, ambassadors, undersecretaries, etcetera, etcetera. They all had a duty to serve the Republic to the very end and to remain with me as long as I was in office. Two or three of them understood this, belatedly, and have returned."[54]

Thousands of persons fearing detention or summary execution took refuge in embassies and legations in Madrid. The number of such refugees has been variously estimated. Norman J. Padelford says that it was calculated to be in excess of five thousand.[55] Aurelio Nuñez Morgada, Chilean ambassador and dean of the diplomatic corps in Madrid, affirms that it exceeded fifteen thousand,[56] while Alvarez del Vayo, who as foreign minister conducted the negotiations for the evacuation of the refugees, gives it as twenty thousand.[57] The last figure is more likely considering that the Norwegian legation alone, which was among the least important of the missions extending asylum to political refugees, housed nine hundred, according to Felix Schlayer, the Norwegian chargé d'affaires.[58]

"We have confirmed something we only knew in theory," wrote a leading anarchist in the welter of these events, "namely, that the Revolution, in which uncontrolled and uncontrollable forces operate imperiously, is blind and destructive, grandiose, and cruel; that once the first step has been taken and the first dike broken, the people pour like a torrent through the breach, and that it is impossible to dam the flood. How much is wrecked in the heat of the struggle and in the blind fury of the storm! Men are as we have always known them, neither better nor worse. . . . They reveal their vices and their virtues, and while from the hearts of rogues there springs a latent honesty, from the depths of honest men there emerges a brutish appetite—a thirst for extermination, a desire for blood—that seemed inconceivable before."[59]

"We do not wish to deny," avowed a prominent anarchist in the region of Catalonia, "that the nineteenth of July brought with it an overflowing of passions and abuses, a natural phenomenon of the transfer of power from the hands of the privileged to the hands of the people. It is possible that our victory resulted in the death by violence of four or five thousand inhabitants of Catalonia who were listed as rightists and were linked to political or ecclesiastical reaction. But this shedding of blood is the inevitable consequence of a revolution, which, in spite of all barriers, sweeps on like a flood and devastates everything in its path, until it gradually loses its momentum."[60]

And a Basque Nationalist, a republican and Catholic, writes:

Blood, a great deal of innocent blood was shed on both sides. . . . But the most radical difference as far as the republican zone was concerned—which does not justify, but at least explains, the excesses—lies in the very fact of the [military] insurrection. The army, almost the entire secret police, the administration of justice, whatever police forces there were, whose duty it was to maintain order, revolted, leaving the legal government defenseless. The latter was compelled to arm the people, the jails were opened to release friendly political prisoners, and the common-law criminals who came out with them acted on their own account. Furthermore, with the stirring up of the lower depths of society the malefactors that exist in every city, in every nation, came to the surface, and found an easy field for their work. In normal times, the police would have kept them under control, but the very insurrection deprived the government of coercive forces and helped the criminals to secure arms. Is it surprising that during the first few days of the revolt these uncontrolled elements did as they pleased? At the same time the extreme left-wing organizations dispensed justice in a rude and elementary fashion, the justice of men who had suffered and had been molded in an atmosphere of hatred. All this does not justify the crimes committed in the republican zone, but it readily explains them.

What cannot be explained, and even less justified, are the crimes, much greater in number and in sadism, that were committed precisely by that army, by that police force, by those educated young gentlemen who lacked for nothing and who boasted of their Catholicism."[61]

"The Revolution," wrote President Azaña sometime later, "commenced under a republican government that neither wished to support it nor could support it. The excesses began to unfold themselves before the astonished eyes of the ministers. Faced by the Revolution, the government had the choice either of upholding it or suppressing it. But even less than uphold it could the government suppress it. It is doubtful whether it had forces enough for this. I am sure it did not. Even so, their use would have kindled another civil war."[62]

Shorn of the repressive organs of the state, the liberal government of José Giral possessed nominal power, but not power itself,[63] for this was split into countless fragments and scattered in a thousand towns and villages among the revolutionary committees that had instituted control over post and telegraph offices,[64] radio stations,[65] and telephone exchanges,[66] organized police squads and tribunals, highway and frontier patrols, transport and supply services, and created militia units for the battlefronts. In short, nowhere in Spain did the cabinet of José Giral exercise any real authority, as prominent adherents of the anti-Franco camp have amply testified.[67]

In spite of the massive and irrefragable evidence that a far-reaching social revolution shattered the republican regime in July 1936, Herbert M. Matthews, *New York Times* correspondent in the left camp during the Civil War and recognized authority on Spain for four decades, made light of these revolutionary changes in his last book on the Civil War published in 1973. After quoting the liberal historian Gabriel Jackson as saying that the "most profound social revolution since the fifteenth century took place in much of the territory remaining in the hands of the Popular Front," he comments: "In more or less strong terms, nearly every historian of the Spanish Civil War makes the same point. I would say that there was a revolution of sorts, but it should not be exaggerated. In one basic sense, there was no revolution at all, since the republican government functioned much as it did before the war."[68]

Proof of the extent and depth of the Revolution is not lacking, even from Communist sources, despite the fact that the Communist International, following the directives of the Kremlin, tried for diplomatic reasons, as will be seen in a subsequent chapter, to screen from the outside world the far-reaching social revolution that had swept the country. "Are the big industrialists who rose against the people still owners of the plants?" asked Jose Díaz, general secretary of the Communist party. "No, they have disappeared and the plants . . . are in the hands of the workers, controlled by the unions."[69] "Today," declared Antonio Sesé, secretary of the Communist-controlled Catalan section of the UGT, "the workers have the plants, the workers have the banks, the workers have the land, and the workers have the arms."[70] Mikhail Koltzov, leading Soviet journalist and Stalin's personal agent in Spain, stated quite early in the war that, according to a rough estimate, approximately eighteen thousand industrial and commercial enterprises were taken over by the workers' unions and by the state, twenty-five hundred of them located in Madrid and three thousand in Barcelona.[71]

Landed properties were seized, some were collectivized, others divided among the peasants, and notarial archives as well as registers of property were burned in countless towns and villages, although the destruction of property records was not acknowledged in the official journal until more than a year later.[72] "In none of the provinces" of the anti-Franco camp, affirmed José Díaz the Communist leader, "do big landowners exist."[73]

Hundreds of seizures made by the agricultural workers' unions affiliated with the UGT and CNT were subsequently registered with the Institute of Agrarian Reform, an agency of the ministry of agriculture, which issued frequent reports listing confiscated properties. The wording of these reports might indicate that the estates had been sequestered by the institute and then turned over to the agricultural workers' unions, but the fact is that, with very few exceptions, the institute merely recorded the expropriations. "I can affirm," writes Rafael Morayta Núñez, secretary general of the institute during the first months of the Revolution, "and this everyone knows, that it was not the government that handed the land to the peasants. The latter did not wait for a government decision, but appropriated the estates and cultivable lands themselves."[74] In the province of Ciudad Real, for example, according to an acute observer, "an overwhelming majority of all the larger estates have been expropriated and collectivized by their hands, and the business of the [Institute of Agrarian Reform] in the whole matter has only been to give a legal *placet.*"[75] The unions saw an advantage in registering their confiscations with the institute, for this tended to legalize their action and rendered the sequestered estates eligible for technical and economic assistance from that agency.[76]

Railways, streetcars and buses, taxicabs and shipping, electric light and power companies, gasworks and waterworks, engineering and automobile assembly plants, mines and cement works, textile mills and paper factories, electrical and chemical concerns, glass bottle factories and perfumeries, food-processing plants and breweries, as well as a host of other enterprises, were confiscated or controlled by workmen's committees, either term possessing for the owners almost equal significance in practice. For example, in the region of Catalonia the telephone system belonging to the Compañía Telefónica Nacional de España, a subsidiary of the International Telephone and Telegraph Corporation, was placed under the control of a joint CNT-UGT committee, with the consequence—according to the testimony of the anarchosyndicalists, who were the dominant influence on that body—that the management was left with practically no other function but to keep an account of income and expenses and was powerless to withdraw funds without the committee's consent.[77] Another example is that of the hydroelectric enterprise, Riegos y Fuerzas del Ebro, a subsidiary of the Barcelona Traction, Light, and Power Company, which was also controlled by a joint CNT-UGT committee. This committee took charge of the company's installations, bank accounts, and other assets with the result that the management, according to an official report, was unable to "exercise effective control over its business and its finances."[78]

Motion-picture theaters and legitimate theaters, newspapers and printing shops, department stores and hotels, deluxe restaurants and bars were likewise sequestered or controlled, as were the headquarters of business and professional associations and thousands of dwellings owned by the upper classes (see Appendix I).

But the economic changes in town and country, as will be seen in the ensuing chapters, were not confined to the property of the wealthy strata of society. With the collapse of the state, all barriers had fallen away, and it was too enticing a moment for the revolutionary masses not to attempt to remold the entire economy to their heart's desire.

"In the early days of radiant optimism," wrote Manuel Azaña after the conflict had ended, "the minds of nearly all Spaniards were fired by a messianic goal. If, in the Nationalist camp, it was Christian civilization in the West they were saving, in the Republican camp the prophets proclaimed the birth of a new civilization. Terrible hyperboles that easily inflame what is visionary in the Spanish soul!"[79]

3. The Revolution Hits the Small Bourgeoisie

To the dismay of thousands of handicraftsmen, small manufacturers, and tradesmen, their premises and their equipment were expropriated by the labor unions of the anarchosyndicalist CNT and often by the somewhat less radical unions of the Socialist UGT.[1]

In Madrid, for instance, the unions not only took over the premises and equipment of shoemakers, cabinetmakers, and other small-scale producers, but collectivized all the beauty parlors and barber shops, establishing the same wages for the former owners as for their employees.[2] In Valencia, a city of over 350,000 inhabitants, nearly all plants, both large and small, were sequestered by the CNT and UGT,[3] while in the region of Catalonia, where the anarchosyndicalists were in almost unchecked ascendancy during the first months of tbe Revolution,[4] collectivization in many towns was carried out so thoroughly that it embraced not only the large factories but the least important branches of handicraft.[5] The collectivization movement also infringed upon another preserve of the middle classes. In Barcelona, the capital of Catalonia, with a population of nearly 1.2 million, the anarchosyndicalist workers collectivized the wholesale business in eggs and fish[6] and set up a control committee in the slaughterhouse, from which they excluded all intermediaries;[7] they also collectivized the principal market for fruit and vegetables and suppressed all dealers and commission agents as such, permitting them, however, to join the collective as wage earners.[8] The milk trade in Barcelona was likewise collectivized. The anarchosyndicalists eliminated as unhygienic over forty pasteurizing plants, pasteurized all the milk in the remaining nine, and proceeded to displace all dealers by establishing their own retail outlets.[9] Many of the retailers entered the collective, but some refused to do so: "They asked for a much higher wage than that paid to the workers . . . , claiming that they could not manage on the one allotted to them."[10] In Granollers, one of the principal market towns of Catalonia and a hive of middlemen before the war, all intermediaries were suppressed or crowded out of the channels of trade, the peasants having no alternative but to dispose of their produce through local supply committees set up by the CNT.[11] The same pattern occurred in countless other localities all over the left camp.[12] In the region of Valencia, the center of the great orange industry, to take yet another example of the invasion by the unions of the field of private trade, the CNT set up an organization for purchasing, packing, and exporting the orange crop, with a network of 270 committees in different towns and villages, elbowing out of this important trade several thousand middlemen.[13] In short, the labor unions impinged upon the interests of the middle classes in almost every field. Retailers and wholesalers, hotel, café, and bar owners, opticians and doctors, barbers and bakers, shoemakers and cabinetmakers, dressmakers and tailors, brickmakers and building contractors, to cite but a few examples, were caught up relentlessly by the collectivization movement in numberless towns and villages.[14]

If some members of the middle classes accommodated themselves to their new situation as workers instead of employers in their former businesses, in the mute hope that the revolutionary fever would quickly burn itself out and that their property would be restored, they were soon to be disappointed; for, after the first few weeks of widespread and uncoordinated seizures, some of the unions began a systematic reorganization of entire trades, closing down hundreds of small plants and concentrating production in those with the best equipment. "Those small employers of labor who are a little enlightened," declared *Solidaridad Obrera*, the principal anarchosyndicalist organ in Spain, "will easily understand that the system of producing goods in small plants is not efficient. Divided effort holds back production. Operating a tiny workshop with handicraft methods is not the same as operating a large plant that utilizes all the advances of technology. If our aim is to do away with the contingencies and insecurities of the capitalist regime, then we must direct production in a way that ensures the well-being of society."[15] In accordance with this outlook, the CNT workers, sweeping along with them those of the UGT, closed down more than seventy foundries in the region of Catalonia and concentrated their equipment and personnel in twenty-four.[16] "In these," a spokesman for the socialized industry declared, "we rectified the defects [in the foundries] of those small employers who did not concern themselves with technical matters, and whose plants were centers of tuberculosis."[17] In Barcelona, the CNT wood-workers' union—which had already set up control committees in every shop and factory and used the former employers as technical managers at the standard wage for workers[18]—reorganized the entire industry by closing down hundreds of small workshops and concentrating production in the largest plants.[19] In the same city the CNT carried out equally radical changes in the tanning trade, reducing seventy-one plants to forty,[20] while in the glass industry, one hundred plants and warehouses were cut down to thirty.[21] Still more drastic was the CNT's reorganization of the barber shops and beauty parlors in Barcelona; 905 were closed, and their personnel and equipment were concentrated in 212 of the largest establishments, the dispossessed owners being given the same rights and duties as their former employees.[22] A similar reorganization, or socialization, as it was called, was effected in the dressmaking, tailoring, metal, and leather goods trades in Valencia,[23] in the shoemaking industry of Sitges,[24] the metal and textile industries of Alcoy,[25] the lumber trade of Cuenca,[26] the brickmaking industry of Granollers,[27] the tanning trade of Vich,[28] the baking industry of Barcelona,[29] and the cabinetmakers' trade of Madrid,[30] and of Carcagente,[31] to give only a few examples. "In all the towns and villages of Catalonia, Aragon, the Levante, and Castile," wrote one observer who had traveled widely in these regions, "the small plants where work was carried on badly under uneconomic and unhygienic conditions were closed down as rapidly as possible. The machinery was gathered together in several workshops, sometimes in a single workshop. In this way, the regulation of production was simplified and coordination of effort was more effective."[32]

It is no wonder then that in the first shock of these revolutionary events the small-scale producers and businessmen looked on themselves as ruined; for even when the anarchosyndicalists respected the small man's property, some among them made it clear that this was only a temporary indulgence while the war lasted. "Once this war has ended and the battle against fascism has been won," warned a prominent anarchosyndicalist in Valencia, "we shall suppress every form of small property and in the way it suits us. We shall intensify collectivization and socialization, and make them complete."[33] To be sure, the anarchosyndicalists claimed that the "accommodating and intelligent behavior of the workers captured the sympathy of many small businessmen and manufacturers who had no objection whatever to socializing their businesses and becoming workers with the same rights and duties as the others,"[34] but only in the most exceptional cases did members of the small bourgeoisie welcome the revolutionary changes,[35] and the goodwill they showed could not afford a real index of what they felt in their hearts. The working class was armed; it was virtual master of the situation, and the small bourgeoisie had no course but to defer to the power of events.

Nevertheless, the more radical workers did not rely entirely upon force or the threat of force to achieve their ends. Sometimes they tried persuasion: "You small shopkeepers who know nothing of social questions, " ran an appeal issued by the Food Section of the Shop Assistants' Union of Barcelona, "are about to be absorbed by developments that will completely transform the present social structure into one more just and more noble, in which the exploitation of man by man will be a thing of the past.

"The groveling existence you have led until now, devoted exclusively to a business at which you work twelve to fourteen hours a day in order to sell four wretched cabbages, two kilos of rice, and three liters of oil, must end. . . . This food section calls upon you to educate yourselves every day with the help of our union, located on the mezzanine of 12, Plaza de Maciá, where, as a result of continual contact with our comrades, you will succeed in freeing yourselves socially and morally from the prejudices that have dominated you until today."[36]

But the middle classes had not schemed and saved for years and struggled to survive the competition of the larger concerns to see their hopes of independence ruined in a day. If they had expected anything from the Revolution, it was freedom from competition and a greater share of the social wealth, not expropriation and a worker's wage. Even before the collectivization movement had struck them with its full force, a profound disquietude had diffused itself among them, and the anarchosyndicalists had tried in vain to allay their fears by painting the future in attractive colors. In the second month of the Revolution *Solidaridad Obrera* said:

News that the small bourgeoisie is deeply alarmed has reached our ears. We were under the impression that the anxiety of the first few days had evaporated, but the uneasiness of the shopkeeper, the businessman, the small manufacturer, the artisan, and small peasant holder persists. They lack confidence in the leadership of the proletariat. . . .

The small bourgeoisie will lose nothing by the disappearance of capitalism. It must not doubt that it will profit many times over. For example, take the daily anxiety of the majority of the shopkeepers and small manufacturers over the payment of bills, rents, and taxes. . . .

When private property and freedom to trade in other people's goods have disappeared, we shall have saved from a nightmare many shopkeepers who live under the constant threat of eviction and distraint. . . .

The Spanish Revolution

The small bourgeoisie must not worry. It must draw closer to the proletariat. It can be quite sure that when private property and trade have been abolished a new mode of life will be introduced, a mode of life that will in no way injure those who may feel themselves affected by these social changes.

The small bourgeoisie should throw off its fears; for once fascism has been crushed, it can look to the future with greater optimism. However, it must identify itself with the proletariat.[37]

4. The Revolution in the Countryside

Just as the artisans, small manufacturers, and small businessmen were exercised by the collectivization movement, so, too, were the peasant owners, tenant farmers, and sharecroppers. While rural collectivization was applied almost without exception to the large estates on which landless peasants had worked as day laborers before the Revolution —a form of cultivation they spontaneously adopted—thousands of small and medium farmers were caught in the sweep of the collectivization movement in the first weeks of the Revolution. Even those who were not immediately affected apprehended in its rapid growth a mortal danger to themselves (see Appendix II); for not only did the collective system of agriculture threaten to drain the rural labor market of wage workers and to create ruinous competition in the production and sale of farm produce, but it also presented a standing threat to the holders who, having appropriated the land, felt that the Revolution had accomplished its mission.

"It is impossible to determine exactly how much land was seized by working-class organizations in Republican Spain," writes Edward E. Malefakis, "because of the shifting lines of battle and because the seizures only gradually found their way into governmental statistics as they were retroactively legalized by the IRA [Institute of Agrarian Reform]. . . . In trying to reconcile the evidence available, I have come to the conclusion that approximately one-third of all lands and (since collectivization occurred mainly on arable land) between half and two-thirds of all cultivated land in Republican Spain were seized. By a cruel irony, the victims were predominately small and medium holders, since most of the latifundio districts had fallen to the Nationalists almost immediately after the outbreak of hostilities and consequently were not included in the IRA reports."[1]

If the individual farmer viewed with dismay the swift and widespread collectivization of agriculture, the farm workers of the anarcho-syndicalist CNT and the Socialist UGT saw it as the commencement of a new era. The anarchosyndicalists, who were the classic revolutionaries of Spain and the main promoters of rural collectivization, regarded it as an essential feature of the Revolution. It was one of their prime objectives and held their minds with a powerful fascination. They believed not merely that it would result in an improvement in the standard of living of the peasant by the introduction of scientific agronomy and mechanical equipment,[2] not merely that it would protect him from the hazards of nature and from the abuses of intermediaries and usurers, but that it would uplift him morally. "Those peasants who are endowed with an understanding of the advantages of collectivization or with a clear revolutionary conscience and who have already begun to introduce [collective farming] should endeavor by all convincing means to prod the laggards," said *Tierra y Libertad*, the mouthpiece of the FAI, the organization, as has already been noted, that exercised a directing influence over the unions of the CNT. "We cannot consent to small holdings . . . because private property in land always creates a bourgeois mentality, calculating and egotistical, that we wish to uproot forever. We want to reconstruct Spain materially and morally. Our revolution will be both economic and ethical."[3]

Collective labor, said another publication of the FAI, banishes hate, envy, and egoism and opens the way for "mutual respect and solidarity because all those who live collectively treat one another as members of a large family."[4]

Collectivization was also a means of uplifting the peasant intellectually. "The greatest disadvantage of individual farming, which occupies all able-bodied members of the family: the father, the mother, the children," Diego Abad de Santillán, a leader of the CNT and FAI, contended, "is the excessive amount of labor. . . . There are no fixed hours of work, and the expenditure of physical energy is unlimited. . . . [The] peasant should not sacrifice himself or his children to the point of exaggeration. It is essential that he should have the time and energy to educate himself and his family, so that the light of civilization can illuminate life in the countryside.

"Work on collective farms is easier and enables members to read newspapers, magazines, and books, to cultivate their minds and open them to every progressive development."[5]

Similar views were held by the Socialist UGT,[6] but a still more powerful reason for CNT and UGT advocacy of collective farming and opposition to the breakup of the large estates lay in their fear that the small landowning peasant might one day become an obstacle and

even a threat to the future development of the Revolution. "Collectivization," said a local secretary of the powerful National Federation of
Land Workers, affiliated with the UGT, "is the only means of making
headway. We must not even think of parcelation at this stage. The soil
is not everywhere the same and some harvests . . . are better than
others. If we were to divide up the land we should relapse into that old
state of affairs when some hard-working peasants had no food while
the lucky ones lived well, and once again we should have masters
and servants."[7] "On no account," declared the executive committee
of the federation, "shall we allow the land, equipment, and livestock
to be divided up, because it is our intention to apply collectivization
to all expropriated estates so that labor and the produce thereof are
shared equally among the peasant families."[8]

"We anarchosyndicalists," declared the organ of the youth movement of the CNT and FAI, "believed from the very beginning that
individual farming would lead directly to large properties, to the
domination of political bosses, to the exploitation of man by man, and
finally to the reestablishment of the capitalist system.

"The CNT did not want this to happen and consequently fomented
industrial and agricultural collectives."[9]

This fear that a new class of wealthy landed proprietors would
eventually rise on the ruins of the old if individual tillage were encouraged was no doubt partly responsible for the determination of
the more zealous collectivizers to secure the adherence of the small
cultivator, whether willing or forced, to the collective system. It is, of
course, true that the official policy of the CNT, as well as that of the
less radical UGT, was, within certain limits, one of respect for the
property of the small republican farmer.[10] "I consider that voluntary
membership should be the fundamental basis of any collective farm,"
said left-wing Socialist leader Ricardo Zabalza, general secretary of
the National Federation of Land Workers. "I prefer a small, enthusiastic collective, formed by a group of active and honest workers, to
a large collective set up by force and composed of peasants without
enthusiasm, who would sabotage it until it failed. Voluntary collectivization may seem the longer course, but the example of the small,
well-managed collective will attract the entire peasantry, who are profoundly realistic and practical, whereas forced collectivization would
end by discrediting socialized agriculture."[11] However, although neither the UGT nor the CNT permitted the small republican farmer to
hold more land than he could cultivate without the aid of hired labor,[12]
and in many instances he was unable to dispose freely of his surplus

crops because he was compelled to deliver them to the local committee on the latter's terms,[13] he was often driven under various forms of pressure, as will be shown later in this chapter, to attach himself to the collective system. This was true particularly in villages where the anarchosyndicalists were in the ascendant. Whereas the Socialist-led National Federation of Land Workers included in its ranks an appreciable number of smallholders and tenant farmers, who had little or no propensity for rural socialization and who had joined the organization because of the protection it had afforded them against *caciques*, landlords, usurers, and middlemen.[14] The anarchosyndicalist peasant unions were composed, at the outbreak of the war, almost entirely of laborers and indigent farmers who had been fired by the philosophy of anarchism. For these zealots, rural collectivization was the foundation stone of the new regime of anarchist, or libertarian communism, as it was called, that they had looked forward to establishing on the morrow of the Revolution. Libertarian communism would be a regime "of human brotherhood that would attempt to solve economic problems without the state and without politics in accordance with the well-known principle, 'from each according to his abilities, to each according to his needs,'"[15] a regime without classes, based on labor unions and self-governing communes, that would be united into a nationwide confederation, and in which the means of production and distribution would be held in common.[16]

"Libertarian communism," wrote Isaac Puente, a prominent anarchist, "is the organization of society without the state and without private property. For that reason it is not necessary to invent anything or create any new form of organization. The nuclei around which our future economic life will revolve are already present in our society: the labor union and the free commune—the labor union, in which the workers of the factories and collectives gather together spontaneously, and the free commune, an assembly with an ancient tradition, in which the people in the villages and hamlets also gather together spontaneously and which offers a solution to all the community problems in the rural areas.

"These two bodies, obeying democratic and federative principles, will make sovereign decisions and will not be controlled by any higher body. Their only obligation will be to unite into industrial federations that will take collective possession of all private property and will regulate production and consumption in each locality."[17]

Although the majority of CNT-FAI members regarded libertarian communism as the final goal of their movement, there were a few "individualist" anarchists who, while opposed to the employment of hired labor, held that an anarchist society should not be limited to one particular system of production. "Anarchism," wrote one of the foremost Spanish libertarians, "must be made up of an infinite variety of systems and of individuals free from all fetters. It must be like an experimental field . . . for all types of human temperament."[18]

Although no hard and fast rules were observed in establishing libertarian communism, the procedure was more or less the same everywhere. A CNT-FAI committee was set up in each locality where the new regime was instituted. This committee not only exercised legislative and executive powers, but also administered justice. One of its first acts was to abolish private trade and to collectivize the soil of the rich, and often that of the poor, as well as farm buildings, machinery, livestock, and transport. Except in rare cases, barbers, bakers, carpenters, sandalmakers, doctors, dentists, teachers, blacksmiths, and tailors also came under the collective system. Stocks of food and clothing and other necessities were concentrated in a communal depot under the control of the local committee, and the church, if not rendered useless by fire, was converted into a storehouse, dining hall, café, workshop, school, garage, or barracks (see Appendix III). In many communities money for internal use was abolished because the anarchists believed that "money and power are diabolical philters that turn a man into a wolf, into a rabid enemy, instead of into a brother."[19] "Here in Fraga [a small town in Aragon], you can throw bank notes into the street," ran an article in a libertarian paper, "and no one will take any notice. Rockefeller, if you were to come to Fraga with your entire bank account you would not be able to buy a cup of coffee. Money, your God and your servant, has been abolished here, and the people are happy."[20] In libertarian communities where money was suppressed, wages were paid in coupons, the scale being determined by the size of the family. "The characteristic of the majority of CNT collectives," wrote a foreign observer, "is the family wage. Wages are paid according to the needs of the members and not according to the labor performed by each worker."[21] Locally produced goods such as bread, wine, and olive oil, were distributed freely if abundant, while other articles could be obtained with coupons at the communal depot. Surplus goods were exchanged with other anarchist towns and villages; money was used only for transactions with communities that had not adopted the new system.

The Spanish Revolution

Although a complete picture of life in all the libertarian towns and villages cannot be given here, a good impression can be gleaned from the following descriptions:

In Alcora, according to an eyewitness, money was no longer in circulation. Everybody can get what he needs. From whom? From the committee, of course. However, it is impossible to provision five thousand persons through a single center of distribution. Hence, there are stores where, as before, one can satisfy one's requirements, but these are mere centers of distribution. They belong to the entire village, and their former owners no longer make a profit. Payment is made not with money but with coupons. Even the barber shaves in exchange for coupons, which are issued by the committee. The principle whereby each inhabitant shall receive goods according to his needs is only imperfectly realized, for it is postulated that everyone has the same needs. . . .

Every family and every person living alone has received a card. This is punched daily at the place of work; hence no one can avoid working, [for] on the basis of these cards coupons are distributed. But the great flaw in the system is that owing to the lack of any other measure of value, it has once again been necessary to have recourse to money in order to put a value on the labor performed. Everyone—the worker, the businessman, the doctor—receives coupons to the value of five pesetas for each working day. One part of the coupon bears the inscription "bread," of which every coupon will purchase a kilo; another part represents a certain sum of money. However, these coupons cannot be regarded as bank bills, as they can be exchanged only for consumer goods, and this in a limited degree. Even if the amount of these coupons were larger, it would not be possible to acquire means of production and become a capitalist, were it only on the most modest scale, for they can be used solely for the purchase of consumer goods. All the means of production belong to the community.

The community is represented by the committee. . . . All the money of Alcora, about 100,000 pesetas, is in its hands. The committee exchanges the products of the community for other goods that are lacking, but what it cannot secure by exchange it purchases. Money, however, is retained only as a makeshift and will be valid as long as other communities have not followed Alcora's example.

The committee is the paterfamilias. It owns everything; it directs everything; it attends to everything. Every special desire must be submitted to it for consideration; it alone has the final say.

One may object that the members of the committee are in danger of becoming bureaucrats or even dictators. That possibility has not escaped the attention of the villagers. They have seen to it that the committee shall be renewed at short intervals so that each inhabitant will serve on it for a certain length of time.

All this has something touching in its naïveté. It would be a mistake to criticize it too harshly and to see in it more than an attempt on the part of the peasants to establish libertarian communism. Above all, one should not forget that the agricultural laborers and even the small tradesmen of such a community have had until now an extremely low standard of living. . . . Before the Revolution a piece of meat was a luxury, and only a few intellectuals have needs that go beyond the bare necessities of life.[22]

In a conversation with some of the peasants of Alcora, this acute observer goes on to furnish what may be regarded as a typical example of the minute control exercised by the committee of each libertarian village over the lives of its inhabitants:

"What happens if someone wants to go to town, for example?"
"That's very simple. He goes to the committee and exchanges his coupons for money."
"So he can exchange as many coupons as he likes?"
"No, of course not."
These good fellows are rather surprised at my difficulty in understanding.
"When is he entitled to money, then?"
"As often as he needs it. He only has to ask the committee."
"So the committee examines the reasons?"
"Of course."
I am somewhat alarmed. This regulation, it seems to me, must allow very little freedom under libertarian communism, and I try to find out on what grounds the committee of Alcora permits traveling. . . .
"If someone has a girl outside the village, can he get money to pay her a visit?"
The peasants assure me that he can.
"As often as he likes?"
"Good heavens, he can go every night from Alcora to see his girl if he wants to."
"But if someone wants to go into town to see a movie, can he also get money?"
"Yes."
"As often as he likes?"
The peasants begin to doubt my common sense.
"On holidays, of course, but there is no money for vice."[23]

Of the libertarian village of Castro, another eyewitness writes:

The salient point of the anarchist regime in Castro is the abolition of money. Exchange is suppressed; production has changed very little. . . . The committee took over the estates, and runs them. They have not even been merged, but are worked separately, each by the hands previously employed on its lands. Money wages, of course, have been abolished. It would be incorrect to say that they have been replaced by pay in kind. There is no pay whatever; the inhabitants are fed directly from the village stores.

Under this system, the provisioning of the village is of the poorest kind; poorer, I would venture to say, than it can possibly have been before, even in the wretched conditions in which the Andalusian *braceros* [farm laborers] are wont to live. The pueblo is fortunate in growing wheat, and not only olives, as many other pueblos of its kind; so there is at any rate bread. Moreover, the village owns large herds of sheep, expropriated with the estates, so there is some meat. And they still have a store of cigarettes. That's all. I tried in vain to get a drink, either of coffee or wine or lemonade. The village bar had been closed as nefarious commerce. I had a look at the stores. They were so low as to foretell approaching starvation. But the inhabitants seemed to be proud of this state of things. They were pleased, they told us, that coffee drinking had come to an end; they seemed to regard this abolition of useless things as a moral improvement. What few commodities they needed from outside, mainly clothes, they hoped to get by direct exchange of their surplus in olives. . . . Their hatred of the upper class was far less economic than moral. They did not want the good living of those they had expropriated, but to get rid of their luxuries, which to them seemed to be so many vices. Their conception of the new order which was to be brought about was thoroughly ascetic.[24]

Puritanism was a characteristic of the libertarian movement. Drinking and smoking were nearly always censured. In the libertarian village of Magdalena de Pulpis, for example, the abolition of alcohol and tobacco was hailed as a triumph.[25] In the village of Azuara, the collectivists closed the café because they regarded it as a "frivolous institution."[26] "An anarchist should not smoke," the anarchist periodical *Revista Blanca* once stated. "An anarchist should never do anything that injures his health, least of all if it costs money." Nor should an anarchist visit the brothel: "The man who frequents houses of ill fame is not an anarchist. . . . If an anarchist is not superior to other men, he cannot call himself an anarchist. . . . He who buys a kiss puts himself on the level of the woman who sells it. Hence, an anarchist must not purchase kisses. He should merit them."[27]

In the anarchist village of Graus, to judge from a Socialist, the standard of living was higher than before the war. "The land, the mills, livestock, business, transport, handicraft workshops, sandalmaking, poultry breeding, and the liberal professions all come under the collective system. The village is an economic unit in the service of the common good. There is work for all. There is well-being for all. Misery and slavery have been driven out. . . . A powerful siren regulates the life of the village: the hours of labor, refreshment, and rest. . . . Men over sixty years of age are exempted from work. . . . This is one of the first principles of the collective. . . . When a collectivist decides to marry, he is given a week's vacation with the usual income, a house is found for him—house property is also collectivized— and he is provided with furniture . . . which he pays off gradually without interest. All the services of the collective are at his disposal. From birth to death he is protected by the collective."[28]

Referring to the village of Membrilla, an anarchist account records:

On 22 July, the big landowners were expropriated, small property was liquidated, and all the land passed into the hands of the commune. The smallholders understood these measures, which freed them from their debts and
their worries regarding the payment of wages.

The local treasury was empty. Among private individuals the sum of thirty
thousand pesetas in all was found and seized. All the food, the clothing, the
tools, etc., were distributed equitably among the population. Money was
abolished, labor was collectivized, property was taken over by the community, and the distribution of consumer goods was socialized. However, it was
not the socialization of wealth but that of poverty. . . .

There is no longer any retail trade. Libertarian communism reigns. The
drugstore is managed by its former owner, whose accounts are controlled by
the commune. . . .

Three liters of wine are distributed to every person per week. Rent, electricity, water, medical attention, and medicines are free. The consultation of a
specialist outside the commune, if it is necessary, is paid for by the committee.
I was seated near the secretary when a woman came in to ask permission to
go to Ciudad Real in order to consult a specialist about a stomach ailment.
Without bureaucratic dilatoriness she immediately received the cost of her
journey.[29]

Far less expeditious was the committee in the libertarian village of
Albalate de Cinca, whose authority to hand out or withhold money
gave it autocratic powers. "A woman wanted to go to Lerida to consult
a specialist," wrote Agustín Souchy, a prominent foreign anarchosyndicalist. "When she arrived at committee headquarters it was seven
o'clock. . . . Its members work in the fields together with the labor
groups, and in their spare time they attend to the affairs of the village
as well as of the [CNT] organization.

" 'To obtain money for the journey you must first secure a doctor's
certificate,' the president explains.

"This reply did not satisfy the old woman. She complained of
rheumatism and tried unsuccessfully to induce the committee to give
her the money without a doctor's certificate.

" 'There are some people,' said the president, 'who take advantage
of the new possibilities that the collective offers. Many never went to
town before. . . . Now that they can travel without cost, they exag-
gerate a little!'

"Perhaps the explanation of the president was one-sided. The doctor could have given a more objective opinion on the matter."[30]

Describing other aspects of life in the libertarian villages he visited,
Agustín Souchy said of Calaceite:

Here there used to be many small cultivators . . . as well as blacksmiths and
carpenters, all of whom had their own little workshops, where they labored

in a primitive way without machinery. The collectivist ideal showed them the path to communal labor. Now there is a large smithy in which ten men work; they have modern machinery, a healthy and bright place to produce in. All the carpenters of the village labor together in a big workshop. . . .

The able-bodied [agricultural] workers have been divided into twenty-four labor groups, each group comprising twenty members. According to pre-arranged rules, they till the village lands collectively. Formerly every man worked for himself; today he works for the community. . . .

The village has two drugstores and a doctor. They belong to the collective, not because they were forced to, but because they wished to. There was trouble with the bakers. They wanted neither to join the collective nor to work under the new conditions, so they left the village. Fresh bakers have not been called in. A temporary solution has been found: the women bake the bread as of old, but the village wants new bakers to come in.

Once the village was poor; today it is happy. Many people used to go hungry, but now they can eat.[31]

Of Calanda, Souchy wrote:

What was once the church is now a food warehouse. . . . The new meat market is in the annex, hygienic and elegant, such as the village has never known. No purchases are made with money. The women receive meat in exchange for coupons without paying anything or rendering any service. They belong to the collective and that is sufficient to entitle them to food. . . .

Collectivists and individualists live peacefully side by side. There are two cafés in the village. One for the individualists, and the other for the collectivists. They can permit themselves the luxury of taking coffee every night. . . .

A splendid expression of the collective spirit is the communal barber shop, where the service is free. The peasants never used to shave. Now nearly all faces are well groomed. Everyone can have a shave twice a week. . . .

Wine is served at the rate of five liters a week. Food is not lacking. . . .

Everything is collectivized with the exception of those small stores whose owners wished to maintain their independence. The drugstore belongs to the collective and so does the doctor, who receives no money. He is provided for like other members of the collective.[32]

With reference to the village of Maella, an article in *Tierra y Libertad* stated: "Money has disappeared. . . . In this village neither doctors nor teachers receive money. With complete unselfishness they have abandoned that ridiculous privilege. Nobody at all receives pay."[33]

In Muniesa, bread, meat, and oil were distributed freely, but in contrast to most libertarian villages some money was in circulation. "Every male worker," commented Souchy, "receives a peseta a day; women and girls receive seventy-five céntimos; and children under ten, fifty céntimos. This money should not be regarded as a wage. It is distributed together with vital necessities so that the population can purchase supplementary goods."[34]

Antireligious as well as anticlerical sentiments were deeply rooted in the Spanish working-class movement, particularly among the anarchists. As far back as 1896, the forerunner of the modern FAI, the Alianza de la Democracia Socialista, had called for "the abolition of cults, the substitution of science for faith, and of human justice for divine justice."[35] Moreover, the Russian anarchist Mikhail Bakunin, from whom the Spanish libertarians derived most of their theoretical arsenal, once declared that "the existence of a god is incompatible with the happiness, the dignity, the intelligence, the moral sense, and the liberty of men, because, if in fact there is a god, my intelligence, however great, my will, however strong, are nothing compared with the divine will and intelligence."[36] In *God and State*, he affirmed that there were three ways whereby the people could escape from their lot: two imaginary and one real. "The first are the tavern and the church, the debauchery of the body and the debauchery of the mind, the third is the social revolution."[37] The attitude of the Spanish anarchists toward religion had not changed since the days of Bakunin and the Alianza: "Humanity," said an article in *Tierra y Libertad*, shortly before the outbreak of the Civil War, "will not enter a new world of justice and liberty as long as it kneels before God and submits humbly to the state."[38] And in the early days of the Revolution, *CNT*, the leading libertarian organ in Madrid, declared editorially; "Catholicism must be swept away implacably. We demand not that every church should be destroyed, but that no vestige of religion should remain in any of them and that the black spider of fanaticism should not be allowed to spin the viscous and dusty web in which our moral and material values have until now been caught like flies. In Spain, more than any other country, the Catholic church has been at the head of every retrograde aim, of every measure taken against the people, of every attack on liberty."[39]

"Catholic mysticism no longer exists [in the village of Mazaleón]," affirmed Souchy. "The priests have disappeared, and the Christian cult has ended. But the peasants did not want to destroy the Gothic building that majestically crowns the mountain. They turned it into a café and an observatory. . . . They broadened the windows of the church and constructed a large balcony where the altar was once located. The view embraces the southern spurs of the Aragonese mountains. It is a place for tranquillity and for reflection. Here the villagers sit on Sundays, taking coffee and enjoying the calm of the evening."[40]

In almost every region of the anti-Franco camp there were ardent spirits who, exhilarated by the initial progress of the collectivist movement in the villages, whether in the virtually all-embracing form of libertarian communism or in the restricted form of collectivized agriculture, continued to drive it forward with boiling energy. They had an apostolic belief in the justice and grandeur of their aims and were determined to bring them to fruition wherever they could and without procrastination. "We are in the thick of the Revolution," declared one zealous libertarian, "and we must destroy all the chains that subject us. If we do not break them now, when can we?

"We must carry out a total revolution. Expropriation must also be total. This is not the time for sleeping, but for rebuilding. When our comrades return from the front, what will they say if we have been idle? If the Spanish worker does not carve out his own liberty, the state will return and will reconstruct the authority of the government, destroying little by little the conquests made at the cost of a thousand sacrifices and a thousand acts of heroism.

"The rear should act energetically so that the blood of the Spanish proletariat is not shed in vain. . . . We must carry out our revolution, our own particular revolution, expropriating, expropriating, and expropriating the big landlords, as well as those who sabotage our aspirations."[41]

At a congress of the collective farms of Aragon, one delegate declared that collectivization should be carried out with the maximum intensity, avoiding the example of those villages where it had been only partially realized.[42] This statement exemplified the mood of thousands of fervent proponents of collective farming, who were unfettered by any fear of alienating those peasant holders and tenant farmers for whom individual cultivation was paramount. They had power in their hands, and they paid no heed to the much-reiterated warnings of their leaders, such as the one uttered during the congress of the CNT Peasants' Union of Catalonia that "to introduce wholesale collectivization would be to invite disaster because it would clash with the love and affection of the peasants for the land they have obtained at such great sacrifice."[43]

Although CNT-FAI publications cited numerous cases of peasant proprietors and tenant farmers who had adhered voluntarily to the collective system,[44] there can be no doubt that an incomparably larger number doggedly opposed it or accepted it only under extreme duress. This aversion to rural collectivization on the part of smallholders and tenant farmers was on occasions conceded by the anarchosyndicalists, although they sometimes claimed that they had overcome it. "What we have been up against most," said the general secretary of the CNT peasants' Federation of Castile, "is the backward mentality of the majority of small owners. Just imagine what it meant for the peasant proprietor, accustomed to his small plot of land, his donkey, his wretched hut, his petty harvest—modest possessions for which he had more affection than for his sons, his wife, and his mother—to have to give up this burden that he has carried with him from time immemorial, and say: 'Take them, comrades. My humble belongings are for everyone. We are all equal. A new life has begun for us.' Yet that is exactly what we have succeeded in getting the Castilian peasant to do. When a child dies in the countryside one no longer hears that heartrending saying once so common: 'Little angels go to heaven.' Under the capitalist system, the peasant used to get furious when his mule or his ass died, but remained quite calm when he lost a child. That was natural. His small property cost him endless sacrifices; not so his child. Often the death of his little children solved his economic problems."[45] Even in Aragon, whose debt-ridden peasants were strongly affected by the ideas of the CNT and FAI, a factor that gave a powerful spontaneous impetus to collective farming, the libertarians themselves have occasionally acknowledged the difficulty they encountered when collectivizing the soil. "It has been an arduous and complicated task," said one of them in reference to the village of Lécera. "More correctly, it still is. We want men to convince themselves, by their own experience, of the justice and the advantage of our ideas."[46]

While rural collectivization in Aragon embraced more than 70 percent of the population in the area under left-wing control[47] and many of the 450 collectives of the region[48] were largely voluntary, it must be emphasized that this singular development was in some measure due to the presence of militiamen from the neighboring region of Catalonia, the immense majority of whom were members of the CNT and FAI. It could not have been otherwise; for after the defeat of the military rising in Barcelona the militiamen had left for Aragon not only to prosecute the struggle against the rebel or Nationalist forces that occupied a substantial part of the region, but to spread the Revolution. "We are waging the war and making the Revolution at the same time," declared Buenaventura Durruti, one of the outstanding leaders of the libertarian movement,[49] himself a commander of a CNT-FAI militia force on the Aragon front. "The revolutionary measures in the rear are not taken merely in Barcelona; they extend from there right up to the firing line. Every village we conquer begins to develop along revolutionary lines."[50] "We militiamen must awaken in these persons the spirit that has been numbed by political tyranny," said an article in a CNT newspaper, referring to the villagers of Farlete. "We must direct them along the path of the true life, and for that it is not sufficient to make an appearance in the village; we must proceed with the ideological conversion of these simple folk."[51] Of the village of Bujaraloz, another article in a CNT newspaper stated: "The change is radical. The initiative in carrying it into effect lay with the peasants, and it was confirmed some days later with the arrival of the first column of Catalan volunteers, that of Durruti, that passed through the village on its march toward Saragossa, giving a fresh impulse to the revolutionary atmosphere."[52]

As a consequence, the fate of the peasant owner and tenant farmer in the communities occupied by the CNT-FAI militia was determined from the outset; for although a meeting of the population was generally held to decide on the establishment of the collective system, the vote was always taken by acclamation, and the presence of armed militiamen never failed to impose respect and fear on all opponents. Even if the peasant proprietor and tenant farmer were not compelled to adhere to the collective system, life was made difficult for recalcitrants; not only were they prevented from employing hired labor and disposing freely of their crops, as has already been seen,[53] but they were often denied all benefits enjoyed by members.[54] In practice, this meant that in the villages where libertarian communism had been established they were not allowed to receive the services of the collectivized barber shops, to use the ovens of the communal bakery and the means of transport and agricultural equipment of the collective farms, or to obtain supplies of food from the communal warehouses and collectivized stores. Moreover, the tenant farmer, who had believed himself freed from the payment of rent by the execution or flight of the landowner or of his steward, was often compelled to continue such payment to the village committee.[55] All these factors combined to exert pressure almost as powerful as the butt of the rifle and eventually forced the small owners and tenant farmers in many villages to relinquish their land and other possessions to the collective farms. As Souchy put it:

"Those instances in which the small owners gave up their property for idealistic reasons were few, although not altogether rare. In some cases fear of seizure by force was the reason for relinquishing their land in favor of the collectives.[56] But nearly always the reasons were economic.

"Isolated and left to his fate, the small owner was lost. He had neither means of transport nor machinery. On the other hand, the collectives had economic facilities that he could never afford. Not all the small owners realized this immediately. Many joined the collectives later on when they were convinced, through their own experience, of the advantages they offered."[57]

The fact is, however, that many small owners and tenant farmers were forced to join the collective farms before they had had an opportunity to make up their minds freely. Although the libertarian movement tended to minimize the factor of coercion in the development of collectivized agriculture or even to deny it altogether,[58] it was, on occasions, frankly admitted. "During the first few weeks of the Revolution," wrote Higinio Noja Ruiz, a prominent member of the CNT, "the partisans of collectivization acted according to their revolutionary opinions. They respected neither property nor persons. In some villages collectivization was only possible by imposing it on the minority. This necessarily occurs in every revolution. . . . The system, to be sure, is good, and satisfactory work has been done in many places; but it is painful to see antipathies created in other localities owing to a lack of tact on the part of the collectivizers."[59]

Referring to Catalonia, a rich and productive region, where the mass of peasants were small proprietors and leaseholders, the leading CNT newspaper, *Solidaridad Obrera*, commented: "Certain abuses have been committed that we consider counterproductive. We know that certain irresponsible elements have frightened the small peasants and that up to now a certain apathy has been noted in their daily labors."[60] Writing shortly afterward about the same region, Juan Peiró, one of the foremost leaders of the CNT, asked:

Does anyone believe . . . that through acts of violence an interest in or a desire for socialization can be awakened in the minds of our peasantry? Or perhaps that by terrorizing it in this fashion it can be won over to the revolutionary spirit prevailing in the towns and cities?

The gravity of the mischief that is being done compels me to speak clearly. Many revolutionaries from different parts of Catalonia . . . after conquering their respective towns have tried to conquer the countryside, the peasantry. Have they tried to achieve this by informing the peasantry that the hour of its emancipation from the social exploitation to which it has been subjected year after year has arrived? No! Or have they tried to accomplish this by carrying to the countryside, to the consciousness of the peasant, the spirit and the moral standards of the Revolution? No, they have not done that either. When they have gone into the countryside, carrying with them the torch of the Revolution, the first thing they have done has been to take away from the peasant all means of self-defense, . . . and, having achieved this, they have robbed him even of his shirt.

If today you should go to different parts of Catalonia to speak to the peasant of Revolution, he will tell you that he does not trust you, he will tell you that the standard-bearers of the Revolution have already passed through the countryside. In order to liberate it? In order to help it liberate itself? No, they have passed through the countryside in order to rob those who throughout the years and throughout the centuries have been robbed by the very persons who have just been defeated by the Revolution.[61]

To compel any person, by whatever means, to enter the collective system was, of course, contrary to the spirit of anarchism. Errico Malatesta, the Italian anarchist whose writings had an important influence on the Spanish libertarian movement, once stated: "One may prefer communism, or individualism, or collectivism, or any other kind of system imaginable, and work by propaganda and example for the triumph of one's ideas, but it is necessary to beware, on pain of inevitable disaster, of affirming that one's own system is the only one, the infallible one, good for all men, in all places, and at all times, and that it should be made to triumph by other means than by persuasion based on the lessons of experience."[62] At another time, he stated: "The revolution has a purpose. It is necessary for destroying the violence of governments and of privileged persons; but a free society cannot be formed except by free evolution. And over this free evolution, which is constantly threatened as long as men exist with a thirst for domination and privilege, the anarchists must watch."[63] But even this surveillance implied, in order to be effective, the existence of armed forces, of elements of authority and coercion. Indeed, in the first large-scale social revolution that occurred after these lines were written—the Spanish Revolution—the CNT and FAI created armed forces to protect the collective system and used them, moreover, to spread it. The fact that these forces were distasteful to some anarchist leaders only emphasizes the cleavage between doctrine and practice.

Theoretically, the anarchists were opposed to the state dictatorship advocated by the Marxists. Rejecting the dictatorship of the proletariat, Bakunin, the Russian anarchist, whose influence on the Spanish libertarian movement was deep-rooted, wrote:

The Marxists . . . console themselves with the belief that this dictatorship will be provisional and short. They say that its only concern and its only aim will be that of educating and elevating the people, both economically and politically, and to such a level that all governments will soon become unnecessary. . . .

They say that the yoke of state dictatorship is a transitional means indispensable for achieving the complete emancipation of the people: anarchy or liberty is the objective, the state or dictatorship, the means. Hence, in order to emancipate the laboring masses, it is first of all necessary to enslave them. . . .

They affirm that only the dictatorship—their own undoubtedly—can represent the will of the people. But we reply: no dictatorship can have any other aim than that of its own perpetuation and it cannot produce and develop among the people who support it anything but slavery. Liberty can be created only by liberty, that is to say, by the rebellion of the people and by the free organization of the working masses from below upward.[64]

In 1920 Lenin wrote, justifying the dictatorship of the proletariat: "The scientific concept, dictatorship, means neither more nor less than unlimited power resting directly on force, not limited by anything, not restrained by any laws or any absolute rules. Nothing else but that."[65] Commenting on this definition of the dictatorship of the proletariat, Bertram D. Wolfe once made the following observation: "This formulation is beautiful in its pedantic clarity, for the first giant step in the establishment of a totalitarian power is the destruction of all the restraints that, even in a nonrevolutionary autocracy, tend to limit power: the restraints of religion, morals, traditions, institutions, constitutions written or unwritten, laws, customs, private conscience, public opinion—in short, anything and everything that may place any limits on power and any restrictions upon an attempt to atomize and remake a people. The history of all totalitarian regimes has proved the rightness of Lenin's 'scientific' definition."[66]

If, theoretically, during the Spanish Revolution, the CNT and FAI were opposed to the state dictatorship advocated by the Marxists, they nevertheless established a multiplicity of parochial dictatorships in countless localities, with the aid of vigilance groups and revolutionary tribunals. While these fell short of the "scientific concept" of totalitarian dictatorship defined by Lenin, the CNT and FAI exercised their power in a naked form not only against priests and landowners, moneylenders and merchants, but in many cases against small tradesmen and farmers.

This was not the first occasion that the Spanish anarchists contradicted their stated principles. The libertarian historian, César M. Lorenzo, writes:

On 18 January 1932, groups of the FAI staged an insurrection in the mining region of the upper Llobregat and Cardoner, where the working conditions were deplorable and the workers were harshly exploited. In Berga, Cardona, Figols, Sallent, Suria, libertarian communism was "proclaimed." But the movement did not spread beyond that part of Catalonia. This permitted the government to crush it easily within five days. . . . In all those places where the libertarians had the situation briefly in hand and attempted to make the social revolution, they ran counter to their principles. Wishing to abolish laws, to institute a society without authority and without restraints, and to give free rein to the spontaneous creativity of the masses, they were compelled to set up executive committees charged with maintaining order and watching over malcontents or opponents. They imposed their rule by force through decrees they modestly called "proclamations." Far from realising "Anarchism," the leaders of the Revolution, armed and supplied with dynamite, established what one would characterize as the "dictatorship of the proletariat" without taking into consideration the views of the peasants and the small bourgeoisie.[67]

Part II
The Rise of the Communists

5. Hope for the Middle Classes

The foregoing chapters have made clear the pessimism, bordering on despair, that took possession of a large section of the urban and rural middle classes from the outset of the Revolution. Confronted by the brute facts, they found cold comfort in the words of the republican jurist, Angel Ossorio y Gallardo, that in view of the "immense social revolution" that had taken place, "the only thing we members of the middle classes can do is to place ourselves alongside the proletariat."[1] Nor could they take comfort in the promises held out by the revolutionaries of a new and better world once private property and trade had disappeared into the limbo of things past; for the immense majority of the small manufacturers, artisans, tradesmen, peasant proprietors, and tenant farmers placed their hopes of a better life, not in the abolition, but in the accumulation of private property. To develop as they wished, they needed freedom of trade, freedom from the competition of the large concerns now collectivized by the labor unions, freedom to produce goods for personal profit, freedom to cultivate as much land as they pleased, and to employ hired labor without restriction. To defend that freedom, they needed above all, a regime in their own image, based on their own police corps, their own courts of law, and their own army; a regime in which their own power would be unchallenged and undiluted by revolutionary committees. But now all hope of such a regime had gone, and the middle classes had no alternative but to withdraw into the background. They were far too prudent to swim against the tide, and they adapted their attire to suit the changed conditions. "The appearance of Madrid," observed a conservative republican, "was incredible: the bourgeoisie giving the clenched-fist salute. . . . Men in overalls and rope sandals, imitating the uniform adopted by the [working-class] militia; women bareheaded; clothes, old and threadbare; an absolute invasion of ugliness and squalor, more apparent than real, of people who humbly begged permission to remain alive."[2] A left-wing observer wrote of Barcelona: "The Ramblas lie sloping gradually upwards for more than a mile to the Plaza de Catalunya. From the other end you looked down on an unending harvest of heads. Today there is not a hat, a collar, or a tie to be seen among them; the sartorial symbols of the bourgeoisie are gone, a proletarian freedom has swarmed in along the Calle del Hospital and the Calle del Carmen from the Parallelo. Or, as Puig suggests, the bourgeoisie have disguised themselves for better safety as proletarians by leaving hat, collar, and tie at home."[3]

Short of risking their liberty or their lives in openly opposing the Revolution, there was nothing the middle classes could do but to adjust themselves to the new regime in the hope that eventually the tide might change. Certainly they could not look for support to any of the right-wing parties that until the outbreak of the war had represented their more conservative layers, for those parties had perished in the flames of the Revolution. Nor could they turn to the liberal republican parties, such as the Izquierda Republicana, the Unión Republicana, and the Esquerra Republicana de Catalunya, the Left Republican party of Catalonia, the strongest middle-class party in that region, for the majority of the leaders were either accommodating themselves to the radicalism of the situation or were characterized by inertia born of fear. "In twenty-four hours, minds that once appeared averse to change have evolved strikingly," wrote a famous anarchist within a few days of the Revolution. "Displaying a remarkable ability to adapt themselves, men who were spiritually very far removed from us have accepted the new order of things without protest. Nobody is startled today to hear of socialization and the disappearance of private property."[4]

Other republican leaders, regarding everything as lost, had either left the country or were fleeing to the ports.[5] Even Manuel Azaña, the president of the Republic, only yesterday the idol of the liberal segment of the middle classes, was paralyzed by pessimism and fear and had plummeted overnight from his summit of acclaimed leadership. From the very first moment, affirms Angel Ossorio y Gallardo, Manuel Azaña felt that the war was lost, and the excesses that had occurred in the early days revolted and demoralized him.[6] True, many of the leaders of the liberal republican parties would have been capable navigators in calm seas, but they were helpless in the midst of the storms that had buffeted the Republic before the Civil War and even more so now in face of the hurricane that had shattered the coercive organs of the state. "The slight resistance we offered to the assaults of other organizations, our silence and our aloofness in face of the daring advances of the audacious led many persons to believe that we no longer existed," declared the president of the Republican

Left party. "They could not understand the noble aim that impelled us to stifle our indignation. The prudence and sense of responsibility that others lacked had to distinguish our behavior, if the wall of resistance we had to erect with arms in our hands against the violent onset of the enemy were not to collapse."[7] But, floundering in the flood of the Revolution, the liberal as well as the conservative members of the middle classes were impressed at the time only by the manifest impotence of their parties and soon began to cast about for an organization that would serve as a breakwater to check the revolutionary tide set in motion by the anarchosyndicalist and Socialist labor unions.

They did not have to search for long. Before many weeks had passed the organization that succeeded in focusing upon itself their immediate hopes was the Communist party.

A minor factor in Spanish politics before the Civil War, with only sixteen seats in the Cortes and an officially estimated membership of forty thousand,[8] the Communist party was soon to mold decisively the course of events in the camp of the anti-Franco forces. Championing the interests of the urban and rural middle classes—a stand few republicans dared to assume in that atmosphere of revolutionary emotionalism—the Communist party became within a few months the refuge, according to its own figures, of 76,700 peasant proprietors and tenant farmers and of 15,485 members of the urban middle classes.[9] "The Republican middle class," writes a Socialist, "surprised by the moderate tone of Communist propaganda and impressed by the unity and realism which prevailed in this party, flocked in great numbers to join its ranks."[10]

That the Communist party's influence among the middle classes went far beyond the aforementioned figures is indubitable, for thousands of members of the intermediate classes in both country and town placed themselves under its wing without actually becoming adherents of the party.[11] From the very outset of the Revolution, the Communist party, like the PSUC, the Partit Socialista Unificat de Catalunya, the Communist-controlled United Socialist Party of Catalonia,[12] took up the cause of the middle classes, who were being dragged into the vortex of the collectivization movement or were being crippled by the disruption of trade, the lack of financial resources, and the requisitions carried out by the working-class militia.

"In a capitalist society, the small tradesmen and manufacturers," declared *Mundo Obrero*, the Communist organ in Madrid, "constitute a class that has many things in common with the proletariat. It is, of course, on the side of the democratic Republic, and it is as much opposed to the big capitalists and captains of powerful fascist enterprises as the workers. This being so it is everybody's duty to respect the property of these small tradesmen and manufacturers.

"We therefore strongly urge the members of our party and the militia in general to demand, and, if need be, to enforce respect for these middle-class citizens, all of whom are workers, and who therefore should not be molested. Their modest interests should not be injured by requisitions and demands that are beyond their meager resources."[13]

Treball, the Communist organ in Catalonia, said:

It would be unpardonable to forget the multitude of small commodity producers and businessmen of our region. Many of them, thinking only of creating what they had believed would be a position of independence for themselves, had succeeded in setting up their own businesses. Then came a change in the situation precipitated by the attempted coup d'etat of the fascists. The immense majority of small commodity producers and businessmen, who had lived completely on the margin of events, are now more confused than anyone because they feel that they are being harmed and that they are at an obvious disadvantage in comparison with the wage earners. They declare that nobody is concerned about their fate. They are elements who might tend to favor any reactionary movement because in their opinion anything would be better than the economic system that is being instituted in our region. . . .[14]

The distressing situation of many of these people is obvious. They cannot run their workshops and businesses because they have no reserve capital; they have hardly enough to eat, especially the small manufacturers, because the wages they have to pay to the few workers they employ prevent them from attending to their own daily needs. . . .

A moratorium must be granted to all those people who have placed themselves at the service of the antifascist militia, so that they do not have to bear the full weight of the requisitions imposed by the war. A moratorium must be granted and a credit should be opened so that their businesses do not go into liquidation.[15]

To protect the interests of the urban middle classes in this region the Communists organized eighteen thousand tradesmen, handicraftsmen, and small manufacturers into the Federación Catalana de Gremios y Entidades de Pequeños Comerciantes e Industriales, Catalan Federation of Small Businessmen, (known as the GEPCI),[16] some of whose members were, in the phrase of *Solidaridad Obrera,* the CNT organ, "intransigent employers, ferociously antilabor," including Gurri, the former president of the Tailoring Trades Association.[17]

Lest the reader believe that the Communists' support of the middle classes was altruistic rather than pragmatic, that they were concerned more with the welfare of these classes than with the strengthening of their position vis-à-vis their anarchosyndicalist and Socialist opponents, he should be reminded of Lenin's words that the enemy can be conquered only "by taking advantage of every, even the smallest opportunity of gaining a mass ally, even though this ally be only temporary, vacillating, unstable, unreliable and conditional. Those who do not understand this do not understand a particle of Marxism, or of scientific modern socialism in general."[18]

In the countryside the Communists undertook a spirited defense of the small and medium proprietor and tenant farmer against the collectivizing drive of the rural wage workers, against the policy of the labor unions prohibiting the farmer from holding more land than he could cultivate with his own hands, and against the practices of revolutionary committees that requisitioned harvests, interfered with private trade, and collected rents from tenant farmers.

The liberal republicans, on the other hand, whose primary concern should have been the defense of the very classes whose interests the Communists were championing, remained cautious to the point of timidity. A consultation of their newspapers offers sufficient proof of this. In fact, they did not venture to raise their voices until April 1937, when the revolutionary tide was receding. "We are tired of remaining silent," declared Miguel San Andrés, the Left Republican deputy. "The plundering of the small manufacturer, of the small farmer, and intellectual, of all those people who have been working year after year in order to save a little money cannot be tolerated. . . . We have seen our interests trampled underfoot, and have remained silent."[19]

Not so the Communists. From the outset of the Revolution they were vociferous in the defense not only of the small businessman but also of the small farmer and did their best to profit from any discontent in the countryside. "In the early days of the military rebellion," wrote Julio Mateu, a member of the central committee of the party, in reference to the province of Valencia, "when an endless chain of committees and more committees tried to make a clean sweep of the entire countryside by immediately converting all small proprietors into agricultural workers, by despoiling them of their land and harvests, there was a real danger of setting the peasants against the antifascist organizations. The modest agricultural producers, who for a long time had been oppressed by the political bosses and reactionary usurers, were once again maltreated, this time because of lack of understanding on the part of those who should have helped them in

their development. The mistake of considering simple Catholic peasants as enemies prompted some organizations to commit such injustices as to collect from the tenant farmers the rents they formerly paid
to the landowners. . . . We have passed through moments of real
danger, having been within an ace of unleashing a civil war in the
rear between the farmers and the agricultural workers. Fortunately,
this has been averted, although at the cost of bursting our lungs in an
intense campaign of political education in the villages aimed at securing respect for small property."[20]

Speaking at a public meeting, Vicente Uribe, a member of the Communist party's central committee and minister of agriculture from
September 1936, declared:

"The present policy of violence against the peasants has two dangers. The first is that it may estrange those who are on our side, on
the antifascist side. The other is still more serious: it will endanger the
future food supply of Spain. . . . It cannot be tolerated that while at
the fronts the soldiers are giving their lives and their blood for the
common cause, there are persons far behind the lines who use rifles
belonging to the people in order to impose by force ideas that the
people do not accept.

"But I tell you, peasants; I tell you, workers of the countryside, that
despite the abuses some persons are committing, despite the barbari-
ties they are perpetrating, your obligation is to work the land and
extract the utmost from it, because you are protected by the government, by parties and by organizations, and because you have at your
side the Communist party. . . . Even though violence is used, it is
your duty as patriots, your duty as republicans, your duty as antifascists to call upon the government, to call upon the Communists,
and you can be sure that, in order that you may cultivate the land
peacefully, we shall be at your side armed with rifles."[21]

Speaking a few days later at another meeting, he stated, in reference to the establishment of libertarian communism by the anarchosyndicalists in some of the villages of Valencia province:

"We know that some committees have set up a certain type of
regime, a regime in which everyone is subjected to the mercy of their
will. We know that they confiscate harvests and commit other abuses,
such as seizing small peasant farms, imposing fines, paying for goods
with vouchers, in other words, a whole series of irregularities. You
know perfectly well that these actions—and listen carefully to this—
can never, never have the approval of the government nor even its
connivance. . . . We say that the property of the small farmer is sacred

and that those who attack or attempt to attack this property must be regarded as enemies of the regime."[22]

It was only natural that the Communists' defense of the interests of peasant owners and tenant farmers should have brought their party a broad wave of adherents. In their campaign they were most successful, of course, in areas where small and medium-sized farms predominated. In the rich orange- and rice-growing province of Valencia, for example, where the farmers were prosperous and had supported right-wing organizations before the Civil War, according to official figures, fifty thousand had by March 1937 joined the Peasant Federation,[23] which the Communist party had set up for their protection in the first months of the Revolution. "The Communist party," complained a Socialist, "devotes itself to picking up in the villages the worst remnants of the former Partido Autonomista, who were not only reactionary, but also immoral, and organizes these small proprietors into a new peasant union by promising them the possession of their land."[24] In addition to providing its members with fertilizers and seed and securing credits from the ministry of agriculture—likewise controlled by the Communists—the Peasant Federation served as a powerful instrument in checking the rural collectivization promoted by the agricultural workers of the province. That the protection afforded by this organization should have induced many of its members to apply for admission into the Communist party is understandable. "Such is the sympathy for us in the Valencia countryside," Julio Mateu, general secretary of the federation, affirmed, "that hundreds and thousands of farmers would join our party if we were to let them. These farmers, many of whom believed in God—and still do—and prayed and in private beat their breasts, love our party like a sacred thing. When we tell them that they should not confuse the Peasant Federation with the party, and that even without a membership card it is possible to be a Communist by working for its political line, they are wont to reply, 'The Communist party is our party.' Comrades, what emotion the peasants display when they utter these words!"[25]

Because the Communist party gave the urban and rural middle classes a powerful infusion of new hope and vitality, it is not surprising that a large part of the copious flow of new members into the party in the months following the Revolution came from these classes. It is almost superfluous to say that these new recruits were attracted, not by Communist principles, but by the hope of saving something from the ruins of the old social system. Furthermore, in addition to defending their property rights, the Communist party defined the social overturn, not as a proletarian, but as a bourgeois democratic revolution. Within a few days of the outbreak of the war, politburo member Dolores Ibárruri, popularly known as La Pasionaria (the Passion Flower), declared in the name of the central committee:

> The revolution that is taking place in our country is the bourgeois democratic revolution that was achieved over a century ago in other countries, such as France, and we Communists are the front-line fighters in this struggle against the obscurantist forces of the past.
>
> Cease conjuring up the specter of communism, you generals, many times traitors, with the idea of isolating the Spanish people in its magnificent struggle against those who wish to turn Spain into a tragic, backward country, a country in which the military, the clergy, and the political bosses would be the absolute masters of life and property! We Communists are defending a regime of liberty and democracy, and side by side with republicans, Socialists, and anarchists we shall prevent Spain from retrogressing, cost what it may. . . .
>
> It is a lie to speak of chaos; a lie to say that a chaotic situation exists here, as do the reports given out by traitors to the Republic!
>
> In this historic hour the Communist party, faithful to its revolutionary principles and respecting the will of the people, places itself at the side of the government that expresses this will, at the side of the Republic, at the side of democracy. . . .
>
> The government of Spain is a government that emerged from the electoral triumph of 16 February, and we support it and we defend it because it is the legal representative of the people fighting for democracy and liberty. . . .
>
> Long live the struggle of the people against reaction and fascism! Long live the Democratic Republic!"[26]

Thus, from the outset, the Communist party appeared before the distraught middle classes not only as a defender of property, but as a champion of the Republic and of orderly processes of government. Not that these classes had complete confidence in its good faith, but they were ready to support it as long as it offered them protection and helped to restore to the government the power assumed by revolutionary committees. That their support was shot through with suspicion and fear was natural, for in the past the Communists had pursued an entirely different policy, as will be seen in the ensuing chapter.

6. The Popular Front

"Our task is to win over the majority of the proletariat and to prepare it for the assumption of power," La Pasionaria had declared toward the end of 1933. "This means that we must bend all our efforts to organize workshop and peasant committees and to create soviets. . . . The development of the revolutionary movement is extremely favorable to us. We are advancing along the road that has been indicated to us by the Communist International and that leads to the establishment of a Soviet government in Spain, a government of workers and peasants."[1]

This policy was in strange contrast to the seemingly moderate goals pursued by the Communist party after the outbreak of the Civil War and Revolution in July 1936. The change that had occurred stemmed from the resolutions passed at the Seventh World Congress of the Communist International in 1935, officially adopting the Popular Front policy.

At the root of this new policy lay the deterioration in German-Soviet relations since Adolf Hitler's rise to power in January 1933 and Joseph Stalin's fear that Germany's revived military strength would ultimately be directed against the USSR. Suffering from the aftereffects of compulsory collectivization and bending every effort to strengthen her political and military system, the Soviet Union was careful not to offer any provocation that would draw her into permanent estrangement from the Nazi regime.

Isaac Deutscher writes:

Hitler's bloody suppression of all domestic opposition and his racial persecutions affected diplomatic routine business between Moscow and Berlin as little as it affected similar business between Paris or London and Berlin. Stalin undoubtedly calculated on the strength of the Bismarckian tradition among the German diplomats, a tradition which demanded that the Reich should avoid embroilment with Russia. In the first year of Hitler's chancellorship he did not utter in public a single word about the events in Germany, though his silence was excruciating to the bewildered followers of the Comintern.

He broke that silence only at the seventeenth congress of the party, in January 1934. Even then he refrained from drawing the conclusions from events which had ended so disastrously for the European Left, and he vaguely fostered the illusion that fascism, "a symptom of capitalist weakness," would prove short-lived. But he also described the Nazi upheaval as a "triumph for the idea of revenge in Europe" and remarked that the anti-Russian trend in German policy had been prevailing over the older Bismarckian tradition. Even so, he was at pains to make it clear that Russia desired to remain on the same terms with the Third Reich as she had been with Weimar Germany.[2]

Indeed, *Izvestiia*, the organ of the Soviet government, declared within a few weeks of Hitler's appointment to the Reich chancellorship that the USSR was the only state that had "no hostile sentiments toward Germany, whatever the form and composition of that country's government."[3] But Russia's advances had been coldly received, and at the end of 1933, Vyacheslav Molotov, chairman of the Council of People's Commissars, complained that during the past year the ruling groups in Germany had made a number of attempts to revise relations with the Soviet Union.[4]

With a view to seeking safeguards against the menace of German expansion and to making her influence felt in the chancelleries of western Europe, the Soviet Union reversed her attitude of hostility toward the League of Nations and joined that body in September 1934. "On entering the League of Nations," said the Comintern organ, *International Press Correspondence*, "it will be possible for the U.S.S.R. to struggle still more effectively and practically against a counterrevolutionary war on the U.S.S.R."[5] But in spite of this move, uneasiness regarding German intentions continued unabated. "The direct threat of war has increased for the USSR," declared Molotov in January 1935. "We must not forget that there is now in Europe a ruling party that has proclaimed as its historical task the seizure of territory in the Soviet Union."[6] As a further move to ward off the German threat to her security, Russia concluded a Pact of Mutual Assistance with France on 2 May 1935. This treaty was favored by the French mainly to remove any links that still remained between the USSR and Germany since the Russo-German rapprochement begun at Rapallo in 1922[7] and to end the opposition of the French Communist party to the national defense program;[8] in fact, it was never supplemented by any positive military agreement between the respective general staffs[9] and from the beginning elicited very little enthusiasm even from government circles.[10]

Some idea of what the French Ministry of Foreign Affairs, even at the time of the French Popular Front government of Léon Blum, thought of the Franco-Soviet pact may be gathered from a memorandum by the acting state secretary of the German Foreign Office relating to a conversation on 1 September 1936 with the French ambassador, François-Poncet. Referring to the proposed meeting of the five Locarno Powers (Great Britain, France, Belgium, Italy, and Germany) to negotiate a new western pact to take the place of the Locarno Agreement, the memorandum stated:

M. François-Poncet was particularly interested in hearing whether we were willing to go to the conference and negotiate on the first points on the agenda without bringing up the fifth point, or whether we wanted to force the French Government now, in advance, expressly to renounce the fifth point, that is, the ties in the east. In other words, did the German Government take the stand that it was possible to start out by negotiating on a Western Pact, leaving the eastern questions open? Or did it demand from the very first that France renounce her eastern ties, before Germany would enter into a discussion concerning a Western Pact? If Germany followed the first course, he believed he could say that the Franco-Russian ties would gradually cool, particularly since they had never been popular with a large sector of the French people; we would then attain our objective slowly but surely. If, on the other hand, we should apply pressure to the French Government now and demand that it give up the Russian alliance, the French Government could only refuse to do so. In a long discourse M. François-Poncet tried to convince me of the rightness of the one alternative and the wrongness of the other, emphasizing solemnly during the course of his statements that there were no special military ties between France and the Soviet Union.[11]

Moscow was fully alive to the possibility that the pact might eventually be disregarded, and it thus became a vital task for French Communists to ensure that France would honor her commitments.

"We can congratulate ourselves on the Franco-Soviet treaty," declared Vaillant Couturier, the French Communist leader, "but as we have no confidence that the French bourgeoisie and the fascist cadres of the French army will observe its clauses, *we shall act accordingly*. We know that whatever may be the interests that lead certain French political circles toward a rapprochement with the USSR, the champions of French imperialism hate the Soviet Union."[12]

Powerful forces both in France and Britain opposed any hard and fast commitments in eastern Europe that might entangle the West in a war with Germany, and these forces seeemed ready to countenance the latter's expansionist aims at the expense of the Soviet Union. "In those prewar years," writes Sumner Welles, who became U.S. undersecretary of state in 1937, "great financial and commercial interests of the Western democracies, including many in the United States, were firm in the belief that war between the Soviet Union and Hitlerite Germany could only be favorable to their own interests. They maintained that Russia would necessarily be defeated, and with this defeat Communism would be destroyed; also that Germany would be so weakened as a result of the conflict that for many years thereafter she would be incapable of any real threat to the rest of the world."[13]

On 6 May 1935, William Dodd, U.S. ambassador to Berlin, made the following notation in his diary regarding a letter he had received from Lord Lothian: "He indicated clearly that he favors a coalition of the democracies to block any German move in their direction and to turn Germany's course eastwards."[14] And in an article entitled "Why Not a Franco-British Alliance?" Viscount Rothermere, one of the British press lords, wrote: "The new bond between France and Britain would have another effect of inestimable importance. It would turn Germany's territorial ambitions in the direction where they can do least harm and most good—towards the east of Europe."[15]

That the Western democracies were confronted with a fateful choice is indubitable. On the one hand, they could oppose and destroy the Nazi regime while it was still weak, leaving the Soviet Union free to develop its resources and become in time, with allied Communist parties, the greatest menace in the world. "I feel that if the Nazi regime in Germany is destroyed then the country will go communist," stated the Marquess of Londonderry, secretary of state for air from 1931 to 1935, in a letter to Winston Churchill on 9 May 1936, "and we shall find a lining-up of France, Germany, and Russia and the menace of communism as the most powerful policy in the world."[16] No less explicit was Thierry Maulnier, who, in an article written after the sacrifice of Czechoslovakia to Nazi Germany at Munich in September 1938, expressed the views of the parties of the French right. "These parties," he wrote, "felt that in the event of war not only would the disaster be tremendous, not only would the defeat and devastation of France be within the bounds of possibility, but, even more, that Germany's defeat would mean the collapse of those authoritarian systems that form the principal bulwark against Communist revolution and that it would perhaps lead to the immediate bolshevization of Europe. In other words, a French defeat would indeed have been a defeat of France, while a French victory would have been less a victory for France than for the principles quite rightly regarded as leading directly to the ruin of France and of civilization itself. It is a pity that the men and parties in France who shared in that belief did not in general admit it, for there was nothing inavowable about it. Indeed, in my opinion, it was one of the principal and well-founded reasons, if not the best-founded, for not going to war in September 1938."[17]

On the other hand, the Western democracies could, though not without opprobrium and extreme peril to themselves, allow the Nazi regime to overrun the nontotalitarian states in central and southeastern Europe lying west of Russia's border in the hope that it would in time come into collision with the rising power of the Soviet Union.

The view of the stuanchest conservative opponent of any policy involving the sacrifice to Nazi Germany of the small states in central and southeastern Europe must be recorded here. Winston Churchill wrote to the Marquess of Londonderry:

We all wish to live on friendly terms with Germany. We know the best Germans are ashamed of the Nazi excesses and recoil from the paganism on which they are based. We certainly do not want to pursue a policy inimical to the legitimate interests of Germany, but you must surely be aware that, when the German Government speaks of friendship with England, what they mean is, that we shall give them back their former colonies, and also agree to their having a free hand, as far as we are concerned, in Central and Southern Europe.

This means that they would devour Austria and Czechoslovakia as a preliminary to making a gigantic Middle-European bloc. It would certainly not be in our interest to connive at such policies of aggression. It would be wrong and cynical in the last degree to buy immunity for ourselves at the expense of smaller states in Central Europe.

It would be contrary to the whole tide of British and United States opinion for us to facilitate the spread of Nazi tyranny over countries which now have a considerable measure of democratic freedom. In my view, we should build up so strong a Federation of Regional Agreements under the League of Nations that Germany will be content to live within her own bounds in a law-abiding manner, instead of seeking to invade her smaller neighbours, slay them and have their farms and homes for themselves.[18]

But in those prewar years there were more powerful voices than that of Winston Churchill. How far British policy toward Germany was determined by the fear of Russia is illustrated by Lord Lloyd, a leading British diplomat. In his pamphlet, *The British Case*, written shortly after the outbreak of war between Britain and Germany in 1939 and given the stamp of official endorsement by the commendatory preface of Lord Halifax, then secretary of state for foreign affairs, Lord Lloyd wrote: "However abominable [Hitler's] methods, however deceitful his diplomacy, however intolerant he might show himself of the rights of other European peoples, he still claimed to stand ultimately for something which was a common European interest, and which therefore could conceivably provide some day a basis for understanding with other nations equally determined not to sacrifice their traditional institutions and habits on the blood-stained altars of the World Revolution."[19]

To prevent the Western democracies from compounding their differences with the Third Reich at the possible expense of Russia, to guarantee that the Franco-Soviet Pact of Mutual Assistance would not fall by the wayside, and, moreover, to conclude similar alliances with other countries, notably Great Britain, it was essential for the Soviet Union that governments hostile to German aims in eastern Europe should be brought into office. With this end in view, the Popular Front line was formally adopted at the Seventh World Congress of the Comintern in August 1935, although some of the sections of the Comintern had, in accordance with the new trend in Soviet foreign policy, been seeking cooperation with other parties before that date. This attempt had been most successful in France.[20]

The foreign political goals of the Soviet Union should not obscure the fact that long before the formal adoption by the Comintern of the Popular Front line, in Spain most of the parties of the left saw a compelling domestic reason for a movement of unity, namely, the defeat of the left by the center-right in the November 1933 elections. The Communists claimed that they initiated the movement of unity in Spain, but this assertion should be discounted.[21]

In its program, the Seventh World Congress of the Comintern decided that one of the immediate tasks of the Communists in all countries was to bring the peasantry and the small urban bourgeoisie into a "wide anti-fascist people's front." This was essential, it argued, because the "dominant circles of the British bourgeoisie support German armaments in order to weaken the hegemony of France on the European Continent . . . and to direct Germany's aggressiveness against the Soviet Union."[22] Certainly, British support of German rearmament in the first half of 1935 alone lent support to these charges.

On 6 February 1935, Sir John Simon, then secretary of state for foreign affairs, had stated in the House of Commons: "Germany's claim to equality of rights in the matter of armaments cannot be resisted, and ought not to be resisted."[23] On 18 June 1935, the Anglo-German Naval Agreement had been signed, giving the German navy 35 percent of British naval tonnage. Criticizing this agreement on 11 July 1935, Winston Churchill declared: "We have condoned, and even praised the German treaty-breaking in fleet-building."[24] "In Russia," wrote Max Beloff, "the [naval] pact was interpreted as a sign of Britain's weakness and of her desire to divert Germany from air preparations to naval building, where she felt stronger. It might also serve to divert Germany's attention eastward and to allow Britain to disengage herself from Europe, so as to salvage her menaced position in the Far East. A new field of activity would be open for British advocates of an entente with Germany. The Germans would not, the Russians argued, observe the agreement, and only welcomed it as a breach in the treaties. It was clear that the German command of the Baltic [the gateway to Russia] would be unassailable. Nor does there seem any reason to doubt that it was the Baltic situation which Herr Hitler had chiefly in mind."[25] Furthermore, in the summer of 1935, Germany reintroduced conscription in violation of the Versailles Treaty. This, too, was condoned by Britain.[26]

With British policy undoubtedly in mind, the Seventh World Congress of the Comintern declared that the struggle for peace opened up the greatest opportunity for creating the broadest united front and that "all those interested in the preservation of peace should be drawn into this united front." This was to be achieved by mobilizing the people against "the plundering price policy of monopoly capital and the bourgeois governments" and against "increasing taxation and the high cost of living."[27] Although the congress reaffirmed the aims of the Communist International, namely, the revolutionary overthrow of the rule of the bourgeoisie and the establishment of the dictatorship of the proletariat in the form of soviets,[28] the policy of unity with the middle classes could not but lead sooner or later to an attempt on the part of the Comintern's various sections to deemphasize their revolutionary goals and to disarm the suspicion with which they were once regarded. The result was that in Spain, as one historian points out, the Communists "very carefully walked a fence between appealing to the revolutionary masses and the moderate republican [middle-class] elements, sometimes contradicting themselves."[29]

7. Camouflaging the Revolution

From the standpoint of Soviet foreign policy, the Popular Front line met with appreciable success. In the early months of 1936, both in France and Spain, the Communists participated in general elections on a broad basis and helped to bring liberal governments into office, uniting not only with the Socialists, their former foes, but also with the moderate parties.

That Germany should have viewed with alarm the success of a policy designed to establish an anti-German front by reinforcing and extending Russia's political and military ties with western Europe is natural, but not until the outbreak of the revolt in Spain in July 1936 did an opportunity arise to counter this threat to her own plans by direct intervention on the side of the rebellion. Contrary to the opinion widely held, no promises of German military aid were given to the organizers of the revolt prior to the oubreak of hostilities. According to the documents relating to Spain in the archives of the German foreign ministry, published in Washington by the Department of State in 1950, Hitler did not promise assistance until several days after the outbreak of the rebellion, when General Franco sent a German businessman resident in Spanish Morocco and the local Nazi leader to Germany to request planes and other support.[1] This request was quickly acceded to, for according to Nazi sources German airplanes were active on the side of General Franco in the first weeks of the war either in transporting Moorish troops and Foreign Legionaries from Spanish Morocco to the mainland or in bombing operations.[2]

At the Nuremberg trials in 1946, Hermann Goering, Hitler's air force chief, stated:

When the civil war broke out in Spain, Franco sent a call for help to Germany and asked for support, particularly in the air. One should not forget that Franco with his troops was stationed in Africa and that he could not get the troops across, as the fleet was in the hands of the communists [the forces of the left]. . . . The decisive factor was, first of all, to get his troops over to Spain.

The Führer thought the matter over. I urged him to give support under all circumstances, firstly, in order to prevent the further spread of communism in that theater and, secondly, to test my young Luftwaffe at this opportunity in this or that technical respect.

With the permission of the Führer, I sent a large part of my transport fleet and a number of experimental fighter units, bombers, and antiaircraft guns; and in that way I had an opportunity to ascertain, under combat conditions, whether the material was equal to the task. In order that the personnel, too, might gather a certain amount of experience, I saw to it that there was a continuous flow, that is, that new people were constantly being sent and others recalled.[3]

In going to the aid of General Franco, Germany had a twofold objective. On the one hand, although fearful of the international complications that might arise from being drawn too deeply into the Spanish conflict[4] at a time when she was not yet ready for a large-scale war, she hoped to secure strategic advantages in preparation for the coming struggle in western Europe. In a communication to the Wilhelmstrasse, dated 1 May 1937, the German ambassador to General Franco wrote: "There is no doubt that, [after] a war won because of our intervention, a Spain socially ordered and economically reconstructed with our help will in the future be not only a very important source of raw materials for us, but also a faithful friend for a long time to come."[5] On the other hand, Germany hoped that the defeat of the Popular Front and the resurgence of the right in Spain would weaken the French Popular Front and strengthen forces in France that were opposed to blocking German expansion eastward and regarded the Franco-Soviet Pact of Mutual Assistance as likely to entangle their country in a struggle that, in the event of a German defeat, would result in the enthronement of communism in Europe. "What Moscow wants," ran an article that was typical of an appreciable segment of French opinion, "is a war between French and German soldiers. At some time or another, on some pretext or another, Russia hopes that she will be able to force us to throw our troops against the [German] frontier and deal a double blow by weakening the dreaded German power and by delivering our country up to a foreign war that would ring in the hour of the Bolshevik Revolution."[6]

Russia was not blind to the dangers of German intervention in Spain. But, anxious not to give body and color to attacks that pictured her as the open patron of world revolution lest she antagonize the moderate parties in the Western democracies on whom she based her hopes of an anti-German front, she formally adhered on 23 August 1936 to the international Non-Intervention Agreement that had been proposed by France to prevent an extension of the conflict[7] and undertook, together with the other countries participating in the accord, not to send arms to Spain. "Had the Soviet Union not agreed to the French proposal for neutrality," commented a Communist newspaper, "it would have very seriously embarras[s]d the [French] Government, and considerably assisted fascists in France and England, as well as the governments of Germany and Italy, in their campaign against the Spanish people. . . . If the Soviet Government took any step which added further fuel to the present inflammable situation in Europe, it would be welcome by the Fascists of all countries and would split the democratic forces, thus directly preparing the way for so-called 'preventive warfare' against Bolshevism as represented by the USSR."[8]

The Soviet Union's concern for Western democratic opinion ill accords with the charge put forward by rebel sources, based on the publication of "secret" Communist documents, that the Communists had been conspiring to set up a soviet regime in Spain in the summer of 1936;[9] for it is obvious that had they attempted to set up such a regime they would have ruined the Kremlin's efforts to establish a firm alliance with the democratic powers. For this reason alone—to say nothing of the fact that they certainly did not have the necessary strength—the charge may be safely discounted. In fact, even José María Gil Robles, the leader of the right-wing Catholic CEDA, writes: "I never believed in the possibility at that time of a Communist uprising, much less in one directly involving the Comintern. . . . Confronted by the Hitlerite threat, Stalin favored a rapprochement with England and France. The Franco-Soviet pact and the resolutions of the Seventh Congress of the Third International [Comintern] testify that he subordinated revolution in Europe to the policy of containment of German imperialism. And nothing could have awakened greater hostility among the European democracies than an attempt to implant a Communist state in Spain. . . . The real danger lay not in a carefully organized Communist insurrection, but in the climate of anarchy that prevailed everywhere. The last time I spoke with Señor Azaña . . . he did not conceal from me his fear of being overwhelmed by the masses of the Popular Front."[10]

The "secret" documents that formed the basis for the charge that the Communists were conspiring to set up a soviet regime in the summer of 1936 have not only been exposed conclusively as forgeries by Herbert R. Southworth, a partisan of the left,[11] but have been recognized as such by one of contemporary Spain's foremost historians of the Civil War, Ricardo de la Cierva, a supporter of the military uprising, who claims that they were written by the Spanish right-wing author Tomás Borrás. "Hence," he affirms, "the documents were born spurious . . . [but] they were utilized with tremendous effectiveness by Spanish and foreign propagandists." He cautions, however, that "to refute their authenticity" is not to deny the danger and the deep fear of communism that existed at the time.[12] Moreover, he produces evidence from Spanish Communist party sources showing that the party had not abandoned its revolutionary goals, and he argues that during the first half of 1936 it contributed "effectively to the intensification of the revolutionary dynamism of the proletariat."[13]

Still, in spite of this evidence, in spite of the seemingly revolutionary character of the language the Communists sometimes employed before the Civil War so as not to lose touch with the radical temper of the anarchosyndicalists and left-wing Socialists, in spite of the fact that they publicly urged the creation of workers' and peasants' alliances as "future organs of power"[14] and acknowledged that the dictatorship of the proletariat was the party's ultimate goal,[15] and in spite of their warnings to the liberal government that the agricultural workers would divide up the estates of the big landed proprietors by force of arms if it did not carry out the agrarian reform more expeditiously,[16] they were careful to maintain their alliance with the moderates. "The Popular Front must continue," wrote José Díaz. "We have still a long way to travel with the Left Republicans."[17] Again, in spite of their demands for the purging of the army[18] and their threat just before the military insurrection that unless the government fulfilled the Popular Front program they would strive for the creation of a government of a "revolutionary popular character,"[19] this language was designed more to propitiate the prevailing revolutionary sentiment and to goad the government into action against the right than to encourage an immediate social overturn. Indeed, during the strike of the Madrid construction workers before the Civil War that seriously embarrassed the government and threatened to develop into a revolutionary confrontation with the employers and the state,[20] the Communists did their best to induce the anarchosyndicalists to terminate it.[21]

That the military insurrection and the far-reaching social revolution it spawned came at an awkward time for the Kremlin there can be no doubt. The dilemma of appealing to moderate opinion both at home and abroad, while not appearing to desert the revolutionary movement in Spain in face of the increasing intervention by Italy and Germany, could not have been more critical. To resolve the dilemma, Stalin, while officially adhering to the Non-Intervention Agreement, decided on 23 August 1936, as we shall see shortly, to embark on a policy of cautious military intervention under cover of his proclamation of neutrality.

Stalin's decision to intervene came late as compared with those of Hitler and Mussolini. It has already been seen that German planes were active on the side of General Franco during the first weeks of the war, either in carrying troops from Spanish Morocco to the peninsula or in bombing operations, although it is now clear that no promise of help had been given by Adolph Hitler to the organizers of the insurrection before the outbreak of hostilities.

As for Italian intervention, which must be examined briefly, according to fascist sources, Italian aircraft were also in operation during the early weeks of the conflict,[22] although no promise of aid had been given by Benito Mussolini either to General Franco or to General Mola prior to the outbreak of the conflict. In fact, in a book first published in 1954, Antonio de Lizarza Iribarren, the Carlist leader, who had been a member of the monarchist delegation that had requested aid from Mussolini in 1934,[23] states that it was not until 27 July 1936, ten days after the start of the military insurrection, that Mussolini decided, after some hesitation, to support the uprising.[24] This was corroborated in 1967 by Luis Bolín, the London correspondent of the Madrid monarchist newspaper *ABC*, who chartered the de Havilland Dragon Rapide that flew General Franco from the Canary Islands to head the revolt in Spanish Morocco on 18–19 July.[25] In his book *Spain: The Vital Years*, Bolín reproduces a hitherto unpublished document signed by General Franco (and countersigned by General Sanjurjo in Lisbon, the leader-designate of the rebellion, just before his ill-fated flight to Spain to head the revolt)[26] authorizing Bolín to negotiate urgently in England, Germany, or Italy for the purchase of aircraft and supplies. Bolín flew to Rome on 21 July, where he was assisted by former King Alfonso's equerry, the Marqués de Viana. Their request for help, although sympathetically received by foreign minister Count Galleazo Ciano, was at first denied by Mussolini, a fact confirmed by Roberto Canatalupo, the Italian ambassador to Franco.[27] Not until some days later did Mussolini agree to help, and, on 30 July, twelve Savoia-81 bombers were dispatched to Spanish Morocco, although only nine arrived safely at their destination.[28]

In 1968, José María Gil Robles published the following version of the purchase of the first Italian planes: "When the rising occurred and it became necessary to establish an aerial bridge for the passage of troops from Morocco to the peninsula, the Italian government gave notice that the contract for the purchase of the planes should be drawn up with one of the signatories of the [Rome] agreement of 1934.[29] It was essential that señores Goicoechea [head of Renovación Española, who had participated in the accord], Sainz Rodríguez, and Zunzunegui leave urgently for Italy with concrete orders from [General] Mola. They conducted the first successful negotiations for the purchase of war material, almost at the very moment that Luis Antonio Bolín, commissioned by General Franco, was experiencing difficulties in his negotiations. During their interview in Rome with Count Ciano on 25 July, the shipment of transport planes was agreed upon. By 1 August there had already arrived in Nador [the Spanish Moroccan airfield near Melilla] fourteen Italian Savoia-Marchetti military planes, and on 2 August, the number at the same airfield was twenty-four. Thus the pact of 1934 was fulfilled."[30] The official (pro-Franco) *Historia de la cruzada*, published in 1940, also claims that, because Bolín's negotiations were meeting with difficulty, General Mola, who was aware of the negotiations in 1934 conducted by Antonio Goicoechea, requested the latter to leave for the Italian capital to assist those who were already there. The Italian government, it added, had certain reservations up to this point about giving help because of lack of information regarding the significance of the rising. "The presence of Goicoechea in Rome, who, already in 1934 had agreed with Ciano on a possible counterrevolutionary movement, dissipated all doubts."[31]

Despite minor discrepancies in dates, the above evidence from four sources refutes the testimony of Pierre Cot, air minister in the French Popular Front government, to the effect that the shipment of Italian airplanes had been decided upon before 17 July, the date of the military uprising.[32] It also disproves the claim made by Yvonne Delbos, the French foreign minister, to the United States chargé d'affaires in Paris on 6 August 1936 "that the Italian air corps personnel who manned the planes had been enrolled for this duty at least as early as 20 July."[33]

The following excerpt from a report dated 18 December 1936 by the German ambassador in Rome to the Wilhelmstrasse on the interests of Germany and Italy in the Spanish Civil War sheds light on the motives of Italian intervention in Spain:

The interests of Germany and Italy in the Spanish troubles coincide to the extent that both countries are seeking to prevent a victory of Bolshevism in Spain or Catalonia. However, while Germany is not pursuing any immediate diplomatic interests in Spain beyond this, the efforts of Rome undoubtedly extend towards having Spain fall in line with its Mediterranean policy, or at least towards preventing political cooperation between Spain on the one hand and France and/or England on the other. The means used for this purpose are: immediate support of Franco; a foothold on the Balearic Islands, which will presumably not be evacuated voluntarily unless a central Spanish government friendly to Italy is set up; political commitment of Franco to Italy; and a close tie between Fascism and the new system of government to be established in Spain. . . .

In connection with the general policy indicated above, Germany has in my opinion every reason for being gratified if Italy continues to interest herself deeply in the Spanish affair. The role played by the Spanish conflict as regards Italy's relations with France and England could be similar to that of the Abyssinian conflict, bringing out clearly the actual, opposing interests of the powers and thus preventing Italy from being drawn into the net of the Western powers and used for their machinations. The struggle for dominant political influence in Spain lays bare the natural opposition between Italy and France; at the same time the position of Italy as a power in the Western Mediterranean comes into competition with that of Britain. All the more clearly will Italy recognize the advisability of confronting the Western powers shoulder to shoulder with Germany—particularly when considering the desirability of a future general understanding between Western and Central Europe on the basis of complete equality. In my opinion the guiding principle for us arising out of this situation is that we should let Italy take the lead in her Spanish policy, but that we ought simultaneously to accompany this policy with so much active good will as to avoid a development which might be prejudicial to Germany's direct or indirect interests, whether it be in the form of a defeat for Nationalist Spain or in the nature of a direct Anglo-Italian understanding in case of further stagnation in the fighting. We surely have no reason for jealousy if Fascism takes the fore in the thorny task of creating a political and social content behind the hitherto purely military and negatively anti-Red label. . . . We must deem it desirable if there is created south of France a factor which, freed from Bolshevism and removed from the hegemony of the Western powers but on the other hand allied with Italy, makes the French and British stop to think—a factor opposing the transit of French troops from Africa and one which in the economic field takes our needs fully into consideration.[34]

While Hitler and Mussolini responded to the appeals for help after only slight hesitation, Stalin moved with extreme caution before committing himself. Walter Krivitsky, the head of Soviet military intelligence in western Europe, who defected to the West at the end of 1937, testifies:

It was late in August when three high officials of the Spanish Republic were finally received by Russia. They came to buy war supplies, and they offered in exchange huge sums of Spanish gold. . . . [To] conceal the operation Stalin issued, on Friday, August 28, 1936, through the Commissar of Trade a decree forbidding "the export, re-export, or transit to Spain of all kinds of arms, munitions, war materials, airplanes and warships." . . . The fellow travellers of the Comintern, and the public, roused by them, already privately dismayed at Stalin's failure to rush to the support of the Spanish Republic, now understood that he was joining Léon Blum's policy of non-intervention. Stalin was in reality sneaking to the support of the Spanish Republic. [At an extraordinary session of the politbureau Stalin said] that neither France nor Britain would willingly allow Spain, which commands the entrance to the Mediterranean, to be controlled by Rome and Berlin. A friendly Spain was vital to Paris and London. Without public intervention, but by an adroit use of his position as the source of military supplies, Stalin believed it possible to create in Spain a regime controlled by him. That done he could command the respect of France and England, win from them the offer of a real alliance, and either accept it or—with that as a bargaining point—arrive at his underlying steady aim and purpose, a compact with Germany.[35]

That was Stalin's central thought on Spanish intervention. He was also moved, however, by the need for some answer to the foreign friends of the Soviet Union who would be disaffected by the great purge and the shooting of his old Bolshevik colleagues. The Western world does not realize how tenuous at that time was Stalin's hold on power, and how essential it was to his survival as dictator that he should be defended in those bloody acts by foreign communists and eminent international idealists. It is not too much to say that their support was essential to him. And his failure to defend the Spanish Republic . . . might have cost him their support.[36]

Because Krivitsky was denounced as an impostor by Communists and Communist partisans[37] when he made his revelations in a series of articles in 1938 and 1939, and later in book form in 1939,[38] and inasmuch as he is cited many times in this volume, it is important to quote the following passage from an article by the renowned and widely respected scholar on Russian affairs, Boris Nicolaevsky, written after Krivitsky's mysterious suicide in Washington, D.C., in 1941:[39]

"[Krivitsky's] competence and intelligence were indeed exceptional. He worked intermittently [in France, Holland, and Italy] in responsible positions in the secret apparatus of the Comintern, in the military intelligence (the so-called Fourth Administration), and in the GPU. . . . There wasn't anybody whom he did not see nor a secret he did not hear during that time. . . . In the course of the last three years [before his defection] Krivitsky worked in the foreign department . . . of the GPU as one of the three responsible representatives of that fearsome organization in western Europe. About that department— its tasks and the nature of its work—there is only a faint notion abroad. He played a very important role in the apparatus of the GPU and exercised very great influence on the whole policy making of the Soviet Union."[40]

The campaign denouncing Krivitsky as an impostor succeeded in creating around him a suspect aura that partially explains the cautious manner in which some historians even many years later treated his evidence. Hugh Thomas, for example, found it necessary to caution his readers in the first edition of his history of the Spanish Civil War, published in 1961, that "Krivitsky's evidence must be regarded as tainted unless corroborated,[41] although in a revised edition, published four years later, he changed this to read, "Krivitsky's evidence can generally be accepted, though his details are sometimes wrong."[42] To this remark it must be rejoined that Krivitsky's revelations have proved to be amazingly accurate, including many of the smallest details, and they constitute a major contribution to our knowledge of Soviet foreign policy aims and Soviet intervention in the Civil War. He was, in fact, the first person to reveal the presence in Spain of General Ian K. Berzin, the principal Soviet military adviser, of Alexander Orlov, the chief NKVD (secret police) operative, of Arthur Stashevsky, the adviser to Juan Negrín, the minister of finance, and to reveal the true name of General Emilio Kléber, the charismatic leader of the International Brigades, as shown later in this volume. But, more important still, he also asserted, as we have seen, that Stalin, while seeking an alliance with Britain and France during the Civil War, had in mind an alternative and apparently more attractive course—a compact with Germany. As early as December 1936, Krivitsky further claimed, Stalin had commissioned his trade envoy in Berlin, David Kandelaki, "to exert every effort toward making a secret deal with Hitler" and that he was in Moscow in April 1937 when Kandelaki brought with him the draft of an agreement with the Nazi government.[43] Although nothing came of these negotiations, Krivitsky's claim, while at variance with Russia's consistent and passionate support of "collective security," was authenticated some years later. "These very secret negotiations," wrote Leonard Schapiro in 1960, "were first disclosed by Krivitsky. That they in fact took place is now confirmed in a personal dispatch from Neurath [German foreign minister] to Schacht [Reichsbank president], dated 11 February 1937, from which it is clear that Kandelaki, in the name of Stalin and Molotov, put out feelers for an agreement with Germany but was rebuffed by Hitler. The document is among the files of the German Foreign Ministry which fell into Allied hands during the Second World War."[44]

Because of Stalin's caution in committing himself to the Spanish venture, the first Soviet artillery, tanks, and airplanes, together with pilots and tank operators, did not reach Spain until October 1936. In spite of all that has been said to the contrary, they did not arrive before then, as confirmed by such military men of high rank as Generals

José Miaja, Sebastián Pozas, and Ignacio Hidalgo de Cisneros, with whom I was able to converse freely after the war. For example, Hidalgo de Cisneros, the chief of the air force, stated that the first Russian bombers, tanks, and artillery reached Spain in October and the first combat airplanes on 2 November. This information was later corroborated by Juan Modesto, a commander of the Communist-controlled Fifth Regiment, who wrote that the first Soviet tanks arrived late in October and that in November Soviet airplanes "put an end to the impunity with which German and Italian aircraft were bombing the capital of Spain."[45]

The German consul general in Barcelona reported to the Wilhelmstrasse on 16 September 1936 that he had learned from a reliable source that thirty-seven airplanes were landed by the Russians in a small Spanish harbor a week before,[46] but there is no evidence in support of this. More cautious was the following report sent to the German foreign ministry by its chargé d'affaires in the Soviet Union on 28 September: "An expert foreign observer has noted that in the Black Sea harbor of Novorossiisk access to the harbor area has been more severely restricted since the summer months. The old entrance permits have been annulled and replaced by new ones. The same observer felt he had grounds for assuming that there was more than food in the heavy crates composing the cargo of the *Neva*, which left Odessa for Spain. So far, however, it has been impossible to obtain reliable proof of violation of the arms embargo by the Soviet government. Since the wide expanse of the Soviet Union, the position of her harbors, and the well-known Soviet system of surveillance and of restricted areas greatly facilitate any camouflage maneuvers, it is quite naturally extremely difficult to obtain such information."[47]

As for other Soviet military aid to Spain, Segismundo Casado, operations chief on the general staff of the war ministry in the left zone, affirms that in the second half of September "there made their appearance at the ministry of war certain Generals and Chiefs of the Soviet Army who were supposed to be 'military technicians' and were known as 'friendly advisers,'" and that from that day onward light arms began to arrive.[48] On the other hand, Vicente Rojo, chief of staff during the defense of Madrid, who worked closely with Soviet military advisers, states that the "Soviet technicians, in the capacity of a military mission, arrived in October before the first shipment of arms."[49]

Although the Russians sent no Soviet infantrymen to Spain, the first units of the International Brigades—which were organized on the initiative of the Comintern[50] and whose leaders, according to Carlo Penchienati, a commander of the Garibaldi Brigade, were, with rare exceptions, all Communists[51]—went into action in the second week of November.[52] Furthermore, the Italian Communist, Luigi Longo, known by the name of Gallo—political commissar of the Twelfth International Brigade and in later years head of the Italian Communist party after the death of Palmiro Togliatti—states that the first five hundred volunteers arrived in Albacete, their training base, on 14 October 1936.[53]

In supplying arms and some of his best foreign cadres, however, Stalin was careful not to become involved in a major conflict with Italy and Germany. Krivitsky attests that Stalin "doubly cautioned his commissars that Soviet aid to Spain must be unofficial and handled covertly, in order to eliminate any possibility of involving his government in war. His last phrase passed down by those at that politburo meeting as a command to all high officers of the service was: *Podalshe ot artillereiskovo ognia!* 'Stay out of range of the artillery fire!' "[54] And, in a speech made after his expulsion from the Communist party, Jesús Hernández, a former member of the Spanish politburo, declared: "To the direct requests of our party [for war material], Moscow replied with vague excuses about the gigantic technical difficulties that surrounded the shipment of arms and with cunning arguments to the effect that the international situation was so tense and delicate that a more overt aid to republican Spain could create very grave complications for the USSR vis-à-vis the fascist powers and frighten the Chamberlains, Daladiers, and Roosevelts, thereby increasing both the isolation of the Spanish Republic and the danger to the USSR. This was the road that was to lead the Soviet Union into collaboration with the monstrous policy of nonintervention."[55]

Because of her fear of involvement in a war with Italy and Germany, Russia limited her aid to bolstering the resistance of the anti-Franco forces until such time as Britain and France, faced by the threat to their interests in the Mediterranean of an Italo-German overlordship of Spain, might be induced to abandon the policy of nonintervention. Russia, moreover, was careful not to throw her influence on the side of the left wing of the Revolution or to identify herself with it. To have done otherwise would have revived throughout the world, among the very classes whose support the Comintern was seeking, fears and antipathies it was striving most anxiously to avoid. It would have given a deathblow to the French Popular Front—in which the cleavage of opinion was already running deep[56]—and rendered sterile of result every effort to establish a basis of agreement with the moderate parties in other countries, particularly in Britain, where the Communists' campaign for a Popular Front was already meeting with opposition from the Labour party.[57] "The People's Front in France," wrote a British Communist, "has driven back the fascist reaction and stands united with the Soviet Union for peace. If we could do the same in Britain, if the criminal opposition to unity could be overcome, if we could combine a corresponding Anglo-Soviet pact with the Franco-Soviet Pact, then we could build a front which could hold in check the fascist war offensive."[58] Indeed, it was for these reasons that, from the very inception of the war, the Comintern had sought to minimize and even conceal from the outside world the profound revolution that had taken place in Spain by defining the struggle against General Franco as one for the defense of the democratic Republic.[59]

The Comintern, writes an authoritative student of the Spanish scene, was particularly anxious that its policy be well propagandized among the Western democracies. "Consequently, all communist front organizations in the various countries and sympathetic observers of the communist policies, such as Louis Fischer in the United States, stressed the bourgeois aspects of the new policy. Louis Fischer, in his pamphlet *War in Spain*, declared: '. . . Some have regarded the Communists' advocacy of democracy in Spain as a tactical maneuver to mislead foreign democracies and bourgeois liberals into supporting the Loyalists. This interpretation is wrong; such a trick would soon become too transparent for use. The democratic slogan means that the Communists have no desire to establish in Spain a dictatorship guided by one party as in Russia. Spanish conditions are different.' "[60]

The Communists and their allies harped on the moderate character of the Revolution with passionate intensity:

"The working-class parties in Spain, and especially the Communist party," wrote André Marty, a member of the Executive Committee of the Comintern, in an article widely published in the world Communist press in August 1936, "have on several occasions clearly indicated what they are striving for. Our brother party has repeatedly proved that the present struggle in Spain is not between capitalism and socialism but between fascism and democracy. In a country like Spain, where feudal institutions and roots are still very deep, the working class and the entire people have the immediate and urgent task, *the only possible task*—and all recent appeals of the Communist party repeat it and prove it—not to bring about the Socialist revolution, but to defend, consolidate, and develop the bourgeois democratic revolution.

"The only slogan of our party that was spread right across *Mundo Obrero*, its daily paper, on 18 July, was 'Long Live the Democratic Republic!'

"All this is well known. Only dishonest people can maintain the contrary. . . . The few confiscations that have been made—for example, the offices and newspapers of the rebels—constitute sanctions against proven enemies and saboteurs of the regime and were made not as Socialist measures, but as measures for the defense of the Republic."[61]

"The Central Committee of the Spanish Communist party," ran a statement issued by the Communist party of France, "has asked us to make known to public opinion, as a reply to interested and fantastic reports in a certain press, that the Spanish people in their struggle against the rebels are not striving for the establishment of the dictatorship of the proletariat, but have only one aim: THE DEFENSE OF THE REPUBLICAN ORDER AND RESPECT FOR PROPERTY."[65] And a manifesto issued by the French Communist party on the same day declared:

"We speak for the Communist comrades, for the Socialists, and for all fighters for freedom in Spain, *when we declare that it is not a question of establishing socialism in Spain.*

"It is simply and solely a question of the defense of the democratic republic by the constitutional government, which, in face of the rebellion, has called upon the people to defend the republican regime."[63]

"The people of Spain," wrote Harry Pollitt, secretary of the British Communist party, a few days later, "are not fighting to establish Soviets, or the proletarian dictatorship. Only downright lying scoundrels, or misguided self-styled 'Lefts' declare that they are—and both combine to help the aims of the fascist rebels."[64]

"Really, people are sometimes surprising," wrote one observer. "Representative members of the PSUC [the communist-controlled United Socialist Party of Catalonia] express the opinion that there is no revolution at all in Spain, and these men with whom I had a fairly long discussion are not, as one would suppose, old Catalan socialists, but foreign communists. Spain, they explain, is faced with a unique situation: the Government is fighting against its own army. And that is all. I hinted at the fact that the workers were armed, that the administration had fallen into the hands of revolutionary committees, that people were being executed without trial in thousands, that both factories and estates were being expropriated and managed by their former hands. What was revolution if it was not that? I was told that I was mistaken; all that had no political significance; these were only emergency measures without political bearing."[65]

Before many weeks had passed, the Communists took advantage of German and Italian intervention to tone down the class character of the war still further. "In the beginning," declared a Spanish Communist party manifesto, "it was possible to describe the struggle simply as one between democracy and fascism, between progress and reaction, between the past and the future. But now it has broken through these bounds and become transformed into a holy war, into a national war, into a defensive war of the people, who feel that they have been betrayed and that their deepest sentiments have been wounded."[66]

8. The Communists Strive for Hegemony

That the Communist party's policy of camouflaging the Revolution could have been initiated only with the acquiescence or active support of other organizations can be open to no doubt; nor can there be any doubt that to ensure the success of its policy it had to become the ruling party in the left camp. This could be accomplished only at the expense of other left-wing movements, especially the left Socialists, who controlled the UGT, the Socialist labor federation, and the influential Madrid section of the Socialist party, the Agrupación Socialista Madrileña, and who, despite the startling growth of the CNT, the anarchosyndicalist labor federation, in the capital before the Civil War, were in all likelihood still the most powerful force in Madrid and in Old and New Castile on the morrow of the Revolution.

It has already been seen that in the months before the Civil War the official relations between the left-wing Socialists and the Communists had been so cordial that Francisco Largo Caballero, the left Socialist leader, in the ingenuous belief that he could absorb the Communists, had given his support to the fusion of the Socialist and Communist labor federations as well as to the merging of the parties' youth organizations. Moreover, the Agrupación Socialista Madrileña, which he controlled, had decided in March 1936 to propose at the party's next national congress the fusion of the Socialist and Communist parties, a merger that the Communists themselves strongly advocated. But, in spite of the smooth course of official relations, the Communists were disturbed by the left Socialist leader's agitation in favor of an immediate social overturn and, in private, characterized his ultrarevolutionary tendencies as "infantile leftist."[1]

In view of the underlying differences between the Communists and the left-wing Socialists, it is not surprising that the outbreak of the Revolution in July 1936 should have thrown their disparate attitudes into sharp focus. "When the Communist party raised the necessity of defending the democratic Republic," declared José Díaz, its general secretary, in a report to the central committee in March 1937, "the Socialists, a large proportion of our Socialist comrades, took the stand that the democratic Republic had no longer any raison d'être and advocated the setting up of a Socialist republic. This would have divorced the working class from the democratic forces, from the petty bourgeois and popular layers in the country. It was natural that our policy of uniting all the democratic forces with the proletariat should have met with certain difficulties owing to the failure of some Socialist comrades to understand that . . . this was not the moment to speak of a Socialist republic, but of a democratic republic with a profound social content."[2]

Although there is no record that any leading Socialist made a public declaration, either oral or written, at the outbreak of the Revolution urging the establishment of a Socialist republic, such a proposal may conceivably have been made in backstage discussions with the Communists. Certainly it would have been entirely consistent with Largo Caballero's prewar revolutionary policy and with the aims of his most ardent supporters up to the very inception of the conflict, and it is significant that the Communist leader's assertion was never voluntarily challenged. Nor indeed did an assertion by André Marty, French Communist leader, member of the Comintern, and an organizer of the International Brigades in Spain, to the effect that the Socialists abandoned their proposal to establish a Socialist republic as a result of Communist influence elicit any spontaneous denial. "When from the first day of the rebellion," he affirmed in 1937, "the Communist party declared that the prime need was the defense of the democratic Republic, many top-ranking Socialist leaders held, on the contrary, that a *Socialist republic* should be immediately established. This would have immediately smashed the Popular Front and led to the victory of fascism. Today, thanks to our influence, many leaders of the Socialist party have changed their attitude and adopted the platform of the Communist party."[3]

And in a speech early in September 1936, Antonio Mije, a member of the politburo, affirmed: "Even those who used to speak of proletarian revolution without taking into account the present situation understand today the correctness of the Communist party line in defending the democratic Republic."[4]

Anxious no doubt to protect Largo Caballero from the stigma of bowing to Communist policy, his supporters avoided any public discussion of his sudden change of stance. In fact, only when questioned many years after the war, Luis Araquistáin, one of the Socialist leader's few intimate associates, dismissed José Díaz's and André Marty's assertions as "pure nonsense" and as a "Communist lie."[5]

By mid-August Largo Caballero had so tempered his earlier revolutionary language—at least to the outside world—as to declare in a letter to Ben Tillett, the British trade-union leader, that the Spanish Socialists were fighting only for the triumph of democracy and had no thought of establishing socialism.[6] Precisely what arguments the Communist leaders may have adduced to sway Largo Caballero were never disclosed, but if their assertions be true, as would seem likely, they no doubt held that the setting up of a Socialist republic would have antagonized the Western powers and destroyed the advantages to be gained from keeping in office the liberal republican cabinet of José Giral that, in view of the policy generally adopted by foreign powers in cases of insurrection against a legitimate government, could rightfully claim that it be allowed to purchase arms freely in the markets of the world.[7]

But however much Largo Caballero may have allowed himself to be influenced by these impelling considerations in behind-the-scenes discussions with the Communists, it is clear from an editorial in his newspaper *Claridad* on 22 August 1936—as well as from his stepped-up agitation against the Giral government—that he had reservations about Communist policy and was not ready to turn his back completely upon the Revolution. "Some persons," the editorial declared, in an unmistakable reference to the Communists, "are saying: 'Let us crush fascism first, let us finish the war victoriously, and then there will be time to speak of revolution and to make it if necessary.' Those who express themselves in this way have obviously not reflected maturely upon the formidable dialectical process that is carrying us all along. The war and the Revolution are one and the same thing. Not only do they not exclude or hinder each other but they complement and support each other. The war needs the Revolution for its triumph in the same way that the Revolution needed the war to bring it into being.

"The Revolution is the economic annihilation of fascism and is consequently the first step toward its military annihilation. . . . The people are not fighting for the Spain of 16 July, that was still dominated socially by hereditary castes, but for a Spain from which those castes have been finally rooted out. The most powerful auxiliary of the war is the complete economic extinction of fascism. That is the revolution in the rear that will make more assured and more inspired the victory on the battlefields."

A no less serious cause of discord between the Communists and Largo Caballero in the weeks immediately following the outbreak of the Civil War was their disagreement over the liberal republican government of José Giral. The Communists did what they could to shore up his shaky administration, for which even in retrospect they have only words of praise: "The historical merit of the Giral government," affirms the official Spanish Communist history of the Civil War, "is that it knew how to accept and acknowledge the new politicosocial realities that were emerging in Spain."[8] But Largo Caballero railed against its "complete ineptitude." "The ministers are incapable, stupid, and lazy," he fulminated on 27 August 1936, according to the illuminating diary of Mikhail Koltzov, *Pravda*'s correspondent and Stalin's unofficial envoy, who interviewed Caballero shortly after the loss of Badajoz, a Socialist stronghold. Koltzov, to whose diary frequent reference is made in this volume, was, according to Arthur Koestler, who worked for the propaganda department of the Comintern and knew him personally, "the most brilliant and influential journalist in the Soviet Union, [and] it was general knowledge that he was a confidant of Stalin."[9] "Nobody listens to [the ministers]," Largo Caballero raged. "None of them is at all concerned with what the other is doing. They don't have the slightest conception of responsibility or of the gravity of the situation. . . . Besides, whom do they represent? All the popular forces are united outside the framework of the government, around the Socialist and anarchist labor unions. The working-class militia doesn't believe in the government. . . . Indeed, what kind of government is this! . . . It is a farce, not a government! It is a disgrace!" The Communists, he argued, were simply increasing popular discontent by helping the government. "The masses hold out their hands to us; they ask us for government leadership, but we remain passive, we avoid responsibility, we remain inactive!"[10]

A former Cortes deputy offers the following version of the simmering crisis that, although lacking direct corroboration, has elements of credibility: At a meeting of his followers in Madrid after the fall of Badajoz, Largo Caballero decided to replace Giral's "impotent" administration by a working-class government and to set up a proletarian dictatorship. This plan was thwarted only by the timely intervention of the Soviet ambassador, who argued successfully that the war should be continued "under the banner of the democratic Republic," thus averting "the danger that the premature establishment of a working-class government and a proletarian dictatorship would have represented."[11] Although denying this version, the official Spanish

The Rise of the Communists

Communist history of the Civil War virtually confirms it: "On the other hand, it is true that Largo Caballero increased his attacks on and sharpened his criticism of the Giral government, especially at the end of August, when the military situation of the Republic had deteriorated. Some of his closest correligionists, such as Araquistáin and [Carlos de] Baráibar, agitated more or less publicly in favor of the idea of eliminating the republican ministers and giving the direction of the country to Caballero with a view to establishing a 'working-class dictatorship.'"[12]

That the government of José Giral would have been helpless without the backing of the Communists and moderate Socialists, who worked within the ministries in unofficial but vital capacities, is certain. Even Indalecio Prieto, the leader of the moderate or center faction of the Socialist party, who for weeks worked assiduously behind the scenes to bolster the government, scorned its impotence. "Indalecio Prieto," wrote Koltzov, who interviewed the Socialist leader on 26 August, "occupies no official position. Nevertheless, he has been given an enormous, luxurious office, as well as a secretarial staff in the ministry of the navy. . . . He is seated in his armchair, an enormous fleshy mass with a pale ironic face. His heavy eyelids are half-closed, but under those lids the most watchful eyes of Spain are peering. He has won the solid, everlasting reputation of a practical politician, very shrewd and even cunning. . . . I ask his opinion of the situation. In ten minutes he makes a careful analysis, penetrating and pessimistic. He derides the impotence of the government."[13]

And Pietro Nenni, International Brigade commissar, and, after World War II, head of the Italian Socialist party, wrote on 14 August 1936: "I have been observing Prieto for several days. More than a man, he is a prodigious machine in operation. He thinks of a hundred things at once. He knows everything. He sees everything. . . . In shirt sleeves, sweating and panting, Indalecio goes from person to person, gives orders, signs papers, takes notes, growls over the telephone, chides one person, smiles at another. He is nothing; he is not a minister; he is only a deputy of a parliament in recess. And yet he is everything; the animator and coordinator of government action."[14]

Although contemptuous of Largo Caballero and his radical policies, Prieto acknowledged that he was the only politician who could head a government at that time. "He is a fool who wants to appear clever," he told Koltzov when interviewed on 26 August. "He is a frigid bureaucrat who plays the role of a mad fanatic, a disorganizer, a meddler who imagines he is a methodical bureaucrat. He is a man capable of ruining everything and everybody. Our political differences during the past few years lie at the heart of the struggle within the Socialist party. But, at least today, in spite of everything, he is the only man or, better still, his is the only name that can appropriately head a new government." Prieto then added that he was ready to join a government headed by Largo Caballero because "there is no other way out either for Spain or for me if I am to be useful to the country."[15]

The Communists, on the other hand, opposed any change in the administration, and for a few days José Giral's teetering government managed to survive. But, faced by the lightning advance of General Franco's forces toward Madrid and tired of presiding over a government to which the power of state belonged on paper only and which lacked the support of the majority of the working class, José Giral, at the suggestion of President Azaña, according to a report in *Claridad*, proposed that the government be broadened to include other Popular Front organizations.[16] Although the report did not state whether Largo Caballero was to head a new cabinet or simply to participate in an expanded administration under Giral, the authoritative Koltzov clears up this dubiety. He noted in his diary on 3 September that at first the cabinet reorganization was to be modest. Two or three Socialists belonging to the Prieto and Caballero factions were to join it. But suddenly the "old man" demanded for himself the war ministry and, almost immediately thereafter, the premiership. This met with general opposition, except from Prieto. It was felt that Caballero's "bluntness, his unsociability, and his impatience" would make "normal cooperation impossible." Alvarez del Vayo—at that time Largo Caballero's trusted adviser but a secret Communist sympathizer[17]—endeavored to convince the Socialist leader that he should take the war ministry and leave the premiership to Giral. Everyone then went over to the central committee of the Communist party so that it could mediate. The central committee also objected to Largo Caballero's becoming head of the government, but he insisted on "all or nothing." The general situation and the pressure of time, Koltzov observed, favored Caballero, for rumors of the crisis were spreading and in wartime such a situation could not be prolonged a single day. "Prieto declared that notwithstanding his relationship with Caballero, which was well known to everyone, he would not oppose him and that he was ready to accept any post in a government headed by him. . . . It was very distressing for everyone to accept a government presided by the old man. . . . In spite of everything, Largo Caballero is, in fact, today, the most venerable and representative figure in the labor movement. . . .

The Rise of the Communists

As for his leftist demagogic extremism, Vayo puts everyone at ease: this will disappear the very day he assumes responsibility for running the country." Feeling himself on firm ground, Koltzov continues, Caballero then presented another demand in the form of an ultimatum: that the Communists enter the cabinet. "The party was against this. It preferred to give the Popular Front government all its support while remaining on the outside; furthermore, it did not want to create unnecessary difficulties of an international nature lest the future government be called Bolshevik, Soviet. The old man stated that all this was nonsense, that he too would decline,[18] that everything could go to hell, and that the [Communist] party would be held accountable for whatever happened."[19] The party's opposition to entering the government is confirmed by César Falcón, editor during the first months of the war of *Mundo Obrero*, its organ in Madrid: "The Communist party maintained a position contrary to that of Caballero. Why change the government when for various reasons the national and international situtation was not opportune for the participation of Socialists and Communists."[20]

In face of Largo Caballero's inflexible attitude and new directives from Moscow that the party should join the government—directives that were received with "no little astonishment," according to former politburo member Jesús Hernández[21]—the Spanish Communist leaders reversed their position, and a new cabinet was formed on 4 September.

The members of the cabinet, the parties to which they belonged, and the portfolios they held, were as follows:[22]

Francisco Largo Caballero	Socialist	Prime Minister and War
Julio Alvarez del Vayo	Socialist	Foreign Affairs
Angel Galarza	Socialist	Interior
Anastasio de Gracia	Socialist	Industry and Commerce
Juan Negrín	Socialist	Finance
Indalecio Prieto	Socialist	Navy and Air
Jesús Hernández	Communist	Education and Fine Arts
Vicente Uribe	Communist	Agriculture
José Giral	Left Republican	Minister without portfolio
Mariano Ruiz Funes	Left Republican	Justice

| Bernardo Giner de los Ríos | Republican Union | Communications |
| José Tomás y Piera | Left Republican party of Catalonia | Labor and Health |

Later in the month Julio Just, a member of the Left Republican party, was made minister of public works.[23] and Manuel de Irujo, a member of the Basque Nationalist party, was appointed minister without portfolio.[24]

"The participation of the bourgeois parties in the Loyalist government is . . . a symbol," wrote Louis Fischer, a supporter at that time of Communist policy. "To capitalists in fascist Spain, and to the outside world, it is intended as an indication that the Republic has no plan now of setting up a Soviet State or a communist regime after victory in the civil war."[25]

The fact that the Catholic Basque Nationalist party, a middle-class organization, had opposed the military rebellion and had agreed to participate in the Largo Caballero government—on condition that the Basque country be granted autonomy[26]—was exploited to the full by the Communists and by fellow travelers in their domestic and foreign propaganda. The following excerpt from a letter reproduced in the pro-Franco newspaper *Heraldo de Aragón* on 10 June 1937 and allegedly written by Alvarez del Vayo to another member of the government, whose identity was not given, is worth quoting in view of its credibility: "How many times I have remembered what you said four months ago in my presence! It was necessary, you said—and you will recall that I immediately assented—to give the outside world the impression of a bourgeois tendency [in the government]. Nothing has favored us so much abroad as unity with the Basque Nationalist party."

Communist praise of José Antonio Aguirre, who became premier of the autonomous Basque government, was at times so extravagant that it embarrassed him. "I must confess," he stated in a report to the central government, "that as far as I am concerned the eulogies and headlines of the newspapers, principally the Communist newspapers, were sometimes so exaggerated, the adjectives so friendly and laudatory, that instead of feeling flattered I blushed with shame. This old tactic has no place in the customs of the Basque people, who are forthright and not doublefaced."[27]

Referring to the composition of the Largo Caballero government, the official Spanish Communist history of the Civil War observes:

The Rise of the Communists

"This was the first time that a Communist party had participated in a coalition government, together with a Socialist party and various middle-class parties. It was also the first time that Communists and Catholics formed part of the same government.[28] In the international arena there was no precedent for such a coalition government with these characteristics."[29] Of greater importance historically is the fact, as Stanley Payne points out, that this unprecedented coalition was "but one of the first of several major features by which the Popular Front governments of wartime Spain anticipated the coalition regimes and 'People's Democracies' that emerged from the wreck of the Second World War in Europe."[30]

Although the Communist party held only two portfolios in the new government, this furnished no real index of its strength in the country, either at the time the cabinet was constituted, when the number of its adherents had swollen far beyond the prewar total of forty thousand,[31] or a few months later, when it became, with an officially estimated membership of nearly a quarter of a million, the strongest political party in the anti-Franco camp. The precise figure, according to José Díaz, its general secretary, in a report to the central committee in March 1937, was 249,140, of which 87,660 (35.2 percent) were industrial workers, 62,250 (25 percent) agricultural laborers, 76,700 (30.7 percent) peasants, that is, peasant owners and tenant farmers, 15,485 (6.2 percent) members of the urban middle classes, and 7,045 (2.9 percent) intellectuals and members of the professional classes.[32]

If a large number of the party's new adherents, such as peasant owners, tenant farmers, tradesmen, small manufacturers, civil servants, army and police officers, doctors, teachers, writers, artists, and other intellectuals, had been members of the liberal republican parties or even right-wing sympathizers before the Civil War and had been attracted to the party by the hope either of rescuing something from the ruins of the old regime or of sharing in the Communists' growing power; if, moreover, an appreciable number had been members of the Socialist party or the UGT before the war, an even greater number had never cast their faith into any political mold and, like the converts from the Socialist movement, had been drawn to the Communist party by its proselytizing zeal, its immensely skillful propaganda, its vigor, its organizing capacity, in both the civilian and military fields, and the prestige it derived from Soviet arms and technicians.

Illustrative of the Communists' success in acquiring new members is the following testimony from a variety of sources:

"The Republican middle class, surprised by the moderate tone of communist propaganda and impressed by the unity and realism which prevailed in this party, flocked in great number to join its ranks," writes the Socialist historian Antonio Ramos Oliveira. "Army officers and officials who had never turned the pages of a Marxist leaflet became communists, some through calculation, others through moral weakness, others inspired by the enthusiasm which animated this organization."[33]

"Actually, bourgeois generals and politicians, and many peasants who approve the Communist party's policy of protecting small property holders, have joined its ranks," wrote Louis Fischer. "I think these people influence and are influenced. But essentially their new political affiliation reflects a despair of the old social system as well as a hope to salvage some of its remnants."[34]

"Whenever Poldi took us along to his many conversations with young officials of the various ministries," writes a Socialist, "I tried to assess them. It struck me that most of them were ambitious young men of the upper middle classes who now declared themselves communists, not, as we had done in Madrid, because to us it meant the party of revolutionary workers, but because it meant joining the strongest group and having a share in its disciplined power. They had leaped over the step of humanist socialism; they were efficient and ruthless."[35]

As for the intellectuals, another Socialist affirms: "Traditional Spanish pride was transformed into humiliation in the hands of the intellectuals. Nearly all of them bowed to the will of the Communist party."[36] Indicative of the efforts made by the Communist party to capture the sympathy of the Spanish intellectuals and scientists were the elaborate measures taken by the Communist-controlled Fifth Regiment to evacuate them from Madrid in the early days of the siege, giving them every comfort and protection.[37]

Fernando Claudín, a former Communist and member of the party for three decades, writes:

The Communist International and the Communist party of Spain understood from the first moment the decisive nature of the military problem. With the help of Soviet technicians and Communist cadres from other countries, the Spanish Communist party concentrated all its energies on the solution of this problem. Its structure, its method of functioning, the training of its cadres, made it particularly adept for this task. . . . The semimilitary features of the Bolshevik model after which it had fashioned itself enabled the Communist party of Spain to convert itself rapidly into the *military party* of the Republic, into the organizational nucleus of the army, that had to be created quickly and without which everything was condemned to death: libertarian

The Rise of the Communists

experiments, the Republican state, parties, and labor unions. The most elementary common sense caused the masses, independently of their political and union predilections, to understand that without an army, without a single command, without discipline, without a war economy, without "iron" unity—as the Communist party put it—in the front and in the rear, without subordinating every other consideration to the urgent necessity of defeating the enemy forces that were advancing, there was no salvation. If the membership of the Communist party and of its great auxiliary the Unified Socialist Youth (JSU) grew very rapidly in the first months of the war as well as its political influence and authority, this was not due to the fact that the proletariat considered the Communist party of Spain "more revolutionary" than the *Caballeristas* and anarchosyndicalists, but more clear-sighted and more capable of handling the crucial problem of the situation. The prestige that the Soviet Union acquired through its help to the Republic had undoubtedly no small influence on the growth of the Communist party of Spain, but the principal factor is the one we have just indicated. It is significant that the membership and influence of the party increased relatively little within the unions of the UGT, without mentioning those of the CNT, in other words, within the organized working class. Numerous petty bourgeois elements joined the Communist party of Spain, attracted by the reputation the party had acquired as the defender of order, of legality, and of small property. And above all, a large number of young men not yet trained in the traditional unions and working-class organizations adhered to the party—or placed themselves under its leadership through the JSU—attracted by the military virtues of the party and by a simplified ideology in which revolution was identified with antifascism intermingled with patriotism.[38]

Hardly inferior to all these factors as a source of Communist strength was the relative weakness or even impotence of other organizations. From the inception of the conflict, the liberal republicans, lacking influence among the masses, had retired into the background—or, as one friend of the Spanish Republic put it, they "remained in a comatose state throughout the war"[39]—ceding to the Communists the delicate work of opposing the left wing of the Revolution and defending the interests of the middle classes. Symptomatic of the change was the favorable publicity given to the Communist party by *Política*, the organ of the Left Republican party. "The change in the attitude of the bourgeois republicans is . . . very interesting," ran an article in *Pravda*. "Previously they tried not to notice the Communist party and spoke of it with animosity and disdain. Now some organs of the republican press devote whole laudatory articles to it."[40]

The Left Republicans not only gave friendly publicity to the Communists, whose declared policy coincided with their own—for example, José Giral, himself a member of the Left Republican party, observed that the coincidence of views between his party and the

Communists was almost identical[41]—but not a few, to quote Indalecio Prieto, the moderate Socialist leader, actually served the ambitions of the Soviet Union.[42]

Furthermore, because of their lack of centralized direction, the anarchosyndicalists, in spite of their numerical strength, were an unequal match for the Communists with their monolithic organization, their cohesion, and, above all, their discipline. According to Ettore Vanni, the Italian Communist and director of *Verdad*, the Communist newspaper in Valencia, Communist discipline was "accepted with a fanaticism that at once dehumanized us and constituted our strength. In face of the demands of the war, everything vanished: the family, the home, the individual. For us there was only one thing: the party— everywhere and always the party."[43]

In its discipline, unscrupulousness, and totalitarian nature lay the principal ingredients of the party's political success. Gerald Brenan writes:

[The Communists] were incapable of rational discussion. From every pore they exuded a rigid totalitarian spirit. Their appetite for power was insatiable and they were completely unscrupulous. To them winning the war meant winning it for the Communist party. . . . But perhaps more serious . . . was their lack of moral or political integrity. Their opportunism extended to everything. They seemed to have no program that could not be reversed if its reversal promised them any advantage, and they were just as ready to use the middle classes against the proletariat as the proletariat against the middle classes. No doubt the historical method of Marxism lends itself to a good deal of stretching: even so their going back on so many of their past tenets recalled the feats of those Jesuit missionaries of the seventeenth century who, the better to convert the Chinese, suppressed the story of the Crucifixion. It is a comparison worth insisting on. By their devotion to an institution rather than to an idea, to a foreign Pope rather than to a national community, they were following the road laid down by Loyola. And their impact on Spain was very similar. Just as the Jesuits from the time of Lainez had turned their backs on the great ascetic and mystical movements of their age and had worked to reduce everything to a dead level of obedience and devotion, so the Communists showed that the great release of feeling that accompanies a revolution was distasteful to them. They frowned on all its impulses, both its cruel and its creative ones, and applied a severely practical spirit to its various manifestations.[44]

Clearly, the anarchosyndicalists could not compete with the monolithic organization of the Communist party, guided and bolstered as it was by some of the best brains from the Communist cadres of other countries.[45] "In defense of the libertarians," writes César M. Lorenzo, himself a libertarian, "it should be stated clearly that the cultural level of the Socialists, Communists, and members of other parties was scarcely higher. Not only did illiteracy weigh heavily on political life, but also the archaism of an education that offered little in the way of scientific disciplines and had always been monopolized by the church (in spite of the efforts of a Francisco Giner de los Ríos among the middle class or of a Francisco Ferrer among the working class) blunted the faculties of educated persons."[46] Even if it is true, as Lorenzo contends, that during the first weeks of the Civil War the CNT played the dominant role in Madrid, this dominance—which is by no means certain—did not last for long.[47] Having no plan for the conquest of power, he affirms, lacking the undisputed hegemony it possessed in Catalonia, Aragon, or Malaga, the CNT could not centralize the conduct of military operations and the organization of the police and judiciary or transform the structure of the economy. "As a result, Madrid was delivered up to indescribable disorder. Each ideological sector formed a state within a state, each had its own militia, its own tribunals, its 'chekas,' its prisons, its own private buildings, its own food and munitions depots; each waged war in its own way and occupied itself solely with its needs. . . . [The] government was incapable of performing the task of unification. Since the Socialists proved too sluggish to assume this responsibility, since the libertarians, because of their doctrines, their extreme antiauthoritarianism, could not or would not assume the responsibility, it was logical that someone else would take their place. This was the Communist party.

"From the very beginning the Stalinists had created a military structure. Their disciplined troops, with their hierarchical makeup, endowed with perfect auxiliary services, soon showed their superiority over all other militia forces. . . . In the months of September and October, they seized the ascendancy from the libertarians, carried other parties along in their wake, and appeared as the best defenders of the capital."[48]

In a later passage, Lorenzo argues that a libertarian revolution in Spain would have been possible only if 90 percent of the population had been favorable to the ideas disseminated by the CNT and FAI, but all social and political groups hostile to the anarchosyndicalists, he confesses, far exceeded in numbers the adherents of the CNT and FAI.

Hence to establish libertarian communism it would have been necessary to coerce a large number of people, to stop them from sabotaging, from calumniating, from provoking disorders: it would have been necessary to arrest their leaders, dissolve their organizations, muzzle their press. In other words,

to establish libertarian communism it would have meant instituting a libertarian Communist dictatorship; it would have meant negating . . . that very
communism that is the antithesis of all political power, of all oppression, of
the police and the army. It would have meant reconstructing the state, transforming organized anarchism into a kind of ruling caste overseeing the rest of
the population, a caste that would become more and more tyrannical and
privileged. (Bakunin, Kropotkin, and Malatesta had clearly shown the danger
of power and had explained the genesis of the state.)

But if the Spanish libertarians had not been held back by these theoretical
considerations and by their devotion to their ideology, could they actually
have taken power? It is very doubtful. . . . Taking power was only possible
by a party that wielded iron discipline, a party organized militarily with a
revolutionary general staff, with a centralized and hierarchical apparatus,
an implacable ideological line, and combat groups possessing unquestioned
leaders. Within the CNT everyone had his own opinion, everyone acted
according to his own judgment, the leaders were ceaselessly criticized and
challenged, the autonomy of the regional federations was inviolable, just as
the autonomy of the local federations and unions was inviolable within the
regional federations. To get a decision accepted . . . a militant had to exhaust
himself making speeches, personal contacts, moving from place to place.
Among the libertarians the ballot was repugnant; the unanimity they sought
required interminable debates. How, under these conditions, could the CNT
have taken power even if its "leaders" had desired it?[49]

At the outbreak of the Revolution, the Socialists—despite anarchosyndicalist claims to the contrary—were in all probability still the
strongest force in the capital and in Old and New Castile. They were
soon undermined by open and secret defections to the Communist
party, for which their own passivity was in some degree responsible.
A leading left-wing Socialist, at one time very much influenced by the
Communist party, confesses that the "dynamic quality of the Communists was very congenial to me as compared with the extreme sluggishness of many Socialists."[50] Another left-wing Socialist writes: "I
had lost all confidence in the Socialist party's power of assuming responsibility and authority in a difficult situation, and my companion,
Torres, an old member of the Socialist Youth Organization, had recently joined the Communists."[51] On 9 March 1937 the moderate
Socialist organ, El Socialista, referred editorially to a letter from a
group of Socialists stating that they were joining the Communist
party because their own party showed no sign of life at the fronts.[52]

The Socialists were entangled in factional strife. In the hands of the
centrists led by Indalecio Prieto, the executive committee of the party
was in a state of irreconcilable belligerence with local units sympathetic to Largo Caballero. "Each provincial federation and division
acted on its own initiative," attests Wenceslao Carrillo, one of the

leading Caballero Socialists in the Agrupación Socialista Madrileña, controlled by the left wing. "Only the Madrid division maintained contact with a number of federations and sections, which asked it for directives."[53] "The life of the socialist movement," writes Gabriel Morón, a prominent centrist, "was reduced to a faint breath, manifesting itself in internal dissensions. . . . In the rear, as at the front, the boldest, the most zealous and unscrupulous imposed their views, made their influence felt, and asserted their personality." Later he attests: "There were no individuals with these moral and temperamental traits left in the Socialist party. On the other hand, the Communist party was filled with them to the point of congestion."[54]

The Communists took full advantage of the divisions within the Socialist party. Referring some years after the war to the dissensions among the leaders of the Socialist party, Jesús Hernández, former politburo member and one of the two Communist ministers in the government, wrote: "We managed to derive the utmost benefit for ourselves from their suicidal antagonisms. One day we supported one man against the other; the following day we did the reverse, and on all occasions we incited them against one another so that they would destroy themselves, a game we played in full view and not without success."[55]

The drive that the Communists initiated to engulf the Socialist movement began under the most promising auspices. That the successes they rapidly achieved, particularly at the expense of its predominant left wing, should have irked Largo Caballero was, of course, inevitable; for when, before the war, he had advocated fusion with the Communists, he may have believed, as he later contended, that he could absorb them,[56] but never had he anticipated the absorption of his own following. His resentment was acute when, within a few days of the inception of the war, the Catalan federation of the Spanish Socialist party led by Rafael Vidiella, hitherto a stout supporter, merged with the Catalan section of the Communist party and two other organizations to form the PSUC, the United Socialist party of Catalonia, which accepted the discipline of the Comintern or Third International[57] and brought the local organization of the UGT under its dominion.[58] But in other parts of the left zone, particularly in Madrid, the stronghold of the left-wing Socialists, the danger to Largo Caballero's influence revealed itself in its full stature. Lacking directives from their own party, which was racked and torn by internal discord, a large number of left Socialist workers, swayed by the dynamism and proselytizing methods of the Communists,[59] were ebbing away and embracing the rival movement. To make matters worse, some of Largo Caballero's most trusted aides, both in the Socialist party and the UGT, had transferred their attachment to the Communists, either in secrecy or without disguise. These included Julio Alvarez del Vayo, foreign minister and vice-president of the Madrid section of the Socialist party,[60] Edmundo Domínguez, secretary of the National Federation of Building Workers and president of the Madrid headquarters of the UGT, Amaro del Rosal, a member of the UGT executive committee, Felipe Pretel, the treasurer of the UGT,[61] as well as Margarita Nelken[62] and Francisco Montiel, two well-known Cortes deputies and intellectuals.

Addressing the plenary session of the central committee of the Communist party in March 1937, Montiel stated: "It is wonderful, for those of us who were outside the Communist party until a few weeks ago, to contemplate how, in the very midst of the revolutionary struggle, one organization that was for many years a powerful political force and had almost a monopoly of the political leadership of the Spanish proletariat was disintegrating, ruined by its mistakes, and how another organization, composed in the early days of little more than a handful of men, but guided to perfection by Marxism and Leninism, could become after 18 July the real force in the struggle against fascism and the real directing force of the Spanish masses."[63]

A still more important development that told on Largo Caballero's political influence was the loss of his authority over the JSU,[64] which was formed three months before the outbreak of the Civil War as a result of the amalgamation of the Union of Young Communists and the Socialist Youth Federation, whose representatives had met in Moscow with the executive committee of the Young Communist International to draw up plans for the fusion of the two organizations.[65] Santiago Carrillo, general secretary of the JSU, claimed in 1937 that its membership that, according to his figures, had been forty thousand at the time of the fusion had risen to one hundred fifty thousand just before the outbreak of the Civil War[66] and to three hundred thousand in April 1937.[67]

The preparatory operations for this merger, writes Luis Araquistáin, Largo Caballero's close collaborator and adviser, or "eminence grise," as his opponents described him, who undoubtedly approved of the negotiations at the time but never acknowledged publicly his participation, were conducted in the home of his brother-in-law, Julio Alvarez del Vayo. "I lived in Madrid, one floor above him, and witnessed the daily visits paid to him by young Socialist leaders for the purpose of inteviewing the Comintern agent then prominent in Spain, a certain Vittorio Codovila, who used the false name of Medina, and spoke Spanish with a strong South American accent. It was there that a voyage to the Muscovite Mecca was organized for them; it was there that it was agreed to deliver the Socialist youth, the new working-class generation of Spain, to communism."[68]

In spite of everything that has since been said to the contrary, Largo Caballero had encouraged the fusion of the two youth movements,[69] although in a joint statement issued in March 1936, before the merger had taken place, it was agreed that until a national congress of unification had determined democratically the principles, program, and definitive structure of the united organization and elected a directive body, the fusion would be effected on the basis on the entry of the Young Communists into the Socialist Youth Federation.[70] Stimulated by Largo Caballero's policy of uniting the working-class movements, however, the fusion of the two organizations took place precipitately, and no congress of unification was held.[71] Largo Caballero had not opposed this because the Union of Young Communists was incomparably smaller than his own Socialist Youth Federation—only three thousand members in contrast with fifty thousand, according to one estimate[72]—and because he had believed that through his supporters he would be able to control the united movement. But in the sequel he was rudely deceived; for within a few months of the inception of the Civil War, Santiago Carrillo, general secretary of the JSU and hitherto a sedulous admirer,[73] quietly joined the Communist party together with other former leaders of the Socialist Youth Federation.[74] Some of them, including Carrillo (who became secretary of the party in exile and returned to Spain in that capacity forty years later after the death of Franco), later became members of its central committee[75] and transformed the JSU into one of the main props for Communist policy. Commenting on this defection, Carlos de Baráibar, the left Socialist leader, who, according to his own confession, was very much influenced by the Communists early in the war, recalls: "A group of leaders of the Unified Socialist Youth [JSU] visited me to inform me that they had decided to join the Communist party en masse . . . I considered it monstrous that such a thing could have happened . . . with no one's knowledge other than that of Alvarez del Vayo who, as I learned later, was informed of every step taken. And all of them were advised by the person whom we used to call the 'eye of Moscow,' the secret representative of the Comintern [Vittorio Codovila]."[76]

In order fully to understand the future course of events, it is essential at this point to emphasize the power that Moscow's foreign representatives—the Comintern "delegates" or "instructors," as they were called—exercised at that time over the Spanish politburo. Vittorio Codovila, an Argentinian, was, in the words of onetime central committee member Enrique Castro, "the real head of the party."[77] Furthermore, according to Eudocio Ravines, a former foreign Communist who knew Codovila personally and who worked on the staff of the Communist organ *Frente Rojo* in Valencia, before the Civil War Codovila had "liquidated politically" the former Spanish party leadership and replaced it with "elements subordinate to his will."[78] According to the same knowledgeable source, Boris Stefanov, a Bulgarian, "one of the few friends of Lenin who had survived the purges" and one of Stalin's closest friends, was also in Spain, using the alias Moreno, and is described by Ravines, who knew him personally, as "the maximum director of the Revolution, the war, the feints, and maneuvers of the Communist party. His word was taken as though it were personally inspired by Stalin."[79] Equally important was the fact that Palmiro Togliatti, the Italian Communist and member of the Executive Committee of the Comintern, who had escaped from Mussolini's Italy in 1924 and became head of the Italian Communist party after World War II, was also active in Spain, especially after the departure of Codovila in 1937, when he became the virtual head of the party, directing strategy and writing many of the speeches of José Díaz and La Pasionaria. Using the aliases Ercole Ercoli and Alfredo, Togliatti remained in Spain with Stefanov until the end of the Civil War.[80]

In his testimony before the U.S. Senate Subcommittee on Internal Security in February 1957, Alexander Orlov, chief NKVD (Soviet secret police) official in Spain from September 1936 until his defection in July 1938, stated: "Palmiro Togliatti was also in Spain . . . with me, and he had been a good friend of mine at that time. He directed the Spanish Communist party and the Spanish Communist military forces on behalf of Moscow. . . . [At] the head of the Italian Communist party [today] stands the most able man in the Communist movement —that means Palmiro Togliatti."[81] Furthermore, in the opinion of the American Communist John Gates, head commissar in 1938 of the Fifteenth Brigade, "Togliatti was the most powerful communist figure in Spain. His responsibility was the whole policy of the Spanish communists. . . . The enormous growth of the Spanish Communist party after the fascist revolt must be attributed in large part to his advice and leadership. . . . Togliatti was a brilliant tactician, probably the most able in the communist world."[82]

The Rise of the Communists

Given the monolithic character of the Comintern apparatus, it is not surprising that these foreign Communists, with their vast political experience in the world movement and wielding power that flowed directly from the Kremlin, had little difficulty in dominating the meetings of the Spanish politburo. Nor is it surprising that the JSU—thanks to the power and influence of Vittorio Codovila and to the help of Santiago Carrillo and other Socialist youth leaders, who had joined the Communist party—soon became an important instrument of Comintern policy.

Shortly after the defection of Santiago Carrillo, the Communists consolidated their hold over the JSU still further. Instead of holding the projected national congress of unification that was to determine democratically the principles, program, and definitive structure of the united organization and to elect a directive body, Santiago Carrillo convened, in January 1937, a national conference. To this he appointed as delegates not only the representatives of the local sections of the JSU, but a large number of young Communists from the fronts and factories, a stratagem that enabled him to control the conference from start to finish and to secure the election of a national committee packed with Communist party nominees.

"Could we," he asked, defending his action from criticism a few months later, "could we, in wartime, and considering the changes that have taken place in our country and in our own organization, hold a congress attended exclusively by the representatives of the local sections? Could we, with our youth at the fronts, hold the same type of congress that we should have held before 18 July, when our youth was not yet defending its liberty with arms? No, we could not have held such a congress. We had to adapt ourselves to the situation. And the situation made it compulsory that our congress, our national conference, should be attended not only by the representatives of the local sections, but also by those young men who were striving with great sacrifice to increase war production in the factories and by those who were giving their blood for our liberty on land, on sea, and in the air; in other words, by that part of our youth, the best part—not in the local sections, but at the front—that has a legitimate right to direct and control the life of its federation."[83]

The following excerpt from a letter sent to the author some years after the war by Antonio Escribano, the delegate to the conference for Alicante province, is of interest: "I remember when the national committee of the JSU was elected. . . . Several veterans of the youth movement met with Carrillo and his associates and elected representatives for each province. Later they read the 'election' of the national committee which everyone approved by acclamation because instructions had been given to agree to everything proposed by the leadership."

In this coup Carrillo had undoubtedly been aided by his liberal praise of Largo Caballero. "It is necessary to say here and now," he had declared in his speech at the confernece, "that as ever, and even more than ever, Largo Caballero enjoys the support of the Spanish youth in the factories and at the fronts. I must also add that Comrade Largo Caballero is for us the same as he was before: the man who helped our unification. He is the man from whom we are expecting much useful advice so that, in the interests of the common cause we are defending, the unity of the Spanish youth may be a reality."[84]

Carrillo also undoubtedly had been aided not only by the fact that few of the young Socialist delegates were aware at the time that he had joined the Communist party, believing that he and other leaders of the JSU were acting in full accord with Largo Caballero and his supporters in the Socialist party, but also by the fact that all debate had been avoided. Antonio Escribano recalls:

Nothing at all was debated [at the conference]. Those who did speak confined themselves to making a report or address, but no discussion followed. A certain Carrasco spoke on behalf of the antitankists on how to destroy tanks; a sailor spoke on his own subject, an aviator likewise, and so on and so forth. The fact is that nothing regarding the unification of the two organizations was debated. On the contrary, everything that had happened was taken for granted. Those of us who were loyal to Caballero did not raise any objections at the conference for two reasons, both fairly ingenuous when I look back on them today, although justifiable at the time. These reasons were: 1. 90 percent of the young Socialists who attended the conference did not know that Carrillo, Laín, Melchor, Cabello, Aurora Arnaiz, etc., had gone over outright to the Communist party. We believed that they were still young Socialists and that, strange as it seemed to us, they were acting in agreement with Caballero and the Socialist party. Had we known that this group of recreants had betrayed us, I can assure you that an entirely different situation would have arisen. But we were taken off our guard. That is the truth of the matter, which, for my part I am not ashamed to confess. 2. The atmosphere and the manner in which the conference was conducted took us by surprise, and when we wished to react the assembly had already come to an end. We members of the Socialist Youth Federation had been accustomed to discuss the agendas of our congresses and assemblies democratically and exhaustively, and had firmly believed that the conference would be conducted in the same way. . . . Nothing of the kind occurred. When we realized what had happened, it was too late. The conference had ended.[85]

The Rise of the Communists

Indeed, not until a few weeks after the conference, when the struggle between Largo Caballero and the Communists had entered upon an acute stage, did the first fissure in the JSU appear. Open letters to Santiago Carrillo were published from two of Largo Caballero's supporters, José Gregori Martínez, general secretary of the provincial committee of the Valencia JSU, and Rafael Fernández, general secretary of the JSU of Asturias, declining the seats on the national committee to which they had been elected at the conference on the ground that their local sections had not been consulted.[86]

If, in conjunction with all these developments, the skill of the Communists in using artifice and subterfuge, in playing one hostile faction against another, in packing pivotal positions with secret party members or with fellow travelers, in bestowing patronage and exerting pressure upon anyone who joined their ranks or served their interests, is taken into consideration, their early emergence as the real power in the anti-Franco camp should be readily appreciated.

[136]

9. The Communists Pilot the Cabinet

The two ministries the Communist party held in the government furnished no real index of its strength in the country nor did they afford a true indication of the influence it wielded in its councils.[1] The real weight of the Communists in the government lay less in the two portfolios they held than in the secret influence they enjoyed over Largo Caballero's foreign minister and man of confidence, Julio Alvarez del Vayo, and over the minister of finance, Juan Negrín.

Though vice-president of the Madrid section of the Socialist party and officially a member of its left wing, Alvarez del Vayo soon came to be regarded by the leading figures in his party as a Communist at heart.[2] A few days before the end of the war, the Madrid section decided to suspend him and to propose to the national executive his expulsion from the Socialist party because of his pro-Communist activity.[3] A supporter of the Soviet Union and of Comintern policy before the Civil War,[4] he had played an important part, as has been shown, in bringing about the fusion of the Socialist and Communist youth movements,[5] and during the war he endorsed the Communists' campaign for the fusion of the Socialist and Communist parties.[6] In spite of this record, some years later, after emigrating to the United States and becoming a member of the editorial staff of the *Nation*,[7] he denied that he had ever advocated a merger of the two parties.[8]

As Largo Caballero's trusted adviser during the early months of the Civil War, he not only possessed his ear on matters of foreign policy, but was appointed by him to head the vital General Commissariat of War that directed the political orientation of the armed forces. In this body, according to Pedro Checa, a member of the politburo, he served the Communist party "scrupulously."[9] Yet, in spite of his many services, there is evidence that in the inner circles of the party he commanded no respect. "He is a fool, but is more or less useful," was the party's opinion, according to a former central committee member.[10] He was also in charge of appointments to the foreign press bureau, which censored the dispatches of correspondents with an eye to opinion abroad. "During the three months that I was director of propaganda for the United States and England under Alvarez del Vayo," wrote Liston Oak, "I was instructed not to send out one word about this revolution in the economic system of loyalist Spain. Nor are any foreign correspondents in Valencia [the provisional seat of government] permitted to write freely of the revolution that has taken place."[11] He appointed the Czech Communist Otto Katz, alias André Simone, as director of the foreign propaganda agency in Paris, the Agencia Española.[12]

But valuable as were Alvarez del Vayo's services to the Communists in helping them to implement their strategy of infiltration and domination in the early stages of the Civil War, the main instrument in bringing their plans to fruition in its final stages was Juan Negrín, son of a wealthy Canary Islands businessman. An adherent, at the outbreak of the conflict, of Indalecio Prieto's anti-Communist center faction of the Socialist party,[13] a professor of physiology at the Madrid School of Medicine, minister of finance in Largo Caballero's government, prime minister from May 1937 to April 1938, and premier and defense minister from April 1938 until the end of the war in March 1939, he was more responsible than any other Spaniard for the later success of Communist policy. A detailed account of Negrín's subservience to the Communists and of his vast contribution, as premier and defense minister, to the success of their policy in the last twelve months of the war lies beyond the scope of the present chapter, but the interested reader can find such overwhelming corroborative evidence in the writings of top-ranking Socialists and in other sources as to leave not a scintilla of doubt.[14] Added to all this is the fact that later in the war Negrín relied heavily upon his personal political secretary, Benigno Rodriguez, a party member and a former editor of *Milicia Popular*, organ of the Communist Fifth Regiment.[15] Like Alvarez del Vayo, Negrín was suspended toward the end of the war from the Madrid section of the Socialist party because of his political conduct.[16] Although he was Prieto's own man and recommended by him to head the ministry of finance in Largo Caballero's government in September 1936,[17] long before the war had run its course, Negrín freed himself, at first secretly and then openly, from the personal and political bonds that tied him to the moderate Socialist leader.

Too many people, anxious not to hurt the cause of the Republic, have appeared blind to Negrín's subservience to the Communists. Claude Bowers, for example, the U.S. ambassador to Spain during the Civil War, claimed that Negrín was "as remote from communism as it is possible to be."[18] His ignorance may be partially attributed to the fact that shortly after the outbreak of the conflict he established his official residence in Hendays, in the south of France, and remained there, like many other members of the diplomatic corps, for the duration of the conflict, but there can be no doubt that his sympathy for the republican cause obscured his judgment.[19]

"Negrín," writes Frank Sedwick, "was to open the doors wide to communist domination of the government and the armed forces. . . . [He] remains today [1963] one of the most controversial figures of the Spanish Civil War. Undeniably he was a strong leader, an indefatigable worker, and a fighter to the end. His courage, self-confidence, resourcefulness, and vigorous personality won him the perpetual praise of Herbert Matthews [of the *New York Times*] and certain other correspondents whose personal involvement with the Loyalist cause may have taken a measure of objectivity from their writing."[20]

It is curious that thirty-four years after the Civil War, notwithstanding all the available evidence corroborating Negrín's pro-Communist activities, Herbert Matthews still denied Negrín's extraordinary services to the Communist cause and remained until his death in 1956 Negrín's principal apologist in the vast bibliography on the Spanish conflict. In his final work on Spain, published in 1973, he wrote: "Mistaken beliefs about Negrín have colored and distorted a great many histories, especially perhaps those of the most scrupulous postwar scholars, hardly any of whom had the opportunity of knowing Dr. Negrín. He was the key figure on the Republican side. Get his character and motives wrong and the history being written will be wrong. Even a scholar as discerning and shrewd as Hugh Thomas, whose portrayal of Dr. Negrín is quite fair and sympathetic, could not allow himself to believe that certain charges against Don Juan—that he yielded to communist demands for instance—were completely false. In his book *The Spanish Revolution*, Professor Payne is wrong in saying: 'That he [Negrín] was dedicated to the cause of a leftist victory irrespective of tactics or consequences seems without question.' Dr. Negrín used and worked with the communists simply for practical reasons which had nothing to do with 'leftism' or any ideology. He had no political coloration or preference for any political party or movement as such."[21]

In spite of Matthews's mild criticism of Thomas, both writers have expressed similar views regarding the supposed independence of Negrín. "[It] would be quite wrong to conclude that Negrín was a mere instrument of Soviet policy," Thomas writes. "It is true that few politicians have successfully used a Communist party, and not been later swallowed by it. But in the 1930s and in Spain the possibility did not seem so far-fetched. Negrín's personal self-confidence and his reserved secret nature perhaps led him to think that he could slough off the communist connection when necessary. . . . Though he was on excellent terms with the Russian economic adviser, Stashevsky, on one occasion (when minister of finance) he had told another Russian not to try to dictate the internal affairs of Spain. Otherwise, added Negrín, 'there is the door.' "[22] The source of this unconfirmed anecdote, however, was Pablo de Azcárate, the republican ambassador in London, who was a perfervid admirer of Negrín's[23] and who, in the words of his former friend and colleague at the League of Nations, Salvador de Madariaga, later abandoned the "strict path of truth" for the "intellectual bog" of communism.[24]

As minister of finance in Largo Caballero's administration, Negrín maintained intimate relations with Arthur Stashevsky, the Soviet trade envoy, to whom Stalin, according to Walter Krivitsky, the head of Soviet military intelligence in western Europe, had assigned the task of "manipulating the political and financial reins of loyalist Spain."[25] Stashevsky, he asserts, discovered in Negrín "a willing collaborator in his financial schemes."[26] Although we have only Krivitsky's word for this allegation, two knowledgeable supporters of Negrín have confirmed the close relationship between the two men. Louis Fischer —who was personally acquainted with most of the leading Russians in Spain, and who, Indalecio Prieto claims, was Negrín's "propaganda agent" abroad and "probable financial director" of that propaganda to judge from the "large sums" he received from Negrín[27]—affirms that Stashevsky "not only arranged Spanish purchases of Russian arms but was Negrín's friendly adviser on many economic problems."[28] Alvarez del Vayo, an unwavering supporter of Negrín's, acknowledges that the Russian with whom Negrín had the most contact was Stashevsky and that they formed a "real friendship."[29] On the other hand, Angel Viñas, the leading authority on republican finances and Spanish gold reserves during the Civil War and as scrupulous a scholar as one could hope for, while confirming that Stashevsky was a "key man in implementing the initial aid for republican Spain" and was directly involved with Negrín in major financial operations relating to the purchase of arms in the Soviet Union,[30] casts some doubt on the manipulative financial role that Stalin allegedly assigned to the Soviet trade envoy.[31]

Krivitsky also asserts that Stashevsky offered to ship the enormous Spanish gold reserves—estimated at that time as the third largest in the world—to the Soviet Union and to supply Madrid with arms and munitions in exchange. "Through Negrín," Krivitsky alleged, "he made the deal with Caballero's government."[32] In contrast, Alexander Orlov, who was the head of the NKVD in Spain from 1936 until his defection in 1938 to the United States[33] and who, as will be seen, was entrusted by Stalin with the arrangements for the actual shipment, affirms that Negrín, "aware of the deteriorating [military] situation," sounded out Stashevsky about storing the gold in Russia. "The envoy cabled Moscow, " Orlov adds, "and Stalin leaped to the opportunity."[34]

On the other hand, two letters from Premier Largo Caballero to Marcel Rosenberg, the Soviet ambassador, formally requesting his government's approval of the shipment that were published thirty-four years later by Marcelino Pascua, Spain's wartime ambassador to Moscow, appear, on the surface at least, to rule out the intervention of Stashevsky. In his first letter, dated 15 October 1936, Largo Caballero stated that in his capacity as prime minister he had decided to request the Soviet ambassador to ask "your government if it will kindly agree to the deposit of approximately 500 metric tons of gold, the exact weight to be determined at the time of delivery,"[35] and in the second letter, dated 17 October, acknowledging Russia's acceptance of the proposal, Largo Caballero stated that "we plan to arrange for the payment of certain orders placed abroad . . . and for transfers of foreign currency to be charged against the gold that your government has agreed to accept on deposit."[36]

Much as these official letters—both of which, according to Pascua, were drafted by Negrín[37]—appear to call in question Stashevsky's role, they do not exclude the possibility that they were simply the result of preliminary discussions between the Soviet trade envoy and the finance minister and that they were subsequently approved and signed by Premier Largo Caballero. The diplomatic language of the letters—the first requesting and the second acknowledging Russia's *approval* of the proposed shipment—may well have been used, at Stashevsky's suggestion, to disguise Stalin's special interest in acquiring the Spanish treasure.

Yet, with Madrid in danger, the question of moving the gold reserves to safer keeping had been considered even by the Giral cabinet,[38] although the idea was not acted upon until Largo Caballero had formed his administration on 4 September, with Negrín as finance minister.

The Rise of the Communists

On 13 September, by a *decreto reservado*—a confidential decree—countersigned by President Azaña, Negrín, in his capacity as finance minister, obtained authority from the cabinet to transfer the gold and silver stocks as well as the paper currency held by the Bank of Spain "to a place that offers in his opinion the maximum security." Article 2 stated that the decree would be submitted "in due course" to the Cortes, but it never was.[39] Within a few days, ten thousand cases of gold coins and ingots were transferred to a large cave at Cartagena.[40]

That Cartagena should have been selected is not surprising. "It was a large naval base," writes Viñas, "armed and adequately defended, somewhat removed from the theater of operations and from which it would be possible, if necessary, to ship the reserves to another place. . . . Perhaps the cabinet may not have anticipated their ultimate destination," he comments. "In fact, immediately after their arrival at Cartagena, it was decided to increase the volume of shipments to France."[41]

Obviously, the purpose of the transfer to Cartagena was not simply to protect the gold reserves from capture by enemy forces, but to accelerate their conversion into foreign exchange for the purchase of urgently needed war material. As Viñas points out—quoting Gordón Ordás, a conservative republican, who was one of several government representatives entrusted with the purchase of arms abroad—the Non-Intervention Agreement rendered the purchase of arms difficult unless there were available "sufficient money on deposit to effect cash payments, since any attempt to buy on credit was fruitless."[42]

To meet this problem, both the Giral and Largo Caballero governments made a number of gold shipments to the Bank of France for conversion into foreign currency, such shipments aggregating about 200 metric tons as compared with a total in gold reserves of approximately 710 metric tons.[43] Most of the shipments to France were made after the transfer to Cartagena.[44] Nevertheless, according to Luis Araquistáin, a Caballero supporter and one of the arms purchasers and largest recipients of funds,[45] grave problems arose because of partial and irregular shipments and because of delays in obtaining authorizations from the Bank of France for the release of the necessary funds, with the result that on some occasions weeks went by without a single purchase being made.[46] Gordón Ordás records that these delays were responsible for the collapse of important transactions and that British banks tried to "delay as long as possible the release of funds to a destination that did not appear desirable to them."[47]

Hardly less disturbing was the angry reaction of the rebel or Nationalist Junta in Burgos, which was accurately apprised of the gold shipments through its agents and friends in Spain and France.[48] By means of official communiqués, radio broadcasts, telegrams, and letters of protest addressed to Western governments, to the Bank of France, and to other central banks, as well as by threats of legal suits, Burgos did what it could to obstruct the sale of the gold, charging that the acceptance of the reserves used by the Bank of Spain to guarantee its currency was "a monstrous complicity with the Marxist gang," that their sale was an act of "pillage" and a violation of the basic banking law, the Ley de Ordenación Bancaria, governing the gold reserves that "form part of the national patrimony just like the territory of the nation."[49]

Although Viñas does not examine in detail the juridical aspects of the depletion of the gold reserves, whose essential purpose was to serve as a backing for the paper currency in circulation, he states that the financing of the war made it essential "to circumvent the strict provisions of the Ley de Ordenación Bancaria, which necessarily precluded the alienation and application of the reserves for such purposes as the purchase of weapons and war materials."[50] On the other hand, Alvarez del Vayo skates over the massive gold shipment to Russia with the bland remark that it "took place strictly in accordance with the Ley de Ordenación Bancaria."[51]

The emotional atmosphere created by the Nationalists' campaign undoubtedly caused misgivings in the minds of Negrín and Largo Caballero and led them to fear that France might eventually block the use of the gold reserves. This apprehension must also have contributed to their decision, whether inspired by Stashevsky or not, to ship the bulk of the reserves to Russia, where they could be used for the purchase not only of Soviet arms and supplies, but also of foreign exchange necessary for the acquisition of arms and supplies in other countries. The principal channel for these transactions in western and central Europe was the Soviet-controlled Banque Commerciale pour l'Europe du Nord in Paris, that was (and still is) under Soviet control, and whose operations were shrouded in absolute secrecy, an undoubted advantage in the prevailing climate,[52] but one that now leaves the bank's accounting open to the charge of possible manipulation since it has never published any records relating to its transactions on behalf of the Republican government.[53]

On 20 October 1936, three days after Largo Caballero had written

his letter acknowledging Russia's agreement to accept the gold reserves on deposit, NKVD chief Alexander Orlov received the following coded telegram from Joseph Stalin:
"Together with Ambassador Rosenberg, arrange with the head of the Spanish Government, Caballero, for the shipment of the gold reserves of Spain to the Soviet Union. . . . This operation must be carried out with the utmost secrecy.

"If the Spaniards demand from you a receipt for the cargo, refuse. I repeat, refuse to sign anything, and say that a formal receipt will be issued in Moscow by the State Bank."[54]

The official, final receipt for 7,800 of the original 10,000 cases of ingots and coins transferred from Madrid to Cartagena (the balance of 2,200 went to France and Valencia between September 1936 and February 1937[55]) was issued on 5 February 1937, bearing the signatures of Marcelino Pascua, the Spanish ambassador in Moscow, G. F. Grinko, people's commissar of finance, and N. N. Krestinski, deputy people's commissar for foreign affairs.[56] The work of opening the 7,800 cases and of counting and weighing the contents of each case was done, the receipt indicated, "in the presence and with the participation of one of the following persons: Arturo Cadela, Abelardo Padin, José Gonzalec [sic] and José Velasco." The weight of the shipment was given as 510,079,529.13 grams or 510.08 metric tons, with a value at that time of $518 million, based on an estimated pure gold content of 460.52 metric tons.[57]

Almost twenty years later—long after Negrín's relations with the Spanish Communists in exile had begun to cool—a copy of the receipt and a large number of other documents in Negrín's possession relating to the gold deposited in Moscow were turned over to the Franco authorities by his son Rómulo as a result of negotiations initiated at Negrín's request, shortly before his death in France on 12 November 1956, by his close friend and former justice minister, Mariano Ansó. The documents, Negrín had told Ansó, were the property of the Spanish state regardless of the form of government in power. Shortly after his death, his son Rómulo, "wishing to carry out the will of his father," turned the papers over to the Spanish consulate general in Paris.[58]

In an accompanying document dated 14 December 1956 that was drafted and signed by Ansó and countersigned by Negrín's son, acknowledging that it reflected faithfully the feelings of his father, Ansó expressed Negrín's "deep concern with the interests of Spain as opposed to those of the USSR" and his fear that "without documentation to support her rights" Spain would be left "defenseless in a necessary settlement of account arising from what was perhaps the largest and most important transaction carried out between two countries."

After listing a number of other matters that "weighed on Negrín's mind"—including the retention by the USSR of "important and numerous units of the Spanish merchant fleet"—Ansó affirmed that in any financial settlement of accounts between Spain and Russia, Negrín felt that it was "his duty as a Spaniard to give his unconditional support to the interests of the nation."[59]

These, of course, were the thoughts and concerns of a man seasoned in later years by gradual disillusionment with the Soviet Union and the Spanish Communists, a man vastly different from the vaguely idealistic professor of physiology and newcomer to government with whom Alexander Orlov arranged, on 22 October 1936, for the shipment of the bulk of the Spanish gold reserves to the Soviet Union. "The finance minister seemed the very prototype of the intellectual— opposed to communism in theory, yet vaguely sympathetic to the 'great experiment' in Russia," Alexander Orlov wrote some years later. "This political naivety helps to explain his impulse to export the gold to that country. Besides, with Hitler and Mussolini supporting the Nationalists and the democracies standing aloof, Russia was an ally, the one great power helping the Spanish Republicans. 'Where are the gold reserves, now?' I asked. 'At Cartagena,' Negrín replied, 'in one of the old caves used by the Navy to store munitions.' Stalin's luck again, I thought excitedly. My problem was immensely simplified by the fact that the cargo was already in Cartagena. That capacious harbor was where Soviet ships were unloading arms and supplies. So not only the ships but also trustworthy Soviet manpower were within easy reach."[60]

Whatever we may think of Orlov's use of the term "political naivety" with regard to Negrín, there can be no doubt that in view of the attitude of the Western powers the gold could not have been mobilized successfully for the war effort if it had not been shipped to Russia. Orlov told Negrín that he would carry out the operation with the Soviet tank soldiers who had recently arrived in Spain. "I wish to stress that, at that time, the Spanish Government . . . was not in full control," he informed the U.S. Senate subcommittee. "I frankly told finance minister Negrín that if somebody got wind of it, if the anarchists intercepted my men, Russians, with truckloads of Spanish gold, they would kill my men, and it would be a tremendous political scandal all over the world, and it might even create an internal revolution.

So . . . I asked him whether the Spanish government could issue to me credentials under some fictitious name . . . as a representative of the Bank of England or the Bank of America, because then . . . I would be able to say that the gold was being taken for safekeeping to America. . . . Negrín did not object. He thought it was a fine idea. I spoke more or less decent English, and I could pass for a foreigner. So he issued to me the credentials of a man named Blackstone, and I became the representative of the Bank of America."[61] In a book written eight years earlier, Alvarez del Vayo mentions this incident, but either did not know or did not wish to reveal the true identity of Blackstone. "On the Russian side," he wrote, "there took part in the operation only an attaché from the Embassy chosen by Ambassador Rosenberg, of whom all we knew was that he was to be called Blackstone. Negrín jocularly baptized him with that name when he was introduced by the Ambassador."[62]

Orlov then left for Cartagena and asked for sixty Spanish sailors to load the gold onto the Soviet ships. Next he arranged to transport the gold from the cave to the piers. "A Soviet tank brigade had disembarked in Cartagena two weeks earlier," he wrote, "and was now stationed in Archena [north of Murcia], forty miles away. It was commanded by Colonel S. Krivoshein, known to the Spanish as Melé. Krivoshein assigned to me twenty of his army trucks and as many of his best tank drivers. . . . The sixty Spanish sailors had been sent to the cave an hour or two in advance. . . . And so, on October 22, in the expiring twilight, I drove to the munitions dump, the cavalcade of trucks behind me." Stacked against the walls were thousands of identical wooden boxes. "The crates held gold ingots and coins— hundreds of millions of dollars' worth! Here was the treasure of an ancient nation, accumulated through the centuries!"[63] The loading took three nights, from 7 P.M. to dawn. On the second or third day, Orlov testified before the U.S. Senate subcommittee, there was a tremendous bombardment and somebody mentioned that if a bomb hit the neighboring cave where thousands of pounds of dynamite were stored they would all be blown to bits. "The health of [Francisco] Méndez Aspe [head of the treasury and Negrín's man of confidence] was a very serious thing. He was a very nervous man. He told us we must discontinue loading or we will perish. I told him we could not do it, because the Germans would continue to bombard the harbor and the ship will be sunk, that we must go on with it. So he fled and left just one assistant, a very nice Spanish fellow, who did the counting of the gold [boxes] for them."[64]

On 25 October, 7,800 cases of gold were shipped to Odessa in four Soviet vessels;[65] they arrived on 2 and 9 November. The extraordinary scene at the Russian port was described to Krivitsky by one of his associates:

"The entire vicinity of the pier was cleared and surrounded by cordons of special troops. Across this cleared and empty space from dock to railroad track, the highest Ogpu [NKVD] officials carried the boxes of gold on their backs. For days and days they carried this burden of gold, loading it onto freight cars, and then taking it to Moscow under armed convoys. He attempted to give me an estimate of the amount of gold they had unloaded in Odessa. We were walking across the huge Red Square. He pointed to the several open acres surrounding us, and said: 'If all the boxes of gold that we piled up in Odessa yards were laid side by side here in the Red Square, they would cover it from end to end.'"[66]

But even more impressive than this imagery is the fact, as the receipt shows, that of the 7,800 cases only 13 contained ingots, while 7,787 contained coins, millions upon millions of gold pieces—American dollars, Argentinian, Chilean, and Mexican pesos, Austrian, Belgian, French, and Swiss francs, Dutch florins, English sovereigns, German marks, Italian lira, Portuguese escudos, Russian rubles, and Spanish pesetas—some of them antique, others rare enough to possess a numismatic value far in excess of their weight in fine gold, coins that, if we borrow the above imagery, would have carpeted the Red Square from end to end.

The Spanish treasury was never credited with the numismatic value of the rare and antique coins. According to Marcelino Pascua, however, extraordinary care was taken in listing coins that were false or contained less than their legal amount of gold, and in each case the particular bag in which they were packed, with the name of the Spanish employee responsible for the packing, was noted on official Russian documents that, because of their length, were not translated.[67] Instead of being credited with the numismatic value of the rare and antique coins, the Spanish treasury was given credit, as its orders for the sale of gold were executed, with the fine gold value of whatever quantities the Precious Metals Department of the People's Commissariat of Finance reported it had melted down and refined.[68] The Russians never revealed what became of the rare and antique coins listed in the official receipt. There were no independent witnesses to the melting and refining. The four Spaniards from the Bank of Spain who accompanied the shipment and who were present at the counting and weighing did not, as far as can be determined, witness the other operations. In any case, they were not allowed to return to Spain. "It is possible," writes Viñas, "that Negrín and Méndez Aspe decided that they should remain in Moscow so that no rumors regarding the destination of the gold would leak out." He describes their plight in the Soviet capital: They were totally unprepared for a long stay and were very worried about their families in Spain and other personal matters. Eventually, their families joined them in Moscow, but their constant desire was to return to Spain.[69] In the course of his extensive research in the Bank of Spain, Viñas was shown "a moving letter" from Arturo Candela, one of the four bank employees who had accompanied the gold to Moscow, addressed to Julio Carabias, vice-governor of the bank, urging him "in a disguised way," to "get them out of here."[70] "In the summer of 1938," testifies Viñas, "Negrín and Méndez Aspe decided to take Pascua's advice and permitted them to leave the USSR. . . . The Soviet government insisted that the strictest silence be maintained, but allowed them to go. For their part, the republicans suggested that they be assigned to Spanish agencies in Stockholm, the U.S.A., Mexico, and Buenos Aires. On 27 October 1938, they left Moscow."[71]

As for the high-ranking Soviet officials who intervened in the gold operation, there is evidence that at least two were shot, although there is no way of knowing whether their deaths were associated directly or indirectly with the gold shipment. According to the authoritative *Who Was Who in the USSR*, G. F. Grinko, people's commissar of finance, and N. N. Krestinski, deputy people's commissar for foreign affairs (both of whom signed the official receipt), were executed on 15 March 1938 on charges of alleged membership in the anti-Soviet "rightist Trotskyite Bloc." Grinko, ironically, was also accused of "efforts to undermine the financial might of the USSR."[72]

Although Angel Viñas, with painstaking meticulousness, arrives at the conclusion that the gold deposit, as such, was virtually exhausted eight months before the end of the Civil War,[73] an important question must be asked. Were the massive amounts of foreign exchange generated by the sale of the gold to the Soviet State Bank and transferred to the Soviet-controlled Banque Commerciale de l'Europe du Nord in Paris, there to be credited to the accounts of the ministry of finance, also used up? Inasmuch as the operations of the Banque Commerciale were shrouded in absolute secrecy and its records of the accounts held by the ministry of finance have never been published, this question must be left unanswered.

However, any objective study of the financial transactions between Spain and the USSR must take into account the Soviet credits extended to the Negrín government in 1938. So far, such an analysis has been made only by Angel Viñas. In his latest work, to be published in 1978, he shows, on the basis of republican documents, that Negrín's strategy was to secure long-term credits from the Soviet Union, so as to retain as much of the remaining gold deposit as possible. This strategy was unsuccessful. In the fall of 1937, Negrín instructed Pascua to request a credit of $150 million, but, on 29 October, the ambassador replied: "I am continuing to press for credits. However, you have no idea how difficult it is to get a quick decision. They [the Russians] are extremely calculating, procrastinating, and at times not absolutely straightforward." The Russians responded, Viñas continues, with an offer of $20 million to be used exclusively for nonmilitary supplies, and insisted that orders for war material be paid for as hitherto by the sale of the gold on deposit, "because, in order to fill them, the USSR must import raw materials, as a result of which it must drain its foreign exchange reserves." Not until March 1938, Viñas reveals, did Stalin grant a credit of $70 million, but only on the most stringent terms: $35 million was to be secured by an equivalent amount in gold and repaid in two years, while the unsecured balance was to be repaid in four years. As the gold deposit was virtually exhausted by the summer of 1938, other credits were undoubtedly extended to pay for the large arms shipments sent to Spain towards the end of the year, but no documentation has yet been found.[74]

Nineteen years later, on 5 April 1957, a few months after Negrín's death, *Pravda* reported not only that the gold deposit was totally depleted, but that the Spanish government still owed $50 million out of a Soviet credit of $85. This figure seems reasonable, even low, if we take into account the arms shipments made towards the end of 1938.

However, with regard to *Pravda*'s claim that the gold deposit was exhausted, Indalecio Prieto was not convinced and responded vehemently: "We are dealing here with a colossal embezzlement. Regardless of my opinion of Juan Negrín, I declare him incapable of perpetrating the macabre hoax before his death of arranging . . . to turn over to Franco a document [the official receipt for the gold] with no material value." After listing various ways in which he claims that Spanish funds were used for the benefit of the French Communist party, including subsidies to the newspaper *Ce Soir* and the purchase of a dozen steamships by France Navigation, a company run by French Communists, Prieto continued: "Even though all those expenses were charged to the gold deposit in Russia, its total depletion is impossible. I repeat: We are dealing with a monumental embezzlement. To protect herself, Russia will falsify whatever substantiative documents she considers necessary. . . . From his grave, Negrín will not be able to deny the authenticity of signatures imitated by expert forgers."[75]

One final question remains. Was the cabinet consulted before the gold was shipped to Russia? Both Negrín and Alvarez del Vayo claimed that it was.[76] Prieto, however, said that it was not. "Senor Negrín, as minister of finance," he wrote, "obtained the consent of the government and the signature of the president of the Republic for a decree [the *decreto reservado* of 13 September[77]] empowering him to take whatever measures he deemed necessary to safeguard the gold of the Bank of Spain. As a member of that government I accept my share of responsiblity for the decree, although neither I nor the other ministers knew of the aim pursued. I do not know whether Largo Caballero, who was then head of the government, was aware of it.[78] The loading was surrounded with great secrecy. I found out about it by pure chance just when the gold was being loaded under the direction of Negrín and Méndez Aspe, having arrived at Cartagena to attend to matters connected with my department."[79] It is hard to believe that Prieto knew nothing about the planned shipment until his arrival in Cartagena, and his claim, as will be seen shortly, is contradicted by Orlov.

Prieto also asserted that Negrín could not disguise his "uneasiness" when he saw him in Cartagena. "He undoubtedly assumed that I had gone there to nose around. He didn't give me any reason for his presence. I knew the motive because the chief of the Naval Base had told me that the finance minister had asked him for sailors to load the gold . . . and that he had consented. I approved the permit and that was the extent of my participation in the matter."[80]

Orlov gives supportive evidence that Prieto was initially unaware of the plan to ship the gold reserves to Russia. In his testimony before the U.S. Senate subcommittee, he stated that before the gold was loaded onto Soviet ships he decided to ask the Spanish government for an order to spread warships along the route in the Mediterranean. "I knew that such an order could not be issued without Prieto, . . . *who did not know anything about the whole plan of the gold operation*. So, I called up the Soviet Ambassador . . . [I] asked him to take it up with Prime Minister Caballero and arrange that the Navy Minister, Prieto, should issue orders to the Spanish warships. . . . In a few days, the Spanish Finance Minister, Negrín, and . . . Prieto came to Cartagena. The orders were issued."[81]

[150]

Alvarez del Vayo also states that Prieto arranged for the necessary naval protection, although he unwittingly contradicts his assertion that Negrín transferred the gold to Russia "only after getting the consent of the whole government."[82] "As it was necessary to assure and protect the transportation by sea," he wrote, "Indalecio Prieto . . . was made *a co-partner in the secret.* He also received the news with gratification, and directly and personally took charge, arranging that a squadron should accompany the convoy nearly to Tunis."[83] Prieto, however, claims not only that he was initially unaware of the plan to ship the gold to the Soviet Union, but that he was not asked to furnish a naval escort and did not offer to provide one.[84] He adduced as evidence a letter from the commander of the destroyer fleet in Cartagena, Vicente Ramírez de Togores, who asserted that not a single Spanish warship escorted the Soviet merchant ships.[85] Mariano Ansó suggests that this letter may have been written just to oblige Prieto.[86] At all events, the assertion runs directly counter to the testimony of Nicolai G. Kuznetsov, the Soviet military attaché, who was charged with the protection of the gold on the high seas and who makes it clear that a naval escort, including the cruiser *Libertad*, accompanied the Soviet ships as far as North Africa.[87]

Prieto also dismissed as a "lie" an assertion by Alvarez del Vayo that "Negrín insisted that President Azaña should be fully informed" and that the president was "pleasantly surprised by the plan."[88] Azaña "knew absolutely nothing about it," Prieto replied. "Largo Caballero and Negrín had acted in the same way toward the head of state as they had toward the ministers, concealing everything from them, even after it was a fait accompli. Azaña was enraged. . . . He told me he was going to resign immediately. Although sympathizing with him I tried to calm him. 'Your resignation,' I told him, 'would mean the collapse of the Republic because it would be used by the other nations to end [diplomatic] recognition in view of the fact that a substitute for the presidency, under existing circumstances, would be constitutionally impossible.'"[89]

From this welter of conflicting statements, the following reasonably safe conclusions can be drawn: (1) Although Negrín obtained the consent of the cabinet and the signature of President Azaña for the decree of 13 September, empowering him to transfer the gold reserves to a place that offered the maximum security, his decision a month later to ship the gold to Russia was made without conferring with the cabinet and without consulting either Prieto or Azaña. (2) Prieto was made a "co-partner in the secret," as Alvarez del Vayo claims, but only after

Negrín and Caballero had decided to transfer the gold to Moscow. (3) Having signed the permit for the Spanish sailors to load the gold onto the Soviet ships, Prieto must have been asked to provide a naval escort, or even offered to provide one, since it would be chimerical to suppose that so important a mission could have been undertaken without his knowledge and consent. Indeed, Marcelino Pascua states that the friendship between Negrín and Prieto was at that time "close, even intimate, one might say," and that Negrín told him that he used to consult Prieto "frequently on various matters because of his greater political experience and their mutual confidence and attachment."[90]

Why, then, did Prieto deny his share of responsibility for the shipment? The answer is that his denial was first made in 1940 when his postwar enmity with Negrín had reached its peak. And why, one may ask, did Prieto, always distrustful of Moscow, cooperate? His thinking in October 1936 could not have been different from that of Largo Caballero who, although sharing Prieto's distrust of Moscow, felt that the attitude of the Western powers left no choice but to ship the gold to Russia.

Largo Caballero has made his own position very clear: it undoubtedly was the same as that of Prieto and of others privy to the shipment. "As the rebels were at the gates of Madrid," he wrote after the Civil War, "[Negrín] asked the government for authority to transfer the gold from the Bank of Spain to a safe place without stating where. This was a natural thing to do in order to prevent the treasure, through misadventure, from falling into the hands of the rebels; for without gold with which to purchase arms the defeat of the Republic would have been inevitable. . . . The first step taken by Negrín was to transfer the gold to [the naval base of] Cartagena. Later, fearing a landing, he decided to send it abroad. Where? England and France were the very soul of 'nonintervention.' . . . Could we have had any faith in them? No. Then, where else could we have sent it? There was no other place but Russia, the country that was helping us with arms and food. . . . With this gold we paid Russia for the war material she was sending us. . . . Also we used what gold we needed for other purchases."[91]

Yet, despite the undoubted military and financial advantages of shipping the gold to Moscow, there was one inescapable drawback: this important transfer, worth at the time over $500 million, was to make the cabinet dependent in large measure on the goodwill of Moscow.

That Stalin was delighted over the safe arrival of the gold reserves there can be no doubt, for he had now begun shipping arms to Spain and only by the physical possession of the gold could he be assured of payment. According to Alexander Orlov—who claims that he and Ambassador Rosenberg "were flabbergasted when . . . told that the Spanish Government was willing to trust Stalin with all the savings of the Spanish nation"—Stalin celebrated the arrival of the gold with a banquet attended by members of the politburo, at which he said, "The Spaniards will never see their gold again, as they don't see their ears," an expression based on a Russian proverb.[92]

In January 1937—two months after the arrival of the shipment— Orlov, according to his own account, received "a very warm letter" from Paul Alliluyeva, Stalin's brother-in-law, congratulating him on having received "the highest decoration of the Soviet Union, the Order of Lenin." Although Orlov did not give the reason for the award, it was in all probability connected with the gold shipment.[93]

Still another factor weighing heavily in favor of Communist influence in the affairs of government was the arrival in September and October 1936 of military advisers and political agents, who exercised, in fact if not in form, the authority of ministers in various departments. "As time went on," writes Colonel Segismundo Casado, operations chief on the general staff in the early months of the war, "Russian influence was increased at the War Ministry. [The Russian military advisers] looked over the plans of the General Staff and through the minister they rejected many technical proposals and imposed others."[94] In a later passage he says: "These 'friendly advisers' exercised authority just as much in the Air Force and in the Tank Corps."[95] Of Russian influence in high places, Luis Araquistáin writes: "The Air Force, directed by the Russians, operated when and where they pleased, without any coordination with the land and sea forces. The navy and air minister, Indalecio Prieto, meek and cynical, made fun of his office to anyone who visited him, declaring that he was neither a minister nor anything else because he received absolutely no obedience from the Air Force. The real air minister was the Russian General Duglas [Yakov Smushkevich]"[96] Later on, he adds: "Behind [the Russian officers] were innumerable political agents who were disguised as commercial agents and were in real control of Spanish politics. . . . They directed the Russian officers, the Communist party and Rosenberg himself [the Soviet ambassador], who in reality was only an ambassador of straw. The real ambassadors were those mysterious men who entered Spain under false names and were working under direct orders from the Kremlin and the Russian police."[97]

The Rise of the Communists

The influence of the Russians cannot be explained on the ground that the Soviet forces in Spain were strong enough to coerce the government by mere numbers. "I am sure," affirms Indalecio Prieto, "that at no time did the Russians in our territory aggregate more than five hundred, including aviators, industrial technicians, military advisers, naval men, interpreters, and secret agents.[98] Most of them were aviators, who, like the Germans and Italians, were relieved after short periods.[99] . . . Russia could not exercise any coercion because of the military forces she sent to Spain. Her ability to do so stemmed from the fact that she was, owing to the attitude of the other powers, our sole purveyor of war material and that her coercive instrument was the Spanish Communist party, the Communists, and the communistoids enrolled in other political organizations, principally in the Socialist party."[100]

In addition, the position of the Communists in the government was greatly strengthened by the fact that they could rely for support in major issues of domestic and foreign policy on the republican and moderate Socialist representatives. José Giral, premier of the government formed on 19 July and minister without portfolio in Largo Caballero's administration, representing the Left Republican party, declared in a speech in March 1937, it will be recalled, that the coincidence of views between his party and the Communists was almost identical.[101] "We have to take into account the attitude of the states that surround us," said El Socialista, that expressed the opinions of Prieto, the moderate Socialist leader. "We still hope that the estimate of Spanish events made by certain democracies will be changed, and it would be a pity, perhaps a tragedy, to compromise these possibilities by an irrepressible desire to accelerate the Revolution."[102] Furthermore, in spite of Russian pressure and the ravages on his following, Largo Caballero maintained tolerable relations with the Communist party during the first months of his incumbency; for, however provoked he may secretly have been, a large measure of agreement still existed between them. In fact, from the day his government was formed, he adopted the Communist viewpoint that it should impress the outside world with its moderation. Not that he or the other non-Communist members of his cabinet were concerned with the broader aims of Russian policy. They simply hoped that by proclaiming respect for legal forms, Britain and France, fearful of an Italo-German vassalage of Spain, would finally raise the arms embargo. It was necessary, Largo Caballero declared, during a private conversation shortly after taking office, "to sacrifice revolutionary language to win the friendship of the democratic Powers."[103] In this respect he was not remiss. "The Spanish Government is not fighting for socialism but for democracy and constitutional rule," he stated to a delegation of British members of Parliament.[104] And in a communiqué to the foreign press he said: "The Government of the Spanish Republic is not aiming at setting up a Soviet regime in Spain in spite of what has been alleged in some quarters abroad. The government's essential aim is to maintain the parliamentary regime of the Republic as it was set up by the Constitution which the Spanish people freely assumed."[105] No less instructive was the moderate tone of his speech when, as premier, he appeared before the rump Cortes on 1 February 1937: "When I assumed this post I renounced nothing, absolutely nothing in my political thinking. I say this before you and before the entire country. . . . But, in view of the danger that confronts our country as a result of the military uprising, I felt it my duty to assume the responsibilities that naturally devolve upon me because of my office by laying aside for a short time the immediate aspirations inherent in the ideology I have always defended."[106]

Illustrative of his cabinet's regard for foreign opinion was the declaration it issued after its first session. Avoiding all reference to the profound revolutionary changes that had taken place or to any social program, it stated:

1. In view of its composition, the government considers itself the direct representative of all those political forces that are fighting at the fronts for the maintenance of the democratic Republic, against which the rebels have taken up arms. . . .
2. The program of the government consists essentially of the firm intention to accelerate victory over the rebellion, coordinating the forces of the people by the necessary unity of action. . . . To this end all other political interests are subordinated, ideological differences being set aside. . . .
4. The government affirms the feelings of friendship of Spain toward all nations and its most devoted adherence to the covenant of the League of Nations, hoping that, in just return, our country will receive from others the same consideration it will give to them. . . .
6. The government greets with the utmost enthusiasm the land, sea, and air forces, as well as the People's Militia who are defending the republican Constitution. Its highest aim is to be worthy of such heroic fighters, whose legitimate desires for social betterment will find in it a determined champion.[107]

Because it was essential for the sake of foreign opinion that legal forms be observed, the Cortes met on 1 October, as stipulated in the Constitution. The director of the Communist organ, *Mundo Obrero*, commented:

The Rise of the Communists

"The deputies of the nation, the legal representatives of the people, the deputies elected by the free will of the people on 16 February, have assembled this morning. The government has appeared before the Congress in accordance with the republican Constitution.

"In the midst of civil war, while the struggle to impose republican legality and the will of the people is proceeding at the fronts, the government is ratified by the chamber. Constituted as the genuine representative of the people, it has functioned as such until today. The head of the state gave it his confidence, and today it reinforces its legal origin . . . with the confidence of parliament. . . . On the one side is the Republic, with its legal organs. . . . On the other are the military traitors, the fascist blackguards, the adventurers of all classes in Spain and abroad. . . . The civilized world has now been able to judge; it is on our side in its entirety. To help the legal authorities of Spain is a duty imposed by international law; to help the rebels is a crime against civilization and against humanity."[108]

After the next session of the Cortes in December, the organ of the Left Republican party declared:

Legality has only one medium of expression. This is what yesterday's session of the parliament of the Republic demonstrated. . . . It was also the most eloquent demonstration of the continuity of the democratic republican regime and of the unshakable determination of the country not to allow the legality of its public life to disappear in the whirlwind of passions and appetites unleashed by this bloody Civil War.

At this time, . . . when the world is contemplating the unique struggle of the people of Madrid and of the Spanish people as a whole, the Republic maintains a rich and vigorous constitutional life. All its basic institutions, allowing for the exigencies of the times and the particular circumstances of a country at war, function normally. Not one has been supplanted. . . .[109]

The session of the Cortes of the Republic that took place yesterday once again destroys the specious arguments of those who, particularly outside Spain, take delight in stridently censuring a people fighting to defend rights that are so legitimate that in countries with an older democratic tradition they are not even mentioned because they are taken for granted. Spain is today waging a struggle for republican and democratic consolidation such as other countries experienced many years ago.

Would it be too much to ask those governments that are tolerating the international crime being committed in Spain by German and Italian intervention to appreciate what this signifies? Face to face with the enemy at home, the Spanish people, victorious in the February elections, would have triumphed over the barbarous rebellion within a few days. But face to face with the military apparatus of Germany and Italy, it has no course but to appeal frankly and sincerely to world opinion.

The same government, or rather a legal continuation of that government, the same Parliament, the same president of the Republic, the same institutions with which every country in the world had maintained friendly and cordial relations until 17 July exercise today, more than four months after the outbreak of the rebellion that is striving to put an end to the legal Constitution of Spain, the same powers and the same functions. Does this mean nothing at all? Or, in face of the inexcusable aggression of which these institutions have been the object, has the world lost all feeling?[110]

After the war the Communists, republicans, and Socialists in exile, still hoping to influence world opinion in favor of the Spanish republican cause, did what they could to conceal the depth of the 1936 Revolution. Some, in fact, even maintained that the republican Constitution had remained inviolate during the Civil War. For example, Pablo de Azcárate, former Spanish ambassador in London and a fervent Negrín supporter, affirmed that "from 16 July 1936 to 5 March 1939 [the date of the overthrow of the Negrín government by a coalition of left-wing organizations] the constitution was in force, *in fact* and *in law*, throughout the territory under the legitimate authority of the Republic, and *in law only* in that ruled by the rebels."[111] It was undoubtedly this sort of political distortion and dishonesty that caused Salvador de Madariaga, who before the Civil War had been Azcárate's friend and colleague at the League of Nations and an admirer of his "capacity, integrity, and intellectual clarity," to become a pungent critic, when he later became "a loyal adjutant of Negrín, who in turn was a loyal adjutant of Stalin" and "abandoned the strict path of truth for the putrid intellectual bog of communism."[112]

To ensure that the Western democracies would continue to recognize the government as the legally constituted authority, it was essential that Manual Azaña, the president of the Republic, should remain in office to sanction its decrees and perform the diverse functions laid down in the Constitution. Whether he could be persuaded to do so indefinitely was open to grave doubt, not only because his hostility to the Revolution was a matter of common knowledge, but because on 19 October 1936—three weeks before the government's transfer to Valencia as a result of the enemy's threatening advance upon the capital—he had decided to move to Barcelona, from where, it was feared, he might cross the border into France and there resign the presidency. "It was arranged with the president," recalls Largo Caballero, "that we should all go to Valencia. . . . First to leave was Senor Azaña. . . . Instead of staying in Valencia, as agreed, he went to Barcelona. It was a means of getting closer to the frontier. He did not consult with us or say a word to anyone."[113]

A reason why he did not cross the border into France and resign the presidency was the pressure that was brought to bear upon him by republicans and particularly by Indalecio Prieto, with whom he was always in close contact. Relating after the war how Azaña informed him in April 1938 of his intention to resign because of his inability to settle a government crisis in accordance with his own wishes, Prieto records his reply as follows: "You cannot resign . . . [because] your resignation would bring down everything and because you personify the Republic, which to a certain degree the countries not allied to Franco respect. If you were to resign, that respect, thanks to which we are still able to exist, would disappear."[114]

When Azaña left Madrid in October 1936, records Frank Sedwick in his biography of the president, the press announced that he was to make a tour of the eastern and Catalonian fronts. "Much has been written of his failure to visit the fronts and of his 'cowardice' in leaving Madrid, although few republicans at that time thought Madrid could hold out. Everything seemed to be disintegrating, and the rest of the government followed Azaña within three weeks. Little was left of the original diplomatic corps; many founders of the Republic and intellectuals like [Gregorio] Marañón, [Ramón] Pérez de Ayala, [José] Ortega y Gasset, and Madariaga either had left Spain already or were soon to make their exit. . . . On leaving Madrid, Azaña went to Barcelona. His enemies say he chose Barcelona so that he could be close to the French border in case of a republican military collapse; his friends say he went to reside there in order, by his presence, to help keep Catalonia in tow."[115]

But few, least of all Azaña, harbored any illusions about the authority of his presidential office or about his power or desire to check the Revolution in the anarchosyndicalist-dominated region of Catalonia. "From the beginning of the war," attests Juan Marichal, the compiler of Azaña's *Obras Completas*, "he saw that his only possible role was the very limited one of representing a symbolic brake on the revolutionary violence."[116]

Like the republicans and Prieto, the Communists and their allies were especially troubled over Azaña's pessimism and the danger that he might at any time resign the presidency. "Reports reaching us regarding the attitude of Señor Azaña . . . were by no means reassuring," testifies Alvarez del Vayo. "We feared that his habitual pessimism, exacerbated by isolation, might lead him to make some irrevocable decision."[117]

In a letter written after the war Azaña frankly acknowledged his pessimism: "No one is unaware of the fact that I did everything possible from September 1936 to influence policy in favor of a compromise settlement because the idea of defeating the enemy was an illusion."[118]

But physical fear as well as pessimism influenced Azaña's wartime conduct. Largo Caballero recalls that whenever he had official business to transact with Azaña in Madrid, the president would ask him when the government planned to leave the capital. "Is it going to wait until the last moment when there will be no escape? I warn you. I have no desire to be dragged through the streets with a rope around my neck."[119]

"Fear that he might fall into the hands of the fascists," writes Ignacio Hidalgo de Cisneros, the Communist chief of the air force, "was a real obsession."[120] And Miguel Maura, the leader of the Conservative Republican party, who was minister of the interior in the first two governments of the Republic in 1931 but remained on the sidelines during the war, while attesting to Azaña's "extraordinary intelligence and august qualities," confirms this fear. "[He] was afflicted with overwhelming physical fear. . . . It was stronger than he and he did the unimaginable to disguise it."[121]

For these reasons—his fear and pessimism as well as his profound revulsion to revolutionary violence—the thought of resignation dominated Azaña's mind from the inception of the conflict. "He had wanted to resign at the very beginning," writes Sedwick, "and almost did resign after the massacre of political prisoners in the Cárcel Modelo (Model Prison) of Madrid in August 1936. On this occasion it was Angel Ossorio [the republican jurist] who dissauded him from renouncing the presidency. On the other critical occasions both during and after the summer of 1936, on the one hand it was Indalecio Prieto and the sincere moderates who importuned Azaña to consider himself and his office as the necessary personification of the Republic abroad, while on the other hand it was those who received from Moscow their orders that the façade of a democratic Spain had to be maintained. Knowingly or unknowingly, Azaña thus became the essential tool of both factions. Brave with the pen, a paper expert in military matters, a classic type of constitutionalist, that sensitive and fastidious intellectual never wanted any role in an actual war, particularly a civil war whose outcome could portend but little hope for his aspirations of a democracy in Spain. Yet he remained at his post."[122]

The pessimism of President Azaña and of many other republican leaders was well known to the Kremlin. In December 1936, Stalin, demonstrating how much he valued their diplomatic utility, gave

The Rise of the Communists

Largo Caballero the following advice: "The Spanish Revolution," he stated in a letter that also bore the signatures of Molotov, the chairman of the Council of People's Commissars, and K. Y. Voroshilov, the commissar for defense, "traces its own course, different in many respects from that followed by Russia. This is determined by the difference in the social, historic, and geographic conditions, and from the necessities of the international situation. . . . It is very possible that in Spain the parliamentary way will prove to be a more effective means of revolutionary development than in Russia. . . . The republican leaders must not be rejected, but, on the contrary, they must be attracted and drawn closer to the government. It is above all necessary to secure for the government the support of Azaña and his group, doing everything possible to help them to overcome their vacillations. This is necessary in order to prevent the enemies of Spain from regarding her as a Communist republic, and, in this way, to avoid their open intervention, which constitutes the greatest danger to republican Spain."[123]

In his reply Largo Caballero stated: "You are right in pointing out that there exist appreciable differences between the development of the Russian Revolution and our Revolution. Indeed, as you yourselves point out, the circumstances are different. . . . But, in response to your allusion [to the parliamentary method] it is advisable to point out that, whatever the future may hold for the parliamentary institution, it does not possess among us, or even among the republicans, enthusiastic supporters. . . . I absolutely agree with what you say regarding the republican political parties. We have endeavored, at all times, to bring them into the work of the government and into the war effort. They participate to a large extent in all organs of administration, local, provincial, and national. What is happening is that they themselves are doing hardly anything to assert their own political personality."[124]

10. Wooing Britain, France, and Germany

Stalin undoubtedly saw great advantages in the continued recognition of the Spanish government as the legally constituted authority. He knew that as long as it was recognized as such by Britain and France, it would not only be in a position to bring the question of Italo-German intervention before the League of Nations, but could demand that, in accordance with the generally accepted rules of international law in cases of insurrection against a legitimate government, it would be permitted to purchase arms freely in the markets of the world.[1] He knew, moreover, that if Britain and France were to abandon their policy of neutrality, the Civil War in Spain might ultimately develop into a large-scale conflict from which he could remain virtually aloof until the warring parties had fought to the point of mutual exhaustion and from which the Soviet Union would emerge master of the European continent.

Already in 1925, Stalin had enunciated his strategy in the event a general war should ravage Europe. In a speech at a plenary session of the central committee of the Soviet Communist party, published for the first time in 1947, he declared: "If war should begin it would not suit us to sit with folded arms. We should have to come out, but we should be the last to do so. And we should come out in order to throw the decisive weight into the scales, the weight that should tip the scales."[2]

Thus, it is not surprising that after the outbreak of the Spanish Civil War, Stalin, to quote Hugh Thomas, "seems to have reached one conclusion, and one conclusion only, about Spain: he would not permit the Republic to lose, even though he would not help it to win. The mere continuance of the war . . . might even make possible a world war in which France, Britain, Germany, and Italy would destroy themselves, with Russia, the arbiter staying outside."[3]

It is interesting to note that Neville Chamberlain, British prime minister from 1937 to 1940, suspected that the "Bolshies," to use his own language, were "chiefly concerned to see the 'capitalist' Powers tear each other to pieces whilst they stay out themselves,"[4] and that this suspicion was also harbored by the French government quite early in the war. On 25 November 1936, U.S. Ambassador William Bullitt reported to the State Department: "The French government is convinced that the Soviet government desires to push the conflict to the bitter end on the theory that even though, in the first instance the Soviet government would suffer defeat through the overthrowing of the Madrid and Barcelona governments [that is, the central adminis-tration and the semiautonomous government of the region of Cata-lonia] by Italian and German troops enlisted in Franco's army, the final result would be an attempt by the Germans to establish a new status in Spanish Morocco and an attempt by the Italians to maintain possession of the Balearic Islands which would result in war between Germany and Italy on one side and France and England on the other. This the Soviet government anticipates would lead to eventual Bol-shevization of the whole of Europe."[5]

But neither Britain nor France wished to be drawn into a general European war from which Russia alone might emerge triumphant. "In no case whatever," affirmed J. L. Garvin, editor of the *Observer*, an influential conveyor of conservative party opinion, "can it be to the interest of Britain and the British Empire that Germany should be overthrown to exalt still further and beyond restraint the Soviet Power of the future, and to make Communism supreme, whether in Europe or Asia."[6] Hence, in spite of the risks involved to themselves of a Spain under possible bondage to Italy and Germany, Britain and France were not to be diverted from the policy of nonintervention, and through mediation they hoped that the entrenchment of Italy and Germany in Spain could be averted.[7]

Although Léon Blum, the Socialist premier of the Popular Front government of France, is alleged to have adopted a neutral stand mainly under strong British pressure,[8] there is also evidence that, despite his personal sympathies for the Spanish left, he was a pacifist who was afraid to endanger the peace of Europe[9] and that the initia-tive for nonintervention came from his cabinet.[10] He had also been subject to pressure from some of the Radical party ministers in his cabinet, from the president of the Republic,[11] from the combined forces of the French right, and from the powerful Radical party[12] that represented a large segment of the middle classes within the Popular Front alliance.

Equally indicative of the opposition of influential quarters in both

Britain and France to any military commitment that might involve them in a war with Germany was their hostility to the Franco-Soviet Pact of Mutual Assistance. If this hostility was undisguised by an important section of French opinion,[13] to say nothing of the antipathy in official quarters,[14] it was no less patent in authoritative British newspapers. "British opinion," said the *Times*, the unofficial mouthpiece of the government, "is not prepared to accept . . . the leadership of France over the whole field of foreign politics, or to admit responsibility for all the liabilities which she had been accumulating . . . in the shape of alliances on the farther side of Germany. . . . The Franco–Soviet Pact is not regarded here as a helpful diplomatic achievement."[15]

"France," wrote "Scrutator" in the *Sunday Times*, "has made alliances in Eastern Europe for power—its motive is still power, even if there is no idea of aggression but only self-defense. Rightly or wrongly—wrongly, as some of us think—she convinced herself that the benefits to herself of an alliance with Russia and the Little Entente outweighed the risk of entanglements in disputes not really her own. In this regard, France's policy is not ours."[16]

"These pacts [the Franco-Soviet and Czech-Soviet treaties]," wrote J. L. Garvin, "mean war and can mean nothing else. If we support them they mean war between Britain and Germany and can mean nothing else. If Britain is to give countenance or patronage to those fatal instruments; if we are to have any lot or part in them whatever; if we are to stand behind France and Czechoslovakia as the potential allies of Russia and Communism against Germany—then the situation becomes inherently deadly to peace, and it is no use talking of anything else. We cannot have it both ways. If we are to interfere with Germany in the East she must ultimately strike us in the West. Nothing else is possible."[17]

If such expressions of opinion were more outspoken than official declarations, they nevertheless corresponded closely to the attitude of the highest levels of the British government, an attitude of which the Kremlin was fully conscious. Indeed, the fear that both Britain and France might arrive at some agreement with Germany at the expense of eastern Europe was deeply grounded in Moscow. In a conversation with Joseph E. Davies, U.S. ambassador to Russia, in February 1937, Maxim Litvinov, Soviet commissar for foreign affairs, did not conceal this disquietude: "He could not understand," Davies informed the secretary of state, "why Great Britain could not see that once Hitler dominated Europe he would swallow the British Isles also. He seemed to be very much stirred about this and apprehensive lest there should be some composition of differences between France, England, and Germany."[18]

The Kremlin redoubled its efforts in Spain with a view to enticing Britain and France from their neutrality. It was motivated by fear that the impetus of German militarism might ultimately be directed against the east rather than against the west, as well as by disappointment over the continued neutrality of Britain and France with regard to the Spanish conflict despite increasing Italo-German intervention,[19] over the failure of the French government to supplement the Franco-Soviet Pact by any positive military agreement,[20] and over the rejection of a Popular Front by the British Labor party.[21]

At the end of January 1937, Juan Comorera, the leader of the PSUC, told the central committee of his party in words that reflected discussions that had taken place with Ernö Gerö, a top-ranking Comintern agent in Spain known as "Pedro,"[22] who had just returned from Moscow,[23] that "the essential thing at this time is to seek the collaboration of the European democracies, particularly that of England."[24]

"In the democratic bloc of powers," Comorera declared two days later at a public meeting, "the decisive factor is not France; it is England. It is essential for all party comrades to realize this so as to moderate [their] slogans at the present time. . . . England is not a country like France. England is a country governed by the Conservative party. England is a country of slow evolution, which is constantly preoccupied with imperial interests. England is a country of plutocrats, a country with a profoundly conservative middle class that reacts with great difficulty. . . . Some persons say that England could never on any account agree to the triumph of Germany over Spain because that would signify a danger to her own vital interests. But we should realize that the big capitalists in England are capable of coming to an understanding at any time with Italian and German capitalists if they should reach the conclusion that they have no other choice with regard to Spain.

"[Therefore] we must win, cost what it may, the benevolent neutrality of that country, if not its direct aid."[25]

That this was to be achieved not merely by accentuating the moderate tendencies initiated by the Communists at the outbreak of the Revolution, but by more tangible means, was evident from a note sent by Alvarez del Vayo, the philo-Communist foreign minister, in February 1937 to the British and French governments offering to transfer Spanish Morocco to these two powers in return for the adoption of measures designed to prevent further Italo-German intervention.

It is significant that during the discussions that "Pedro" held with the PSUC leaders at the end of January upon his return from Moscow approximately two weeks before the offer was made, he spoke of the advisability of offering Spanish Morocco and the Canary Islands, also in the hands of General Franco, to Britain and France in order to win the support of these two powers. During her revolution, he argued, Russia had also been compelled to make territorial sacrifices.[26]

Jesús Hernández, politburo member and minister of education, affirmed, after he had ceased to belong to the Communist party, that the note was inspired by the Russians, although, according to Pablo de Azcárate, the philo-Communist Spanish ambassador in London,[27] the memorandum was inspired and drafted by him with the approval of Alvarez del Vayo.[28] "Litvinov [the Soviet foreign minister] in Geneva and Rosenberg in Spain," Hernández alleges, "persuaded Alvarez del Vayo . . . to make 'certain offers' favorable to Great Britain and France in Spanish Morocco in exchange for the help of both powers to the Republic."[29] Because this territory was in the hands of General Franco, and there had recently been insistent reports that Germany was fortifying the coast opposite Gibraltar,[20] it must have been obvious to Moscow that no such assignment could have been made in favor of Britain and France and accepted by them without the risk of precipitating an international conflict. In fact, Hernández affirms that if these two countries, "that had more than ample motives for anxiety over the prospect of a violent change of the status quo in Morocco, had been lured by the seductive offer, the friction between the democratic powers and Germany and Italy would have reached white heat, creating favorable conditions for Soviet plans to push the two blocs into a war far removed from Russia's borders."[31]

It is doubtful, however, whether the majority of the members of the republican government were aware of the wider objectives of Soviet policy in Spain or even of the Moroccan proposal at the time it was made. Indalecio Prieto asserts that no proposal relating to Morocco was ever submitted to the cabinet and that if it had been, he would have "opposed any step in favor of such an impractical idea." Curiously, he asserts that he never heard of the proposal while serving as a cabinet minister. "There must have been something to it," he observes, "although I was unaware of it."[32] Yet a copy of the note, which fell into the hands of General Franco's administration,[33] was published in full in the enemy press,[34] and excerpts or summaries appeared in the major newspapers of Britain and France in the succeeding days. Signed by Alvarez del Vayo, the note stated in part:

I

1. The Spanish government wishes Spain's future foreign policy, as far as western Europe is concerned, to assume the form of active collaboration with France and the United Kingdom.

2. To this end, Spain would be ready to take into consideration, both in the matter of economic reconstruction and in her military, naval, and air relations, the interests of these two powers, insofar as this is compatible with her interests.

3. In the same manner, Spain would be ready to examine, in conjunction with these powers, the advisability or otherwise of modifying the present status of North Africa (Spanish Morocco) on condition that such modification is not made in favor of any power other than Great Britain and France. . . .

II

If these proposals, which are made in a spirit of full international collaboration, are appreciated at their true worth by the British and French governments, these governments would henceforth be responsible for the adoption of any measures within their power designed to prevent further Italo-German intervention in Spanish affairs, in view of the fact that the interests of peace, which are synonymous with the national interests of the Western democracies, demand the effective prosecution of this aim.

If the sacrifices the Spanish government is willing to make prove insufficient to prevent the further supplying of men and material to the rebels by Italy and Germany, and if, in consequence, the republican government is compelled to fight the rebel generals, aided by two foreign powers, until victory is attained, then the proposals made in the first part of this note will be considered null and void, in view of the fact that their essential aim, which is to spare the Spanish people further suffering, would be frustrated.[35]

"The Spanish memorandum," writes Alvarez del Vayo in reference to the note, "gave the most conclusive proof of the Republic's desire for an understanding with Great Britain and France. Though it could not, in view of the existing circumstances, take the form of a pact of mutual assistance or an alliance, it was to all intents and purposes the same."[36] In a later passage, he says:

Neither of the two governments received the Republican initiative favorably,[37] and the international "leakage" by which the text of the Spanish memorandum was made known to the public gave evidence of an active hand behind the scenes which was doing everything possible to frustrate attempts to help the cause of the Spanish government. . . .

Although the February memorandum was an official statement of the Republic's foreign policy during the war, it must not be thought that it represented the extent of our efforts to persuade Great Britain and France to adopt

[166]

an attitude more in keeping with their own interests. By every relevant argument, by communicating reports on Italo-German activity to both governments, by the submission of concrete proposals for combating the Italian menace in Majorca—by every means in our power we endeavored to bring about a change of attitude in London and Paris.[38]

We were not crying for the moon. We made no request for armed assistance. We only asked that in strict accordance with the policy of non-intervention—which Great Britain and France had imposed on us and should for that very reason have enforced—"Spain should be left to the Spaniards"; and that if those two democracies did not feel able to prevent Germany and Italy from continuing to intervene in Spain, they should make honorable recognition of the failure of their policy and reestablish in full the right to freedom of trade. In a word, we asked that international law should be respected.

The way in which the British and French governments ignored our warnings, suggestions, and requests was truly heartbreaking."[39]

Notwithstanding these disappointments, Russia continued to bolster the resistance of the anti-Franco forces in the stubborn belief that Britain and France could not permit an Italo-German vassalage of Spain and would sooner or later be forced to intervene in defense of their own interests, undermining or destroying Germany's military power before she had time to prepare for war in eastern Europe.

Moscow, affirmed Boris Stefanov, the Comintern delegate, "will try by every means to avoid being isolated, to force the Western democracies to fight Hitler, if there is no other course but war."[40]

"We want [the democratic states] to help us," declared José Díaz, the general secretary of the Spanish Communist party, "and believe that in this way they will be defending their own interests. We try to make them understand this and to enlist their help. . . . We know full well that the fascist aggressors find bourgeois groups in every country to support them, such as the Conservatives in England and the rightists in France, but fascist aggression is going forward at such a pace that national interests, in a country like France, for instance, must convince all men who desire the liberty and independence of their country of the necessity of standing up to this aggression. And today there is no more effective way of doing this than by giving concrete help to the Spanish people."[41]

"Moscow tried to do for France and England what they should have done for themselves," Juan Negrín, prime minister during the last two years of the war, declared after the end of the conflict. "The promise of Soviet aid to the Spanish Republic was that ultimately Paris and London would awake to the risks involved to themselves in an Italo-German victory in Spain and join the USSR in supporting us."[42]

The Rise of the Communists

At this stage it is important to anticipate the course of events to the time after the loss of Catalonia in February 1939, a few weeks before the close of the war, when the anti-Franco forces had been deprived of the French border and the area of their resistance had been reduced to the central and southeastern parts of Spain. Moscow—prior to taking the drastic step of negotiating a nonaggression pact with Germany in a last endeavor to turn German military might against the West—still clung to the belief, though much diminished, that Britain and France would reverse their policy of neutrality.

Although it has now been confirmed, as Krivitsky revealed in 1939, that quite early in the Civil War, Stalin had conducted secret negotiations with the Nazi government,[43] it was not until the overthrow of the Communist-dominated government of Juan Negrín in March 1939, a few weeks before the end of the war, that he threw out the first open hint of his desire for a rapprochement with Germany. "Marshal Stalin in March, 1939" testified the former Reich foreign minister, Joachim von Ribbentrop, during his trial at Nuremberg, "delivered a speech in which he made certain hints of his desire to have better relations with Germany. I had submitted this speech to Adolf Hitler and asked him whether we should not try to find out whether this suggestion had something real behind it. Hitler was at first reluctant, but later on he became more receptive to this idea. Negotiations for a commercial treaty were under way, and during these negotiations, with the Führer's permission, I took soundings in Moscow as to the possibility of a definite bridge between National Socialism and Bolshevism and whether the interests of the two countries could not at least be made to harmonize."[44]

The extremely cautious manner in which both sides broached the question of a political settlement from the time of Stalin's speech, as revealed by documents found in the archives of the German foreign office,[45] stemmed no doubt from the fact that each side feared that the other might use any concrete proposal for a political agreement to strengthen its own bargaining position vis-à-vis Britain and France. In fact, up to the end of July 1939, less than four weeks before the signing of the German-Soviet Non-Aggression Pact and the secret Protocol that preceded the attack on Poland and World War II, these documents indicate that matters had not gone beyond vague soundings. Although Stalin did not open formal negotiations with Hitler until July, he was not backward during the Spanish Civil War—apart from the negotiations during the early months of the war revealed by Krivitsky—in letting Hitler know that it would be to Germany's advantage to have him as a partner rather than an enemy. This is borne out by the testimony of Alexander Orlov: "The fourth line of Soviet intelligence," he wrote, "is so-called *Misinformation*. . . . Misinformation is not just lying for the sake of lying; it is expected to serve as a subtle means of inducing another government to do what the Kremlin wants it to do. . . . During the Spanish Civil War . . . the Misinformation desk was ordered to introduce into the channels of the German military intelligence service information that the Soviet planes fighting in Spain were not of the latest design and that Russia had in her arsenal thousands of newer planes, of the second and third generation, possessing much greater speed and a higher ceiling. This was not true. Russia had given Spain the best and the newest she had (though in insufficient quantities). This misleading information greatly impressed the German High Command. . . . Evidently, Stalin wanted to impress on Hitler that the Soviet Union was much stronger and better armed than he thought and that it would be wiser for Germany to have Russia as a partner rather than an opponent."[46]

Stalin's foreign policy in the Western world, affirmed Krivitsky in April 1939, was predicated upon a profound contempt for the "weakling" democratic nations and upon an equally profound respect for the mighty totalitarian states, as exemplified by the Nazi regime. "Stalin was guided by the rule that one must come to terms with a superior power. [His] international policy during the last six years [1933 to 1939] has been a series of maneuvers designed to place him in a favorable position for a deal with Hitler. When he joined the League of Nations, when he proposed the system of collective security, when he sought the hand of France, flirted with Poland, courted Great Britain, intervened in Spain, he calculated his every move with an eye upon Berlin, in the hope that Hitler would find it advantageous to meet his advances."[47]

Nevertheless, even after the loss of Catalonia in February 1939 and the renewal of Stalin's wooing of Hitler, Moscow had not entirely abandoned the hope that Britain and France might reverse their policy of neutrality, and the Spanish Communists and the Communist-dominated Negrín government were instructed to continue the struggle in the hope that the latent antagonisms between the Western powers might finally burst into flame. On 23 February 1939 the politburo of the Spanish Communist party declared:

It is a profound error to believe that we can hope for nothing or for very little from abroad and that the democratic countries, which have allowed Catalonia to be invaded by the Germans and Italians, will not help us now that we have lost such an important position. The international situation has never been more unstable than it is today. Furthermore, the successes of the fascist invaders in Catalonia have increased their boldness, encouraging them to reveal still more clearly their plans of conquest, plunder, and war, and this in turn opens the eyes of those who until now have not wanted to face reality and increases the possibilities of direct and indirect aid for the Spanish people. On the side of the Spanish Republic is the Soviet Union, that powerful country, the firm defender of liberty, justice, and peace throughout the world. The working class, as well as the sincerely democratic countries, have until now given Spain very substantial material aid and will continue to do so. What they have not been able to do, partly because of lack of unity and determination in the struggle and partly because they have not yet completely understood the importance to them of a just solution of the Spanish problem, is to change radically in our favor the policy of their governments. But what has not been achieved up to now can still be accomplished if we increase our resistance.

For all these reasons, we say that resistance is not only necessary but possible, and we affirm that, as on previous occasions when many persons believed that everything was lost . . . , our resistance can change the situation. It will permit new factors to develop, both in Spain and abroad, that will redound to our advantage and will open the prospect of victory.[48]

It would be untrue to suggest that only the Communists placed their hope of victory in the reversal of British and French policy and in the eventual outbreak of a European conflict, for this hope was also privately entertained by the other forces of the left. Referring to the occupation of the Basque provinces and Asturias by General Franco and by his Italian and German allies in the summer and autumn of 1937, Wenceslao Carrillo—a prominent supporter of Largo Caballero and father of JSU leader Santiago Carrillo, who after the war fiercely denounced his anti-Communist parent—wrote:

"Nevertheless, the hope of victory that the Communist party and the Negrín government held out to us, based on the possibility of world war, had not disappeared. Neither France nor England, they argued, can consent to an out-and-out triumph of fascism in Spain because that would put them in a critical position in the Mediterranean. As I am ready to tell the whole truth, I refuse to conceal the fact that, in the beginning, I too shared this belief. If France and England had created the Non-Intervention Committee in their desire not to become involved in a war, surely they could not go to the extreme of providing their possible enemies with the means of opposing them with a greater chance of success. But I did not think of profiting from war; nor was I in the service of interests other than those of my country."[49]

When the Civil War had ended, Alvarez del Vayo wrote: "Not a day passed until almost the end, when we did not have fresh reasons to hope that the Western democracies would come to their senses and restore us our rights to buy from them. And always our hopes proved illusory."[50]

But if these expectations were disappointed, it was not because those who determined policy in Britain and France were blind to the possible dangers of a Franco victory or because they contemplated lightly the extension of Italian and German influence on the peninsula; it was because the purview of their foreign policy went beyond the situation in Spain and embraced the whole of Europe. If they refused to challenge Germany in Spain; if, moreover, they willfully sacrificed Austria and Czechoslovakia to Nazi totalitarianism: if, finally, the British government under the premiership of Neville Chamberlain secretly proposed—before being outmaneuvered by the Hitler-Stalin Non-Aggression Pact of 23 August 1939 and the secret Protocol to divide up Poland—a political settlement with Germany that would have freed Britain from her guarantee to go to Poland's assistance if attacked, this was because the long-range goal of British "appeasement" was to avoid a conflict in western Europe by encouraging German penetration eastward.

Chamberlain's secret proposals for a political settlement with Germany at the expense of Poland were the zenith of the "appeasement" policy, pursued clearly and consistently ever since Britain had openly encouraged German rearmament in 1935.[51] The proposals were recorded by Herbert von Dirksen, German ambassador to London, in a memorandum written after the outbreak of World War II and found on his estate at Groditzberg by the Soviet army. The authenticity of the memorandum is beyond question, for Dirksen himself later confirmed the proposals in every important detail,[52] and they have not been challenged by leading British historians.[53] Although not directly related to the Spanish Civil War, the memorandum sheds more light than any other document on the basic objective of British appeasement—to turn German aggression eastward—and thereby helps to explain why British leaders were unwilling to risk involvement in the Spanish conflict and a possible conflagration in western Europe. Dirksen testifies:

When Herr [Helmut] Wohlthat [emissary of Goering] was in London for the whaling negotiations in July [1939], Wilson [Sir Horace Wilson, Chamberlain's chief collaborator and adviser] invited him for a talk, and, consulting prepared notes, outlined a program for a comprehensive adjustment of Anglo-German relations. . . .

In the political sphere, a non-aggression pact was contemplated, in which aggression would be renounced in principle. The underlying purpose of this

The Rise of the Communists

treaty was to make it possible for the British gradually to disembarrass themselves of their commitments towards Poland, on the ground that they had by this treaty secured Germany's renunciation of methods of aggression. . . .

The importance of Wilson's proposals was demonstrated by the fact that Wilson invited Wohlthat to have them confirmed by Chamberlain personally, whose room was not far from Wilson's. Wohlthat, however, declined this in order not to prejudice the unofficial character of his mission. . . .

In order to avoid all publicity, I visited Wilson at his home on August 3 and we had a conversation which lasted nearly two hours. . . . Again Wilson affirmed, and in a clearer form than he had done to Wohlthat, that the conclusion of an Anglo-German entente would practically render Britain's guarantee policy nugatory. Agreement with Germany would enable Britain to extricate herself from her predicament in regard to Poland on the ground that the non-aggression pact protected Poland from German attack; England would thus be relieved of her commitments. Then Poland, so to speak, would be left to face Germany alone.

Sir Horace Wilson, on my insistence, also touched on the question of how the negotiations were to be conducted in face of the inflamed state of British public opinion [a reference to the aroused state of public opinion following Hitler's seizure of Czechoslovakia in March 1939]. . . . He admitted quite frankly that by taking this step Chamberlain was incurring a great risk and laying himself open to the danger of a fall. But with skill and strict secrecy, the reefs could be avoided. . . .

The tragic and paramount thing about the rise of the new Anglo-German war was that Germany demanded an equal place with Britain as a world power and that Britain was in principle prepared to concede. But whereas Germany demanded immediate, complete and unequivocal satisfaction of her demand, Britain—although she was ready to renounce her eastern commitments, and therewith her encirclement policy, as well as to allow Germany a predominant position in east and south-east Europe and to discuss genuine world political partnership with Germany—wanted this to be done only by way of negotiation and a *gradual* revision of British policy. This change could be effected in a period of months, but not of days or weeks.[54]

Although Sir Horace Wilson's proposals came to nothing, largely because Hitler's foreign minister Joachim von Ribbentrop favored a pact with Stalin that offered immediate territorial gains at the expense of Poland rather than a pact with Britain that would have required a period of uncertain negotiation because of the inflamed state of British public opinion, they were the culminating effort, the final desperate gamble of the British government to direct Germany's course eastward and away from western Europe.

The British historian A. J. P. Taylor has questioned whether the British and French governments intended that Nazi Germany should destroy the "bolshevik menace." "This was the Soviet suspicion, both at the time and later," he adds. "There is little evidence of it in the official record, or even outside it. British and French statesmen were far too distracted by the German problem to consider what would happen when Germany had become the dominant Power in eastern Europe. Of course they preferred that Germany should march east, not west, if she marched at all. But their object was to prevent war, not to prepare one; and they sincerely believed—or at any rate Chamberlain believed—that Hitler would be content and pacific if his claims were met."[55] If this be so, then the policy of the British government of consistently encouraging German rearmament from the beginning of 1935, conniving at the German reoccupation of the Rhineland in 1936, wantonly abandoning Austria and Czechoslovakia in 1938, and being willing to sacrifice Poland to Germany in 1939, makes positively no sense. It is impossible to believe that the so-called policy of "appeasement" did not take into account, at some time or another, once Germany had achieved her aims in central and southeastern Europe and had devoured Poland, what might happen when the Nazis had established a common border with Russia. At all events, there is ample evidence, as we have seen, that powerful forces in Britain and France hoped to use Germany as a counterpoise to Russia and to purchase immunity for the West at the expense of eastern Europe.[56]

The attitude, then, of the controlling forces in Britain and France toward the Spanish Civil War was determined not merely by their hostility to the revolutionary changes, of which they were fully apprised in spite of the efforts to conceal them behind the façade of a "democratic Republic,"[57] but by the whole field of foreign politics. Hence, no attempt at dissimulation and persuasion on the part of successive Spanish governments, prompted mainly by the Communist party, no attempt even at curbing the Revolution, could have altered their policy with regard to the Spanish conflict.

Nevertheless, despite the doubts that may occasionally have assailed them, the Spanish Communist leaders executed the directives of the Kremlin without apparent hesitation even though these directives meant antagonizing irreversibly other parties of the left and eventually undermining the war effort and the will to fight. "Those of us who 'directed' the Spanish Communist party," declared Jesús Hernández in a speech delivered some years after he had been expelled from the party, "acted more like Soviet subjects than sons of the Spanish people. It may seem absurd, incredible, but our education under Soviet tutelage had deformed us to such an extent that we were completely denationalized; our national soul was torn out of us and replaced by a rabidly chauvinistic internationalism that began and ended with the towers of the Kremlin."[58]

The Rise of the Communists

Yet the leaders of the Spanish Communist party did not necessarily understand the Kremlin's purely pragmatic aims in rendering aid to the anti-Franco zone. "I sincerely believed," writes Valentín González, more commonly known as "El Campesino," a much-publicized Communist and somewhat charismatic figure during the war, "that the Kremlin sent us its arms, its military and political advisers, and the International Brigades under its control as a proof of its revolutionary solidarity. . . . Only later did I realize that the Kremlin does not serve the interests of the peoples of the world, but makes them serve its own interests; that, with a treachery and hypocrisy without parallel, it makes use of the international working class as a pawn in its political maneuvers, and that in the name of world revolution, it tries to consolidate its own totalitarian counterrevolution and to prepare for world domination."[59]

Part III
Curbing the Revolution

11. Anarchism and Government

The efforts of the Communists from the outset of the Civil War to gain the support of Great Britain and France and to ensure the continued recognition first of the Giral and later of the Caballero government as the legally constituted authority necessarily had an important effect on the course of the Revolution. If these two countries were to be influenced even in the smallest measure, the government would have to reconstruct the shattered machinery of state not upon revolutionary lines but in the image of the deceased Republic. Moreover, if the Caballero administration were to be a government in essence rather than in name, it would have to assume control of all the elements of state power appropriated by the revolutionary committees in the first days of the Civil War.[1] On this point all members of the cabinet were of one mind, and there can be little doubt that they would have been so irrespective of the need to impress foreign opinion.

But the work of reconstructing state power could not be achieved, or at least would be extremely difficult to achieve, without the participation in the government of the extreme wing of the Revolution, the powerful anarchosyndicalist or libertarian movement, as it was more frequently called, represented, as we have seen, by the anarchist-oriented CNT and by the FAI, its ideological guide, whose mission was to protect the CNT from deviationist tendencies[2] and to lead the trade-union federation to the anarchist goal of libertarian communism.[3] Formed in 1927 as a clandestine organization, the FAI's initial purpose was to aid in the struggle against the Primo de Rivera dictatorship inasmuch as the CNT, formed in 1911 and outlawed by Primo, had virtually ceased to function. César M. Lorenzo writes:

It was only at the beginning of 1929, when the CNT was partially reconstructed, that [the FAI] started to become known. . . . Organized very loosely on the basis of autonomous groups [known as "affinity" groups because of their common place of work or residence, as in the case of Communist cells] and comprising on the average about ten men, it had a peninsular committee . . . that served as a connecting organ. . . . [The] FAI's real cohesion derived from the ideological intransigence of its members, who were ferocious enemies of authority, hierarchy, politics, the state, legal action, and compromise.

Curbing the Revolution

The "Faistas" undertook the conquest of the CNT, imposing themselves by their radicalism, their violent language, their ceaseless criticism, forever predicting that the social revolution would arrive the very next day. . . . The FAI, it should be stressed, was in reality only a faction, in prodigious expansion, of the CNT; it was not an alien force attempting to control it, like the Communist party, for example, which failed very quickly in its efforts at penetration, but an appendix, an outgrowth of the CNT itself, formed by the latter's own militants already organized in the unions. Its true epicenter was Catalonia, the cradle and ever-turbulent seat of the libertarian movement. It was not long before it became a "state within a state" inside the CNT.[4]

"[What] is clear and beyond question," Federica Montseny, a leading member of both the CNT and the FAI, wrote many years after the war, "is that the CNT was founded by the most devoted and most dynamic segment of the anarchists and attracted the working class to itself precisely because of this dynamism and devotion. . . . And one other thing that no one should forget is that, if the CNT saved itself on various occasions from falling into the hands of other political organizations, it was precisely because of the . . . unfailing vigilance and activity of the [anarchist] comrades within its ranks. In this way, it protected itself from the influx of Marxists in the years that followed the Russian Revolution."[5]

The FAI attempted to accomplish its directive mission by virtue of the fact that its members, with few exceptions, belonged to the CNT and held many positions of trust. It was an established principle that any person belonging to a political party should not occupy any official position in the trade-union organization.[6] The FAI, moreover, kept a close and constant supervision over the unions of the CNT, often threatening to use force to prevent deviationist trends when argument failed. To be sure, this domination—or at least attempted domination—by the FAI was not always openly acknowledged by the CNT and FAI and indeed was at times emphatically denied,[7] but it was frankly admitted after the Civil War by the more independent leaders of the CNT.[8] It is true, however, as José Peirats, the libertarian historian, points out that while the FAI exerted considerable influence over the CNT—"watching closely for heresies of CNT leaders who were not FAI members"—the CNT in turn exerted a powerful influence over the FAI.[9] Nevertheless, his assertion that the FAI was "in reality" directed by the CNT runs counter to other testimony.[10]

Although views were divided in the cabinet as to the advisability, from the standpoint of foreign opinion, of allowing the libertarians to participate in the government,[11] the advantages of having them share responsibility for its measures were indubitable. "The entry of representatives of the CNT into the present Council of Ministers would certainly endow the directive organ of the nation with fresh energy and authority," said *Claridad*, Largo Caballero's mouthpiece, on 25 October 1936, "in view of the fact that a considerable segment of the working class, now absent from its deliberations, would feel bound by its measures and its authority." But would the anarchosyndicalists wish to become ministers in the central government and join in the reconstruction of the state? This was questionable even though quite recently they had, in violation of venerable principles, joined the Catalan regional government.[12]

Rootedly opposed to the state, which they regarded as "the supreme expression of authority of man over man, the most powerful instrument for the enslavement of the people,"[13] the libertarians were equally opposed to every government whether of the right or left, including the Soviet government that had destroyed the anarchist movement in the first years of the Russian Revolution. "The entire dialectic of the officials of the Russian government," said *Tierra y Libertad* of Barcelona, the FAI organ, two weeks before the outbreak of the Civil War, "cannot erase one palpable, one evident fact regarding the Russian experiment: that the route of the state is the route of the counterrevolution. We have always maintained that this is so, and the study of the last nineteen years of Russian events has provided a most eloquent demonstration of the correctness of our view. In proportion as the Soviet state became stronger the revolution perished in the iron grip of decrees, bureaucrats, repressive machinery, and taxation. The revolution is a thing of the people, a popular creation; the counterrevolution is a thing of the state. It has always been so, and will always be so, whether in Russia, Spain, or China."[14]

Anarchist opposition to all forms of government found vehement expression in polemics during the latter half of the nineteenth century between Bakunin, the great Russian anarchist, whose writings had a far-reaching influence on the Spanish working-class movement, and Karl Marx. In the words of Bakunin, the "people's government" proposed by Marx would simply be the rule of a privileged minority over the huge majority of the working masses. "But this minority, the Marxists argue, would consist of workers. Yes, I dare say, of *former* workers, but as soon as they become rulers and representatives of the people they would cease to be proletarians and would look down upon all workers from their political summit. They would no longer represent the people; they would represent only themselves. . . . He who doubts this must be absolutely ignorant of human nature."[15]

Curbing the Revolution

And the Italian anarchist, Errico Malatesta, whose influence on the Spanish libertarian movement was appreciable, stated: "The primary concern of every government is to ensure its continuance in power irrespective of the men who form it. If they are bad, they want to remain in power in order to enrich themselves and to satisfy their lust for authority; and if they are honest and sincere they believe that it is their duty to remain in power for the benefit of the people. . . . The anarchists . . . could never, even if they were strong enough, form a government without contradicting themselves and repudiating their entire doctrine; and, should they do so, it would be no different from any other government; perhaps it would be even worse."[16]

The establishment of the democratic Spanish Republic in 1931, following the fall of the Monarchy and the Berenguer dictatorship, did not cause the libertarians to modify their basic tenets: "All governments are detestable, and it is our mission to destroy them."[17] "All governments without exception are equally bad, equally contemptible."[18] "All governments are destroyers of liberty."[19] "Under the Monarchy and the Dictatorship," wrote an anarchist at the time of the republican-Socialist coalition in 1933, "the workers suffered hunger and a thousand privations, and they continue to do so today under the Republic. Yesterday it was impossible to satisfy their most urgent needs, and today conditions are the same. We anarchists say this without fear that any worker will contradict us, and we say more. We say that at all times, under whatever type of government, the workers have been tyrannized and have had to wage bitter struggles so that their right to live and enjoy themselves after exhausting hours of labor would be respected."[20] Just as the libertarians made no distinction between governments of the left and governments of the right, they made no distinction between individual politicians: "For us, all politicians are equal—in electoral demagogy, in filching the rights from the people, in their desire for fame, in their opportunism, in their ability to criticize when in the opposition, and in their cynicism when justifying themselves once in power."[21]

In contrast to other working-class organizations, the CNT and FAI shunned parliamentary activity.[22] They held no seats in central or local governments, refrained from nominating candidates for parliament, and, in the crucial November 1933 elections that brought the parties of the right to power, they had enjoined their members to abstain from voting. "Our revolution is not made in Parliament, but in the street," *Tierra y Libertad* had declared[23] a month before the elections. "We are not interested in changing governments," Isaac Puente, an influential anarchosyndicalist, had written at the time. "What we want is to suppress them. . . . Whatever side wins, whether the right or the left, will be our enemy, our jailer, our executioner, and will have at its disposal the truncheons of the assault guards, the bullying of the secret police, the rifles of the civil guard, and the outlook of prison wardens. The working class will have just what it has today: somber jails, spies, hunger, welts, and lacerations."[24] And a few days before the elections, *Tierra y Libertad* declared:

Workers! Do not vote! The vote is a negation of your personality. Turn your backs on those who ask you to vote for them. They are your enemies. They hope to rise to power by taking advantage of your trustfulness. Urge your parents, your children, your brothers and sisters, your relatives, and your friends not to vote for any of the candidates. As far as we are concerned they are all the same; all politicians are our enemies whether they be republicans, monarchists, Communists, or Socialists. Honorio Maura is just as shameless as Rodrigo Soriano and [Herrán] Barriobero. Largo Caballero and Prieto are just as cynical and despicable as Balbontin and his associates. . . . We need neither a state nor a government. The bourgeoisie needs them in order to defend its interests. Our interests lie solely in our working conditions, and to defend them we require no parliament. No one should vote. . . . Do not be concerned whether the rightists or the leftists emerge triumphant from this farce. They are all diehards. The only left-wing organization that is genuinely revolutionary is the CNT, and, because this is so, it is not interested in Parliament, which is a filthy house of prostitution toying with the interests of the country and the people. Destroy the ballots! Destroy the ballot boxes! Crack the heads of the ballot supervisers as well as those of the candidates![25]

In the February 1936 elections, however, the CNT and FAI changed their posture; for, while opposing the Popular Front program—which they regarded as a "profoundly conservative document" out of harmony with "the revolutionary fever that Spain was sweating through her pores"[26]—they decided not to urge their members to abstain from voting, not only because the left coalition promised a broad amnesty for thousands of political prisoners in the event of victory,[27] but because a repetition of the abstentionist policy of 1933 would have meant as great a defeat for the libertarian movement as for the parties that adhered to the Popular Front coalition.[28] This change of posture ensured the victory of the Popular Front coalition, but did not imply any fundamental change of doctrine. The anarchosyndicalists' impressive background of hostility to all governments and to all politicians makes it hard to conceive that they would join the cabinet of Largo Caballero, especially as, for many years before the outbreak of the Civil War, they had been at sword's point with the Socialist leader and his rival trade-union organization, the UGT.

12. The Anarchosyndicalists Enter the Government

As leader of the Socialist UGT, Largo Caballero's relations with the anarchosyndicalists in the years before the Civil War had been marked by constant enmity. During the dictatorship of General Primo de Rivera (1923–30) he had served as councillor of state in the dictator's cabinet, partly with the object of protecting and strengthening his own organization and partly in the hope of gaining ground from the anarchosyndicalists, whose unions had been proscribed by the dictator. During the preceding years, writes Gerald Brenan in his classic work, the CNT had been increasing its numbers very rapidly. "With the aid of its *sindicato único* and the prestige of its great strikes it had not only swept away all the recent gains of its rival in the Andalusian campo, but it had invaded the socialist preserve of the center and north. Here it had seized half the builders' union in Madrid, which was one of the first strongholds of the UGT, had drawn off many of the railwaymen and planted itself firmly in the Asturias, in the port of Gijón and in the great iron foundries of Sama and La Felguera.

"To Caballero, who had the whole organization of the UGT in his hands, this was a serious matter: the fear of losing ground to the CNT was almost an obsession with him. As a Marxist he felt the supreme importance of the unification of the proletariat. He sensed therefore in the Dictatorship a good opportunity for making some progress in this direction. Possibly the UGT would be able to absorb the CNT altogether.

"This hope was not fulfilled." By using the arbitration boards of the dictatorship as a starting point, Brenan continues, the UGT greatly increased its strength in the country districts, especially in Estremadura, Granada, Aragon, and New Castile, but it failed completely in Catalonia and made no progress among the industrial proletariat. "The anarchosyndicalists preferred to enter the reactionary *sindicato libre*, which they knew would break up with the fall of the Dictatorship."[1]

The Anarchosyndicalists Enter the Government

At one time the CNT had likewise hoped to monopolize the entire trade-union movement. At an anarchosyndicalist congress held in 1919, a resolution was passed giving the workers of Spain a period of three months in which to enter the CNT, failing which they would be denounced as scabs.[2] But nothing came of this attempt to absorb the rival movement.

When, a few years later, Largo Caballero became a councillor of state in the dictator's cabinet and used the arbitration boards to increase the strength of the UGT, he became the object of the CNT's unsparing criticism. Nor did relations between them improve with the advent of the Republic in 1931, when he became minister of labor; for he again used his powers to augment the influence of the UGT at the expense of the rival organization and clashed with the CNT over his defense of state interference in labor disputes. Brenan writes:

The Minister of Labor, Largo Caballero, had introduced a series of laws regulating the rights of the working classes in their dealings with capital. The most important of these, the law of December 24, 1931, laid down the conditions which all contracts between workers and employers must fulfil in order to be valid. A special tribunal was set up to decide alleged infractions. Another law, the *Ley de Jurados Mixtos*, established tribunals at which labor disputes were to be compulsorily settled. . . . Another law required eight days notice to be given of every strike. Apart from the fact that these laws ran contrary to the Anarcho-Syndicalist principles of negotiating directly with the employers and interfered with the practice of lightning strikes, it was clear that they represented an immense increase in the power of the State in industrial matters. A whole army of Government officials, mostly Socialists, made their appearance to enforce the new laws and saw to it that, whenever possible, they should be used to extend the influence of the UGT at the expense of the CNT. This had of course been the intention of those who drew them up. In fact the UGT was rapidly becoming an organ of the State itself and was using its new powers to reduce its rival. The Anarcho-Syndicalists could have no illusions as to what would happen to them if a purely Socialist Government should come into power.[3]

Unlike the UGT, the CNT rejected the labor courts, or *jurados mixtos*, of the Republic, not only because they increased the power of the state in disputes between labor and management, but because their purpose, in the opinion of a prominent CNT-FAI member, was "to castrate the Spanish proletariat in the interests of 'class conciliation.' "[4] Not conciliation, but continual and implacable war between labor and management was what the CNT wanted, and direct action was its method: violent strikes, sabotage, and boycott.[5] This was not simply a means of improving the standard of living of the workers; above all, it was a method of agitation, of stimulating and keeping alive a spirit of revolt in preparation for the day of insurrection. "Direct action," declared the International Workingmen's Association (AIT) with which the CNT was affiliated, "finds it highest expression in the general strike, which should be a prelude to the social revolution."[6] Famed for their frequent uprisings in the years before the military rebellion, the anarchosyndicalists were the classic force of Spanish insurrection. It mattered little whether these uprisings, invariably confined to a few localities, failed for lack of support elsewhere; what was important was that they should rouse the revolutionary temper of the working class. Today they might fail, but tomorrow they would be victorious. "If yesterday ten villages revolted," wrote Isaac Puente, "one thousand villages must rise tomorrow, even if we have to fill the holds of a hundred [prison] ships like the *Buenos Aires*. Defeat is not always failure. The future does not always belong to those who triumph. We never play our last card."[7]

The sharp divergence between the CNT and UGT was not in any way lessened by Largo Caballero's leftward swerve in 1933,[8] for the anarchosyndicalists continued to regard him with unrelenting animosity. Nor did his advocacy of the dictatorship of the proletariat, through the instrumentality of the Socialist party[9] and of the unification of the CNT and UGT[10] a few months before the outbreak of the Civil War, temper this animosity; for they held that Largo Caballero was a "dictator in embryo," who favored "the absolute hegemony of the Socialist party on the morrow of the triumphant insurrection of the working class,"[11] and that under the cover of unification his "crooked aim" was to absorb the CNT in localities where the UGT was stronger.[12] No practical discussions to bring about the fusion ever took place, and the somewhat more cautious attitude adopted by the leadership of the UGT toward the developing strike movement, just before the military insurrection,[13] tended to increase still further the hostility of the CNT, which was sweeping the rank and file of the UGT along with it in several places. "The mass of workers were desperate," wrote an acute observer, "and were prepared to follow the most ardent leaders."[14] "In Madrid," *El Sol* reported, "we are witnessing the amazing spectacle of the CNT . . . declaring general strikes, continually organizing partial strikes, and inspiring intransigent and rigid attitudes that cause the government to despair."[15]

Then came the Civil War and the Revolution, creating fresh points of friction between the two trade-union federations.[16]

Yet, in spite of this discord, in spite of the traditional antigovernment stand of the anarchosyndicalists and of their distrust of him personally, Largo Caballero tried, when forming his cabinet at the beginning of September 1936, to secure their participation in the belief, as his organ *Claridad* later put it, that they "would feel themselves bound by its measures and its authority."[17] But much as he needed them to share the responsibilities of office in order to forestall any criticism of his government's decrees, he offered them only a single seat without portfolio,[18] a meager reward for what would have entailed a flagrant breach of principle. That offer, commented the Madrid anarchosyndicalist organ, *CNT*, some weeks later, was "neither generous nor enticing" and was "absolutely disproportionate to the strength and influence of the CNT in the country."[19]

To be sure, the CNT, if smaller than the UGT in Madrid province, yielded nothing to it in the majority of provinces within the left zone, such as Albacete, Guadalajara, Jaen, and Toledo (to mention but a few where the two federations had approximately the same number of adherents), and, in addition to being more powerful in the regions of Aragon, Catalonia, and Valencia, had, in all probability, more members than its Socialist rival in the total area controlled by the left-wing forces.[20]

Nevertheless, the national committee of the CNT accepted Largo Caballero's offer, subject, however, to ratification by the regional federations.[21] A national plenum of regional federations met on 3 September, but the delegates rejected the offer.[22] Two days later, after Caballero had already formed his cabinet, *CNT* in Madrid declared: "Perhaps many wonder how it is that the CNT, one of the principal forces preparing for the victory of the people at the front and in the rear . . . does not form part of this government. Undoubtedly, if the CNT were inspired by political ideas, the number of its seats in this government would have to be at least as large as that of the UGT and the Socialists." In other words, the CNT would have required the same number of seats as both the Largo Caballero faction of the Socialist party, which the paper identifies with the UGT because of its control of the trade-union executive, and the Prieto faction, which controlled the party executive. "However," the article continued, "the CNT once again affirms its unshakable adhesion to its antiauthoritarian postulates and believes that the libertarian transformation of society can take place only as a result of the abolition of the state and the control of the economy by the working class."[23]

Although the delegates to the CNT national plenum rejected Largo Caballero's offer of a single seat—some of them even opposing collaboration with the Socialist leader altogether—they adopted, after "long and tumultuous debates," a compromise resolution accepting government participation in principle and providing for the restructuring of the government and the state.[24]

According to the resolution, "auxiliary commissions" were to be set up in each ministry comprising two representatives of the CNT, two of the UGT, two of the Popular Front parties, and one government delegate.[25] This project would have spared the CNT the embarrassment of direct participation in the cabinet, but would nonetheless have given it representation in every branch of government. According to Lorenzo, its rejection by Caballero was hardly surprising, for the commissions would have been "veritable organs of power," and the ministers would have been reduced to "simple executors" of the will of the two trade-union federations.[26]

Although the libertarian movement could not join the cabinet without striking at the very roots of official doctrine, some of its leaders were loath to leave the affairs of government entirely in the hands of rival organizations. Among the most resolute of these advocates of intervention in the government was the secretary of the national committee of the CNT, Horacio M. Prieto, a pragmatic libertarian, who, viewing as "unrealistic" the resolution of 3 September and feeling that "time was pressing ruthlessly," demanded that the CNT enter the government "with several ministers openly and without shame."[27] The CNT, he observed some years later, "should not have declined [to enter the government] in view of the important role we were playing in the war . . . , but fear of violating the ideological principles of the movement, respect for its ideas, for its tenets, and fear of shouldering this responsibility acted as a brake on initiative with the result that indecision prevailed."[28]

Because of this indecision, because of the fear of violating doctrinal scruples, but feeling that they could not leave the central government entirely in the hands of rival organizations, the delegates of the regional committees of the CNT tried a novel approach. At a plenary assembly held on 15 September they decided that the government should be replaced by a national council of defense composed of five members of their own organization, five of the UGT, and four members of the republican parties.[29] The national council of defense, of course, would have been a government in everything but name, although the title would have been less offensive to the libertarian movement.

The anarchosyndicalists certainly wanted to enter the government, wrote one libertarian after the war, "but they demanded that it should change its name to national council of defense. The purpose of this purely nominal change was to reconcile their fervent desire to enter the government with their antistate doctrine. What childishness! A movement that had cured itself of all prejudices and had always scoffed at mere appearances tried to conceal its abjuration of fundamental principles by changing a name. . . . This behavior is as childish as that of an unfortunate woman, who, having entered a house of ill fame and wishing to preserve a veneer of morality, asks to be called a hetaera instead of a whore."[30]

As César M. Lorenzo, the son of Horacio M. Prieto, the secretary of the CNT national committee, observes: "The CNT had entered the Catalan government and fervently wished to enter the Basque government. Then why differentiate between a regional and a national government? . . . A municipal councillor, a judge, or a policeman was just as much an element, a part of the state, as a minister. Exercising authority in a village was neither more nor less antianarchist than exercising it in a nation. A vast territory can be administered very democratically, whereas a locality can be subjected to tyranny."[31]

Foreign anarchists, who later criticized the Spanish libertarians for entering the government, had previously approved of the idea of a national council of defense. "It is a curious thing," wrote Helmut Ruediger, representative in Spain of the International Workingmen's Association, with which the CNT was affiliated, and director of the German-language papers, *CNT-FAI-AIT Informationsdienst* and *Soziale Revolution*, both published in Barcelona, "that nearly all the dissenting comrades [abroad] accepted the program providing for the direction of the antifascist movement by a national council of defense. . . . Let us be frank. *This was also a program for the exercise of power*, the only difference being that the *name* was a little more pleasant to our anarchist comrades in other countries."[32]

In the hope of avoiding any resistance to the proposed council on the part of Communists, Socialists, and republicans because of possible repercussions in moderate circles abroad, the delegates of the CNT regional committees to the plenary assembly held on 15 September proposed that Manuel Azaña continue as president of the Republic.[33] "Our position abroad," declared *Solidaridad Obrera*, the leading newspaper of the CNT, "cannot deteriorate as a result of the new structure we propose; for it must be borne in mind that the decorative figures that characterize a petty-bourgeois regime would be retained so as not to frighten foreign capitalists."[34]

Nevertheless, the CNT's campaign in favor of a national council of defense elicited no support from any of the parties in the government and, on 28 September, at another plenary assembly of the regional committees of the CNT, Horacio Prieto, secretary of the national committee, assailed the project as a waste of time since it was unacceptable to the political parties and, in his opinion, "evidenced a total lack of realism, taking into account foreign powers and the international aspect of the war." He hammered away at his arguments in favor of government participation "pure and simple," demanded that the delegates "put an end to so many scruples, moral and political prejudices, so many denials of reality, and so much semantic fuss," pleading that "it was necessary to act quickly, that every day that passed aggravated the position of the CNT."[35]

Although shaken by Prieto's words, the delegates still clung to their proposed solution. For several weeks the CNT waged a ceaseless campaign in favor of the national council of defense,[36] but its efforts were unavailing. Largo Caballero was adamant in his opposition. His attitude, which was identical with that of the Communists and republicans,[37] found expression in the following passage taken from an editorial in his mouthpiece, *Claridad*: "A radical transformation of the organs of the state would occasion a loss of continuity, which would be fatal to us. Furthermore, we are waging a battle in Geneva [at the League of Nations], which, in the event of victory, could have far-reaching consequences for us because the scales would be tipped in our favor in view of the fact that we should obtain the material elements indispensable for winning the war. What would be the repercussions of the leap outside the bounds of the Constitution peremptorily demanded by the comrades of the CNT? We fear that it would put things just where our enemies want them."[38] A month later, another editorial in *Claridad* declared: "Quite as important as attending to the purely military needs of the Civil War—perhaps even more so—is to give to the institutions of the regime a form that will awaken the least suspicion in foreign countries."[39] That these editorials reflected the personal views of Largo Caballero was confirmed by Mariano Cardona Rosell, who became a member of the national committee of the CNT at the end of September 1936 and was one of the members of that body who conducted the negotiations with the premier.[40]

Faced by Largo Caballero's unbending attitude and by opposition from other quarters, Horacio Prieto decided to "put an end to the last remnants of opposition" within the CNT and convoked a plenary session of the regional federations for 18 October. This time his arguments prevailed. The plenum accorded him full powers to conduct negotiations "in his own way" in order to bring the CNT into the government.[41] "I was convinced," he wrote after the war, "of the necessity of collaboration, and I smothered my own ideological and conscientious scruples."[42]

Explaining the libertarian movement's new line, *CNT* declared: "We are taking into consideration the scruples that the members of the government may have concerning the international situation, . . . and for this reason the CNT is ready to make the maximum concession compatible with its antiauthoritarian spirit: that of entering the government. This does not imply renouncing its intention of fully realizing its ideals in the future; it simply means that . . . in order to win the war and to save our people and the world, it is ready to collaborate with anyone in a directive organ, whether this organ be called a council or a government."[43] In their negotiations with Caballero the CNT representatives asked for five ministries, including war and finance, but he rejected their demand.[44] Finally, on 3 November, they accepted four: justice, industry, commerce, and health, none of which, however, was vital; moreover, the portfolios of industry and commerce had previously been held by a single minister.

The composition of the reorganized government was as follows:

Francisco Largo Caballero	Socialist	Prime Minister and War
Julio Alvarez del Vayo	Socialist	Foreign Affairs
Angel Galarza	Socialist	Interior
Anastasio de Gracia	Socialist	Labor
Juan Negrín	Socialist	Finance
Indalecio Prieto	Socialist	Navy and Air
Jesús Hernández	Communist	Education and Fine Arts
Vicente Uribe	Communist	Agriculture
Juan García Oliver	CNT	Justice
Juan López	CNT	Commerce
Federica Montseny	CNT	Health and Public Assistance
Juan Peiró	CNT	Industry
Carlos Esplá	Left Republican	Propaganda
José Giral	Left Republican	Minister without portfolio

Curbing the Revolution

Julio Just	Left Republican	Public Works
Bernardo Giner de los Rios	Republican Union	Communications
Jaime Aiguadé	Left Republican party of Catalonia	Minister without portfolio
Manuel de Irujo	Basque Nationalist	Minister without portfolio[45]

It was not without foreboding that the CNT representatives crossed the unfamiliar threshold of ministerial responsibility. Indeed, according to one libertarian writer, they knew, when they took possession of their departments, that they could not influence the Revolution.[46] To be sure, Largo Caballero's decision to give the CNT four portfolios instead of one was neither an act of sympathy nor of generosity. There is evidence that he was motivated partly by his desire to invest his government with greater authority[47] at a time when he was planning to transfer his government to Valencia in the belief that at any moment Franco's forces might seize the capital. "[The] moment had arrived," he wrote later, "to leave the capital. The enemy had concentrated large forces and might make a surprise attack any night and enter Madrid."[48] He also feared, whether with grounds or not, that if the cabinet should leave Madrid without first admitting representatives of the libertarian movement, the CNT and FAI might set up an independent administration. "In Madrid's critical situation," writes Alvarez del Vayo, "had the anarchists not been allowed to share the government's responsibility, it is more than likely that they would have seized the opportunity afforded by the government's departure for Valencia to try to set up a local junta of their own. This would have only produced confusion and disaster throughout the loyal territory."[49]

Whether warranted or not, this concern does not appear to have been an issue with President Azaña who, after his flight from Madrid two weeks earlier,[50] was now installed in Barcelona with his presidential guard, conveniently close to the French border. Still savoring his presidential powers that, in the final analysis, he now derived not from the rule of law, as embodied in the Constitution, but from his tenuous role as constitutional cover for the Revolution, he refused at first to sanction the decrees appointing the libertarian ministers. He did not see, writes Largo Caballero, the effect that the revision of Spanish anarchism would have upon the future. "From terrorism and direct action, it had moved to collaboration and to sharing the responsibilities of power. . . . It was a unique event in the world and would not be sterile. I told him that if he did not sign the decrees I would resign. He signed them, although with reservations."[51]

Azaña, records Alvarez del Vayo, raised serious objections to the appointment of two of the four candidates proposed for the ministerial posts—Federica Montseny and Juan García Oliver, both members of the FAI. "In different circumstances the natural course would have been to yield to the will of the President or to give him time to change his mind. But in those dark days through which Madrid was passing, any indecision would have been fatal. Already the prospective ministers, two of whom had come expressly from Barcelona, had begun to suspect that their entry into the government was not well considered in high places, and were talking about returning to Catalonia and breaking off relations between the CNT and the government. Twice I had to leave the Prime Minister's study in order to quiet and reassure them. A telephone conversation between the President of the Republic and the Prime Minister, not lacking in a certain dramatic quality, put an end to an embarrassing situation. Although we were unable to hear his voice, the rest of us could almost feel the exasperation of Señor Azaña coming over the wires. Within a few moments, however Señor Largo Caballero was given authorization to send to the official gazette the notice of the appointment of the four CNT members, duly sanctioned by the President."[52]

Mindful of posterity, Azaña wrote in his memoirs some six months later: "Not only against my judgment, but against my most angry protest, was the cabinet reorganization of November incorporating the CNT and the anarchists into the government—which the republicans themselves considered inevitable and useful—forced upon me."[53]

In connection with this episode, the then mayor of Barcelona, Carles Pi Sunyer, a member of the Catalan Esquerra and confidant of Azaña, relates in his memoirs that the president telephoned him one evening, saying that he wished to speak to him. "I went there immediately. I found him shattered, his morale in ruins. Even his intelligence, so brilliant, appeared dull, half-extinguished. He told me he wanted to go away, to leave Spain, to resign the presidency of the Republic. . . . What had happened? Largo Caballero had telephoned him to say that he was going to form a government with four CNT ministers. Azaña had objected, but, in spite of his objection, the decrees appointing them had appeared under his name in the official gazette. But he did not wish to ratify the appointments. . . . We spoke for a long time.

Curbing the Revolution

When, finally, I left him, very late, he seemed to have resigned himself to remaining in the office to which destiny had tied him."[54]

Shorly after the names of the CNT ministers appeared in the *Gaceta de Madrid* of 5 November, Largo Caballero raised the question of transferring the seat of government to Valencia. Indalecio Prieto, the moderate Socialist and navy and air minister, who according to one of his own supporters was convinced like Largo Caballero that within three to six days the enemy would seize Madrid,[55] testifies:

Francisco Largo Caballero assembled his ministers in order to propose that the government should leave Madrid . . . without a moment's delay. Weeks before I had proposed that the government should leave, but with publicity. . . . I didn't want the transfer to take place at the last moment unexpectedly, which would give the impression of a flight. It was advisable, I felt, that the people of Madrid should be psychologically prepared so that they would find the measure justifiable and would bid us farewell with affection rather than vilify us as fugitives if we did not advise them in advance. But the premier disregarded my proposal.

The subsequent debate on his proposal was most dramatic. The four members of the National Confederation of Labor who had just joined the government considered that they were victims of a deception. Believing that they had been made ministers solely in order to implicate them in this grave decision, they refused to approve it. After considerable discussion they suggested that we should all leave except the four who would remain in Madrid. I joined in the debate, vigorously opposing that formula. "Either we all leave," I said, "or no one leaves. It would be unacceptable if some were to be branded as cowards and others hailed as heroes. Either we are all cowards or all heroes. . . ."

The CNT ministers requested permission to discuss the matter among themselves and left the conference room. . . . After considerable delay they returned to say that they would approve the proposal. Largo Caballero announced that the new residence would be Valencia and not Barcelona as had been expected, where the president of the Republic had moved. He demanded secrecy of everyone and stated that anyone could leave whenever he wished. I could count on two passenger planes that were to undertake the flight at dawn and were capable of carrying all those ministers who wished to fly. No one accepted my invitation at the time. Some believed that it was too long to wait.

No sooner had the cabinet meeting ended [on 6 November] than Largo Caballero took to the highway and passed through the town of Tarancón that lay across the direct route to Valencia. Tarancón was occupied by the Rosal Column, composed of anarchists and convicts from the San Miguel de los Reyes Penitentiary in Valencia, who had been freed at the outset of the rebellion.[56] When news of the government's agreement reached Colonel Rosal he decided that no one should proceed to [Valencia]. Julio Alvarez del Vayo, the foreign minister, was the object of gross abuse.[57] Juan Peiró and Juan López, the CNT ministers, were turned back. They presented themselves at my house in the middle of the night, and I took them with me by plane.[58]

Also turned back was Pedro Rico, the rotund mayor of Madrid. Upon his return to Madrid, writes Indalecio Prieto, instead of rejoining the City Council, he took refuge in the Mexican embassy. "His stay in the embassy, where all the refugees with the exception of himself were rightists, was most disturbing to Pedro Rico. He could not return to the City Hall, where his attempt to flee had been condemned. Fearing reprisals, he did not dare sleep at home, even less walk the streets. . . . [The] prospect of again confronting the militiamen at Tarancón terrified him. I suggested that he should travel in the trunk of an automobile as I and several Socialists had done in 1934 when we had [escaped] to France. . . . It required the help of God to stuff him into the trunk. His fatness, greater than mine, and his awkwardness made it very difficult to pack him in. This provided an enjoyable spectacle to all those Franco supporters who witnessed the operation in the patio of the Mexican embassy."[59]

Indalecio Prieto's account of the government's furtive departure from Madrid is fully confirmed in all essentials by the famous anarchist militia leader, Cipriano Mera, later commander of the Fourteenth Division and the Fourth Army Corps, who hastened to Tarancón to protest the government's flight. There he found ministers, undersecretaries, and other government officials, as well as top military men, all detained by the Rosal Column. Horacio M. Prieto, the secretary of the CNT national committee, soon arrived, also on his way to Valencia with the other members. He defended the committee's departure on the grounds that it had to be close to the government "in order to be fully informed of events and to determine its policy accordingly"; Mera replied that the national committee of the CNT should not abandon Madrid, especially when everyone was fleeing. "Its presence in Madrid," he argued, "can be of great moral value to the people and can help to change the situation in our favor. . . . The departure of the government . . . is a shameful flight, because hardly eight hours ago it told the people of Madrid that it would share its fate."

But the decision to leave Madrid had been made, and Mera, declaring that he would organize a thousand men to defend the capital—"to show these people that, while they flee, we shall defend what they have abandoned"—returned to Madrid without shaking the hand of the national secretary "because I regarded him as a weakling and unworthy of the important post he held in a revolutionary organization such as ours."[60]

The decision of the anarchosyndicalist ministers to leave Madrid had immediate reverberations in the libertarian movement. When they arrived in Madrid to take up their posts, writes César M. Lorenzo, the CNT leaders asked his father, Horacio M. Prieto, to instruct them how to act as ministers. Horacio Prieto replied that they had had sufficient experience as militants to know what to do in the interests of the CNT. A libertarian, even a national secretary, he told them, ought not to give orders to other libertarians or subject them to any special kind of discipline. The CNT was not the Communist party. They should act according to their good conscience. The latitude Prieto gave them, Lorenzo adds, was soon to turn against him, for when the question of the government's transfer to Valencia was debated the ministers agreed without consulting the national committee. "Horacio Prieto could not . . . demand the resignation of the four ministers . . . and thus provoke a government crisis. The departure of the government for Valencia, which entailed the departure of the national committee,[61] provoked the anger of the militants of the CNT. They held Horacio Prieto responsible, accusing him of cowardice and calling him a 'liquidator.'" As a result, on 18 November, Horacio Prieto, at a special national plenum covened by him, tendered his "irrevocable resignation" and was succeeded by Mariano Vázquez as secretary of the national committee.[62]

But more important than the CNT ministers' departure from Madrid and the resignation of Horacio Prieto was the profound stir created in the libertarian movement by the decision of its leaders to enter the central government. Not only did this decision represent a complete negation of the basic tenets of anarchism, shaking the whole structure of libertarian theory to the core, but, in violation of democratic principle, it had been taken without consulting the rank and file.[63]

From the day the cabinet was reorganized, the leading anarchosyndicalist newspaper, *Solidaridad Obrera*, in an attempt to overcome the scruples of the purists, sought to justify the decision by minimizing the divergence between theory and practice.

"The entry of the CNT into the central government is one of the most important events in the political history of our country. Both as a matter of principle and by conviction, the CNT has been antistatist and an enemy of every form of government.

"But circumstances . . . have transformed the nature of the Spanish government and the Spanish state.

"At the present time, the government, as the instrument that controls the organs of the state, has ceased to be a force of oppression against the working class, just as the state no longer represents a body that divides society into classes. And both will oppress the people even less now that members of the CNT have intervened."[64]

In subsequent months, as the friction between the "collaborationist" and "abstentionist" tendencies in the libertarian movement increased, some supporters of government collaboration argued that the entry of the CNT into the cabinet had marked no recantation of anarchist ideals and tactics,[65] while others frankly acknowledged the violation of doctrine and contended that it should yield to reality. "The philosophicosocial conceptions of anarchism are excellent, wonderful, in theory," wrote Manuel Mascarell, a member of the national committee of the CNT, "but they are impractical when confronted with the tragic reality of a war like ours. The conduct of anarchists and anarchosyndicalists should be inspired by and should be in harmony with our anarchist ideology, but when circumstances, when particular events demand a modification of tactics, anarchists should not confine themselves to the limited framework of what, theoretically, in normal times, was held to be their line of action, because to cling obstinately to principles, to follow a rigid line without departing one iota from what is laid down in anarchist textbooks and declarations is the most comfortable attitude one can adopt in order to justify doing nothing or risking nothing."[66]

As for the opponents of government collaboration, one libertarian historian writes: "I believe . . . that there was tacit consent on the part of many militants, enemies of collaboration, who uttered pious cries of wrath, but who allowed the others to have their way."[67]

Whatever the varied reactions within the libertarian movement, the CNT-FAI leaders had not entered the government without an inner struggle with conscience and principle. Not all of them admitted this conflict, but the confession of Federica Montseny, the minister of health and a member of the Peninsular Committee of the FAI, gave unerring expression to the doubts and misgivings that had assailed a large segment of the libertarian movement. At a meeting of the CNT after she had ceased to belong to the cabinet she declared:

As the daughter of veteran anarchists, as the descendant, I might say, of a whole dynasty of antiauthoritarians, with an achievement, with a record, with a life of struggle in continual defense of the ideas I inherited from my parents, I regarded my entry into the government, my acceptance of the post to which the CNT assigned me, as having more significance than the mere appointment of a minister. Other parties, other organizations, other sectors cannot appreciate the struggle inside the movement and in the very consciences of its members, both then and now, as a result of the CNT's participation in the government. They cannot appreciate it, but the people can, and if they cannot then they should be informed. They should be told that for us—who had fought incessantly against the state, who had always affirmed that through the state nothing at all could be achieved, that the words "government" and "authority" signified the negation of every possibility of freedom for men and for nations—our intervention in the government as an organization and as individuals signified either an act of historical audacity of fundamental importance, or a rectification of a whole work, of a whole past, in the field of theory and tactics.

We do not know what it signified. We only know that we were caught in a dilemma. . . .

When I was appointed by the CNT to represent it in the government, I was in the Regional Committee of Catalonia; I had lived through the whole epic from 19 July to November without a stain. . . .

What inhibitions, what doubts, what anguish I had personally to overcome in order to accept that post! For others it could have meant their goal, the satisfaction of their inordinate ambitions. But for me it implied a break with my life's work, with a whole past linked to the ideals of my parents. It meant a tremendous effort, an effort made at the cost of many tears. But I accepted the post. I accepted it, conquering myself. I accepted it, ready to clear myself of responsibility before my own eyes for what I considered to be a rupture with everything I had been, on condition that I always remained loyal, upright, honest, always faithful to the ideals of my parents and of my whole life. And that is how I entered the government.[68]

In a letter to me after the war, Severino Campos, who was secretary of the Regional Committee of Anarchist Groups of Catalonia and was present at the meeting of CNT-FAI leaders at which the entry of the CNT into the government was decided upon, said that Federica Montseny at first vigorously opposed her appointment as one of the four ministers, but finally yielded to pressure. The other appointees, he said, were not present at the meeting. After the war, Montseny wrote to me stating that the four persons designated to represent the CNT in the government were selected by Horacio Prieto, secretary of the national committee. Juan Peiró and Juan López, she pointed out, represented the right wing and Juan García Oliver and herself the left. "[Horacio Prieto]," she added, "hoped that I would check the opposition of the puritans."[69]

In an article written several years after the war, Montseny affirmed that she personally "never had any illusions" as to the possibility of achieving anything in the government. "I knew, we all knew," she averred, "that in spite of the fact that the government was not at that time a real government, that power was in the street, in the hands of the combatants and producers, [government] *power would once again be coordinated and consolidated* and, what is worse, with our complicity and our help, and that it would ruin many of us morally."[70]

Such a complete departure by the CNT and FAI from their antigovernment creed could have been determined only by very powerful motives. Of these motives, the following given by leading members of the CNT were undoubtedly among the most important:

"We were compelled by circumstances," Montseny herself declared shortly after entering the cabinet, "to join the government of the Republic in order to avoid the fate of anarchist movements in other countries that, through lack of foresight, resolution, and mental agility, were dislodged from the Revolution and saw other parties take control of it."[71]

"At that time," she affirmed at a later date, "we only saw the reality of the situation created for us: the Communists in the government and ourselves outside, the manifold possibilities, and all our conquests endangered."[72]

"Were we going to entrust the interests of the workers . . . exclusively to the political parties?" asked Juan López, CNT minister of commerce. "On no account!"[73]

"The CNT," wrote Manuel Villar, director early in the war of *Fragua Social*, the CNT newspaper in Valencia, "was compelled to participate in the government for the specific purpose of . . . preventing an attack on the conquests of the workers and peasants . . . , of preventing the war from being conducted in a sectarian manner and the army from being transformed into an instrument of a single party, of eliminating the danger of dictatorship, and of preventing totalitarian tendencies in every aspect of our economic and social life."[74]

Another reason was given by García Oliver, CNT-FAI minister of justice. To secure military aid from the "international bourgeoisie," he asserted, after he had left the cabinet, it was necessary "to give the impression that not the revolutionary committees were in control but rather the legal government."[75]

And, finally, according to Juan López, the minister of commerce, one of the CNT's fundamental objectives in entering the government was to regulate the political life of Spain by giving legal validity to the revolutionary committees that had sprung up in the first months of the Civil War.[76]

But the diverse explanations given by representatives of the libertarian movement as the rationale of the CNT's entry into the government would be incomplete if they did not include those adduced by Horacio Prieto, the principal advocate of collaboration. His son, César M. Lorenzo, writes:

The reasons that made the participation of the CNT in the central government necessary were presented by Horacio Prieto in numerous speeches, lectures, debates, and discussions. They can be summarized as follows: "The liber-

Curbing the Revolution

tarians were not equipped psychologically or materially to impose their will in the republican zone, even less to win the war against fascism. Even in the most unlikely event that they were to triumph over the fascists and the other antifascists, the Revolution would be suppressed by the economic blockade and armed intervention of foreign powers. Furthermore, the republican government was leading the loyalists to disaster through its political blindness and military incapacity and was also devoting its efforts to combating the working class, its militia, and its revolutionary work. Hence, it was necessary, within the framework of an advanced democratic state, to save the gains of socialization, to centralize the conduct of [military] operations, and neutralize the pressure of the great powers. Finally, the de facto politicalization of the libertarians from the first days of the Civil War, through their participation in all local or regional organs of administration, and the desire of the popular masses to see created a true union of antifascists, had to be consummated in the sharing of supreme responsibility."[77]

13. Against the Revolutionary Committees

While the anarchosyndicalist leaders fostered the hope that the libertarian movement's participation in the cabinet would enable it more successfully to defend its revolutionary conquests, the Communist leaders, on the other hand, their eyes turned toward the Western democracies, hoped that this participation, by enhancing the government's authority among the rank and file of the CNT and FAI, would facilitate the reconstruction of the shattered machinery of state, and would enable them, under cover of a democratic superstructure, to gather into their hands all the elements of state power appropriated by the revolutionary committees at the outbreak of the Civil War. They further hoped that the CNT's entry into the government would hasten the supplanting of these committees—which, in addition to assuming powers of state, had superseded the normal functions of the municipalities and of other local governing bodies—by regular organs of administration that had either been thrust into the shade or had ceased to function from the first day of the Revolution.[1]

This policy represented a radical change for the Communists, who, at the time of the left-wing rising in the Asturias in 1934, had called for the substitution of the republican state by revolutionary organs of power.[2] It also contrasted with the policy pursued by the Russian Bolsheviks in 1917; for whereas the latter had directed their efforts during the first months of the Revolution to supplanting the old governing bodies by the soviets, in the Spanish Revolution the Communists strove to replace the revolutionary committees by regular organs of administration. "An epidemic of exclusivist committees of the most varied shades and performing the most unexpected functions has broken out," complained the Communist organ, *Mundo Obrero*, early in the war. "We declare that each and every one of us should be interested in the defense of the democratic Republic, and for this reason all bodies should reflect accurately the composition of the [Caballero] government as well as the aims that inspire it, aims we have all undertaken to support and defend. This is a prerequisite for winning the war, imposed by numerous factors, both of a national and international character, and to which we must adapt our step."[3]

The Communist view—shared by Socialists and republicans—was that the committees, which in most cases were dominated by the more radical members of the CNT and UGT and whose authority was practically unlimited in their respective localities, should give way to regular organs of administration, in which all the parties forming the government would be represented and whose powers would be circumscribed by the laws of the state. The anarchosyndicalists contended that these revolutionary bodies should, on the contrary, become the foundation stones of the new society. "The committees," declared *CNT*, the principal libertarian newspaper in Madrid, "are organs created by the people to oppose the fascist insurrection. . . . Without these committees, which replaced the municipal and provincial administrations as well as many other organs of bourgeois democracy, it would have been impossible to resist fascism. They are revolutionary committees that the people created in order to make the Revolution. . . . By this we do not mean to say that Spain should be split up by the work of hundreds of scattered committees. We want the reconstruction of Spanish society . . . to be based on the organs that have sprung up from the people, and we should like them to work in agreement with one another. Our prime motive in defending them is to prevent the resurgence of those bourgeois organs and norms that were shipwrecked so pitifully on 19 July."[4]

Inside the cabinet, however, the CNT-FAI ministers yielded step by step to their opponents, who applied constant pressure to end the power of the committees on the ground of placating foreign opinion and enhancing the government's prospects of securing arms from the Western powers. Writes Federica Montseny, one of the four anarchosyndicalists in the cabinet: "The arguments of the Communists, Socialists, and republicans were always the same: It was essential to give an appearance of legality to the Spanish Republic, to calm the fears of the British, French, and Americans. As a consequence, the state recovered the positions it had lost, while we revolutionaries, who formed part of the state, helped it to do so. That was why we were brought into the government. Although we did not enter it with that intention, we were in it, and therefore had no alternative but to remain imprisoned in the vicious circle. But I can state positively that, although we lost in the end, we defended our ground inch by inch and never voted for anything that curbed the conquests of the Revo-

[200]

lution without first being authorized by the national committee of the CNT, on which there was a permanent representative of the FAI."[5]

In February 1937, Juan Peiró, CNT minister of industry, acknowledged his fear that Britain and France would not reverse their stand on the matter of supplying arms to the government, but stated that victory depended on these two powers, "on condition that we prosecute the war and not the Revolution." This, he added, did not imply renouncing the Revolution. "The road to follow is this: We must wage the war, and, while waging it, limit ourselves to preparing for the Revolution by means of a conscientious and discreet control of the factories, for this is equivalent to taking up revolutionary positions and equipping ourselves in a practical way for the final assault on capitalist society after the end of the war."[6] A prominent member of the left wing of the libertarian movement wrote: "It was feared that we would lack the 'help' of the 'democratic' nations, if they were to see us driving ahead with the Revolution, and with this argument the politicians succeeded in causing the promoters of the movement for liberty in Spain to hesitate."[7]

As a result, the government, with the acquiescence of the CNT members, approved decrees that, far from giving legal validity to the committees as the CNT had hoped on entering the cabinet,[8] provided for their dissolution and replacement by regular provincial and municipal councils, in which all the parties adhering to the Popular Front as well as the trade-union organizations were to be represented.[9] In addition, a decree was published providing for the suppression of all controls on highways and at the entrance to villages set up by local committees and by parties or trade-union organizations and for the taking over of their functions by the police forces under the ministry of the interior.[10] All of these measures, of course, threatened the predominant position of the anarchosyndicalists in numberless towns and villages and threw the more extreme spirits into a position of antagonism to the leadership of the CNT and FAI.

That Largo Caballero, despite his revolutionary stand before the war and the fact that the UGT, which he controlled, held a dominant position on the committees in many towns and villages, should have found common ground with the Communists and other members of the government on the matter of their dissolution is understandable, if only because of his concern for foreign opinion. When, shortly after taking office, he had declared that it was necessary to sacrifice revolutionary languuge in order to win the friendship of the democratic powers,[11] he must have realized that his efforts to secure Anglo-

Curbing the Revolution

French aid could not be confined solely to verbal adhesions to the republican Constitution and that it would be necessary to dissolve the revolutionary organs that had assumed state functions. But, apart from the question of foreign opinion, the supporters of the government had other cogent motives for opposing the committees, chiefly the fact that they impinged on its authority and obstructed its work in almost every sphere.[12] "At the present time," commented *Claridad*, the mouthpiece of Largo Caballero, "these organs can only serve as impediments to a function that belongs solely and exclusively to the Popular Front government, in which all parties and labor organizations in the country participate with full responsibility."[13] And the Communist *Mundo Obrero* declared: "There may be some doubt as to whether or not the numerous bodies created at the beginning of the Civil War in the towns and villages of loyalist Spain were necessary. But there can be no doubt that at the present time they . . . greatly hinder the work of the government."[14] Criticism of the committees on this score came not only from the Communists and Socialists; even Juan Peiró, the anarchosyndicalist minister of industry, avowed that they interfered with government functions. "The government issues an order," he declared at a public meeting of the CNT a few weeks before the promulgation of the decrees, "but the local committees interpose their directives. While it tries to put order into things, they disorganize everything. (Murmurs from the audience.) Either the government is superfluous or the committees. (Cries of 'Yes!') What do these interjections mean? That the committees are superfluous? (More cries of 'Yes!' 'No!' 'Yes!') . . . The committees are not superfluous, but they must become auxiliary bodies of the government."[15]

Because of the cleavage in the libertarian movement on the question of dissolving the committees, it was a far cry from the promulgation of the decrees to their actual implementation, and in a large number of localities, where the anarchosyndicalists were in undisputed ascendancy, and even in some where the less radical UGT was dominant, the committees subsisted in the teeth of government opposition.

It should be noted, however, that according to the anarchosyndicalists, the delay in setting up the new municipal councils in some places was due to the efforts of the Popular Front parties to secure a representation out of proportion to their strength. "In spite of the time that has elapsed since the promulgation of the decree providing for the formation of the new municipal councils," wrote the FAI organ *Castilla Libre*, with regard to the province of Ciudad Libre (previously Ciudad Real), "they have been set up in only three or four localities.

The Popular Front, which represents no one, wants to appropriate the majority of posts. We want proportional representation."[16]

"Those who defend the existence of a network of committees of all kinds," the Communists remonstrated, "forget one important thing: that at the present time nothing can be more prejudicial to us than the division of power. We know that the comrades who uphold the committees do not want Spain to be atomized by the scattered efforts of hundreds of these committees. On the other hand, they consider that the democratic organs [of the Republic] are useless at the present time. This is an error. As we have to defend the democratic structure of the state because it conforms to the present period of the Revolution and because it is a vital requisite for winning the war, it is inexplicable that anyone should think of converting that structure and the organs that give it life into a mere decoration."[17]

But persuasion alone could not ensure the enforcement of the decrees. Only by reconstructing the police corps of the Republic could the government impose its will and centralize in its hands all elements of state power assumed by the revolutionary committees. And of this the cabinet of Largo Caballero had long been conscious, as will now be seen.

14. The Police

Early in this volume it was shown that the police power of the Republic crumbled under the impact of the military rebellion and the social revolution. The Civil Guard, the Assault Guard, and the secret police disintegrated as a result of wholesale desertions to the rebel cause and the taking over of police functions by vigilance committees and militia units improvised by the left-wing organizations.[1] These forces, declared Angel Galarza, minister of the interior in the Largo Caballero government, "either well or badly, efficiently or inefficiently, some in absolute good faith, others driven by base ambitions and evil instincts, performed a function in the rear . . . , [and] were the only forces that at one time could be used against the fascists in the towns and villages."[2] "Fascism in the rear areas," wrote *Política*, the organ of the Left Republican party, "has been put down principally as a result of the intelligent and skillful work of the militia."[3]

With only the bare remnants of the republican police corps at its disposal, the liberal government formed by José Giral on 19 July 1936 was impotent in the face of the revolutionary terror exercised by the working-class organizations, whose police squads and patrols carried out searches, arrests, and summary executions. In Madrid, according to Arturo Barea, a Socialist, each of the branches and groups of the trade unions and political parties set up "its own police, its own prison, its own executioners, and a special place for its executions."[4]

Nor could the Giral cabinet or any government that succeeded it hope to curb this terror and establish its authority in the eyes of the Western world without reconstructing and expanding the police forces under its control. On this point the Communists, Socialists, and republicans were of one mind, although each had its own view as to who should ultimately control the reorganized police corps.

The first significant step in the reconstruction of the regular police forces was taken on 31 August 1936, when the Giral cabinet promulgated a decree providing for the purging and reorganizing of the Civil Guard, henceforth to be known as the National Republican Guard.[5] Under the Largo Caballero government, thousands of new members were recruited for this corps;[6] the same was true of the Assault Guard, whose numbers increased by twenty-eight thousand at the beginning of December, according to Angel Galarza, the left-wing Socialist minister of the interior.[7] No less important was the growth of the *carabineros*, or carabineers, a corps composed of customs and excise officials and guards dependent on the ministry of finance, which, like the assault and civil guards, had fallen to pieces under the blow of the military insurrection and the Revolution. Although the Giral government planned to reorganize and use the corps as a force of public order against the extreme wing of the Revolution, its reconstruction and expansion were not seriously undertaken for this purpose until Juan Negrín assumed control of the ministry of finance, when the Largo Caballero cabinet was formed in September 1936. The *carabineros*, who before the war had numbered approximately fifteen thousand in the entire country,[8] were reported in April 1937 to total forty thousand men in the left camp alone, that is, in about half the area of Spain.[9] Some of them were serving at the front, but it was well known that the major part was kept in the rear.[10] That this corps was reorganized partly with an eye to the left wing of the Revolution was emphasized by the threatening tone of a speech by Jerónimo Bugeda, Negrín's undersecretary, addressed to a body of carabineers: "You are," he declared, "the guardians of the state that Spain wishes to create for herself, and those visionaries who believe that a chaotic situation of social indiscipline and licentiousness is permissible are utterly mistaken because the army of the people, as well as you *carabineros*, who are a glorious part of that army, will know how to prevent it."[11]

The anarchists did not conceal their fears that the carabineers would eventually be used against them.[12] In a dispatch from Valencia published in the *New York Herald Tribune*, James Minifie reported: "A reliable police force is being built up, quietly but surely. The Valencia government discovered an ideal instrument for this purpose in the *carabineros*. . . . The anarchists have already noticed and complained about the increased strength of this force 'at a time when we all know there's little enough traffic coming over the frontiers, land or sea.' They realize that it will be used against them."[13]

Concurrently with the reconstruction of the police corps, the government of Largo Caballero took steps to bring the independent squads and patrols of the working-class organizations under its control. Shortly after taking office, it published a decree providing for their incorporation into a Vigilance Militia, under the authority of the ministry of the interior, to collaborate with the official police forces in the maintenance of internal order.[14] All militiamen performing police functions who did not belong to the new corps were to be regarded as "disaffected elements," while the members were given priority if they wished to enroll in the regular police forces.[15] The decree soon proved to be but a preparatory step toward the incorporation of the squads and patrols of the working-class organizations into the armed forces of the state.[16] Members of the Communist, Socialist, and republican parties were quick to avail themselves of the opportunity to enter the official police corps, but the anarchosyndicalists held back and in many places clung tenaciously to their own police squads and patrols in defiance of the government. Far from acquiescing in the absorption of their own militia by the state, some of the more resolute elements demanded that the government police corps should be dissolved and their members be incorporated into the militia of the working-class organizations.[17] But it was a vain demand; for the government, strengthened by the reorganized police corps and by the absence of any apparent protest by the CNT-FAI ministers, was beginning to disarm and arrest recalcitrants and take over the administration of public order in one locality after another, where the anarchosyndicalists had been in control since the first days of the Civil War.[18] Some of the measures taken by the police in different localities were in accordance with instructions issued by the minister of the interior to local authorities under his jurisdiction to collect arms in the possession of all persons not belonging to official bodies under the control of the ministries of finance, interior, justice, and war.[19]

Parallel with the reconstruction of the government police corps, important changes were taking place in the field of justice. The revolutionary tribunals set up by the working-class organizations in the early days of the war[20] were gradually being displaced by a legalized form of tribunal composed of three members of the judiciary and fourteen members of the Popular Front parties and trade-union federations, two representing each organization.[21] Although decrees providing for the creation of the new courts were promulgated by the Giral government at the end of August 1936, they did not begin to function in all the provinces of the left camp until several weeks after the CNT had entered the Caballero government in November.[22]

While the reorganization of the regular police corps was gradually taking place, the Communists were making full use of their skill in proselytism, defamation, and infiltration to secure for themselves a position of predominance.[23] Moreover, aided by both overt and covert supporters in high places, by the timidity if not the complaisance of many leading Socialists and republicans, they secured pivotal positions in the reconstructed police apparatus. For instance, Lieutenant Colonel Ricardo Burillo, an open Communist, became police chief of Madrid; Justiniano García and Juan Galán, also members of the party, were made chief and subchief respectively of the Servicios Especiales, the intelligence department of the ministry of the interior,[24] while two others were appointed to vital posts in the police administration, one being made commissar general in the Department of Security, Dirección General de Seguridad, in charge of the appointment, transfer, and discipline of the police, and the other becoming head of the training center of the Secret Police School, the Escuela de Policía, that formed the cadres of the new secret police corps.[25]

From the time of its creation this corps, ultimately more important than any of the uniformed forces of public order, became a mere arm of the Soviet secret police, which, because of the paramount position Spain now occupied in Soviet diplomacy, had established itself in the left camp quite early in the war. According to Walter Krivitsky, an emergency conference was held in Moscow on 14 September 1936 at which Sloutski, head of the foreign division of the Soviet secret police, was present. "From [Abram] Sloutski," he adds, "I learned that at this conference a veteran officer of his department [Alexander Orlov] was detailed to establish the OGPU [NKVD][26] in Loyalist Spain. He was Nikolsky, alias Schwed, alias Orlov."[27] The fact that the first three names were revealed by Krivitsky in 1939, long before they were published elsewhere, is proof of his inside knowledge of the NKVD, a knowledge already confirmed by two men of high integrity —Boris Nicolaevsky and Paul Wohl—who knew him intimately.[28] Nikolsky was Orlov's party name, according to *The Legacy of Alexander Orlov*, which was prepared by the U.S. Senate Subcommittee on Internal Security after his death in the United States in 1973,[29] where he had resided since his defection in 1938;[30] Schwed was the "code name," as Orlov himself confirmed in 1966, that Stalin employed to communicate with him regarding the shipment of Spanish gold to Russia,[31] and Lyova was yet another alias, according to Louis Fischer, who met him in Madrid in mid-September 1936 and revealed this information in 1941.[32]

In reply to a questionnaire prepared by Stanley G. Payne,[33] Orlov stated on 1 April 1968 that he had been appointed by the Soviet politburo on 26 August 1936 and that the date given by Krivitsky of 14 September is false. The discrepancy is not important; indeed, what is important is Krivitsky's knowledge of this top-secret appointment, considering the massive campaign against him as an impostor. Orlov also stated, in response to the same questionnaire, that Krivitsky had never held a high office in the Soviet secret police, but served only as an NKVD "letter drop" in the Hague—"the lowliest denomination on the operative scale." This statement can be dismissed as a belated attempt to denigrate Krivitsky, who exposed, as we shall see, the repressive role of Orlov's apparatus in republican Spain, for in none of his books, articles, or testimony before the U.S. Senate subcommittee did Orlov make this charge. Nor could anyone supposedly so low on the scale of command have had such far-ranging and accurate inside knowledge as did Krivitsky.[34]

Within a few months of Orlov's appointment by the politburo to head the NKVD in Spain, the Soviet secret police, operating in intimate association with Spanish and foreign Communists, with crypto-Communists in the ranks of Socialists and republicans, and with the Communist-controlled Spanish secret police, became the decisive force in determining the course of events in the anti-Franco camp.[35]

In reference to my book, *The Grand Camouflage*, Herbert L. Matthews, former *New York Times* correspondent in the left-wing zone, wrote on page 113 of his last work on Spain, *Half of Spain Died*: "Bolloten claims that the secret police in Spain became 'a mere arm' of the Soviet secret police apparatus and that the Russian OGPU quickly 'became the decisive force in determining the course of events in the anti-Franco camp.' This is a wild exaggeration. Governmental power at no time got out of the hands of Spanish republican leaders." Yet, on page 110, he observes: "As early as September 1936 the communists, under the direction of the Russian NKVD representative, Alexander Orlov, began filling prisons with hundred of *their*—not necessarily the republican government's—enemies, torturing and killing many of them. There was not, as Burnett Bolloten, the former United Press correspondent on the Franco side [actually I was on the left-wing side from 18 July 1936], claimed, 'an independent Russian police system' dominating all of Loyalist Spain throughout the war. There were many police organizations (Hugh Thomas counted nine) including *some legitimate ones*."[36] It is, of course, true, as I have already pointed out earlier both in this volume and in *The Grand Camouflage*, that in the first months of the war police powers were exercised by a multiplicity of police squads, militia units, and patrols belonging to the various trade-union and political organizations. If, in fact, as Matthews concedes, there were many such units, including "some legitimate ones"

—implying that there were many that escaped the authority of the government—if, moreover, as he allows, the Communists under the direction of the NKVD began filling prisons with "hundreds of their enemies . . . torturing and killing many of them," it is difficult to reconcile these statements with his assertion that "governmental power at no time got out of the hands of the Spanish republican leaders."

In all his written and oral testimony, Orlov invariably describes his functions in Spain somewhat inoffensively as those of "chief Soviet adviser to the republican government on intelligence, counter-intelligence, and guerrilla warfare"[37] and avoids any reference to his secret police functions and repressive role in the internal affairs of the left camp. On the other hand, Louis Fischer describes Orlov as "chief of the GPU [NKVD] agents in Loyalist territory,"[38] a simple and unadorned title that expresses more bluntly the power he exercised over the lives of Spanish citizens. "The Ogpu [NKVD],"[39] Krivitsky affirmed, "had its own special prisons. Its units carried out assassinations and kidnappings. It filled hidden dungeons and made flying raids. It functioned, of course, independently of the Loyalist government. The ministry of justice had no authority over the Ogpu, which was an empire within an empire. It was a power before which even some of the highest officers in the Largo Caballero government trembled. The Soviet Union seemed to have a grip on Loyalist Spain, as if it were already a Soviet possession."[40]

15. Nationalization versus Socialization

If, in order to impose the will of the government, it was necessary to reconstruct the regular police corps and dissolve the revolutionary committees that had assumed functions formerly belonging to the state, the Communists, Socialists, and republicans believed it was also necessary to break the power of the revolutionary committees in the factories by bringing the collectivized enterprises, particularly in the basic industries, under the control of the government.

A preliminary step in this direction was taken at the outset of the Revolution by José Giral's liberal republican government. With a view to strengthening its position vis-à-vis the revolutionary committees and to giving an aura of legality to their expropriations, it approved a decree on 2 August, proposed by the republican minister of industry and commerce, Plácido Alvarez Buylla, providing for the sequestration by the state of industrial and commercial enterprises whose owners or managers had abandoned them at the outbreak of the Civil War. If these owners and managers, the decree stipulated, failed to present themselves for work within forty-eight hours of the publication of the decree, the state would proceed with the sequestration of their firms in order to guarantee their continued operation.[1]

Although government intervention during the early months was very limited and did not extend beyond the appointment of a representative of one of the Popular Front parties to each of certain officially designated industrial and commercial enterprises in Madrid,[2] the decree was nevertheless the first significant step taken by the central government with a view to controlling industry and trade.

Other decrees followed shortly afterward.

"By the decrees of 14 and 20 August and 1 September 1936," writes the official Communist history of the Civil War and Revolution, "the Giral government appointed a series of state advisers to various electric power companies and formed a Consejo General de Electricidad, Board of Electricity, with powers to intervene in technical and administrative questions in these companies. The executive committee of this council had a Popular Front composition: the republican Elfidio Alonso; the Socialist Amador Fernández, the Communist Luis Cabo Giorla; the UGTista Manuel Lois, etc.

"There arose in the Spanish economy a very special kind of state capitalism. It was not the kind of state capitalism utilized or manipulated by the financial oligarchy. It was a state capitalism in which control was exercised through the representatives of the Popular Front parties, which assured no small influence to the working class. The Giral government, despite its limitations, carried out revolutionary measures that until that time no bourgeois government in Spain had undertaken. And one can only speak of it with respect and admiration."[3]

State capitalism or nationalization, the Communists knew, would eventually enable the central authority not only to organize the manufacturing capacity of the anti-Franco camp in accordance with the needs of the war and to control the output and allocation of war material, often assigned by the labor unions to their own locals or militia units,[4] but also to weaken the left wing of the Revolution at one of the principal sources of its power. They did not, of course, openly acknowledge the political motive of their desire for nationalization and defended it only on military and economic grounds.[5] In their campaign they were aided by the fact that collectivization suffered from palpable defects. In the first place, the collectivized enterprises appeared unconcerned with the problems of provisioning and distributing skilled labor, raw materials, and machinery in accordance with a single and rational plan of production for military needs. "We have been satisfied with throwing out the proprietors from the factories and putting ourselves in them as committees of control," declared Diego Abad de Santillán, CNT-FAI leader in Catalonia. "There has been no attempt at connection, there has been no coordination of economy in due form. We have worked without plans and without real knowledge of what we were doing."[6] Furthermore, nonessential civilian goods and even luxury items were being produced simply because they yielded a high profit, with the resultant waste of raw materials and human effort.[7] And, finally, some enterprises lacked proper accounting and control, the workers distributing to themselves as wages everything they received from sales without allowing for replacement of stocks and depreciation of capital.

"When the war broke out," Juan Negrín, minister of finance, told Louis Fischer, "working-men's committees, often anarchist, took over the factories. . . . They paid themselves in wages everything they took in from sales. Now they have no money. They are coming to me for running expenses and for raw materials. We will take advantage of their plight to gain control of the factories."[8]

Although the Communists made good use of these deficiencies to press their campaign in favor of nationalization, the CNT and FAI, contrary to general belief, had their own plans for the coordination of industrial production. To remedy the defects of collectivization, as well as to iron out discrepancies in the living standards of the workers in flourishing and impoverished enterprises, the anarchosyndicalists, although rootedly opposed to nationalization,[9] advocated the centralization—or socialization, as they called it—under trade-union control, of entire branches of production.[10] This was the anarchosyndicalist or libertarian conception of socialization, without state intervention, that was to eliminate the wastes of competition and duplication, render possible industrywide planning for both civilian and military needs, and halt the growth of selfish actions among the workers of the more prosperous collectives by using their profits to raise the standard of living of the workers in the less favored enterprises.[11] Already in the early months of the war, the leaders of some of the local CNT unions had undertaken limited forms of socialization, confined to a branch of industry in a single locality, such as the cabinetmakers' trade in Madrid, Barcelona, and Carcagente, the dressmaking, tailoring, metal, and leather goods trades in Valencia, the shoemaking industry in Sitges, the metal and textile industries of Alcoy, the lumber trade of Cuenca, the brickmaking industry of Granollers, the tanning trade of Barcelona and Vich, to mention but a few examples.[12] These partial socializations were not regarded as ends in themselves but rather as transitional stages in the integration of atomized branches of production into a Socialist (that is, a libertarian) economy under trade-union control.

This work of socialization, however, could not go forward as rapidly as the libertarian planners desired. They encountered the opposition of many concerns in a privileged position, controlled by workers of the UGT as well as by those of the CNT, who did not wish to sacrifice any of their profits to help the less successful collectives.[13] In addition, the leadership of the Socialist UGT, like the Communist party, advocated government ownership and control of the basic industries,[14] and opposed the confiscation of the property of the small bourgeoisie,[15] on which complete Socialist planning, in accordance with the ideas of the CNT leaders, depended.

"The divergence of outlook between the CNT and UGT on economic matters was constant," testifies Mariano Cardona Rosell, a member of the national committee of the CNT, "owing to the fact that while the CNT advocated a more and more effective socialization it met with lack of cooperation on the part of the national, regional, and local leaders of the UGT, who paid little or no attention to this vital problem. As a result, the rank and file of the UGT followed the directives of the CNT in many localities."[16] These divergent attitudes rendered the establishment of a centrally coordinated industry impossible, either through libertarian socialization or nationalization, and perpetuated the prevailing state of economic chaos.

Yet another obstacle to the integration of industry into a Socialist or libertarian economy lay in the fact that a large number of firms controlled by the CNT were in a state of insolvency or semi-insolvency and were compelled to seek government intervention to secure financial aid. They could not in general have recourse to the banks, for these were controlled by the UGT Bank and Stock Exchange Employees' Union, the Sindicato de Trabajadores de Banco y Bolsa,[17] affiliated with the Federación Nacional de Trabajadores del Crédito y Finanzas, National Federation of Employees of Credit and Finance, a fief of left-wing Socialist Amaro del Rosal, a Communist supporter.[18]

So desperately did some of the CNT-controlled enterprises need funds that government intervention was openly recommended by CNT minister of industry, Juan Peiró.[19] This is hardly surprising, for, in January 1937 alone, eleven thousand requests for funds were made to his ministry.[20] According to the official Communist history, the CNT ministers of industry and commerce "tried by every means to legalize and consolidate the dominion of the CNT over the greater part of the economy, utilizing state funds to finance the 'syndicalized' enterprises in a state of bankruptcy."[21]

But the efforts of the CNT to obtain government aid to salvage these enterprises and to extend the collective system were unsuccessful. Juan Peiró, writes José Peirats, the anarchosyndicalist historian, tried to draft a decree providing for the collectivization of all industries, but Largo Caballero made him desist, warning him that England, France, and Belgium, which owned substantial economic interests in Spain, would withdraw diplomatic recognition from the republican government. Peiró then redrafted his decree, but the cabinet opposed it and made certain changes. From the cabinet the decree went to a ministerial commission that, according to Peirats, converted it into a skeleton. "But the calvary is not over. To put the decree into effect money is necessary, that is, a credit must be granted by the minister of finance. He haggles like a usurer and finally grants an insignificant sum. . . . Finally, the Industrial Bank intervenes, which reduces the amount still further." The outcome, concludes Peirats, was that the government crisis of May 1937—discussed later in this volume—occurred before the minister of industry could put into effect this "eminently conservative" decree and that the first act of the new government, in which the CNT was not represented, was to "rescind the decree purely and simply."[22]

The Communists took full advantage of the economic strife to further their campaign in favor of government ownership and control of industry and against collectivization and socialization. Referring to the "premature experiments in collectivization and socialization," party secretary José Díaz declared: "If, in the beginning, these experiments were justified by the fact that the big industrialists and landlords had abandoned their factories and estates and that it was necessary to continue production, later on they were not. . . . At first it was understandable that the workers should take possession of the abandoned factories in order to continue production at all costs. . . . I repeat that this was understandable, and we are not going to censure it. . . . [But] today when there is a government of the Popular Front, in which all the forces engaged in the fight against fascism are represented, such things are not only inadvisable, but they have the opposite effect from that intended. Today we must coordinate production rapidly and intensify it under a single direction so as to provision the front and the rear with everything they need. . . . To rush into these premature experiments in 'collectivization' and 'socialization' when the war is still undecided and at a time when the internal enemy, aided by foreign fascism, is violently attacking our positions and endangering the future of our country, is absurd and is tantamount to aiding the enemy."[23]

16. "A Democratic and Parliamentary Republic of a New Type"

At the root of the Communist party's opposition to the CNT's plans for the libertarian socialization of industry lay the fact that socialization was a threat to its own program of nationalization, and also that, to be effective, it must impinge on the property of the middle classes, whose support the Kremlin needed for the success of its foreign policy. To counter this danger, the Spanish Communists argued that the attempts to further the Revolution at the expense of the middle classes were due to the workers' lack of political understanding. "In the first days of the rebellion," declared a Communist leader, referring to Valencia, "many workers fell into a mania of confiscating and socializing because they believed that we were in the midst of a social revolution. Nearly all industries were socialized. . . . This fever of 'socialization' not only laid hold of factories and workshops abandoned by bosses who supported the rebellion but even encroached on the small property of liberal and republican employers. . . . Why have the workers fallen into these errors? Mainly owing to a lack of understanding of the present political situation that leads them to believe that we are in the midst of a social revolution."[1]

Federico Melchor, a member of the executive committee of the JSU, the Communist-oriented Unified Socialist Youth Federation, affirmed:

"We are not making a social revolution today; we are developing a democratic revolution, and in a democratic revolution, the economy . . . cannot be launched into Socialist channels. If we are developing a democratic revolution and say we are fighting for a democratic Republic, how can we attempt in the economic field to introduce methods of a totalitarian Socialist type? . . . Comrade Alvarez del Vayo said the other day, 'In order to triumph, a correct political line is necessary.' To that we should add: a correct political line based on a clear economic line, on a correct economic line, is necessary. These economic aberrations, these economic trends, these experiments that are carried out in our country, are not due to any accident; they stem from a whole ideology, from the ideological deformation of a broad section of the working-class movement that is trying to carry forward the economic development of our country without adapting itself to the stages that this economic development requires."[2]

To argue along these lines in the prevailing state of revolutionary exultation was for the Communists a heavy task; for they had to contend not only with the libertarian movement, but also with the more radical members of the UGT, of the Socialist party, and of the JSU. From this task they did not shrink. "At a time of the greatest revolutionary effervescence," recalled Antonio Mije, a member of the politburo, "we Communists did not blush on the platforms of Madrid and the rest of Spain, when we came out in defense of the democratic Republic. Whereas some people were afraid even to mention the democratic Republic, we Communists had no objection to explaining to impatient elements, who did not understand the situation, that politically it was advisable to defend it against fascism."[3]

"We are fighting for the democratic Republic, and we are not ashamed to say so," declared Santiago Carrillo, the secretary of the JSU, in a speech at the national conference in January 1937 in which he outlined, for the first time since the fusion of the Socialist and Communist youth movements, the policy of the united organization. "Confronted by fascism and the foreign invaders, we are not fighting at the present time for the Socialist revolution. There are some who say that at this stage we should fight for the Socialist revolution, and there are others who even say that we are practicing a deception, that we are maneuvering to conceal our real policy when we declare that we are defending the democratic Republic. Nevertheless, comrades, we are fighting for a democratic Republic, and, furthermore, for a democratic and parliamentary Republic. This is not a stratagem to deceive Spanish democratic opinion, nor to deceive democratic opinion abroad. We are fighting sincerely for the democratic Republic because we know that if we should commit the mistake of fighting at this time for the Socialist revolution in our country—and even for some considerable time after victory—we should see in our fatherland not only the fascist invaders but side by side with them the bourgeois democratic governments of the world that have already stated explicitly that in the present European situation they would not tolerate a dictatorship of the proletariat in our country."[4]

Failure to protect foreign capital, affirmed Federico Melchor, "would be an error in international relations because then England would decisively intervene against Spain not on our side but with Franco, because England has economic interests in our country to defend."[5]

Although there is no record that any democratic government ever threatened to intervene, the fear of incurring the open hostility of the democratic powers no doubt carried considerable weight among the rank and file of the JSU. Nevertheless, dissatisfaction with the policy adumbrated at the conference was not long in manifesting itself; for, within a few weeks, it was denounced by Rafael Fernández, general secretary of the JSU of the Asturias, as "anything but Marxist."[6] This was more than a personal opinion. It was the opinion of a substantial number of Socialists in the JSU, who felt themselves betrayed by what they regarded as a rightward swing, and their mood is accurately reflected in the following protest sent from the battle front:

"I have read several times in different newspapers the speeches made by Carrillo . . . to the effect THAT THE UNIFIED SOCIALIST YOUTH IS FIGHTING FOR A DEMOCRATIC AND PARLIAMENTARY REPUBLIC. I believe that Carrillo is completely mistaken. As a young Socialist and revolutionary I am fighting for the collectivization of the land, of the factories, of the entire wealth of Spain, for the benefit of everyone, for the benefit of humanity.

"Do Carrillo and the others who aim at leading us along that prejudicial and counterrevolutionary road believe that the militants of the JSU are sheep? No, we are not sheep; we are revolutionaries!

"What would our comrades who have perished on the battlefields do if they could raise their heads and see that the JSU had been an accomplice in betraying the Revolution for which they gave their lives? They would do only one thing. They would spit in the face of the culprits."[7]

If it was difficult for the Communists to convince the radical members of the JSU of the correctness of their policy, it was still more difficult to convince the libertarian movement. Yet, the success of that policy depended on the compliance, if not the wholehearted approval, of this powerful movement. With this end in view, Soviet diplomatic representatives, according to Federica Montseny, anarcho-syndicalist minister of health, held frequent conversations with CNT-FAI leaders. "The advice they gave us," she wrote, "was always the same: it was necessary to establish in Spain a 'controlled democracy' (euphemistic term for a dictatorship); it was not advisable to create the impression abroad that a profound revolution was being carried out; we should avoid awakening the suspicion of the democratic powers." The behavior of the Russians, she adds, was very courteous. "I never heard them utter a threatening word. . . . When I went to Geneva in January and February of 1937 to attend the Congress of Hygiene, Rosenberg [the Soviet ambassador] urged me to go to Russia, saying, 'Comrade Stalin would be very happy to meet you. Go there, Federica! You will be received like a little queen.' [The Russians] never made any concrete offer that would have forced me to break relations with them. They were too subtle for that. But on various occasions, Rosenberg suggested that I send my daughter to Valencia to live with his wife and children in a villa they occupied on the outskirts. When I heard these suggestions the blood froze in my veins."[8]

If the CNT-FAI ministers felt compelled to make political concessions to Soviet policy at the expense of the Revolution in the hope of influencing the democracies, they did not adhere undeviatingly to the Communist slogan of the democratic Republic.[9] If, on entering the government, they had agreed to adopt it, this was, according to Juan López, CNT minister of commerce, "in order to produce an impression beyond the frontiers, but never to strangle the legitimate revolutionary conquests of the working class."[10]

The libertarian movement as a whole accepted the Communist slogan of the democratic Republic less than did the CNT-FAI ministers, as was clearly reflected in its press:

"The thousands of proletarian combatants at the battle fronts," declared the *Boletín de Información*, "are not fighting for the 'democratic Republic.' They are proletarian revolutionaries, who have taken up arms in order to make the Revolution. To postpone the triumph of the latter until after we win the war would weaken considerably the fighting spirit of the working class. . . . If we wish to raise the enthusiasm of our fighters and inject the antifascist masses with revolutionary zeal, we must drive the Revolution forward with determination, liquidate the last vestiges of bourgeois democracy, socialize industry and agriculture, and create the directing organs of the new society in accordance with the revolutionary aims of the proletariat.

"It should be clearly understood that we are not fighting for the democratic Republic. We are fighting for the triumph of the proletarian revolution. The Revolution and the war are inseparable. Everything that is said to the contrary is *reformist counterrevolution*."[11]

CNT exclaimed: "'Democratic revolution.' 'Parliamentary republic.' 'This is not the moment for carrying out the social revolution.' Here are a few slogans worthy of the political program of the republican parties but degrading to the working-class organizations. . . . [If] the

Socialist and Communist parties as well as their youth movement had honored their Socialist principles 'the entire apparatus of the old bourgeois state' (Marx) and the structure of capitalist economy would have been destroyed. In the *Communist Manifesto* Marx and Engels never referred to a transitional period of a 'democratic and parliamentary republic.' . . . For this reason, the Marxism of all the Spanish Marxist parties is a Marxism that has nothing in common with revolutionary Marxism but much with social-democratic reformism, against which Lenin directed his revolutionary theories outlined in *State and Revolution.*"[12]

To counter the embarrassing denunciations of their policy in the CNT and FAI press, the Communists—who, at the beginning of the Civil War, as has already been seen, had likened the revolution taking place in Spain to the bourgeois democratic revolution that had been achieved over a century before in France,[13] were compelled, for the purposes of home consumption, to modify their language. "What do the comrades of *CNT* accuse us of?" asked *Mundo Obrero* in reply to the anarchosyndicalist organ.

According to them, we have diverged from the path of revolutionary Marxism. Why? Because we defend the democratic Republic. . . . [We] should like to define the character of the republic in our country at the present time. . . . First, the working class, the peasants, and the small bourgeoisie have ALL THE ARMS; second, the peasants have the land: the agricultural laborers are working the former large estates collectively or individually, and the tenant farmers now possess their own land; third, working-class control has been established in all factories, and the big political bosses who joined the military rising have been expropriated and therefore deprived of their social and political power; fifth, the greatest influence, the principal directing influence in the development of the democratic revolution is in the hands of the entire working class; sixth, the former army of oppression has been destroyed and we have a new army of the people. Hence, our republic is a special type; it is a democratic and parliamentary republic with a social content that has never existed before. And this republic . . . cannot be considered in the same light [as those republics] where democracy is a fiction, a democracy based on the absolute hegemony of the exploiters. This point having been established, we must inform the comrades of *CNT* that by defending democracy and the republic we do not abjure or contradict the doctrines of revolutionary Marxism. It was Lenin who taught us that to be revolutionary one should not jump into space. It was Lenin who taught us that to be revolutionary one should always bear in mind the concrete situation of a given country so as to apply to it the most suitable revolutionary tactics.[14]

At the plenary session of the central committee of the Communist party in March 1937, José Díaz declared:

Curbing the Revolution

We are fighting for the democratic Republic, for a democratic and parliamentary republic of a new type and with a profound social content. The struggle taking place in Spain is not aimed at the establishment of a democratic republic like that of France or of any other capitalist country. No. The democratic Republic for which we are fighting is different. We are fighting to destroy the material foundations on which reaction and fascism rest; for without their destruction no true political democracy can exist. . . .

And now I ask: To what extent have [they] been destroyed? In every province we control big landowners no longer exist. The church, as a dominant power, has likewise ceased to exist. Militarism has also disappeared, never to return. Nor are there any big bankers and industrialists. That is the reality of the situation. And the guarantee that these conquests will never be lost lies in the fact that the arms are in the hands of the people, of the genuine antifascist people, of the workers, the peasants, the intellectuals, and the small bourgeoisie, who were always the slaves of those castes. That is the best guarantee that the past will never return. And precisely for that reason, because we have a guarantee that our conquests will not be lost, we should not lose our heads . . . by trying to introduce experiments in "libertarian communism" and "socialization." . . . The present stage of political development in Spain is that of the democratic revolution, the victory of which depends on the participation of all the antifascist forces, and these experiments can only serve to drive them away and estrange them.[15]

But the efforts of the Communists to convince their critics were unavailing; for the adherents of the libertarian movement, particularly of its extreme wing, the Libertarian Youth, were in their immense majority immovably hostile to Communist slogans and, in distinction from the CNT-FAI leadership, were becoming more and more skeptical as to whether any advantage could be gained by making concessions to foreign opinion. Some hint of the temper of the movement may be gleaned from the following quotations. In an attack on the Communist-led JSU that in January 1937 had officially espoused the cause of the democratic Republic, *Juventud Libre*, the leading organ of the Libertarian Youth, declared:

The strongest argument that the Unified Socialist Youth can put forward in order to defend the democratic and parliamentary Republic is that we should desist from speaking of revolution so as not to make our position with regard to the European democracies more difficult. Childish argument! The European democracies know only too well who we are and where we are inevitably going; they know, just as the fascist countries know, that in Spain practically all the soldiers who are fighting against fascism are revolutionaries and will not permit this magnificent occasion for making the Revolution . . . to be snatched from them. Whether we speak either of the democratic and parliamentary Republic or of the Revolution, the European democracies will help us only if it suits them. . . .

[220]

"A Democratic and Parliamentary Republic of a New Type"

To deceive our soldiers, who are dying heroically on the battlefields, to deceive our peasants and workers, who are laboring in the rear areas, with a democratic and parliamentary Republic, is to betray the Spanish Revolution. . . .

The economic wealth of the country as well as the arms are in our hands. Everything belongs to us. . . . We are defending everything we have against the international fascist criminals. The traitors who try to steal what belongs ot us should be denounced as fascists and shot without mercy.[16]

"Anyone who comes to us at this time, when we have the possibility of transforming Spain socially, with the story that this transformation would not be approved of by the international bourgeoisie, is a joker," declared José García Pradas, director of *CNT*. "From the very moment that he aspires to make a revolution with the license of the international bourgeoisie, he has no authority to tell us what to do.

"If we have to refrain from making the Revolution in order to prevent the international bourgeoisie from clashing with us, if we have to conceal our every aim, if we have to renounce our every aim, then why are our comrades fighting? Why are we all fighting? Why have we thrown ourselves into this struggle, into this war without mercy against Spanish and foreign fascism?"[17]

And *Fragua Social*, the CNT organ, stated:

"At the very moment when our country is being lashed by a tempest, by a real social revolution that has changed everything, the Communist party comes out with the demand for a parliamentary republic, a republic that has already been left far behind by the march of events. Paradoxically, this results in a situation where the Communists form the extreme right wing of Loyalist Spain, the last hope of the small bourgeoisie, which sees its world going under. However strange it may appear, the Communists are the nerve center of a policy and of a campaign of propaganda aimed at pushing us back to the first years of the bourgeois republic, a policy that ignores the existence of a triumphant and regenerating 19 July."[18]

It was, of course, incorrect to ascribe to the Communists the intention of rolling back the Revolution to before 19 July. All their propaganda for abroad notwithstanding, they could not return to the days of the 1931 Republic without restoring the property of the big landowners and industrialists, in other words, without giving them a share in the affairs of state. This would have been incompatible with the Kremlin's purpose in Spain that, under cover of a democratic superstructure, was to control her domestic and foreign policy in conformity with its own diplomatic needs. By curbing the Revolution, the Communist party aimed not at restoring the property of the big landowners and industrialists but at finding a backing for itself among the middle layers of the population and at using them, as long as it suited its purpose, to offset the power of the revolutionary segment of the anti-Franco camp. If this was its policy in the field of industry and trade, it was no less so in the field of agriculture, as will be seen in the succeeding chapter.

17. Balancing the Class Forces

Aided by the ministry of agriculture that they controlled, the Communists were able to influence substantially the course of events in the countryside. By far the most resounding of the decrees issued by Vicente Uribe, the Communist minister, was that of 7 October 1936, by which all rural properties belonging to persons who had intervened either directly or indirectly in the military insurrection were confiscated without indemnity and in favor of the state.[1] "This decree," commented *Mundo Obrero*, the Communist party organ, "breaks the foundation of the semifeudal power of the big landlords who, in order to maintain their brutal caste privileges and to perpetuate salaries of two pesetas a day and labor from dawn to dusk, have unleashed the bloody war that is devastating Spain."[2] Under the terms of the decree, the estates that had been cultivated directly by the owners or by their stewards or had been leased to large tenant farmers were given in perpetual usufruct to organizations of peasants and agricultural workers to be cultivated individually or collectively in accordance with the wishes of the majority of beneficiaries. Small cultivators who had leased estates were promised the permanent use of their holdings, not to exceed thirty hectares in dry sections, five in irrigated districts, and three in fruit-growing areas.[3] The decree of 7 October, affirmed the Communist organ, *Frente Rojo*, "is the most profoundly revolutionary measure that has been taken since the military uprising. . . . It has abolished more than 40 percent of private property in the countryside."[4]

Although the language of the decree gave the impression that the government had taken the initiative in confiscating the properties of supporters of the military insurrection, in point of fact the measure merely set the seal of legality on expropriations already carried out by agricultural laborers and tenant farmers. The Communists, however, frequently represented the measure as having been instrumental in giving the land to the peasants. "In Communist newspapers," wrote Ricardo Zabalza, left-wing Socialist and general secretary of the powerful National Federation of Land Workers, the Federación Nacional de los Trabajadores de la Tierra, affiliated with the UGT, "we have read such things as this: 'Thanks to the decree of 7 October, a measure of a Communist minister, the peasants have the land today.' Such statements no doubt make very effective propaganda among the ignorant, but they cannot convince anyone who is half-acquainted with the facts. . . . Before any Communist minister was in the government, the peasant organizations, on instructions from our federation, had already confiscated de facto all the land belonging to the rebels."[5] And, in an article written after the Civil War, Rafael Morayta Nuñez, secretary general of the Institute of Agrarian Reform during the first months of the conflict, writes: "I can state positively, and this everyone knows, that it was not the government that handed the land to the peasants. The latter did not wait for a government decision, but appropriated the estates and cultivable lands themselves. . . . Hence the much-vaunted decree of 7 October, which a certain political party practically claims to be exclusively its own creation, did not give those estates to the peasants or to anyone else; for the peasants were already working them several months before, and the only thing the decree accomplished—a decree that was, of course, approved by the government—was to give legal status to those expropriations."[6]

Because the decree applied only to the estates of persons charged with participating directly or indirectly in the military revolt and thereby exempted from legal confiscation the properties belonging to republican and other landowners who had not identified themselves with General Franco's cause, the anarchosyndicalists considered that it was inadequate to the situation. *CNT* commented:

The minister of agriculture has just promulgated a decree confiscating in favor of the state all rural properties whose owners intervened directly or indirectly in the fascist insurrection of 19 July. As usual, of course, the state arrives late. The peasants did not wait for such a vital problem to be settled by decree: they acted in advance of the government, and from the very beginning . . . they seized the property of the landowners, making the revolution from below. With a real understanding of the land problem, they were more expeditious than the state. They expropriated without making any distinction between owners who had intervened and owners who had not intervened in the rebel conspiracy. . . . The expropriation, as a punishment, only of those who have intervened directly or have helped the fascists, leaves the supreme problem of the Spanish Revolution unsolved.

Our authorities should understand once and for all that the nineteenth of July destroyed the regime of unjust privileges and that a new life is springing up all over Spain. As long as they do not understand this, as long as they cling to institutions and methods that became obsolete on 19 July they will always lag behind the conquests of the people.[7]

Criticism of the limitations of the decree came also from the National Federation of Land Workers, controlled by the left-wing Socialists. At a national conference held in June 1937, the federation demanded that the decree should be amended so as to include within its scope not only persons implicated in the military uprising, but also those who had been regarded as enemies of the working class for having "violated labor contracts, discharged workers unjustly because of their ideas, denounced them [to the police] without good reason, [and] encouraged strike breaking."[8]

But the Communist party could not countenance such an amendment. Seeking support among the propertied classes in the anti-Franco camp, it could not afford to repel the small and medium proprietors who had been hostile to the working-class movement before the Civil War, and, indeed, through the Ministry of Agriculture and the Institute of Agrarian Reform, which it controlled, it seconded, on the basis of the limitations of the decree of 7 October, many of their demands for the restitution of their land. "I can tell you about the Castilian countryside," declared a leader of the libertarian youth movement, "because I am in daily contact with all the agricultural districts of Castile, districts to which the delegates of the Ministry of Agriculture go . . . with the object of returning to the bourgeoisie, to the fascists, to the landowners, the property they once possessed. The minister of agriculture claims that these are small proprietors. Small proprietors, with a splendid number of acres! Are the political bosses of the villages and those who used to conspire against the workers small proprietors? Are those who have twenty or twenty-five workers and three or four pairs of bullocks small proprietors? I must ask where the policy of the minister of agriculture is leading and just what is the limit to the term 'small proprietor.'"[9]

The protection the Communist party gave even to farmers who had belonged to right-wing parties before the Civil War—particularly in the province of Valencia, where it organized them into the Peasant Federation[10]—irrevocably antagonized a large segment of the rural population. "The Communist party," complained a Socialist, referring to the Peasant Federation, "devotes itself to picking up in the villages the worst remnants of the former Partido Autonomista, who were not only reactionary, but also immoral, and organizes these small proprietors into a new peasant union by promising them the possession of their land."[11]

There can be no doubt that the Communist party's championship of the small, to say nothing of the medium proprietor, irrespective of his political antecedents, was one of the many important reasons for the bitter strife that soon developed between itself and the left wing of the Socialist party, which controlled the National Federation of Land Workers.[12] The Communists demanded that collectivization be entirely voluntary,[13] thereby implying that the property of the right-wing as well as of the republican farmer should be respected. The left-wing Socialists, while against the compulsory collectivization of the land of the small republican farmer,[14] were opposed to sacrificing the growth of the collective farm movement to the small owner who had been in open conflict with the rural wage worker before the Civil War. "The loyal small proprietor," declared the left Socialist paper, *Claridad*, the mouthpiece of the UGT, "should not be forced to enter the collective farms, but generous technical, economic, and moral aid should be given to every spontaneous initiative in favor of collectivization. When we say 'loyal small proprietor' we deliberately exclude both the small owners, who were brazen enemies of the working class, and the venomous and petty political bosses, who are now sniveling and trying to keep in the background and who constitute a real Fifth Column in the rural areas. As for these, we must draw their teeth and claws. It would be a veritable catastrophe if, on the basis of these elements, an attempt were made to create an organization of kulaks, while ignoring the courageous peasants fighting at the front who suffered imprisonment, torture, and misery in the past."[15]

In their efforts to win the support of the middle layers of the rural population, both right-wing and republican, the Communists were forced to restrain the collectivist tendencies even in their own youth movement. "Not only have we seen certain organizations advocate collectivization," said Santiago Carrillo, general secretary of the JSU, "but in the beginning we also saw our own youth defending it through failure to understand the character of the present struggle. However, the comrades of Badajoz and other peasant provinces know very well that when the federation told them they were pursuing the wrong policy and that when they started to follow the correct one the situation in the countryside began to change. . . . It is hardly necessary for us to point out how the only country in the world that has made the revolution, the Soviet Union, began to collectivize the land after nine years of proletarian power. How, then, in a democratic Republic are we going to do what the Soviet Union did after nine years of workers' power? We declare that, as long as the situation in our country does not permit any other course, our line for a long time to come will be the defense of the small peasant, the defense of the legitimate interests of the small proprietor of the countryside."[16]

The policy of the Communists, as expressed by the minister of agriculture's decree of 7 October and by its practical application, was criticized for other reasons than those given in the foregoing pages. Ricardo Zabalza, general secretary of the National Federation of Land Workers that enrolled small tenant farmers as well as farmhands, affirmed, when interviewed about conditions in the province of Albacete: "There are many landowners whose properties have not been confiscated, either because they are adherents of the left or because they have passed themselves off as such. Their tenants are compelled by law to continue the payment of rent, and this is an injustice because the tenants of rebel landowners are freed from such payment."[17] Zabalza also criticized the decree on the ground that it prevented a distribution of land in favor of the village poor. This criticism was based on the fact that the tenant farmers and sharecroppers who benefited from the decree were legally entitled to retain all the land they had cultivated before the Revolution, provided that it did not exceed the specified limits, and were therefore unwilling to cede any portion of their holdings to the rural wage workers. "As a result," Zabalza argued, "the wage workers remain without land in many places or have to content themselves with the worst soil or with that farthest from the villages because the rest of the land, or nearly all of it, is in the hands of small owners and tenant farmers. This makes friction inevitable, for it is impossible to accept the galling injustice of a situation whereby the sycophants of the former political bosses still enjoy a privileged position at the expense of those persons who were unable to rent even the smallest parcel of land because they were revolutionaries."[18]

But more important still as a source of friction in the countryside was the fact that the Communists used the decree to stimulate the personal interest of those tenant farmers and sharecroppers who, before its publication, had been caught up by the collective farm movement or had agreed to a redistribution of land in favor of the agricultural laborers.

"Then came the decree of 7 October," declared the National Federation of Land Workers, "offering tenant farmers the possibility of retaining in perpetual usufruct all the land they formerly cultivated, provided that it did not exceed thirty hectares in dry sections, five in irrigated districts, and three in fruit-growing areas. This represented

Curbing the Revolution

. . . a guarantee that no lessee, provided that he was not an open supporter of the rebellion, could be dispossessed of his land. . . . And
the practical effect of this decree has been to create, among the tenant
farmers and sharecroppers who had accepted the new order of things,
a desire to recover their former parcels."[19]

Encouraged by the support they received from the Communists,
many right-wing tenant farmers and sharecroppers who had accepted
collectivization in the first months of the Revolution demanded the
return of their former parcels. At the peak of their offensive against
the collective farms, Ricardo Zabalza declared: "Our most fervent aim
today is to guarantee the conquests of the Revolution, especially the
collective farms that were organized by the different branches of our
federation and against which a world of enemies is rising up, namely,
the reactionaries of yesterday and those who held land on lease because they were lackeys of the political bosses, whereas our members
were either denied land or evicted from their wretched holdings. Today these reactionaries protected by the famous decree of 7 October,
and enjoying unheard-of official aid, are endeavoring to take by assault the collectivized estates with the object of dividing them up,
distributing their livestock, their olive trees, their vineyards, and their
harvests, and of putting an end to the agrarian revolution. . . . And
in order to do this they are taking advantage of the absence of our
best comrades, who are at the front and who would weep with rage if
they should find on their return that their efforts and sacrifices had
served only to enthrone their eternal enemies, who, to increase the
mockery, are now protected by membership cards of a working-class
organization."[20]

In their campaign against the collective farms, the Communists also
endeavored to mobilize the agricultural laborers. Early in April 1937,
Mariano Vázquez, who, in November 1936 had succeeded Horacio
Prieto as secretary of the national committee of the CNT,[21] accused
them of going to areas where the CNT and UGT had established collective farms by mutual agreement and of "stirring up egotistic impulses
. . . by promising personal advantages to the laborers and inciting
them to divide up the land that they were working collectively."[22]
Nor did the Communists limit themselves to this procedure; for Vázquez also charged that they had assassinated dozens of anarchosyndicalists in the province of Toledo,[23] and, a few months later, the
general secretary of the CNT Peasants' Federation of Castile declared:
"We have fought terrible battles with the Communists, especially
with brigades and divisions under their control that have assassinated

[228]

our best peasant militants and savagely destroyed our collective farms and our harvests, obtained at the cost of infinite sacrifice."[24]

It was inevitable that the attacks on the collectives should have had an unfavorable effect upon rural economy and upon morale, for while in some areas collectivization was anathema to the majority of peasants, in others collective farms were organized spontaneously by the bulk of the peasant population. Ralph Bates, noted author, assistant commissar of the Fifteenth International Brigade, and an authority on Spain and the Spanish Revolution, wrote to me after he had severed his ties with the Communist party: "The C.P. drive against collectivization was absolutely wrong, for while there were plenty of abuses, forced collectivization, etc., there were plenty of good collectives, i.e., voluntary ones." In Toledo province, for example, where even before the war rural collectives existed,[25] 83 percent of the peasants, according to a source friendly to the Communists, decided in favor of the collective cultivation of the soil.[26]

As the campaign against the collective farms reached its height just before the summer harvest—a period of the year when even the more successful farms were beset with economic difficulties—a pall of dismay and apprehension descended upon the agricultural laborers. Work in the fields was abandoned in many places or carried on apathetically, and there was danger that a substantial portion of the harvest, vital for the war effort, would be left to rot.

The Communists then suddenly changed their policy.

The first intimation of this about-face came early in June 1937, when the minister of agriculture issued a decree promising various forms of aid to the collectives so that they could carry out "as satisfactorily and as speedily as possible the agricultural labors appropriate to the season."[27] This did not mean that no assistance had been given in the past. According to the Communist organ, *Frente Rojo*, the Institute of Agrarian Reform—which was controlled by the minister of agriculture, and, under the decree of 7 October, had been charged with the task of apportioning aid to the beneficiaries—had since that date provided collective farms with fifty million pesetas in credits, farm implements, seeds, and fertilizers.[28] This is not unlikely. But this assistance must have gone solely to collectives that accepted the intervention of the institute; for the CNT, which rejected state intervention because it threatened the autonomy of its collectives, charged that the latter were denied all help from the minister of agriculture.[29] But, according to Mariano Cardona Rosell, a member of the national committee of the CNT and its representative on the executive commission of the National Service of Agricultural Credit, although the Institute of Agrarian Reform was not empowered to extend credits and assistance to collectives outside its jurisdiction, such collectives could apply for aid from the National Service without any danger of control other than that arising from the credit transactions involved.[30] But this service, which operated under the auspices of the ministry of agriculture, and on whose executive commission there were representatives of the CNT and UGT as well as officials of that department,[31] did not begin to function properly until late in the summer of 1937. Moreover, although, according to Cardona Rosell, it extended very substantial credits to collective farms that applied for assistance, some CNT collectives did not take advantage of it for a long time owing to their suspicion of official bodies and the fear that these might curb their independence.

The preamble to the minister of agriculture's decree of June 1937, previously mentioned, promising various forms of aid to the collectives, stated that help was necessary to avoid "economic failures that might chill the faith of the land workers in the collective form of cultivation they chose freely when they confiscated the land of the rebel exploiters." Said Article I of the decree: "For the purposes of assistance by the Institute of Agrarian Reform, all collective farms set up since 19 July 1936 are considered legally constituted *during the current agricultural year*,[32] and no claim will be handled by the subsidiary departments of the Institute of Agrarian Reform for the return of land occupied by the said collectives . . . even in cases where it is alleged that errors have been made of a legal character or in defining the political status of the former owner or beneficiary of the collectivized land." "This means," commented *Frente Rojo*, the Communist organ, "that the only thing that counts in guaranteeing the legality of the collectives is the very act, the revolutionary act of having formed them, and that they are thus saved from any legal or political stratagem that might be devised against them." It did not mention the fact that the status of legality had been conceded only temporarily. "[The decree]," it asserted, "grants to the agricultural collectives formed since 19 July 1936 an indestructible legal position. . . . What began as a spontaneous impulse among a large section of the agricultural workers has now been converted by virtue of the decree into a legal form of agricultural labor."[33] Nevertheless, many months later, in a program of common action, the CNT and UGT found it necessary to demand that the collective farms be legalized.[34] This did not change matters, for toward the end of the Civil War *CNT*, the anarchosyndicalist organ in

Madrid, was still insisting that they be legalized.[35] In fact, Vicente Uribe, who remained in charge of the ministry of agriculture until the end of the conflict, never granted a permanent status of legality to the collectives.

Although the decree of June 1937 offered no guarantee of legality beyond the current agricultural year, it produced a sense of relief in the countryside during the vital period of the harvest, and in that respect achieved its purpose.

But no sooner had the crops been gathered than apprehension again set in. On 19 August, the central government—which in May had been reorganized without the participation of the CNT[36]—dissolved the anarchist-dominated Defense Council of Aragon that had been set up early in the war to control the Revolution in that part of Aragon occupied by the anti-Franco forces, predominantly libertarian. In a report to Largo Caballero in November 1936, in which he justified the creation of the council, Joaquín Ascaso, its anarchist president, stated that the absence of all governing organs in the three provinces of Aragon and the occupation of part of this region by militia, "not all subjected to the necessary and desirable discipline," had given rise to a chaotic situation that threatened economic ruin in the rear and disaster at the front. For these reasons, he added, it had been essential to create a body that would assume all the functions exercised by the former organs of administration, "a body adequate both in its structure and functioning to the present situation."[37]

Initially, the council had been made up solely of representatives of the CNT and FAI and had operated as a completely independent entity. "The creation of an autonomous organ of power that was exclusively libertarian could not satisfy a central government formed of representatives of all the political parties," writes César Lorenzo, the son of Horacio Prieto, who, it will be recalled, was secretary of the national committee of the CNT until November 1936 and one of the principal advocates of CNT participation in the government. "Nowhere else in the loyalist zone was there a local body in the hands of one single segment of opinion. . . . The Council of Aragon thus became a choice target of the republicans, Socialists, and the Communists, who did not hesitate to denounce it as a camouflaged dictatorship and to accuse it of cantonalism.[38] The disapproval was so widespread that even the leaders of the CNT proclaimed their dissatisfaction." Lorenzo adds that they thought the creation of the council not only rendered their efforts to join the government more difficult, but the council itself was "illegal" because it had been created without the approval of the CNT national committee and had not been ratified by any plenum or regular congress. The Aragonese anarchists, he affirms, were not slow to recognize the problems created by their "high-handed conduct." They realized that in order to survive they must obtain the authorization of the government at all costs. "Benito Pabón, the well-known leader of the Syndicalist party[39] and a great friend of the CNT, devoted his efforts to persuading them to . . . request openly the legalization of the council even at the cost of their own pride. He showed them that the complexity of the international situation required a total reorganization of the council because the great powers would not help the Republic if the predominance of the extreme left were advertised ostentatiously, and he convinced them that it was essential to maintain certain bourgeois democratic appearances."[40]

As a result, the Defense Council of Aragon agreed to give representation to other organizations in return for recognition by the central government.[41] The CNT and FAI nevertheless retained in their hands the key posts: presidency, public order, propaganda, agriculture, economy, transport, and supplies.[42] Although the Communists were given two seats, they could not live with an archrevolutionary body that fomented libertarian communism in the countryside and pursued a policy of all-out collectivization of the holdings of the small proprietor and tenant farmer.[43] But only after the power of the CNT and FAI had been broken in the neighboring region of Catalonia in May 1937—a subject treated later in this volume—and Largo Caballero had been replaced by Juan Negrín in the premiership and by Indalecio Prieto in the war ministry was it possible for the central government, in which the CNT was no longer represented, to take action against the council. After the Communists had prepared the way for its dissolution by a short though fierce campaign at the beginning of August,[44] the Eleventh Division under the command of the Communist Enrique Líster, acting on instructions from Indalecio Prieto and with the full knowledge and approval of the cabinet, moved into the region and dissolved the council.[45] So as not to arouse suspicion, the division has been instructed to proceed to Aragon to "rest and reorganize" after the battle of Brunete on the central front, and a dissolution decree, secretly approved by the central government, was published only after the council had been dissolved.[46] "Hated by the people, the Council of Aragon collapsed without the firing of a single shot," writes Líster. "And when the next day the dissolution decree appeared in the *Gaceta* the council had ceased to exist."[47] Commenting on the decree, *Adelante*, mouthpiece at that time of the moderate Socialists

in the government, said: "Perhaps the change that took place yesterday in Aragonese territory may not have extraordinary repercussions
abroad. No matter. It deserves to have them because by this action
the government offers the firmest testimony of its authority."[48]

Concurrently with the publication of the decree, José Ignacio Mantecón, a member of the Left Republican party, but a Communist sympathizer, who after the Civil War joined the party,[49] was appointed
governor general of the region. "From the first day," writes Líster,
"we understood each other perfectly and we gave him all our collaboration and help in his difficult task."[50] Backed by the military power
of the Eleventh Division, Mantecón ordered the breakup of the collective farms and the arrest of militants of the CNT.[51] According to a
report of the Aragon CNT, the land, farm implements, horses, and
cattle confiscated from right-wing supporters were returned to their
former owners or to their families; new buildings erected by the collectives, such as stables and hen coops, were destroyed, and in some
villages the farms were deprived even of the seed necessary for sowing, while six hundred members of the CNT were arrested.[52]

After the war, José Duque, one of the two Communist members of
the Defense Council, stated, when he was no longer a member of the
party but still a critic of the council's radical agrarian policies, that in
his opinion Líster's measures were more severe than they need have
been.[53] Manuel Almudí, the other Communist on the council, agreed,
speaking as a Communist: "Líster's measures in Aragon were very
harsh. He could have acted with greater discretion. Great ill feeling
was aroused as a result of his conduct."[54] Of this repression the tenant farmers and small owners who had entered the collective farms in
the early weeks of the Revolution, when the power of the CNT and
FAI in Aragon was undisputed, took full advantage. They divided up
the land as well as the crops and farm implements, and, with the aid
of the assault guards and Communist military forces, even raided
those collectives that had been established in accordance with the
wishes of their members.

The situation became so serious that the Communists, although
evading personal responsibility, later acknowledged that a dangerous
policy had been adopted. José Silva, general secretary of the Institute
of Agrarian Reform and a Communist party member, wrote:

It was in Aragon where the most varied and strange experiments in collectivization and socialization were made, where undoubtedly the most violence
was used in order to compel the peasants to enter the collective farms, and
where a manifestly false policy tore open serious breaches in rural economy.

Curbing the Revolution

When the government of the Republic dissolved the Council of Aragon, the governor general tried to allay the profound uneasiness in the hearts of the peasant masses by dissolving the collectives. This measure was a very grave mistake and produced tremendous disorganization in the countryside. Under cover of the order issued by the governor general, those persons who were discontented with the collectives—and who had good reason for being so, if the methods employed in forming them are taken into account—took them by assault, carrying away and dividing up the harvest and farm implements without respecting the collectives that had been formed without violence or pressure, that were prosperous, and that were a model of organization, like the one in Candasmo.

It is true that the governor's aim was to repair injustices and to convince the workers of the countryside that the Republic was protecting them, but the result was just the opposite from that intended. The measure only increased the confusion, and violence was exercised, but this time by the other side. As a result, labor in the fields was suspended almost entirely, and a quarter of the land had not been prepared at the time for sowing.[55]

"The danse macabre of the Communists and reactionary owners resulted in the ruin of agriculture in Aragon," José Peirats charges. "The collectivists who were not in jail were either persecuted or took refuge in other regions or sought protection in the CNT divisions. In these circumstances the hour arrived to prepare the soil for the next harvest. The small owners who had been triumphant could not work with their own hands the properties they had occupied. [On the other hand], the dispossessed peasants—intransigent collectivists—refused to work under a regime of private property, or, worse still, to hire themselves out for wages."[56]

To redress this situation the Communist party had once again to change its policy, and some of the dismantled collectives were restored. "The recognition of the rights of the collectives," said Silva, the Communist general secretary of the Institute of Agrarian Reform, "and the decision to return what had been unjustly taken away from them, together with the efforts of the governor general of Aragon in this direction, brought things back to normal. Tranquillity returned, and enthusiasm was revived among the peasants, who gave the necessary labor for sowing the abandoned land."[57]

According to Peirats, although there is no complete information on the effect of Communist repression on what he calls the "second stage of collectivization," the comparative figures of delegates who attended the two congresses of collectivists held in Aragon in 1937—five hundred in February, before the breakup of the collective farms, and two hundred in September, after their dissolution and the subsequent reversal of Communist policy, when some of the dismantled collectives had been restored—are significant. "It is very possible," he concludes, "that this second stage of collectivization reflected more faithfully the sincerity of its adherents. They had been subjected to a hard test, and those who had been capable of withstanding it were collectivists inured to all adversities. However, it would be foolish to characterize all those who abandoned collectivization during the second stage as anticollectivist. Fear, official coercion, and uncertainty of the future weighed heavily in the decisions of an important segment of the Aragonese peasantry."[58]

But, while the situation in Aragon improved in some degree after the Communists had modified their policy, the hatreds and resentments generated by the breakup of the collectives and by the repression that followed were never wholly dispelled. Nor was the resultant disillusionment that sapped the spirit of the anarchosyndicalist forces on the Aragon front ever entirely removed, a disillusionment that no doubt contributed to the collapse of that front a few months later. Peirats writes: "The collective farms were once again authorized. The prisoners were released. Collectivization got under way. The new sowings were prepared. But this time it was Franco who reaped the harvest. . . . One cannot play the game of demoralizing a front and its rear with impunity."[59]

After the destruction of the collective farms in Aragon, the Communist party was compelled to modify its policy and to support collectives in other regions against former owners who sought the return of confiscated land.[60] This change was caused not only by the damage inflicted on rural economy and on morale at the front and in the rear by its previous policy, but by another important factor: much as the Communist party needed the backing of the small and medium tenant farmer and proprietor in the anti-Franco camp, it could not allow them to become too strong, lest, under the leadership of the liberal republicans and moderate Socialists, they should, in conjunction with the urban middle classes, endeavor to take the affairs of state into their own hands. In order to guide domestic and foreign policy in accordance with Russia's diplomatic needs, the Communists had to be supreme. They could be so only by a careful interplay of the pieces on the board; for their influence rested not only on the inherent strength of their own party, powerful though it was, but on a careful balancing of class forces that, because of their mutual antagonisms, could not combine against the arbiter that stood between. Hence, if in the beginning it was essential for the Communists to destroy the power of the extreme left by an alliance with the middle strata of the population, it was no less important at a later stage to prevent these layers from acquiring too much strength and threatening the supremacy of their party.

But no attempt on the part of the Communists to balance one class against another could succeed for long unless they could gain control of the armed forces, both at the front and in the rear, unless they could incorporate the independent revolutionary militia into a regular army under the command of a staff of officers and political commissars amenable to their wishes. And this they recognized from the first days of the Revolution.

Part IV

From the Revolutionary Militia to a Regular Army

18. The Revolutionary Militia

The reader will remember that the government of liberal republicans formed by José Giral at the outset of the Civil War inherited an officer corps whose cohesion had been shattered by the military insurrection and social revolution.[1]

In an attempt to counter the rebellion, the government issued a decree releasing the enlisted men from all oaths of service and obedience to their officers. But the decree, wrote President Azaña, was not heeded in cities that were controlled by the military. It was observed in the garrisons of Madrid, Barcelona, Cartagena, Valencia, and other cities, where the rebellion had been thwarted.

The men left their barracks and nearly all of them went home. An appreciable number joined the volunteer units that, under improvised leadership and with limited weapons, went to fight at the fronts. The few units that could be kept in their barracks were virtually useless. The rebellion had undermined discipline everywhere. The professional officers were suspect, and the ranks, composed mainly of workingmen, preferred to listen to the directives of their unions or parties than to those of their commanders. In Madrid, whose garrison consisted of thirteen regiments, it was a hard job, during the first few days, to organize four to six infantry units and a battalion of engineers for service in the Sierra.

The republican government gave arms to the people in order to defend the approaches to the capital. Several thousand rifles were handed out. But in Madrid, and especially in Barcelona, Valencia, and other places, the masses stormed the barracks and carried off the arms. In Barcelona they occupied all the military establishments. War material, which was already scarce, disappeared. They burned the draft records; they burned the horses' saddles. In Valencia the horses of a cavalry regiment were sold to the gypsies for five or ten pesetas each. At the beginning of a war that threatened to be terrible the deluded masses destroyed the last remnants of the military machine, a machine that was going to be so badly needed. These deeds, and others that were no less deplorable, were due to the following reasons: few people gauged the importance of the rebellion and the gravity of the situation. Many welcomed it as a favorable event.[2]

Because the government lacked the necessary forces with which to combat the military insurrection, the weight of the struggle at the fronts fell upon the labor unions and proletarian parties that organized militia forces under commanders appointed or elected from among the most resolute and respected of their men. These militia units, or "columns," as they were generally called, to which army officers were attached under the watchful eye of party or union representatives, were controlled exclusively by the organizations that had created them, the officers assigned by the war minister possessing little or no authority.[3]

"When, out of absolute necessity, [the working-class organizations] had to make use of us," complains a republican army officer, "they employed only the minimum of loyal officers strictly indispensable to their needs; these were kept under constant vigilance and were, in addition, menaced because of their alleged fascist sympathies."[4]

In order to create a counterpoise to the revolutionary militia, no less than to organize additional armed units for service at the front, the liberal republican government of José Giral decided, during the last days of July, to call up two years of conscripts,[5] a measure that met with trifling response, not only because many of the men were already in the militia, but also because the government lacked any coercive machinery for enforcing the draft.

In addition, during the first few days of August, the government published a decree providing for the creation of "volunteer battalions,"[6] and two weeks later, in a still more significant move, it issued a series of decrees aimed at the formation of a "volunteer army" that was to be raised from among men in the first-line reserve, with cadres composed of retired officers and of noncommissioned officers not then on active service, whose loyalty had been attested by a Popular Front organization.[7]

But the effect of these measures, too, was negligible because, as President Azaña testifies, "thousands upon thousands of volunteers preferred to enlist in the popular militia organized spontaneously by the unions and parties."[8] Moreover, the idea of an army under the control of the government—a government whose premier, José Giral, and war minister, Hernández Sarabia, were both stalwart supporters of the moderate-minded Azaña—was viewed with alarm not only by the anarchosyndicalists of the CNT[9] but also by the left-wing Socialists of the UGT, whose secretary, Largo Caballero, had several violent interviews with José Giral on this account.[10] In an editorial published two days after the promulgation of the decrees, *Claridad*, the mouthpiece of Largo Caballero, declared that they could not be justified either on the ground that the militia forces were not large enough numerically to carry on the war or on the ground that they lacked efficiency; that the number of men incorporated in them or who desired to join them could be considered "virtually unlimited"; and that as far as their military efficiency was concerned, "it could not be greater and we doubt whether it could be surpassed by any other armed organization." Furthermore, *Claridad* affirmed, the reserve soldiers who had not yet volunteered for service in any other force were "not animated, however great their loyalty to the Republic, by the same political and combative ardor that had induced the militiamen to enlist," and the preferential right—granted them under the terms of one of the decrees—to enroll in the regular army units to be organized after the war would not stimulate the fighting zeal of the militia. Having disposed of the military arguments in favor of the volunteer army, the editorial continued:

"The new army, if there must be one, should have as its foundation the men who are fighting today and not merely those who have not yet fought in this war. It must be an army that is in keeping with the Revolution . . . to which the future state will have to adjust itself. To think of replacing the present combatants by another type of army that, to a certain extent, would control their revolutionary action, is to think in a counterrevolutionary way. That is what Lenin said (*State and Revolution*): 'Every revolution, after destroying the state apparatus, shows us how the governing class attempts to reestablish special bodies of armed men at "its" service, and how the oppressed class tries to create a new organization of this type capable of serving not the exploiters but the exploited.'"[11]

Unlike the left-wing Socialists, the Communists entertained no misgivings about the projected army, and, indeed, aided the Giral cabinet in implementing its decrees.[12] Yet, if as has already been shown, their championship of this government sprang from the need to keep it in office as a democratic veil to influence the Western world,[13] if, in particular, their support of the military decrees was inspired by the need to create a centralized force of greater combat efficiency than the militia, the Communists also had a more subtle motive; for they not only regarded the decrees as a step toward a permanently organized army of the state, over which they hoped, in the course of time, by systematic and adroit penetration, to establish their supremacy, but they knew that as long as the unions and parties possessed their own armed units and as long as these units had not been merged into a regular army whose pivotal positions they themselves controlled, their own party could never be master of the anti-Franco camp.

In their endeavors to quiet the fears of the Caballero Socialists with regard to the creation of the volunteer army, the Communists were careful to conceal the political motive of their support under the sole and powerful argument of military efficiency and to refrain, as yet, from calling for the fusion of the militia into a government-controlled army, a demand that was soon to become an important item in their declared program.

Their central organ, *Mundo Obrero*, wrote:

We believe that all the parties and organizations belonging to the Popular Front will agree with us on the necessity of creating in the shortest possible time an army with all the technical efficiency required by a modern war. There can be no doubt that the cornerstone of our army is our heroic popular militia. But it is not enough to romance about its self-sacrifice and heroism. We must give thought to the measures that should be put into effect immediately with a view to increasing the efficiency of the people in arms. . . .

Some comrades have wished to see in the creation of the new volunteer army something like a detraction from the role of the militia, possibly because the decree lacks sufficient clarification. Undoubtedly the militia should enjoy all the advantages conceded to the volunteer army, and we do not entertain the least doubt that the government will say so immediately because no one under present circumstances could think of creating anything that runs counter to our glorious popular militia. Actually, the aim of the decree is to complement and reinforce the popular army, to give it greater efficiency, and to end the war as soon as possible.[14]

But the issuance of a further decree granting militiamen the same preferential right as conceded to members of the volunteer army[15] did nothing to remove the uneasiness that the government's project had created in the minds of the left-wing Socialists. The appointment of Diego Martínez Barrio—who had formed the ill-starred cabinet of conciliation on the morning of 19 July, and whose party, the Unión Republicana, stood on the right flank of the Popular Front coalition—to head the commission charged with the organization of this army[16] only tended to deepen their suspicion of the government's intentions. It was this suspicion, superimposed upon the imminent threat to Madrid consequent upon the rapid advance of General Franco's forces—an advance that had carried them more than 230 miles in twenty days after their capture of Badajoz on 14 August—that impelled José Giral, weary of presiding over a government that had power only on paper and lacked the support of the majority of the working class, to propose that the government be broadened to include other Popular Front organizations.

It was in these circumstances, as has already been shown, that a new government was formed on 4 September, with Largo Caballero as premier and war minister.

Whether Largo Caballero would carry out the thoroughgoing military reorganization that the Communists envisioned was by no means certain in view of his antipathy to the entire concept of militarization expressed not only in the above-quoted editorial in *Claridad*, but in the following interview given to Mikhail Koltzov, Stalin's unofficial envoy, on 27 August, one week before he entered the war ministry. Koltzov noted in his diary:

Largo Caballero himself is dressed in workman's overalls, a revolver in his belt. He is tanned by the sun and wind, very vigorous and hearty for someone who is nearly seventy years of age. Alvarez del Vayo has set up the appointment and acts as translator. . . . Without preliminary remarks of any kind, Largo Caballero fulminates against the government. . . . The working-class militia doesn't believe in the government, it doesn't believe in the war ministry, because the ministry makes use of the services of shady people, of former reactionary monarchist generals, of career officers, who are obvious traitors. . . . To the question why there is such a delay in converting the militia units into a regular army and whose fault it is, he gives no precise answer and renews his attack on the government. He regards as dangerous the recently published decree laying the foundations for the volunteer army. . . . [He] sees in the decree a contempt for the working-class combatants and a bestowal of special privileges on career soldiers: "The military caste is being resuscitated"!

I try to make him see the value of reserves for the army, especially in a country like Spain, without military training, that has done hardly any fighting. He predicts that the regular army will wrest from the people the arms that have cost them so dearly.

A long and lively discussion ensues regarding the advantages of the army and the militia. . . . Largo Caballero cites passages from *State and Revolution* by Lenin regarding the people in arms. I remind him that it was Lenin himself who created the workers' and peasants' army, granting it absolute priority over the heterogeneous militia groups, columns, and detachments. The fusion of the best elements among the lesser officers, carefully selected, with the advanced revolutionary workers, comprises the alloy from which a powerful antifascist popular army can be forged. Whenever units of the army and detachments of militia or guerrillas exist side by side with equal rights, sooner or later a contradiction emerges that later degenerates into a conflict, and the army, being on a much higher level, always wins. Then why prolong this period of contradictions? The fusion of all the antifascist armed forces into a single military organism must be accelerated.

Again he offers no direct objections, but he censures the Communists for wanting "to organize everything, to place leaders everywhere, to give everything a title, a label, a number." He attributes this to the youthfulness of their leaders, to the party's self-confidence, which is based not on its own successes and its own experiences but on those of the Russian Communists. He says that by helping the [Giral] government the Communists are doing harm, that they are inviting catastrophe, and are increasing popular discontent. The working-class parties must sweep away the functionaries, the bureaucrats, the whole ministerial system of operation and adopt new, revolutionary forms of leadership. . . .

All this gushes from Largo Caballero with vehemence and irritation, with the stubborn force of conviction. It is difficult to comprehend the source of this belated radicalism, this maximalism, in a man who, for decades, defended the most conciliatory and reformist positions within the working-class movement, who entered into agreements and even coalitions with extreme right-wing bourgeois governments, including the reactionary monarchist dictatorship of Primo de Rivera. But Alvarez del Vayo and many others affirm that the "old man" has in fact changed enormously deep down within himself, that the struggle in Asturias [in 1934] and [the experiences] of the entire subsequent period have caused him to revise his political course. . . .

We speak for another hour and a half. Caballero refers several times to the incapacity and lack of loyalty of the republican generals, personal friends of Azaña, all those Sarabias [a reference to Hernández Sarabia, minister of war]. Later, when we are alone, Alvarez del Vayo and I . . . enter a small bar. He is very pleased with the interview and the conversation. He is confident that the "old man" is now in complete agreement with the need for a regular people's army. "He did not tell you this frankly; that's his way, but you will see; he will come out in favor of the army. The old man is favorably disposed toward the Soviet Union and the experience of the Russian Revolution."[17]

But only time would tell how far Largo Caballero, in his new capacity as war minister, would travel with the Communists and their Russian aides in creating the type of army they had in mind.

The first major problems that confronted him in his new capacity were undoubtedly the defects of the militia system; for, in spite of *Claridad*'s claim that the efficiency of the militia could not be greater, these defects were indubitably among the principal reasons for General Franco's swift advance up the Tagus Valley toward the Spanish capital. True, they did not spring from any lack of combativity, for in street fighting or in small battles against a localized enemy, the militiamen showed great courage; they sprang rather from lack of training and discipline, from the absence of any effective unity, either of conception or of action, among the militia units, and from the rivalry existing between the various organizations.

President Azaña recalls:

There were republican, Socialist, Communist, CNT, UGT, FAI, and other battalions and brigades, as well as units formed by workers belonging to the same trade, without any plan, each one leaving happily for the front, with commanders selected by the militiamen, and with political and strategic objectives of their own creation. No one was subject to military discipline. . . . The war ministry [under Hernández Sarabia] tried to put order into all this confusion. It officially recognized the militia units, tried to arm them, gave them professional leadership, when they were willing to accept it, and assigned tactical and strategic missions to them in accordance with the most urgent needs. Whether these missions were carried out or not depended on the mood of the men, the whims of the subordinate officers, or the directives of the political organizations. The personnel reports prepared by the war ministry every day . . . reveal the incredible heterogeneity of that army and the varied composition, in number and quality, of its units. . . . At any rate, the commander of each sector of the front was a professional officer appointed by the war ministry. There were other professional officers in subaltern command posts. . . . They were all in a difficult position. Their authority was not always respected. They had to convince their subordinates that orders should be obeyed and take care that they did not arouse any suspicion of disloyalty. If the men retreated in disorder, if they disobeyed, or fulfilled an order badly, the commander could not deal harshly with them.[18]

"It is hardly necessary to say," wrote a left-wing observer, "that these troops made every mistake that can be made. Night attacks were launched with *vivas* for the Revolution; artillery was often placed on the same line as the infantry. Sometimes there were really grotesque incidents. One day a militiaman told me that after lunch a whole detachment went into a neighboring field to eat grapes; when it returned its position was occupied by the enemy."[19] Referring to the offensives launched by Catalan militia forces against the besieged town of Huesca, in the region of Aragon, Manuel Aznar, a supporter of General Franco, writes: "In the early days, the attacks of the Catalan columns, nearly all of which were made up of anarchist militia, were so completely uncoordinated and so divorced from the norms of military technique that their movements resembled the arbitrary efforts of disintegrated hordes rather than genuine military operations. As a result, Nationalist headquarters gained two to three months in which to assemble reinforcements, to learn from their own weaknesses, to concentrate war material, and to prepare for the transition from an elastic to a rigid defense. Furthermore, it could be seen from the concentration of artillery fire, the disposition of machine guns, the preparation of assaults, the bad organization of the troops, the irresolution of the subaltern commanders, and from the weakness of the offensives that the besieging army lacked the most essential psychological and technical elements for war."[20]

On the same front, according to Jesús Pérez Salas, a professional officer and a loyal republican who commanded the Macià-Companys column in the early months of the war, it was impossible to carry out a combined operation involving different units.

Whenever the staff decided upon an operation of this kind, . . . it was obliged to call the [militia] commanders to headquarters and explain to all of them the fundamental objective of the operation and the role that each column was to play. Thereupon, a debate was initiated, during which the militia commanders expressed their agreement or disagreement, often forcing a change in the original plan by their vetoes. After a great struggle, an agreement was reached but always with respect to an operation on a reduced scale and of much smaller scope. Even so, it was never carried out, because when the time came for undertaking the operation there was always somebody who acted tardily, upsetting that coordination which is the key to success.

This was due to the fact that orders, even within each sector, were never carried out precisely, and that, as forces of very distinct ideology existed on the front, each one of them looked upon the failure of the others with a certain degree of satisfaction. The CNT, which formed the bulk of the forces, wished for the defeat of its political enemies of the POUM and the PSUC with all its heart. These, in their turn, held the men of the CNT in abomination.[21]

"Sectarianism, differences in outlook, and proselytizing zeal," wrote a prominent member of the CNT and FAI, "resulted not only in the militia units being indifferent to one another's existence and forgetting that they had a common foe, but also, on many occasions, in really dangerous situations arising between them."[22]

"Party pride seemed stronger than the feeling of common defense," affirms the Socialist writer Arturo Barea, who was in frequent contact with militiamen returning from the Madrid front. "A victory of an Anarchist battalion was paraded in the face of the Communists; a victory of a Communist unit was secretly lamented by the others. The defeat of a battalion was turned into ridicule for the political group to which it belonged. This strengthened the fighting spirit of the individual units, but also created a hotbed of mutual resentment damaging the military operations as a whole, and circumventing a unified command."[23]

But the most striking overall account that may be regarded as typical of the situation obtaining on most of the fronts in the early months of the Civil War is given by the republican officer Major Aberri, who was sent from Barcelona to assist in the reorganization of the Aragon front:

On approaching Sariñena [headquarters of the militia forces], I came across a truck halted on the other side of the highway, and, at the request of a group of soldiers, I stopped my car. Their truck had broken down, but they did not know what was wrong with it. . . .

"Where are you going?" I asked them with surprise.

"To Barcelona, to spend the Sunday there."

"But aren't you supposed to be at the front?"

"Sure, but as there's nothing doing we are going to Barcelona."

"Have you been given leave?"

"No. Can't you see we are militiamen?"

They did not understand my question because it was the most natural thing in the world for them to leave the front when it was quiet. They knew nothing of discipline, and it was clear that nobody had bothered to instruct them on the subject. After a forty-hour week at the front they got bored and left it. . . .

Once [in Sariñena] I reported to the commander of the [Aragon] front [a professional officer] and informed him of my assignment. I told him what plans I had in mind, what I thought it necessary to do. He looked at me pityingly, and then replied:

"We shall see. We shall see. Things are not what they used to be, and you have to be pretty smart to get along with these fellows. At any rate I am having a conference with the heads of the [militia] columns very soon, and you will have an opportunity to judge for yourself. Meanwhile, stay and have lunch with me. . . ." We spoke at length during the meal and he told me about his tragedy; he had no authority and could not make himself obeyed by anybody. The leaders of the columns were demigods who accepted neither orders, advice, nor suggestions.

"You will see for yourself! The war cannot be waged in this way. I have no supplies; war material is distributed by the parties and trade unions; arms are not sent where they are most needed, but where [these organizations] decide. . . ."

The leaders of some of the columns arrived. . . . The majority of them had never served in the army. Some were accompanied by professional officers, who were called technicians, but who unfortunately were without authority. Their role was an auxiliary one, and their advice was to no purpose. Also to no purpose were the mortifications we officers had to suffer in spite of the fact that we had been loyal to our oath and had risked our all. Nobody had any confidence in us: any Tom, Dick, or Harry thought he had a right to spy on us and ignore our suggestions. . . .

The commander of the Aragon front recommended that a decisive operation be launched against Huesca. Everything pointed to the fact that this historic Aragonese town was almost without protection, and that with an intelligent and well-coordinated attack it would have fallen into the hands of the Republic. . . . Those present listened to his plan, which was discussed in detail, but unfortunately they finally decided to consult their respective trade-union organizations before accepting anything. In the end the discussion took a very regrettable turn because the commander's request that some of the columns should hand over to other units the additional material they needed was rejected out of hand. In other words, the commander of the front had absolutely no authority to decide on the disposition of men and arms.

I point these things out, even though briefly, since they accurately reflect the predicament of a people who, because of a lamentable indiscipline and a tremendous lack of equipment, had to perform prodigies of heroism in order to resist a regular army. . . . What could they not have achieved with good leaders, with sufficient war material, and with military discipline? I saw this later when I visited the different sectors of the front. There were no fortifications at that time. A position was taken by sheer courage, but since nobody bothered to fortify it, it was lost during the next enemy counterattack. The employment of war material was equally absurd. I was once in a position where there were several 10.5 guns, but there were no munitions. These were in the possession of a nearby column, which refused to part with them although it had no artillery itself. . . .

The system of trenches was also in keeping with the situation. At some points parapets had been thrown up with an eye to a neighboring column that belonged to a different political organization. There was a certain amount of satisfaction when a rival got a beating from the enemy. . . .

During my mission on the Huesca front, I had to pass a night very near the enemy lines. I was tired and I lay down to sleep, but shortly after wrapping myself up in my blanket, I heard someone singing at the top of his lungs. I got up and found a sentinel singing a jota for all he was worth.

"Listen," I said. "Don't you know that a sentinel should keep quiet?"

"Who the hell cares? That's what things were like in the past."

"No, man, no! They should be the same now. Don't you realize that they could spot you and plug a bullet into you from the other side?"

"Nuts! We have agreed not to plug one another. Besides, if I don't sing, I'll fall asleep."

In face of such reasoning I retired to my improvised "dormitory"—a blanket, the earth, and the grass—ready to sleep when this yokel of a guard had finished his repertoire. But no sooner had he stopped singing than I heard him speaking with a loud voice, as though carrying on a discussion with someone at a distance. I got up from my nook again and saw with amazement —afterward nothing amazed me—that our sentinel was talking to the sentinel on the fascist side of the lines, who was asking him what he had eaten for dinner. Our man, laying it on thick, gave him a pantagruellian menu. Lucullan had eaten at his own table.

"You've eaten that!" retorted the other. "You've only eaten potatoes and you've had to be thankful for them!"

"You mean that's all you've had, and things are going to get even worse for you. We have everything we want here. Come over and you'll soon see."

Turning down this offer, the other fellow replied with an invitation to a certain member of his enemy's family, whom he qualified in not very academic language [your whore of a mother],[24] to come over to his own lines, adding, "And shut up, you starving rat!"

"Starving rat!" exclaimed our sentinel. "Just to show you that we have more food here than we need, here's a sausage for you."

And without further ado, he flung a hand grenade over the parapet. The result was inevitable. Within a few seconds the firing became general along the entire front. Hand grenades, rifles, and machine guns performed their fantastic symphony for a good quarter of an hour.

Then silence fell, but only after several thousand cartridges had been wasted stupidly.[25]

In addition to all the aforementioned defects, the militia system had other notable shortcomings. There was, for example, no central general staff in the proper sense of the word. Martín Blázquez, an officer in the war ministry, first under Hernández Sarabia and then under Largo Caballero, writes: "There was, of course, no general staff, but its functions were partly fulfilled by the intelligence department, which received all cables and [radio] messages. . . . Most of the other departments of the general staff were not created until after . . . Largo Caballero became minister of war."[26] It is worthy of remark that the war ministry under Hernández Sarabia had to rely upon the working-class organizations for much of its information. "In the offices of the UGT in Madrid," writes Alvarez del Vayo, "a permanent information bureau was set up, and this for some time was the war ministry's finest news agency. From every province, from every village where a representative of this organization was installed, the slightest movement of rebel troops was telephoned immediately to the central office."[27]

Still, there was no central military body that could review the situation on all the battle fronts, formulate a common plan of action, and decide on the allocation of available supplies of men, munitions, arms, and motor vehicles in such a way as to produce the best results on the most promising front. In the first months of the Revolution the war ministry exercised hardly any authority in the field of transportation and had to rely upon a National Committee of Road Transport, dominated by representatives of the CNT and UGT.[28] Not only did the committee pay scant heed to the demands of the war ministry,[29] but its own orders were for the most part disregarded by militia units, committees, trade-union branches, and local party headquarters that retained what vehicles they could for their own use without regard to general requirements.[30]

To make matters worse, each party and labor union had its own military headquarters that, in most cases, attended to the requirements of its own militia without any knowledge of or regard to the needs of other units on the same or neighboring sector, least of all on distant fronts, and, frequently, supplies of one unit were stolen by another.[31] Alejandro García Val, a commander at one time of the Communist party's Fifth Regiment, acknowledged after the war that the regiment often stole vehicles from the CNT to compensate for its own deficiency.[32]

Whereas the strength of General Franco's forces during the first few months of the war lay largely in the Moors and Foreign Legionaries with their stern discipline, training, and professional cadres[33] and in the modern aircraft that had been arriving from Italy and Germany since the first weeks of the war,[34] the militia units, with few exceptions, had no staff of officers they would trust to lead them into the field; were, for the most part, ignorant of the organization of war, of cooperation between sections and companies, of the use of cover and camouflage, of the digging of trenches; were subject to the orders of no central military authority; had little or no discipline; and had no modern aircraft to protect them until the adversary reached the very gates of Madrid at the beginning of November.[35] In such circumstances, they were not only incapable of any sustained offensive action in the first months of the war, and at many points wasted month after month in fruitless sieges,[36] but they often crumbled under the onset of the enemy. "It is a phenomenon of this war," declared García Oliver, the anarchist leader, "that when towns held by the fascists are attacked they hold out for a long time and that [when we are attacked] we do not resist at all. They surround a small town, and after a couple of days it is taken; but when we surround one we spend our entire life there."[37]

19. Discipline and the Anarchosyndicalist Militia

Of the manifold defects of the militia system that General Franco's victories forced to the front during the first weeks of the war, none was more hotly debated or called for more urgent correction than the lack of discipline. Although this problem beset all the militia units, whatever their ideology, its solution encountered a philosophical impediment only in those formed by the libertarian movement, for the liberty of the individual is the very core of anarchism, and nothing is so antipodal to its nature as submission to authority. "Discipline is obedience to authority; anarchism recognizes no authority," said *La Revista Blanca*, a leading anarchist journal, in an issue published beore the Civil War.[1]

The CNT-FAI militia reflected the ideals of equality, individual liberty, and freedom from obligatory discipline integral to the anarchist doctrine. There was no officers' hierarchy, no saluting, no regimentation. "A CNT member will never be a disciplined militiaman togged up in a braided uniform, strutting with martial gait through the streets of Madrid, and rhythmically swinging his arms and legs," said an article in *CNT*.[2] And a resolution approved at a regional congress of the Valencia CNT stated: "When a comrade enters the CNT barracks, he must understand that the word barracks does not signify subjection to odious military regulations consisting of salutes, parades, and other trivialities of the kind, completely theatrical and negating every revolutionary ideal."[3] If there was no discipline in the CNT-FAI militia units in the early days of the Civil War, there were also no military titles, badges, or distinctions in the way of food, clothing, and quarters, and the few professional military men whose services were accepted acted only in an advisory capacity.[4] The basic unit was the group, composed generally of ten men;[5] each group elected a delegate, whose functions were somewhat akin to those of a noncommissioned officer of the lowest rank, but without the equivalent authority. The groups formed a century that elected its own delegate, and any number of centuries made up a *columna*, or "column"[6] at whose head stood a committee of war.[7] This committee was likewise elective and was divided into various sections in accordance with the needs of the column.[8] The gradation into group and century delegates and a committee of war did not imply the existence of any permanent staff with special privileges since all delegates could be removed as soon as they failed to reflect the wishes of the men who had elected them.[9] "The first impression one gets," ran a CNT-FAI account, "is the total absence of hierarchy. . . . There is no one giving orders by authority."[10] Nevertheless, duties had to be assigned, and in such a way as to avoid friction. In the anarchist Iron Column, for example, lots were drawn by the militiamen to decide who should stand guard at night and who in the early morning.[11]

But so serious were the drawbacks of this antiauthoritarian system, particularly in the field of battle, that a widespread call for discipline soon arose. "On repeated occasions we have stated that we do not believe in the discipline of the convent or of the barracks," declared *Solidaridad Obrera*, "but that in actions in which a large number of persons participate a precise coincidence of views and a perfect coordination of effort are indispensable.

"In the course of the last few days we have witnessed certain things that have broken our hearts and made us somewhat pessimistic. Our comrades act independently and in a great number of cases ignore the slogans issued by the [directing] committees [of the CNT].

"The Revolution will escape from our hands; we shall be massacred from lack of coordination if we do not make up our minds to give the word discipline its real meaning.

"To accept discipline means that the decisions made by comrades assigned to any particular task, whether administrative or military, should be executed without any obstruction in the name of liberty, a liberty that in many cases degenerates into wantonness."[12]

Gaston Leval, the well-known anarchist writer, maintained that it was incongruous to try to wage war on the basis of anarchist ideas because "war and anarchism are two conditions of humanity that are mutually repugnant; one is destruction and extermination, the other is creation and harmony; one implies the triumph of violence, the other the triumph of love." There were in the rear, he said, a large number of comrades who at first had rejected discipline altogether and then had accepted self-discipline, but "if self-discipline results in an effectual collective discipline in a particular column, this does not justify dangerous generalizations, because this is not the case in the majority of militia forces, and, to avoid disasters, a discipline imposed from without is essential."[13] The following anecdote appeared in an anarchosyndicalist refugee periodical about Buenaventura Durruti, the most revered of anarchist leaders during the Civil War, who was killed on the Madrid front in October 1936 and was regarded as a purist in matters of doctrine. A group of young militiamen belonging to the column he commanded had left the Aragon front in panic with the object of returning to Barcelona. Apprised of their intention, Durruti hastened to intercept them: "Springing out of his car, and brandishing his revolver, he cowed them and made them face the wall. Meanwhile, a militiaman from the locality arrived on the scene and asked him for a pair of shoes, to which he replied vigorously, 'Look at the shoes these fellows are wearing; if they are all right you can have the pair you like. There's no need for the shoes to rot in the soil!' It was very far from Durruti's mind to shoot those youngsters because he was accustomed to say: 'Here no one is under compulsion. Those who are afraid to remain at the front can return to the rear.' But he was so convincing that all of them asked to return to the front, where they fought with unexampled heroism."[14]

In spite of the persuasiveness of the CNT's widespread call for discipline, it was no easy task to secure the acceptance of ideas that slashed at the roots of anarchist doctrine, and not a little ingenuity was at times necessary. In an article that appeared in the organ of the peninsular committee of the FAI, a leading anarchist argued: "If the war is being prolonged, this is due not only to the material help the rebels receive from the fascist countries, but also to the lack of cohesion, discipline, and obedience of our militia. Some comrades will object, 'We anarchists cannot accept the command of anyone.' To these we should reply that anarchists also cannot accept any declaration of war, yet we have all accepted the declaration of war against fascism because it is a question of life and death and involves the triumph of the proletarian revolution.

"If we accept war, we must also accept discipline and authority because without them it is impossible to win any war." Then, criticizing a statement made by a delegate at a recent FAI congress to the effect that anarchists had always been enemies of discipline and that they should so continue, he said: "The Tarragona delegate starts from a fundamental error. We anarchists have encouraged indiscipline against the institution and power of the bourgeoisie, not against our own movement nor against our own cause and our own interests. To lack discipline where the general interests of our antifascist movement are concerned is to condemn ourselves wittingly to failure and defeat."[15]

On static fronts the idea of obligatory discipline was slow in taking root among the CNT-FAI militia. But on the fluid central front, where the advantages of General Franco's superior military organization were presented in dramatic terms, the breakdown of traditional anarchist principles had gone so far by the beginning of October that the CNT defense committee of Madrid, which was in charge of the Madrid CNT-FAI militia, was able to introduce regulations that included the following articles: "Every militiaman shall fulfill the regulations issued by battalion committees and century and group delegates.

"He shall not act on his own account in matters of war and will accept without discussion any post and any place to which he is assigned, both at the front and in the rear.

"Any militiaman not obeying the regulations issued by battalion committees and century and group delegates will be punished by his group, if the offense is slight, and by the battalion committee, if the offense is serious.

"Every militiaman must understand that, although he joined the militia voluntarily, he now forms part of it as a soldier of the Revolution and that his duty is to take orders and to execute them."[16]

Although many libertarians yielded to the idea of discipline as "one of the great sacrifices that the victory of redemptive ideals imposes,"[17] others saw in the acceptance of the concept of authority by the libertarian movement a blow so deadly to anarchist principles, a threat so real to the future course of the Revolution, that they could not conceal their anxiety. "We know," stated a propaganda committee of the anarchist youth movement, "that present circumstances have compelled us, for the time being, to forget some of our dearest principles . . . but do not let us forget that the basic tenet of anarchism is antiauthoritarianism, and that if we sail along with the authoritarian current by which some comrades have already been carried away nothing will remain of anarchist ideas. Let us remember that other revolutions were arrested in their ascending movement and were brought to disaster when they were warped by the authoritarian disease that every revolution breeds. . . . No, comrades, for the sake of the ideals that animate us all, for the sake of the Revolution, the anarchist youth begs of you not to follow this path. The authoritarian germ will lead to hatred, and we must not forget that hatred in our midst is the worst enemy of the Revolution."[18]

20. The Fifth Regiment

For the Marxist organizations, particularly for the Communist party, whose members were indoctrinated with the principles of leadership and control, the problem of military discipline caused no heart searching. This is not to suggest that indiscipline did not exist in the ranks of the Communist militia;[1] rather, no conscientious scruples had to be overcome, no ethical principles had to be laid aside, as in the case of the anarchosyndicalists, before the problem could be solved. The Civil War had been in progress but a few days when *Mundo Obrero*, the Communist organ, affirmed that every militiaman should get used to the idea that he belonged to a militarized corps. "Discipline, Hierarchy, and Organization," it demanded. "Every man must obey his group, each group the body directly above it, and so on and so forth. In this way our victory will be assured."[2] The Communists saw in military discipline and organization the central problem of the war. They lost no time in vesting the commanders of their militia with adequate powers to enforce discipline, and they undertook, through their Fifth Regiment, the training of military cadres and the formation of units with technical staffs and specialized departments.

The Fifth Regiment was their outstanding military achievement. "We had to create an army and staff at once, for most of the armed forces were with the rebels," the Italian Communist and chief political commissar of the regiment, Vittorio Vidali[3]—known in Spain as Carlos Contreras or Comandante Carlos—told a foreign reporter.

We had at first just groups of comrades, old and young, men and women, many of whom did not even know how to use a rifle. . . . We had only enthusiastic, determined people, seizing any weapons they could find, following any leaders that arose, rushing to any front which they heard it was necessary to seize from the enemy.

In those days we took anyone who knew anything and made him an officer. Sometimes it was enough just to look into a face and see that the eyes were intelligent and determined, and say to the man: "You are a captain. Organize and lead these men."

After two days we occupied the Salesian Convent—six hundred of us, of whom two hundred were communists. We decided to organize and the war department said: "You will be the Fifth Battalion; already we have four other applications."

"No," we said, "we shall be the Fifth Regiment, for we shall get at least a thousand men."

Well, those first four battalions remained on paper, but the fifth had six thousand men in less than ten days. During this time the [Giral] government wrote us: "Comrades of the Fifth Battalion," and we answered back: "We of the Fifth Regiment." After we got six thousand men they admitted that we were a regiment. . . .

We decided to create a special company which should give an example of discipline. We called it the "Steel Company." . . . For this company we established special slogans designed to create an iron unity. "Never leave a comrade wounded or dead, in the hands of the enemy," was one of these. "If my comrade advances or retreats without orders, I have the right to shoot him" was another.

How Madrid laughed at that. The Spaniard is such an individualist that nobody will accept such discipline, they said. Then our first Steel Company —mostly communists and metalworkers—paraded through the city; it made a sensation.[4] After that we created twenty-eight such companies of picked men, besides the ordinary muster of our regular Fifth Regiment militia.[5]

So successful was the Fifth Regiment in its recruiting of Communists, Socialists, and republicans and of nonparty workers and peasants that at the peak of its development in December 1936 it claimed that it had sixty thousand men serving on different fronts.[6] Although Enrique Líster, who became commander in chief of the regiment in September 1936, claimed during the war that it comprised 130,000 men,[7] his book, published many years after the war, names the more sober figure of 69,600.[8] On the other hand, Ramón Salas Larrazábal, who although a supporter of the right has produced in his four-volume history of the Popular Army by far the most objective study of this subject, claims that the total number of men enrolled in the regiment including the units trained in its induction and training centers in Albacete, Alicante, Almeria, and Guadix, as well as in Madrid, never exceeded 30,000. "To reach the figure of 60,000 claimed by the Communists," he affirms, "it would be necessary to include in the Fifth Regiment the International Brigades, which initially used the seal of the regiment's headquarters."[9]

According to Enrique Castro, the first commander in chief of the Fifth Regiment, it quickly became metamorphosed into "a great center of political and military education."[10] Out of this center, which supervised every aspect of the volunteers' lives, political and spiritual, as well as economic and domestic, there flowed a large number of units possessing uniformity of method and organization. "They were parts of a building set," wrote one authority, "which could be rebuilt into an army when the time came. Their officers had precise rank and their orders received the backing of a disciplinary code which the volunteers accepted on enlistment. At the same time the political enthusiasm of the combatants was watched over and fostered by the political commissars."[11]

One of the great assets of the Fifth Regiment was the collaboration not only of professional military men who had been Communist party members before the war—such as Lieutenant Colonel Luis Barceló, a commander of the regiment,[12] and head of the Inspección General de Milicias, the Office of the Inspector General of Militias, to which the militia units were required to apply for whatever arms and funds they needed from the war ministry[13]—but also of other professional officers, who, though far removed from Communist ideology, were attracted to the party because of its moderate propaganda,[14] superior discipline, and organization and because it alone seemed capable of building an army that could carry the war through to victory.

In the prevailing wartime atmosphere, the discipline of the Communist party was undoubtedly one of its principal assets:

"The Communist party must be granted the credit of having set the example in accepting discipline," wrote a non-Communist professional officer. "By doing so it enormously increased not only its prestige, but its numbers. Innumerable men who wished to enlist and fight for their country joined the Communist party.

"It often happened that, when I came across a man who was just leaving for the front, I asked him:

"'But why did you join the Communist party? You were never a Communist, were you? You were always a republican.'

"'I joined the Communists because they are disciplined and do their job better than anybody else,' was the answer."[15]

The party's discipline and the adherence of professional officers, as well as the collaboration of the foreign Communists with military experience, who were associated with the regiment for varying periods before helping to organize the International Brigades, were advantages.[16] Most important was the preferential treatment the regiment received, as compared with other units, in the distribution of Soviet arms. Referring to the light arms that began to arrive in September, Segismundo Casado, who was operations chief on the war ministry general staff when Largo Caballero became minister of war, writes: "I noticed that these were not being given out in equal quantities, but that there was a marked preference for the units which made up the so-called Fifth Regiment."[17] Enrique Líster, the commander of the regiment, boasted in January 1937, at the time of its dissolution and fusion into the regular army, that it had thousands of machine guns and hundreds of pieces of artillery.[18] Although these figures were undoubtedly inflated for wartime propaganda purposes—to judge from the incomparably smaller number of machine guns estimated by Líster himself thirty years later[19]—it is nevertheless true, as Ralph Bates, assistant commissar of the Fifteenth International Brigade, stated, that the units of the Fifth Regiment received "the cream of the weapons."[20] Because of this preferential treatment, the opportunity given to a large number of men of the regiment to train in Russia as tank operators,[21] and the attraction of the Communists' efficiency, the regiment was able to recruit heavily from non-Communist sources.

The influx of many Socialists and republicans would appear to support the Communists' contention that the Fifth Regiment was not a Communist force but a force that belonged to the Popular Front as a whole. "The story has been spread by interested persons that the Fifth Regiment was the military organization of the Communist party, a military force of the party," wrote its commander in chief. "No, the fact that a large number of the officers were Communists does not mean that the Fifth Regiment was an auxiliary of the Communist party, and anyone affirming this would be departing from historical truth. The Fifth Regiment was this: the military organization of the Popular Front. Its political composition was as follows: Communists 50 percent; Socialists 25 percent; republicans 15 percent; without party affiliation 10 percent."[22]

Nevertheless, as the Communist *International Press Correspondence* attested: "From the beginning the Fifth Regiment was recruited and politically influenced by the Communist party."[23] In truth, it was under the rigid and all-embracing control of the party and was to all intents and purposes the principal element of its armed power during the first six months of the Civil War.

21. The Communists and the Popular Army; Soviet Officers and Civilians and the NKVD

Important though the Fifth Regiment was to the Communist party as an element of armed power, there were potent political as well as military reasons why the Communists soon proposed that the independent party and trade-union militia should be incorporated into a government-controlled force. They knew that the war could not be carried through to victory without a single command that could decide on the disposition and manner of employment of all the fighting forces—in default of which there could be neither an organized army nor any planned strategy. They knew, too, that as long as the parties and labor unions possessed their own militia under the control of their own leaders and these forces were not fused into a regular army consolidated by the power of discipline and authority—an army of whose levers of command they aimed to secure control—they could never be the ruling force in the anti-Franco zone, determining, behind the curtain of democratic institutions, domestic and foreign policies.

During the life of the Giral cabinet, it will be recalled, the Communists had refrained from calling for the merging of the militia into a government-controlled army because of the Caballero Socialists' distrust of that cabinet's intentions,[1] but once Largo Caballero himself was at the helm and in charge of the war ministry, they could do so without equivocation.[2] Indeed, the insistence of the two Communist ministers and the Soviet military advisers who, in urging their demands, made full use of the succession of defeats on the central front —highlighted on 27 September by the capture of Toledo, fifty-one miles from the capital—caused measures to be promulgated providing for the militarization of the militia and the creation of a military force, or Popular Army, as it was called, on a conscripted basis and under the supreme command of the war minister.[3] "Largo Caballero," writes Louis Fischer, whose personal contact with most of the leading

Revolutionary Militia to Regular Army

Russians in Spain gives his testimony particular authority, "long resisted the idea of a regular army, and it was only with difficulty that his Soviet military advisers persuaded him to abandon the popular but inefficient form of party armies."[4] But it was a long way, as events will show, from the publication of the military measures approved by Largo Caballero to their thoroughgoing execution, and, in succeeding months, the Communists, in barracks and trenches, in public harangues, and in the cabinet itself, pressed unremittingly for their enforcement.[5]

To set an example, the Communist party progressively broke up its own militia, the Fifth Regiment,[6] whose battalions, together with other forces, were welded into the "mixed brigades"[7] of the embryonic regular army. The Communist Enrique Líster, head of the regiment at the time, was made commander (with a Soviet officer at his side)[8] of the First Brigade.[9] Because they took the lead in disbanding their own militia, the Communists, according to Carlos Contreras, the regiment's chief political commissar,[10] secured for themselves the control of five of the first six brigades, the majority of whose members had received their baptism of fire with the regiment.[11] Enrique Castro stated some years later that, in addition to Enrique Líster of the First Brigade, José María Galán, commander of the Third, and Miguel Gallo, commander of the Sixth (not to be confused with Luigi Gallo, or Longo, of the International Brigades) were party members, and that José Martínez de Aragón and Arturo Arellano, commanders of the Second and Fourth Brigades respectively were Socialists with close ties to the Communist party. Fernando Sabio, the commander of the Fifth Brigade, was described by Castro as a Socialist, but he did not indicate to what degree, if at all, he was under the influence of the Communist party.[12] Líster gives the names of the five other commanders, but does not mention their political affiliation, except that of Martínez de Aragón, whom he describes simply as a "republican." He points out, however, that all were professional officers who had served either with the army or with the *carabineros* before the war.[13]

While they were thus gathering into their hands the control of the first units of the Popular Army, the Communists were not neglecting its commanding summits. Indeed, during the early weeks of Largo Caballero's tenure of the war ministry, they had already secured a promising foothold. This they were able to do partly because their relations with the war minister, notwithstanding his many grievances, were still of a tolerable nature (as a result, two of their adherents, Antonio Cordón and Alejandro García Val, were appointed to the operations section of the general staff[14]), but mainly because in key positions in the war ministry they possessed men of supposedly unquestioned loyalty to Largo Caballero. These included such professional officers as Lieutenant Colonel Manuel Arredondo, his aide-de-camp, Captain Eleuterio Díaz Tendero, the head of the vital information and control department[15]—who in the months before the Civil War was the principal organizer of the UMRA, the left-wing Unión Militar Republicana Antifascista, which the Communists claim was an amplification of their Unión Militar Antifascista formed in 1934[16]—and Major Manuel Estrada, the chief of the war ministry general staff,[17] who, unknown to Largo Caballero, were being drawn or had already been drawn into the Communist orbit.[18]

By the same open and disguised occupation of directing posts, the Communists became firmly embedded in the vital general commissariat of war, set up for the purpose of exercising politicosocial control over the armed forces through the medium of political commissars or delegate commissars, as they were officially called.[19] The custom of installing commissars in the militia units had been adopted by the different parties and labor organizations at the outbreak of the Civil War with the object of keeping a constant vigil over the morale of the militiamen and the reliability of the professional officers. "Many of the militia battalions," attests Lieutenant Colonel Esteban Rovira, chief of the Forty-second Brigade, "were led by commanders who, conniving with the enemy, deserted at the first opportunity. This resulted in a natural distrust on the part of the men for their officers and made it necessary for them to have their own delegate in the military command in order to guarantee the loyal conduct of the officers. These delegates were the first political commissars."[20] In October 1936, in accordance with the general tendency toward centralization, a government body was created to regularize this practice. While the commissar was still expected to guard against disloyalty on the part of professional officers,[21] he was also expected to establish concord between the officers and men of the new regular army and to uphold the former's prestige and authority.[22] In addition to these duties and to the tasks of enforcing discipline[23] and watching over the morale of the soldiers,[24] the commissar had other responsibilities. "The commissar is the soul of the combat unit, its educator, its agitator, its propagandist," said Carlos Contreras. "He is always, or should be always, the best, the most intelligent, the most capable. He should occupy himself with everything and know about everything. He should interest himself in the stomach, in the heart, and in the brain of the soldier of the people. He should accompany him from the moment he enlists and receives his training until he leaves for the front and returns from it; he should interest himself in how he eats, how he sleeps, how he educates himself, and how he fights. He must see that his political, economic, cultural, and artistic needs are satisfied."[25] To be sure, not all commissars conducted themselves as they were expected to. "There are political commissars," affirmed Contreras, "who do not maintain close contact with the mass of the soldiers, who are not with them in the trenches, and who only want to be near the commanding officer."[26]

Because of the influence the commissar could exert upon the ranks, to say nothing of the opportunity his position gave him to sway the minds and hearts of the officers—he should engage in "political agitation among the officers and infuse them with the same spirit that animates the men," said the Communist leader Antonio Mije, a member of the politburo[27]—it is not strange that predominance in the commissariat of war was for the Communist party a vital factor in its bid for control of the regular army. It was well assured of this predominance to some extent because Mije occupied the subcommissariat of organization—the most important of the four subcommissariats created[28]—but principally because Felipe Pretel, the secretary general, and Julio Alvarez del Vayo, the commissar general, both of whom Largo Caballero had nominated because they possessed his unstinted confidence, secretly promoted the interests of the Communist party.[29] Before long, the party increased its influence still further owing to the appointment of José Laín, a JSU leader and recent Communist convert, as director of the school of commissars[30] and to the illness of Angel Pestaña, the leader of the Syndicalist party,[31] who had occupied one of the four subcommissariats and who was replaced by Gabriel García Maroto, a friend of Alvarez del Vayo's and a left-wing Socialist with pronounced Communist leanings, although critical of some of the party's methods. As Largo Caballero was not apprised until some months later of the defection of Alvarez del Vayo and Felipe Pretel and of the consequent extent of Communist penetration of the commissariat of war,[32] the Communist party and its allies were able to exploit their privileged position without hindrance by appointing an overwhelmingly large number of Communist commissars at the expense of and to the extreme displeasure of other organizations. For example, Gabriel García Maroto stated that, at the beginning of 1937, on the central front, Socialist battalions frequently complained to him that Communist commissars had been appointed to them and that they found this intolerable. He also said that Alberto Fernández Ballesteros, a Caballero Socialist, who held the position of inspector-commissar on the southern front, had protested that Antonio Mije, in appointing thirty commissars for that front, had selected only Communists.[33]

Because of the Communist party's control of the commissariat of war, such complaints could not reach Largo Caballero through the commissariat itself and did so, eventually, only through independent channels.[34]

Since the precise functions and powers of the political commissar were not strictly delimited by law, he possessed a broad measure of independence, which the Communist commissar—who was instructed to be "the organizer of the party in his unit, boldly and systematically recruiting the best elements from among the best fighters and recommending them for positions of responsibility"[35]—used to the full in helping to extend his party's dominion over the armed forces. Even before the creation of the general commissariat of war, the Communists had not neglected party activity at the front. "Teams of agitators must be created to inform militiamen of the attitude of the party with regard to all problems. . . . The Communists should take upon themselves the task of recruiting for the party the best fighters at the front."[36]

Jesús Hernández, Communist minister in the Largo Caballero government, declared, in a speech delivered some years later, after he had ceased to belong to the party:

Dozens, hundreds of party and JSU "organizers" invaded the fronts and military units, and our officers were given categoric instructions to promote the maximum number of Communists to higher ranks, thus reducing the proportion of promotions open to members of other organizations. But it is my duty to state that while this reckless policy was being carried out the Communists did not cease fighting the enemy, and their resolution and discipline at the fronts showed them to be better than the best, a fact that facilitated the proselytizing work we had undertaken. . . . The zeal of some Communist officers and commissars was so unbridled and so undiplomatic that it went to the unspeakable extreme of removing officers and of sending men to the front line for refusing to become members of the Communist party or of the JSU.

By this procedure the strength of the party was "reinforced" at the fronts by thousands of new adherents, but at the same time . . . the party destroyed unity, spread discord, and inflamed rivalry among military units of a different political complexion.

That was the practical result of the policy we were ordered to carry out and were stupid enough to follow.[37]

Revolutionary Militia to Regular Army

Indalecio Prieto, the moderate Socialist leader, alleges that the Communists actually assassinated at the front Socialists who refused to join their party.[38] And Jesús Pérez Salas, a professional officer and a loyal republican writes: "In accordance with their usual tactics and with the slogans they received, the Communist commissars, who formed the majority, endeavored to increase their party membership by ceaseless propaganda among the men in their units who did not share their ideas. They employed every means at their disposal, from the promise of future promotions to the threat of execution for offenses that had not been committed. This could not be viewed favorably by the other parties, inasmuch as they observed a continual reduction in the number of their members, who were compelled to change their party cards in order to avoid victimization. As a result of all this, a contest ensued between commissars representing different political views, with consequent prejudice to the armed forces."[39]

The atmosphere created by the conduct of the Communist political commissars was certainly the very opposite from what Largo Caballero had hoped would be encouraged when the commissariat of war was formed. "When at the battle fronts or in the barracks and other places where the troops are billeted," ran a circular order signed by him, "disagreements or conflicts arise between soldiers or militiamen belonging to different trade-union organizations, delegate commissars shall act with perfect equanimity and in such a way that brotherly acts shall efface all divergences of opinion between the combatants as well as all selfish aims of individuals or groups."[40]

In addition to the work of the Communist political commissars and officers and to the help of crypto-Communists and philo-Communist Socialists in promoting the influence of the party in the armed forces, yet another factor of greater consequence militated in its favor: this was the arrival, first of Soviet officers, then of Soviet arms.

"Shortly after [Largo Caballero's] government had been formed in September 1936," writes Luis Araquistáin, friend and political associate of the premier for many years, "the Russian ambassador presented to it a serving Soviet general [Vladimir Gorev], stating that he was military attaché of the embassy and offering his professional services. Later on fresh 'auxiliaries' sprang up spontaneously without being requested, and they introduced themselves *motu proprio* into the military staff and army corps, where they gave orders at will."[41] It would be incorrect, however, to infer that the principal Soviet military advisers arrived in Spain without the approval or at least the knowledge of the war minister. In point of fact—to judge from the exchange of letters between Soviet leaders and Largo Caballero, referred to later in this chapter—the war minister himself, through the Soviet ambassador, Marcel Rosenberg, actually requested the aid of Russian military advisers. On the other hand, it appears that not infrequently they acted on their own accord without the consent of the war ministry, disregarding its views and conducting themselves independently and highhandedly. Colonel Segismundo Casado, the chief of operations on the war ministry general staff and an opponent of the Communists, affirms that "their influence reached such a point as to control every project of the general staff and often entirely to reverse technical plans, replacing them with their own. These generally contained some political end; in questions of organization, appointing commanders; in news, in making propaganda in a party sense; in operations, putting on one side incontrovertible tactical and strategical considerations in order to impose their policy."[42] And the war minister himself testifies: "The Spanish government, and in particular the minister responsible for the conduct of operations, as well as the commanding officers, especially at headquarters, were not able to act with absolute independence because they were obliged to submit, against their will, to irresponsible foreign interference, without being able to free themselves from it under pain of endangering the assistance that we were receiving from Russia through the sale of war material. Sometimes, on the pretext that their orders were not being carried out as punctually as they desired, the Russian embassy and the Russian generals took the liberty of expressing to me their displeasure, stating that if we did not consider their cooperation necessary and fitting, we should tell them so plainly so that they could inform their government and take their departure."[43] On the other hand, General Vicente Rojo, chief of the central general staff from May 1937 to the end of the war, who enjoyed the support of the Communists throughout the conflict, later vehemently asserted that such charges were "false, absolutely false," and that the directives for planning operations and the orders to execute them were *always* conceived and drafted by the chiefs of the republican general staff."[44]

The behavior of the Russian civilians, to say nothing of the NKVD, was no less imperious than that of the military, if I may generalize from my own personal knowledge of Mirova, the Tass news agency representative in Valencia, and from the conduct of the Soviet ambassador—dealt with later in this chapter—as well as from that of Mikhail Koltzov, leading Soviet newspaper correspondent, who was influential in the Kremlin. Toward the end of 1936, Koltzov established himself in the Madrid commissariat of war, where, according to the Socialist Arturo Barea, then in charge of censoring the reports of foreign newsmen—a function that Koltzov placed arbitrarily under the control of the commissariat—he "intervened in most of the discussions on the authority of his vitality and arrogant will."[45]

In his last work on Spain, *Half of Spain Died*, to which reference has been made on several occasions,[46] Herbert Matthews, the *New York Times* correspondent during the Civil War and widely accepted authority on Spain for four decades, deliberately ignores the above-quoted testimony of Largo Caballero that appeared in my book *The Grand Camouflage*[47] and asserts: "Burnett Bolloten wrote of 'the minatory and imperious behavior of the Russian officers' and even of civilians like Mikhail Koltzov, the *Pravda* correspondent, who seemed to have the equivalent of a 'hot line' to Stalin. If so, this was behind the scenes and it never reached the stage of being high-handed with men like premiers Largo Caballero and Juan Negrín."[48] Matthews also ignored the fact that on one memorable occasion, mentioned in *The Grand Camouflage* and later in this volume, Largo Caballero, incensed by the Soviet ambassador's demands, expelled him from his office.[49]

There can be no doubt that the minatory and imperious behavior of the Russian officers accelerated the deterioration of Largo Caballero's relations with the Communists that had already set in as a result of their absorption of the Socialist movement in Catalonia, of the JSU, and of many of his followers in the UGT and the Socialist party.[50] While, for a time, these relations showed no manifest impairment, a significant crack in the smooth surface appeared when he appointed General José Asensio to the undersecretaryship of war on 22 October 1936.

As a commander during the first weeks of the war of the militia forces in the Sierra de Guadarrama, defending the northwestern approaches to Madrid, Asensio, at that time a colonel, had so inspired the confidence of the Socialist leader that when Largo Caballero became premier and war minister in September, he had made him a general and placed him in charge of the threatened central front in command of the Army of the Center. The Communists, who had already been striving to win Asensio's adherence to their party, acclaimed his promotion and new assignment, praised the military accomplishments of "this hero of the democratic Republic"[51] under whose direction their steel companies in the Sierra had "won victory after victory,"[52] and made him an honorary commander of their Fifth Regiment.[53] All these attentions, a prominent Communist acknowledged later, were designed to wean Asensio from Largo Caballero.[54] In the succeeding weeks, when Asensio showed no inclination to follow the trajectory of other professional military men who had yielded to the courtship of the Communists, and even evinced for them a profound antipathy, they demanded his removal from the command of the central front.[55]

The tactics the Communists employed toward Asensio were their standard practice. Colonel Segismundo Casado writes:

I may as well point out here what tactics the Communist party usually followed in their relationships with the commanders of the People's Army. They treated as subordinate those commanders who were affiliated to their party, demanding simply that their orders should be carried out in whatever way best served their party ends, often in contradiction to their duty as soldiers. These officers generally obeyed blindly, paying more attention to the orders of the party than to those of the military high command. Other commanders on many occasions opposed their plans and rejected suggestions which sounded more like orders, or refused to take part in activities which would not have left them with a clear conscience. [The Communists] pretended to show the greatest consideration to those, but only for a short time, and in a wholly superficial way. They asked them to dine, they told them of the great admiration they had for them, for their intelligence or bravery. In a word, they attempted to stir their private ambitions, but when they were convinced that it was not possible to captivate them by such means, they started an insidious campaign of libel against them, so that the high command was obliged to relieve them. More than one commander lost his life or his freedom through simply doing his duty.[56]

"The commander who accepted Communist party membership without hesitation," wrote the organ of the moderate Socialists as the war was nearing its end, "soon acquired, in the Communist press, military qualities superior to those of Napoleon and Alexander, while those who dared to reject a membership that they had not requested were obliquely or openly criticized."[57]

The Communists' demand that Asensio be ousted from the command of the central front was aided by the military disasters that brought General Franco's forces close to the gates of Madrid during the month of October 1936. Yet, in spite of these defeats, the more balanced appraisals of Asensio concur in the view that he possessed great military capabilities and exceptional mental gifts[58] and that the debacle was inevitable in view of the defects of the militia system and the lack of tanks, artillery, and aircraft.[59] These, it is true, did not arrive from Russia until the end of October, while the International Brigades under Communist leadership that were to play a cardinal role in the defense of Madrid entered the field only in the second week of November, as will be seen later in the chapter.

Alvarez del Vayo, the pro-Communist foreign minister and commissar general of war, approved the rough draft of a letter written by Louis Fischer to Largo Caballero on 11 October questioning the loyalty of Asensio,[60] at the very time when the Communists were demanding his removal from the central front, and later voted in the cabinet for his dismissal from the undersecretaryship of war.[61] But he contends that Asensio was "unquestionably one of the most capable and intelligent officers in the Republican army" and that he could "have become the greatest military genius."[62] It is noteworthy that the day before he approved Fischer's letter to Largo Caballero, Alvarez del Vayo had written the following lines in a note to Asensio: "I am aware of the very important operation due to begin at dawn. To know that you will be there personally directing it adds very much to my hopes. Owing to recent bitter experiences, we can only trust in your skill. For that reason I have decided to send you these intimate lines, which under all circumstances should remain between us."[63]

Although for a time Largo Caballero refused to remove Asensio, he finally yielded. But while propitiating the Communists with one hand, he diminished their victory with the other by elevating him to the undersecretaryship of war.[64] His determination to pursue an independent course found practical expression in two further moves. He reinstated Segismundo Casado, whom he had dismissed from his post as chief of operations at the pressing instance of the Communists. Casado attributes his dismissal to the fact that he had warned the high command that the marked preference with which Russian arms were being distributed to the Fifth Regiment would cause suspicion and jealousy among the men and would soon bring about the accession to power of the Communist party. "This party," he adds, "observing what my opinion was, with the underhandedness which characterized it, started a campaign of discredit against me and convinced the minister of war that I was not the most suitable person to fill the office of operations chief because I had the faults of violence and pessimism."[65]

In addition to defying the Communists by reinstating Segismundo Casado, Largo Caballero removed Manuel Estrada, the chief of the war ministry general staff—who had recently joined the Communist party[66]—and replaced him by General Toribio Martínez Cabrera, a friend of Asensio's. In the whirl of events, these shifts passed almost unnoticed by the general public, but they gave the Communists cause for disquiet and convinced them of the rough weather ahead with Largo Caballero.

But while strengthening Largo Caballero's authority within the war ministry, the shifts did nothing in the long run to curtail the influence of the Communists on the vital central front. General Sebastián Pozas, whom Largo Caballero appointed to succeed Asensio as commander of the Army of the Center, soon succumbed to their advances, as will be seen shortly, and on the evening of 6 November, with the enemy already in the outskirts of the capital, the cabinet hastily abandoned the imperiled city.

That same evening Mikhail Koltzov visited the deserted ministries. In his diary,[67] he noted:

I made my way to the war ministry, to the [general] commissariat of war. . . . Hardly anyone was there. . . . I went to the offices of the prime minister. The building was locked. I went to the ministry of foreign affairs. It was deserted. . . . In the foreign press censorship an official . . . told me that the government, two hours earlier, had recognized that the situation of Madrid was hopeless . . . and had already left. Largo Caballero had forbidden the publication of any news about the evacuation "in order to avoid panic." . . . I went to the ministry of the interior . . . The building was nearly empty. . . . I went to the central committee of the Communist party. A plenary meeting of the politburo was being held. . . . They told me that this very day Largo Caballero had suddenly decided to evacuate. His decision had been approved by the majority of the cabinet. . . . The Communist ministers wanted to remain, but it was made clear to them that such a step would discredit the government and that they were obliged to leave like all the others. . . . Not even the most prominent leaders of the various organizations, nor the departments and agencies of the state, had been informed of the government's departure. Only at the last moment had the minister told the chief of the central general staff that the government was leaving. . . . The minister of the interior, Galarza, and his aide, the director of security Muñoz, had left the capital before anyone else. . . . The staff of General Pozas, the commander of the central front, had scurried off. . . . Once again I went to the war ministry. . . . I climbed the stairs to the lobby. Not a soul! On the landing . . . two old employees are seated, like wax figures, wearing livery and neatly shaven . . . , waiting to be called by the minister at the sound of his bell. It would be just the same if the minister were the previous one or a new one. Rows of offices! All the doors are wide open. . . . I enter the war minister's office. . . . Not a soul! Further down, a row of offices—the central general staff, with its sections; the general staff, with its sections; the general staff of the central front, with its sections; the quartermaster corps, with its sections; the personnel department, with its sections. All the doors wide open. The ceiling lamps shine brightly. On the desks there are abandoned maps, documents, communiqués, pencils, pads filled with notes. Not a soul![68]

There can be little doubt that the government's precipitate and furtive departure—a departure that both Indalecio Prieto and the Communist ministers had urged the premier to organize and publicize ahead of time so as to avoid the "impression of a flight"[69]—did much to tarnish Caballero's reputation and to enhance the prestige of the Communist party. The latter, aided by its Fifth Regiment, by the presence of Soviet arms and military advisers, and by the arrival on 8 November of the Communist-controlled Eleventh International Brigade, the first of the International Brigades to enter the field, took the lead in defending the beleaguered city.

On the morning of 7 November, while the machinery of government, with its functionaries and files, was still en route to Valencia, *Mundo Obrero*, the Madrid Communist daily, declared: "[Thousands] upon thousands of men, of workers, whose future depends upon their courage, have rushed to the city's defense. The [locals of the] labor unions and of all the antifascist and working-class organizations are crammed with men ready to fight."[70] And the organ of the Communist Fifth Regiment declared: "The fate of Madrid will be determined in a matter of hours. Thousands of militiamen are fighting the Moors and Foreign Legionaries, whose aim is to crush the people of Madrid. This is the historic hour, the hour of the decisive battle. It has been said again and again for many days that Madrid will be the tomb of fascism, and now the moment has arrived to turn those words into a reality. . . . The guns are thundering at our gates. Every Madrileño should be on his feet, ready to win, regardless of the price."[71]

Before leaving for Valencia on the evening of 6 November, General Asensio, the undersecretary of war, had handed sealed orders, approved by Largo Caballero, to General Pozas, the commander of the Army of the Center, and to General José Miaja, who had just been appointed commander of the Madrid military district, inscribed: "Very confidential. Not to be opened until 6 A.M." Both generals decided not to wait until the designated hour to read their instructions. Had they done so, they contended, twelve precious hours would have been wasted.[72] Moreover, on opening their envelopes they found that they had been addressed incorrectly and that each had been given the other's assignment, a mistake that, in the opinion of Major Vicente Rojo, Miaja's chief of staff, might have "multiplied the probabilities of defeat," had it not been discovered in time.[73]

Pozas was given orders regarding the tactical movement of his battered forces and the establishment of new headquarters,[74] while Miaja was instructed to set up a Junta de Defensa or Defense Council, with

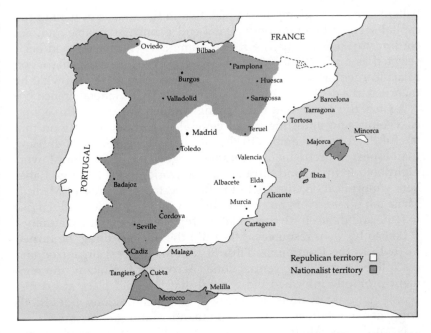

FRANCE

Oviedo · Bilbao

· Pamplona

· Burgos · Huesca

· Valladolid · Saragossa · Barcelona

Tarragona

Tortosa

· Madrid · Teruel · Minorca

· Toledo · Majorca

PORTUGAL · Valencia

· Ibiza

Badajoz · Albacete · Elda

· Murcia · Alicante

· Cordova

· Seville · Cartagena

· Cadiz · Malaga

Republican territory ☐

Nationalist territory ■

Tangiers · Cueta

· Melilla

Morocco

Division of Spain, 7 November 1936

himself as president, comprising members of all parties in proportion to their representation in the government, and to defend Madrid "at all costs." If all efforts to save the city should fail he was to retreat toward Cuenca "to establish a line of defense at a place indicated by [General Pozas], the commander of the Army of the Center."[75]

"No one in the government," affirmed Zugazagoitia, the director of *El Socialista* and a close associate of navy and air minister Indalecio Prieto, "believed that Madrid could be defended, the prime minister even less than the ministers, for he was only too well aware of the state of military confusion and disintegration. . . ."[76] Reluctantly, the war minister left Madrid convinced like Prieto that within three to six days it would be taken by the enemy."[77]

The battlefront was virtually nonexistent, writes Vicente Rojo, Miaja's chief of staff. "The columns that had been containing the enemy on the Toledo and Estremadura highways were destroyed. Of the 3,500 men comprising one column, barely 300 could be found."[78]

That Miaja should have resented General Asensio's and Largo Ca-

Revolutionary Militia to Regular Army

ballero's action in giving him a task that in those days of peril to the capital seemed to augur only a fatal end is understandable and, according to Zugazagoitia, he realized immediately that he had been selected as a scapegoat.[79] In fact, General Pozas asserted that when Miaja learned of his assignment he nearly wept with rage at what he regarded as a deliberate attempt to sacrifice him to General Franco.[80]

Against this background of seemingly impending doom, this aging, easygoing, and undistinguished general—to whom nothing on that fateful day of 6 November 1936 could have appeared more enticing than a peaceful retirement—became a legendary figure almost overnight both in Spain and throughout the world, much to Largo Caballero's mortification, thanks to the unexpected resistance of Madrid. Miaja felt no sense of gratitude to the war minister for his sudden rise to fame and thenceforth their relationship was one of mutual enmity.

Left to his own resources, Miaja did the obvious thing: he turned for help to the Communist Fifth Regiment, the best organized and disciplined force in the central zone. According to Koltzov, the regiment promptly informed the general that it would place at his disposal "not only its units, its reserves, and its munitions, but also its entire general staff, as well as its commanders and commissars."[81]

Nevertheless, Madrid's defenders were in the main poorly armed and organized. An account of that historic event follows:

The battle of Madrid, which began on 7 November 1936, pitted an ill-armed, unorganized but numerically far superior mass of Madrileños against an army of Moroccans and legionaries, fully trained, properly equipped and numbering roughly 20,000. The Madrileños had some Russian tanks and aircraft in support and Franco's troops were supplemented by German and Italian men and equipment. . . .

Now, as the grey, uncertain dawn broke on 7 November, the ancient city of Madrid heard the thunderous beginning of an artillery bombardment such as it had never encountered before . . . , but to everyone's surprise, as the shells burst, houses collapsed, men, women and children were buried beneath the debris and a great film of dust rose above the city like a ghost presence, there were very few scenes of real panic. The propagandists within the city had done their work well. Flaming speeches, powerfully written pamphlets, moving exhortations on the radio and a number of poems charged with stirring imagery had created an atmosphere in Madrid where heroism came naturally in the least expected person. . . . Workers of all kinds answered the radio call for recruits and moved towards the front lines, some completely unarmed but fanatically prepared to take up the arms of the killed and wounded. Women and children toiled all day building barricades and a group of women presently demanded and began to organize a women's fighting battalion. . . .

And then, on the misty morning of 8 November, a strange new band of fighters, disciplined men they seemed to the Madrileños, wearing corduroy uniforms and steel helmets, came marching, in good order, along the Gran Vía towards the front.[82]

This was the Eleventh International Brigade—the "International Column" as it was first called by the Spanish press—under the electrifying leadership of the Soviet General Emilio Kléber. Hugh Thomas writes:

By the evening of 8 November the brigade was in position. The Edgar André and the Commune de Paris battalions were sent to the Casa de Campo. The Dombrowsky battalion went to join Líster and the Fifth Regiment at Villaverde. Kléber took command of all the Republican forces in the University City and the Casa de Campo. He immediately startled the Spanish commanders with his efficiency. . . . It has often been argued that the International Brigade saved Madrid. This XIth International Brigade, however, probably comprised only about 1,900 men. The XIIth International Brigade, which eventually arrived at the Madrid front on about 12 November, comprised about 1,550. This force was too small to have turned the day by numbers alone. Furthermore, the militia and workers had checked Varela [the enemy commander] on 7 November, before the arrival of the Brigade. The victory was that of the populace of Madrid. The bravery and experience of the Brigades was, however, crucial in several later battles. The example of the International Brigades fired the militiamen to continue to resist, while giving to the Madrileños the feeling that they were not alone. . . . [On 9 November] Valera, checked in the Casa de Campo, mounted a new attack . . . in the Carabanchel sector. But the street-fighting baffled the Moroccans, who made no progress. In the Casa de Campo, Kléber assembled the whole of the International Brigade. In the misty evening they launched an attack. "For the Revolution and Liberty—forward!" Among the ilex and gum trees, the battle lasted all night and into the morning of 10 November. By then, only Mount Garabitas in the Casa de Campo was left to the Nationalists. But one third of the International Brigade was dead.[83]

Robert Colodny, in his account of this epic, is more emphatic than Thomas on the importance of the role played by the Eleventh International Brigade. "Madrid was saved," he writes, "when the three battalions of the Eleventh International Brigade, the Edgar André, the Commune de Paris and the Dombrowski, under the command of General Kléber, deployed in the Casa de Campo, and with the support of Soviet tanks and planes, halted the charge of Varela's veterans. The appearance of the foreign volunteers stiffened the resistance of the militia and won the time necessary to organize, train and equip the Republican brigades."[84]

Meanwhile, Major Vicente Rojo, whom Largo Caballero had appointed as Miaja's chief of staff just before his departure on 6 November,[85] had put together a general staff to defend Madrid, composed, in accordance with his instructions, of members of the "available personnel" of the war ministry general staff,[86] whose chief, General Toribio Martínez Cabrera, with other senior officers had, like the war minister, abandoned the capital for Valencia. According to Captain Antonio López Fernández, Miaja's aide, Rojo's staff was formed of men whom the war ministry had not deemed sufficiently important to take to Valencia, but who were "officers of the highest order who until then had vegetated, almost ignored, in posts of the lowest category in the general staff."[87] Among these neglected officers was Major Rojo himself, who, in the words of one authority, had been "widely recognized as the best military strategist in the Army."[88] According to the right-wing historian Ramón Salas Larrazábal, in his monumental four-volume study of the Popular Army, Rojo enjoyed "great prestige," was regarded as "one of the most competent members" of the Spanish army, and was "liked and esteemed by all his comrades in arms." During the war, he adds, even though he may have lost the affection of many of his comrades, "he retained the respect of all."[89]

On 10 November, the fourth day of the battle for Madrid, the ubiquitous and influential Koltzov, who was better acquainted with the military situation than any other journalist in Spain, wrote in his diary: "Miaja is very little involved in operational details; he even knows little about them. These are matters he leaves to his chief of staff and to the commanders of columns and sectors. Rojo wins the confidence of the men by his modesty, which conceals his great practical knowledge and an unusual capacity for work. This is the fourth day that he has remained bent over the map of Madrid. In an endless chain, commanders and commissars come to see him, and to all of them, in a low, calm voice, patiently, as though in a railroad information office, sometimes repeating himself twenty times, he explains, teaches, indicates, annotates papers, and frequently draws sketches."[90]

Nevertheless, it was General Miaja, the president of the Defense Council, who made the headlines. Of Vicente Rojo, his chief of staff, the press said nothing. On 20 December, Koltzov noted in his diary: "For some reason not a line about Vicente Rojo has appeared in a single newspaper in Madrid or in any other newspaper in Spain. The reporters go into raptures in their descriptions and portrayals of commanders and commissars, of quartermasters and medical corpsmen. They publish enormous portraits of singers and dancers who work in hospitals, but of the man who, in fact, directs the entire defense of Madrid they write not a word. I imagine this is not due to enmity or antipathy, but simply to the fact that 'it hasn't occurred to them. Here at times the most obvious things do not occur to one. It is difficult not to notice Vicente Rojo. Without exaggeration . . . he is accessible twenty-four hours a day. . . . As chief of the general staff of the defense of Madrid [he] holds in his hands all the threads of the complex web of units, groups, batteries, isolated barricades, sapper crews, and air force squadrons. Without resting, without sleeping, he follows carefully every movement of the enemy in every single one of the myriad sectors into which the battle line is divided."[91]

Not until 16 January 1937 did Koltzov note in his diary that the silence of the press had been broken. "Now they mention him. He is cited in second place in the list of leaders and heroes in the defense of Madrid. I cannot help but rejoice at having contributed to this by speaking of Rojo in the press before anyone else. *El Socialista* says in an editorial article: '. . . We are grateful to Mikhail Koltzov for the discovery he has made, for having shown us a man who in the seclusion of his modest office devotes all his powers to saving Madrid.'"[92] "With his journalistic vision," writes Alvarez del Vayo, Koltzov "discovered on General Miaja's staff a modest but extraordinarily competent officer, Vicente Rojo. . . . Koltzov called Rojo to the attention of the journalists of the Madrid press and his name began to be mentioned. Koltzov was alert to everything."[93]

Because of the conspicuous role played by General Miaja as president of the Defense Council and the vital though less conspicuous part played by Vicente Rojo, his chief of staff, it is of special interest to record that in the convulsive months before the Civil War, when political loyalties were shifting rapidly, they had secretly joined the UME, the right-wing Unión Militar Española. A documentary work published by General Franco's government states:

In order to appreciate the lack of sincerity in the conduct of these two officers, who were caught at the time of the [insurrectionary] movement in territory dominated by the Red Government, it is sufficient to bear in mind that both were enrolled in the Unión Militar Española (UME), which had been formed . . . with the patriotic aim of throwing up, at the opportune moment, a dike capable of protecting Spain from the Communist tide. But once this moment had arrived and the Nationalist rising in Madrid had failed, General Miaja and Major Rojo—who had seen the fate that had befallen so many general and lesser officers of the army, a large number having been assassinated precisely because they had belonged to the UME—instead of siding with their comrades, hastened to offer their services to the Popular Front. But, as their consciences were not clear, and inasmuch as they believed that, by doing away with the file cards recording their membership in this organization, all trace of their previous conduct would disappear, General Miaja . . .

went, on 18 July 1937 to the [police department in charge of political records] and demanded that both his card and that of Vicente Rojo . . . be shown to him. Once in his possession, he put them away in his pocket.[94]

A photostatic copy of a document signed by officials of the republican police department, testifying to the incident, is published in Appendix X of the same work. The authenticity of the document was confirmed by the highly reliable republican army officer, Colonel Jesús Pérez Salas.[95] Miaja's and Rojo's membership in the UME is attested by Largo Caballero, who saw the official list of members that was found during a search of the UME's headquarters in Madrid.[96]

Although there is no evidence that either Miaja or Rojo was involved in any way in the military conspiracy, their precautionary adherence to the UME before the war, in the midst of the internecine turmoil, and the rumors of an impending army coup would explain why, at the inception of the conflict, Rojo, who had been highly esteemed by the army chiefs,[97] offered his services to the government only after being warned by a friend that if he failed to do so he might be shot,[98] and why Miaja, then commander of the Madrid military district, who had long been regarded as a loyal republican,[99] entered Martínez Barrio's "government of conciliation" as war minister,[100] in the belief that it would capitulate to the demands of the insurgent generals.[101] This indeed was also the assessment of the left, to judge from its violent reaction.[102] Miaja's precautionary step in joining the UME before the war would also explain why, after the collapse of Martínez Barrio's government, he refused to join the cabinet of José Giral as war minister because he believed, as he confessed, that the victory of the insurrection was inevitable.[103] It is noteworthy that when interviewed by me after the war, he stated that he refused to join the government because it had neither an army nor a police force with which to combat the rebellion.

This was only the beginning of Miaja's checkered Civil War career. Shortly after the collapse of Martínez Barrio's government he was appointed commander of the Valencia military district, then placed in charge of the Cordova front, where, at the head of a heterogeneous force, he failed to capture the ancient Moorish capital, raising among the militiamen the question of his loyalty to the regime—the lot of many a professional officer at the inception of the Civil War. At the end of August he returned to head the Valencia military district only to be relieved a few weeks later. He then disappeared mysteriously, and the war ministry instructed a judge Lola of the army juridical corps to investigate his case.[104] But he soon reappeared, and the investigation was dropped. Finally, toward the end of October, as the enemy was speeding toward the capital, he was reappointed military commander of the Madrid district, which adds substance to the view that even before he was named president of the Defense Council on 6 November and ordered to defend the capital "at all costs" he had been chosen as a scapegoat.

Yet, in spite of his unheroic past, a singular twist of fortune and a well-directed campaign of propaganda by the Communist party that needed a front behind which it could maneuver freely, made Miaja the most glorified figure in the defense of Madrid. As Gustav Regler, the former German Communist and political commissar of the Twelfth International Brigade put it, "Republican propaganda needed a hero to put on a pedestal. . . . As a matter of policy, as well as from a sense of tact, we endorsed this glowing picture when talking to the foreign correspondents and even to the Spanish people."[105]

"Thanks to his great prestige as a result of his achievement," wrote Pedro Martínez Cartón, a lesser member of the politburo of the Communist party, "General Miaja became the best loved general in Spain."[106] Miaja quickly became intoxicated by his new-found popularity. "When I am in my car," he told Julián Zugazagoitia, "women call out to me, 'Miaja!' 'Miaja!' And they scream to each other, 'There goes Miaja! There goes Miaja!' . . . I greet them and they greet me. They are happy and so am I."[107] And Colonel Segismundo Casado attests: "I managed to apply a cold douche to lower the fever which he had caught from the people, the press, and above all, the clique which surrounded him and which brought him to a state of actual danger. More than once he told me that the popular enthusiasm had reached such a pitch that women even kissed him in the streets."[108]

But after the war, when Miaja had parted company with the Communist party following his participation in the National Council of Defense, which revolted against the Communists and the Negrín government in March 1939, the party in exile did what it could to explode the myth it had diligently created. "In order to distort the true situation regarding the defense of Madrid," wrote Antonio Mije, a member of the politburo, "there have been and there still are persons interested in attributing it to the traitor Miaja. Those who have made and continue to make such propaganda know nothing of what happened, nor of the military 'fruits' Miaja is capable of giving. He never knew more than what he was told as to what was going on in Madrid. He never felt the terrible and difficult situation in its full intensity. The tragedy of those days in Madrid could not penetrate the skull of a dull-witted general, lacking any knowledge of the people."[109]

Nor has Miaja's image fared much better over the years at the hands of Soviet Communists who knew him personally. Ilya Ehrenburg, noted writer and *Izvestia*'s correspondent during the Civil War, describes the general in his memoirs as a "sick old man, overburdened by events" and as a figurehead.[110] Rodion Malinovsky, later the famous Marshal Malinovsky and Soviet defense minister, known in Spain as Colonel Malinó, affirms that Miaja had nothing at all to do with Madrid's defense.[111]

Still, during the war, when the Communists needed a malleable and self-indulgent figure behind whom they could operate at will, they not only glorified the general in their press, but pampered him and pandered to his vanity. Among those who served the party assiduously in this task through blatant flattery and attention, to judge from the reminiscences of Enrique Castro, a witness and a member at that time of the party's central committee, was María Teresa León— the wife of the famous Communist poet Rafael Alberti—who became "the almost constant companion of the general, whom she dazzled and distracted, thus helping the others to do what had to be done without the old soldier getting in their way."[112] And Herbert L. Matthews, the *New York Times* correspondent in Madrid, says of Miaja: "The picture of the loyal, dogged, courageous defender of the Republic—a picture built up from the first days of the siege of Madrid—was a myth. He was weak, unintelligent, unprincipled."[113]

For his part, Miaja needed the Communists as a protective shield— "other men had been bumped off at the beginning of the war for much less [than membership in the UME]," Caballero acidly observed some years later.[114] Prodded by Francisco Antón, the secretary of the Madrid Communist party organization and inspector-commissar of the central front, his principal activator and mentor,[115] Miaja soon entered the Communist fold. "General Miaja," wrote Louis Fischer, "carried a Communist party card though he probably knew as much about communism as Francisco Franco. Communist propaganda had inflated him into a myth."[116]

Miaja's espousal of the Communist cause was no secret at the time. Even the Comintern organ, *International Press Correspondence*, stated in an article datelined Madrid, 28 January 1937, that he was then a member of the party.[117] In May 1937, President Manuel Azaña noted in his diary: "Miaja has succumbed to the temptation of 'converting' to communism. The idea is laughable. From where did Miaja get his communism? Four years ago when I was war minister he told me that he was a staunch republican, but that he could not compromise with the Socialists and they should be shot! It is most likely that he has embraced the Communists as a precautionary measure to gain the support and protection of a political party. Nothing more disagreeable could have happened to Largo, who is at daggers drawn with the Communists and who rages against them and their Russian mentors and inspirers. According to Largo, the result of Miaja's 'communism' is that all the important military posts in Madrid are given to Communists and that the units they command get all they ask for, whereas supplies to other units are curtailed."[118]

Just as important to the Communist party as its influence over General Miaja, the president of the Defense Council—which because of the exodus of many of the outstanding political figures was composed, according to Vicente Rojo, mainly of "young men who had voluntarily decided to remain in the city ready to participate actively in its defense"[119]—was the party's control of most of the council's key posts, although José Díaz, the party secretary, was careful to emphasize that the junta functioned "in agreement with and under the direction of the government."[120] Its composition and the affiliation of its members, as published in *Mundo Obrero*, the Communist party organ,[121] were as follows, the true political allegiance of its members, however, if different from the given affiliation, being indicated in brackets:

Géneral José Miaja	Communist	President
Fernando Frade	Socialist [Communist]	Secretary[122]
Antonio Mije	Communist	War
Santiago Carrillo	JSU [Communist]	Public Order[123]
Amor Nuño	CNT	War Industries
Pablo Yagüe	UGT [Communist]	Supplies[124]
José Carreño	Left Republican	Communications and Transport
Enrique Jiménez	Republican Union	Finance
Francisco Caminero	Syndicalist	Civil Evacuation
Mariano García	Libertarian Youth	Information and Liaison

Interestingly enough, Rojo—who accuses me of "irresponsibility" in *El gran engaño*, the Spanish translation of *The Grand Camouflage*, for referring to matters of which I have "no knowledge" while "silencing" what I know,[125] denies that the Defense Council—the overwhelming evidence to the contrary notwithstanding—was directed by the Communist party.[126]

In addition to controlling the Defense Council through its occupation of key posts, the Communist party was assured not only of the political allegiance of General Miaja, its president, but of the active support of Vicente Rojo, his chief of staff. Although there is no evidence at all that Rojo ever joined the party, his constant and intimate association with the Communist military leaders in Madrid and with General Vladimir Gorev, the Soviet adviser—officially the Soviet military attaché—in organizing the defense of Madrid, enabled him to live down an ambiguous past and to establish himself in Russian favor. This is evidenced not only by Mikhail Koltzov's praise of him during the war itself, but by that of other Soviet participants many years after the war had ended.[127] It is also evidenced by the place reserved for him in the Spanish Communist party's history of the Civil War, published in Moscow in 1966. "Vicente Rojo," it states, "enjoyed great prestige in the army owing to his extensive knowledge of military science. A man of profound religious convictions, he dedicated himself with exemplary loyalty to the cause of the people and the Republic. Through his sangfroid and courage, through his capabilities as a strategist and organizer, he very soon won general respect."[128]

Rojo first emerged as a public figure in the scenario of the Civil War in September 1936, when he brought terms of surrender to Colonel José Moscardó, the defender of the besieged Alcázar in Toledo, Spain's prestigious Infantry Academy, where before the war he had been highly regarded as a professor of military history and where, during the first days of the rebellion, 1,800 men, women, and children had taken refuge. According to Cecil Eby's dramatic chronicle of the siege, Rojo's position was ambiguous. After Moscardó had rejected the conditions of surrender, someone asked Rojo why he did not remain with the defenders. "Rojo became pensive. 'If I did, this very night my wife and children in Madrid would be killed,' he said. Not until afterwards did anyone note that Rojo had avoided telling them whether he wanted to stay with them or not. Before being blindfolded again [prior to being escorted from the fortress], Rojo dumped the contents of his tobacco pouch on the desk and said, 'This is the best memento I can give you.' As the bandage was tightened around his eyes, he suddenly cried out '*Viva España!*' as a soldier might do if he were facing a republican firing squad. Though this was a monarchist cheer, it was ambiguous—which Spain was Major Rojo alluding to?" Again, on the matter of the mines that were being dug in order to destroy the fortress, Rojo muttered as he was leaving the building, " 'For the love of God, keep hunting for the entrance to the mines.' "[129]

Whatever may have been the real political sympathies of Vicente Rojo, the truth lies buried with him in Spain, where he was allowed to return many years after the Civil War had ended and where he died in June 1966. Even Carlos Contreras, who, as chief political commissar of the Communist Fifth Regiment, knew him well, acknowledged that the Communist party was never absolutely sure of his true allegiance.[130] Koltzov, too, while zealous in his praise of Rojo's military talents, expressed certain doubts about his politics. "It is said of Vicente Rojo," he wrote in his diary on 20 December 1936, "that he is too reserved, that he says little about political matters, that he remains silent on burning issues, that perhaps he is keeping something to himself. I would like to think that this is not true. For the moment the defense of Madrid is to a very large extent his accomplishment. This carries more weight than the resounding and frequently empty utterances of revolutionary upstarts who come from the old aristocratic army. Rojo teaches the men, he creates cadres of officers from the people. . . . New books will be written on the new military art of the Spanish people in their struggle for liberty. Vicente Rojo will write them. Books will also be written about him."[131] Whatever may have been Rojo's private political beliefs, there can be no doubt that his outstanding military ability, his total dedication to his work, and, above all, his readiness to cooperate with the Spanish Communists in securing positions of control in the army, especially as the war advanced, overrode all other considerations. From the rank of major, he was soon promoted to lieutenant colonel, then to general in May 1937, when he became chief of the central general staff, in which post, according to the testimony of one professional colleague whose work is beyond question, he did what he could to promote Communist predominance in the army.[132] He remained in this post until after the fall of Catalonia in February 1939 and the flight of tbe left-wing forces across the border into France. Convinced that the war was lost, he refused to accompany the Communist-dominated Negrín government to the central zone. This was his only major disagreement with the Communist party during more than two years of quiet but close collaboration.

A factor that may have caused some historians to overlook Rojo's pro-Communist stance during the war[133] was his Catholic faith, which he openly avowed despite great danger to himself.[134] Moreover, Martín Blázquez, who knew Rojo personally before the war, says that he had no liking for Azaña and that "his political views were obviously far removed from the left."[135]

His unusual case is explained in part by Enrique Castro, a former member, as we have seen, of the Communist party's central committee and onetime commander in chief of the Fifth Regiment: "Politically Rojo could never have been with the party. He accepted the party because he understood that it was not only a political force but also a military force; he accepted it because he knew that as long as he acted correctly the party would defend him against everyone and everything. But he was not a Communist nor could he ever have been. He believed blindly in God, and he was a man of such faith, with such a sense of dignity, that he did not conceal his faith in spite of the fact that being a militant Catholic placed him at that time in mortal danger."[136]

While it is no doubt true that Rojo never joined the Communist party, it is no less true that a man can often serve its interests better without an identifying label. When, early in the war, as commander in chief of the Fifth Regiment, Castro ordered a militiaman to take care of Rojo, he added, "'We need him. He can be very useful to the party.' 'But . . . he is a Catholic,' the militiaman objected. 'For that reason perhaps,' was Castro's telling answer."[137]

Rojo's immense contribution to the defense of Madrid was overshadowed not only by the publicity given to Miaja, but also by the dramatic entrance upon the scene of the charismatic General Emilio Kléber at the head of the Eleventh International Brigade.

Kléber's real name, according to an article in the Bulgarian Communist newspaper, *Sovietskaia Bukovina*, of 10 February 1965,[138] was Manfred Zalmanovich Stern, his nom de guerre being derived from that of the famous general of the French Revolution, Jean Baptiste Kléber. This, apparently, was the first time in almost thirty years of official Soviet silence that his full name was ever revealed by any Soviet source, although in 1939 the Soviet defector Walter Krivitsky correctly gave Kléber's last name as Stern.[139] It is now clear, as we shall see later, that he was not, as some historians have erroneously believed, the General Gregoriy M. Shtern or Stern, who served as the chief Soviet military adviser in Spain from May 1937 under the assumed name of General Grigorovich.

According to Carlos Contreras,[141] chief political commissar of the Fifth Regiment, who knew Kléber well, the general arrived in Spain from Russia in September 1936, worked with the regiment for a while, then proceeded to Albacete, where he helped to organize the first of the International Brigades, and arrived in Madrid on 8 November. There he was assigned to the most seriously threatened sectors of the front—the University City and Casa de Campo. Within a few days his popularity surpassed Miaja's. "The Madrileño, who found his face attractive," writes Julián Zugazagoitia, the director of *El Socialista* of Madrid, "learned his name without any phonetic difficulty. As he pronounced it, he endowed him, by autosuggestion, with the maximum virtue and the maximum ability. His name effaced all others."[142] On arriving in Madrid a few days after Kléber, Ludwig Renn, the German Communist writer and commander of the Thälmann Battalion of the Twelfth International Brigade, found that the newspapers "were full of the Eleventh Brigade and General Kléber who, unknown a week before, was now the most popular man in Spain. He had driven back Franco's best troops, the Moors and Foreign Legionaries."[143] The foreign press was also unstinting in its praise. "He was the man of the hour then," recalls Herbert Matthews, "and we all played him up sensationally—as he deserved."[144]

Walter Krivitsky wrote:

Kléber was presented to the world, in interviews and sketches, as the strong man of the hour, fated to play a momentous role in the history of Spain and the world. His physical appearance lent color to the legends. He was big in stature, his features were heavy and his shock of grey hair belied his forty-one years. Kléber was introduced to the world as a soldier of fortune, a naturalized Canadian, a native of Austria, who, as an Austrian was prisoner in Russia, had joined the White Guards in their fight against the Bolsheviks, only to become converted finally to communism. . . . I had known Kléber and his wife and children and brother for many years. His real name was Stern. He was a native of Bukovina. . . . During the World War he served as an officer, was taken prisoner by the Czar's troops, and sent to a camp at Krasnoyarsk, Siberia. After the Soviet revolution he joined the Bolshevik Party and the Red Army. . . . Then he attended the Frunze Military Academy, from which he was graduated in 1924. For a while we worked together in the Intelligence Department of the General Staff. In 1927 Kléber was assigned to the military section of the Comintern. . . . He went to China for the Comintern on confidential missions. Kléber had never been to Canada and never associated with the White Guards. This bit of fiction was used to cover up the fact of his being a staff officer of the Red Army. It made his role as leader of the International Brigade more plausible. In reality, despite the dramatic part assigned to him, he was without power in the Soviet machine.[145]

According to Contreras, Kléber's rise to fame in the defense of Madrid immediately aroused Miaja's and Caballero's jealousy. "It was his popularity among the people," he asserted, "that killed him."[146] What he did not disclose, however, was that Spanish Communist leaders, as the evidence will show, also resented Kléber's popularity and in all probability were equally responsible for his fall. And in this resentment, shared by all those Spaniards who saw their place in history dimmed by Kléber's sudden radiance, not only personal jealousy but national pride was a powerful ingredient. "[The] national pride of the Spanish Republicans," writes Verle Johnston in his history of the International Brigades, "soared with the successful defense of Madrid, and Miaja and the General Staff did not appreciate the spotlight being focused with such intensity upon a foreigner. It seems to have been for this reason that the Political Commissariat of the International Brigades, either on the request or at least with the concurrence of the Spanish Communist Party, removed Kléber from Madrid very suddenly early in January [1937]."[147] On the other hand, Contreras claimed that General Gorev, the Soviet military adviser to Miaja and Rojo, proposed that Kléber be removed.[148] The two versions are by no means incompatible inasmuch as the decision may have been arrived at by Gorev, in deference to Spanish pride, in agreement with the Spanish Communist party and the Political Commissariat of the International Brigades, whose chief commissar, André Marty, the French Communist deputy, was, according to Louis Fischer—then quartermaster of the brigades—"at daggers drawn" with General Kléber.[149]

It is now known that the offensive against Kléber was initiated, though not necessarily inspired, by Vicente Rojo who, to judge from his own guarded testimony, seems to have enjoyed the quiet support of Gorev in the Kléber incident,[150] and who, until Koltzov brought him into public view in January 1937, had remained unnoticed by the Spanish press. This omission must have been extremely painful to a man who had contributed much to the organization of Madrid's defense and explains why he totally ignores Kléber in his book, *España heroica*, published in 1942, which nevertheless names the Spanish commanders on the various sectors of the Madrid front.[151] Rojo, of course, could not have forgotten Kléber. Indeed, in a letter to General Miaja dated 26 November 1936—only eighteen days after Kléber's arrival in Madrid, but published for the first time in 1967 in his book, *Así fué la defensa de Madrid*, thirty-one years later—he condemned the "exaggerated" publicity given to Kléber, his "artificial" popularity, and "false" gifts of leadership. "His men," he contended, "are fighting well, but nothing more, and this many others are doing who are not commanded by Kléber." In addition, he accused Kléber of making false reports on the military situation, of insubordination and political ambitions, and warned Miaja against "an underhanded maneuver that may oust you from the functions that, as all your subordinates can see, you are performing with enthusiasm."[152]

Whether Rojo acted on his own initiative or with the foreknowledge and even at the prompting of Spanish Communist leaders may never be proved, but it is significant that Spanish Communist memoirs and histories barely mention Kléber's important contribution to the defense of Madrid. In fact, neither Enrique Líster, the most publicized Communist militia commander on the Madrid front, nor Dolores Ibárruri (La Pasionaria), the famed Communist leader, so much as mention him in their memoirs, although they devote considerable space to the capital's defense.[153] Even the official Spanish Communist history of the Civil War, published in 1967, thirty-one years after the event, which is generous in its praise of Rojo,[154] devotes less than one line to Kléber.[155] All this evidence lends support to the suspicion that Spanish Communist leaders had more to do with his removal than has hitherto been supposed. Hence, it is not easy to subscribe to the version by Franz Borkenau, written in 1937[156] and echoed many years later by several historians without due credit or substantiating evidence,[157] that Kléber's downfall was due to a coalition of Largo Caballero, Miaja, and the anarchists, who suspected that he was planning a Communist coup d'etat with the backing of the International Brigades. The idea that this comparatively small body of men might leave the front to stage a coup against the government—at the very time when Stalin was counseling Largo Caballero in his letter of December 1936 to do everything possible "to prevent the enemies of Spain from considering her as a Communist republic"—simply does not jibe with the Communists' more subtle designs in Spain for seizing the reins of government. Even Borkenau, who gives no sources, seems to question the validity of his own version.[158]

After his removal from Madrid, Kléber went into temporary retirement in Valencia, was later offered a minor post by Largo Caballero on the rapidly disintegrating Malaga front—which he refused[159]—then appeared in the summer of 1937 on the Aragon front, without the previous publicity, at the head of the Forty-fifth Division, from which he was soon removed by Rojo, then chief of the central general staff. According to Carlos Contreras, "Rojo found some reason to remove Kléber. He did not want to leave, was very upset and wept."[160] Shortly thereafter he was recalled to the Soviet Union. Although it was rumored that he was shot,[161] it was not until the publication of the above-mentioned article in *Sovietskaia Bukovina*, twenty-eight years later, that his liquidation was confirmed by any source behind the Iron Curtain. "His fate was tragic," said the article. "During the period of the Stalin cult he was unjustly accused and convicted. He died in a [labor] camp and was [posthumously] rehabilitated."

Neither Kléber's evanescent glory in the most difficult days of Madrid's defense nor Rojo's invaluable organizational work behind the lines should obscure the role of General Gorev, the Soviet military adviser, who controlled the Russian artillery, tank, and air force units on the central front. According to Louis Fischer, who had easy access to the Soviet officers in Spain,[162] Gorev was the real hero of Madrid. "On November 15 [1936]," he wrote after the war, "I went to the War Office to see General Gorev who had taken command of the military situation. . . . He had organized the defense of Madrid. More than any one man he was the savior of Madrid."[163] This, too, was the view of Carlos Contreras.[164] On the other hand, Koltzov's diary, from which all reference to Gorev, whether open or disguised, was either excluded by the author or excised by Soviet censors—no doubt because at the time of its publication in 1938 the general had disappeared in Stalin's purges[165]—gives generous recognition to Rojo.[166] By contrast, Ilya Ehrenburg, *Izvestia*'s correspondent, in his memoirs published in 1963, ten years after Stalin's death, makes only passing reference to Rojo, but reserves a conspicuous place in history for Gorev. "Vladimir Yefimovich Gorev," he writes, "seldom looked in at the cellars of the [war] ministry; he spent most of his time at the front. He was under forty but had great military experience. Intelligent, reserved, and at the same time passionate—I could even call him poetical—he won everybody's esteem. To say that the people had faith in him would be an understatement: they believed in his lucky star. Six months later the Spaniards had learned how to wage war, they had talented commanders—Modesto, Líster and others less well known. But in the autumn of 1936, with the possible exception of chief of staff Rojo, there were few men of vigor and military knowledge among the commanders of the Republican army. In the November days Gorev played a tremendous role, helping the Spaniards halt the Fascists in the suburbs of Madrid."[167] Even Rojo, who emphatically denies that Gorev "or any other foreigner" was in charge of the defense of Madrid, acknowledges that the general "cooperated efficaciously," was in "close contact" with him "a large part of the time," and was a "very valuable auxiliary in the difficult hours of the battle for Madrid when Soviet matériel began to arrive quite heavily."[168]

Thus it seems clear from the evidence available that credit for the organization of Madrid's defense—without detracting from Kléber's vital contribution in the field of battle—belongs both to Rojo and Gorev, working together in close cooperation.

Because many years of Soviet silence has frequently led to the confusion of Gorev with General Ian K. Berzin, the principal Soviet military adviser in Spain[169]—known during the war as General Grishin[170]—it is important to note that their separate identities have now been positively established as a result of a number of books published in the Soviet Union between 1965 and 1971 that show that Gorev was both military attaché at the Soviet embassy in Madrid and adviser to General Miaja, and hence to Vicente Rojo, whereas Berzin was the overall senior Soviet military adviser.[171]

In the defense of Madrid, Gorev was assisted by a group of high-ranking Soviet officers: G. Kulik, his immediate superior, known in Spain as General Kuper or Kupper, and adviser to General Pozas, commander of the central front;[172] D. G. Pavlov, who, under the pseudonymn of General Pablo, commanded the Soviet tank corps;[173] N. Voronov, known as Volter, who was in charge of Soviet artillery;[174] and Yakov Smushkevich, known as General Duglas or Douglas,[175] commander of the Soviet air force units and adviser to the Spanish air force chief, Ignacio Hidalgo de Cisneros, a moderate Socialist and son of an aristocratic family from the province of Alava, who, together with his wife, Constancia de la Mora, a granddaughter of the famous conservative prime minister, Antonio Maura, joined the Communist party early in the war because of its discipline and efficiency and the help received from the USSR.[176]

Referring to the important battle of the Jarama in February 1937, the Communist commander Enrique Líster says of Pavlov: "From the sixth to the thirteenth he was the real organizer of republican resistance. General Pablo was a man of great energy, was intelligent, courageous, and quick in his decisions; he enjoyed great prestige among those of us who knew him. A valuable collaborator of the general was Captain Antonio, his interpreter-adjutant-secretary and I don't know what else besides, whom I had known at the Lenin School, where he was called Pintos, and who in his own country after the war, under the real name of Kravchenkov, won the high award of Hero of the Soviet Union."[177] And of Yakov Smushkevich, Major General of Aviation G. Prokofiev writes, "[He] was the soul of the organization of the massive actions of the republican aviation."[178]

Berzin, Gorev, Pavlov, Smushkevich, and E. S. Ptukhin, who succeeded Smushkevich in May 1937,[179] as well as Gregoriy M. Shtern or Stern, known in Spain as General Grigorovich,[180] who succeeded

Berzin on the same date, perished in Stalin's purges between 1937 and 1941. "During this time," declared Nikita Khrushchev, secretary of the Soviet Communist party, in his famous denunciatory speech against Stalin in February 1956, "the cadre of leaders who had gained military experience in Spain and in the Far East was almost completely liquidated."[181] According to Ilya Ehrenburg, who managed to survive the purges, many of the Soviet commanders in Spain "fell victim to the abuses of power in later years."[182] Louis Fischer attributes their execution to the "long history of angry rivalry" between the NKVD and the Red Army, which resented "being spied upon by unknown members of their units who collected information or misinformation and purveyed it to headquarters for misuse. . . . This situation long antedated the Spanish civil war but was exacerbated by it. Soviet army officers in Spain told me they were being 'pushed around' and 'spied upon' by the NKVD. They carried their complaints to Stalin and they were executed."[183]

The fate of Soviet journalists in Spain was no better. Of the three outstanding journalists who covered the Spanish Civil War—Ehrenburg of *Izvestia*, Mirova of the Tass news agency, and Koltzov of *Pravda*, all of whom were Jews—only Ehrenburg survived. Mirova was arrested upon her return to Moscow in 1937[184] and was not heard from again, while Koltzov, both a brilliant journalist and a literary figure and Stalin's personal representative in Spain, was, according to the authoritative *Who Was Who in the USSR*, arrested in 1938, died in imprisonment on 4 April 1942, and was posthumously rehabilitated.[185] It is of special interest that although a biography of Koltzov is included in the *Bolshaia sovietskaia entsiklopediia*, the Great Soviet Encyclopedia, Volume 33, published in 1938, his name was left out of the second edition, Volume 22, prepared before Stalin's death in 1953. His collected works appeared between 1933 and 1936, when he was still in high favor, but were not republished until 1957, four years after the dictator's death. In a biography of Koltzov in *Sovetskie pisateli* (Soviet Writers), Volume 1, published in Moscow in 1959 during the Khrushchev "de-Stalinization" era, B. E. Efimov, a close friend, says that he "perished by the foul hand of the concealed enemies of the people."[186] *Russkie sovetskie pisateli-prozaiki* (Soviet Russian Prose Writers), published in Leningrad between 1959 and 1966, is more explicit: "Koltzov's literary and social activity," it states, "was suddenly brought to an end in December 1938, when he became a victim of the tyranny that reigned in the years of Stalin's personal cult."[187] However, the third edition of the Great Soviet Encyclopedia, Volume 12, published in 1973, while reinstating Koltzov, makes no reference to his death, reflecting the softer attitude toward Stalin during the post-Khrushchev era.

Koltzov was not arrested immediately upon his return to the Soviet Union in 1938, for he visited Louis Fischer in May. "He was still 'all right,'" Fischer wrote in 1941. "That is why he dared to come. He was purged the same year [1938]. His articles and books are no longer published and most of his friends think he has been shot. Next to Radek he was probably the most influential Soviet journalist. Koltzov, incidentally, is the 'Karkov' of Ernest Hemingway's *For Whom the Bell Tolls*. Koltzov was very emotional about Spain. But when talking to strangers he wrapped himself in a smoke-screen , which consisted of equal parts of brittle *Pravda*—editorial prose and literary spoofing. That made him seem pompous and cynical."[188] Claud Cockburn, the British writer, alias Frank Pitcairn, who was a reporter of the London *Daily Worker* during the Spanish Civil War, drew the following portrait of Koltzov in his autobiography, written after he had left the Communist party:

I spent a great deal of my time in the company of Mikhail Koltzov, who then was editor of *Pravda* and, more importantly still, was at that period the confidant and mouthpiece and direct agent of Stalin himself. He was a stocky little Jew . . . with a huge head and one of the most expressive faces of any man I ever met. What his face principally expressed was a kind of enthusiastically gleeful amusement—and a lively hope that you and everyone else would, however depressing the circumstances, do your best to make things more amusing still. He had a savagely satirical tongue [he had once been the editor of *Krokodil*, the Moscow satirical weekly][189] and an attitude of entire ruthlessness toward people he thought either incompetent or even just pompous. People who did not know him well—particularly non-Russians—thought his conversation, his sharply pointed Jewish jokes, his derisive comments on all kinds of Sacred Cows unbearably cynical. . . . To myself it never seemed that anyone who had such a powerful enthusiasm for life . . . could possibly be described properly as "cynical." Realistic is perhaps the word—but that is not quite correct either, because it implies, or might imply, a dry practicality which was quite lacking from his nature. . . . As the Spanish war ground its way to its gruesome conclusion and all over Europe people who had supported the Republic became truly cynical, despairing, without faith or enthusiasm for anything, I found myself looking forward more and more eagerly to conversations with Koltzov. . . . He was a man who could see the defeat for what it really was, could assume that half the big slogans were empty and a lot of the big heroes stuffed or charlatans, and yet not let that bother him at all or sap his energy and enthusiasm. . . . Koltzov had appointed me London correspondent of *Pravda*. This position I held only for a short time because very soon after that came the news of his disappearance.

As his personal appointee, I had to be quietly dropped. I do not know to this day what Koltzov had done or was supposed to have done in Moscow. His fall—and, one presumes, execution—came at the height of his power there, and a lot of people when they heard of it could not believe it. They spread stories that he had been sent to China as a top secret agent under another name. A lot of his friends went on believing that for years, as a kind of wishful thinking to soften their grief. Others were thrown into total disarray by the news, became despairing and totally cynical.[190]

Of the top-ranking Soviet officers who served in Spain between 1936 and 1937 in the highest advisory capacities, only Berzin and Gorev—both of whom were recalled to the Soviet Union in 1937—perished during the war itself. Others perished later.

According to *Who Was Who in the USSR*, Berzin was arrested by the NKVD in late 1937 and died that year in imprisonment.[191] Although his liquidation was not confirmed by Soviet sources until many years later—by Ilya Ehrenburg in 1963,[192] by *Komsomolskaya Pravda* of 13 November 1964.[193] and by the Soviet-published work *Bortsy Latvii v Ispanii, 1936–1939* in 1970[194]—Walter Krivitsky had announced his disappearance as far back as 1939.[195] In the light of what is now known of the unchecked power of the NKVD and of Krivitsky's extraordinary knowledge of the Soviet secret police, his disclosures—which, it will be recalled, were denounced at the time as lies because of the Communist campaign against him as an imposter—have unassailable credibility today. Indeed, they offer the most likely explanation thus far for Ian Berzin's liquidation and for that of Arthur Stashevsky, Juan Negrín's adviser on financial matters, who, it seems, shared Berzin's opposition to the NKVD's activities in Spain. Krivitsky wrote:

> General Berzin had served for fifteen years as chief of the Military Intelligence of the Red Army. A native of Latvia, he led, at the age of sixteen, a guerrilla band in the revolutionary struggle against the Czar. . . . Berzin joined the Red Army under Trotsky and rose to a powerful position in the high command. Large-framed, already grey-haired, given to few words, crafty, Berzin was selected by Stalin to organize and direct the Loyalist Army [in Spain].
> Stalin's chief political commissar in Spain was Arthur Stashevsky. He was of Polish extraction. Short and stocky, he looked like a business man, and nominally he was the Soviet trade envoy in Barcelona. But Stashevsky, too, had served in the Red Army. He resigned from the military service to take up the task of reorganizing the Russian fur industry. . . . His success was brilliant. . . . Stalin now assigned to him the job of manipulating the political and financial reins of Loyalist Spain. . . .
> In March 1937, I read a confidential report from General Berzin to the Commissar of War, Voroshilov. It was also read by Yezhov [chief of the NKVD].

. . . He stated that our OGPU [NKVD][196] agents were compromising the Soviet authority in Spain by their unwarranted interference and espionage in government quarters. He concluded with a demand that [Alexander] Orlov, [chief NKVD operative in Spain] be recalled from Spain at once. "Berzin is absolutely right," was Sloutski's comment to me, after I had read the report. Sloutski, chief of the Foreign Division of the OGPU, went on to say that our men were behaving in Spain as if they were in a colony, treating even Spanish leaders as colonists handle natives. When I asked him if anything would be done about Orlov, Sloutski said it was up to Yezhov.

Yezhov, grand marshal of the great purge then under way, himself looked upon Spain as a Russian province. Moreover, Berzin's associates in the Red Army were already being seized all over the Soviet Union, and Berzin's own life was no safer than any. With so many of his comrades in the nets of the OGPU, any report from him would be viewed with suspicion at the Kremlin.

In April, Stashevsky arrived in Moscow to report to Stalin personally on the Spanish situation. Though a rock-ribbed Stalinist, a rigidly orthodox party man, Stashevsky also felt that the conduct of the OGPU in the Loyalist areas was an error. Like General Berzin, he opposed the high-handed colonial methods used by Russians on Spanish soil.

Stashevsky had no use for dissenters or "Trotskyists" in Russia, and approved the OGPU method of dealing with them, but he thought that the OGPU should respect the regular Spanish political parties. Cautiously he intimated that Stalin might perhaps change the Spanish policy of the OGPU. The "Big Boss" pretended to agree with him, and Stashevsky left the Kremlin quite elated.[197]

A few months later both Stashevsky and Berzin were recalled to Moscow and disappeared in Stalin's purges. Krivitsky gives the date of their recall as July 1937 and states that Stashevsky's wife, who was in Paris at the time, informed him that her husband and General Berzin "had come through, but had stopped only between trains, proceeding to Moscow in great haste." "The execution of the leading commanders of the Red Army," Krivitsky adds, "portended ill for Berzin. Like Stashevsky, he had been intimately associated with the purged commissars and generals since the beginning of the Soviet revolution, nearly twenty years before. Against that fact his achievements in Spain and his strict and obedient loyalty would count for nothing."[198] Although Krivitsky appears to link Berzin's and Stashevsky's fate, at least partially, to their criticism of the NKVD's methods in Spain, it is perhaps significant that Orlov, who had undoubtedly read Krivitsky's charges against him after his defection to the United States in 1938, avoids any reference to the accusations in his book, The Secret History of Stalin's Crimes, although it will be remembered that he made a special point of denigrating Krivitsky in his reply to the questionnaire presented to him by Stanley Payne in 1968.

Revolutionary Militia to Regular Army

As for General Gorev, Ehrenburg discovered his "fate" when he arrived in Moscow in December 1937,[199] while Nikolai G. Kuznetsov, the Soviet naval attaché and adviser to the Spanish Republican Fleet in 1936–37, known as Kolya,[200] states in his book published in Moscow in 1966 that Gorev was "suppressed," but gives no date.[201] "It is interesting to note," writes Orlov, "that General Gorev was arrested only two days after Kalinin, the President of the Soviet Union and member of the politburo had presented him with the Order of Lenin in a special ceremony in the Kremlin for his outstanding services in the Spanish Civil War. This episode showed that even the members of the politburo did not know who was on the death list, and that the matters of executions were being decided by two men only: by Stalin and Yezhov [chief of the NKVD]." In addition to confirming the arrest and execution without trial of Gorev and Berzin, Orlov gives the names of brigade commanders Kolev and Valua who, he says, "helped the Spanish government create the Republican Army" and were among the "many Soviet commanders" in Spain who were recalled to Moscow in 1937 and executed.[202]

With the exception of Berzin and Gorev, who were purged in 1937 —and with the further exception of Voronov, who lived to become president of the Soviet Artillery Academy,[203] and Kuznetsov, who became commander in chief of the naval forces of the USSR and first deputy minister of the navy[204]—most of the other top-ranking officers who served in Spain between 1936 and 1937 were liquidated in 1941, the year of Germany's invasion of Russia and two years after the Civil War. According to *Who Was Who in the USSR*, Shtern and Smushkevich died in imprisonment in October, while Ptukhin was executed in June.[205] According to the same source, all three were posthumously rehabilitated.

In a book published in Moscow in 1972, Alexander Yakovlev, the famous Soviet airplane designer, makes the following observations about Soviet aircraft during the Civil War that throw some light on Smushkevich's liquidation. "Despite their high manoeuvrability our fighters proved to be inferior to the German machines in regard to speed and especially in regard to the caliber and range of their weapons. Our SB bombers could not fly without fighter escort, but our fighters, being weaker than the German could not provide effective cover. However great the heroism of the republican fliers, what counted in the long run was the quality of combat *matériel*. What happened came as an unpleasant, one might even say an inexplicable surprise, especially coming as it did after the dazzling string of records in aviation. Yet there it was: we were definitely lagging behind Hitler Germany, our potential adversary. . . . Stalin took our reverses in Spain very much to heart. And he vented his displeasure and wrath on those who were only quite recently looked upon as heroes and were enjoying the honors they fully deserved. The first victims were Smushkevich and Rychagov, both twice Heroes of the Soviet Union, and undeservedly as it turned out subsequently."[206]

Also in 1941, according to Hugh Thomas, General Kulik, known in Spain as Kuper, was purged[207] as was Pavlov,[208] who was among those who were "destroyed," as Ehrenburg put it, "for no reason at all by their own people."[209]

As for the lesser officers who served in Spain in different advisory and technical capacities, how many perished in Stalin's purges is unknown, but some attained high rank and even eminence in the Soviet Union years later. For example, P. Batov, I. Eremenko, M. Iakushin, S. Krivoshein, A. Novak, G. Prokofiev, and A. Rodimtsev became general officers of various grades,[210] while R. Malinovsky and K. A. Meretskov attained the rank of marshal, Malinovsky becoming Soviet defense minister and Meretskov Red Army chief of staff.[211]

Meretskov arrived in Madrid in October 1936 and returned to Moscow in June 1937. He served as adviser to Enrique Líster in the First Mixed Brigade for a brief period, then as adviser to General Martínez Cabrera, the chief of the war ministry general staff, at which time he was known as Petrovich, and finally as adviser, for a short time, to General José Miaja.[213]

Another of the lower-ranking officers who survived the purges was the guerrilla war specialist Mamsurov, known in Spain as Hajji or Jadji, who later became a general. "At Gaylord's, a Madrid hotel, Hemingway met our army men," recalls Ilya Ehrenburg. "He liked Hajji, a man of reckless courage, who used to penetrate behind the enemy lines (he was a native of the Caucasus and could easily pass himself off as a Spaniard). Much of what Hemingway says about the activity of guerrillas in his book *For Whom the Bell Tolls* he heard from Hajji. (What a good thing that at least Hajji survived. I met him once later and was overjoyed.)"[213]

Not all the lesser officers were as fortunate. The former German Communist Gustav Regler, political commissar of the Twelfth International Brigade, tells of a party he attended in February 1937 at the invitation of Koltzov, where officers of the Russian delegation were assembled:[214]

Revolutionary Militia to Regular Army

Gorkin, an engineer, was the first to greet me. He had set up searchlight installations for us, the only defense we possessed against night air attacks—the A.A. guns had still to be bought abroad. Now he had been recalled to Russia, and this was his farewell party. He was beaming with satisfaction. His work had been approved of, and in Moscow he would get his reward. . . .

The next day Koltzov visited Arganda. He found me on the balcony of the staff building. Pointing to the searchlight beside me, he asked, "What's that?"

"A legacy from Gorkin," I replied. . . .

He laughed cuttingly and said: "A legacy? That's the literal truth!"

"Has something happened to him on his journey?" I asked.

"No," said Koltzov. . . . "But something will happen to him when he arrives. . . . He'll be arrested when he reaches Odessa."

For some moments I was dumbfounded. Then I asked:

"How do you know? Is it something political?"

"Yes," said Koltzov and it was as though another world was speaking as he went on: "Why are you so surprised? Because of the farewell party? We knew all about it. In fact, that's why we gave him a party. . . . The French give a man rum before they lead him out to the guillotine. . . . In these days we give him champagne."

"I'm going into the line," I said. "I don't feel well."

"It's not easy for a European to get used to Asiatic customs," said Koltzov.

"I prefer American customs," I said. "I'm going to join Hemingway [who had just arrived in Spain and was visiting the front]. . . . One can breathe more freely in his neighborhood, if you'll forgive me for saying so."

"I'll come with you," said Koltzov. . . . "Perhaps I need a breath of western democracy too!"

(I assume that it was this humanity which . . . caused his death in a Stalin gaol.)[215]

It is worth adding here the following incident Regler told Ernest Hemingway that resulted in the two becoming friends: Two volunteers had lost their heads in an engagement near the Escorial, seeing enemies everywhere in the mist, and had shouted to the others to run.

I had them arrested and brought to headquarters. . . . I decided to send them to a sanatorium, and I reported this to Marty [political commissar of the International Brigades]. He replied promptly that he knew of a suitable place, near Alcalá de Henares. They were taken there, and two days ago I had heard that they had been shot in the castle by a Russian execution squad. "Swine!" said Hemingway, and spat on the ground. The gesture made me his friend, and thereafter I lost no opportunity of proving the fact. I told him the inside stories of operations and crises which I had witnessed earlier. I let him know our losses and gave him advance information whenever I could, feeling certain that he really understood what it was all about. I gave him secret material relating to the Party which he respected, because it was fighting more actively than any other body, although he despised its Martys. He used my material later in *For Whom the Bell Tolls*, and countless readers learned from the brutal interpolations in a work of romantic fiction about things that they would not listen to in real life. He depicted the spy-disease, that Russian syphilis, in all its shameful, murderously stupid workings, writing with hatred of the huntsman for the poacher.[216]

In spite of the liquidation of an undetermined number of Soviet officers of various ranks after their return from Spain, the Soviet general staff derived what knowledge it could from the Spanish conflict as did its German counterpart. Indeed, a book published by the Red Army high command in 1939 on the Spanish experience referred to "several crucial matters vital from a practical standpoint in preparing the Red Army for action."[217] But it should not be overlooked that while the Civil War allowed the USSR to test new weapons and techniques in the field of battle, it also served as a testing ground for new weapons and techniques in the field of politics. As one left-wing opponent of Soviet policy in Spain wrote: "It has been repeatedly said that the Spanish Civil War was a general rehearsal for the Second World War; what is not clearly understood is that it was also the first testing ground for 'popular democracy,' perfected forms of which we have been obliged to witness in a dozen countries during the postwar period. The men and methods used to convert these countries into Kremlin satellites were tested in Spain. For this reason, among many, the Spanish experience had and continues to have historical and universal significance."[218]

Although the Comintern delegates and NKVD agents who executed Soviet policies in Spain arrived without the approval of Largo Caballero, the same cannot be said of the principal Soviet military advisers. In fact, the letter sent by Stalin, Molotov, and Voroshilov in December 1936 to Largo Caballero—from which a passage has already been quoted in this volume—stresses that the advisers were sent to Spain as a result of his "repeated requests" transmitted through Marcel Rosenberg, the Soviet ambassador.[219] Furthermore, in his reply of 12 January 1937, Largo Caballero refers to the comrades "requested by us," acknowledging that they were rendering a "great service" and were "discharging their duties with real enthusiasm and extraordinary courage."[220]

Still, in spite of this seemingly friendly exchange of correspondence and Stalin's assurance to Largo Caballero that the advisers had been "categorically ordered not to lose sight of the fact that . . . a Soviet comrade, being a foreigner in Spain, can only be really useful if he adheres strictly to the functions of an adviser and an adviser only,"[221] the power that the Soviet officers necessarily wielded eventually exasperated the war minister and explains his later censure of "irresponsible foreign interference."[222]

Some idea of the friction that soon arose between Largo Caballero and Miaja as a result of the latter's virtual dependence on the Russians may be gained from a telegram sent by the war minister to the general on 17 November 1936, reminding him that the only orders he should obey were those issued by the government, and from Miaja's reply, in which, after taking cognizance of the fact that Largo Caballero had found it necessary to remind him of the most elementary principle of discipline and subordination, which, in his long military career he had never forgotten, he asked to be relieved by someone worthy of Largo Caballero's confidence.[223] Because of the prestige he had acquired, Miaja no doubt anticipated that the war minister would not act upon his request. And he was right.

That the Soviet advisers operated to all intents and purposes independently of the war and air ministries has been confirmed by the Spanish chief of the air force, Hidalgo de Cisneros, a Communist party member,[224] by Luis Araquistáin, Largo Caballero's close political associate,[225] and by the war minister himself.[226] Furthermore, Colonel Segismundo Casado, chief of operations on the war ministry general staff, affirms: "I can state clearly that during the whole war neither the air force nor the tank corps was controlled by the minister of national defense, nor in consequence by the central general staff. The minister and his staff were not even aware of the quantity and types of their machines and only knew the situation of those which were used in actual operations. In the same way the minister and his staff were not aware of the situation, and even of the existence of a great number of unknown [airfields] maintained in secret by the 'friendly advisers' and certain of the aviation chiefs who were entirely in their confidence."[227]

Perhaps even more galling to Largo Caballero than the autonomy of the Soviet advisory staff was the growth of Communist influence in the armed forces, particularly in the central zone. Here the presence of Soviet officers, the marked favoritism shown to the Communists in the distribution of arms and supplies from Russia,[228] the intrepid role of the International Brigades, their superior efficiency, as well that of the Spanish Communist units,[229] all helped to swell the influence of the party and to attract into its orbit an imposing number of regular army officers.

Although some Spanish opponents of the Communists have underrated the importance of the efficiency of the International Brigades as a model for Spanish units,[230] it has nonetheless received ample recognition. *Claridad*, for example, stated on 11 November 1936: "Our proletarian and peasant masses, weighed down by centuries of oppression and ignorance—the work of social castes that have demonstrated their absolute incapacity for organization—must make superhuman efforts to equal these comrades from other nations. Intelligence is sharpened in school. The militiamen of the International Column have had opportunities of cultivating their intelligence during their childhood and youth. Our masses, on the other hand, have had no such opportunities. But when we triumph, we shall have them, and our children shall have even more. For this we are fighting; for this we are dying."[231]

"An indication—and a very important one—of the effectiveness of the Communist party's war work," wrote the correspondent in Spain of the London *Daily Worker*, "is offered by the fact that today the majority of the loyal generals, not to mention the younger loyal officers, have applied for and received membership in the Communist party."[232] And the Socialist historian Antonio Ramos Oliveira, a supporter of Juan Negrín, wrote: "Army officers and officials who had never turned the pages of a Marxist leaflet, became Communists, some through calculation, others through moral weakness, others inspired by the enthusiasm which animated this organization."[233]

Among the high-ranking officers who joined the party, General José Miaja, the president of the Defense Council, figured prominently, as did the liberal and aging General Sebastián Pozas, the commander of the Army of the Center, whose Soviet adviser was General Kulik, later Marshal Kulik, known in Spain as Kuper.[234] To Jesús Hernández, former politburo member, Kulik was "coarse but congenial," "impressively strong and tall who reminded one of a polar bear."[235] To Enrique Castro he was "large and crude. . . . His shaven head and enormous brutal face were impressive. But even more so were his shouts and hands, which moved as though they were the sails of a La Mancha windmill. His staff stood in dread of him."[236] By contrast, the aging Pozas was phlegmatic, nay, effete. No match for the overpowering Kulik, he was quite content to let the Russian general run the show and never bothered to adjust his peacetime schedule to meet the exigencies of a relentless war. "It wasn't until late in the morning that he would be roused from his sleep," recalls General Kulik's aide, Rodion Malinovsky, a future marshal of the Soviet Union and defense minister whose ashes are now immured in the Kremlin walls.[237] "His toilet and breakfast occupied several hours. Later on he would receive his chief of staff, a colonel, who was as old as he. They would exchange pleasantries, after which the audience would end. Out of respect for the truth it must be said that in his convictions he was absolutely loyal to the republicans, a matter of far-reaching importance. But the traditions of the old military routine weighed heavily upon him."[238]

After the February 1936 elections, Pozas had been appointed inspector general of the Civil Guard and had incurred the hostility of the right-wing army chiefs because of his efforts to ensure the loyalty of this corps to the Republic.[239] At the outbreak of the Civil War he became minister of the interior in the Giral cabinet and urged the arming of the people.[240] After assuming command of the Army of the Center in October 1936, he discreetly joined the Communist party,[241] and, in May 1937, when in command of the Eastern Army, he also joined the PSUC, the Communist-controlled United Socialist party of Catalonia.[242] But despite his membership he was simply a name with propaganda value without a shred of influence in the inner circles of the party.

Whereas a large number of officers joined the party, influenced by all the factors enumerated previously as well as by the knowledge that membership would enable them to secure for their units supplies of Russian war material,[243] others were swayed by its moderate propaganda. Colonel Jesús Pérez Salas, a professional officer with genuine republican sympathies, writes:

It cannot be denied that the Communists were masters in the art of propaganda, as a result of which they managed to deceive everybody. This propaganda consisted principally in affirming that their only aim was to defeat Franco and put into effect once again the laws of the Republic. All their leaders, especially La Pasionaria, made loud protestations of loyalty to the regime and to the Constitution, which they claimed they were endeavoring to reestablish. To achieve this end it was necessary, they said, to organize an efficient and disciplined army that would replace the undisciplined militia of the CNT. So well did they carry out that slogan that they managed to deceive everybody. Some professional military men fell into the snare, and not a few, out of enthusiasm for Communist propaganda, thoughtlessly joined the party.

As for myself, who had no other desire than that of winning the war, I believed that the Communists' seemingly fine aims were necessarily a step in that direction. Unfortunately, this was not so. By their propaganda, they aimed only at gaining supremacy in the army in order to use it for their own personal advantage, subordinating to the latter the war against Franco. This was the reason that impelled me to oppose them.[244]

Some officers, particularly those without political affiliation before the war, were drawn to the party for strictly personal motives.

"There were," writes Bruno Alonso, a moderate Socialist and chief political commissar of the republican fleet, "few, very few professional military leaders, without party affiliation before 18 July, but loyal to the Republic, who did not bow to the predominant political influence, some from inclination, others out of weakness of will, and many out of fear lest their lack of political antecedents should result in some arbitrary and irreparable act against them."[245]

"Let me remind you," the Communist Antonio Cordón warned a fellow officer in the war ministry, "that we are living in strange times, when people are killed for nothing at all. I seriously advise you to join the Communist party. It needs you, and you need it."[246]

If the growth of Communist influence at all levels in the army finally told upon the patience of the war minister, still more provoking, especially to a man of Largo Caballero's temperament—who even in dealings with his own colleagues was obstinate and irascible, and who, according to General Asensio, his undersecretary, wished to direct and control everything personally[247]—was the importunity of his opponents. Time and again the obduracy with which he withstood the pressure to which he was constantly submitted led to fierce clashes with the Russian generals[248] and with the Soviet ambassador, Marcel Rosenberg.

"More than as an ambassador," testifies Luis Araquistáin, intimate of Largo Caballero, "[Rosenberg] acted like a Russian viceroy in Spain. He paid daily visits to Largo Caballero, sometimes accompanied by Russians of high rank, military or civilian. During the visits, which lasted for hours on end, Rosenberg tried to give the head of the Spanish government instructions as to what he should do in order to direct the war successfully. His suggestions, which were practically orders, related mainly to army officers. Such and such generals and colonels should be dismissed and others appointed in their place. These recommendations were based, not on the competence of the officers, but on their political affiliations and on the degree of their amenability to the Communists."[249]

"[Rosenberg]," writes Ginés Ganga, a left-wing Socialist Cortes deputy, "used to carry in his pocket a collection of notes couched in the following or similar terms: 'It would be expedient to dismiss X, chief of such and such a division, and replace him by Z'; 'A, employee of such and such a ministry, does not fulfill his duty. It would be advisable to replace him by B'; 'It is necessary to imprison M and bring him to trial for disloyalty,' and so on, ceaselessly."[250]

It is most likely that among the Soviet civilians of high rank who, according to Araquistáin, sometimes accompanied Rosenberg on his daily visits to Largo Caballero, was Alexander Orlov, who undoubtedly kept the attitudes of top-ranking Soviet diplomats under careful scrutiny, a task greatly simplified by the fact that his own headquarters were located in the Soviet embassy. Hence, it may be assumed that if Rosenberg failed to execute Soviet policy with sufficient vigor or ventured to criticize NKVD methods in Spain, as Krivitsky stated that General Berzin and Arthur Stashevsky had done, his aberrant behavior was immediately reported to Moscow. This may explain why Orlov made no reference whatsoever in his book, *The Secret History of Stalin's Crimes*, or in any other written or oral testimony, during the thirty-five years he lived in exile in the United States, to the recall to Moscow of Rosenberg, of Stashevsky, or of Leon Gaykis, Rosenberg's successor in May 1937, all of whom mysteriously vanished without a trace. The only reference I have been able to find in Soviet sources to the violent death of any of these three men is in Ehrenburg's *Eve of War, 1933–41*, who says that he learned of Rosenberg's "fate" when he arrived in Moscow in December 1937.[251] As for Stashevsky and Gaykis, President Azaña noted in his diary on 29 July 1937 that Negrín had read telegrams to him that day from Marcelino Pascua, the Spanish ambassador in Moscow, stating that he was unaware of Gaykis's "situation" or of that of "another important person who was involved in commercial and financial matters," [an obvious reference to Stashevsky].[252] On 6 August Azaña wrote: "There is still no knowledge of the whereabouts of Gaykis . . . who went to his country on a leave of absence."[253]

Orlov's complete silence on the fate of these top-ranking officials, with whom he was in frequent if not daily contact, must of necessity raise two questions. Why did he not consider their recall to Moscow and ultimate disappearance important enough even to mention? Was he perhaps directly responsible for their recall and, hence, indirectly, for their disappearance and ultimate liquidation?

Whatever Rosenberg's private thoughts may have been on the attitude of the NKVD in Spain, he appears, on the surface at least, to have executed Soviet policy as vigorously as his conscience permitted. Although we do not know, of course, what the innermost thoughts of this extremely cultured and apparently sensitive diplomat[254] may have been regarding the policy pursued by Stalin and by his chief

NKVD agent in Spain, his encounters with Largo Caballero were matched in ferocity only by Largo Caballero's encounters with the Communist ministers.

According to Indalacio Prieto, who, as a member of the government, must be regarded as an important witness, "a situation of unbelievable tension" arose between the two ministers and the premier. "Very violent scenes occurred during cabinet meetings, and, in addition, Largo Caballero had tumultuous discussions with the ambassador of the USSR, Señor Rosenberg. I cannot make out whether the attitude of Señor Rosenberg was a reflection of the anger of the Communist ministers or whether the anger of the latter was a reflection of the attitude of the Russian ambassador. What I do know . . . is that the action of Russian diplomacy on the premier, or better still, against the premier, and the pressure of the Communist ministers were simultaneous and alike."[255]

In this situation of mounting conflict with the Russians and their Spanish aides, Largo Caballero, faced by the depredations on his following, by the traditional enmity of the moderate wing of his own party, and by the silent animosity of the liberal republicans, looked to the anarchosyndicalists for support against his tenacious adversaries. The novel relationship thus established between Largo Caballero and his former opponents of the CNT and FAI was a potent factor in disposing him to a policy of conciliation toward them. In particular, it deterred him from carrying out, at the pressing instance of the Communists, a thoroughgoing militarization of the anarchosyndicalist militia on the basis of mixed brigades as a step toward the creation of a regular army, an army to which he himself had never been especially partial[256] and which he well knew was anathema to the libertarian movement.

22. The Libertarian Movement and the Regular Army

"We do not want a national army," cried *Frente Libertario*, the newspaper of the anarchosyndicalist militia on the central front. "We want the popular militia, which incarnates the will of the masses, and is the only force that can defend the liberty and the free social order of the Spanish people. As before the Civil War, we now cry, 'Down with chains.' The army is enslavement, the symbol of tyranny. Away with the army."[1] Juan López, the CNT leader, declared shortly before entering the cabinet of Largo Caballero, "We do not want a uniformed and disciplined militia organized into military units."[2]

The anarchosyndicalists could not accept a regular army without violating their antiauthoritarian principles. True, the exigencies of an implacable struggle had forced them to recognize that their militia units needed some measure of restraint on individualism, but that was entirely different from accepting an out-and-out militarization involving the rigorous subordination of these units to government control, the restoration of rank and privilege, the appointment of officers by the war ministry, the introduction of differential pay rates, heavy disciplinary punishments, and the compulsory salute. "When this word [militarization] is uttered—why not admit the fact?—we feel uneasy, disturbed; we shudder because it calls to mind the constant assaults on dignity and the human personality," avowed *Nosotros*, the anarchist organ in the region of Valencia. "Until yesterday, to militarize implied—and for many people it still implies—regimenting men in such a way as to destroy their wills by breaking their personality in the mechanism of the barracks."[3]

But if the CNT and FAI had ethical motives for their hostility to militarization and the regular army, they had powerful political motives as well. At a congress of the CNT two months before the outbreak of the Civil War, a resolution was approved to the effect that a standing army—and by this was meant any standing army organized after the overthrow of the old regime—would constitute the greatest threat to the Revolution, "because under its influence a dictatorship would be forged that would necessarily deal it a mortal blow." Drafted by a commission composed of some of the outstanding leaders of the libertarian movement, the resolution stated that the greatest guarantee for the defense of the Revolution would be the armed people. "There are thousands of workers," it added, "who have passed through the barracks and have a knowledge of modern military technique. Every commune will have its arms and [other] elements of defense, for they will not be destroyed and transformed into instruments of labor until the Revolution has been finally consolidated. We urged the necessity of holding onto airplanes, tanks, armored cars, machine guns, and antiaircraft guns because it is from the air that the real danger of foreign invasion exists. If that invasion should occur the people will mobilize themselves rapidly in order to oppose the enemy and will return to their work as soon as they have accomplished their defensive mission."[4]

It is no wonder, therefore, that the attempt of José Giral's moderate government in the first weeks of the war to create volunteer battalions and, later, a volunteer army under its control should have been viewed with suspicion by the libertarian movement.[5] *Solidaridad Obrera*, the leading CNT newspaper in Spain, declared with regard to the first of these two measures that even before the military rebellion had been defeated the middle classes were thinking of the regime to be established on the day of victory. But, it affirmed, the workers would not rest on their laurels and would not allow their triumph to be snatched from them.[6] García Pradas, director of the principal anarchosyndicalist organ in the central zone, *CNT*, declared that no one should enlist in the volunteer army because such an army would result in the creation of a new caste that would try to settle accounts after the victory over fascism. The people, he added, had shown that they did not need to join an army in order to win the war and should therefore not allow themselves to be deceived.[7]

Hence, it is not at all surprising that when, a few weeks after entering the war ministry, Largo Caballero promulgated measures providing for the militarization of the militia and the creation of a regular army, anxiety grew in the movement and mounted into alarm when the Communists made manifest progress in penetrating the military apparatus.

In an effort to still the fears of the libertarian youth organization as to the Communists' intentions regarding the army, Santiago Carrillo, the general secretary of the Communist-run Unified Socialist Youth, declared : "I know . . . there are comrades of the Unified Socialist Youth who desire unity with the young libertarians in order to win the war, but that they believe in their heart of hearts that, when the war is over and the armies return from the front, we are going to use these armies to crush, to destroy, to liquidate our brothers, the young libertarians. . . . But I tell you, comrades, that such ideas must be discarded because they are mistaken, because when we call for unity with the young libertarians we do so sincerely. We know that our libertarian comrades are a force necessary to victory, and we are also convinced that after victory they will collaborate with us in building up a strong, free, and democratic Spain. That is our belief, and all we ask of them is that on their part they should abandon their sectarian prejudices, that they should not regard us as passing friends of today and enemies of tomorrow, but as friends today, tomorrow, and always."[8]

Neither the anarchist youth organization nor the libertarian movement as a whole, however, was under any illusions as to the nature of the threat presented by the Communists. The CNT-FAI leaders had proposed in September 1936 that a "war militia" be created on the basis of compulsory service and under the joint control of the CNT and UGT partly in hope of parrying that danger.[9] But neither of these two proposals had evoked a responsive echo, and with the Communist threat still uppermost in their minds, the anarchosyndicalist leaders had finally decided to solicit representation in the cabinet and thus secure for the libertarian movement some measure of influence in the military machine. This, to be sure, had meant jettisoning not only their antigovernment creed, but also their antimilitarist principles that, in the opinion of Manuel Villar, director early in the war of the CNT newspaper, *Fragua Social*, had proved inimical to the libertarian movement. For, he contended, whereas many anarchosyndicalists had regarded the holding of commanding posts with repugnance, the Communists had embarked on an unbridled drive to occupy all they could.[10] "Were we in a position to be squeamish about doctrines?" he asked. "If the CNT had allowed the levers of revolutionary action to escape from its hands, the Revolution itself would have suffered from the lessening of our influence. And as the Revolution was the objective, and the CNT one of its most powerful determining factors, the most revolutionary course was to take those steps that would keep us in the political, military, and economic center of gravity."[11]

But the role the CNT-FAI ministers were able to play in the counsels of the cabinet, particularly in regard to military matters, fell far short of their expectations; for they found, to use the words of Juan Peiró, the anarchosyndicalist minister of industry, that they had no rights or responsibilities regarding the direction of the war.[12] Hoping to remedy this situation, they proposed that a kind of inner cabinet be created to handle military affairs, in which the CNT would be given representation.[13] This proposal—supported by the Communists no doubt in the belief that the new body would enable them to subject Caballero's actions to closer scrutiny and control[14]—materialized in the decree of 9 November, establishing a Higher War Council that was empowered to "harmonize and unify everything related to the war and its direction."[15] The council was composed of Largo Caballero, the war minister, Indalecio Prieto, the moderate Socialist leader and minister of air and navy, Vicente Uribe, the Communist minister of agriculture, Julio Just, the Left Republican minister of public works, García Oliver, the CNT-FAI minister of justice, and Alvarez del Vayo, the philo-Communist minister of foreign affairs and general commissar of war.[16]

In spite of its official aim, this new body was condemned to futility from the outset owing to the dissensions between Largo Caballero and the Communists as well as to the rivalry between the premier and Indalecio Prieto that deprived it of any unanimity and also of the most relevant military information essential to the proper discharge of its functions. The Communists soon had grounds for open dissatisfaction since the Higher War Council met only on rare occasions owing to the resolve of the war minister not to relinquish to his opponents what remained of his authority,[17] while the anarchosyndicalists, who had hoped that it would serve to augment their influence in military affairs, found that their voice had scant effect amid the strength of their opponents.

As a result of all this, the libertarian movement was unable to use its participation in the government to increase its say in the military field or even to curb the progress of the Communists, but rather was obliged in the end to circumscribe its efforts to maintaining control of its own militia units and securing arms from the war ministry. This was no easy task, for the latter had decided that weapons would be withheld from militia forces that were unwilling to transform themselves into regular units with the prescribed cadres. At the regional congress of the Valencia CNT, held in November 1936, the representative of the Alcoy paperworkers declared: "There is the case of a [CNT] column organized in Alcoy with more than one thousand militiamen, which the government does not arm because it has no officers; on the other hand, the Socialists, who are less in number, have been able to organize a column and obtain the necessary arms because they conform to the government's conditions."[18]

To circumvent these stipulations the anarchosyndicalists decided that their units should stimulate acquiescence by adopting military names, an expedient that was employed by most of the CNT-FAI units, including those on the central front, in which, to quote the director of the anarchist *Castilla Libre*, "everything save the nomenclature remained unchanged."[19] At the CNT regional congress, the Alcoy delegate declared that rather than be left without arms it would be better to meet the government's demands by introducing officer rank and insignia. "But," he added meaningfully, "as far as we are concerned, a century delegate is nothing more than a century delegate."[20] This stratagem did not help the libertarian units to secure the arms they needed, and, in the long run, they were forced to yield to the concept of militarization.

It was not only the need for military supplies that finally induced the libertarian movement to bow to the concept of militarization: it was also—and this was no doubt the most important consideration— the need to overcome the defects of the militia system.

One of the most serious of these defects is adequately illustrated by the following unpublished article written by a regular army corporal, who was posted by a CNT-FAI column on the Madrid front: "In the column we found a professional army captain . . . who secretly advised Ricardo Sanz [its anarchosyndicalist leader] on everything he thought should be done. Sanz, who had common sense, always accepted his counsel; but every time a decision had to be taken he had to convene a general assembly of the militiamen and make the captain's advice appear as if it were his own, cleverly inculcating it into the assembly so that it would look like the fruit of debate."[21] Captain Alberto Bayo, the titular head of the invasion of the Balearic Islands by Catalan militia, records the following conversation he had with the members of the anarchist militia committee when giving them orders for the invasion of Majorca:

"'Now, just a minute,' one of the big chiefs replied. . . . 'We only take orders from the leaders of the CNT and we cannot carry out your orders without their approval.'

"'Nevertheless, they will have to be carried out without their knowledge,' I retorted energetically, 'because they are in Barcelona and the landing is a military secret that I cannot risk sending by cable, radio, or even by code, and it must be undertaken tomorrow morning without vacillation and without delay.'

" 'We are very sorry,' they replied, 'but we cannot participate if it is to be carried out tomorrow. We risk our men only when ordered by our leaders.' . . .

"Over and over again I held my patience; I reasoned with them, I ordered them angrily, I beseeched them. . . . Finally they agreed to discuss among themselves whether they would carry out the landing the next day or wait until they received orders from their central committee."[22] The disadvantages of this democratic, antimilitaristic procedure soon made themselves apparent. "Those in charge would order an operation," declared Federica Montseny at a public meeting, "and the militiamen would meet to discuss it. Five, six, and seven hours were lost in deliberation, and when the operation was finally launched the enemy had already attained his objective. Such things make one laugh, and they also make one weep."[23]

But they did something else as well: they caused the anarchosyndicalist militia leaders, especially on the central front, where the pressure of the enemy was unremitting, to turn their backs on their traditional attitude toward militarization. "It was [after the capture of Aravaca and Pozuelo outside Madrid] that all my ideas regarding discipline and militarization were shattered," Cipriano Mera, the anarchist militia leader—who eventually became commander of the Fourteenth Division and then of the Fourth Army Corps—confessed some months later. "The blood of my brothers shed in the struggle made me change my views. I understood that if we were not to be definitely defeated, we had to construct our own army, an army as powerful as that of the enemy, a disciplined and capable army, organized for the defense of the workers. Henceforth I did not hesitate to urge upon all combatants the necessity of submitting to new military principles."[24]

Just as the CNT-FAI units on the Madrid front had, under the spur of necessity, introduced a modicum of discipline, so, under the same impulsion, they began to substitute a military for a militia structure and to urge the creation of cadres. *Frente Libertario*, the organ of the Madrid anarchosyndicalist militia, declared that all prejudices should be laid aside and that the CNT should send to the military training academies a large number of comrades, who should begin to see that the military profession was as honorable and as essential as the trades that had calloused their hands. "The Popular Army now in formation," it added, "requires military technicians, and this need, which is of a national character, is felt especially by our organization, which must watch over the constant development of its power."[25] The Madrid anarchosyndicalist militia was influenced not only by political considerations and by the rigor of the struggle around Madrid, but also by the example of the International Brigades, whose more efficient military organization soon asserted its superiority over the militia system. Little by little, affirms the director of the anarchist *Castilla Libre*, the change that at first had been purely nominal went deeper. "The International Brigades have been observed fighting, and it has been proved that, given the same heroism and expenditure of energy, organization results in greater efficiency. In our militia, cadres appear formed in accordance with the regulations of the war ministry. The battalion leaders become majors; the century delegates become captains, the first corporals and sergeants make their appearance."[26]

That this was not altogether a titular change was clear from statements made by many of the leading figures in the libertarian movement, who, having done with their antiauthoritarian past, became assiduous promoters of militarization. Cipriano Mera, for example, considered military discipline so important that he decided "to discuss matters only with generals, officers, and sergeants."[27] "One of the things that has done us most harm in the army," he declared at a later date, "is the excessive familiarity between officers and men who once belonged to the militia."[28] And Juan García Oliver, who before becoming minister of justice had been regarded as a pure anarchist, now enjoined the students of one of the officers' training schools, with whose organization and administration he had been entrusted, to bear in mind that enlisted men "should cease to be your comrades and become the cogwheels of our military machine."[29]

García Oliver's assignment as chief organizer and administrator of the officers' training schools—an assignment sought by the CNT-FAI ministers upon entering the government in the hope of preventing the Communists from gaining control of the schools and thereby impeding the graduation of officers sympathetic to the CNT and FAI[30] —had been given to the anarchist leader by the Higher War Council because its members, owing to the enmity between Largo Caballero and his rivals, had been unable to agree upon any other candidate. In a speech in May 1937, when he was no longer a member of the council, García Oliver affirmed that he had received the genuine collaboration of the war minister and that the degree of confidence the latter had placed in him was due to the fact that he had not used his assignment for the benefit of his own organization.[31] Undoubtedly, one of the principal reasons for Caballero's support of the anarchist leader was his desire to keep the officers' training schools out of the hands of the Communists. Nevertheless, the assignment did little to help the CNT and FAI, for the anarchosyndicalists who enrolled in the schools were in a minority owing to the resistance by the rank and file of the libertarian movement to the creation of a regular army.[32] "This resulted in my bringing the matter up seriously before the national committee of the CNT," testifies García Oliver, "and in an agreement being reached and carried into practice whereby all the [CNT] Regional Committees of Defense were to pay special attention to the recruiting of students for the training schools." Referring to the existing hostility to officer rank, he attests: "When we sent lieutenants to assist the leaders of our CNT militia, who at that time were still opposed to militarization, they were made to dig trenches with pick and shovel in order to humiliate them." But he adds, "After the fall of Largo Caballero, when the CNT was no longer in the government, and when militarization was carried forward, those very comrades who had previously humiliated the lieutenants showed a very keen interest in attaining the upper ranks of the Republican army."[33]

As head organizer and administrator of the officers' training schools, García Oliver earned the admiration even of his ideological opponents. "[Antonio] Cordón and I," writes Martín Blázquez, a professional officer in the war ministry, "made contact with him, but all we were left to do was to carry out his instructions. Quarters, instructors, equipment, and all other requirements were immediately supplied. Oliver was indefatigable. He arranged and supervised everything himself. He went into the smallest details, and saw to it that they were properly provided for. He even took an interest in the students' timetables and the kitchen arrangements. But above all he insisted that the new officers should be trained in the strictest discipline.

"I, who do not believe in improvisation, was astonished at the organizing capacity shown by this Catalan anarchist. Observing the ability and assurance of all his actions, I realized that he was an extraordinary man, and could not but deplore that so much talent had been wasted in destructive activity."[34]

The startling about-face by some of the most prominent members of the libertarian movement was mirrored in the CNT press. Military bearing was commended,[35] and anarchosyndicalist commissars were urged by the movement to impose "condign punishment, even the heaviest and most drastic" on men guilty of offenses.[36] On 12 February 1937—in the midst of the crucial battle of the Jarama, south of Madrid—an editorial in *CNT* had declared that militiamen should obey the orders of their commanders on pain of death.[37]

But it was not easy to secure general acceptance of the new rules by men who had been taught by their leaders to look upon all armies as the symbol of tyranny, who believed themselves emancipated for all time from the will of autocratic officers, and who had not only introduced the elective principle into their units, but had also lived on terms of equality with group and century delegates. Referring to the above-quoted statement by García Oliver urging the cadets to bear in mind that enlisted men "should cease to be your comrades and become the cogwheels of our military machine," a CNT-FAI member wrote: "When ideas of emancipation, when libertarian conceptions and revolutionary thoughts are seething within us, . . . we cannot understand how our comrade ministers can express themselves in such terms."[38] And writing about the militarization of the militia in Asturias, Solano Palacio, a prominent anarchosyndicalist, avers: "What revolted the militiamen more than anything else was the fact that they were compelled to salute their officers, whom they had hitherto regarded as comrades."[39] The misgivings created among the men on the question of differential pay rates were reflected even in an anarchosyndicalist newspaper that accepted militarization: "Economic differences create classes, and there should not be any in the Popular Army. In this army, everyone, from the militiamen to the generals, has the same needs and the same right to satisfy them. Differences will bring about an estrangement between those who command and those who obey, and the class feelings they engender will have repercussions contrary to the interests of the people. As we are fighting against all privileges, we cannot tolerate the existence of any in the army."[40]

"I should be guilty of insincerity if I were to say that resistance did not have to be overcome," writes Miguel González Inestal, a member of the peninsular committee of the FAI. "In the libertarian camp every single militant had his share of scruples to conquer, of convictions to be adapted—and why not admit it?—of illusions to be buried. This was so not only because of our respect for a traditional attitude, consecrated by experience, but also because we feared, quite reasonably, that the resurrection either in part or in whole of the old army would bring about caste privileges, the deformation of youth, the resurgence of the past, the suppression of all social rights, and, above all, that it might end in that army's becoming the devourer of the Revolution, the instrument of a party."[41]

[310]

It was not because the CNT and FAI feared the latter contingency, no less than because they had no project, as did the Communists, for honeycombing the entire military edifice, that they were determined to maintain the integrity and homogeneous character of their armed units. Thus, although they had decided to convert these units into brigades of uniform military structure and merge them into the regular army under their own commanders, they were opposed to diluting them with nonlibertarian forces by forming mixed brigades[42] under the control of officers appointed by the war ministry, a plan that was mainly of Russian provenance[43] and of which one of the important political aims was undoubtedly to nullify anarchist influence in the armed forces. In fact, Martín Blázquez, the professional officer in the war ministry already quoted, once remarked to General José Asensio, the undersecretary of war, that "as soon as we have created our mixed brigades [anarchist] influence will vanish."[44]

Although Largo Caballero, for political and technical reasons, had approved the militarization of the militia on the basis of mixed brigades,[45] his present desire for easy relations with the CNT, stemming from his growing antipathy to the Communists, inhibited him from attempting seriously to enforce the measure. As a result, the anarchosyndicalist units, while submitting to the general staff for the purpose of military operations, remained under the exclusive control of the CNT and were composed of men and officers belonging to that organization.

In a report dated 8 May 1937, Helmut Ruediger, representative in Spain of the International Workingmen's Association (AIT), with which the CNT was affiliated, stated: "There is now in the central zone a CNT army of thirty-three thousand men perfectly armed, well-organized, and with membership cards of the CNT from the first to the last man, under the control of officers also belonging to the CNT. Furthermore, there are many comrades in mixed units, but the CNT aims at concentrating them all in CNT units." On a later occasion, he wrote: "The CNT understood that it should undertake its own militarization. This was an excellent means of organizing a strong CNT army that would not only prosecute the war against Fascism, but would safeguard the Revolution later on."[46]

The homogeneous character of the anarchosyndicalist units at this stage of the war has been amply confirmed by some of the leading figures in the libertarian movement, including Cardona Rosell, a member of the national committee of the CNT, and García Pradas, director of the anarchosyndicalist daily, *CNT*, and member of the anarchosyndicalist Defense Committee of Madrid that controlled the CNT-FAI armed forces on the central front.[47] García Pradas testifies:

When the militarization of the militia was decreed, our forces in the central zone agreed to it only on the condition that they maintained a certain independence, a condition that included the retention of their own commanders. The government of Largo Caballero and succeeding ones, as well as the Defense Council of Madrid, were not willing to assent to this condition, but they were obliged to "swallow" it, because we would have preferred rebellion to submission. As time went on, we had to admit ordinary recruits into our units. These were never compelled to become members of the CNT, but we always refused to concede to the government the absolute right to appoint commanders on its own account. In general, what happened was that the defense committee proposed to the ministry of war the names of persons it considered suitable, giving the requisite information, and the ministry, with this information in its possession, approved the recommendations and published the appointments. It was advisable to act in this way for various reasons, one of which was to obtain the high pay allowed to commanders. Our commanders in the central zone, after collecting their pay, turned over the greater part of it to the defense committee, which consequently had millions of pesetas at its disposal for aiding agricultural collectives. There were times when, with the acquiescence of our national committee in Valencia or Barcelona, the government wanted to impose certain commanders on us, but neither Eduardo Val, nor Manuel Salgado, nor myself—for a long time in charge of the defense committee—agreed to such a thing, and thanks to our attitude it was possible for us to maintain until the very end those forces with which we were able to crush the Communist party [in Madrid] in March 1939.

That Largo Caballero had assented to and had not simply connived at the evasion of the rigorous form of militarization agreed upon with the Russians is proved by the fact that General Martínez Cabrera, the chief of the war ministry general staff, who enjoyed his entire confidence, authorized the committee of war of the anarchist Maroto Column in February 1937 to organize a brigade composed entirely of that column's members. That this was done either without the knowledge or in defiance of Meretzkov, Martínez Cabrera's Russian adviser, a future marshal of the Soviet Union and Red Army chief of staff,[48] can be open to little doubt. In a report to the general commissariat of war dated 12 March 1937, Alberto Fernández Ballesteros, inspector-commissar of the southern front and a left-wing Socialist Cortes deputy, stated that the committee of war of the Maroto Column alleged that it possessed written instructions from Martínez Cabrera to form a brigade out of members of the column and that both "the commander of the Granada sector, Colonel [Eutiquiano] Arellano, and Lieutenant Colonel Salazar certify having read said orders."[49]

The Libertarian Movement and the Regular Army

The same dispensation to organize a brigade consisting entirely of CNT-FAI members was granted to the anarchist Iron Column, as will be seen in the next chapter. Significant, too, is the fact that the following interview on the question of militarization and the mixed brigades, given by Mariano Vázquez, the secretary of the national committee of the CNT, to *Nosotros*, the mouthpiece of the Iron Column,[50] was published without a dissenting comment from the war ministry:

Nosotros: "Will our columns disappear?"
Vázquez: "Yes, they will disappear. It is necessary that they disappear. [The national committee has already decided] that our columns, like all the others, should be transformed into brigades. . . . Now this transformation does not imply—although it might appear otherwise—any fundamental change because those who were previously in command of the columns will now command the brigades. This means that our comrades, who feel affection for the men in charge of operations, can be sure that they will not be compelled through capricious appointments to accept men whose ideology and, consequently, whose personal treatment they dislike. Furthermore, the political commissars, who are the real chiefs—don't let the word frighten you—of the brigades, will be appointed by the CNT to whom they will be answerable at all times. . . ."
Nosotros: "It has been said—and this is another point that worries our men—that these brigades will be mixed, that is to say that they will be composed of regular Marxist and CNT battalions. Is it true?"
Vázquez: "There is some truth in it, for that is one of the proposals in connection with the formation of the brigades. However, we have our own proposal: the future brigades, which logically it is for us to form, must be composed of comrades belonging to the CNT and FAI and also be under the control of these two organizations, although subject to orders—another world unpleasant to our ears—from the unified command, which all the forces accept voluntarily."[51]

Although the attenuated form of militarization accepted by the CNT-FAI leadership enabled the anarchosyndicalist units to maintain their virtual independence, it was nevertheless stubbornly resisted by the more extreme spirits of the libertarian movement, who clung passionately to their anarchist beliefs. No account of this dramatic struggle between principle and practice, between the rank and file and the leadership, is complete unless it includes the story of the famed Columna de Hierro or Iron Column.

23. The Iron Column

"There are some comrades who believe that militarization settles everything, but we maintain that it settles nothing. As against corporals, sergeants, and officers, graduated from the academies, and completely useless in matters of war, we have our own organization, and we do not accept a military structure." Thus spoke a delegate of the Iron Column at a CNT congress in November 1936.[1]

No column was more thoroughly representative of the spirit of anarchism, no column dissented more vehemently from the libertarian movement's inconsistencies of theory and practice and exhibited a more glowing enmity for the state than the Iron Column that occupied a sector of the Teruel front during the first seven months of the war. "Our entire conduct must not aim at strengthening the state, we must gradually destroy it, and render the government absolutely useless," declared the above-quoted delegate. "We accept nothing that runs counter to our anarchist ideas, ideas that must become a reality, because you cannot preach one thing and practice another."[2] Nor, in carrying out the social revolution, did any anarchist militia unit inspire more fear among middle and small peasants, among landowners, merchants, and shopkeepers. Mainly recruited from among the more fiery elements of the libertarian movement, its three thousand members[3] included several hundred convicts from the San Miguel de los Reyes Penitentiary. "[The prisoners] had to be set free and someone had to face the responsibility of taking them to the front," ran a report issued by the column's committee of war. "We, who have always held society responsible for its own defects, regarded them as brothers. They joined us and risked their lives, fighting at our side for liberty. Imprisonment had earned them the contempt of society, but we gave them their freedom and the opportunity of rehabilitating themselves. We wanted them to help us, and at the same time we wished to offer them the possibility of social regeneration."[4] But these former convicts soon brought opprobrium upon the Iron Column; for, although some of them had been moved to embrace anarchist ideals in the course of their internment, the immense majority were hardened criminals, who had suffered no change of heart and had entered the column for what they could get out of it, adopting the anarchist label as a camouflage.[5]

The notoriety that these malefactors visited upon the Iron Column created considerable friction between its committee of war and the regional committee of the Valencia CNT.[6] But a more important reason for discord lay in the fact that, whereas the regional committee supported the policy adopted by the national leaders of the CNT and FAI, the Iron Column criticized that policy on the grounds that the entry of the libertarian movement into the cabinet had helped to revive the authority of the state and had given added weight to the government's decrees. Such censure—accompanied on occasions by the threat of force if the column's views on certain matters were not adopted[7]—was mortifying to the regional committee and explains in large measure why it did little or nothing to assist the column in securing either men or supplies.

This boycott was a serious matter for the Iron Column. In the early months of the war it had been able to rely upon its own recruiting campaigns and upon confiscations carried out with the aid of anarchist-controlled committees in villages and towns behind the lines.[8] But a decline in revolutionary fervor and the discredit into which the column had fallen in libertarian circles meant that its appeals for volunteers were incapable of furnishing it with an adequate supply of fresh recruits for the relief of the men at the front. Furthermore, the committees were being supplanted by regular organs of administration, in which the more revolutionary elements were no longer the preponderant force. Even more serious was the fact that the war ministry had not only decided to withhold arms from all militia units declining to reorganize themselves along the prescribed lines,[9] but had decreed, although in carefully selected language, that the pay of all combatants—which in the case of the militia had previously been handed to each column in a lump sum without supervision and irrespective of its structure—would henceforth be distributed through regular paymasters stationed only in battalions. As the decree made no mention of paymasters in units that had not adopted a military framework, it was clear that if the Iron Column were to hold fast to its militia structure the time would soon arrive when all pay would be suspended.

The decree in question was submitted to the government by Largo Caballero and after approval was published in the *Gaceta de la Republica* on 31 December 1936. Although its language was discreet, its aims were clear. In this connection, Martín Blázquez made the following statement to General Asensio, when he apparently suggested to him that such a measure be adopted: "I now propose that we decree that those who decline to transform themselves from militiamen into soldiers should get no pay. If we give every battalion a paymaster who will only pay men who obey orders, and if the paymasters of every mixed brigade are subordinate to the quartermaster attached to every brigade command, the brigades, and consequently the whole army, can obviously be organized at once. At the same time it will do away with abuses such as take place in the 'Iron Column,' which numbers barely three thousand men, but receives pay for six thousand every month."[10] In connection with these abuses, according to information given to Alberto Fernández Ballesteros, left-wing Socialist Cortes deputy and inspector-commissar of the southern front, the CNT-FAI militia forces in Malaga inflated their payrolls to such an extent that in a single fortnight they obtained four hundred thousand pesetas more than they were entitled.[11] But it should not be supposed from the foregoing that the padding of payrolls was limited to the CNT-FAI militia, for the Communists, who exaggerated the size of their Fifth Regiment, indulged in the same practice.[12]

In spite of the Iron Column's earlier intransigence with regard to militarization, the committee of war, better informed than the rank and file of the column's plight, now realized that an uncompromising stand was no longer expedient. They knew that the column could not hold out against the pressure of the government and the hostility of the CNT-FAI leadership and that it would either have to assent to the limited form of militarization advocated by the national committee of the CNT or be left without the material support essential to its existence. But could the column be brought to heel? Unrest and demoralization were spreading, and there were already murmurings and threats among the more rebellious spirits that they would leave the front if militarization, even in the mildest form, were introduced. On 22 December alone, ninety-seven men had abandoned the front and were denounced as deserters by the committee of war.[13]

At this crucial juncture, at the end of January 1937, when dangers pressed in upon the column from every side, the committee of war issued a significant report to its members:

[In the beginning], the state was a phantom to which nobody paid any attention. The working-class organizations of the UGT and CNT represented the only guarantee for the Spanish people, . . . [but] almost without noticing it our own dear CNT itself became a sapless and lifeless phantom, having injected into the state its own power and prestige. It is now just another appurtenance of the state and another extinguisher of the flames of the revolution.

Once strengthened, the government began the work of reorganization, and at the moment it has at its disposal an army, like any other state army, as well as several coercive bodies of the old kind. Just as formerly, the police now take action against those workers who attempt to do anything useful from a social point of view. The people's militia has disappeared, and, in a word, the social revolution has been strangled.

If we had the help of the government and also of our organization—we refer to the responsible committees—we should have had more war material and more men for the relief of our comrades. But things turned out differently, and we had to allow our men to wear themselves out month after month behind their parapets. Such self-sacrifice is unknown, nor can it be expected of anyone, and every day tremendous problems arise. . . . We admit the internal problems of the column are difficult to solve, and before anything serious should occur, before demoralization and fatigue should spread and deal a violent blow at what has been conquered and maintained at the cost of unparalleled sacrifice, before all this should happen, we repeat, a formula satisfactory to everyone must be found. . . . If all the anarcho-syndicalist columns are militarized, and we stand out in opposition to the decision of the CNT and FAI as the only column that does not accept militarization, we shall be deprived of help not only from the government, but also from our own organization. With the necessary aid, our column could maintain intact the revolutionary principles that are in keeping with our character, but owing to the absence of that help we must acknowledge that our method of warfare has failed.

We know that the overwhelming majority of our comrades will be furious with those responsible for this, but we should like to point out that their protests will be suffocated violently by the state. There is no longer any possibility of organizing anything against its wishes, for it is sufficiently strong to crush whatever stands in its way. Furthermore, these days of utmost gravity impel us to silence our indignation. Once more we must imitate Christ.

We know the disadvantages of militarization. It conforms neither to our temperament nor to that of others who have always had a fine conception of liberty. But we are also aware of the inconveniences of remaining outside the orbit of the ministry of war. Sad indeed it is to admit that only two courses are now open to us: the dissolution of the column or its militarization. Any other course would be futile. [14]

At the end of the report the committee of war had expressed the hope that the question of militarization would be discussed at an assembly of the column then in progress. But, although the matter was debated, no decision was reached. It was therefore no accident that *Nosotros* published about this time the interview with the secretary of the national committee of the CNT, quoted in the last chapter, in which he was at pains to show that the transformation of the militia columns into mixed brigades along the lines agreed upon by the national committee would not involve any fundamental change. But even this assurance did not modify the intractability of the more zealous opponents of militarization, who constituted the majority of the members of the column.

At the beginning of March, however, matters were suddenly jolted into a climax.

In a ministerial order aimed particularly at accelerating the militarization of the Iron Column and undoubtedly issued after consultation with his CNT-FAI colleagues in the cabinet, Largo Caballero announced that the militia on the Teruel front would be made subordinate to the war ministry from 1 April and appointed José Benedito, commander of the anarchosyndicalist Torres-Benedito Column, to the organizational section of the general staff for the purpose of effecting the necessary changes.[15] At the same time the Iron Column was notified, according to Martín Blázquez, that the decree of 30 December, providing for the distribution of pay through battalion paymasters subordinate to the paymaster general, would be enforced.[16]

Whatever the committee of war's private opinion may have been with regard to these developments, it was submerged by the indignation that swept the column. In a general assembly the men refused to submit to military reorganization and to the new financial regulations, and a large number decided to leave the front in protest.

Of this, Martín Blázquez, who claims to have inspired the decree, writes: "A part of the anarchist 'Iron Column' before Teruel revolted against the imposition of my decree concerning the financial organization of the army. They maintained that the government was turning into a counter-revolutionary government and that it was organizing an army of mercenaries to deprive the people of its conquests of July 1936, when the army and the police forces had disappeared. They demanded that the money for the whole column should be paid *en bloc* as before, and refused to submit either to the organization of battalions or to the new financial arrangements."[17]

On their way to the rear several centuries of the column became embroiled in an armed struggle between assault guards and anarchists in the village of Vilanesa. "When the small incident was settled," ran a report issued a few days later by the left-wing Socialist minister of the interior, Angel Galarza, "the police, for some inexplicable reason . . . were attacked and had to be reinforced. Without instructions from the responsible elements [of the CNT and FAI], members of a certain organization ordered a kind of general mobilization, which occurred in several villages of the province, an attempt being made to cut communications and to impede the circulation of traffic as well as the entry into the villages of the police forces."[18] After a battle that cost both sides a number of dead and wounded, more than two hundred anarchists were taken prisoner, of whom ninety-two, according to *Nosotros*, were members of the Iron Column.[19]

Fearful lest this defiance might give the war ministry an excuse for drafting the members of the column for service in the regular army or lest the Valencia CNT might try to incorporate them into other units of the libertarian movement, the committee of war issued the following guarded notice: "The Iron Column has neither been dissolved nor does it contemplate dissolution. In accordance with the resolution approved by all its members, it has asked to be relieved so as to rest and reorganize itself. That is what is now happening. At the present moment only about three centuries remain to be relieved. When this has been effected, an assembly of the whole column will be convened, . . . wherein, with our customary seriousness and sense of responsibility, the position of the column and the road to be followed will be decided upon. Hence, until then, comrades must not enlist in other organized units . . . , for, as they belong to a column that at the present moment is resting, no one can compel them to do so."[20]

Nevertheless, the Iron Column was now in a state of virtual disintegration. The Communists would no doubt have had Largo Caballero draft its members forthwith into units of the regular army. "It is necessary to put an end to what remains of party and trade-union militia and autonomous columns, and to create a single army," said a manifesto issued by the party's central committee.[21] But Largo Caballero shunned a step that would have been regarded by the CNT-FAI leaders as a precedent dangerous to the independence of other libertarian units. In this way, the committee of war was given a breathing spell in the days before the proposed assembly that was to determine the column's future in which to win support among the men for the restricted form of militarization approved by the national committee of the CNT. While matters were in this posture, it is significant that the following article, written by a member of the column, appeared in the anarchist newspaper, *Nosotros*.[22]

I am an escaped convict from San Miguel de los Reyes, that sinister penitentiary which the Monarchy set up in order to bury alive those who, because they weren't cowards, would never submit to the infamous laws dictated by the powerful against the oppressed. I was taken there, like so many others, to wipe out an offense; namely, for revolting against the humiliations to which an entire village had been subjected; in short, for killing a political boss.

I was young and am still young because I entered the penitentiary when I was twenty-three and was released, thanks to the anarchist comrades who opened the gates, when I was thirty-four. For eleven years I was subjected to the torment of not being a man, of being a merely a thing, a number!

Many prisoners, who had suffered as I had from bad treatment received since birth, were released with me. Some of them, once in the streets, went their own way; others, like myself, joined our liberators, who treated us like friends and loved us like brothers. With them we gradually formed the Iron Column; with them, at a mounting tempo, we stormed barracks and disarmed ferocious [civil] guards; and with them we rudely drove the fascists to the peaks of the Sierra, where they are now held. . . .

Hardly a soul has ever bothered about us. The stupefaction of the bourgeoisie when we left the penitentiary is still being shared by everyone; and instead of our being attended to, instead of our being aided and supported, we have been treated like outlaws and accused of being uncontrollable because we did not subordinate the rhythm of our lives, which we desired and still desire to be free, to the stupid whims of those who, occupying a seat in some ministry or on some committee, sottishly and arrogantly regarded themselves as the masters of men, and also because, after expropriating the fascists, we changed the mode of life in the villages through which we passed, annihilating the brutal political bosses who had robbed and tormented the peasants, and placing their wealth in the hands of the only ones who knew how to create it: the workers. . . . The bourgeoisie—there are many kinds of bourgeois individuals and they are in many places—wove ceaselessly with the threads of calumny the evil slanders with which we have been regaled because they, and they alone, have been injured and can be injured by our activities, by our rebelliousness, and by the wildly irrepressible desires we carry in our hearts to be free like the eagles on the highest mountain peaks, like the lions in the jungle.

Even our brothers, who suffered with us in the fields and factories and were vilely exploited by the bourgeoisie, echoed the latter's terrible fears and began to believe, because they were so informed by persons who wish to be regarded as leaders, that the men fighting in the Iron Column were merciless bandits. . . .

On some nights, on those dark nights when armed and alert I would try to penetrate the obscurity of the fields and the mystery of things, I would rise from behind my parapet as if in a dream . . . , gripping my rifle with a frenzied desire to fire, not merely at the enemy sheltered barely a hundred yards away, but at the other concealed at my side, the one who called me comrade. . . . And I would feel a desire to laugh and to weep and to run through the fields, shouting and tearing throats open with my iron fingers, just as I had torn open the throat of that filthy political boss, and to smash this wretched world into smithereens, a world in which it is hard to find a loving hand to wipe away one's sweat and to stop the blood flowing from one's wounds on returning from the battlefield tired and wounded. . . .

One day—a day that was mournful and overcast—the news that we must be militarized descended on the crests of the Sierra like an icy wind that penetrates the flesh. It pierced my body like a dagger. . . .

[320]

The Iron Column

I have lived in barracks, and there I learned to hate. I have been in the penitentiary, and it was there, strangely enough, in the midst of tears and torment, I learned to love, to love intensely. In the barracks, I was on the verge of losing my personality, so severe was the treatment and the stupid discipline they tried to impose upon me. In prison, after a great struggle, I recovered that personality, for every punishment made me more rebellious. There I learned to hate every kind of hierarchy from top to bottom; and, in the midst of the most agonizing suffering, to love my unfortunate brothers. . . .

As a result of this experience . . . when, in the distance, I heard murmurs of the militarization order, I felt my body become limp, for I could see clearly that the guerrilla fearlessness I had derived from the Revolution would perish . . . and that I would fall once again into the abyss of obedience, into the animal-like stupor to which both barrack and prison discipline lead. . . .

There was never any relief for us, and worse still there was never a kind word. Everyone, fascists and antifascists, and even members of our own movement—what shame we have felt!—have treated us with aversion. We have never been understood . . . [because] during the war itself, we wished to lead a life based on libertarian principles, while others, both to their own misfortune and to ours, have remained yoked to the chariot of state. . . .

History, which records the good and the evil that men do, will one day speak, and it will say that the Iron Column was perhaps the only column in Spain that had a clear vision of what our Revolution ought to be. It will also say that of all columns, ours offered the greatest resistance to militarization, and that there were times when, because of that resistance, it was completely abandoned to its fate. . . .

Our past opposition to militarization was founded on what we knew about officers. Our present opposition is founded on what we know about them now. . . . I have seen . . . an officer tremble with rage or disgust when I spoke to him familiarly, and I know cases today of battalions that call themselves proletarian, whose officers, having forgotten their humble origin, do not permit the militiamen on pain of terrible punishment to address them as "thou."[23]

We used to live happily in the trenches . . . [because] none of us was superior to the other, all of us were friends, all comrades, all guerrillas of the Revolution. The delegate of a group or century was not imposed upon us; he was elected by us. He did not regard himself as a lieutenant or as a captain, but as a comrade. Nor were the delegates of the committees of the column colonels or generals; they were comrades. We used to eat, fight, laugh, and swear together. . . .

I don't know how we shall live now. I don't know whether we shall be able to accustom ourselves to abuse from corporals, from sergeants, and from lieutenants. I do not know whether, after having felt ourselves to be men in the fullest sense of the word, we shall get used to being domestic animals, for that is what discipline leads to and what militarization implies. . . .

But the hour is grave. We have been caught . . . in a trap and we must get out of it; we must escape from it as best we can. . . . The militarists, all the militarists—there are fanatical ones in our own camp—have surrounded us. Yesterday we were masters; today they are. The popular army, which has nothing popular about it except that the people form it, . . . does not belong to the people but to the government and it is the government that commands, it is the government that gives orders. . . .

Caught as we are in the militarists' net, there are only two possible roads. The first road leads . . . to the dissolution of the Iron Column, the second to its militarization. . . .

[But] the column, that Iron Column that caused the bourgeoisie and the fascists to tremble from Valencia to Teruel must not be dissolved; it must continue to the end. . . .

If we were to break up the column, if we were to disband and were later drafted, we should have to march, not with those whom we choose, but with those with whom we are ordered to march. . . .

Whatever we be called, column, battalion, or division, the Revolution, our anarchist and proletarian Revolution, to which we have contributed glorious pages from the very first day, bids us not to surrender our arms and not to abandon the compact body we have constituted until now.

Sunday, 21 March, the day fixed for the holding of the assembly that was to vote on the future of the Iron Column, was a portentous one for all its members. In the past weeks the committee of war had been urging the acceptance of militarization as the only alternative to dissolution, and now that passions had spent their force and disintegration was upon the column, it was obvious that the proponents of militarization were certain to have their way. The arguments used by the committee during the assembly in favor of converting the column into a brigade—that the men belonged to age groups then being drafted by the government; that, even should they decide to disband, they would be inducted shortly afterward into the regular units organized by the state; that the war ministry had agreed to all of the four battalions of the proposed brigade being formed of members of the column and that only the artillery would be in the hands of professional officers[24]—were sufficiently powerful to ensure the favorable vote of the assembly.

A few days later, the committee of war announced to the members of the Iron Column that the unit was to become the Eighty-third Brigade of the regular army.[25]

24. Largo Caballero Breaks with Moscow

For all its seriousness, the episode of the Iron Column added but a ripple to the whirlpool of discord that for weeks had been swirling in Valencia, the seat of government.

Early in February 1937, enmities had acquired fresh malignancy with the fall of the strategic port of Malaga, from where the loosely organized and inadequately equipped militia columns, divided by dissensions and mutual suspicions, had been rolled back in precipitous confusion for more than eighty miles along the coast by an overwhelmingly superior enemy force composed of Spanish and Italian units. Copies of two important documents dealing with the loss of Malaga have been preserved.[1] No one wishing to apportion responsibility fairly can afford to ignore them, for they form, together with the valuable data in General Asensio's book, *El General Asensio: Su lealtad a la república*, in Ramón Salas Larrazábal's *Historia del ejército popular de la república*,[2] and in José Manuel Martínez Bande's *La campaña de Andalucía*,[3] the basis of any serious study of this subject. One is a detailed account of the disaster given on 12 February 1937 to members of the Higher War Council by Colonel José Villalba, a professional officer with no party ties, in charge of the Malaga sector of the southern front; the other is a report dated 18 February 1937 to the commissariat of war by the left-wing Socialist, Alberto Fernández Ballesteros, inspector-commissar of the southern front. These documents refer to the absence of military discipline and organization on the Malaga sector, the muddle and disorder in the rear, the irresponsibility of professional officers and militia leaders, the struggle between the different factions to the prejudice of military operations, the proselytizing efforts of the Communist party, the appointment of an excessive number of Communist political commissars by Cayetano Bolívar, chief political commissar of the Malaga sector, the wanton neglect of defensive works, the treachery of the two commanders in charge of fortifications, Romero and Conejo, who deserted to the

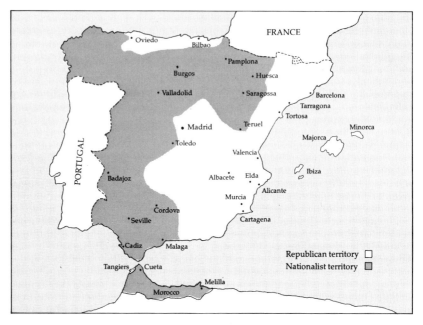

Division of Spain, 8 February 1937

enemy, the inadequate supplies of rifles, guns, and ammunition, the lack of assistance from the fleet and air force, and, finally, the failure of the war ministry to respond to the reiterated appeals of Colonel Villalba and other leaders for reinforcements and supplies. One of the most unlucky figures in the disaster was Villalba himself, who was assigned to the Malaga sector after enemy forces had pierced the eastern defenses at Estepona and when everything was fusing into disaster. Undoubtedly selected by the war ministry as a scapegoat,[4] he was later arrested and imprisoned.[5] After more than a year's internment, however, he was exculpated from any blame for the disaster and rehabilitated.[6]

Of the Malaga debacle the Communists made what use they could to advance their military policy. Day after day and week after week they had been urging that the military measures adopted by the government during the first months of its existence be put into effect,[7] and now the loss of Malaga gave dramatic import to their words. To be sure, the agitation upon which they throve was not without self-interest, for they saw in the rigid implementation of those measures a means, not only of bringing the war to a successful issue, but also of creating a military machine that, if harnessed to their party, would ensure their ascendancy in the affairs of state. They were therefore impatient of Largo Caballero's indulgence toward the anarchosyndicalist militia and particularly of his dilatoriness on the matter of conscription, especially as voluntary recruiting had fallen off and a continuous stream of fresh men was needed to replace losses. They were also impatient of his laggard record regarding other matters and of his ingrained prewar habits. "Papers of the utmost military importance accumulate in enormous stacks unattended to, unexamined," Koltzov noted in his diary. "Regardless of what is happening Caballero retires at nine P.M. and no one dares to awaken the old man. Even if Madrid should fall in the middle of the night, the head of the government would learn of it only in the morning."[8] There was no power nor circumstance, writes K. A. Meretskov, onetime Soviet adviser to the chief of the central general staff, General Martínez Cabrera, that would make Caballero change his long-established routine. "Whenever he went to sleep all contact with the outside world was severed and all access to him was cut off."[9]

There is no doubt an element of exaggeration in these Soviet observations, for even the staunch Spanish Communist, Antonio Cordón, who was the head of the technical secretariat of the undersecretaryship of war under Caballero, acknowledged that the war minister established a "rational work schedule" in the ministry. "He kept rigidly to his own schedule, which began at 8 A.M. sharp . . . and ended at 8 P.M., with a very brief interval for food. At 8 o'clock, he retired, and no one was allowed to disturb him unless the matter was very serious and urgent."[10]

Still, whatever Caballero's habits, the Communists and their Soviet allies could have lived with them, as they managed to live with those of such other prominent Spaniards as General Pozas and Juan Negrín, who were more amenable to their wishes. But, as Cordón observes, "I soon found out that the firmness of character of the Socialist leader, which so many used to admire, including myself, was based on obstinacy, and was frequently transformed . . . by an exaggerated opinion of his own importance and qualifications into a negative trait."[11] With such men, to be sure, the Communists found it hard to deal. Moreover, as Koltzov observes in his diary, Largo Caballero had "crude ways." "From time to time he shouts; he does not permit objections. As minister of war, he resolves military problems personally."[12]

Revolutionary Militia to Regular Army

As far back as September 1936 the government had decided, largely as a result of Communist pressure, to call up the 1932 and 1933 classes,[13] but this decision had remained on paper, partly because Largo Caballero, as we have seen, believed in the superior morale and greater combat efficiency of volunteers,[14] and partly because he knew that the anarchosyndicalists, whose support he needed, were opposed to the enrollment of their members in government units.

Although a CNT national congress decided to agree to the mobilization of the two classes announced by the government, it did so on the understanding that all men with anarchosyndicalist membership cards should be drafted by the CNT for service in its own militia units. In Catalonia, the regional committee of the CNT stated with reference to this decision: "As it would be very childish to hand over our forces to the absolute control of the government . . . the national congress has decided that all persons in the [two mobilized] classes who belong to our trade-union organization should present themselves immediately to the CNT barracks or, in the absence thereof, to the trade-union or [CNT] defense committees [of their locality] that will take note of their affiliation, their age, their employment, the class to which they belong, their address, and all the necessary facts. A report will be sent to the Regional Committee of Defense, Nicolás Salmerón, 10. This committee will issue militia cards that will be sent to the inscribed comrades, who, of course, will henceforth be at the disposal of the Regional Committee, which will assign them to the column or front selected."[15]

When taken to task in February 1937, shortly after the fall of Malaga, by a delegation of the Communist-dominated Defense Council of Madrid for not enforcing the draft, Largo Caballero retorted that the government had neither barracks in which to house the conscripts nor money and arms with which to pay and drill them.[16] Moreover, a few days earlier, in response to Communist demands for the implementation of the draft, he had declared somewhat disingenuously, in reference to the decree of 29 October 1936 that rendered all able-bodied men between the ages of twenty and forty-five liable to conscription,[17] that compulsory military service was in force "de jure and de facto." "What the government and the war minister demanded," he continued, "is that organizations and unions of all kinds should impose on their members the discipline this measure requires so that when the military authorities deem it necessary to employ the services of men of military age they will encounter no obstacles. It is in this way, the minister considers, that those who wish to cooperate in the defense of national territory against the foreign invasion should carry on their propaganda and not by making demands on the government in connection with problems that have already been made the subject of legal measures, such as the decree of 29 October 1936."[18]

But, in truth, this was evasive sophistry designed to conceal the nonenforcement of the draft, and a few days later the Communist ministers, backed by the republican and moderate Socialist representatives in the cabinet, compelled Caballero not only to repeat the call-up of the 1932 and 1933 conscripts, but to include in the same draft the 1934 to 1936 classes.[19] This, however, did not change matters substantially for the libertarian movement. At the beginning of March, the regional committee of the CNT of Aragon, while taking cognizance of the government's mobilization orders, urged the workers in that region to present themselves at the recruiting depots of the CNT for enlistment in anarchosyndicalist units.[20] On 15 March, the day when several of the mobilized classes were to present themselves at their induction centers,[21] the national committee of the CNT, the peninsular committee of the FAI, and the peninsular committee of the libertarian youth issued a joint manifesto enjoining the workers to "form themselves into brigades" and place themselves at the disposal of the "bodies directing the war"[22]—a reference, of course, to the defense committees of the CNT and FAI. In view of all this, it is hardly surprising that *Frente Rojo*, the Communist organ, should have affirmed a few weeks later that in several villages in the region of Estremadura it had been able to prove that men who should have enlisted in the regular army in compliance with the government's mobilization orders had been urged not to do so, and were being formed into battalions of a "certain political or trade-union character."[23]

Meanwhile, the Communist party strove to utilize the Malaga debacle in another way: it demanded the purging of all positions of command. Although directed ostensibly against members of the officer corps who were suspect or incompetent,[24] this demand soon proved to be aimed specifically at those appointees of Largo Caballero who were opposing its permeation of the armed forces. In the words of Enrique Castro, a former member of the party's central committee, this demand represented one more step toward the attainment of hegemony by the party.[25]

That the Communists' chief target should have been General José Asensio is natural; for, as undersecretary of war, he held the most important position in the war ministry next to Largo Caballero, a position to which, it will be recalled, the minister, in a defiant gesture, had elevated him in reply to their demand that he be removed from the central front. The offensive against General Asensio was "unspeakable," wrote Largo Caballero some years later. "I had already been forced to relieve him of his command of the Army of the Center. . . . Now [the Communists] were determined to oust him from the ministry. 'Why?' I asked them. 'Because he is a traitor!' 'Give me proof, evidence!' . . , but they never produced any. At every session of the cabinet the [Communist] ministers raised the same issue: the undersecretary must be dismissed from office; he is a danger in the ministry. I asked them for proof; they offered to furnish it, but they never did. Innocent oversight! . . . When they became convinced that by accusing him of being a traitor they got nowhere, they accused him of being a drunkard and a philanderer. I replied that I had never seen him drunk and that I was surprised they should denounce a Spanish general because he liked women, whereas I knew for certain that they had enrolled *homosexuals* in their party."[26]

But the Communists were undaunted by Caballero's obstinacy. Asensio had now become such an impediment to their plans for hegemony that the Russian ambassador, Marcel Rosenberg, personally demanded his dismissal. To this demand, Largo Caballero, afire with indignation, replied by expelling the Soviet diplomat from his office.

This signal event, confirmed by several colleagues of the premier and by Largo Caballero himself,[27] is colorfully recorded by the left-wing Socialist Cortes deputy, Ginés Ganga, who affirms that Rosenberg threatened to withdraw Soviet aid unless the demand for the removal of the undersecretary of war were heeded. He writes:

Those of us who used to frequent the ministry of war were at first struck by the daily visit, to which we finally became accustomed, of his Excellency, the Soviet ambassador, who spent several hours every day in the office of Largo Caballero, premier and war minister. . . . Rosenberg was usually accompanied by an interpreter, but what an interpreter! Not a secretary of the embassy, but the minister of foreign affairs of the Republic, Don Julio Alvarez del Vayo! . . .

One morning the visit behind closed doors had already lasted two hours when suddenly "old man" Caballero was heard shouting. The secretaries gathered around the door of the office, not venturing to open it out of respect. Caballero's shouting increased in intensity. Then, all of a sudden, the door opened, and the aged premier of Spain, standing in front of his table, his arms outstretched and his shaking finger pointing to the door, was heard saying in a voice tremulous with emotion: "Get out! Get out! You will have to learn, Señor Ambassador, that although we Spaniards are very poor and need help from abroad very much, we are too proud to let a foreign ambassador attempt to impose his will on the head of the government of Spain!

And as for you, Vayo, it would be better to remember that you are a Spaniard and minister of foreign affairs of the Republic and that you should not combine with a foreign diplomat in putting pressure on your prime minister."[28]

After expelling the Soviet ambassador, Largo Caballero remained alone with Alvarez del Vayo. "I rebuked him for playing the Communist game," he recalls. "All he could reply was that since people were saying, even if unjustly, [that Asensio was a traitor] he should be removed from office. A fine argument! But who were the people who were saying this? The Communists and no one else!"[29]

It is indeed curious that Amaro del Rosal, a member of the UGT executive and former partisan of Largo Caballero, who joined forces with the Communists quite early in the war, should have stated many years later, when still a Communist supporter, that "the campaign against Asensio was unfair," that it was "motivated by selfish professional ambitions," and that Asensio was a "great military figure, a fact that disturbed other military men,"[30] for this was an obvious reference to Lieutenant Colonel Antonio Cordón, who, as he himself avows, was frequently at odds with Asensio.[31] While personal intrigue and ambition no doubt played a role in Asensio's downfall, and Cordón's fellow Communists must have used this ambitious young officer—who a year later became undersecretary of war under defense minister Juan Negrín—to undermine Asensio, it goes without saying that the campaign against the general served first and foremost the political ends of the party rather than Cordón's personal ambitions in the war ministry.

The relations between Largo Caballero and the Soviet ambassador had deteriorated dramatically, as demonstrated by the Asensio episode. In reply to the question posed by Stalin, Molotov, and Voroshilov in their letter of December 1936,[32] "Is the Spanish government satisfied with [Rosenberg] or is it necessary to replace him with another representative?" Largo Caballero had answered reassuringly as recently as 12 January 1937, just a few weeks before ejecting the ambassador from his office, "We are satisfied with his behavior and activity. Everyone here likes him. He is working hard, excessively, at the expense of his enfeebled health."[33]

Perhaps because of this friendly response or because they may have hoped that Largo Caballero's stormy scene with the ambassador was just a passing incident, Moscow and the Spanish Communists did not entirely despair of manipulating the Socialist leader. Indeed, they still hoped that they could use his influence to facilitate the fusion of the Socialist and Communist parties, as it had facilitated the unification of the two youth movements. "The Russian plan, passionately adhered to throughout the war, was to fuse the two parties," testified Luis Araquistáin, the left Socialist leader, whose intimate relations with Caballero invest his words with special authority, and who, like Caballero, had personally supported the fusion before the war. "The new party would be called the Unified Socialist party, as in Catalonia, but in reality it would be a Communist party, controlled and directed by the Communist International and the Soviet authorities. The name would deceive the Spanish workers, and it was hoped that it would not alarm the Western powers. Stalin fervently desired that Largo Caballero should use his power in the government and his enormous authority in the Socialist party to impose the absorption of the latter by the Communist party."[34]

But although the influential Madrid section of the Socialist party, the Agrupación Socialista Madrileña, which Caballero controlled and to which Araquistáin belonged, had advocated the merging of the two parties before the war,[35] his experiences had stamped out the last spark of his enthusiasm for amalgamation. After he had been maneuvered out of office in May 1937,[36] Caballero gave another reason for his changed attitude toward the question of fusion. "The only thing I ask," he declared, "is that those who at one time wished to carry out this fusion should keep to the same program that we had, namely, that it should be realized on the basis of a revolutionary program. I remember very well that when we used to speak of this question the Communist party posed as a condition—because it had been so agreed in Moscow—that we should break relations with all the bourgeois parties." This remark was a reference to a letter addressed before the war to the Socialist party executive by the central committee of the Communist party, proposing the fusion of the two organizations. Written during the early phase of the Popular Front period and couched in language designed to appeal more to the radicalism of the numerically superior left Socialists headed by Largo Caballero than to the moderate Socialists led by Indalecio Prieto, who controlled the executive committee, the letter posed, inter alia, the following conditions: "Complete independence with regard to the bourgeoisie"; "complete rupture of the social democratic bloc with the bourgeoisie"; "recognition of the need for the revolutionary overthrow of bourgeois domination and for the establishment of the dictatorship of the proletariat in the form of soviets."[37] "Do the [Communists] insist now, as they once did," Largo Caballero continued, "that we should break relations with all the bourgeois parties? No, on the contrary. The slogan they now have is that we should return to the days before 18 July."[38]

Whatever may have been the real weight of this issue in determining the changed attitude of Caballero and of other left Socialist leaders toward the fusion of the two parties, there can be no doubt that it was not so much their dislike of the moderate tone of the Communist party's present policy as its depredations of the Socialist movement and the fear that it would eventually absorb the Socialists that put the matter entirely out of court. This is suggested by the following account of a conversation among a group of leading left-wing Socialists that took place in January 1937.

Rodolfo Llopis, undersecretary to the premier, recalls:

The conversation turned to what was, for all genuine Socialists, one of the most dramatic of subjects, namely, the disloyalty of the Communists. Someone present drew a picture that was only too familiar to all of us: the campaigns waged by the Communists at the front and in the rear; their drive to remove the Socialists from various organizations; . . . their barefaced proselytism, in which they unscrupulously employed the most reprehensible of methods; their constant disloyalty toward us. He spoke of the behavior of the Socialist youth leaders who had gone over to the Communist party, and of the "conquest" that the Communists had made of the two Socialist deputies, Nelken and Montiel.[39] . . . Meanwhile, he added, our party gave no sign of life; the executive committee [controlled by the moderate Socialists] remained silent. . . .

Several other comrades spoke. Caballero likewise. He said just a few words, but they were clear and emphatic. "What is this about absorption?" he asked. "Nobody will ever absorb me. The party has a tradition as well as potentialities that cannot be thrown overboard. . . . The party cannot die. As long as I live there will be a [Socialist] party!"[40]

Even before the outbreak of the Civil War, when he had briefly harbored the illusion that through the fusion of the two parties he could absorb the Communists, Largo Caballero had grown wary of the idea of amalgamation, and no enticement laid before him by the Spanish politburo and the Comintern, not even a promise that he could head the united party,[41] could induce him to yield to their importunity. "[The Communist International]," he writes, referring to the prewar period, "wanted to fuse the Communist and Socialist parties and put them in its bag, but it encountered one great difficulty: the Communist party did not have men of authority and prestige for such an important task. . . . Unfortunately, they focused their attention upon me. In the Communist press, I was the only Marxist Socialist, a revolutionary, the legitimate representative of the Spanish proletariat, the devoted friend of the workers, the only hope of the future, the Spanish Lenin! My photograph was displayed in newspapers, in movie theaters, in store windows, in Spain and abroad, even in Russia. They wanted to awaken in me those evil instincts that always dwell in the hearts of men: vanity and ambition, but those emotions were fast asleep in the very depths of my being. They didn't know me, otherwise they would not have thought of such stupidities." Vittorio Codovila, the Comintern delegate, known in Spain as Medina, visited Largo Caballero, pressing him for the fusion of the two parties: "I would be the head of the new party and hence the master of Spain because once fusion had been achieved all the workers would join the party and it would become an invincible force." Caballero did not yield: "[I] had already acquired too much experience to allow myself to be influenced by those siren calls." After he became premier in September 1936, pressure was resumed. "[I] replied courteously in the negative." Undeterred, Codovila again visited Largo Caballero. "My visitor told me that this was the psychological moment to carry out the fusion of the two parties; that all the workers were demanding the *Single Party*; that since I occupied the premiership, it would be a success, and that it was advisable to achieve it as soon as possible because in that way the war would be won. In short, he insinuated that I could and should carry out a coup d'etat. Restraining my indignation I replied that it was not true that all the workers were asking for fusion, and that, even if they were, I would not lend myself to the maneuver. I requested him not to mention the matter again. If anyone wanted the union of the workers all he had to do was to join the UGT and the Socialist party. . . . [I] was not ready to stain my modest political and trade-union history with the treachery he proposed. . . . Looking as red as a pomegranate, Medina withdrew. . . . I had placed the premiership, the war ministry, all the posts I held as well as my future tranquillity, in jeopardy." In spite of this rebuff, a final effort was made to persuade the left Socialist leader. Marcelino Pascua, the Spanish ambassador to Moscow, arrived unexpectedly in Valencia with an urgent request. "[He] asked me *on behalf of Stalin* if the fusion of the parties would be carried out. My reply to him was 'No!' "[42]

This unequivocal expression of Caballero's intractability just a few days after he had expelled the Soviet ambassador from his office finally convinced the Russians of the futility of further attempts to knead the Socialist leader to their purpose and became the signal for the launching of a whispering campaign to undermine what remained of his authority. Insidiously, the words "stupidity," "ineptitude," and "senility" were bandied from mouth to mouth,[43] presaging the greatest political battle of the war, a battle that would eventuate in the political demise of the man who had been the most influential and popular of the left-wing leaders at the start of the fighting. Observing, as a Communist, the gradual development of this historic battle against the party's former allies, "against the oldest working-class party in the country, against its unquestioned leader Francisco Largo Caballero," Enrique Castro, then a member of the party's central committee, confesses that he "smiled and rubbed his hands with satisfaction," as the following thoughts occupied his mind:

"We shall win the battle. We shall win the battle against the Socialist party and against Largo Caballero. With the help of the masses, with the help of the other parties and organizations! And with the help of the Socialist party itself! Ya. Ya. Marvelous! Absolutely marvelous! What does it matter that idiots accuse us of disloyalty to our allies? Isn't the party doing what it is supposed to do? Is a proletarian revolution possible without a powerful Communist party in control? The imbeciles should not be astonished! What we are doing to conquer the masses, to achieve the true revolution, the Socialist revolution, is nothing new. Here are the texts of Lenin and Stalin! Texts that are within the reach of anyone who wants to know what they contain, of anyone who wants to know our aim, our method, our tactics and strategy. There is nothing new, nothing new! What is happening is that you, all of you, have been so dumb that you have not bothered to learn who we are and what we are. But that is not our fault. The fault is yours! . . . The political stupidity of our allies is without a doubt one of our best allies."[44]

He adds: "Spain had never witnessed a great political funeral. Now it would. And before very long. Largo Caballero, the politician, had entered his death agony. He was unaware of this, just as he was unaware of many important things during his lifetime. . . . [But] it made his political death the more terrible, a death that would come brutally and by surprise and in an atmosphere of almost complete political isolation."[45]

"Why was this campaign waged [against me]? Do you know why?" Largo Caballero asked his audience at a public meeting some months after he had left the government.

Because Largo Caballero did not want to be an agent of certain elements in our country, and because Largo Caballero defended national sovereignty in the military field, in the political field, and in the social field. And when these elements learned, very late, to be sure, that Largo Caballero could never become an agent of theirs, the line changed and the campaign against me started. But I can affirm that until shortly before this campaign commenced, I was offered everything that could be offered to a man with ambition and vanity: I could have been the head of the unified Socialist party; I could have been *the* political figure of Spain; I would have had the support of those who approached me; but only on the condition that I carried out their policy. And I replied that on no account would I do so.

As I was saying, they got to know me very late. They should have understood from the very first moment that Largo Caballero has neither the temperament nor the substance of a traitor. I categorically refused [to carry out their policy], with the result that on one occasion . . . I had a very violent scene with official representatives of a certain country whose duty it was to be more discreet, but who did not fulfill that duty. And I told them—in the presence of one of their agents, an agent, however, who held a ministerial portfolio [a reference to foreign minister Alvarez del Vayo]—that Largo Caballero would not tolerate any kind of interference in the political life of our country.[46]

25. Largo Caballero Hits Back

Undeterred by the Soviet ambassador's failure to secure the dismissal of General Asensio from the undersecretaryship of war, the Communists applied pressure from other directions. Without actually naming him, *Mundo Obrero*, their Madrid daily, which enjoyed a wide diffusion at the front, gave a brief biography that left no doubt as to the real identity of the "organizer of defeats," who had "furnished grounds for imposing the maximum penalty."[1] At a cabinet meeting held a few days later, the Communist ministers formally demanded Asensio's removal. Foreign minister Alvarez del Vayo, despite his personal conviction that the general was "unquestionably one of the most capable and intelligent officers in the republican army"[2] gave the demand strong support. "Having decided that the fundamental factor was not one's own personal trust in the general," he explains, "but the suspicion which he inspired in a large section of the troops, I was one of the cabinet ministers who stood out most firmly for his dismissal. . . . The fight waged by Caballero against what he thought was an injustice done to his undersecretary had a certain greatness. He deeply resented the fact that I, for the first time, took a position different from his, and from that day, to my great regret, I ceased to be his most trusted minister."[3] In spite of Largo Caballero's bold defense of General Asensio, he was defeated by a broad opposition spanning the political spectrum from the anarchosyndicalist to the Left Republican ministers. This was confirmed by Federica Montseny in a letter to me after the war. Her honesty is particularly appreciated because of the reluctance of several of her former cabinet colleagues to furnish me with serviceable information regarding their respective attitudes. The stand of the Left Republican ministers during the debate was reflected in a derogatory allusion to Asensio in large type on the front page of *Política*, the national organ of their party,[4] the same day that Asensio's resignation was published in the official gazette.[5]

If Alvarez del Vayo had done much to undermine Largo Caballero's position in this crisis, the hostile attitude of the CNT and FAI toward the general, both in cabinet meetings and in their press, was also important.[6] A strict disciplinarian who had employed stern measures against retreating militiamen when in command of the central front and had ordered the execution, according to one authority, of several militia leaders who had refused to obey his orders to attack,[7] Asensio had long been distrusted in libertarian circles, where in the early days opposition to professional officers and to militarism in all its forms had been an article of faith. Hence, the CNT and FAI had been easily sucked into the campaign against the general, and, without consciously desiring it, had thereby facilitated the workings of the Communists against Largo Caballero. In the above-mentioned letter to me regarding Asensio, Federica Montseny avowed that she later considered that the libertarian movement's opposition to the general was a mistake, not only because of his exceptional ability, but because it helped to weaken Largo Caballero in relation to the Communists.

But Largo Caballero was not to be easily divested of a collaborator in whose technical ability he had the maximum confidence, and, with the object of using him in some capacity in the war ministry, instructed him to remain in Valencia under his direct orders.[8] At the same time, provoked by the struggle over Asensio, he took vigorous action against Communist influence in the war ministry. He assigned Lieutenant Colonel Antonio Cordón, a member of the Communist party and head of the technical secretariat of the undersecretaryship of war,[9] to the Cordova front,[10] dismissed his aide-de-camp, Lieutenant Colonel Manuel Arredondo, on account of his sympathy for the party,[11] and posted him, along with Captain Eleuterio Díaz Tendero —the philo-Communist chief of the vital information and control department and chief organizer before the war of the left-wing officer organization, the UMRA[12]—to the Basque front.[13]

Referring to these and other dismissals from the war ministry, Martín Blázquez, who at the time was one of Antonio Cordón's aides, writes: "Whether because my services were regarded as more essential, or because I was believed to be less a sympathizer with the Communist party, I was not dismissed from the ministry as so many others were. . . . Some of my colleagues, including Caballero's aide-de-camp Arrendondo and Díaz Tendero, were sent to the Army of the North at Bilbao. I confess I was alarmed at the prospect of being vindictively sent there myself. I was very pessimistic about the prospects on that front. I had made frequent requests for supplies for Bilbao, but they had all been rejected. 'We shall send nothing to the Army of the North,' I had been told. 'Let the Basques look after themselves! What have they got an independent Republic for?' In view of this shortsighted policy, being sent to the Army of the North obviously meant a very good chance of ending up before a fascist firing-squad."[14]

In this purge the Communists' greatest loss was undoubtedly that of Díaz Tendero, the head of the information and control department that investigated the political antecedents of every man before he could enter the army.[15] Without actually being a member of the Communist party, Díaz Tendero, to quote Margarita Nelken, the left Socialist Cortes deputy, who knew him personally and switched her own allegiance to the Communists in December 1936, "did wonderful things for the party."[16] His ability to advance the interests of the Communists was undoubtedly enhanced by the central role he played in a special officer classification committee, whose task it was—so Stanley Payne attests—to categorize all available officers according to their political reliability.[17] Thus he wielded considerable discretionary power, and his removal by Largo Caballero dealt a severe blow to the Communists' plans to dominate the war ministry, the more so as, according to Asensio, they had previously proposed, with the support of representatives of other organizations, that Díaz Tendero succeed him in his high office.[18]

In addition to the dismissal of Díaz Tendero and the other officers from their key posts, Largo Caballero—in a move that seemed to offer an even greater threat to Communist plans for hegemony—appointed six inspectors, all of them trusted left-wing Socialists,[19] to scrutinize the work of generals, of the lesser officers and noncommissioned officers, of the top officials in the commissariat of war,[20] and of political commissars of every rank.[21]

Cowed momentarily into discretion by this vehement reaction, the Communists ventured a mild criticism only of the latter measure[22] and refrained from condemning in their press the removal of their men from key positions in the war ministry, lest they exacerbate Caballero's anger still further. Through the ingenuity of Díaz Tendero they contrived a means of denouncing these dismissals and of preventing Caballero from retaining Asensio in any capacity in the war ministry. As head of the information and control department, Díaz Tendero had been in contact with all organizations, and was able—because his allegiance to the Communists was barely known outside the war ministry—to use the columns of *Nosotros*, the mouthpiece of the Iron Column,[23] whose dislike for Largo Caballero was untempered by the political considerations that restrained the language of the less extreme libertarian organs that, in spite of their attacks on

Asensio and their hostility to the Socialist leader before the war, were conscious of his present value as an ally against the Communists. On 25 February, *Nosotros*, inspired and documented by Díaz Tendero, published under the caption, "How the purging of the army is being carried out," an article containing one list of "sincere republican officers" dismissed from their posts and another of officers appointed in their stead, who had "never been known for their republican sympathies" and were "either disloyal or just indifferent." The first list included the above-mentioned Communist and pro-Communist officers—Antonio Cordón, Manuel Arredondo, and Díaz Tendero—who had been removed from the war ministry, and the second included the name of Lieutenant Colonel Fernández, who had succeeded Díaz Tendero in charge of the information and control department, and who was, according to *Nosotros*, a great friend of Asensio's. But more interesting than all these facts, the paper affirmed, was that although the impression had been created that General Asensio had been removed, he had, in reality, been relieved of all responsibility and placed behind the scenes as technical adviser to the minister and the new undersecretary. "Moreover, his appointment has been made by a simple ministerial order, whereas assignments and appointments of generals, whatever their status, should be made by decree on the proposal of the government and with the signature of the head of state."

Although there is no corroborative evidence that such a ministerial order was ever issued by Largo Caballero—and, indeed, Asensio himself later denied its existence[24]—the war minister certainly did hope to use the general's services, as the latter himself has conceded.[25] Nevertheless, no formal appointment of the kind suggested was made and it may be safely assumed that the allegation was designed to forestall any attempt to revive Asensio's authority in the war ministry.

In addition to the article inspired by Díaz Tendero, *Nosotros* came out with the following invective against the war minister:

"Largo Caballero is old, too old, and does not possess the mental agility necessary for solving certain problems upon which our own lives as well as the lives and liberty of the whole people depend.

"When the newspapers, all the newspapers—with the exception of those inspired by the war minister himself—accuse one man; when in the trenches, in the barracks, in the committees, in the streets, and in the ministries themselves, it is whispered or openly stated that General Asensio either through ineptitude or treachery has gone . . . from defeat to defeat; when it is common knowledge that on the very night the news of Malaga's fall was received, the general, now adviser to Largo Caballero, got drunk in a cabaret just like any individual who thinks only of wallowing in the mire and debasing himself, the minister should not . . . send letters to the press and adopt tragic airs with the idea of silencing such things." This last was a reference to two open letters written by Largo Caballero, one to Carlos Esplá, the Left Republican minister, the other to the national executive of the Left Republican party, protesting the following allusion to Asensio's successor, Carlos de Baráibar, on the front page of the party organ, *Política*, of 21 February: "If in the dismissals we can discern victory, do not let us invite defeat as a result of the appointments." In the first of these letters Largo Caballero asked Esplá whether *Política* was about to begin "a new campaign of a disruptive character such as the one that has compelled me to deprive myself of an able collaborator?" and urged him to use all his influence to stop it from developing.[26] In his letter to the national executive, he declared that he was not prepared to tolerate the initiation of a campaign by an official organ of a Popular Front party that might create "disagreeable situations" for his trusted collaborators.[27] In reply, *Política* contended somewhat meekly that the words to which Largo Caballero objected had been set up in type before the name of Asensio's successor was known,[28] while the national executive—no less sheepishly—affirmed that it did not see in them any attack on Carlos de Baráibar.[29]

"With hostile eyes the people see that they are being fooled," *Nosotros*'s invective against Caballero continued. "The resignation of Asensio is a trick because behind their backs he is extolled, having been elevated to a position of greater confidence at the side of the minister. . . . The minister of war, comrade Largo Caballero, should bear in mind that he is old, and, what is more, that he is becoming senile and that senile men should neither govern nor be allowed to govern."[30]

Angered by this abusive language and by the allegation regarding Asensio's appointment—an allegation that compelled him to abandon all idea of using his services, even unofficially, in the war ministry, lest he be accused of flouting public opinion and the will of the cabinet—Largo Caballero had Angel Galarza, left-wing Socialist minister of the interior, suspend the publication of *Nosotros*.[31] That same day the minister announced—without mentioning Díaz Tendero by name—that a regular army officer suspected of inspiring several articles had been arrested and that about two hundred copies of *Nosotros* had been found in his home.[32]

Revolutionary Militia to Regular Army

It is noteworthy that *Nosotros*'s attack on Largo Caballero had been embarrassing to the national leaders of the CNT. This was clear when, a few days later at the extraordinary congress of the Catalan CNT, the secretary of the national committee opposed and succeeded in defeating a motion of the Catalan organization that a protest should be made against the suspension of the paper.[33] Some months later, in reference to the attacks on Largo Caballero that had appeared in other libertarian newspapers, Helmut Ruediger, representative in Barcelona of the AIT with which the CNT was affiliated, wrote: "We all knew Caballero's past, but not all the editors of the CNT provincial papers knew that several months ago Caballero had become an opponent of Communist influence and that, consequently, to demand his removal was to do the work of the Communist party."[34]

A few months after the fall of Largo Caballero in May 1937, when the Communists had strengthened their position still further, Asensio was indicted for neglecting to supply the Malaga front with the necessary arms and munitions and was imprisoned pending trial.[35] In May 1938, he was released and rehabilitated, partly because of the intervention of influential friends, including Diego Martínez Barrio, the vice-president of the Republic, and of Vicente Rojo, then chief of the general staff, who was personally convinced of his innocence,[36] partly because he could have made a powerful case against his chief accusers, and partly because of the problem—having regard to the Communists' desire at that time to avoid widening still further the gulf between themselves and the left Socialists—of placing him on trial without impeaching his chief, Largo Caballero, to whose orders he was, as undersecretary of war, directly subordinate.

The *Nosotros* incident was the crowning indignity and injury that Largo Caballero had suffered at the hands of the Communists. For months he had watched their stealthy permeation of the Socialist movement and of the armed forces that had resulted in the loss of a substantial part of his own following, including many intimate associates. But no doubt fearing to forfeit Soviet supplies and also fearing to reveal to the outside world—particularly to Britain and France, which he still hoped might be enticed to raise the arms embargo—the depth of Communist penetration behind the republican façade,[37] he had been inhibited from making any public statement against his tireless adversaries. In fact, it was not until October 1937, five months after the fall of his government, that he ventured any open criticism. He claimed that he waited so long because he did not wish it to be said that he had made any statement that had adversely affected

Spain's position at Geneva or had demoralized the soldiers at the front. "I can assure you," he added, "that one of the greatest sacrifices I have ever made in my life was to keep silent during these past five months. But I am not worried, for, although the calumniators have thrust tooth and nail into my flesh, my conscience is satisfied that my silence was in the interests of Spain and in the interests of the war."[38] These considerations, apparently, also explain his forbearance during his incumbency.

Nevertheless, incensed by the *Nosotros* incident, he could no longer suppress his anger. Issuing from his silence on 26 February, he hit back with a public declaration, in which his diatribes against "fascist agents" were unmistakable allusions to the Communists.

On Sunday, 14 February, he stated, large contingents representing antifascist Spain marched through the streets of Valencia affirming their adhesion to the government and to the republican Constitution. (This referred to a demonstration in his support organized after the fall of Malaga by the provincial secretariat of the Valencia UGT, which was controlled by the left-wing Socialists. In a notice inviting all the trade-union, political, and cultural organizations in Valencia province to participate, the secretariat stated that it wanted the government to see by the demonstration that it had the support of the working people. The Communists accepted the invitation, and, at a gathering of the leaders of the local organizations, succeeded, thanks to the propitious atmosphere created by the fall of Malaga, in securing the adoption of a proposal that a ten-point petition be presented to Largo Caballero on the day of the demonstration embodying, among other things, the following demands: compulsory military service and the cleansing of all responsible military posts. That the Largo Caballero Socialists resented the petition is clear from the following lines in an editorial published in their newspaper the day before the demonstration: "We should not ask for compulsory military service, but should present ourselves when we are called up. . . . We should not ask for anything, but should give everything."[39] Owing to the participation of the Communists and to the petition, with which great play was made, the left-wing Socialists were unable to use the demonstration, as they had intended, to bolster Largo Caballero's authority. On the contrary, the Communists succeeded in using it very much to their own advantage.)

Largo Caballero's statement continued:

While [the demonstrators] were expressing their willingness to give the government unqualified support, and while as a result of this clamorous demonstration the position of republican Spain and its legal government was strengthened in the eyes of the world, fascist agents redoubled their efforts to such an extent that they found in the midst of traditionally republican and working-class organizations a certain response and even help for their aims and intrigues. Disguised among us, and favored by our proletarian and republican kindness, they sowed confusion, stirred up passions, and encouraged indiscipline in our ranks. . . . The authorities know that fascist agents, with membership cards of the republican parties, the Socialist party, the Communist party, and the UGT and the CNT, have been operating freely in loyalist Spain and that their criminal acts have succeeded in disorienting many republican soldiers and even civilians, whose clear and self-sacrificing past certify to their good faith and loyalty. . . . A section of the press and of the antifasicst parties and organizations, responsible members of those bodies, and well-intentioned yet thoughtless people, have become involved in the enemy's dark plot and facilitate his work. So well organized is espionage among us that I affirm in all sincerity that intrigues and passions are coiled around our feet like reptiles. . . .

A whole apparatus has wedged itself between the people and the government, perverting the consciences of many individuals and encouraging the darkest appetites, an apparatus that works consciously or unconsciously—in both ways I believe—against our cause, with the result, as I have already stated, that around the feet of those who should march, and are ready to march at the head of the democratic and working people, serpents of treason, disloyalty, and espionage are coiled.

I am not prepared to tolerate this state of things an hour longer.[40]

Although the Communists publicly described this veiled assault upon themselves as the "toads and snakes" manifesto in a denunciatory speech by politburo member Jesús Hernández, they did so on 28 May 1937, three months later, after the fall of the left Socialist leader.[41] When Largo Caballero issued his statement at the end of February, they were careful not to identify themselves publicly as the object of the assault and gave the statement a discreet reception in their press.[42] They also joined with other organizations at a meeting called by the premier in assuring him publicly of their support.[43]

Nevertheless, at the beginning of March, according to Hernandez, in his book, *Yo fuí un ministro de Stalin*, written some years after he had left the party, a politburo meeting of "far-reaching importance" was held in Valencia, attended by the Moscow delegation comprising Stefanov, Codovila, Gerö, and Togliatti, and by Marty, organizer of the International Brigades. Also present were Orlov, head of the NKVD in Spain, and Gaykis, the Soviet chargé d'affaires, who, Hernández points out, were attending a Spanish politburo meeting for the first time. "In short," he says acridly, "more foreigners than Spaniards." At the meeting, he claims, the overthrow of Largo Caballero was presented by Togliatti as the primary short-term objective. His account of this meeting has been ignored by the official history of the Civil War prepared under the auspices of La Pasionaria,[44] herself a member of the politburo, but was vigorously assailed by Orlov.[45] A summary is given here, since it offers the only testimony we have, although unconfirmed, of behind-the-scenes disagreement with the Moscow delegation over the propposed removal of Largo Caballero.

At the beginning of the meeting, Hernández states, José Díaz, the party secretary, gave his reasons why the Communists should not destroy Largo Caballero: They would incur the enmity of the majority of the Socialist party, would be accused of striving for political and military hegemony, and would isolate themselves from other anti-fascists. "I saw my comrades beset by doubts," Hernández comments, "filled with vacillation and fear . . . panic-stricken by the thought of having to wage a political struggle—for the first time!—against the representatives of Moscow." Hernández claims that he supported José Díaz, arguing that Caballero had behaved loyally toward the Communists, that he had helped them gain predominance in the army, that he had not hindered them from receiving the best arms, that thanks to him they had been able to organize the Popular Front and unite the Socialist and Communist youth, that he had been "docile" to the Soviet advisers, and that he was the Communists' main support for the fusion of the Socialist and Communist parties. To break with Caballero, he added, would be the greatest victory they could hand to General Franco.

"Uribe, Checa, Pasionaria, and Mije [the other members of the politburo, Pedro Martínez Cartón, the sixth member, being at the front] were petrified. They were waiting to hear the voice of Moscow before venturing an opinion." Then Stefanov spoke. Díaz and Hernández, he said, were defending a bad cause. It was not Moscow but "history" that condemned Caballero. Marty complained that Caballero rationed gasoline for the International Brigades and did not provide enough automobiles for his headquarters. " 'The trouble with you,' retorted Díaz, 'is that you have too large a bureaucratic machine.' 'I'm no bureaucrat!' Marty bellowed, thumping his chest with his fist. 'I'm a revolutionary, yes sir, a revolutionary!' 'So are we all,' replied Díaz. 'That remains to be seen,' answered Marty. 'You are a boor,' Hernández interposed, 'and neither your age nor your past history permit you to treat us with disrespect.' 'And you are a lump of shit,' Marty responded. Rising from his seat Díaz shouted, 'You are a guest at this meeting. If you are dissatisfied, there's the door!' "

Uproar followed. "Some were speechless . . . others incensed and rabid. Orlov, imperturbable, smoked in his armchair. Togliatti, cold and impenetrable, contemplated the scene with feigned serenity. Codovila . . . tried to calm Marty. Gueré [Gerö], open-mouthed, looked from one to the other with astonishment. Gaikins [Gaykis] ran a comb through his hair as though unaffected. Pasionaria, nervous and beside herself, shrieked 'Comrades! Comrades!' like a cracked record."

Gaykis spoke: " 'Caballero is withdrawing himself from Soviet influence. A few days ago he practically threw Rosenberg out of his office.' " Then came the turn of those members of the politburo who had not yet expressed themselves. " 'It won't make any difference,' " Hernández thought. " 'They'll sit where the sun is warmest.' . . . One after the other they rose . . . to condemn Largo Caballero and signify their agreement with the Soviet delegation. 'I can see,' Díaz said sarcastically, 'that the majority of the politburo agrees with the line expressed by the delegation, which I shall accept only out of discipline, putting on record my dissenting opinion.' " Togliatti, whom Hernández describes as the "heavy artillery" of the delegation, then spoke. "As could be expected his words were not designed to argue or convince. They were orders, devoid of tact or euphemism. . . . 'I propose that the campaign to soften up the position of Largo Caballero start at once. We shall begin with a large meeting in Valencia, at which Comrade Hernández will be the speaker.' " Hernández says that at first he objected, but, prompted by Díaz, yielded to party discipline. Concluding the meeting, Togliatti stated: " 'As for Largo Caballero's successor . . . I believe we should proceed by a process of elimination. Prieto? Vayo? Negrín? Of the three, Negrín may be the most suitable. He is not anti-Communist like Prieto, nor stupid like Vayo.' "[46]

There is a flaw in Hernández's account of this meeting that cannot be ignored. He claims that Orlov was present. This is unlikely, not because Orlov himself has denied his presence,[47] but because Hernández's description of him as a man "almost two meters tall, elegant, and polished,"[48] is totally inaccurate. This false portrayal may possibly be explained by an experience of mine that leads me to believe that Hernández was referring not to Orlov, but to Belayev, his second in command.

I met Orlov and another high-ranking operative of the NKVD, whom I am now persuaded was Belayev, in the spring and early summer of 1937, when I was a United Press correspondent in Valencia. Unfortunately, I do not recall the names by which they were introduced, but I discovered Orlov's identity many years later, when, after his death in 1973, the U.S. Government Printing Office published a booklet on Orlov together with a photograph taken in 1933.[49] Thanks to this photograph and to my clear recollection of the man, I can state beyond peradventure that far from being "almost two meters tall, elegant, and polished," Orlov was short and inconspicuous and could have passed unnoticed in virtually any crowd.[50] Belayev's physical appearance, I can personally attest, matched so closely the one that Hernández attributes to Orlov that he was undoubtedly the man Hernández had in mind.

Orlov and Belayev, to judge from the evidence available, worked in close cooperation, their names being linked together on three separate occasions, although the spelling of Belayev's name varies. Louis Fischer stated that, in September 1936, the Soviet ambassador in Madrid introduced him to "two Embassy secretaries, Orlov and Belayev," whom he guessed were "GPU [NKVD] men";[51] Julián Gorkin, the POUM leader,[52] who was arrested in June 1937 on the orders of the NKVD, gives the name of the Russian "next in rank" to Orlov, as Bielov,[53] the source of his information being the former Communists Enrique Castro and Valentín González (El Campesino);[54] and, finally, Hernández refers to a certain Vielayev, who, it would appear from the context, was intimately associated with Orlov.[55] Since Bielov and Vielayev are so close to Belayev in pronunciation, especially if we take into account the similarity in the sound of the Spanish B and V, there can be no doubt that they relate to the same person.

It is possible, though by no means certain, that Hernández's erroneous identification stemmed from the fact that he may have known Orlov only by his alias, Schwed, the "code name" Stalin employed to communicate with him in Spain regarding the gold shipment to Russia.[56] In his book published in 1953, Hernández frequently refers to Orlov by this name,[57] but that was fourteen years after Krivitsky had publicly disclosed that Orlov was the head of the NKVD in Spain and after the information had become common knowledge.

It will also be recalled that Alvarez del Vayo in his account of the gold shipment gives no inkling that he was aware—although he may have been—that the man whom Negrín "jocularly baptized" with the name of Blackstone was Orlov.[58] I must confess that from 1939, when I first read Krivitsky's disclosures, to the time I saw Orlov's photograph in 1973, I had surmised that the tall, elegantly attired, and dour individual, with the special air of authority, whom I had met in Valencia in 1937 and whom I now identify as Belayev, was the NKVD chief in Spain. Not for a moment had I suspected that the other man I knew—the short, inconspicuous individual, with the pleasantly disarming smile—was the real Orlov.

All this, perhaps, may help to explain Hernández's false identification, but not entirely; for there are elements of mystery in his frequent reference to Orlov that may never be satisfactorily explained. Witness, for example, the long dialogue he reproduces in his book between himself and Orlov, in which he uses the latter's name more than a dozen times.[59]

In his rebuttal to Hernández's account of the politburo meeting, Orlov claims that Togliatti was not present: "Hernández committed still another factual error, which completely demolishes his story. According to his narrative, this meeting [took place] in March 1937. . . . However, from the biography of Palmiro Togliatti, written by Marcella and Maurizio Ferrara [the Italian Communist writers],[60] we know that Palmiro Togliatti . . . arrived in Spain to take up his duties as representative of the Comintern in June 1937 [actually, July, according to the biography], i.e., *after* Largo Caballero had already resigned from the government. . . . Therefore, Togliatti could not have been at the meeting described and argued that Caballero must go. With Togliatti out, the imaginary meeting, with all of Hernández's fantastic trimmings, collapses."[61]

This part of Orlov's rebuttal, however, does not rest on solid ground, for, according to the Spanish Communist writer Adolfo Sánchez Vázquez, Togliatti was in Spain as a Comintern delegate during "practically" the entire conflict "from 1936 to 1939."[62] In fact, Hernández gives details regarding two other important meetings, held as early as August and November 1936, in which Togliatti participated, as well as another in Madrid, just before the fall of Largo Caballero, during which a large-scale offensive in Estremadura was discussed.[63] More important still is the testimony of Julián Gorkin, the POUM leader, who has researched this matter more thoroughly than any other person: "With regard to the date of Palmiro Togliatti's arrival in Spain and his personal and direct intervenion at the head of the Communist apparatus, a polemic began, principally in Italy, that has not yet ended. . . . His official biographers, Marcella and Maurizio Ferrara [*Conversando con Togliatti*], assert that he did not arrive in Spain until July 1937. . . . On the basis of numerous depositions, of which I have preserved only those of former Spanish Communist leaders and agents of Moscow, who collaborated with him, I can prove the following: a) As head of the Latin section of the Comintern, Togliatti intervened in the affairs of Spain even before the proclamation of the

Republic. . . . b) Togliatti belonged to the commission appointed in Prague, on 26 July 1936, to direct Spanish activities. . . . c) [It was Togliatti] and Duclos [the French Comintern representative] who imposed in Madrid (in September 1936) the line the Spanish Communist party was to follow. d) In Spain or during frequent trips to Paris and Moscow, Togliatti was delegate number one of the Comintern and, as such, intervened directly in all important decisions."[64]

In a letter to me, Gorkin affirms: "Palmiro Togliatti had his friends, the Ferrara couple, write that biography, after I had denounced him at a meeting in Rome for his role in Spain and had the important daily newspaper, *Il Messagero*, publish long extracts from the book by Jesús Hernández." Although Hernández does not give the exact date of the politburo meeting at which the fate of Largo Caballero was decided, he does say that it took place a few days before the plenum of the central committee of the Communist party.[65] This was held in Valencia on 5–8 March 1937.[66] The public meeting at which he spoke was not a special meeting in the Tirys movie theater, as he seems to imply,[67] but a public session of the plenum held in that location on 7 March,[68] which I personally attended.

Just before addressing the crowd, he claims that José Díaz said to him, "Pluck up your courage. The decision to destroy Caballero has been made. If you don't comply, it could mean your political downfall. And that should not happen on any account."[69]

"Both inside and outside the government," Hernández writes, "I served as a battering ram against Largo Caballero and against the undersecretary of defense, General Asensio, his man of confidence in military affairs. My name inspired odium. No one could perceive my personal drama, silent and disguised. And naturally I was judged on the basis of my conduct. This was neither the first nor the last time that I was compelled to stifle my personal feelings in order to obey Moscow. . . . The conflict between my conscience and my public actions was a silent, painful, and hidden duel. The party flattered me, and our followers acclaimed me as a hard-hitting orator, as the 'strong man' of the party leadership. The more my popularity grew, the more I saw myself sinking inexorably into the quagmire of the policy we were ordered to follow . . . and did follow. The fact that I was fully aware of what I was doing converted my duplicity into a moral torment."[70]

Although the overthrow of Largo Caballero was now Moscow's primary short-range objective, it was not until two months later that a suitable opportunity arose to oust him from the premiership. Meanwhile, the Communists continued to press their efforts to strip the military summits of all officers who were an impediment to their plans for hegemony. In this they were aided by an offensive launched on 8 March by General Franco's Italian allies on the Guadalajara sector of the Madrid front.

On the fifth day of the enemy's advance, when it seemed that nothing could arrest his triumphant progress, the two Communist ministers, Hernández and Uribe, supported by the majority of the cabinet, forced Largo Caballero to request the chief of the war ministry general staff, General Martínez Cabrera—whom he had appointed at the end of 1936 in place of the Communist Manuel Estrada[71]—to resign, and demanded that the Higher War Council be immediately convened to decide on his successor.[72] The Communists did not claim credit at the time for the removal of the general, but Hernández publicly declared after the fall of the Largo Caballero government that his party had been instrumental in removing him.[73]

Although *Mundo Obrero*, the Communist organ, had urged some days earlier, with Martinez Cabrera and other officers in mind, that the council should meet regularly to discuss all questions pertaining to the war, such as "the appointment and control of officers and the cleansing of the army of all hostile and incompetent elements,"[74] no action had been taken by Caballero. But now the demand of the Communist ministers could not be denied. Under the chairmanship of Caballero, the council met and voted on the proposal of Uribe, the Communist representative and member of the politburo—who, according to Enrique Castro, was constantly advised by Soviet technicians[75]—that Martínez Cabrera should be succeeded by José Miaja's chief of staff, Lieutenant Colonel Vicente Rojo.[76] Although within a few hours of this meeting a dramatic counteroffensive that transformed the Italian advance into a confused flight made it expedient to cancel Rojo's appointment so that he could remain at his post on the central front,[77] Martínez Cabrera was not suffered to continue in office.[78]

"What was the reason for depriving me of men who could be useful to me in the war ministry?" Largo Caballero asked some years later, referring to both José Asensio and Martínez Cabrera. The reason, he said, was threefold. (1) They had refused to fall into line and enter the Communsit party as Miaja had done. (2) The Communists wanted to fill the vacant posts with their own supporters "in order to know in detail what was going on in the war ministry." (3) The Communists wanted him to "get bored and to relinquish the portfolio of war."[79]

The removal of Martínez Cabrera was swiftly followed by another victory over Caballero; for no sooner had the general been ousted than the Communist ministers and their allies in the cabinet secured the appointment of Vicente Uribe, the Communist minister of agriculture, and of Alvarez del Vayo, the pro-Soviet foreign minister, as government representatives on the general staff.

"Experience has proved to us," stated *Mundo Obrero* on 18 March, "that the subordination of the highest military body to the minister of war is insufficient. Infinitely more just is the direct representation of the government in all the deliberations of the general staff. In this way, the officers who form the latter have at all times the help and advice of the government itself. . . . On the other hand, the arduous task of the holder of the portfolio of war requires this direct help of the two ministers. Our sincere congratulations to the government on this magnificent agreement."

While the Communists were thus registering triumphs in the cabinet and in the Higher War Council, Soviet representatives in Spain were endeavoring to undermine Caballero's influence still further by winning the unconditional adhesion of Carlos de Baráibar, who had succeeded General Asensio in the undersecretaryship of war. A left-wing Socialist belonging to Caballero's intimate circle, Baráibar had been deprived, owing to serious illness, of a firsthand knowledge of the events that had recently extinguished Caballero's enthusiasm for the unification of the Socialists and Communists. The information he had received was derived, according to his own account, solely from pro-Communist sources, Largo Caballero himself having confined his conversations with Baráibar to the latter's state of health and refrained from troubling him with political developments.[80] As a result, Baráibar affirms, he took up his new post inclined to work for the fusion of the two parties. "I frankly avow," he writes, "that there was a moment when I, of all the left-wing Socialists, was the most influenced by the Communists—allowing for the unsurpassable exception of Alvarez del Vayo—and that I understood my resumption of work should distinguish itself by a continual and positive labor in favor of the immediate fusion of the two parties in order to rescue our own from the catastrophe into which its inefficiency was plunging it and at the same time to demonstrate the superiority of Communist methods."[81] In another article, he acknowledges that the "dynamic quality" of the Communists was "very congenial" to him as "compared with the extreme sluggishness of many Socialists."[82]

Notwithstanding the accusations Baráibar heard from the lips of

Socialist colleagues when he was about to resume work that "on the very fronts, even in the field hospitals, the Socialists, just because they were Socialist, were receiving disgraceful treatment, whereas the Communists were favored in everything and even monopolized glory for themselves," and that a Socialist or an anarchist battalion could be seen "barefooted and in tatters at the side of another battalion of the same brigade, but of Communist affiliation, that was equipped as if for a military parade," he was disposed to make allowance for exaggeration.

"The impression I received was so shocking," he writes, "that I honestly believed that there had been considerable exaggeration in all I had heard. Furthermore, the extremely artful replies made in various speeches by Socialists, such as Vayo, who, as we learned later, had long been in the service of the Communist party, appeared so impregnated with revolutionary Marxist fervor, so inspired by the great ideal of unification, so ardently desirous of eradicating whatever might be true in those accusations by means of a far-reaching policy, through which the Socialists and Communists, united more closely every day, would devote themselves to winning the war, that although I no longer lived in the state of ingenuousness that I did when I was cut off from active politics, I nevertheless believed that the evil could not be as great as it appeared, so heinous did it seem to me. For this reason, I felt inclined to continue working for that broad policy of unification, together with men who were incapable of committing such injustices—injustices that conformed to a carefully prepared plan."[83]

But once in the undersecretaryship of war, Baráibar changed his mind. "In that observatory . . . the impression I received was the most disagreeable of my life and shattered the dearest illusions I had cherished during my illness. I gradually discovered to what degree I had been credulous and had run the risk of letting myself be seduced by rose-colored spectacles that were as odious as they were distorting. In the short period during which I held that post, it was necessary to change the administration of the health and transport services and prepare for changes in the quartermaster corps."[84] As the control of this corps was in Communist hands, Baráibar testifies elsewhere, "this terrible weapon of corruption and proselytism was employed unscrupulously in the commission of abuses ranging from the petty fraud of giving a friend a special voucher to the enormous infamy of granting or not granting, as the case may be, food and clothing to an entire unit, depending on its political coloring or that of its commander."[85]

"I learned that on some fronts," writes Largo Caballero, "an annoying preference was shown for the Communists; they were given shoes, clothing, tobacco, and food. The others were treated as stepchildren—that is, when they were not shot in the back. I likewise learned that in some hospitals—just as the priests and nuns had once acted toward noncommunicants—non-Communists were not taken care of. They were neither treated properly nor fed properly; all the attention was given to Communist party members and future prospects."[86] "It is a lamentable thing to have to acknowledge the fact that in order to get rope sandals a soldier must be a Communist," declared the left-wing Socialist Carlos Rubiera early in the war. "In the [military] hospitals the same thing goes on as in the days of the nuns, when, in order to get a stew or chicken, or whatever there was, you had to wear and venerate the scapular or the cross. Now you need the hammer and sickle."[87] And even the moderate Socialists, who were cooperating with the Communist party as closely as they dared against Largo Caballero, their common enemy, condemned the privileged position enjoyed by the Communists at the front.[88]

"Without any desire to offend those persons who occupied positions of maximum responsibility," Baráibar testifies, "I must declare that all the levers on which they relied—the exceptions are so few that they are not worth mentioning—were in the hands of Stalinists who ran the services of the army with the utmost unscrupulousness and profited from its funds and perquisites of office, concerned only with the growth of the Communist party, with the reinforcement of its power, and, in some cases, only with personal gain. And what happened in the departments of the undersecretaryship of the war ministry also occurred in the different sections of the general staff. By means of a fantastic web of intrigue and in spite of the honesty of many persons who held technical posts of the greatest responsibility, and who were not members of any political party, . . . the Communists cornered all the commanding positions, and, protected by them, waged a campaign of proselytism as barefaced as it was menacing."[89]

A few weeks after the fall of Largo Caballero, *CNT* declared, "The Communist party orders officers who are subject to its control to use military discipline in order to make converts, with the result that we find thousands of cases where a military commander employs his prerogatives and the military code not in order to fight fascism, but to annihilate revolutionary organizations and weaken the power of other antifascist bodies."[90]

From the moment he entered the undersecretaryship, Baráibar was regaled by the Russians in the Hotel Metropol, Soviet headquarters in Valencia, and received regular visits from them at the war ministry, during which they endeavored to seduce him from his allegiance to Caballero.[91] Although he does not refer in detail to these occasions, he nevertheless reveals: "I received all manner of flattery and was conceded the honor of being the only Socialist—next to Alvarez del Vayo, of course—capable of appreciating the urgent need . . . for the fusion of the working class. In short, I was being tenderly cultivated for the role of traitor to Largo Caballero."[92] But Baráibar refused to forsake the Socialist leader, and from the day he gave the Soviet ambassador to understand that he would not assume the role the Russians and their Spanish aides expected of him, he ceased to be the object of their cajolery.[93] His rebuff came as a rude surprise, for his recent support of the idea of Socialist-Communist unification, particularly at a time when its luster had begun to tarnish before the eyes of many of his own colleagues, had encouraged the Communists to believe that he would advance their interests in the war ministry. Far from fulfilling these expectations, Baráibar became a prop for Caballero's policy and, in the succeeding weeks, helped the war minister to carry out his most rigorous assault on Communist positions in the armed forces. By the end of March this assault had acquired such amplitude as to elicit a public denunciation by the politburo: "The unity of all antifascists necessary for winning the war is being hindered by a whole series of acts, especially during the last few days, such as the transfer or removal from commanding positions of officers and commissars—*just because they are Communists*—who have given repeated proofs of their abilities and talents."[94]

Largo Caballero's anger had undoubtedly been inflamed by the Communists' behavior in the war ministry and by the practices of their political commissars now being brought to his attention. These practices ranged from the withholding of non-Communist newspapers from the front[95] to the coercing of soldiers to join their party.[96] He also had recently learned of the sectarian conduct of the general commissariat of war that, it will be remembered, had been set up in October 1936 to regularize the appointment of commissars and had passed under the control of the Communists owing to the secret defection of Alvarez del Vayo and Felipe Pretel, whom the war minister had selected because they enjoyed his highest confidence.[97] On 25 November he had issued instructions whereby all commissars were to be appointed by him on the proposal of Alvarez del Vayo, the general commissar, whose recommendations were to be submitted through Felipe Pretel, the secretary general.[98] Although these instructions gave no authority to the commissariat to permit candidates to take up their proposed assignments before formal ratification by the war minister, the candidates recommended by Alvarez del Vayo, as well as by Mije, the Communist head of the subcommissariat of organization, to whom the former frequently delegated his powers, had been allowed to assume their duties "provisionally," a procedure that had greatly benefited the Communist party.[99]

"One of those most responsible," writes Largo Caballero, "was Alvarez del Vayo . . . , who until then had professed to be my trustworthy friend. He labeled himself a Socialist, but was unconditionally in the service of the Communist party and abetted all its maneuvers. . . . I summoned [him]; reprimanded him for his conduct and for appointing more than two hundred Communists without my knowledge and signature. He turned pale as he listened to me and with an absolutely deadpan expression replied that the appointments were of company commissars and that he had made them because he thought he had the authority. With the law in my hand I showed him that there were no exceptions whatsoever."[100]

Shortly after the war Alvarez del Vayo gave the following defense on the question of the commissariat: "When it was formed in Spain, the Spanish Communists . . . took a greater interest in its development and expansion than the other political parties. The latter, for whom it had no particular meaning and who looked on it at first as something rather exotic and unnecessary, contented themselves with presenting lists of candidates drawn up with no special care. The Communists, on the other hand, sent their most active members right from the day of its inception. This inequality grew during the critical period of the defense of Madrid. The situation on that front during the months of November and December 1936 made it necessary to increase the number of commissars. Hundreds of provisional nominations were made, and these only served to increase the existing disproportion."[101]

More than thirty years later, Alvarez del Vayo affirms that the most painful attacks upon him were those that pictured him as having "betrayed" Largo Caballero. "I had loved Don Francisco," he protests, "like no other of my chiefs. I was unquestionably one of the Socialists in whom he confided most at the start of the war. I was already his Foreign Minister and when the time came to create a War Commissariat he insisted that I become the general commissar. . . . Largo Caballero filled me with immense respect. He was an exemplary Socialist, completely at harmony with the working class, from which he had come. . . . With a noble face and youthful blue eyes, Largo Caballero easily won the affection of the masses, among whom, at the start of the war, he was much more popular and beloved than any other leader. I was completely devoted to him. . . . .I appointed [the political commissars] without paying any attention to their political affiliation. . . . Their party or political affiliation made no difference to me. In the end it turned out that the Communists were greater in number than the commissars who belonged to other parties. Largo Caballero was immediately informed by the Socialists who surrounded him (and some of them owed their posts to me) that I 'had delivered the War Commissariat to the Communists.'"[102]

Feeling himself cheated in the trust he had placed in Alvarez del Vayo and realizing how very greatly the commissar general was under the spell of Communist influence, Largo Caballero decided to apprise Manuel Azaña, but although the president of the Republic authorized Alvarez del Vayo's dismissal from the cabinet, Caballero, oddly enough, retained him in office.

"One day in 1937," testifies Indalecio Prieto, the moderate Socialist minister, who was in constant and intimate communication with Azaña during the war, "the premier—Largo Caballero—telephones from Valencia to Barcelona, asking President Azaña for an urgent interview, which is held halfway in Benicarló. Largo Caballero loses no time in declaring: 'I have asked for this conference because I must tell you, and I could not do so by telephone, that one of my ministers is betraying me.' Azaña is surprised. Largo Caballero continues: 'The minister belongs to my own party; he is a Socialist, the foreign minister.' The prime minister then informs the president of the Republic of the disloyal conduct of Julio Alvarez del Vayo. . . . Azaña authorizes Largo Caballero to discard Alvarez del Vayo, but the prime minister does not use the authority granted him, just as a few weeks earlier he did not take advantage of an opportunity I gave him to get rid of that Communist puppet when, in the very midst of a cabinet meeting, I told Alvarez del Vayo that his conduct was more befitting a Soviet official than of a Spaniard who was a minister in the government. Annoyed by my words, Alvarez del Vayo resigned,[103] but Largo Caballero, far from accepting his resignation, retained him in office. . . . There are some men with a reputation for firmness who are given to absurd weaknesses."[104]

The element of inconsistency in Caballero's action in all likelihood derived partly from his hesitation to disrupt Alvarez del Vayo's work and diplomatic connections at the League of Nations[105] and partly from his fear of how Russia, the sole purveyor of arms, might react to Alvarez del Vayo's removal. But his action must also have stemmed in some measure from a knowledge of the frailness of his position should the dismissal of his foreign minister provoke a cabinet crisis. For, while it is certain that Caballero and his followers could rely upon the CNT in the event of a government shake-up, divided though they were by differences of principle and practice, it is no less certain that the Communists and their allies, the moderate Socialists and republicans, whatever the differences between them, were united as one man in their hostility to the left Socialist leader. Thus, rather than risk ejecting Alvarez del Vayo from the government or even from the commissariat of war, Largo Caballero issued, on 17 April, a sensational executive order curbing the powers of that influential body. Not only did he subordinate it to himself in the matter of orientation, but all nominations, removals, and promotions were henceforth to be decided directly by him, while any commissar whose appointment and rank had not been confirmed by 15 May was to consider himself dismissed from the corps of commissars.[106]

This order provoked a hurricane of protest from the Communist party. "It is quite clear," objected *Frente Rojo*, "that the political commissar does not have everybody's sympathy and appreciation. . . . Who are those persons who are attempting to restrict his functions and who would even suppress them, were that possible? They are men with antiquated ideas who are still among us, men who counteract the creative work of our people with the foul practices of the old school. These are the enemies of the political commissars. . . . Far from restricting the work of the commissars and giving them a one-sided orientation, it is necessary for our army that their sphere of activity be broadened and that they be given ample means, as well as the necessary stimulus, for accomplishing their tasks."[107] The following day it asked: "Who can feel hostile to this corps of heroes? Who can feel antagonistic to the forgers of the people's army? Only the declared enemies of the people; only those who are irreconcilably opposed to the antifascist army; only the blind or the insensate who are driven by a torrent of passion to commit the worst infamies. Our commissars are the pride of our army! We must defend them as we would our own children!"[108]

"There are some persons," affirmed La Pasionaria, "who want to kill the commissar's initiative by subjecting him to bureaucratic regulations that will tend to render his magnificent work ineffective and to transform him into a man without enterprise, fearful of any bold action on which the commanding officer may frown.

"But this must not be allowed. The commissar cannot on any account be deprived of his distinguishing characteristics, he cannot be placed in subjection and politically castrated without inflicting grave damage on the organization and the discipline of our Popular Army.

"That would nullify all the constructive work, all the cleaning up that was effected in order to create the Popular Army, the genuine army of the people.

"It would mean leaving our soldiers at the mercy of officers who could at a given moment disfigure the character of our army by returning to the old days of barrack discipline.

"Commissars, stick to your posts!"[109]

"The war minister's recent order concerning the commissariat," retorted Caballero's mouthpiece, *Adelante*, "in no way restricts its functions. On the contrary, it invigorates them and places them within the bounds of the commissariat's aim, which is not to practice political sectarianism . . . but to create the moral atmosphere and sense of responsibility that will carry our army to victory under the supreme control of the man who, at this historic hour, is undertaking the tremendous and glorious task of directing the destinies of Spain."[110]

In its rejoinder, *Frente Rojo* declared: "The war minister can give the commissariat whatever orders he likes, but control must rest in the hands of the commissariat itself. If that is not so, why was it created? For the purpose of making another department of the war ministry? In that case the commissariat would be superfluous."[111]

Adelante contended:

Nobody, least of all the minister of war . . . seeks to diminish the prestige of the [commissariat]. We have already pointed out the aim [of the order], an aim that, of course, will be carried out, namely, that the commissariat of war shall not be used by any party belonging to the Popular Front government coalition for the purposes of propaganda. It is essential that we all act with honesty and with loyalty. On behalf of the Socialist party, we declare that certain commissars belonging to the Communist party have misused their posts in order to make political converts. . . . We affirm that individuals of scant ideological stability and frivolous political behavior, who should have entered the corps of commissars as Socialists, republicans, or anarchists, have, contrary to their intimate convictions, submitted to pressure from commissars of a higher rank belonging to the Communist party and have asked to become members of that organization. And because pressure and coercion, if these did not have the desired results, were followed by a crescendo of defamation and threats, [the premier and war minister] decided . . . to put an end to a state of affairs that would necessarily have led to disaster, to an unbridgeable chasm of distrust and sectarianism being created between the soldiers belonging to different political and trade-union organizations.[112]

Largo Caballero's order had, of course, the unqualified support not only of the left-wing Socialists, but also of the anarchosyndicalists, who had long been exercised by the activities of the Communist political commissars. Back in December, *Frente Libertario*, organ of the CNT armed forces on the Madrid front, had stated that the editors had received countless letters complaining that in many units composed of members of different organizations the noncommissioned officers and commissars were devoting themselves to making political converts and were using coercive measures to this end.[113] And now *CNT*, the Madrid anarchosyndicalist organ, declared: "The war minister, adopting a firm and just attitude that we all praise, has cut short the maneuvers through which the Communist party was planning to secure the political control of the entire Popular Army, maneuvers that included the appointment of a number of commissars utterly out of proportion to the size of its forces at the front. We all laud . . . the mission of the general commissariat of war, but no one can allow this body, which was to guarantee the revolutionary character of our army to bring to the battle fronts not only the same frenzied partisanship that the Communist party practices behind the lines, but also its intolerable plans for hegemony."[114]

The polemic that had raged in the press between the Communists and left-wing Socialists over the commissariat of war assumed a more rancorous character every day as mutual recrimination was stimulated by the presence of other barbed issues in the military field. These included the creation of reserves, which the Communists considered were being organized at too leisurely a pace;[115] the removal from the army of alleged traitors; a decree of Largo Caballero (16 February 1937) limiting the highest rank to which civilian militia leaders could rise to that of major,[116] regarded by the Communists as a hindrance to their plans to gain control of the regular army through the cadres trained in their Fifth Regiment;[117] a subsequent decree issued by Caballero denying admission to the officers' training schools of anyone lacking a recommendation from the CNT or UGT, viewed by the Communists as an attempt to "depoliticalize" the army and convert it into "a monopoly of the two labor federations";[118] and finally, the designation by the Higher War Council, over Largo Caballero's objections, of the Communist ministers of education and agriculture, Jesús Hernández and Vicente Uribe, to discharge missions of military significance in Madrid and the Basque Country. With regard to this matter, in mid-March the council had appointed Jesús Hernández and Julio Just, Left Republican minister of public works, to represent the government in Madrid. Their object was to establish closer relations with the Defense Council and to study the needs of the central front. When the appointments came up for ratification by the government, Largo Caballero, fearing the additional influence that the Communists might gain from the presence of one of their ministers in Madrid, took exception to a proposal that the mission of the two ministers should be permanent. Owing to disagreement, the cabinet never defined the precise duties of the two ministers or settled the length of their stay in the capital, and when they returned temporarily to Valencia, *Adelante*, Largo Caballero's mouthpiece, declared that their mission had terminated.[119] Debate was still gyrating around this issue when the Higher War Council designated Vicente Uribe, its Communist representative, to undertake an investigation into the situation in the north, where a large-scale offensive had been opened on 1 April by General Franco's forces and his German and Italian allies. The war minister viewed this assignment with no less hostility than that given to Hernández, particularly as Uribe was accompanied by Gorev, the Soviet general.

But though important in themselves, these issues were for the most part only symptomatic of the fundamental cleavage between the two factions.

Adelante wrote:

For some time we have been consuming our reserves of patience in face of the sly insinuations and the malevolent criticisms that the newspapers and agitators of the Communist party have been directing . . . against members of the Spanish Socialist party and especially against the work of its most prominent figure. . . .

The Communist organ [*Frente Rojo*] inclines toward a monstrous abuse of criticism. Everywhere it sees defects, shortcomings, and lack of foresight. The time has come to silence these irresponsible statements by asking whether or not the inspirers, who see so many motes in the eyes of others, do not have a beam in their own. And on this matter, what can be said of the activities of the Communist party representatives in the government? The activity of the minister of agriculture is certainly not in all respects the most adequate to our national requirements. Nor is the behavior of the minister of education, as far as the functions entrusted to him by the government are concerned, the kind circumstances demand. In the whole of loyalist Spain the problems of agricultural production and distribution are still without a solution capable of guaranteeing the tranquillity of the rear. Thousands upon thousands of children are left without proper care by the minister of education.

Reserves? . . . Thousands of young Spaniards in the barracks are integrated into the war machine. The fundamental reserves, however, are based on the regulation of agricultural production and distribution. That is the matter that lies within the competence of the minister of agriculture!

Reserves? The most important reserves of the Spanish people are the children, the younger generation. What care are they receiving? What attention is being paid to them?

It is advisable to remind every member of the government that he has precise functions limited to the problems affecting his ministry. It is stupid, for instance, for a minister of education and fine arts, or for a minister of agriculture, to attempt to solve war problems. The ministers should confine themselves to their specific tasks and not meddle in business foreign to their own departments—except at cabinet meetings. They have enough to do solving their own problems. . . . We are not prepared to tolerate any further attempt to disturb the rear by negative criticisms and hypocritical assertions aimed at a systematic disparagement of those who are facing the rigors of the war with that silent and modest heroism with which great deeds are accomplished.

Enough silly talk! An end to high-sounding slogans that are not carried out and to appeals for cordiality, unity, and fraternity that are put into effect with mental reservations and with a view to personal advantage! . . . We Socialists raise above everything else the banner of the Spanish Revolution, a revolution that, thanks to the sacrifice of our martyrs and heroes and to our Spanish slogans and leaders, has been achieved in a Spanish way.[120]

Frente Rojo argued:

Do the comrades of *Adelante* really believe that the ministers are mere trade-union secretaries who should concern themselves only with the "business" of their respective unions? The Communist ministers represent their respective organizations in the government, as do the Socialist, republican, and anarchist ministers, and are, and should be, as much concerned as anyone else about the problems and situations created by the war. Or does *Adelante* believe that the war is being waged only by the war minister and that the question of victory or defeat affects him alone? The war and the administration of the country are conducted by the Popular Front, by all the parties and organizations comprising the Popular Front, and the men who represent them in the government have the same right and obligation to concern themselves with questions affecting the entire country as well as the lives and future of all Spaniards. From where does *Adelante* get its absolutist conceptions?

Our ministers intervened in the north and in Madrid at a very serious moment . . . and the results of their work inspire confidence. We do not say that they alone have solved the difficulties; they have contributed to their solution in a large degree, and their efforts, all the things they have accomplished, have the frank and full support of our party. . . .

Adelante demands that Hernández organize child reserves. It is true that the children have to be prepared for life as well as for the kind of society that will stem from our victory, but first we have to equip our army with the necessary reserves for attaining that victory. . . .

Revolutionary Militia to Regular Army

The comrades of *Adelante* should let us know whether they want a Popular Front policy or a policy based on a personal dictatorship.

Finally, is it not strange, having regard to the fact that the whole people—anarchists, Socialists, Communists, and republicans—have been demanding for months and months the cleansing of the commanding army posts, that this cleansing should begin with the political commissars? How many commissars have passed over to the enemy, we should like to know? How many officers have deserted and are still deserting? Here is a concrete task for the person concerned with the fate of our army. . . .

We do not quite understand the reiteration of the adjective "Spanish" in *Adelante*'s article. What is it insinuating? No one is more Spanish, profoundly and fervently Spanish, than the Communist party and its leaders, and it was precisely our party that characterized the present war as a war of national independence, as a war for the maintenance of Spanish sovereignty.[121]

Adelante declared:

The Communist party says it is supporting a Popular Front policy, but avails itself of every seasonable opportunity to pursue its own policy and to spread propaganda that must of necessity irritate non-Communists. In this way it only succeeds in achieving something quite distinct from what it brags about every day; in other words, it sows suspicion and sectarianism among the workers, rendering difficult the organic unity of the proletariat for which the Socialist party has been fighting for so long, and especially Largo Caballero, against whom the rage of four or five petty, resentful leaders is now concentrated . . . , leaders who are incapable of understanding that a man who is all self-sacrifice and determination can work modestly for seven long months while heaps of nonsensical slogans are spread about the rear with no better result than that of creating confusion. . . . Where are the wits of those who disparage the leader of the Spanish working class? Do they think it is such an easy matter to destroy his prestige by a blustering political campaign? Do they not realize that Largo Caballero is not a political boss as *Frente Rojo* insinuated the night before last, nor an apprentice in dictatorship, nor even a potential dictator. He is the incarnation of a whole revolutionary movement. He is the personification of the history of the Spanish working class and the Marxist movement in Spain. He is the embodiment of forty years of exemplary conduct in our trade-union and revolutionary struggles.[122]

Part V
The Communist Triumph

26. The Communist Party Cultivates the Moderate Socialists

Thwarted by Largo Caballero's opposition to their plans for military hegemony and by his refusal to promote the political supremacy of their party through the fusion of the Socialist and Communist parties, the Communists now decided to ally themselves with the moderate or so-called center faction of the Socialist party and to exploit its internal rivalries in order to undo the left Socialist leader.[1]

Before the Civil War, the center faction, which controlled the executive committee of the party, had been intensely hostile to the Communists. It had condemned their campaign for the fusion of the two parties as the "fraud of unification"[2] and had denounced the coalescence of the two youth movements—which had been achieved thanks to the naïve support of Largo Caballero[3]—as the "absorption of the Socialist youth by the Communist party."[4] Indeed, the executive committee had viewed the Communists with such suspicion and dislike that it had refused to answer a proposal they had made to set up a liaison committee between the two parties. "The Communist party," wrote José Díaz in April 1936, "has proposed to the Socialist party the formation of a contact committee with a program designed to facilitate the development of the democratic Revolution and to carry it to its final consequences. This proposal has been left unanswered by the present reformist and centrist leadership. On the other hand, it has been welcomed by the left wing. The masses of the Socialist party repudiate the attitude of the present reformist executive and see in the line of Largo Caballero one that approaches most the revolutionary path, the path of the Communist party and the Communist International."[5]

While publicly extolling Largo Caballero, the leader of the left wing, the Communists excoriated Prieto, the leader of the center faction. A masterful character, who enjoyed immense prestige in moderate circles, Prieto had infinitely more in common with the liberal and even conservative republicans than with the left wing of his own party.[6] Thus, when he declared to *L'Intransigeant* of Paris in the spring of 1936 that Spanish individualism could not conform to the "methods of Moscow" and that he favored Socialist collaboration in the republican government, *Mundo Obrero*, the Communist organ, suggested that inasmuch as he had repudiated not only the "violent struggle for power" but the "essence of Marxism" by advocating "old-style working-class collaboration with the bourgeois Republic," he should "voluntarily resign from the Socialist party and join any of the republican parties."[7] Yet, despite this taunt, in the spring of 1936, the Communists were secretly more in sympathy with Prieto's moderate stance than with Largo Caballero's ultrarevolutionary posture, which they obliquely or privately censured,[8] but they knew that the center faction represented only a small section of the Socialist movement and that they had much to gain from publicly associating themselves with the powerful left wing as long as their friendship with Largo Caballero lasted.

Although collaboration between the Communists and the center faction of the Socialist party had not been feasible before the Civil War, it now appeared practicable largely because of Prieto's unexpected friendliness toward Marcel Rosenberg, the Soviet ambassador,[9] and toward General Smushkevich, alias Duglas, the head of the Russian air force units in Spain, to whom he offered every facility in his capacity as navy and air minister. "Prieto was at first on excellent terms with the Russians," testified Hidalgo de Cisneros, the Spanish chief of the air force, at one time an intimate of Prieto's,[10] who joined the Communist party quite early in the war.[11] "He said that we should do everything we could to encourage them to help us. He urged the Russians to send us war material. He made two or three speeches to the Russian pilots, one of which he made in Albacete, thanking them for coming to Spain and saying that their country was the only one that had helped the Republic. He spoke like a Communist. He was on excellent terms with Duglas and Rosenberg."[12]

In the same uncharacteristic spirit of cooperation with the Communists, Prieto assured Codovila, the Comintern delegate, of his readiness to work for the fusion of the Socialist and Communist parties,[13] an intention he also conveyed to Pietro Nenni, International Brigade commissar and later head of the Italian Socialist party, during a conversation on 3 March 1937.[14]

Although Prieto's expression of friendly intentions was in strident contradiction with his past, he undoubtedly had inner reservations, to judge from his vigorous resistance to the Communists after he became defense minister some months later. The following episode, recounted by Prieto, which occurred after he succeeded Largo Caballero in the war ministry, is worth recording: "One night, at an unaccustomed hour, Gaisky [Leon Gaykis, the Soviet ambassador, who succeeded Rosenberg] brought me some welcome news: an important shipment of war material that I felt might be decisive was about to leave Russian ports. The ambassador showed pleasure at my display of satisfaction. Two days later he came back to see me and asked me to support the fusion of the Socialist and Communist parties. I refused, and he repeated his demands almost threateningly. He insisted with tenacity, hinting that he was carrying out orders from Moscow and that I would be rewarded or punished according to the attitude I adopted. He did not sway me. During a third visit, but without referring in any way to our earlier conversation [Gaykis] informed me that the much-needed war material that had been offered would not be shipped. That was the punishment I received."[15]

But in the spring of 1937, Prieto still needed the Communists, as they did him, to compass the ruin of Caballero. Prieto had not forgiven his opponent for preventing him from assuming the premiership in May 1936.[16] In fact, the relations between Prieto and Caballero even before that date had been so strained by mutual rivalry and antagonism that they barely spoke to one another.[17] After the outbreak of the Civil War, according to air force chief Hidalgo de Cisneros, although they formed part of the same cabinet, they avoided each other as much as possible and used intermediaries to discuss affairs jointly affecting their respective ministries.[18] Like the Communists, Prieto was animated by hostility to the left wing of the Revolution[19] and by the hope that a moderate course would induce Britain and France to abandon their policy of neutrality. On 4 October 1936, *El Socialista*, which expressed Prieto's viewpoint, had stated: "We have to take into account the attitude of the states that surround us. . . . We still hope that the estimate of Spanish events made by certain democracies will be changed, and it would be a pity, a tragedy, to compromise these possibilities by accelerating the Revolution."[20] But between Prieto and the Comintern, which directed Spanish Communist policy, there was a profound divergence of aim; for whereas the Comintern was concerned first and foremost with the advantages that Russia's strategic position would derive from the raising of the arms embargo,[21] Prieto—like Azaña and many other liberal republicans who looked to the moderate Socialist politician for leadership—was interested solely in the Spanish scene. To his mind, Anglo-French aid would counteract the mounting influence of Russia, which he attributed largely to their neutrality: "The Western democracies," he declared after the war, "fearful of communism, did not realize that this movement grew in Spain as a result of their own lack of assistance. To the extent that these countries denied us help, popular sympathy went openly to Russia when it was learned that she was supplying us with the means of defense."[22]

Yet, because he now needed the Communists for his own purposes and little realized that, like Caballero, he would eventually become their victim, Prieto did not allow the misgivings their growth and proselytizing methods—which were the subject of sharp and even violent criticism in *El Socialista*[23]—were causing him to interfere with the close association they were establishing with the executive committee of the party, over which he still preserved a directing influence through its secretary, Ramón Lamoneda, and its president, Ramón González Peña. Nor did the Communists allow their past distrust of Prieto to impede their courtship of the moderate Socialist leader and his center faction. As Stefanov, the Comintern delegate, told Eudocio Ravines, the foreign Communist, in reference to Prieto: "For us, as you well know, there are neither friends nor enemies; there are persons who serve and persons who do not."[24]

In a statement reflecting the rapprochement between the center faction and the Communists, as well as the breach with the left-wing Socialists, the politburo of the Communist party declared at the end of March:

"Having regard to the fact that the relations between the Communists and Socialists are becoming closer every day owing to a correct understanding of the policy of the Popular Front, and that the hostility to the Communist party is not due to the opposition of the Socialist party itself, but to a few isolated individuals who do not interpret the correct feelings of the masses, the politburo considers it necessary to strengthen its ties with the Socialist party. It therefore invites the executive committee to hold a joint meeting with a view to examining the present situation and establishing on a permanent basis closer relations than have existed until now by the setting up of coordinating committees of a local and national character that will facilitate the discussion and adoption of measures leading to unity of action and AS QUICKLY AS POSSIBLE TO THE FUSION OF THE SOCIALIST AND COMMUNIST PARTIES INTO A GREAT SINGLE PARTY of the Spanish working class.

The Communist Party Cultivates the Moderate Socialists

"With this aim in view, the politburo has apointed a delegation to establish relations immediately with the leadership of the Socialist party."[25]

As a result of the negotiations that took place during the month of April, a national coordinating committee was formed, in which Ramón Lamoneda represented the Socialist party and José Díaz the Communist party. Its first action was the issuance of instructions to all units of the two organizations to set up similar liaison committees in their respective localities.[26] In the succeeding months the idea of fusing the two parties was extolled, theoretically and rhetorically, with only slightly less enthusiasm by the Prieto Socialists[27] than by the Communists, but it never became a reality. Nonetheless the close relations that the Communists and Prieto Socialists had now established were destined to exercise a fateful influence on the course of events during the decisive days ahead; for, behind the public agreement to work for the fusion of the Socialist and Communist parties, there lay, as events will testify, a secret compact to oust Largo Caballero from the premiership and war ministry.

27. Catalonia: Revolution and Counterrevolution

Strengthened by their secret agreement with the moderate Socialists —an agreement to which some of the Left Republican leaders were also privy[1]—the Communists required but a suitable opportunity to bring the conflict with Largo Caballero to a head.

This came with the eruption on 3 May 1937 of an armed conflict in Barcelona, the capital of the semiautonomous region of Catalonia. Tensions had been mounting ever since the defeat of the rebel garrison in July 1936, by the combined efforts of the assault and civil guards and by the left-wing organizations,[2] had left the CNT and FAI virtual masters of the city, the largest and most heavily industrialized urban center on the peninsula.

Following the defeat of the military insurrection, the CNT and FAI, by far the most powerful of the working-class organizations in Catalonia, seized post offices and telephone exchanges, formed police squads and militia units, and through their factory, transport, and food committees established their dominion over the economic life of the city as well as over a significant share of the economy of the region.[3] In August 1936, Jaime Miravitlles, a Catalan Left Republican, wrote: "Capitalism no longer exists in our region. . . . It is the labor unions that . . . control the large metallurgical and textile plants and public utility corporations."[4] Furthermore, the CNT and FAI assumed command of most of the Franco-Spanish border,[5] a prerogative reserved to the central government. Madrid had been empowered by Article 9 of the Statute of Catalan Autonomy of September 1932 to take control of internal order if the interests of the state were threatened, but, itself a prey to revolution, it had neither the will nor the strength to exert authority.

Just as the republican Constitution of 1931 had become an empty formula, so, too, had the Catalan Statute. Not since the Middle Ages had Catalonia been so completely free from Madrid; but it was a freedom hardly satisfying to the middle classes, the principal advocates of Catalan autonomy, for while the Revolution had destroyed the coercive power of Madrid, it had also shattered the political structure upon which the free enterprise system and the security of private property reposed. The statute had given Catalonia a parliament and an executive council—the government of the Generalitat—in which the Esquerra Republicana de Catalunya, the Republican Left of Catalonia, the strongest party of the Catalan middle and lower middle classes, was dominant, but the practical significance of these two bodies had all but disappeared in the whirlwind of the Revolution.

On 20 July, immediately after the defeat of the military insurrection, Luis Companys, president of the autonomous region and head of the Esquerra, made the following conciliatory statement to a group of triumphant anarchosyndicalist leaders including Juan García Oliver, minister of justice in Caballero's government a few months later:[6] "Today you are the masters of the city and of Catalonia . . . and I hope you will not take it amiss if I remind you that you have not lacked the help of the loyal men of my party whatever their number, as well as that of the guards and Mozos [Mozos de Escuadra, a special defense corps of the government of the Generalitat][7]. . . . You have conquered and everything is in your power. If you do not need me or do not want me as president of Catalonia, tell me now, and I shall become just another soldier in the struggle against fascism. If, on the other hand, you believe that in this post . . . I and the men of my party . . . can be useful in this struggle . . . you can count on me and my loyalty, both as a man and as a politician, who is convinced that today a shameful past has ended, and who sincerely desires that Catalonia shall march at the head of the most socially advanced countries."[8] Although the authenticity of President Companys's statement has been challenged by Major Federico Escofet, who was general commissioner of public order in Catalonia at the time of the events,[9] it has been accepted without question by Angel Ossorio y Gallardo, the republican jurist, in his laudatory biography of Companys and by Carles Pi Sunyer, the mayor of Barcelona and close political associate of the president.[10]

The anarchosyndicalist leaders had gone to the Generalitat Palace in response to a request by President Companys. "We were armed to the teeth with rifles, machine guns, and revolvers," recalled García Oliver. "Companys received us standing, visibly moved. . . . The formalities were brief. We sat down with rifles between our legs."[11] "During the interview," testifies Diego Abad de Santillán, another leading anarchosyndicalist who was also present, "some of the members of the government of the autonomous region were pale and trembling."[12]

This was by no means Companys's first encounter with the leaders of the CNT and FAI. In the days of the Monarchy he had won prominence as their defense lawyer. He had little in common with them, for in all essential characteristics they were worlds apart, as shown by his abandonment of his legal profession to organize politically the Catalan middle and lower middle classes. As one of the founders of the Esquerra and of the Unió de Rabassaires, he represented the small manufacturers, artisans, and businessmen, as well as the tenant farmers and sharecroppers of the region. This did not endear him to the CNT and FAI, and a remark in 1933 by *Solidaridad Obrera*, the anarchosyndicalist organ, that he was "cut from the same cloth as other politicians,"[13] epitomized their feelings toward him. Their relations did not improve when in 1934 he was elected president of the Generalitat of Catalonia, and his government, faced with a critical period of social unrest, closed down the headquarters of the CNT and FAI and proscribed their press. *"Solidaridad Obrera,"* wrote Abad de Santillán, "was unable to appear for more than a few months in 1934 notwithstanding the fact that it had the second largest circulation in the region. The trade-union activities of the CNT were carried on in complete clandestineness. Our locals, our clubs, and cultural centers were not opened throughout 1934, and the sole concern of the Generalitat government was the destruction of the CNT and the extermination of the FAI."[14]

But now the anarchosyndicalists were at the helm.

In his propitiatory statement to the CNT-FAI leaders, Companys, to use the words of García Oliver, was "flexible" and "realistic." "[He] employed the language that circumstances dictated and rose to the very difficult occasion with a unique gesture of dignity and understanding . . . as a Catalan who realized that the great hour of his country had struck and as a very advanced liberal who had no fear of the boldest social changes."[15]

No doubt the protection Companys had given the anarchosyndicalists in the past now helped to predispose them in his favor. No doubt, too, their revived confidence was reinforced by his later statements. "The militant workers," he declared at a public meeting in October, "are, of course, those who must pay the greatest attention to the work of the Revolution. We, the representatives of the small bourgeoisie who must be respected and heard, should ease the way for the workers. We must either go along with them or behind them, but in the long run, it is they who must dictate the law. It would be useless to try to avoid the future of the workers by stratagem or by force."[16]

A supple politician with a reputation for maudlin demagoguery, yet with a touch of genuine compassion for the underdog, he was quick to adapt himself to the prevailing mood. "There were few republicans," writes Abad de Santillán, "who had acquired such a perfect understanding of the situation created on 19 July, and there were few who expressed themselves with such clarity and with such force in favor of the new social regime controlled by the workers."[17] Clearly, Companys was too shrewd a politician to oppose the CNT and FAI at a time when they were in the full tide of victory. He knew that resistance would be perilous and that his party must choose between going under or being borne along by the storm until it might reassert its sway. But loyalty to his followers and a humane impulse to protect even persons suspected of being sympathetic to General Franco prevented him from suffering in silence the violent forces set in motion by the Revolution. Indeed, pleas for restraint and censures of violence marked most of his public statements,[18] and his personal intervention enabled many persons whose lives were threatened to leave the country. "When, after July 1936, [Luis Companys] was overwhelmed by the Revolution," a Catalan scientist told Angel Ossorio, "and all of us had to run to the Generalitat to protect friends and institutions, I saw that he did everything possible to save all those he could, although at times without success. I know that many of our right-wing politicians . . . , such as Abadal, Ventosa y Calvell, Puig y Cadafalch, Count Montseny, high dignitaries of the church, innumerable priests, and many industrialists, who were able to escape, saved their lives thanks to the intervention of Gassol [councillor of culture in the Catalan government] and España [councillor of the interior], who acted at the request of and in full agreement with Companys."[19]

Yet Companys was careful to censure excesses and disorder in the name of the Revolution and refrained from criticizing the changes it had wrought.[20] This, too, was the attitude during the first few months of the Civil War of other leaders of the Esquerra[21] as well as of *La Humanitat*, their party organ,[22] and if they ventured to criticize the Revolution they did so by innuendo rather than by frank dissent.

"In twenty-four hours, minds that once appeared averse to change have evolved strikingly," wrote Federica Montseny. "Displaying a remarkable ability to adapt themselves, men who were spiritually very far removed from us have accepted the new order of things without protest."[23]

"We could have been supreme, imposed an absolute dictatorship, declared the Generalitat government a thing of the past, and instituted in its place the real power of the people," wrote Abad de Santillán. "But we did not believe in dictatorship when it was exercised against us, nor did we wish to exercise a dictatorship ourselves at the expense of others. [We decided that] the Generalitat government should remain at its post with President Companys at its head."[24] And García Oliver affirmed: "The fate of Spain . . . was being decided in Catalonia between libertarian communism, which would have been equivalent to an anarchist dictatorship, and democracy, which signifies collaboration. . . . The CNT and FAI decided in favor of collaboration and democracy, renouncing the revolutionary totalitarianism that would of necessity have led to the throttling of the Revolution by an anarchist and anarchosyndicalist dictatorship."[25]

Although opposition to dictatorship was the rationale most frequently used by the anarchosyndicalists to explain their decision not to impose their will in Barcelona,[26] they nevertheless established in the rural areas a multiplicity of parochial dictatorships with the aid of militia groups and revolutionary tribunals. Although they did not balk at the use of force in instituting collectivized agriculture and libertarian communism in countless villages,[27] they had no program, as did the Communists, for concentrating the power of government in their own hands.

This problem was acknowledged by Major Escofet, general commissioner of public order at the time of the military insurrection and a member of the moderate Esquerra. When on 20 July, he recalls, the CNT in Barcelona found itself "virtually in control of the streets, the arms, and transportation, in other words, with power in its hands, its leaders, who were bold and energetic and experienced fighters, were disoriented. They had no plan, no clear doctrine, no idea what they should do or what they should allow others to do. The CNT concept of libertarian communism was devoid of realism and was silent as to the road it should follow in a revolutionary period."[28]

The political paralysis of the CNT was also acknowledged by Helmut Ruediger, representative in Barcelona of the International Workingmen's Association (AIT), with which the CNT was affiliated. In response to criticism by foreign anarchists, he wrote: "Those who say that the CNT should have established its own dictatorship in 1936 do not know what they are demanding. . . . The CNT would have needed *a government program, a program for exercising power; [it would have needed] training in the exercise of power, an economic plan centrally directed, and experience in the use of the state apparatus.* . . . The CNT had none of these. Nor do those who believe that the CNT should have implanted its own dictatorship have such a program, either for their own country or for Spain. Do not let us delude ourselves! Furthermore, had it possessed such a program before 19 July, *the CNT would not have been the CNT; it would have been a bolshevik party,* and, had it applied such methods to the Revolution, it would have dealt anarchism a mortal blow."[29]

Lacking a program of their own for the seizure of government power, the CNT-FAI leaders decided to allow the Generalitat government to remain standing. But the war and revolution in Catalonia could not be directed by a government without influence over the largest and most radical segment of the working class. Nor could the anarchosyndicalist leaders reinvigorate the government with their own authority without violating their antistate principles. Hence, a Central Anti-Fascist Militia Committee was created, in which the CNT and FAI appropriated the key departments of war, public order, and transportation.[30] According to García Oliver, the committee was created at the suggestion of President Companys.[31] This is most likely, for no one could have realized more clearly than Companys that if the war were to be waged successfully, that if some of the values and institutions of the republican regime were to be saved from the hurricane of the Revolution and the revolutionary terror subjected to even a modicum of control, some kind of central governing body was necessary—a government in essence if not in name, in which the CNT-FAI leaders could participate without loss of face and that could prosecute the war until such time as the nominal government might regain the essential elements of real power. If his conciliatory statement to the anarchosyndicalist leaders was but a first step in this direction, then, far from representing a surrender to the FAI, it was, as Angel Ossorio y Gallardo, republican jurist and biographer of the president, put it, an act of "supreme dexterity" designed to make the FAI surrender to Companys. "It should not be assumed," he added, "that he wished to deceive the FAI. The fact is that there is no greater dexterity than sincerity. What the president undoubtedly wanted to say was this: 'Practically speaking, I have only the nominal power. The real power is in your hands. . . . But don't you agree that your efforts require a directive body? If you do not have one you will easily fall into disorder and impotence. Use me then in a governing and leadership capacity.'"[32]

Although President Companys may have conceived of the role of the Central Anti-Fascist Militia Committee as that of an auxiliary body of the Generalitat government, the committee immediately became the de facto executive body in the region. Its power rested not on the shattered machinery of state, but on the revolutionary militia and police squads and upon the multitudinous committees that sprang up in the region during the first days of the Revolution. The work of the militia committee, attests Abad de Santillán, himself a member, included the establishment of revolutionary order in the rear, the creation of militia units for the front, the organization of the economy, and legislative and judicial action. In sum: "The militia committee was everything; it attended to everything."[33] "The Central Anti-Fascist Militia Committee," he wrote on another occasion, "became the real and only power, the absolute, revolutionary power."[34]

Not that the Generalitat government was destitute of power, for it could rely upon the remnants of the regular police corps—the assault and civil guards—and upon the militia organized by the moderate parties, but these were vastly outnumbered by the armed forces of the CNT and FAI. The council of finance of the Catalan government exercised control over the banking system of the region[35]—a source of power neglected by the anarchosyndicalists inasmuch as they had always advocated the abolition of money and credit—but it served mainly as a rubber stamp for the Revolution, since one of its principal functions was to meet the financial needs of the militia committee and advance sums to collectivized plants and other enterprises to enable them to pay wages. To be sure, the government appeared to issue decrees or executive orders like a sovereign power, but most of those published in its official journal, the *Butlletí Oficial*,[36] were simply legislative acknowledgments of accomplished facts. Witness, for example, the decree suspending the Catalan municipal councillors belonging to parties that opposed the Popular Front;[37] the decrees establishing the forty-hour week and raising wages 15 percent;[38] the decree suspending eviction proceedings against militiamen;[39] the decree confiscating the property of the church and of persons implicated in the rising;[40] the executive order making compulsory the reinstatement of workers discharged on political grounds;[41] and the executive orders issued by the councillor of labor relating to the new working conditions established by the unions in various branches of industry.[42] "On 24 July 1936," wrote *Luz y Fuerza*, a CNT periodical, "the workers of the

Sociedad General de Aguas de Barcelona and of the Empresa Concesionaria de Aguas Subterráneas del Río Llobregat confiscated both concerns and took over administrative and technical control. . . . The following day, the government of the Generalitat recognized the validity of the confiscation, and a government comptroller [*interventor*] joined the committee of control."[43] "The government of the Generalitat," said a CNT-FAI report on the sequestration of the Metro Transversal subway by the anarchosyndicalists, "has appointed a comptroller who as been accepted, in principle, by the workers, but whose function is entirely passive. Effective control is in the hands of the revolutionary committee of the enterprise."[44]

Obviously, the urban middle- and lower-middle classes were not satisfied with the inferior position of the Catalan government and the power of the anarchosyndicalists to collectivize at will;[45] nor were the tenant farmers and sharecroppers of the Unió de Rabassaires, which represented the majority of the peasant population in the region. Having seized the land, they felt that the Revolution had accomplished its mission. Not so the extreme spirits. In those villages where anarchosyndicalist laborers were predominant, or where the influx of CNT-FAI militiamen weighted the scales in their favor, individual cultivation was abolished, often at the expense of rural production. "Certain abuses have been committed, which we consider counterproductive," confessed *Solidaridad Obrera*, the leading CNT newspaper. "We know that certain irresponsible elements have frightened the small peasants and that the latter are showing a lack of interest in their daily labors."[46] On another occasion it stated: "News that the small bourgeoisie is deeply alarmed has reached our ears. We were under the impression that the anxiety of the first few days had evaporated, but the uneasiness of the shopkeeper, the businessman, the small manufacturer, the artisan, and small peasant holder persists. They lack confidence in the leadership of the proletariat."[47]

Neither in the towns nor in the villages could the intermediate classes turn to the Esquerra, hitherto their unfailing defender, for most of its leaders were timorous to the point of self-effacement. In contrast, the Catalan Communists, who controlled the PSUC, the Partit Socialista Unificat de Catalunya, boldly defended—in consonance with the policy of the Spanish Communist party—the interests of these classes that were being dragged into the whirlwind of the collectivization movement or threatened with extinction by the disruption of trade, by the lack of financial resources, and by the requisitions carried out by the CNT and FAI. "It would be unpardonable," said *Treball*, the PSUC organ in Barcelona, "to forget the multitude of small commodity producers and businessmen in our region. . . . They declare that nobody is concerned about their fate. They are elements who tend to favor any reactionary movement because it seems to them that anything would be better than the economic system that is being instituted in our region. . . . The distressing situation of many of these people is obvious. They cannot run their workshops and businesses because they have no reserve capital; they have hardly enough to eat, especially the small manufacturers, because the wages they have to pay to the few workers they employ prevent them from attending to their own daily needs."[48]

And a PSUC manifesto declared: "We demand an economy freed from naive experiments and the ingenious plans of individuals who are operating today on the bleeding body of Catalonia with the recklessness and irresponsbility of a madman in a laboratory encircled by flames. We demand an economy freed from the influence or pressure of so many committees that have sprung up everywhere . . . [and] that sap the magnificent vitality of Catalonia."[49]

It was the PSUC, not the Esquerra, that opposed the revolutionaries of the CNT and FAI, defended the interests of the *rabassaires* and organized eighteen thousand tradesmen, artisans, and manufacturers into the GEPCI, the Catalan Federation of Small Businessmen and Manufacturers.[50] Because the PSUC allowed the GEPCI, many of whose members were employers of labor, to enter the Catalan UGT, which it controlled,[51] it was criticized by Juan J. Domenech, the CNT leader, who charged that, to increase its size, the UGT in Catalonia did not object to enrolling speculators, shopkeepers, and merchants or to their exploiting the workers.[52]

A small party at the outset of the Civil War, the PSUC was the result of the fusion of four minuscule organizations aggregating approximately 2,500 members—the Unió Socialista de Catalunya, the largest component, which appealed strongly to Catalan nationalist sentiments, the Federacío Catalana del Partit Socialista Obrer Espanyol, the Catalan section of the Spanish Socialist party, the Partit Comunista de Catalunya, and the Partit Catalá Proletaria. From information furnished me by Miguel Serra Pamies, secretary, before the war, of the Socialist Union and subsequently a member of the PSUC's central committee, and from data provided by other sources, I arrive at the following numerical breakdown: Socialist Union of Catalonia, between 1,200 and 1,500 members; Catalan Federation of the Spanish Socialist party, between 600 and 700 members; Communist party of

Catalonia, less than 400 members; Catalan Proletarian party, approximately 80 members. Miguel Valdés, the PSUC leader, put the initial membership of the united party at around three thousand.[53] On the other hand, Luis Cabo Giorla, a member of the central committee of the Spanish Communist party, gave the figure of 5,000 as the initial membership.[54] Negotiations for the fusion of the four groups had been proceeding inconclusively before the outbreak of the Civil War as a result of the insistence of the Communists that the united party be linked to the Communist or Third International and of the demand by the Catalan Federation of the Socialist party that it be associated with the Labor and Socialist International. The prospects of breaking the deadlock were not improved by the attitude of Juan Comorera, the president of the Socialist Union, who at first opposed any connection with either International, particularly the Third. He is alleged to have told members of the executive committee of his party that it was essential to prevent the Communists from capturing the new organization.[55] But under the impact of the Revolution these differences melted away. The leaders of the four parties knew that the emergence of the CNT and FAI as masters of the situation left them scant hope of survival unless they united their forces. After a heated debate, Juan Comorera and Rafael Vidiella (president of the Catalan Federation of the Socialist party and at that time a loyal supporter of Largo Caballero) withdrew their objections to adherence to the Communist International, and the new party was formed.[56]

By March 1937, only nine months after its formation, the PSUC claimed fifty thousand adherents. "Fifty thousand militants in Catalonia is a sort of miracle," declared Juan Comorera, who became PSUC secretary at the time of the merger. "In Catalonia there is no Marxist tradition. Forces diametrically opposed to Marxism have been and still are active, namely, the great mass of the peasantry, the segment of the working class that is anarchist by tradition, and the other segment also linked by tradition and by its slow development to the petty bourgeois republican parties. . . . To have created a party of fifty thousand militants in an atmosphere without any [Marxist] tradition, faced as we are by powerful adversaries who have done everything they could to hinder us, is a great triumph."[57] The figure of fifty thousand does not appear to be greatly exaggerated. The recruits that flocked to the party came from many sources: manual and white-collar workers from the Catalan section of the UGT, government officials, police, teachers, tradesmen, artisans, small manufacturers, as well as small and medium-sized farmers, tenant farmers, and sharecroppers, many of whom had formerly held Esquerra membership cards. "The PSUC," said Severino Campos, a CNT-FAI member, "devotes itself to making converts of persons who are not inspired by the slightest Marxist or, least of all, revolutionary sentiment."[58] However, speaking in July 1937, one year after its formation, at a time when the PSUC was at pains to deemphasize its middle-class composition, Comorera claimed that 60 percent of its members were industrial workers and 20 percent agricultural laborers. "If to these percentages," he continued, "we add those of officials, clerks, teachers, and of all other salaried workers, we can affirm that 97 percent of our party is composed of wage earners." The balance, he stated, was made up of "comrades in the liberal professions and of a negligible, an insignificant number of elements of the small bourgeoisie."[59] As no mention was made of the *rabassaires*, many of whom, according to Victor Colomer, the agrarian secretary of the PSUC, joined the party,[60] it must be assumed that these tenant farmers and sharecroppers were classified somewhat loosely as agricultural laborers.

From the time of its formation, it will be recalled, the PSUC adhered to the Communist International. Shortly thereafter the Communists became the ruling nucleus. In addition to controlling its organizational work, its press, and trade-union activities, they were in charge of internal vigilance, as all records were in the hands of Joaquín Olaso, the head of the party's control commission. "Pedro"—the Comintern delegate, whose real name was Ernö Gerö and who, after World War II, became a member of the Soviet-controlled Hungarian government—was placed at Comorera's elbow, and Spanish Communist leaders were sent regularly to Barcelona with directives.[61] Within a few months, both Comorera and Rafael Vidiella, who before the fusion was the president of the Catalan Federation of the Socialist party and a staunch supporter of Largo Caballero, reinforced their ties with the Spanish Communist party, when they were made members of its central committee.[62]

The PSUC was directed behind the scenes with extraordinary energy, tact, and efficiency by "Pedro." He watched over *Treball*, the party organ and, aided by a perfect knowledge of Catalan, smoothed over differences in the inner circle of the party resulting from the Catalan nationalism of some of its leaders and their reluctance to accept the centralizing aims of the Spanish Communists. Several times in the course of the war, the friction created by the nationalist sentiments of some of its leaders and the centralizing tendencies of the Spanish Communist party threatened to erupt in open conflict, and only the tremendous tact and personal authority of "Pedro" succeeded in bringing the *Catalanistas* to heel.[63] After the war the Spanish Communist party in exile gave the following version of the friction within the PSUC: "From the moment the PSUC was formed all the healthy and loyal elements who had come from the four parties . . . with Comrade Juan Comorera at the head, looked for support and help to the [Spanish] Communist party. But, from the very first moment, some elements also came to the PSUC to begin an undeclared struggle against the line of the Communist International. . . . These wretched elements . . . fought against the Communist orientation of the party from the day of fusion, using their positions in both the central and executive committees to this end."[64]

In addition to keeping the recalcitrants in line, "Pedro" dominated the meetings of the party's executive committee, personally inspected the smallest units of the party, and, in short, exercised a close and constant supervision over almost every detail.[65] High in the confidence of Moscow, he even monitored the activities of Vladimir A. Antonov-Ovseenko, the Soviet consul general in Barcelona.[66]

Before many weeks had passed the PSUC had gained sufficiently in self-confidence to press for the dissolution of the Central Anti-Fascist Militia Committee and the concentration of power in the hands of the Catalan government. In this it was aided not only by President Companys, but by pressure from the central government, which discountenanced a revolutionary body that exposed to the world at large that its authority in Catalonia was ineffectual. "We were told time and again," affirms Abad de Santillán, "that as long as we persisted in maintaining [the committee] . . . arms would not reach Catalonia, that we would not be given foreign currency with which to purchase them abroad or raw materials for our industry." There was, therefore, no course, he asserted, if they were not to lose the war, but to dissolve the committee and join the Catalan government.[67]

In the new administration, formed on 28 September by José Tarradellas, the shrewd and extremely able confidant of President Companys, the anarchosyndicalists held three out of twelve portfolios. In July, Companys had appointed Tarradellas (who, forty-one years later, in 1977, was to become the first president of the Generalitat after the death of General Franco) to serve as government representative on the militia committee and now, in accordance with his powers under the Catalan constitution, he delegated to him his executive functions by naming him first councillor or premier in the Generalitat government. The twelve seats in the government, or "council," as the antistatists preferred to call the new Catalan administration, were apportioned among the various organizations as follows:

José Tarradellas	Esquerra	First Councillor and Councillor of Finance
Artemio Aiguadé	Esquerra	Internal Security
Ventura Gassol	Esquerra	Culture
Juan P. Fábregas	CNT	Economy
Antonio García Birlan	CNT	Health and Public Assistance
Juan J. Domenech	CNT	Supplies
Juan Comorera	PSUC	Public Services
Miguel Valdés	PSUC	Labor and Public Works
Andrés Nin	POUM	Justice
Felipe Díaz Sandino	Independent (liberal republican)	Defense
José Calvet	Unió de Rabassaires	Agriculture
Rafael Closas	Acció Catalana Republicana	Councillor without portfolio

Although the dissolution of the militia committee strengthened the authority of the Generalitat government, it did not end the division of power in the region; for the revolutionaries maintained their own police squads—the *patrullas de control*, or patrols, under the authority of the CNT-dominated Junta de Seguridad—and their armed militia, both in the rear and at the front—under the authority of the CNT-controlled Secretariado de Defensa—as well as a vast network of defense, transport, and food committees that covered the length and breadth of the region. On the other hand, the Generalitat government, through the councillor of internal security, Artemio Aiguadé, and his *comisario general de orden público*, or police commissioner, Martín Rauret, both Esquerra members, could rely on the assault and republican guards, as well as on the militia of the moderate parties under the somewhat loose authority of the councillor of defense, Lieutenant Colonel Felipe Díaz Sandino, a liberal republican air force officer.

To end this division of power in the region became the goal of the PSUC and the Esquerra in the coming months. A careful distinction, however, should be made between their respective tactics and aims; for whereas Companys and Tarradellas hoped to end the political dichotomy by subtle manipulation of the CNT and FAI and by turning to account their political artlessness and inexperience, thus avoiding encroachment by the central government and the Spanish Communist party on the autonomy of the region, the PSUC—despite the Catalanist sentiments of some of its leaders—looked to the central government and the Spanish Communists for help to end the division of power, regardless of the inevitable impingement on Catalan autonomy. Furthermore, as one left-wing historian of the Revolution puts it: "[Companys] saw from the viewpoint of his middle-class policy that the time had arrived to 'domesticate' the CNT, but he did not wish to destroy it for it served as a counterweight to the PSUC, which was stealing his clientele."[68]

The political arena in Catalonia was complicated by the presence of the POUM, the Partido Obrero de Unificación Marxista (the Workers' Party of Marxist Unification), formed in 1935 through the fusion of Andrés Nin's Izquierda Comunista (Communist Left) with Joaquín Maurín's Bloque Obrero y Campesino (Worker and Peasant Bloc).[69] Although small by anarchosyndicalist standards and possessing little more than a skeleton organization outside Catalonia, it was nonetheless a force to be reckoned with in the region.

A vigorous advocate of Socialist revolution independent of Moscow, an unrelenting critic of Communist policy in Spain and of Stalin's trials and purges, the POUM was denounced as "Trotskyist." Although some of its leaders, including Andrés Nin, the party secretary, and Juan Andrade, a member of the executive, had once been disciples of Trotsky, the POUM was not a Trotskyist party, and it frantically attempted to prove that it was not in numerous articles and speeches.[70] Nevertheless, in accordance with the tactic used by Stalin at the Moscow trials of amalgamating all opponents under a single label, the Communists denounced the dissidents of the POUM as Trotskyist agents of Franco, Hitler, and Mussolini.[71]

The truth is that Trotsky had profound differences with the POUM even before the war,[72] and within a few months of the outbreak of hostilities, his handful of followers, the Bolshevik Leninists, organized the exiguous Spanish section of his Fourth International. "The POUM was never Trotskyist, i.e., a Bolshevik party," declared *Unser Wort*, the organ of the Fourth International. "The POUM leaders defended themselves desperately against the 'accusation' of Trotskyism and did not shrink even from the most contemptible means. Not only did they expel Trotskyists from their ranks, but, what is more, the POUM published these expulsions in the most provocative way."[73]

The Communist Triumph

Bertram D. Wolfe, a defender of the POUM at the time, wrote in 1939:

The simple facts in the case are:

1. The P.O.U.M. is not Trotskyist. Its membership and leadership come predominantly from the Communist Party, the Catalonian section of which was expelled in bloc during the ultra-left wave of 1929, for rejecting union-splitting, for advocating the tactics of the united front, for opposing the stupid theory that the rest of the working class was "social fascist", for objecting to the mechanical transference of tactics to Spain which had no connection with Spanish realities. Its outstanding leader was Joaquín Maurín, repeatedly and bitterly attacked by Trotsky as "centrist", "opportunist", "petty-bourgeois", "main misleader of the Spanish proletariat", "Menshevik traitor" and similar choice epithets. . . . In his gentler moods, Trotsky pronounced "Maurinism . . . a mixture of petty bourgeois prejudices, ignorance, provincial science and petty politics", and concluded that ". . . the first step on the road to a revolutionary party in Spain must be to denounce the political vulgarity of Maurinism. In this, we must have no mercy. . . ."

2. Two of the leaders of the P.O.U.M., Andrés Nin and Juan Andrade, were former followers of Trotsky. They broke with him almost five years ago when they rejected his instructions to enter the Second International. . . . Since then, Trotsky has variously honored them as "a mere tail of the 'left' bourgeoisie", "the traitors Nin and Andrade" . . . and has declared that "in Spain, genuine revolutionists will no doubt be found who will mercilessly expose the betrayal of Maurín, Nin, Andrade and Co., and lay the foundation for the Spanish Section of the Fourth International."

3. The Trotskyites are not members of the P.O.U.M. The P.O.U.M. has a standing order for the expulsion of all Trotskyites. *La Batalla* [the party organ] has carried a number of articles polemizing against Trotskyism, not in the "merciless", arrogant and insulting tone with which only Russians like Stalin and Trotsky can write of even their best political elements if they do not happen to serve their factional purposes in the party feud in the Soviet Union, but in a factual and theoretical form which both Trotskyites and Stalinites alike have long given up or forgotten.[74]

The Trotskyists inveighed against the POUM for entering the Catalan government, in which Andrés Nin occupied the post of councillor of justice. "Any form of coalition government on the basis of a common program with the bourgeoisie and the reformists is outright treason to the revolutionary program," they declared. "The essential task is the total destruction of the bourgeois state and its substitution by a government of workers, namely committees or soviets."[75]

In its polemic with the Trotskyists the POUM argued that its presence in the Catalan government was a transitional step toward complete working-class power and that its slogan had always been and continued to be "a workers' government, committees of workers, peasants and combatants, and a Constituent Assembly."[76] The Trotskyists rejoined that this slogan was inconsistent with the POUM's participation in a government that, shortly after its formation, decreed the dissolution of the workers' committtees and their replacement by local councils, giving representation both to middle-class and working-class parties. They also censured the POUM for merging its trade-union organization, the FOUS, the Federación Obrera de Unidad Sindical,[77] with the PSUC-controlled Catalan UGT instead of with the revolutionary CNT, alleging that the POUM's purpose was to avoid friction with the anarchosyndicalist leaders.[78] The POUM argued that it had made this move in the hope of giving the UGT a "revolutionary injection," thus making the fusion with the CNT more practical.[79] Andrés Nin, the POUM leader, for his part, claimed that if the FOUS had entered the CNT it would have been only a small minority, whereas in the UGT it hoped to make its opinions prevail.[80] These hopes were quickly disappointed, for the UGT leadership prevented any free expression of opinion by refusing to hold general assemblies and expelled POUM members from prominent positions.[81] These expulsions, alleged *La Batalla*, the party organ, were "demanded for the most part by those petty bourgeois elements in the UGT who before the war had clashed with the revolutionary workers in the chambers of commerce and employers' associations."[82]

The Communists ignored the dissensions between the Trotskyites and the POUM, for the latter was only slightly less outspoken in its criticism of the Soviet Union and of Soviet policy in Spain than were the Trotskyists.

On 27 August, the POUM protested the execution of Grigorii E. Zinoviev and Lev B. Kamenev and of other old Bolsheviks by Stalin.[83] "The CNT, Socialists and republicans did not understand the significance of what was happening in Moscow," writes Victor Alba, at one time a member of the POUM. "They gave little information and made no comment. The CNT, which should have seen in the trials a warning, treated them as though they were just a family quarrel."[84] The Trotskyists accused the POUM of "minimizing or hiding as far as possible the news about Stalin's trials and assassinations."[85] This was only partially true because, although there was a strong current of opinion in the POUM that feared to exasperate the Communists by denouncing the trials, this fear did not prevail.[86]

The opening of the new Moscow treason trial in January 1937 added fresh acerbity to the press polemics between the POUM and the Communists, when the POUM declared that the accused were innocent. Replied *Frente Rojo*, the Communist organ:

The Communist Triumph

"*La Batalla*, the organ of the band of counterrevolutionaries and *provocateurs* who direct the POUM, has at last exposed itself. The occasion for throwing off the mask is the trial in Moscow of the second gang of Trotskyist terrorists, spies, and assassins, accomplices of the Gestapo, who are directed, like the POUM, by Trotsky himself."[87] To this *La Batalla* retorted: "Stalin knows perfectly well that, with the exception of one or two of the accused, the others are not Trotskyists. . . . We also are accused of being Trotskyists. We are not. . . . The defendants in Moscow are also accused of several other things. They are agents of the Gestapo, they are in the service of fascism and foreign espionage. The same is said of us. . . . Fortunately Spain is not Russia, but an attempt is being made to put Spain under Russian tutelage and control, which, of course, we oppose with the utmost vigor. And that is what Stalin and his domestic and foreign bureaucrats do not forgive us. They do not forgive us for raising high the banner of Marx and Lenin, which they have abandoned and betrayed. They do not forgive us for proclaiming the truth about their domestic and foreign policies. They do not forgive us for fighting in Spain for the Socialist revolution."[88]

During the following months the polemics raged with increasing virulence. On 25 April *Treball*, the PSUC organ, declared: "The Trotskyists . . . know that they are definitely discredited among the masses; they know that the masses now recognize them as the most obvious enemies of the working class; they know that everyone realizes that they are not only assassins—this is proved by the case of Kirov [the Russian Communist leader, whose assassination was officially laid to a Trotskyist conspiracy]—but saboteurs and warmongers. They have seen that the workers reject them, that they spit in their faces, denounce them as the most disgusting of their enemies. Naturally, they dare not show their true face, but instead camouflage and disguise themselves. The Trotskyist Gorkin [Julián Gorkin, international secretary of the POUM, a member of its executive committee, and director of *La Batalla*, who wrote most of its editorials[89]] uses the same method. But his explanations prove at least one thing: that the Catalan masses flee from Trotskyism as from the plague and that the POUM leaders are anxious to deny what they really are."

From the outset, the POUM had excoriated the Communists and Socialists for supporting the democratic Republic: The international bourgeoisie, wrote *La Batalla*, was fully aware "that the issue in Spain is one of revolution or counterrevolution, of socialism or fascism. The Socialists and the Communists in their efforts to deceive the republican bourgeoisie at home and abroad only deceive the working class."[90]

To this type of criticism Santiago Carrillo, the secretary of the Communist-controlled Unified Socialist Youth, responded: "There are some who say that . . . we are practicing a deception . . . when we declare that we are defending the democratic Republic. . . . This is not a stratagem to deceive Spanish democratic opinion nor to deceive democratic opinion abroad, . . . because we know that if we should commit the mistake of fighting at this time for the Socialist revolution . . . we should see in our fatherland not only the fascist invaders, but side by side with them the bourgeois democratic governments of the world. . . . [The] Trotskyist elements know full well that if we were to call for social revolution as an immediate goal, we would be playing the game of Franco and Mola, [which] is to represent the legal government as a government of reds, as a government of Communists."[91]

On 18 November 1936, *La Batalla* declared that the leaders of the Communist International did not want a proletarian revolution in Spain. "A new victorious proletarian revolution in Europe, not under the sole auspices of the Third International, would mean the transfer of the center of gravity of the international working-class movement from Moscow to where that revolution was being carried out. For that reason . . . the Stalinist leaders in Spain must liquidate the organizations that do not submit blindly to their discipline. That applies to us as well as to the CNT and FAI. They consider that we are more difficult to destroy in the theoretical field and wish to destroy us first. As for the anarchists they think they can destroy them afterward."

On 24 November, in a document presented to the CNT councillors, the PSUC proposed the exclusion of the POUM from the cabinet and the formation of a new government "with plenary powers."[92] The anarchosyndicalists refused to countenance these proposals. On 8 December, President Companys, without publicly defining his position on the question of the POUM, declared that "a strong government with plenary powers capable of imposing its authority on everyone" was necessary.[93] To this the CNT replied that "a 'strong government' would simply be a dictatorship."[94] The Esquerra organ, *La Humanitat*, hitherto extremely circumspect,[95] ventured to object that the CNT's reaction was "inexplicable. . . . [We] cannot see what advantages a 'weak government' could offer in this hour of war and revolution because war and revolution are waged and won exclusively on the basis of iron discipline, of unity and action, . . . which are only feasible with a strong government . . . that imposes its authority inexorably. On everyone. Absolutely everyone."[96]

The Communist Triumph

No headway was made in resolving the differences between the opposing sides, and on 12 December, Premier Tarradellas officially announced that the cabinet was in a state of crisis. On the same day, Juan Comorera, the PSUC leader and councillor in the outgoing cabinet, publicly demanded the ouster of the POUM, charging that it had been disloyal to the government—its leaders having attacked the government's decrees—and that it had waged an anti-Soviet campaign at a time when the Soviet Union "had placed itself on the side of our people and given us tremendous help." In addition, he demanded the suppression of the CNT-dominated Secretariado de Defensa and the Junta de Seguridad that controlled the revolutionary militia and the patrols, so as to give "plenary powers" to the councillors and to establish "an iron discipline within the government apparatus."[97] There were juntas and committees, he said later, that "govern more than the government itself."[98] On the other hand, the POUM, which had its own patrols and militia, argued that the junta and secretariado, in both of which it was represented, were "organs of revolutionary expression" that prevented the state "as presently constituted" from being turned into "a police state against the proletariat."[99] "Can the revolutionary working class in Catalonia," it asked, "allow these levers [of control] to be snatched from it? Not on any account. To agree to that would be to take a very dangerous step backward on the road of the Revolution."[100]

For more than three weeks the anarchosyndicalist leaders resolutely opposed the PSUC's demands, but, not feeling personally endangered or especially sympathetic toward the POUM because of its attempts to penetrate the CNT before the Civil War[101] and because of its criticism of their policies, they finally acquiesced in its exclusion from the government. In exchange, the PSUC dropped its demand for the suppression of the junta and the secretariado and agreed to give the council of defense to the CNT in return for the council of justice vacated by the POUM.

From this solution of the crisis the POUM concluded that the PSUC's prime concern all along had been its removal from the cabinet. But, it warned: "Now that the [PSUC] has obtained its immediate goal, does anyone believe that it will renounce its aims? . . . With our elimination it has won its preliminary objective. For the moment it does not feel strong enough to go any further."[102]

To help the CNT to rationalize its sacrifice of the POUM—a sacrifice that one prominent foreign anarchist later attributed to a threat from the Soviet ambassador that further military aid would be denied unless the POUM were ousted[103]—the PSUC agreed to withdraw officially from the cabinet. But this was only a nominal concession, for the PSUC representatives, Comorera, Valdés, and Vidiella, simply appeared in the new government with UGT labels, although they were well-known members of the PSUC executive and within a few weeks were to become members of the central committee of the Spanish Communist party.[104]

The composition of the new government was as follows:

José Tarradellas	Esquerra	First Councillor (Premier) and Councillor of Finance
Antonio María Sbert	Esquerra	Culture
Artemio Aiguadé	Esquerra	Internal Security
José Calvet	Unió de Rabassaires	Agriculture
Juan Comorera	UGT [PSUC]	Supplies
Miguel Valdés	UGT [PSUC]	Labor and Public Works
Rafael Vidiella	UGT [PSUC]	Justice
Francisco Isgleas	CNT	Defense
Diego Abad de Santillán	CNT	Economy
Juan José Domenech	CNT	Public Services
Pedro Herrera	CNT	Health and Public Assistance

Solidaridad Obrera hailed what appeared to be the preponderant trade-union character of the new government as a victory for its syndical ideas and a defeat for the political parties as represented by the PSUC and the POUM. "With this solution of the crisis," it continued, "we feel that no one has cause for complaint or reproach of any kind. The two antagonists, the POUM and the PSUC, whose conflict has brought us to our present pass, have been excluded from the council of the Generalitat. Both are represented in the UGT . . . ; both stem from the same ideological branch, although slight differences of attitude and tactics separate them. In our opinion, neither has the right to cry out in protest."[105]

The POUM, however, was bitter. "Our elimination has been carried out," said Juan Andrade, a member of its executive, "not because of the casuistic claim that we are represented in the UGT, but because we hold intransigently revolutionary positions. . . . Anarchosyndicalism has always been guilty of paying more attention to form than to content. . . . The CNT leadership has opted for a course that is extremely dangerous. . . . It has preferred to yield to the antirevolutionary tendencies that desire our elimination . . . rather than maintain the uncompromising, revolutionary line of the rank and file."[106] And Jordi Arquer, the political commissar of the POUM militia, declared: "We have been defeated MOMENTARILY not by the PSUC-UGT, but by a power that lies behind these organizations and is responsible for the maneuver . . . raising before those who oppose its will the specter of abandoning us and leaving us without arms and munitions in face of the criminal hordes of Franco."[107]

A notable consequence of the December crisis and of the political victory of the PSUC was the growth in self-confidence and pugnacity of some of the Esquerra leaders, as evidenced by a public meeting of their party on 28 December, the first since the outbreak of the Civil War. Although they refrained from publicly gloating over the ouster of the POUM, there can be little doubt that they perceived in its removal a significant setback for the Revolution. In fact, so belligerent were their speeches, so suffused with veiled and even open threats to the future of the Revolution,[108] that President Companys, who still believed that the presence in the cabinet of the CNT and FAI was essential if the libertarian movement were to be "domesticated" and gradually divested of its armed power, felt impelled to inject a note of caution. While criticizing the "confused network of committees and juntas," urging the centralization of all administrative authority in the hands of the government, and warning that "a revolution that does not have a disciplined, energetic, and responsible government is condemned to failure," he offered the following pacifier to the CNT and FAI: "Some republicans believe, even dream, that in the future a political and social system will be established equal to or similar to the one that existed before 19 July. This simply demonstrates their blindness and lack of loyalty because this is not possible. Nor would it be right or legitimate. I have said and I say it again that the time has come for political power to pass into the hands of the working classes. For this reason they should be the most interested in watching over the purity, the honor, the effectiveness, and wisdom of the work of government."[109] These words seemed to placate the libertarian leaders, who firmly believed in Companys's early commitment to the Revolution. Said *Solidaridad Obrera*: "Luis Companys is in agreement at the present time with the proletarian organizations . . . especially with the CNT, and reveals a political vision that is more perceptive, more sincere, and more loyal than that of some of his correligionists."[110]

But no amount of subtle statecraft or artful treatment of the CNT and FAI by President Companys and Premier Tarradellas could appease the more impatient members of the middle classes, who were faced with immediate or gradual economic ruin. They longed for a rapid end to anarchist power and saw in the dynamic leadership and aggressive policies of the PSUC the only hope of salvaging some of their possessions from the wreckage of the Revolution. No wonder that they continued to flock to the rival party in growing numbers. Companys and Tarradellas, on the other hand, undoubtedly believed, as one admirer of the premier capsulized his thinking, that "the time of the Esquerra would come when anarchosyndicalism, through political immaturity, would collapse of its own accord," and that it was far wiser, at least for the time being, to pursue a policy of accommodation with its leaders than to force them into intransigent positions.[111]

For this reason, Tarradellas, while urging the centralization of all administrative authority in the Generalitat government and the enforcement of the government's decrees, frequently defended the CNT and FAI from Communist attack. On one occasion, for example, when an armed clash threatened to erupt in the town of Granollers, he endeavored to prevent the dispatch of government reinforcements by the Communist police commissioner, Eusebio Rodríguez Salas.[112] On another, he sided with the CNT when the PSUC criticized the functioning of the anarchist-dominated Commission of War Industries, over which he presided,[113] and, on yet another, he vigorously defended the CNT councillor of defense, Francisco Isgleas, and his undersecretary, Juan Molina, against Communist charges of procrastination in implementing the government's decrees.[114] For his frequent defense of the libertarians Tarradellas received their glowing praise.[115]

His cautious policy, backed by Companys and by some of the other leaders of the Esquerra and Acció Republicana, a small Catalan middle-class party, irked the PSUC, but not until after the war did the party criticize the premier openly. "These bourgeois leaders," ran a PSUC document, specifically referring to Tarradellas, "collaborated directly and indirectly with the counterrevolutionary policy of anarchism in the secret hope of precipitating its ideological collapse and then taking into their hands the political and economic power of the [region]."[116]

To the dismay of the Esquerra leaders, the PSUC was able to exploit their prudent tactics to attract to itself not only the more restless segment of the urban middle classes, but also large numbers of sharecroppers and tenant farmers of the Unió de Rabassaires and adherents of the CADCI, the union of office workers and retail clerks, both of which organizations had been inviolable preserves of the Esquerra before the outbreak of the Civil War.[117]

No sooner had the PSUC achieved its goal during the cabinet reshuffle in December than it turned its attention to the revolutionary committees that had assumed control of the wholesale food trades at the outset of the Revolution.[118] In an attempt to reestablish freedom of trade, Juan Comorera, the PSUC secretary and councillor of supplies in the new cabinet, decreed their dissolution. The committees, he alleged, shortly before issuing his decree, had replaced the middlemen, "to the prejudice of society," and were responsible for the enormous increase in the cost of food.[119] Although the anarchosyndicalists argued that the committees prevented the rich from speculating at the expense of the workers, it is clear from the CNT and POUM press that the committees "in the name of 'Liberty and the Revolution'" were guilty of "a thousand and one abuses"[120] and "in most cases perpetuate the vices of the bosses and speculate just like them."[121] Nevertheless, the real point at issue was not so much the abuses as the political and economic power of the committees.

But it was a far cry from the publication of Comorera's decree to its enforcement as long as the armed power of the revolutionaries remained intact. To undermine this power, the PSUC applied unremitting pressure after the December crisis to end the duality of police powers in the region. These were divided, as we have seen, between the patrols, on the one hand, under the authority of the CNT-dominated Junta de Seguridad, and the assault and national republican guards, on the other, under the control of the Esquerra councillor of internal security, Artemio Aiguadé. One important by-product of the crisis was the appointment by the pro-Communist Aiguadé[122] of Eusebio Rodríguez Salas, a PSUC member, as *comisario general de orden público*, or police commissioner, in place of the less aggressive, yet anarchophobic Martín Rauret, a prominent member of the Esquerra. Next to Comorera, Rodríguez Salas soon became the libertarians' principal object of execration. A former anarchist, who in 1917 had lost an arm in a raid on the Bank of Tarragona, he had since abjured his libertarian creed, joined Maurín's Bloque Obrero y Campesino, and finally allied himself before the war with the small Catalan Communist party, bringing to the PSUC the fearlessness and daring that had characterized his activity as an anarchist.

Shortly after the December crisis, the Catalan UGT, which now officially represented the PSUC in the government, proposed that all the forces of public order—patrols as well as assault and national republican guards—be dissolved and their members incorporated into a single internal security corps.[123] The CNT rejected the proposal. "The patrols should not only be maintained; they should be increased," said *Solidaridad Obrera*. "All those attacks directed against them are directed at the very heart of our revolution."[124] Nevertheless, with the backing of the UGT-PSUC and Esquerra councillors, the government approved a series of decrees providing for the dissolution of the various forces of public order and their reorganization into a single internal security corps, in which, significantly, the positions of command were to be held mainly by the officers of the dissolved assault and national republican guards.[125]

As the libertarian movement—whose representatives in the government had approved some of the provisions or had been outvoted on others,[126] but had nonetheless observed the principle of cabinet solidarity—did not denounce the decrees, the POUM declared: "If other organizations have not perceived clearly the trend of events and have not reacted as the situation demands, they will make themselves responsible before history. . . . The fate of the Revolution is in the balance. That is what these organizations that express their loyalty to the Revolution day by day do not appear to understand. . . . [Their] policy, which tends to maintain a unity that in no way benefits the Revolution, profits only reformism. . . . Our party has only one mission with regard to these decrees: to denounce them publicly and tirelessly, to work unremittingly and indefatigably for their abrogation, and to see that the working class imposes its own order and its own police forces."[127]

To this attack *Solidaridad Obrera* responded: "We state frankly in plain language and without beating about the bush that the decree relating to public order does not satisfy us. Our representatives in the council of the Generalitat have done the impossible, trying to polish it by removing all those features of a reactionary character. They have only partially succeeded. Although, as a disciplined organization, we respect the legislation, this does not mean that we renounce our efforts to substitute it for a new legal instrument reflecting more closely the true revolutionary political situation in our region. . . . [We] regard the creation of that single security corps, [which is] completely alien to the struggles and aspirations of the working people, as a mistake."[128]

During the next few days, open and furtive agitation against the decrees reached such intensity that, on 16 March, the regional committee of the CNT, to assuage the fears of the rank and file, announced that the government had agreed to postpone discussion of the decrees.[129] This confounded Tarradellas. There was "certainly some misunderstanding," he said, "as the decrees in question, which were undoubtedly well received by public opinion, were approved by the government and published in the *Diari Oficial* on 4 March." What had actually happened, he explained, was that the government had agreed to postpone the appointments to the key positions in the new corps.[130] This was true. In fact, because of the agitation, the appointments, which were to have been confined mainly to members of the assault and national republican guards, were never made, and the legislation died on the pages of the *Diari Oficial*, leaving the duality of police powers in the region unchanged.

Meanwhile, the PSUC was agitating for the implementation of other measures, such as compulsory military service and the fusion of the militia into a regular army. Although the Catalan government had approved the mobilization of the 1934–35 classes in October,[131] the measure had remained unheeded, for the CNT held that it would be "very childish to hand over our forces to the absolute control of the government" and that its members should be drafted only by the CNT for service in libertarian units.[132] Even after the CNT took over the defense council in December, the anarchosyndicalists continued to oppose the draft and strove to maintain the integrity and homogeneous character of their armed forces under the control of their own revolutionary leaders. Thus, while the PSUC pressed for the fusion of the militia into a regular army "in the service of the republican government"[133]—by which it meant, of course, an army and a government subject to its will—the CNT urged that the militia be organized into an army "in the service of the Revolution."[134] There, in a nutshell, lay the irreconcilable conflict between the opposing sides.

In this dispute, the position of the POUM, which had its own militia forces, was clear: "The only guarantee that the working class can have as to the fate of the Revolution is its own army. And the army of the working class can be no other than . . . an army recruited from the militia. . . . It is absolutely necessary that control be maintained by the revolutionary organizations. . . . In short, our party declares itself resolutely in favor of a regular army, but of a regular army that is the living expression of the Revolution."[135]

Intensifying its agitation for a regular army under government control, the PSUC set up a Committee for the Popular Army that on

28 February held an impressive demonstration and military parade. To the CNT the committee presented a grave challenge. On the ground that it usurped his authority, the CNT defense councillor, Francisco Isgleas, threatened to resign. To avert a cabinet crisis, the Esquerra, prompted by Tarradellas and Companys, urged that the activities of the committee be suspended "despite every good intention," inasmuch as they might result in a "usurpation of functions and initiatives properly belonging to the Generalitat council."[136] A compromise was reached: the Committee of the Popular Army was officially constituted as an auxiliary body of the defense council, with Isgleas as vice-president and Companys as president.[137] This was nonetheless a victory for the PSUC. Through the machinery of the committee, now recognized as an official body, it was able to increase its agitation and to exert even greater pressure on the defense councillor. Mirroring the consternation of the libertarian movement, *Tierra y Libertad*, the leading mouthpiece of the FAI, declared that behind the PSUC's campaign for a regular army there lay "a policy of aggression against anarchism."[138]

Simultaneously, Isgleas was under mounting pressure from the central government, which had long opposed the independence of the Catalan militia on the neighboring Aragon front and the military independence acquired by Catalonia as a result of the Revolution. But not until the beginning of March did the Generalitat government, hungry for arms and funds, agree to submit to Valencia's military decrees and to subordinate the Catalan militia to the war ministry.[139] As a result, on 18 March, Isgleas—who, with Tarradellas, had negotiated the financial and military accords on behalf of the Catalan government—was compelled to set firm dates for the call-up of the 1932–36 classes.[140]

On 23 March, *La Batalla* published an article by Enrique Adroher, a POUM member and delegate on the CNT defense council, denouncing Valencia's military policy toward Catalonia as "a cheap piece of blackmail" and charging that it had used money and arms and military defeats to gain control of the Catalan army. "Catalonia has lost her military independence. The Catalan proletariat has lost its army," he added. "How can those who have been calling themselves nationalists and even separatists [a reference to the Esquerra autonomists and the separatists of the small Estat Catalá party] face the Catalan people? How can the CNT councillors face their comrades fighting on the battlefields of Aragon? How can they all justify this shameful capitulation to the central government. . . . It is incomprehensible that the anarchist comrades, who would rather allow themselves to be killed than permit a revolver to be taken away from them, should quietly agree to surrender the army, which, in the last analysis, is the real weapon of the working class."[141]

Not all the anarchists had quietly submitted to the demands of Valencia; for early in March—as in the case of the Iron Column described earlier in this volume—nearly one thousand militiamen stationed in Gelsa on the Aragon front left in protest against the militarization decrees, fearing that these measures would transform the militia into an instrument of the state under the rigid control of the government. In Barcelona, they set up "The Friends of Durruti"—named after the famous anarchist, Buenaventura Durruti, killed in November on the Madrid front—to combat the "counterrevolutionary" policy of the leadership of the CNT and FAI. Officially constituted in mid-March with Félix Martínez and Jaime Balius (director at the time of the CNT newspaper *La Noche*) as secretary and vice-secretary respectively,[142] the organization increased its membership, according to Balius, to between four and five thousand by the beginning of May.[143] None of its adherents, Balius affirmed, belonged to the Bolshevik Leninists, despite numerous claims to the contrary—for example, by Frank Jellinek, the *Manchester Guardian* correspondent in Spain, who alleged, as did the Communists, that the organization was "penetrated and controlled" by Trotskyists.[144] However, Manuel Grandizo Munis, a foreign leader of the minuscule group of Spanish Bolshevik Leninists, a former secretary general of the Trotskyist Communist League of Mexico, says: "We worked fraternally with the workers of the Friends of Durruti and they helped us in the sale and distribution of our newspaper."[145]

Whether the withdrawal from the front of so large a group of militiamen had any effect on the anarchosyndicalist leadership cannot be said with certainty, but it is noteworthy that only a day after the first draftees were due to present themselves at their induction centers, in compliance with the military decrees, the CNT councillors, led by Francisco Isgleas, walked out of the Generalitat government, provoking a cabinet crisis.[146]

The PSUC and CNT were now deadlocked over every crucial issue. The libertarian movement had tried to protect the independence of its armed forces by temporizing or by feigning acceptance of the government's decrees, but the pretense could not be continued, and an open split in the cabinet was inevitable. As a condition for resolving the crisis, the libertarians demanded that the legislation on public order "undergo such a fundamental change that only the title remain" and that the defense council should be authorized to prevent "by every means at its disposal military parades and demonstrations and whatever prejudices or undermines revolutionary morale and the will to fight."[147] The PSUC, on the other hand, declared that it had not provoked the crisis and had done everything possible to avoid it. "A government must be formed that will not allow any segment or group constantly to obstruct [its] work in favor of the war. A government must be formed that will honor its commitments and implement the decrees that have been approved unanimously but have not yet been put into effect."[148] Furthermore, it insisted that the anarchosyndicalists sign a pledge that the military and public order decrees approved by the previous government would be executed "without modification" and that all the measures of the new government would be fulfilled.[149] But the CNT was not about to set its signature to any document that might later be used against it, and that, in its opinion, "ran counter not only to the ideological principles that inspire our organization but to the very essence of the Revolution and to the conquests achieved by the working masses since 19 July."[150]

The crisis was now entering its second week with no solution in prospect. On 3 April, President Companys put together, as a last resort, a makeshift cabinet comprising six councillors:

José Tarradellas	Esquerra	First Councillor (Premier) and Councillor of Finance and Education
Artemio Aiguadé	Esquerra	Internal Security
Juan Comorera	PSUC	Public Works, Labor, and Justice
José Calvet	Unió de Rabassaires	Agriculture and Supplies
Francisco Isgleas	CNT	Defense
Juan J. Domenech	CNT	Economy, Public Services, and Health

No one regarded the new government as anything but a stopgap, least of all Companys, who, expressing his growing impatience with the CNT at the outset of the crisis, had called for a "government that can govern and can impose its will on those who obstruct its work."[151]

On 7 April, the PSUC and UGT launched a "Victory Plan" for Catalonia. "The whole problem at the present time," ran the preamble, "hinges on the question of power, on the question of authority. Without authority there can be no army. Without authority there can be no war industry. . . . Without authority there can be no victory." Its main points were: (1) The rapid creation of a regular Popular Army of Catalonia as an integral part of the republican army. (2) Immediate organization of five divisions on the basis of the 1932–36 classes. (3) Nationalization of the basic war industries and the militarization of transport. (4) Rapid creation of the single internal security corps in compliance with the decrees approved by the previous government of Catalonia. (5) Concentration of all arms in the hands of the government.[152]

The entire plan was in conflict with the revolutionary aims of the CNT. "We have already made too many [concessions]," warned *Solidaridad Obrera*, "and believe that the time has come to turn off the spigot."[153]

Andrés Nin, the POUM leader, welcomed this stand: "On 19 July the working class had power in its hands. . . . It allowed the opportunity to pass. . . . The proletariat still holds in its hands important positions. . . . If today we do not take advantage of the situation to take power peacefully, tomorrow we shall have to resort to a violent struggle to put an end to the bourgeoisie and the reformists. . . . With great anxiety we have watched the vacillations and doubts of the CNT leadership. Too many concessions have been made to the counterrevolution. . . . For this reason we welcome with pleasure the CNT's present stand. . . . The CNT has declared: 'Here we stop! Not a single step backward!' "[154]

On 10 April, *Tierra y Libertad*, the FAI organ, reflecting the mood of the more radical spirits, declared: "CRUSH THE COUNTERREVOLUTION, COMRADES! That is your mandate. Our duty is to make it a reality." Despite this mandate, the CNT leaders continued their negotiations with the PSUC and Esquerra representatives in the Generalitat Palace in search of a modus vivendi that might stave off open warfare between the opposing camps. But the streets outside seemed paved with dynamite as sporadic clashes proliferated and the danger of civil war loomed more ominously with every passing hour.

On 16 April, President Companys set up another stopgap government to tide things over. A few weeks later he recorded:

For a long time the councillor of [internal] security Aiguadé had been demanding additional forces [from the central government]; those of the Generalitat were insufficient [to meet the needs of the situation]: Only two thousand armed assault guards, six hundred others unarmed, and few national guards. The policy of unity and tact had to go hand in hand with an

[396]

effort to increase the authority of the government by taking action in specific cases involving so-called uncontrolled groups and coercive measures directed against the government's orders. This I had been demanding with insistence not only because of the pressure of public opinion, but also because of the very demands of the Ministry of the Interior and other authorities of Madrid, and the comments in the foreign press regarding the frontier, etc., etc. The complexity of the situation made reinforcements necessary, because even with the utmost tact it was anticipated that a clash might occur. The government of the Generalitat was exhausting its resources for resolving the situation and public opinion was pressing. The power of the government was growing constantly, but the majority of the people in Catalonia were irritated to such a degree that there was a danger that the government might lose public confidence and that the forces of public order in the service of the Generalitat might become demoralized.[155]

The new cabinet set up by Companys on 16 April possessed the same political composition as the one formed in December, although with a few minor changes:

José Tarradellas	Esquerra	First Councillor (Premier) and Councillor of Finance
Antonio Mariá Sbert	Esquerra	Culture
Artemio Aiguadé	Esquerra	Internal Security
José Calvet	Unió de Rabassaires	Agriculture
José Miret	UGT [PSUC]	Supplies
Rafael Vidiella	UGT [PSUC]	Labor and Public Works
Juan Comorera	UGT [PSUC]	Justice
Francisco Isgleas	CNT	Defense
Andrés Capdevila	CNT	Economy
Juan Domenech	CNT	Public Services
Aurelio Fernández	CNT	Health and Public Assistance

Like the makeshift cabinet formed on 3 April, the new government was stillborn. Its members could not agree on a common program, and the festering problems of military and police control remained in all their intractable complexity.

The POUM characterized the patched-up crisis as a mockery—"a mockery that is all the more intolerable because three weeks have passed—exactly three weeks—and then things are left exactly as they were." Again it criticized the CNT. "The comrades of the National Confederation of Labor did not know what attitude to adopt [at the outset of the war] toward the problem of power. . . . [Instead] of urging the working class to seize power completely, they preferred to regard it as a simple question of collaboration. . . . We are certain that the mass of CNT workers will view the solution of the present crisis with the same disfavor as we do. . . . [This] solution is no solution . . . because it has resolved nothing. . . . The problems of the Revolution . . . will be posed again in the future sooner than many believe. . . . The reformists will not abandon their aims. If the comrades of the CNT do not realize this, so much the worse for them and so much the worse for all of us. Because what is at stake is not the future of this or that organization, but the future of the Revolution."[156]

The next day the Barcelona committee of the POUM declared: "The government that has just been formed is an attempt to establish a truce, no matter how brief, in the struggle between the Revolution and the counterrevolution. The small bourgeoisie and the reformists will take advantage of this breathing spell that has been given them to gain and consolidate new positions. The working class has the historic duty to prepare itself for a definitive solution [of the crisis] . . . by instituting a Workers' and Peasants' Government."[157]

Although the CNT leadership had agreed to paper over the crisis, the real mood of the libertarian movement was reflected in its press. "The CNT," said *Solidaridad Obrera* on 17 April, "accepts the solution of the conflict on the understanding that the course followed by the previous council has been cut short and with the conviction that this course will be substituted by a just policy that respects and consolidates the revolutionary gains of the proletariat." "[The CNT]," ran another article in the same issue, "has on many occasions appeared flexible and accommodating in the extreme. But beware! Let no one mistake its meaning or think that the Spanish anarchists will allow themselves to be trampled underfoot with impunity by their so-called comrades!"

The same day, *Ruta*, the organ of the Libertarian Youth, declared: "[The counterrevolution] is attempting to take possession of the state apparatus. Yesterday it asked for a large, single security corps. . . . Today it proposes a regular army devoid of revolutionary content. What is the aim of these rascally maneuvers? . . . To be able to rely on forces that will serve it without question, so that tomorrow it can drown the social gains of the proletariat in blood. How can this plan be frustrated? . . . By forging the military organization of the Revolution. . . . To [the young men in the rear] we make an ardent appeal: FORM THE CADRES OF THE REVOLUTIONARY YOUTH BATTALIONS!"

And another article in the same issue threatened: "The time has come to make the counterrevolution retreat. The FAI and the Libertarian Youth . . . have stated that . . . they will have to fight to put an end to those people who are incapable of being loyal and, even less, of feeling the cause of antifascism and the Revolution to the full. . . . [The] way to prevent the sacrifices of our comrades from being reduced to naught is . . . to create an army that will guarantee victory in the war and the Revolution and to remove from the public life of Catalonia, Comorera, Aiguadé, Rodríguez Salas, etc." And, finally, on the same day, *Tierra y Libertad* declared in banner headlines: "FOR CERTAIN POLITICAL PARTIES THE ESSENTIAL THING IS NOT THE DESTRUCTION OF FASCISM. WHAT OBSESSES THEM IS THE ANARCHIST MOVEMENT. WHAT CONSUMES THEIR BEST ENERGIES IS THEIR CAMPAIGN AGAINST THE CNT AND FAI. . . . IF THEY WANT TO REPEAT IN SPAIN WHAT THEY HAVE DONE IN OTHER COUNTRIES, THEY WILL FIND US ON A WAR FOOTING."

In the midst of the heightening tension came an abortive attempt, on 24 April, on the life of the Communist police commissioner, Rodríguez Salas.[158] Then came the murder the next day of Roldán Cortada, a PSUC member and secretary of the UGT Municipal Workers' Federation. A shiver of apprehension passed through the region. The assassination, which Rodríguez Salas attributed to "uncontrollables"[159] —a term now commonly used to characterize all refractory elements of the CNT and FAI, who were opposed to government collaboration and sought the adherence of the libertarian movement to its antistatist principles—added fresh heat to the simmering conflict. "AN END TO IMPUNITY!" cried *La Humanitat*, the Esquerra organ. "Public order must be organized rapidly and under the command of a single person, who must put an end, rapidly and relentlessly, to [these] criminal deeds that occur all too frequently. No longer can we permit groups of individuals who have been given the name of uncontrollables to impose by force their own will and their own law upon the majority of citizens."[160] "Isn't it a disgrace," asked the *Diari de Barcelona*, the mouthpiece of the separatist Estat Català, "that there are still uncontrollables and *agents provocateurs*? . . . And the decrees on public order approved some time ago by the Generalitat, why have they not been implemented? What purpose do the authorities serve?"[161]

And a joint manifesto issued by the PSUC and UGT demanded: "An end to the assassination of militant workers! . . . An end to provocations against antifascist and proletarian unity! War against *agents provocateurs* in the pay of national and international fascism! The people demand justice and are prepared to impose it at all costs."[162]

On 27 April, the day of Cortada's funeral, the PSUC organized a giant procession. "[It] was not merely a funeral; it was a plebiscite," said *Treball*, the party organ. "Thousands upon thousands of workers, of antifascists, marched through the streets of Barcelona . . . united fraternally in sorrow, but also in protest. . . . The grandiose funeral has demonstrated that the Catalan people are resolved to put an end to the murderers and nests of bandits who want to frustrate our victory over fascism. A plebiscite has been held. And the figures of the plebiscite tell us that what we have experienced up to now we cannot tolerate a day longer; that the antifascist masses must unite . . . against the enemy within, against those we call uncontrollables."[163]

While the CNT protested that it was "repugnant" to "make political capital out of a painful event that has cost the life of an antifascist comrade,"[164] the POUM declared that the funeral was a pretext for "a counterrevolutionary demonstration." "Through the unions large numbers of Catalan workers were mobilized . . . [moved by] sympathy for the death of a militant worker fallen in the struggle in the rear. . . . The essential political aim of demonstrations like that of yesterday is to create among the reactionary small bourgeoisie and among the most backward layers of the working class a POGROM atmosphere against the revolutionary vanguard of the Catalan proletariat: CNT, FAI, and POUM. A psychological climate is being created preparatory to actions of greater magnitude."[165]

Fast on the heels of Roldán Cortada's assassination came the slaying of Antonio Martín, the anarchist president of the revolutionary committee in the border town of Puigcerdá, during an encounter with assault and national republican guards in the neighboring village of Bellver.[166] Shortly thereafter truckloads of carabineers, dispatched from Valencia by finance minister Juan Negrín, began seizing the frontier posts along the Franco-Spanish border hitherto controlled by revolutionary committees.[167] Two weeks earlier, on 16 April, an order issued by Negrín, assigning certain reorganized carabineer units for duty on the border,[168] had given advance warning of Valencia's intention to recapture this vital element of state power essential to the control of foreign trade and to the flow of arms.

Knowledge of the death of Martín, of the seizure of frontier posts by the carabineers, of attempted disarmings by assault and national republican guards, and of raids by Rodríguez Salas, the Communist police commissioner, into the anarchist stronghold of Hospitalet,[169] to flush out Roldán Cortada's alleged killers, caused the storm clouds gathering in Barcelona to darken and thicken perceptibly.

On 29 April, groups of armed men mobilized by the local committees of the CNT and FAI occupied the streets of the Catalan capital.

All had rifles and some wore hand grenades around their waists. At 6 P.M. the government met, but, after a brief session, announced that it would not continue its work under the pressure of groups who were "trying to impose their will by force and to compromise the war and revolution." "The government is therefore suspending its meeting and hopes that all persons not subject to its direct authority will immediately leave the streets so as to make it possible for the state of disquiet and alarm that Catalonia is presently experiencing to quickly disappear. At the same time the council of the Generalitat has taken the necessary steps to ensure the strict fulfillment of its orders."[170]

May Day was approaching. The negotiations that had been proceeding between the UGT and the CNT for a joint demonstration had to be abandoned.[171] The widening chasm between the opposing sides prevented any slogan from being found that was broad enough to bridge their differences even for a day.

In the explosive atmosphere the new ultraradical anarchist organization, the Friends of Durruti, became extremely active. In the last days of April, they plastered Barcelona with their slogans. "We accept their program," wrote Juan Andrade, one of the more radical members of the POUM executive, "and are ready to agree to whatever proposals may be made to us. There are two points in those slogans that are also the fundamental ones for us: All power to the working class, and democratic organs of the workers, peasants, and combatants, as an expression of proletarian power."[172]

On 1 May, the POUM executive declared:

For two days, the workers have been standing guard. [They] . . . have been watching day and night over the fate of the Revolution. . . . They are neither uncontrollables nor *provocateurs*. They are the same workers who fought in the streets on 19 July. . . .

Bearing arms, they are keeping vigil because their patience is exhausted. They are tired of so much political capitulation, of paper governments based on impotent compromises. . . .

We have no confidence in the members of the government. For this reason we keep watch in the streets. . . .

We can no longer tolerate the real uncontrollables. We want control, but absolute control. At the front and in the rear. Control by the working class. . . .

But our action must not degenerate into a sporadic movement, into a suicidal "putsch," that would jeopardize the triumphant march of the working class. No, not the action of groups only [but] the action of all the workers with a concrete program and a clear understanding of the needs and possibilities of the moment.

And for this a Revolutionary Workers' Front [is needed] formed by the proletarian parties and organizations committed to winning the war and leading the Revolution to its final consequences.

The Communist Triumph

And a government [is needed] that is the expression of those who work and those who fight, a workers' and peasants' government, elected democratically by the workers and peasants and by the combatants.[173]

Meantime, the assault and national republican guards were increasing their efforts to disarm the anarchosyndicalists in the streets. On 2 May, *Solidaridad Obrera* warned: "THE GUARANTEE OF THE REVOLUTION IS THE PROLETARIAT IN ARMS. TO ATTEMPT TO DISARM THE PEOPLE IS TO PLACE ONESELF ON THE WRONG SIDE OF THE BARRICADES. NO COUNCILLOR OR POLICE COMMISSIONER, NO MATTER WHO HE IS, CAN ORDER THE DISARMING OF THE WORKERS, WHO ARE FIGHTING FASCISM WITH MORE SELF-SACRIFICE THAN ALL THE POLITICIANS IN THE REAR, WHOSE INCAPACITY AND IMPOTENCE EVERYBODY KNOWS. DO NOT, ON ANY ACCOUNT, ALLOW YOURSELVES TO BE DISARMED!"

28. Barcelona: The May Events

The dynamics of the political conflict in Barcelona were now leading inexorably toward open warfare, toward that bloody episode and turning point in the Spanish Revolution known as the May days or May events.

Seizing the initiative, Rodríguez Salas, the PSUC police commissioner, made a daring move. At 3 P.M. on Monday, 3 May, accompanied by three truckloads of assault guards, and acting in concert with Aiguadé, the Esquerra councillor of internal security, he raided the central telephone exchange, which the CNT had occupied since the defeat of the military in July and regarded as a "key position in the Revolution."[1] Swiftly entering the ten-story building, the assault guards occupied the ground floor, but were stopped when they reached one of the upper floors.[2]

In accordance with the Catalan government's decree on collectivization and workers' control of 24 October 1936 that legalized the sequestration or control of the larger commercial and industrial concerns seized by the unions during the first days of the Revolution, the telephone exchange, owned by the Compañía Telefónica Nacional de España, a subsidiary of the International Telephone and Telegraph Corporation, was controlled by a committee of the CNT and UGT. On this body the anarchosyndicalists were the dominant force, and their red and black flag, which had flown from the tower of the building ever since July, attested to their supremacy.

Although, in accordance with the decree, the committee was presided over by a government delegate, his presence merely created an illusion of official control where in reality none existed. "Serious things were going on there that the government had to end," declared Juan Comorera, the PSUC secretary. "All the interior controls of the telephone exchange were in the service, not of the community, but of one organization, and neither President Azaña nor President Companys, nor anyone else, could speak without an indiscreet controller overhearing."[3] This was no exaggeration. It was precisely for the purpose of intercepting conversations that the CNT had placed "interventors" or controllers in the building. President Companys himself, in his notes on the May events, testifies that "all the telephone calls of the Generalitat authorities, of the President of Catalonia and of the President of the Republic were intercepted."[4] If this interception was not a prerogative bestowed by law, it was nonetheless, in the opinion of the CNT, an indefeasible right conferred by the Revolution. In its ability to interpose its veto, to intercept, as the FAI leader, Abad de Santillán, puts it, "compromising messages and conversations" and to overhear persons "conspiring to whittle away the people's rights,"[5] the CNT possessed a vital element of real power, that neither the PSUC nor the Esquerra could permit for long if they were ever to be masters of the region.

Thus, when Rodríguez Salas raided the central telephone exchange with an order signed by Aiguadé,[6] it is not unlikely that he had the tacit if not formal approval of most of the members of the government except those belonging to the CNT.[7] One other notable exception, however, was the shrewd and extremely circumspect premier of the Catalan government, José Tarradellas. According to President Azaña —who, it will be recalled, had fled to Barcelona in October 1936 in order to be near the French border[8]—Tarradellas told him on the first night of the fighting that he had learned of the raid only after the order had been given and that he considered the decision "hazardous," because the government lacked resources with which to subdue any resistance it might encounter.[9] "He criticized Aiguadé a lot," Azaña further testifies, "for having launched a battle without preparing for it, and Companys for talking so much about doing battle, as a result of which he had alarmed the anarchists. He believed that ultimately everything would be settled through negotiation."[10]

On learning of the raid, the CNT councillors demanded the removal of both Rodríguez Salas and Aiguadé, but to no avail.[11] "The intransigence of the other parties," writes José Peirats, the anarchosyndicalist historian, "and especially the opportunist attitude of the president of the Generalitat, who resolutely opposed this punishment, provoked a general strike followed by an outbreak of hostilities."[12]

In a retrospective account of the May events, Manuel Cruells, a staff reporter at the time on the *Diari de Barcelona*, the organ of Estat Catalá, representing the small separatist movement among the Catalan middle classes, states: "If Companys had adopted an energetic attitude by removing his councillor of the interior and the general commissar of public order, as logically he should have done, there would have been no tragic week of May in Barcelona. . . . It is somewhat difficult to understand the attitude of President Companys under the particular circumstances. . . . Either he was badly informed and did not realize how grave the situation might become as a result of his refusal, or he was well informed and acquiesced in provoking the serious situation. . . . Why did the president not insist on the proposed resignations? Had he allowed himself to be carried away by the anti-FAI hysteria that had already begun to manifest itself in the streets? Did he wish to be loyal, as on other occasions, to certain friends in his own party? It is difficult to explain the real cause of the president's attitude, but we can affirm that it was decisive in sparking the conflict, suffused with hate, that Barcelona had to endure."[13]

As news of the raid on the telephone building became known, anger swept through the working-class districts, mainly anarchosyndicalist. "Hundreds of comrades occupy the streets," wrote an anarchist eyewitness. "They wish to go to the center of the city and make a CLEAN SWEEP of those who want to repeat the fascist provocation of 19 July. They are restrained with difficulty. The comrades . . . know what the aggressors are seeking. . . . What they want is to strangle the Revolution, destroy the conquests of the revolutionary workers, and simply reestablish the bourgeois democratic Republic. To achieve this goal it is necessary to provoke the anarchists into a conflict, declare them enemies of the 'Popular Front' government, destroy their organizations, open the way to intervention by the democratic capitalist powers, and drown the onward march of the revolutionary Spanish workers in blood. The so-called 'workers' fatherland' is an accomplice in this executioners' job against the Revolution and is sacrificing the future liberty of the Spanish people for the help the democratic capitalist powers offer against the fascist threat to its existence."[14]

Hundreds of barricades were rapidly erected. "The building of these barricades was a strange and wonderful sight," wrote George Orwell, an eyewitness in the Ramblas, one of the main avenues. "With the kind of passionate energy that Spaniards display when they have definitely decided to begin upon any object of work, long lines of men, women, and quite small children were tearing up cobblestones, hauling them along in a handcart that had been found somewhere, and staggering to and fro under heavy sacks of sand."[15]

Before nightfall Barcelona was an armed camp. "Thousands upon thousands of workers have returned to the streets with arms in their hands," declared the POUM executive. "Plants, machine shops, warehouses have stopped work. The barricades of liberty have risen again in every part of town. The spirit of July has once more taken possession of Barcelona."[16]

In a great ring around Barcelona extending from the working-class suburbs to the edge of the commercial and official section of the city, the anarchosyndicalists were masters of the situation. Inside the business and political enclave, however, the opposing forces were fairly evenly matched. For example, in the Plaza de Cataluña, the central square, where the anarchosyndicalists held the *telefónica*, the PSUC was entrenched in the Hotel Colón, its headquarters, which it had sequestered in July, and from whose windows almost the entire square could be swept by machine-gun fire.

In the working-class suburbs of Sarriá, Hostafrancs, and Sans, as well as the maritime quarter of Barceloneta, the assault and national republican guards were powerless.[17] Some surrendered without resistance, while others remained in their barracks, waiting to see how the crisis would run its course. "Instantaneously, nearly the whole of Barcelona was in the power of our armed groups," affirms the FAI leader Abad de Santillán. "They did not move from their posts, although they could have done so easily and overcome the small centers of resistance."[18] Had the CNT and FAI been interested in taking power, he asserted, their victory would have been complete, "but this did not interest us, for it would have been an act of folly contrary to our principles of unity and democracy."[19]

Near the Catalan Parliament building, where President Azaña had recently established his official residence, intermittent firing was going on. At 8 P.M., he instructed his secretary general, Cándido Bolívar, then in Valencia, to request Premier Largo Caballero for reinforcements to bolster his presidential guard. Caballero had retired even earlier than usual, and Bolívar brought the ruffled premier out of bed at 8:30 P.M. After urging him to dispatch additional forces without delay, Bolívar departed, little suspecting that his request would remain unheeded.[20] Shortly afterward interior minister Galarza informed Caballero that Aiguadé had asked for the "urgent dispatch of 1,500 guards, indispensable for suppressing the movement."[21]

At 11 P.M. Premier Tarradellas, acting on behalf of President Companys, visited Azaña to offer his apologies for the state of turbulence. The normally short trip of only a few minutes from the Generalitat Palace to the Parliament building had taken an hour and a half. "He had been obliged to descend from his car at every barricade . . . to parley at length, and had been humiliated," Azaña notes in his memoirs. "When he began to make excuses [for the turmoil], stressing the fact that, as a Catalan, he felt ashamed, I interrupted him and repeated the remarks I had made to Bolívar to pass on to the prime minister. 'Don't make excuses! Suppress the insurrection! As far as I am concerned, guarantee my safety and my freedom of movement.'" Tarradellas then took leave of the president, who heard nothing more from the Catalan government during the rest of the fighting. "No one in the Generalitat asked about me, or tried to speak to me, or concerned himself with my position," he remarks bitterly. "It was more than a scandalous discourtesy; it was an act of silent hostility." Nor did Prime Minister Largo Caballero concern himself with the president's plight. "He neither called me nor sent me any message."[22]

"The whole night [3–4 May] the rebels were masters of the city," Azaña continues. "They raised barricades, occupied buildings and important points without anyone interfering with them. . . . I was not worried, but I was disturbed by the position they had put me in. I perceived vaguely that the conflict did not directly involve me, and I even thought that if things got worse it might help to achieve peace [in Spain]. What disgusted me and annoyed me was the scandal the rebellion would create abroad, the benefit the other rebels would derive from it, and its repercussions upon the war."[23]

That same night the executive committee of the POUM met with the regional committees of the CNT, FAI, and Libertarian Youth. Julián Gorkin, a member of the executive, recalls: "We stated the problem in these precise terms: 'Neither of us has urged the masses of Barcelona to take this action. This is a spontaneous response to a Stalinist provocation. This is the decisive moment for the Revolution. Either we place ourselves at the head of the movement in order to destroy the internal enemy or else the movement will collapse and the enemy will destroy us. We must make our choice; revolution or counterrevolution.' [The regional committees] made no decision. Their maximum demand was the removal of the [police] commissioner who had provoked the movement. As though it were not the various forces behind him that had to be destroyed! Always the form instead of the substance! . . . Our party placed itself on the side of the movement, even though we knew it was condemned to failure."[24]

The following morning, Tuesday, 4 May, Aiguadé repeated his request for fifteen hundred assault guards, but interior minister Galarza, acting on instructions from Largo Caballero, gave only a temporizing reply. "I have ordered the concentration of [police] forces in Castellón, Murcia, Alicante, and Valencia," he responded, "and, in case of necessity, should serious clashes occur in Catalonia . . . the necessary

The Communist Triumph

forces will be placed at your disposal. But the *premier and I agree that while everything should be prepared* the intervention of forces not stationed in Catalonia is undesirable, so long as those already there do not have to be employed to the full and have not been proved inadequate."[25] By temporizing, Largo Caballero hoped that the fighting would subside without government intervention. Waging a political battle for survival against the Communists, he was not inclined to antagonize the CNT and FAI or to strengthen the hand of his opponents in Catalonia by sending reinforcements to the region.

Meanwhile, the situation in Barcelona was deteriorating. The rattle of machine-gun fire, the explosion of hand grenades and dynamite, and the fire of mortars merged into a single roar. This "devilish noise," wrote Orwell, "echoing from thousands of stone buildings, went on and on and on, like a tropical rainstorm. Crack-crack, rattle-rattle, roar—sometimes it died away to a few shots, sometimes it quickened to a deafening fusillade, but it never stopped while daylight lasted."[26] Although isolated attempts were made to capture enemy strongholds, there was comparatively little fighting in the open. Most of the combatants remained in buildings or behind barricades and blazed away at their enemies opposite.[27]

"We realized that what was happening was that everybody's house was burning," declared Abad de Santillán some days later, "and that the only hope under the circumstances was to extinguish the flames and end the bloody slaughter."[28] A few months later, however, he had second thoughts: "Perhaps . . . we allowed ourselves to be guided much more by a sense of loyalty and generosity than by a precise understanding of the plot that had been hatched against us."[29]

At 2 P.M. the CNT and FAI appealed over the radio for a cease-fire: "Workers! . . . We are not responsible for what is happening. We are attacking no one. We are only defending oursleves. . . . Lay down your arms! Remember, we are brothers! . . . If we fight among ourselves we are doomed to defeat."[30]

But there were forces intent on stoking the conflict. Not only were Rodríguez Salas's men initiating new offensive actions, but the tiny Trotskyist group of Bolshevik Leninists and the dissident anarchists of the Friends of Durruti, joined by a few of the more militant members of the POUM, were extremely active.

The attitude of the POUM leaders, on the other hand, was pessimistic. As Julián Gorkin recalled, "We placed ourselves on the side of the movement, even though we knew it was condemned to failure."[31] "We did not feel ourselves spiritually or physically strong enough to take the lead in organizing the masses for resistance," a member of the executive acknowledged.[32] And George Orwell, a participant in the fighting and a POUM sympathizer, corroborates: "Those who were in personal touch with the POUM leaders at the time have told me that they were in reality dismayed by the whole business, but felt that they had got to associate themselves with it."[33]

The leadership did not publicly display its pessimism and on the surface appeared combative despite its unsuccessful overtures to the regional committees of the libertarian movement on the night of 3 May for joint, aggressive action. The next morning, *La Batalla* urged the workers to remain in "a state of permanent mobilization" and to "prosecute and intensify the offensive that has been initiated as there is no better means of defense than attack. It is imperative to demand and obtain the resignation of the general commissioner of public order. . . . It is imperative to demand and obtain the abrogation of the decrees on public order adopted by reaction and reformism. To achieve all this and to continue the revolutionary action, broadening its scope every day and carrying it to its ultimate consequences, it is imperative that the working class, remaining in a state of mobilization and on the offensive, should form the Revolutionary Workers' Front and should proceed immediately with the organization of committees in defense of the Revolution."[34]

In Valencia, that same morning, Tuesday, 4 May, Premier Largo Caballero, fearing that the Communists might exploit the fighting to topple his government, summoned the CNT ministers. Aiguadé, the Catalan councillor of internal security, he told them, had asked the minister of the interior to dispatch fifteen hundred assault guards. "The government," he argued, "could not do that because it would mean placing forces in the service of the person who may possibly have had something to do with the conflict. Before acceding, he would take over the administration of public order as provided in the Constitution."[35] He therefore suggested that representatives of the national committee of the CNT and of the executive committee of the UGT should leave for Barcelona immediately to try to end the hostilities.[36] A meeting of the national committee was then summoned, at which it was decided to send representatives to Barcelona "so as to avoid the taking over of public order by the central government."[37] Mariano Vázquez, CNT secretary, and García Oliver, CNT minister of justice, were designated by the committee, while Carlos Hernández Zancajo and Mariano Muñoz Sánchez, both supporters of Largo Caballero, were appointed by the UGT executive.[38]

At 11 A.M. the central government met. Backed by Indalecio Prieto and by the Left Republican ministers, the Communists pressed the premier to take immediate action, demanding not only that reinforcements be dispatched to Catalonia, but that the government assume control of public order and of military affairs in the region. Succumbing to the threat of a cabinet crisis, Caballero reluctantly agreed to adopt these measures, but only if the situation did not improve by evening.

At 1:10 P.M. President Companys—who had undoubtedly instructed Aiguadé to request the fifteen hundred assault guards from Valencia—informed Largo Caballero that the situation was "very serious," that the police forces were "inadequate for rapid action and are becoming exhausted."[39] Caballero replied: "I deem it my duty to inform you that . . . all [the ministers] have decided that if the situation does not improve *by an early hour this evening*, the government will assume control of public order in accordance with the Statute [of Catalan Autonomy]. Tell me if you have any objection."[40] This was an extremely delicate question for President Companys—the chief custodian of regional autonomy—who certainly would have preferred the dispatch of reinforcements to the sacrifice of Catalan autonomy. But, fearful lest he be denied the much-needed forces unless he surrendered the control of public order, he responded: "*I believe that [the central government] should cooperate in strengthening the available forces* of the councillor of internal security." But, then, with resignation, he added, "In view of the danger that the [state of public order] may get worse the government of the Republic can adopt the measures it deems necessary."[41]

In a written statement, signed on 9 August 1946 in the presence of several Catalan refugees, Jaime Antón Aiguadé, the nephew of Artemio Aiguadé, alleges that his uncle told him that President Companys surrendered the control of public order to Valencia without either consulting him or the Catalan government. He further alleges that, according to his uncle, Companys's pleas for reinforcements were inspired by Juan Comorera, the PSUC leader, who, "during those days did not move for a single moment from Companys's side, giving him advice and taking advantage of the moral depression of the president to propose solutions that suited the interests of the PSUC." It was Comorera, the document claims, who suggested to Companys that he "accept the solution proposed by the government of Valencia."[42]

However this may be, there can be little doubt that President Companys had the tacit support of other leaders of the Esquerra, including that of Aiguadé himself, when he agreed to surrender the control of public order to Valencia, and that the document in question was a palpable attempt—during a period of postwar dissensions within the Esquerra—to lay the historic responsibility for the loss of Catalan autonomy solely at the door of Companys and the PSUC.

Despite Companys's go-ahead, Premier Largo Caballero was not yet willing to act. He was still hoping that his emissaries in Barcelona might end the bloodshed by mediation. But Indalecio Prieto, his Socialist rival and navy and air minister, did wish to take action. An irreconcilable opponent of the CNT and FAI, he believed from the inception of the Revolution, according to his own account, that the most important task of the republican government was to recover the reins of power.[43] He instructed air force chief Ignacio Hidalgo de Cisneros to proceed to the Catalan air base at Reus with a detachment of ground forces for its defense and with two bomber and two fighter squadrons "for operations against the region in the event the insurrectionists should win."[44] Furthermore, in reply to a succession of teletyped messages from Manuel Azaña requesting with "hysterical insistence"—as one witness put it—that steps be taken for his personal protection,[45] Prieto ordered two destroyers, the *Lepanto* and *Sánchez Barcaiztegui*, to sail for Barcelona with marines to evacuate the president. "I have already stated," Azaña records in his memoirs, "that the prime minister did not attempt to communicate with me either directly or indirectly. Nor did he inform the ministers of my situation. Prieto got in touch with me by telegraph on Tuesday, mid-morning. He was aware of the tumult in Barcelona, but . . . he could not fully appreciate my position without seeing it. He told me that he was sending two destroyers to the port of Barcelona . . . to be placed at my disposal; that twenty airplanes would leave for Reus and Prat; that the ministries of the interior and war were sending two armed units, and that one thousand air force soldiers were being flown to Reus. He was very alarmed and ready to crush the rebellion."[46]

All day Tuesday the government in Valencia remained in continuous session. In the late afternoon Largo Caballero's opponents reminded him of the commitment he had made earlier in the day to assume control of public order and military affairs in Catalonia if the situation did not improve by the evening. During the entire day, the CNT and FAI in Barcelona had kept up their appeals for a cease-fire. At 3 P.M. they had exhorted over the radio: "Workers of the CNT, workers of the UGT! Do not put up with deceit and trickery. Above all let us unite. Lay down your arms! Heed only one slogan: Everyone back to work to defeat fascism!"[47] Despite these appeals, wrote Agustín Souchy, the AIT representative in Casa CNT-FAI, anarchosyndicalist headquarters, the hostilities could not be contained. "Rancor increased on all sides."[48]

While the cabinet debate in Valencia was still in progress, *Frente Rojo*, the Communist evening newspaper, declared: "For a long time we used to attribute anything that occurred to gangs euphemistically called 'uncontrollables.' Now we see that they are perfectly controlled . . . but by the enemy. This cannot be tolerated any longer. . . . There has been enough indulgence already. There is a limit to patience. When the existence of Spain as an independent nation is at stake, when the liberty of the Spanish people and the well-being and future of the popular masses is in jeopardy, we cannot allow ourselves to be stabbed in the back. . . . There can be no more discussion on these matters. We must act. And with the severity that circumstances demand. . . . All those who attempt, in one form or another, with some aim or another, to disturb [order] or break [discipline] should immediately feel the ruthless weight of popular authority, repression by the government, and punitive action by the popular masses."[49]

Inside the cabinet the debate assumed a rabid character. "Comrade Federica Montseny," said the CNT, "led the opposition for four hours against the Communists and republicans who supported the taking over of public order and defense. It was a tumultuous debate, which we lost when the vote was taken."[59] It was decided, however, that the measures would not be put into effect until the last moment,[51] a condition wrung by Montseny and Caballero from their opponents in the belief that the CNT and UGT representatives now en route to Barcelona might negotiate a peaceful settlement.

On their arrival, the emissaries from Valencia joined the Catalan leaders in the Generalitat Palace in appealing for a cease-fire. Mariano Vázquez, the CNT secretary, urged his embattled followers to remember the neighboring Aragon front, where "the fascists might attack at any moment."[52] García Oliver, the CNT-FAI leader and minister of justice, declared: "Think of the pain, think of the anguish . . . of those antifascist workers in that part of Spain dominated by the whip of Hitler and Mussolini when they learn . . . that in [Catalonia] we are killing one another. . . . All of you should remain in your respective positions . . . but should cease firing, even though provoked by persons not interested in finding a solution to this conflict. . . . [I] declare that the guards who have died today are my brothers. I kneel before them and kiss them. . . . [All] those who have died today are my brothers. I kneel before them and kiss them."[53]

That some libertarians were incensed by their leaders' appeals for a cease-fire is confirmed by anarchist sources. "It should not surprise anyone," observed an eyewitness, "that when our representatives, who went to the Generalitat [Palace] to arrange a settlement, gave the order 'Cease Fire!' there were some comrades who felt, in their indignation, that it was a form of treachery to allow those assassins [a reference to the PSUC members and assault guards firing near Casa CNT-FAI] to escape without just punishment."[54]

There was also dissension among the leaders. Helmut Ruediger, vice-secretary of the AIT, who was active in Barcelona at the time of the May events, testifies:

The problem as to whether the CNT should "go the whole way," taking into its own hands the reins of power, or should continue to collaborate was raised several times after the militants had decided in favor of collaboration on 19 July. The decision of 19 July was unanimous, although spontaneous. Not everyone realized what it signified. But it was during the May days, in particular, during the stormy meetings in Casa CNT-FAI in Barcelona, while the deafening noise of rifle and machine-gun fire could be heard on every side, that more than once the question—which finally received a negative response—was raised: "Should we or should we not *take power*?" It was in these terms that the representatives of the organization summed up the problem during those bloody days. But being *anarchists*, what did they mean by "power"?

Let us first agree as to what they definitely *did not* mean. Anarchism and revolutionary syndicalism have never seen in state power, in government, with its administrative and repressive machinery, the means of realizing the social changes they desire. Nor were they of the opinion that the basic condition of Socialist construction should be the erection of a new fascist-Stalinist style totalitarian superstate. They maintained that the social revolution should dispense with *both* the bourgeois state and the new totalitarian superstate, and that social reorganization, like the defense of the Revolution, should be concentrated in the hands of *working-class organizations*—whether labor unions or new organs of spontaneous creation, such as free councils, etc., which, as an expression of the will of the workers themselves, from *below up*, should construct the new social community, thus discarding all conventional forms of authoritarian "power" exercised from above.

But in view of the fact that on 3 May the CNT, representing the majority of the Catalan industrial workers, was in open conflict with *all* organizations comprising the other social layers . . . (the small bourgeoisie, the intellectuals, the *immense mass* of the Catalan peasants, namely, the *rabassaires* [sharecroppers], white-collar workers, technicians, etc.) the question of "power" meant *whether the CNT at that time should crush them all, concentrate the leadership of public affairs in its own hands, and create its own repressive apparatus necessary to prevent the "crushed" from returning to public life.* The reply was "no," but the decisions of those tragic days later provoked a whirlwind of discussions, mutual recriminations, and struggles within the Spanish and international libertarian movement.[55]

At about 9:30 Tuesday night, shortly after the appeals for a cease-fire had been broadcast from the Generalitat Palace, the emissaries from Valencia met with members of the Catalan government under the chairmanship of Companys. "We proposed the formula that a provisional council [government] should be set up, composed of four representatives, [Esquerra, CNT, UGT, and Unió de Rabassaires] in which no one who had belonged to any of the previous governments should participate," said the CNT. "In this way, we would remove Aiguadé and Rodríguez Salas, because we stipulated that the new councillor of internal security should assume absolute [that is, personal] control of public order." This proposal was accepted. But when the CNT suggested that the new government should be formed immediately "so that . . . public opinion would know that the conflict had been resolved," the Communists maintained that "it was first of all essential that the firing in the streets should cease." The CNT representatives tried to hold their ground. "We believed it was necessary to gain time to prevent the [central] government from having to assume control of public order, but no agreement was possible. Although the Esquerra and the Unió de Rabassaires did not join in the debate, they supported the Communist point of view. Finally, at 2 A.M. [Wednesday, 5 May], the meeting ended with a decision to announce over the radio . . . that we had reached agreement and that firing should cease completely in order to normalize the situation. . . . When the meeting was over we informed the [central] government that things were going well."[56]

Encouraged by this news, Largo Caballero announced before dawn that the government had approved "the necessary decrees for rapidly resolving the situation in Catalonia, but believes that their implementation will not now be necessary and that order will be restored in Barcelona today."[57] Vain hope! "During the remainder of the night," observed President Companys in his personal notes, "hard fighting continued in the streets, and the rapid dispatch of reinforcements was demanded by [the council of] internal security, by the Presidencia [the office of President Companys] and also by Vidiella [the PSUC leader]."[58]

The CNT leaders redoubled their efforts early Wednesday morning to quiet their following. "We threw into the balance all our influence, constantly sending delegations to the places where incidents were occurring."[59] But their efforts were not always well received. "I heard some comrades cry with rage over the telephone," recalls Abad de Santillán, "when they telephoned the [CNT-FAI] committees and the latter told them not to shoot, even though they were being attacked by machine-gun fire."[60]

Meanwhile, the Bolshevik Leninists and the Friends of Durruti did what they could to keep tempers afire and to give some direction to the fighting.[61] "No compromise!" declared a leaflet distributed on the barricades by the Bolshevik Leninists. "This is the decisive moment. Next time it will be too late. . . . Long live the unity of action of the CNT-FAI-POUM."[62] "A revolutionary junta!" demanded a leaflet signed by the Friends of Durruti. "Shooting of those responsible. . . . No surrender of the streets. The Revolution before everything. We greet our comrades of the POUM who have fraternized with us on the streets. *LONG LIVE THE SOCIAL REVOLUTION! DOWN WITH THE COUNTERREVOLUTION!*"[63]

The next day, *La Batalla* printed the leaflet of the Friends of Durruti on its front page with the comment that it was of "really extraordinary interest" and that "we are very pleased to reproduce it."[64] But beyond this guarded comment, the POUM leadership kept a respectable distance between itself and the Friends of Durruti. Only the most radical elements of the party collaborated with it, but without the authority of the POUM executive. Although the executive did not join other organizations in appealing over the radio for a cease-fire,[65] it did not dissociate itself publicly from the efforts at pacification of the CNT-FAI leadership. True, *La Batalla* had urged the workers in its issue of 4 May to remain in "a state of permanent mobilization" and to "prosecute and intensify the offensive that has been initiated,"[66] but these exhortations were not repeated in subsequent issues, for the POUM felt helpless in face of the passionate and repeated appeals for a cease-fire by the anarchosyndicalist leadership.

"For four days," stated the *Spanish Revolution*, the English-language bulletin of the POUM, "the workers stood ready, vigilant and awaiting the CNT's order to attack. The order never came. . . . The National Confederation of Labor [CNT], held by the workers as the mass organization of the Revolution, recoiled before the question of workers' power. Caught up in the reins of the government, it tried to straddle the fence with a 'union' of the opposing forces. That is why the revolutionary workers' fight of May 3 to 7 was essentially *defensive* instead of *offensive*. The attitude of the CNT did not fail to bring forth resistance and protests. The Friends of Durruti group brought the unanimous desire of the CNT masses to the surface, but it was not able to take the lead."[67]

According to Felix Morrow, the American Trotskyist, one of the most vitriolic critics of the leadership of the POUM and the CNT, this radical language was for "export purposes" only. "In general," he added, "*Spanish Revolution* has given English readers who could not follow the POUM's Spanish press, a distorted picture of the POUM's conduct; it has been a 'left face.'" "Instead [of putting itself at the head], the POUM leadership . . . put its fate in the hands of the CNT leadership. *Not* public proposals to the CNT for joint action made before the masses, but a behind-the-scenes conference with the regional committee.[68] Whatever the POUM proposals were, they were rejected. You don't agree? Then we shall say nothing about them. And the next morning . . . *La Batalla* had not a word to say about the POUM's proposals to the CNT, about the cowardly behavior of the CNT leaders, their refusal to organize the defense, etc."[69]

In the interest of objectivity, it is important at this stage to quote from "Senex," one of the principal foreign defenders of anarchosyndicalist policy during the May events. In response to Felix Morrow's criticism of the CNT leadership in his book, *Revolution and Counter-Revolution in Spain*, he wrote:

It is often alleged by the revolutionary romantics of the Fourth International that had the Spanish workers struck out boldly for an uncompromising revolutionary line, they could have dispensed with Russian aid; the response of the international proletariat would have been so spontaneous, direct and overpowering in its effect that no government would dare to halt the flow of armaments to revolutionary Spain.

This point is brought out by Felix Morrow in his analysis of the May events in Barcelona in 1937. . . . The CNT, according to our author, should have taken up the challenge of the Stalinist and bourgeois forces and made the ensuing struggle the starting point not only of a thoroughgoing social revolution in Spain itself, but of a revolutionary world conflagration triumphantly sweeping the major countries of Europe. In other words, the CNT workers, upon whom rested the tremendous historic responsibility of holding the first line of defense against the fascists, should have thrown caution to the winds, indulged in a grandiloquent historic gesture, plunged recklessly into the adventure of breaking up the antifascist front, thus opening wide the gate to the fascist avalanche—and all in hope of immediately bringng about the world revolution. . . .

For—much to the astonishment of all of us—we are assured that the European revolution was so palpably near during the May events that it was only the reformist degeneracy of the Spanish anarchists that stopped it from proceeding along the "inevitable" stages of development envisioned by Felix Morrow and other revolutionary strategists.

It is interesting in this connection to trace the logical steps in the glib reasoning employed by the latter in order to conjure up the vision of a triumphant European revolution just waiting around the corner, ready to burst forth at the historic opportunity afforded by the May events, but hopelessly bungled up by the Catalonian anarchists.

Had the anarchist and POUM workers of Barcelona kept up their resistance against Stalinist aggression during the May days—Mr. Morrow assures us—the entire loyalist Spain would have been swept by a triumphant social revolution.

"Any attempt by the bourgeois-Stalinist bloc to gather a proletarian force would have simply precipitated the extension of the workers' state to all Loyalist Spain." But—the reader will ask—what of the well-armed communist police and military units, the flying corps mainly controlled by the Stalinists, the assault guards, the carabineros, the civil guards, many of the socialist controlled military units, the bourgeois sectors, the navy controlled by the right socialist Prieto? Would they give up without any fight? Would all those units, many of whom were drilled and trained for the specific purpose of exercising a check upon the revolutionary workers, disintegrate at the first clash with the latter? And how about the International Brigades, the preponderant majority of whom were firmly controlled by the Stalinists?

That the workers supported by the CNT units stood a good chance of victory in the case of this new civil war, can be readily granted. But this would be a Pyrrhic victory at best, for it is clear that a civil war behind the front lines resulting in the demoralization of the front and the withdrawal of the troops for the participation in this new civil war would open wide the gates to the triumphant sweep of the fascists. . . .

No one with the least knowledge of the situation will say that . . . the French and British masses of people were ready to go to war for the sake of Spain. Nor will he readily concur with Felix Morrow that had the revolutionary forces of Catalonia ousted the bourgeois parties and socialist and Stalinist elements, "the French bourgeoisie would open its borders to Spain, not for intervention but for trade enabling the new regime to secure supplies—or face immediately a revolution at home." In order to do full justice to the profundity of such a statement, one has only to bear in mind that almost half of the French proletarian organizations are under the thumb of the Stalinists and the rest are swayed by the socialists. . . . How could a civil war waged against the socialists and the Stalinists of Spain, in the face of the terrific danger of a fascist break-through at that, fire the socialist- and communist-minded workers of France to the extent of having them lay down an ultimatum to [their] own bourgeoisie demanding arms for the anarchist workers of Catalonia? And, of course, the ultimatum would have to be laid down in the face of the frenzied opposition of the trade-union leadership (socialist and communist), of both parties who would use all powerful means at their disposal to slander, villify, distort the nature of the struggle waged by the revolutionary forces of Spain.[70]

But no amount of debate on the May events will ever settle the disputes between the opposing factions. One week after the fighting had ended, a resolution of the secretariat of the Fourth International declared: "Owing to lack of serious revolutionary leadership the workers have been betrayed."[71] In June, the executive committee of the Spanish Bolshevik-Leninists stated: "The POUM leadership was not even capable of an independent policy: it clung timidly to that of the CNT and slavishly repeated its defeatist slogans."[72] And, after the war, a foreign Trotskyist wrote: "Betrayed by their organizations, abandoned and handed over to the Stalinist scoundrels, the Barcelona workers made a last heroic attempt in May 1937 to defend the conquests of 19 July. . . . Once again, a revolutionary party had a magnificent opportunity to join the rising revolutionary movement, to drive it forward and lead it to victory. But while the leading anarchists placed themselves right from the start on the other side of the barricades, the POUM joined the movement only to hold it back. In this manner, victory was presented to the Stalinist hangmen."[73]

The Communists and their supporters, on the other hand, both in Spain and abroad, in a synchronized campaign, represented the POUM's conduct differently. No sooner had the fighting ended than José Díaz, the Communist party secretary, declared that the "Trotskyists" of the POUM had inspired the "criminal putsch in Catalonia."[74] *Pravda*'s correspondent in Valencia sounded the same note, alleging that the anarchist workers had been "deceived by the Trotskyist-fascist *agents provocateurs*,"[75] while the pro-Communist John Langdon-Davies, writing in the liberal *News Chronicle* of London, stated: "This has not been an anarchist uprising. It is a frustrated putsch by the 'Trotskyist' POUM working through their controlled organizations, 'Friends of Durruti,' and the Libertarian Youth."[76] For months the campaign continued unabated. In November 1937, Georges Soria, of the French Communist *Humanité*, wrote: "The POUM was anxious to maintain the state of disorder as long as possible, for this was the order [it] had received from General Franco." The POUM, he alleged, wanted to weaken the resistance of the people so that Catalonia could not go to the aid of the Basques, then under attack by Franco's German and Italian allies. "It was further hoped that it would be possible to organize widespread propaganda abroad against Republican Spain. And it actually happened that in those days the reactionary and fascist press abroad wrote about 'chaos' in Catalonia, and about a 'rebellion of the people against the Soviet dictatorship.' At the same time the insurgent radio transmitters in Salamanca and Saragossa broadcast unceasingly day and night orders couched in the same terms as those of the POUM: 'Hold your rifles ready, do not give up the fight at any price, combine with your brothers at the front, throw the Russian dictators out of your country.' "[77]

The Communist interpretation of the events was so well propagandized that, years later, the ingenuous Claude Bowers, U.S. ambassador to Spain, who during the Civil War was stationed in Hendaye, France, on the Franco-Spanish border, gave the following version: "In early May, the loyalist government moved against [the anarchists] with cold steel. A crisis had been provoked by the anarchists and the POUM, which was composed of Trotsky communists. It was generally believed that many of these were Franco agents. In factories, they were urging the seizure of private property and strikes to slow down production in the midst of war."[78]

The continuance of serious fighting on Wednesday, 5 May, brought the CNT leaders to the Generalitat Palace at an early hour. "The firing continues," wrote *Fragua Social*, the CNT organ in Valencia. "The streets of Barcelona are bathed in blood. The danger that our rear might crumble increases from hour to hour."[79]

"As the morning advanced," *Solidaridad Obrera* reported, "the fighting continued in various districts of the city and became general in the Plaza de Cataluña [where the telephone exchange was located], in the Calle de Clarís, Layetana [renamed Vía Durruti, where Casa CNT-FAI and the general commissariat of public order were uncomfortably close neighbors], and in the vicinity of the Generalitat Palace and the Avenida del 14 de Abril, increasing the number of wounded. . . . In several places . . . groups of individuals who could be described as *agents provocateurs* . . . devoted their time to firing their weapons and to arresting peaceful citizens, taking their union cards away from them. . . . One of the most lamentable activities of the *agents provocateurs* . . . [was sniping from housetops] in order to spread alarm in those districts where calm prevailed."[80]

On arriving at the Generalitat Palace the CNT leaders insisted that no time be lost in forming the new government. They were aware that Caballero could not hold out much longer against his adversaries and that, failing a settlement through mediation, he would be forced to implement the measures he had approved under duress the previous day. "Our efforts were unavailing," said the CNT, "for at 11:30 the session was adjourned. . . . When we reconvened, the Communists . . . argued that the [new government] should not be formed for three hours. We were [still] deliberating when we were informed that the central government had decided to take over public order and defense[81]. . . . We clearly observed the veiled satisfaction with which everyone welcomed the government's decision."[82] Furthermore, the *Boletín de Información* of the CNT and FAI alleged: "Companys and Tarradellas, as well as the UGT [PSUC] representatives, did everything possible to delay all the negotiations, so that the fighting would continue. Their pleasure could be seen whenever the fratricidal struggle increased in intensity and, on the other hand, they looked dismayed whenever they noted any pacification."[83]

At noon, after a meeting lasting only thirty minutes, the central government issued a statement announcing the public order and military decrees approved the previous day.[84] Colonel Antonio Escobar of the national republican guard was named delegate of public order, while General Sebastián Pozas was made military commander of the region—officially the Fourth Organic Division—and of the so-called Eastern Army in neighboring Aragon, where the CNT and FAI were dominant. These appointments nullified the Catalan councils of defense and internal security and, along with them, the cherished autonomy of the region.

Although, at its party congress held in June 1937, the Esquerra criticized Valencia for not responding immediately to the Catalan government's requests for reinforcements and denounced the delay as a "manuever" to force Catalonia to surrender her autonomy,[85] none of its leaders protested at the time. Indeed, the tone of the official announcement by the Generalitat Palace suggests that President Companys and the other Esquerra leaders accepted Valencia's decision with relief and that their fear of the CNT loomed larger at the time than their devotion to the autonomy of the region. "[The] government of the Republic, on its own initiative, has taken charge of public order in Catalonia," ran the announcement. "With resources superior to those available to the Generalitat, the government of the Republic can meet the needs of the present situation. This is no time for comment. All we can recommend and should recommend, if we wish to serve the interests of the war against fascism, is loyal and determined collaboration with the government of the Republic. Long live the Republic! . . . We urge everyone to lay down his arms and to end the turmoil in the streets."[86]

To be sure, Companys—like Premier Taradellas—would have preferred a gradual erosion of anarchist power to any impingement on Catalan autonomy, but once the fighting had erupted and his requests for reinforcements had been denied, he bowed without protest to Valencia's decision to assume control of public order. Haunted by the fear that he would be held accountable before history for the surrender of Catalan autonomy—a fear that became an obsession in later months[87]—Companys made numerous attempts after the power of the CNT and FAI had been broken to regain control of public order, but always without success.[88]

Until the May events, the faith of the anarchosyndicalist leadership in Companys had been virtually unquestioning. "In all his words and in all his actions," wrote Abad de Santillán, "there was but a single attitude, a moral and spiritual purpose, that we shared almost completely. There were few republicans who had acquired such a perfect understanding of the situation created on 19 July and there were few who expressed themselves with such clarity and such force in favor of a new social regime controlled by the workers. . . . The May events suddenly presented him to us in a different light. From that time on we began to doubt the sincerity of the president's past conduct. Was he or was he not implicated in the provocation of the bloody events? . . . While we played all our cards in an attempt to end that fratricidal bloodletting, we lacked the support of Companys for the first time since the July days. . . . Companys should explain to the Catalan working class, which supported him in very difficult times, if his role was that of an accomplice or of a prisoner in the May provocation and the subsequent invasion of the autonomous region."[89]

In accordance with the CNT's proposal of Tuesday night, a provisional government was finally set up on Wednesday, composed of four councillors: Carlos Martí Feced of the Esquerra, Valerio Mas, the secretary of the CNT Regional Committee, Antonio Sesé, the secretary general of the PSUC-controlled Catalan UGT, and Joaquín Pou of the Unió de Rabassaires. Although the question of Artemio Aiguadé's removal from the council of internal security was automatically resolved as a result of the taking over of public order by Valencia, Rodríguez Salas remained in charge of the general commissariat, pending the arrival of Antonio Escobar, the delegate of public order appointed by Valencia.

Fresh appeals were now broadcast from the Generalitat Palace. CNT secretary Mariano Vázquez again begged the workers to leave the streets. "We tell you that this situation must end. . . . We do not want this stigma to fall upon the Spanish anarchists. . . . This is not the moment, in front of piled-up corpses, to discuss who is right. It is essential that you disappear with your weapons from the streets. . . . We must not wait for others to do so. We must do so ourselves. Afterward we shall talk. If you decide, when you discuss our conduct at our next assembly, that we deserve to be shot, then you may shoot us, but now you must obey our slogans."[90] But Vázquez's stentorian lungs could not prevail against the aroused rank and file, and the struggle continued unabated.

Two incidents exacerbated the situation: Antonio Sesé, the newly designated PSUC-UGT councillor, was shot and killed when proceeding to the Generalitat Palace.[91] Who was responsible was never known, although accusations were plentiful. "It was alleged that he had been fired on from the [CNT] Public Entertainments Union," said the national committee of the CNT, "[but] it was subsequently proved that the bullet that cost him his life was not fired from the union building."[92] The Communists charged that he had been assassinated by "Trotskyist aggressors in the service of fascism,"[93] while Agustín Souchy, the CNT-FAI spokesman, declared that the shot had been fired "from a barricade belonging to Sesé's own party comrades."[94] That same day, Colonel Escobar, the newly appointed delegate of public order, was seriously wounded, when shot at on his arrival in Barcelona to occupy his new post.[95] As a result, Valencia named Lieutenant Colonel Alberto Arrando as the new delegate of public order.[96]

Up to now the only armed forces to arrive in Barcelona from Valencia were the marines dispatched by Indalecio Prieto on board the destroyers *Lepanto* and *Sánchez Barcaiztegui* to evacuate the president, but they were unable to reach the Catalan Parliament building.[97] Azaña was beside himself, furious over the "glacial indifference" and "insolent behavior" of Largo Caballero, and fearful of "perishing unjustly and tragically in Barcelona."[98]

In a telegraphed message to Prieto on Wednesday morning, complaining that for forty-eight hours he had not been able to discharge his presidential functions, he threatened to make a decision of "incalculable consequences" unless the government remedied the situation, and he told Prieto to give his message to Martínez Barrio, the speaker of the Cortes.[99] This was an obvious threat to resign, one of several made during the war, but never carried out owing largely to the efforts of Prieto, who, although contemptuous of the president's faintheartedness, valued him most highly as a constitutional cover for the Revolution.[100]

This was not the first time that Prieto had witnessed Azaña's faintheartedness. In October 1936, when the president was urging the government to leave Madrid,[101] he asked Prieto, "Does the government want the fascists to catch me here?" Irritated by Azaña's hurry to depart and by his concern over his personal safety, Prieto remarked to air force chief Hidalgo de Cisneros, "That cowardly fairy is acting like a hysterical whore."[102] Known as one of the most eloquent orators of the Republic, Prieto also had a reputation for vulgar language in private conversation.

"Prieto was very alarmed, seriously concerned," Azaña noted in his diary. "He did what he could to help me, but, even so, he did not quite understand the situation. The proof is that he told me that very morning that, in the government's opinion, *it was advisable that I leave for Valencia.* . . . 'The problem,' I said, 'is not that I am against going to Valencia, but that I cannot go into the street.' Martínez Barrio went to the telegraph and read the tape. It made such an impression upon him that, without waiting for the end of the conversation, he rushed off to see Caballero. He quickly returned, saying the government was going to do this, that, and the other, and I should be calm. I answered appropriately, and there was no further discussion."[103]

On Thursday morning, during a break in the fighting, the commander of the *Lepanto*, accompanied by five or six marines, presented himself in the Parliament building.[104] Azaña thought that any attempt to depart would be foolhardy. "Prieto continued to press me to take advantage of ten minutes of calm to leave for the port,"[105] but none of his suggestions appeared feasible to the president. "There was a faint smile of skepticism on Prieto's face," writes Zugazagoitia, a Prieto intimate and later minister of the interior. "He was sure that with a little courage any of his suggestions could be carried out successfully, preferably evacuation by sea. The distance from the Catalan Parliament building to the port was very short, and the journey could have been made by car in four minutes. But Don Manuel preferred four days of fears and insecurity to four minutes of resolution."[106] Finally, according to Azaña, after another conversation with Prieto, "more pressing than ever, during which he expressed the thought that perhaps I was balking at taking the risk, I decided to go." But just as he was about to leave the Parliament building, Azaña relates, the fighting resumed "with greater violence than ever," causing him to postpone his departure for Valencia until the following day.[107]

Meanwhile, it was clear from the heavy fighting on Wednesday that the calls for a cease-fire had not met with the unanimous approval of the rank and file. "Fighting had already been going on for three days," wrote Souchy, "and there was no sign of peace. . . . At about 5 P.M., the Regional Committee of the CNT made the following proposals: 'Hostilities to cease. Every party to keep its positions. The police and the civilians fighting on its side are asked to agree to a truce!'"[108] But these proposals passed unheeded. The Friends of Durruti brought out a fresh leaflet: "A revolutionary junta has been formed in Barcelona. All elements responsible for the subversive assault maneuvering under cover of the government must be shot. The POUM must be admitted to the revolutionary junta because it has placed itself on the side of the workers."[109] The revolutionary junta, however, was never formed.[110] The regional committees of the CNT and FAI denounced the Friends of Durruti as *agents provocateurs* and declared that the leaflet was "absolutely intolerable and in conflict with the policy of the libertarian movement. . . . Everybody must fulfill the slogans of these committees. Now that the Council of the Generalitat has been formed, everybody must accept its decisions inasmuch as everybody is represented in it. All arms must leave the streets."[111]

"One more terrible blow against the embattled workers," wrote Felix Morrow, the Trotskyist critic of the POUM already quoted. "The regional committee of the CNT gave to the entire press . . . a denunciation of the Friends of Durruti as *agents provocateurs*. . . . The POUM press did not defend the left-wing anarchists against this foul slander."[112] The fact that the Friends of Durruti had publicly proposed that the POUM be admitted to the revolutionary junta was undoubtedly embarrassing to the POUM leadership, the more so as a rumor was in the air that the entire responsibility for the events was to be placed at the party's door. "I dimly foresaw," wrote George Orwell, "that when the fighting ended the entire blame would be laid upon the POUM, which was the weakest party and therefore the most suitable scapegoat."[113]

At about 8:30 Wednesday evening the provisional government appealed to "all the workers and people of Catalonia to lay down their arms and to forget their rancor and their enmities."[114] Other appeals were made. "Do not listen to the aggressors, to the Trotskyists who want the struggle to continue," the PSUC declared. "Let us unite around the government of the Generalitat."[115] Miguel Valdés, the PSUC leader, exhorted: "Workers of Barcelona, comrades of the CNT, we must not waste our energies a moment longer. We must put an end to the Trotskyist criminals, who in their newspapers continue inciting the antifascists of Catalonia to kill one another."[116]

Jacinto Toryho, the director of *Solidaridad Obrera*, an FAI member, also spoke. Referring to the "wave of collective insanity" that was destroying all the achievements of the first ten months of the Revolution as well as the "hope of the international proletariat," he stated: "This behavior, comrades of the CNT and UGT, comrades of the PSUC and FAI, comrades of the assault and national republican guards, is unbelievable; it is despicable, despicable because it is degrading to all of us. . . . In Barcelona the workers are assassinating one another. . . . This state of insanity that has transformed the most sensible people into madmen must end. . . . Just think that there is a front nearby. Just think that this front may become demoralized if it should learn of this hecatomb. . . . Comrades of the police, return to your barracks! Comrades of the CNT, return to your locals! Comrades of the PSUC and UGT, return to your centers! Let peace return!"[117]

Throughout the evening a joint appeal of the CNT and UGT was broadcast urging the workers to return to work. "It is necessary to return to normality. To continue this industrial inactivity at the present time when we are waging a war against fascism is equivalent to collaborating with our common enemy."[118]

As a result of these appeals, the fighting abated early Thursday morning, 6 May. Disconcerted by the attitude of their leaders, the anarchosyndicalists' ardor had begun to wane and many of them abandoned the barricades. But, as the morning advanced, fighting flared up again. The national committee of the CNT said:

The transport union ordered a return to work, but as the tracks were damaged, the repair cars had to be sent out before the streetcars could leave their depots. During the morning they had to return because they were fired upon. . . . The metro had to suspend its service because at some entrances the Communist police and members of Estat Català surrounded the passengers. . . . In some places large numbers of CNT cards were torn up. In others, our comrades were attacked. Our locals were besieged. . . . In the afternoon . . . the situation was more serious than ever. The comrades were ready to take matters into their own hands regardless of the consequences. [But] in spite of the many provocations . . . we could not close our eyes and wage the final battle. [It was perfectly clear] that we had played our enemies' game. They wanted us to go into the street; they wanted public order to pass into the hands of the [central] government. . . . We understood only too well the tragedy of those comrades who had been provoked and cornered and who had seen their comrades and friends fall. But, above all, it was necessary to prevent the entire struggle of the Spanish proletariat since 19 July from being suddenly reduced to naught.[119]

The POUM, feeling that further resistance was useless, instructed its followers to leave the barricades and presented the situation as optimistically as it could. "In view of the fact that the counterrevolutionary maneuver has been repulsed," declared the executive in a statement published in *La Batalla* on Thursday morning, 6 May, "the

[425]

workers should withdraw from the struggle and return to work today, without fail and with discipline, to continue laboring with enthusiasm for the rapid defeat of fascism. The POUM orders all its armed militants to withdraw from the barricades and from the streets and to resume work, but to maintain a vigilant attitude." At the same time, *La Batalla* claimed that the proletariat had "obtained an important partial victory. . . . It has smashed the counterrevolutionary provocation. It has brought about the removal of those directly responsible for the provocation. It has dealt a serious blow to the bourgeoisie and the reformists. It could have achieved more, very much more, if the leaders of the predominant working-class organizations in Catalonia had risen to the occasion as did the workers. On the repeated orders of their leaders the masses have begun to withdraw from the struggle thus evidencing a great spirit of discipline. Nevertheless, the proletariat should remain vigilant. It should stand guard, bearing arms. It should keep watch over the activities of the bourgeoisie and the reformists and be ready to thwart their counterrevolutionary maneuvers." And a few days later, after the fighting had ended, the party's central committee declared: "As the workers fighting in the streets lacked concrete aims and responsible leadership, the POUM had no alternative but to organize and direct a strategic retreat, . . . avoiding a desperate action that might have degenerated into a 'putsch' and resulted in the complete destruction of the most advanced section of the proletariat. The experience of the 'May days' shows unequivocally that the only progressive solution to the present problem lies in the seizure of power by the working class and that it is therefore essential to coordinate the revolutionary activity of the working masses through the formation of a revolutionary workers' front, uniting all organizations ready to fight for the total destruction of fascism. This can be accomplished only through military victory at the front and the victory of the revolution in the rear. The central committee considers that the policy pursued by the party during the events was absolutely correct and fully endorses the line of the executive committee, convinced that it has defended the interests of the Revolution and the broad working masses."[120]

On Thursday evening, 6 May, news was received in Casa CNT-FAI that fifteen hundred assault guards had reached the outskirts of Tortosa, one hundred miles south of Barcelona. Both Federica Montseny, the CNT minister of health, who had arrived the previous day to help terminate the fighting, and Mariano Vázquez, the CNT secretary, hurried to the Generalitat Palace to communicate with Valencia. Not without reason were they apprehensive lest the assault guards en route to Barcelona might provoke every anarchist-controlled community in their path to insurrection. It fell to García Oliver, the CNT minister of justice, now back in Valencia, and to Angel Galarza, Largo Caballero's minister of the interior, to persuade Vázquez and Montseny to facilitate the passage of the assault guards through Catalonia and to restore peace to the embattled city before the arrival of reinforcements. The secret discussions that took place by teletypewriter to put an end to the fighting form part of Companys's notes and documents on the May events,[121] the essential portions of which are reproduced here:

[García Oliver]: This is the ministry of the interior, Valencia. Is the minister of health there?

[Montseny]: Yes . . . Listen García, Mariano is going to speak to you and then we shall talk to Galarza. . . .

[Vázquez]: This morning it looked as though the situation would soon clear up. . . . At midday, the situation began to deteriorate, because the police were preparing to attack union buildings. . . . The fact that Arrando [the new delegate of public order, who had replaced the wounded Escobar] has retained Rodríguez Salas as police commissioner has had a decisive influence on the situation. He is still in charge of the police and has no doubt instructed them to assume the attitude they are adopting. In many places the tearing up of CNT membership cards has been systematic. . . . Five comrades belonging to the bodyguard of Eroles [Dionisio Eroles, the anarchist chief of services, in the general commissariat of public order] have been taken from their homes and murdered. As a result of these and similar occurrences the comrades have taken steps to defend themselves. The atmosphere became more tense when news was received that 1,500 guards had arrived at Tortosa. It is impossible to foresee at this time what is going to happen. . . . [If] there is not a rapid change in the attitude of the police and in their leadership it will be impossible to prevent the fighting from becoming general again. . . . The impression should not be created that reprisals are going to be taken against [our] organization and militants. . . . If the police coming from Valencia continue to advance, it will be impossible to avoid flareups in the villages through which they have to pass and where there has been no trouble up to now.

[García Oliver]: This is García Oliver. . . . The minister of the interior has ordered the immediate dismissal of Rodríguez Salas. He is ready to resolve the situation in Catalonia in the fairest possible way. It is imperative that the assualt guards who are on their way to Barcelona reach their destination to relieve the police [who are] extremely exhausted, nervous and inflamed by the conflict. . . . You must understand this and make it clear to the committees and comrades. It is also imperative that you make it clear to the comrades and villages through which these impartial, absolutely impartial forces of appeasement have to pass. [The] government knows that without this strict impartiality the conflict, far from being resolved, would become worse, and would spread to the whole of Catalonia and the rest of Spain, and would

The Communist Triumph

result in the government's political and military downfall. . . . [The] minister of the interior [is considering] the advisability of dispatching these forces by other means than by road, which is too long and full of [potential] obstacles that may be spread in their path by all those aggressors interested in prolonging the present situation in Barcelona and bringing about the collapse of the government. As the administration of public order has now been taken over, I repeat that it is advisable that you immediately instruct the comrades in the villages not to place any obstacles in the way of these forces of appeasement. On the contrary, they should give them every kind of assistance and receive them with affection, because otherwise the danger exists . . . that if they are attacked en route they will become angered, as a result of which we should only have succeeded in transforming the problem of Catalonia into a national bonfire in which inevitably we would all be rapidly consumed. Above all, pay immediate attention to the province of Tarragona, where the POUM and the separatists [a reference to Estat Catalá] have many supporters, with the object of preventing them from mixing with [our] comrades and inciting them to armed resistance against the forces of public order. . . .

[Vázquez]: [Although we understand] the undeniable advantage of relieving the police in Barcelona, we should recognize that the problem here does not require the intervention of the police. The position is such that if they were merely to receive orders to return to their barracks for a few hours normality would return completely. It is imperative that the police should not attack or do anything at all for a period of three to four hours. This period would be sufficient to restore confidence as a result of which barricades would disappear and the police would abandon the buildings and places they occupy. . . .

[Galarza]: This is the minister of the interior. On learning at 7:30 P.M. that police commissioner Rodríguez Salas was still in command, I made the following statement [to Arrando], which I copy from the tape I have in front of me: "There should immediately be placed at the head of the administration of security a police commissioner, who is a member of the regular police corps, a man in whom you have more confidence; and the representatives of the unions and parties should stop intervening in public order." [Arrando] replied as follows: "I absolutely agree and shall obey your instructions immediately." . . . [Regarding] the time you require [to restore confidence], I have no objection to the following: At 10 P.M., the police will receive orders not to fire a single shot and to refrain from attacking any building. Only those forces necessary for vigilance will remain on the streets, but without searching for arms or making arrests for a period of three hours. You will undertake the responsibility of seeing that your people in the street and in [their] locals withdraw to their homes during this period and do not fire a single shot. I am going to issue these orders. Obviously, you understand that if they are not observed loyally by both sides nothing will be gained. The Premier is calling me. Wait a moment. . . . [Here] is García Oliver. . . .

[Montseny]: García, what Galarza says we can accept on condition that the truce is called tomorrow from 6 to 9 A.M., so as to give us time to organize a mass peace demonstration attended by the whole of Barcelona, and headed by the representatives of the organizations with their banners bound together. We shall suggest this to the UGT and are sure it will agree. . . .

[Galarza]: With regard to those three hours . . . I have no objection to their being between 6 and 9 A.M. As for the demonstration, provided there are no aggressors, it appears to me to be a very good idea, but I fear that these elements may take advantage of the general state of tension and that the demonstration may begin well but end badly. Perhaps it would be better to hold it on Sunday instead of tomorrow [Friday] and announce it in a joint statement of the two labor organizations. I am going to give orders to the police to observe the maximum prudence during the night. Leave it to me to see that after 9 A.M. tomorrow new and relaxed forces will be there with a person of my absolute confidence in command. [This was a reference to Lieutenant Colonel Emilio Torres Iglesias of the assault guards, who was appointed police chief of Barcelona].[122] . . .

[Montseny]: Very well, Galarza. . . . The truce may prove to be a salvation, but bear in mind that I do not know up to what point your orders will be obeyed if the same persons remain in charge of public order. . . .

[Galarza]: Tomorrow, other officers will be there.[123] . . . But keep this absolutely to yourself lest there be someone interested in repeating the Escobar incident. Tell your people that some of them should try withdrawing to their homes after midnight, and if, as I hope, nothing prevents them from doing so and everyone else does the same, then three hours will not be necessary tomorrow for this operation. It will be very easy to make the test. However, this implies such responsibility for me that I hope not only that I can rely upon your help, but that you will understand that this is the last attempt I can make at this type of solution. Do not announce any of these agreements over the air, but give them to your men of confidence in writing and with your signature. Does this sound all right to you?

[Montseny]: We shall endeavor to make a test at night, although we cannot promise anything owing to the difficulty of getting around at night and orienting [our] people personally. . . . Mariano asks me to tell you that we should agree on 6 A.M. to 9 A.M., as this will give us time to work and will be much easier.

In accordance with their understanding with Galarza, Vázquez and Montseny worked feverishly throughout the night to arrange the truce. "We informed the Catalan organization of the agreements we had reached," said the national committee of the CNT, "and ordered the comrades to prepare to withdraw at 6 A.M."[124] Furthermore, directives were sent to the villages and towns on the main road to Barcelona to allow the assault guards to proceed without hindrance. In Tortosa, where fighting had erupted on Tuesday,[125] the local CNT was instructed not to offer any resistance to the assault guards. "Our comrades acted accordingly," said *Solidaridad Obrera*, "thereby displaying their discipline and respect for the directives of the organization."[126]

In Barcelona, several hours before dawn on Friday, 7 May, there were signs that the ardor of the anarchosyndicalists had finally spent itself. A feeling that it would be futile to continue the struggle against the will of their leaders had overwhelmed them, and disillusionment was widespread. Many withdrew from the barricades and disappeared into the darkness. At dawn, the local committees of the CNT and UGT issued a joint appeal: "Comrades, everybody return to work!"[127]

That evening the assault guards from Valencia, accompanied by a force of carabineers sent by finance minister Juan Negrín, entered the city unopposed. Reinforcements, equipped with the latest weapons, continued to arrive by land and sea, and within a few days the number in the region was estimated at twelve thousand.[128]

The power of the anarchosyndicalists in Catalonia, the citadel of the Spanish libertarian movement, had now been broken. What would have appeared inconceivable a few months earlier, in the heyday of the CNT and FAI, had now become a reality and the most portentous victory of the Communists since the beginning of the Revolution.

29. The Overthrow of Largo Caballero

Having achieved their immediate objective in Catalonia, the Communists now brought their struggle with Largo Caballero to a head.

Exploiting the upheaval, they demanded that the government suppress the POUM, which they held responsible for the bloodshed and whose leaders they had long been denouncing as Trotskyists and fascist agents. Every instrument of propaganda at their disposal was immediately set in motion to force acceptance of their will, and their agitation assumed a frenzied character.

José Díaz declared at a public meeting on May 9:

Our principal enemies are the fascists. However, the fascists have their agents who work for them. Of course, if these agents were to say, "We are fascists and we want to work among you in order to create difficulties," they would immediately be eliminated by us. For this reason they have to give themselves other names. . . . Some call themselves Trotskyists, which is the name used by many disguised fascists who talk of revolution in order to spread disorder. I therefore ask: If everyone knows this, if the government knows it, why does it not treat them like fascists and exterminate them pitilessly? . . .

Every worker must know about the trial of the Trotskyists that has taken place in the USSR. . . . It was Trotsky himself who directed the gang of criminals that derailed trains in the Soviet Union, carried out acts of sabotage in the large factories, and did everything possible to discover military secrets with the object of handing them over to Hitler and the Japanese imperialists. And, in view of the fact that all this was revealed during the trial and that the Trotskyists declared that they had done these things under Trotsky's direction and in complicity with Hitler and the Japanese imperialists, I must ask: Is it not perfectly clear that the Trotskyists are not a political or social organization of a definite tendency like the anarchists, Socialists, or republicans, but a gang of spies and *provocateurs* in the service of international fascism? The Trotskyist *provocateurs* must be swept away!

That is why I stated in my speech at the recent plenary session of the central committee not only that this organization should be dissolved in Spain and its press suspended, but that Trotskyism should be swept out of all civilized countries, that is, if we really want to get rid of this vermin. . . .

In Spain itself, who but the Trotskyists inspired the criminal putsch in Catalonia? *La Batalla* in its 1 May edition was full of brazen incitements to revolt. . . . Well, this paper is still coming out in Catalonia. . . . Why? Because the government cannot make up its mind to seize it as every antifascist demands.

If, after ten months of war, a strong policy is not instituted to make the rear worthy of some of the fronts, I shall be forced to conclude, and I am sure every antifascist will be too, that unless this government imposes order in the rear another Popular Front government will have to do so.[1]

Behind the scenes the Communists—who had recently established close relations with the Socialist Party leadership[2]—met with the Socialist executive in order to chart "a common course of action." "The two parties," affirms the official Communist history, "were in agreement regarding the gravity of the political situation and on the necessity of finding a solution to the simmering crisis."[3] That the republicans were privy to these talks there can be no doubt. President Azaña, who, with Prieto's help, had been evacuated by air from Barcelona on 7 May,[4] states that the former premier and Left Republican leader José Giral visited him in Valencia that same day on behalf of the republican parties: "He told me that the republicans as well as the Socialists and Communists were convinced that the situation could not continue. The Communists had decided to do battle with Largo Caballero at the next cabinet meeting. . . . Giral added that the republicans, Socialists, and Communists formed a bloc that would facilitate a solution. . . . Although [he] did not give any further explanation I understood that the conversations between the three parties were well advanced. The Communists, he told me, would take the initiative at the next cabinet meeting by demanding a change of policy and, if they were not successful, would resign from the government. The Socialists and republicans would support their demand."[5]

Earlier in the day Largo Caballero had visited the president. Although Azaña was still enraged by the prime minister's "glacial indifference" to his plight in Barcelona,[6] he decided not to mention the matter. "[Caballero] arrived smiling and affable with a portfolio of decrees," he relates. "He did not say one word about Barcelona. . . . He began the conversation as though we had seen each other every day or I had just returned from a pleasure trip. . . . I had thought over very carfully what I should do during this first interview. My natural impulse was to ask him to explain his behavior. But upon reflection, I refrained from doing so and [decided] that if he did not speak of it, I, too, would say nothing. I was sure that if I were to raise the matter things would become so entangled that he would not be able to depart as prime minister. And I was determined . . . not to relieve him of his functions by a unilateral decision, especially as it might be regarded as an attempt to satisfy my justifiable anger. I remained silent."[7]

Thus, when the republican, Socialist, and Communist leaders visited him on 7 and 8 May to voice their combined opposition to the government, Azaña was careful not to take sides openly in the dispute. "I listened to them all," he wrote, "but tried not to disclose my own opinion regarding the conduct of the government. On the other hand, of course, I could not approve it. In the first place, I told them that I considered their visits to be of an informative nature, but that on no account would I allow the inference to be drawn that I was giving them permission to mount an offensive against the government." He reminded them that contrary to his advice the Giral cabinet had resigned in September to make way for the Caballero government, "hailed as the government of victory," and that "the cabinet reorganization in November, involving the entry of the CNT and the anarchists, which the republicans themselves had deemed inevitable and useful," had been carried out "not only against my advice, but in face of my most angry protest. Now, after a few months," he added, "the very people who had elevated Largo and admitted the FAI [into the government] could not abide them" and were turning to him to resolve the problem. He had not created the Largo Caballero "myth." If a change of policy was now considered necessary, this was because the parties had changed their attitude, "not because the president of the Republic has changed his opinion, which he has not."[8]

A few days later, on 13 May—just two days before the deadline when all political commissars whose appointment and rank had not been confirmed by Largo Caballero were to consider themselves dismissed from the corps of commissars[9]—Jesús Hernández and Vicente Uribe, the two Communist ministers, demanded, at a tempestuous meeting of the cabinet, an immediate change in the premier's policy in the areas of war and public order. They also demanded the dissolution of the POUM in terms that left no room for compromise. The meeting, attests Azaña, who had been apprised of the proceedings by Giral and Prieto, was marked by "unusual violence and vulgarities. . . . Largo called the Communists 'liars and slanderers' and six hours were wasted in this way. The [moderate] Socialists, through Negrín, supported the arguments of the Communists, and the republicans also said something."[10]

In the course of his acrimonious exchanges with the Communist ministers, Largo Caballero vehemently dissented from their view that the POUM was a fascist organization and declared that he would not dissolve the party, that he had not entered the government to serve the political interests of any of the factions represented in it, and that the courts of law would decide whether or not a particular organization should be dissolved.[11] Failing to receive satisfaction, the Communist ministers rose and left the room.[12] "The anarchist-POUM rising . . . in Barcelona," writes Jesús Hernández, "gave us . . . an excuse to provoke the crisis of the Largo Caballero government."[13]

"When the split in the cabinet occurred," testified Indalecio Prieto at a public meeting after the war, "Largo Caballero intended to continue the dispatch of routine matters. I was sitting next to him . . . and said: 'Look here, Caballero, something serious has happened. The ministerial coalition has been broken because one of the parties in the government has withdrawn from it. I therefore think it is your duty, without continuing this meeting, to tell the president of the Republic what has happened and resolve the situation with him.'"[14]

"The opinion expressed by Prieto," writes Julián Zugazagoitia, himself a moderate Socialist and minister of the interior in the succeeding government, "surprised Largo Caballero, who believed that the cabinet could nevertheless continue its deliberations. . . . Prieto's viewpoint, which was perfectly constitutional, was [later] condemned as part of the maneuver begun by the Communists to overthrow Largo Caballero."[15]

It was not until some years after the war that Prieto, reconciled with Caballero, publicly denied the charge that he had acted in secret agreement with the Communists. "Not until now," he declared, "have I bothered to contradict the mistaken assumption that I had dealings with the Communists in order to oust Largo Caballero. Apart from a rule that has guided my conduct toward them ever since the first unfortunate split in our party in 1921, a rule that has always kept me at a distance from them, I am incapable, because of my moral temper, of acting disloyally toward a coreligionist and a friend, who, as premier, was charged at that time with such delicate and complicated functions."[16] On the other hand, Vicente Uribe, one of the two Communist ministers who precipitated the crisis, declared in a speech in exile: "Prieto participated in the plan to remove Caballero from the leadership of the government, although without revealing himself openly. . . . [He] wanted to take revenge on Largo Caballero, whom he had not forgiven, among other things, for frustrating his ambition to become head of the government in May 1936."[17] Furthermore, Gabriel Morón, a onetime supporter of Indalecio Prieto and director general of security, also alleges that Prieto was in agreement with the Communists "to oust Largo Caballero."[18] In any event, the view expressed by Prieto that the withdrawal of the Communist ministers had broken the ministerial coalition was an important factor in shaping the course of events, for Caballero decided to suspend the cabinet meeting and to tender his resignation to the president.

It is noteworthy, however, that according to Azaña, Caballero may have had no intention of resigning and was hoping that the president would "simply authorize him to replace the two Communist ministers."[19] "Largo," he recalls, "stressed to me the untimeliness of the crisis inasmuch as there were reasons of national interest that made it advisable for the government to continue to function in order to execute very important plans . . . whose suspension would be catastrophic."[20] The first of these was a plan to foment a rebellion in Spanish Morocco against General Franco, a plan conceived by Carlos de Baráibar, Caballero's undersecretary of war, and dismissed by Azaña as a "harebrained adventure."[21] The second was a large-scale offensive in the region of Estremadura, originally planned by Baráibar's predecessor, General José Asensio, and by General Martínez Cabrera, former chief of the war ministry general staff, both of whom, it will be recalled, had been forced out of office under Communist pressure.[22] "Largo told me," Azaña writes, "that he was thinking of going to Estremadura *to direct the operation in person*, so as to prevent the rivalries among the officers from ruining everything. I assumed that in reality he would direct nothing and that in fact he would restrict himself to signing the orders submitted by the general staff. There can be no question that he was very much sold on the project, from which he undoubtedly expected to derive the military advantages explained by his advisers and the political and personal advantage of appearing, in the eyes of the general public, as the director of a victorious operation."[23]

Largo Caballero's supporters have claimed, perhaps with excessive optimism—although it is noteworthy that Salas Larrazábal, a supporter of General Franco, in his meticulously documented study of the Popular Army, rated the "feasibility" of the Estremadura offensive very highly[24]—that the operation might have been the turning point in the war had the Communists and their Soviet advisers not opposed it. "Its aim," writes Luis Araquistáin, the left Socialist leader and intimate of the premier and war minister, "was to cut the rebel army's lines of communication with the south, whence it received steady reinforcements of Italian and Moroccan troops. The success of that operation, by splitting the enemy into two unconnected parts and depriving him of the foreign troops and war material that were entering through the ports near the Strait of Gibraltar, could have changed the course of the war completely. The north would have been saved; the whole of Andalusia would have been recovered. Probably the war itself would have been won. . . . At any rate, Franco's victory would have been neither so quick nor so decisive, and at least there would have been time and favorable circumstances for negotiating a diplomatic peace."[25]

The projected operation, placed under the overall command of the regular army officer Lieutenant Colonel Enrique Jurado, was, according to Salas Larrazábal, to involve a total of one hundred thousand men, the largest number yet deployed in a single operation.[26] Scheduled for the beginning of May, the launching of the offensive was delayed on various pretexts by General Miaja, who for reasons of personal glory was not anxious to shift the main theater of operations from Madrid to another front. Behind his dilatory maneuvers, however, were the Communists and their Soviet allies, who feared the possible success of an operation that might delay their plans, now well advanced, for the overthrow of Largo Caballero.[27]

Miaja opposed the projected offensive from the very beginning and when ordered to send several units from Madrid to the Estremadura sector, he at first refused.[28] "His disobedience," affirms Araquistáin, "was inspired by the Communists, who were then Miaja's real chiefs and who made of him—an officer of limited ability—a great international figure. In the end Miaja had to abandon his insubordination in face of the energetic attitude of Largo Caballero."[29]

This, however, was not the end of Communist resistance to the offensive. Colonel Segismundo Casado, chief of operations on the war ministry general staff and until September 1936 commander of Azaña's presidential guard, testifies: "[Miaja] realized that after the orders he had received he must proceed at once to move the forces under his command to the positions assigned to them. But during the afternoon of the same day a general, a 'friendly Russian adviser,' came to my office telling me that no aircraft could take part in the action against Merida [Estremadura], because it was needed on other fronts. For several days past I had realized the possibility that the communists were trying to hold up this action, and after listening to the 'friendly adviser' I was convinced that it could not be carried out."[30]

According to Largo Caballero, the Russians had initially approved the project: "[They] proposed the names of brigade commanders, all of them Communists, to head the units that were to take part in the operation. But the general staff and I had already appointed men to these posts. . . . I gave orders to the effect that a memo be requested from the real chief of the air force [Soviet General Yakov Smushkevich or 'Douglas'] regarding the number of machines that could be assigned. He replied that we could count on ten airplanes. Ten airplanes for an offensive involving forty thousand men! I interpreted this as a reprisal for not having given the commanding posts to the Communists. We were tired of seeing the Communists assigned to places where they could receive all the laurels and the others where they received only the enemy's bullets."[31]

Jesús Hernández asserts that he personally argued in favor of the Estremadura offensive during a meeting at the headquarters of Soviet military adviser Kulik, after instructions had been received from Moscow to oppose the "Asensio plan," and was accordingly rebuked by Comintern delegate Togliatti. Although he also affirms that Largo Caballero's resolve to carry out the offensive "finally collapsed" when the Russians informed him at the beginning of May that they would not provide him with the necessary aircraft,[32] it is clear from Caballero's conference with Azaña two weeks later, when he tendered his resignation, that he still hoped to execute the plan.

Partly because Azaña felt that it would be impolitic to give the impression that he was eager to accept Largo Caballero's resignation and partly because the premier regarded the Estremadura offensive as a question of "national interest," Azaña told him that he would ponder the matter of his resignation overnight and give him a decision the next morning (14 May).[33]

The next day, Martínez Barrio, leader of Unión Republicana, visited the president. "[He] told me," Azaña relates, "that he considered the crisis very dangerous because of the attitude the unions might adopt in the event Caballero were removed. . . . In short, he favored postponing the crisis because it might mean a leap into the unknown. I did not share these fears entirely, save for the danger of a disturbance of public order by some unions and the anarchists. Largo was credited with much greater power in the UGT than he actually had. And people, in general, were tired of abuses and incompetence. In any case, I had decided not to give Largo and his supporters the impression that I personally viewed his defeat as inescapable or that his inevitable fall and replacement were due to anger or antiproletarian bias on the part of the president. This point was of interest because already in March or April Largo had told me that he foresaw 'another expulsion of the workers from power as in 1933.' It was essential, in the public interest, that those who might feel that they had been 'expelled' from power should be expelled as a result of the well-known opposition of others [the Communists] who, because they wore the same labels, could speak in the name of the workers." After "carefully weighing the pros and cons" and concluding that "the fruit was not yet ripe enough" for him, Azaña told Caballero that he believed that the crisis should be postponed for a few days and that because the premier "had invoked reasons of national interest" he did not wish to hinder him from carrying out the Estremadura offensive. "It would not be hard to convince the Communists to rejoin the government," he added, "if [Caballero] were to explain to them the reason for the postponement. Should the Estremadura plan be successful . . . the situation would improve appreciably, and he would have a decisive argument with which to confound his critics. He agreed immediately."[34]

Largo Caballero gives a somewhat different version: "[The president] suggested that I should withdraw my resignation and proceed with the projected operation. If this turned out well, the political atmosphere would improve. Afterward we would talk about the matter again. I opposed the president's suggestion because I was convinced that the maneuvers against the government were at their height and that any postponement would be useless. He insisted, speaking to me of sacrifices and other things, and I reluctantly agreed to withdraw my resignation."[35]

To Azaña's surprise, Caballero made no attempt to bring the Communists back into the government or to inform them of the decision to postpone the crisis. "[Largo Caballero] must have thought that his omission . . . was very astute," Azaña writes. "But precisely because of this omission his Socialist opponents entered the scene to force his hand and to prevent him from using the postponement as a means of escape."[36] Azaña does not explain how they had learned of his agreement with Caballero, but Araquistáin suggests that it was "perhaps through Azaña himself, who used to be in constant touch with Indalecio Prieto."[37]

"We were preparing to leave that afternoon [for Estremadura]," Caballero recalls, "when Lamoneda [secretary of the Socialist executive], Negrín, and de Gracia [two of the three moderate Socialist ministers] presented themselves in my office at the war ministry. Prieto did not go; he remained behind the scenes. They informed me that in view of the resignation of the Communists, the three Socialist ministers named by the party executive had resigned. I replied that their solidarity with the Communists was incomprehensible. . . . Negrín replied that it was a decision of the executive and they had to respect it."[38]

At a meeting of the national committee of the Socialist party in July 1937, Bugeda, a Prieto Socialist, confirmed that the executive committee had taken the view that the Socialists could not remain in the government after the Communists had withdrawn their collaboration.[39]

"The maneuver was clear," wrote Araquistáin. "The three ministers of the center [Prieto] faction joined hands with the Communists in order to oust Caballero. It was essential to prevent the Estremadura offensive from being carried out, lest it prove successful. This view was expressed by Juan-Simeón Vidarte, a Socialist deputy belonging to the Prieto faction, in the following frank and criminal words: 'If Caballero should succeed in this offensive, no one will be able to throw him out of the government.'"[40] In his memoirs, many years after the war, Vidarte did not reply to this accusation, but he did say the following about the Estremadura offensive: "I spoke to Prieto about Asensio's plan. He told me that the whole thing was nothing but an illusion harbored by Asensio and Caballero. Miaja had stated clearly that to provide eight or ten divisions would be to leave Madrid in grave danger. Prieto, as air minister, could not provide more than eight or ten airplanes. The operation . . . was unrealizable."[41]

It was because of the resignation of the moderate Socialist ministers, a resignation that could have been avoided had Indalecio Prieto so desired in view of the influence he still exercised over Ramón Lamoneda, the secretary, and González Peña, the president of the Socialist executive, that the suspicion that he had acted in secret concert with the Communist ministers hardened into positive belief. Moreover, it had not been forgotten that Lamoneda had carried out, at Prieto's bidding, the subtle maneuver that had resulted in Caballero's removal from the executive before the outbreak of the Civil War.[42]

Upon learning of the resignation of the Socialist ministers, Largo Caballero visited President Azaña. "I told him what Lamoneda, Negrín, and de Gracia had said, and his reply was that he did not understand the attitude of these Socialists. As I insisted on resigning, he decided to begin consultations."[43] Azaña continued to hide his animosity: "I extended to him a few words of courtesy and personal consideration . . . ill-deserved, as they were, coming from me and after all that had happened."[44] This "polite affability," as he describes it,[45] served its purpose during the delicate negotiations that lay ahead, for Largo Caballero harbored only an occasional doubt with regard to the president's true attitude toward him.[46]

During the round of conferences that Azaña held on 15 May with a view to forming a new ministry, the concurrence of the Socialist executive and the Communist party was no less apparent than at the outset of the crisis. "The Communists and the Socialists," attests Azaña, "lashed out at the incompetence of Largo, at his camarilla, at his lack of communication with the government and the Higher War Council, at his distrust of the Russians, etcetera, etcetera. The Communists told me that . . . they would agree to his retaining the premiership . . . but on no account the war ministry. . . . It was clear that the main point of contention would be the assignment of the portfolio of war and its separation from the premiership. . . . I called Largo Caballero and asked him to form a government. He appeared very pleased."[47]

On 17 May, Caballero submitted to the president his list of ministers. "In his proposal," writes Azaña, "the premier, that is to say, he personally, not only retained the portfolio of war, but he appropriated the portfolios of navy and air!" Considering that the crisis had arisen, Azaña observes, because Largo Caballero was not wanted in the war ministry, this "devouring" of defense portfolios could be construed as an attempt on his part to render a solution impossible and to leave the government. "But . . . on no account did Largo wish to withdraw from the government." It was one more step toward the "absorption of government functions" and "a way to exploit the crisis by throwing Prieto out of a leading ministry." " 'Are you going to dispense with Prieto?' " Azaña asked Caballero. " 'In spite of the services he has rendered and the prestige that he enjoys?' No, he was not going to dispense with him. He wanted to appoint him minister of agriculture, industry, and commerce! . . . It was obvious, without any further analysis of the proposal, that Largo would not be able to form a cabinet."[48]

Even before submitting his plan to President Azaña, Largo Caballero had been aware that it would encounter stern opposition from the Communists and Prieto Socialists, for although they had made no overt objection to his being premier, they had not concealed their determination to exclude him from the war ministry. For their part the Communists had publicly insisted that the prime minister in the new government should occupy himself exclusively with the affairs of his own office. Another condition that was equally significant—in view of the decree that was to have gone into effect on 15 May, whereby all political commissars whose appointment and rank had not been confirmed on that date were to consider themselves dismissed from the corps of commissars—was that the commissariat of war should enjoy autonomy in all matters connected with the appointment and political direction of the commissars.[49]

The Socialist executive demanded that Indalecio Prieto should head a new department known as the ministry of national defense,[50] a department that was to combine not only the navy and air ministry, which he had held in the outgoing government, but also the ministry of war. These demands were undoubtedly formulated in accordance with a prior agreement between the Communist and moderate Socialist leaders. After the war, Vicente Uribe, a member of the politburo, wrote: "Prieto was appointed minister of national defense by mutual agreement and on the understanding that he would correct the errors of Caballero, strengthen the unity of the people, and tighten the bonds between the Communists and the Socialists. I myself raised these matters with Prieto several times before he became defense minister, and he always told me that he was agreeable and would do nothing prejudicial to the unity of the Socialists and the Communists."[51]

Clearly, the demands of the Communists and Socialists were tantamount to rejecting Largo Caballero not only as war minister, but also as premier, for the Prieto Socialists and the Communists understood well the psychology of the left Socialist leader; they knew that he would voluntarily relinquish no part of his authority, that in his heart there existed an indestructible pride, and that he would refuse to become an ornamental figure in a cabinet in which Prieto, his perennial adversary, would assume control of the most vital ministry. Indeed, even before they had publicly made known their views, the UGT executive, controlled by the left-wing Socialists, declared that it would give no support of any kind to a government in which both the premiership and the war ministry were not held by Largo Caballero.[52]

This statement had undoubtedly been inspired by Caballero himself, for it corresponded to his own position throughout the crisis. "With stubborn energy," recalls Azaña, "Largo had stated several times that he would not return to the government under any circumstances unless he personally held the ministry of war, because he considered that his presence in that office was in the national interest."[53] "You will remember," Caballero wrote to a Socialist colleague after the war, "that the Communists wanted to throw me out of the war ministry and to leave me as a figurehead in the premiership. . . . I declared at the time that, as a Socialist and as a Spaniard, it was my duty to remain in the war ministry, and that otherwise I would not accept the premiership; but I did not say that because I considered myself irreplaceable, nor anything of the kind, but because I had the firm intention of fighting it out with the Communist party and all its accomplices; this I could do only from the war ministry."[54] And on another occasion he wrote: "What was truly senseless was that the other parties united with the Communist party to oust me from the war ministry. Did they not see the danger to the war itself in that party's exclusivist conduct? . . . Moreover, were they so blind that they did not perceive the tremendous desire of the Communists to direct the policy of Spain?"[55]

In his efforts to retain both the war ministry and the premiership, Largo Caballero received the full backing of the CNT. While editorials in the anarchosyndicalist press declared that the working class wanted him to remain in office as a guarantee for the proletarian revolution,[56] that it saw in him "the most capable and honorable person for presiding over the government that must carry us to victory,"[57] and that his presence in the premiership and war ministry was "the most solid guarantee for the proletariat that the character of the struggle being waged against international reaction will not be distorted by anybody or anything,"[58] the national committee declared emphatically that it would not collaborate with any government in which he was not both premier and war minister.[59] Yet, in spite of this support, Caballero did not even bother to consult the anarchosyndicalists when drafting his plan for a new government and, indeed, offered them only two seats, as compared with four in the previous cabinet.[60] This treatment was intensely galling to the CNT, and, in reply, it declared that, although it did not aim at increasing its representation in the government, it could not accept fewer portfolios than before or agree on any pretext to parity with the Communist party, which had likewise been offered two seats, and which, it affirmed, had provoked the crisis, and had not collaborated in the government with the same degree of loyalty as itself.[61]

If Largo Caballero had drafted his plan for a new government without regard for the views of the CNT, even less had he taken into account the opinion of the Communists. Far from heeding their demand that the premier should occupy himself exclusively with the affairs of his own office, he had defiantly claimed for himself not only the control of the land forces, but also the control of the fleet and air force and of arms production.[62] One may wonder whether he really expected that the Communists and their allies would consent to this proposal. If so, his expectations were quickly disappointed; for while José Díaz replied that the plan revealed no inclination to take into account the wishes of the central committee, wishes that were those of the Spanish people as a whole, and that the Communists could not form part of the government on the proposed terms,[63] Ramón Lamoneda declared, in the name of the Socialist executive, that his party could not accept representation in the government because the plan neglected to take into consideration the executive's demands and also because the Communist party had replied in the negative.[64]

Likewise united with the Communists in opposition to Caballero's proposal was the Left Republican party, which echoed the Communist demand that the premier in the new government should concern himself solely with the affairs of his own office.[65]

For the sake of appearances, President Azaña attempted to iron out the differences between Caballero and the Communists and even admonished José Díaz for his intransigence.[66] But the Communist party remained adamant, as was to be expected, and the Prieto Socialists and the Left Republicans stood behind the party, so Caballero was forced to abandon his attempt to form a government.[67]

Thereupon, President Azaña charged a new man with the task of organizing a cabinet. This was Juan Negrín, minister of finance in the outgoing government. Son of a wealthy middle-class family, a Cortes deputy representing Indalecio Prieto's center faction of the Socialist party, he was also a professor of physiology at the Madrid School of Medicine. "I decided to entrust Negrín with the formation of the government," writes Azaña. "The public had expected that I would name Prieto. But it was better to have Prieto head the ministry combining the armed forces, for which there was no other possible candidate. In the premiership, his sudden changes of mood, his 'tantrums,' could be inconvenient. I felt that it would be preferable . . . to take advantage of the quiet energy of Negrín."[68] Prieto believed that Azaña had another reason for passing him over in favor of Negrín: "Azaña explained to me that he had not appointed me to head the cabinet because I was too much of an opponent of the Communists to preside over a coalition in which they were represented. I was very grateful for the explanation and even more grateful that I had been left out of [a post] in which I could not serve and did not want to serve."[69]

Just before Azaña appointed Negrín to form a new ministry, the Socialist executive told Prieto that it had decided to ask Azaña to entrust him with the premiership. "Anything but that," he replied, according to a member of the executive. "I get along badly with the

The Communist Triumph

Communists and my relations with the CNT are not cordial. . . . [The Communists] are already broadcasting the name of Negrín in all directions as Caballero's successor. I believe that he has more support than I at the present time. He also has a calmer and more accommodating disposition. I definitely do not want to accept the premiership under these circumstances, not even if I could count on the benevolent support of Caballero, which I did not have [in May 1936] when I could have been premier and could possibly have averted the catastrophe. I commend the name of Negrín to you."[70]

Although Prieto eschewed the premiership, some believed that he hoped to control the government through Negrín, his intimate and votary, whom he had recommended to head the ministry of finance in September 1936. But those who believed that Prieto would become "the real head" of the government "deceive themselves," wrote Azaña, "not only because Prieto is too intelligent to overstep his role, but because the character of Negrín does not lend itself to that situation."[71] In any event, it is unlikely that Prieto realized, in May 1937, to what extent Negrín was harkening to the call of the Spanish Communists, for even Prieto, a vociferous anti-Communist before the Civil War, was finding it expedient to maintain friendly relations with Soviet and Comintern representatives.[72]

Prieto and Negrín first met in 1931 in the Cortes, where Negrín represented the Canary Islands. In an intimate portrayal of Negrín, Prieto recalls:

We became very friendly, but later we became political adversaries. The differences that gave rise to our enmity were due to the fact that, while head of the government, he allowed himself to become subservient to the Communists, a subservience that has been fully proved, although he insisted on denying it. . . .

Juan Negrín was a man of very exceptional physical and intellectual vigor and possessed a cordiality and charm that were captivating. His capacity for work was as enormous as his disorganization. He was just as likely to work at his desk for twenty-four hours at a stretch as to leave it without a trace for a week. . . .

At the League of Nations in Geneva, where he appeared in 1937, and where they must have thought that the government of the Republic was made up of ruffians, he sparkled with his winning manners, his culture, and command of foreign languages. But in a normal parliamentary regime, he could never have become a prime minister, nor even a minister, since he lacked oratorical gifts. His method of reading or reciting his speeches—they were written for him—was unsuitable to our Parliament, where very often it was essential to improvise.

He ate and drank as much as four men, but to avoid witnesses to these excesses, he dined two or three times at different places. Many evenings he had his first dinner at my home, then a second in a restaurant, and later a third, if all went well, in some night club. Educated in Germany, he acquired certain habits redolent of Nero's Rome, such as emptying a full stomach, rinsing his mouth, and continuing to gorge himself with food and drink.

At the end of 1936, the official in the finance ministry who audited small accounts questioned the superintendent closely because of the unbelievable sums expended on aspirin. The explanation of the superintendent was in absolute accord with the truth. The new minister would frequently ask for aspirin, open the container, put it to his lips, and swallow all the tablets in one gulp.[73]

Easygoing and a bon vivant, infinitely more pliable than the austere and stubborn Caballero, and presumed to be more acceptable to the Western democracies than the left Socialist leader because of his moderate background, Negrín had long been selected as Caballero's successor in the premiership by Arthur Stashevsky, the Soviet trade representative. "In my conversations with Stashevsky in Barcelona in November [1936]," wrote Walter Krivitsky, whose revelations on Soviet activities in Spain later proved, as we have seen, to be extraordinarily accurate, "Stalin's next moves in Spain were already cropping out. Stashevsky made no secret to me of the fact that Juan Negrín would be the next head of the Madrid government. At that time, Caballero was universally regarded as the favorite of the Kremlin, but Stashevsky had already picked Negrín as his successor."[74] It is noteworthy that Miguel Serra Pamies, a member of the central committee of the Communist-controlled PSUC, stated after the war that in February 1937, three months before the crisis, "Pedro," the Comintern agent in Catalonia, had told him and other leaders of his party that Negrín was favored as Largo Caballero's successor.[75]

Juan Negrín had all the makings of a bureaucratic politician, Krivitsky affirmed. "Though a professor, he was a man of affairs with the outlook of a businessman. He was just the type to suit Stalin's needs. . . . He would impress the outside world with the 'sanity' and 'propriety' of the Spanish Republican cause; he would frighten nobody by revolutionary remarks. . . . Doctor Negrín, of course, saw the only salvation of his country in close cooperation with the Soviet Union. It had become obvious that active support could come only from that source. He was ready to go along with Stalin in everything, sacrificing all other considerations to secure this aid."[76]

Whether Negrín was willing to abandon all moral and political scruples to secure Soviet aid as early as May 1937 is not entirely certain, although there is no doubt of his willingness to compromise with his principles once he had become installed in the premiership,

The Communist Triumph

and, in April 1938, in the defense ministry.[77] Salvador de Madariaga may be right when he argues that it is not sure "whether at this early stage Negrín was aware" of the part for which he was being coached by the Communists nor even whether he would have acquiesced in it if he had. "It may still be found on closer scrutiny," he adds, "that in ousting Señor Largo Caballero, the Communists, both Russian and Spanish, were the only actors who knew the script of the whole play, while Don Indalecio Prieto and Dr. Negrín knew little more than some cues and the hard fact that they were getting rid of their rival in the Socialist party."[78]

Especially important to Moscow was the fact that Negrín had no official ties with the Communist party. That Negrín himself must also have been aware that this public nonalignment was essential to his Communist promoters and that he would eventually be forced to choose between his loyalty to Prieto and Soviet demands is suggested by the following dialogue that allegedly occurred when, on behalf of the politburo, Jesús Hernández visited Negrín to offer his party's support:

"Doctor," I said, plunging into the purpose of the interview, "the politburo wishes to propose your candidacy for the premiership to the president of the Republic."

I observed Negrín. He did not show the slightest sign of surprise or emotion at this abrupt announcement of our intention. No doubt he knew more than I about what I was saying. . . .

"You realize that I am little known, least of all popular."

"Don't let that concern you. . . . Popularity is manufactured! If there is anything we Communists have that is well organized it is our agitprop section," I said, laughing.

"But I am not a Communist."

"That's an advantage. If you were a Communist we could not propose you for the premiership. We want a premier who is a *friend* of the Communists—nothing more, but nothing less," I said knowingly. . . .

"Many aspects of Communist policy seem appropriate and wise to me," said Negrín.

"You won't have much support within your own party if your replace Caballero. . . ."

"Little, very little."

"But you will be able to count on the power of the Communists," I affirmed.

"Only in that way shall I be able to govern," Negrín commented.

"Then you shall govern."

"I would not want you to interpret my acceptance as my consent to becoming your 'man of straw.' Don't expect that of me. Besides, I wouldn't be useful to your party, to myself, or to anyone else," Negrín commented, preoccupied.

"I understand and share your scruples, but I can assure you that our support will be as discreet as it will be staunch and respectful. But one thing cannot be avoided—you will be labeled a 'communistoid,'" I explained.

"That's inevitable. . . . Who do you plan to support as defense minister?" he inquired.

"We shall not object to Prieto."

"Prieto isn't much of a friend of yours," observed Negrín.

"True, but his personal prestige more than outweighs all the harm his anti-communism might do."

In making this statement about Prieto, I had in mind the tactic that we had decided to follow regarding the future defense minister. When the politburo had discussed the pros and cons of accepting Prieto as head of the defense ministry, we took into account his great prestige in moderate political circles at home and abroad. In this respect Prieto was useful to us. We also took into consideration the negative side of his character. He was a pessimist; he had no faith in victory. To entrust him with the maximum responsibility for prosecuting the war was an anomaly. . . . The members of the politburo hesitated to support his candidacy. Togliatti [the Comintern delegate] gave us the following advice: "By supporting the candidacy of Prieto we shall bring him under our control. If he doesn't agree to serve us, we shall exploit his notorious and self-proclaimed pessimism to bring about his removal, whenever it is convenient for us. . . . [We] shall try to envelop him in such a heavy shroud of disrepute that he will be rendered useless as an outstanding Socialist leader. One enemy less."

"Personally, I hold [Prieto] in great esteem; but you will have problems with him," Negrín insisted.

"We shall try to 'neutralize' him," I replied, smiling.

"How?"

"The undersecretaryship is just as important as the ministry and, at times, more so, because of its technical aspects. When Prieto becomes minister we shall ask for the undersecretaryship of war and air. . . . The commissariat of war is virtually in our hands. And with your friendship. . . ."

"And that of the Russians," Negrín added, laughing.

"Agreed, Doctor?"

"Agreed."[79]

With the elevation of Juan Negrín to the premiership, Largo Caballero had been defeated and the Communists had triumphed. During the incredibly short period of only ten months, the man who had enjoyed more real influence and popularity than any left-wing politician at the outbreak of the Civil War had been nullified politically and virtually reduced to impotence. Not only had he lost control of the UGT of Catalonia and the Federation of the Spanish Socialist party in the region, not only had he been despoiled of his authority in the powerful Unified Socialist Youth Federation, but he had lost control to the Communists of *Claridad*, his organ in Madrid, and had been betrayed or forsaken by many of his closest collaborators as well as by countless supporters holding commanding positions in the UGT and in local Socialist units. And now, in a final agony, he had been ousted from the premiership and war ministry and soon would be assailed by the Communists as enemy number one of the working class. "From the moment I left the government," he recalled some years later, "Largo Caballero was no longer the same person. He had been transformed. He was no longer a Socialist and even less a Marxist. He was enemy number one of the working class. They called me arrogant, ambitious, intransigent, an anarchist, and other idiotic names. [My] photographs disappeared from everywhere. The idol they had created, they themselves delighted in destroying."[80]

On the other hand, the Communists, through the prestige derived from Soviet arms, through their own self-discipline, cohesion, and ruthless energy, and through their adroit permeation of the entire machinery of state, had risen within the same short period of only ten months from a position of relative insignificance to one where they virtually controlled the destinies of the anti-Franco camp.

But this power they themselves could never have achieved without the active support, the connivance, the unsuspecting good faith, and the obtuseness of others. As "El Campesino," the former Spanish Communist, quoted earlier in this volume,[81] asks:

With few exceptions, especially during the early part of the war, how many Spanish politicians and military men were there who did not welcome the Communist agents with open arms and refuse to play their game? At least I was a convinced Communist, and my attitude had some logic to it; but what logic was there in the attitude adopted by the others? Without the lack of understanding and the complicity that were almost general would it have been possible, in the course of a few months, for a party, as weak numerically as the Communist party, to penetrate—and nearly dominate—the whole government apparatus? . . .

I am not trying to excuse my mistakes, but I should like everyone else to confess his own. If we Spanish Communists were guilty of abuses and iniquities and established our rule completely or were on the point of doing so, it was because the others, with few exceptions, did not rise to the occasion. . . .

The Communist parties [of the world] are strong in proportion as the other parties and trade-union organizations are weak and vacillating and play their game. That was the lesson of Spain and that, today, is the lesson of Europe and the world. If they understand this lesson, they will save themselves, but if they do not, then they are lost.[82]

Part VI
Epilogue

30. The Demise of the Revolution

The period embracing the rise of Juan Negrín in May 1937 to the end of the Civil War falls into two parts. The first is distinguished by the continuing decline of the Revolution, by the efforts of the new defense minister Indalecio Prieto to curb the military power of the Communist party, and by his ouster from the government under Communist pressure in April 1938. The second is marked by the reorganization of the cabinet, by Negrín's assumption of both the premiership and defense ministry, and by the high-water mark of Communist power, followed in the final months of the war by overwhelming military defeats, by the collapse of the party's influence, and by the overthrow, in March 1939, of Negrín and his Communist supporters through a coalition of left-wing and moderate forces, who vainly attempted to negotiate with General Franco a settlement without reprisals.

The composition of the Negrín cabinet formed on 17 May 1937 was as follows:[1]

Juan Negrín	Socialist	Premiership and Finance
Indalecio Prieto	Socialist	Defense
Julián Zugazagoitia	Socialist	Interior
Jesús Hernández	Communist	Education and Health
Vicente Uribe	Communist	Agriculture
José Giral	Left Republican	Foreign Affairs
Bernardo Giner de los Ríos	Republican Union	Public Works
Manuel de Irujo	Basque Nationalist	Justice
Jaime Aiguadé	Esquerra	Labor and Social Welfare

Comprising only nine members as opposed to eighteen in the Largo Caballero government, and divested of left-wing Socialists and anarchosyndicalists, the new cabinet increased the relative strength of the Communist party. Condemned by its opponents as counterrevolutionary, the cabinet was acclaimed by its protagonists as a government of national union. On 31 May, President Azaña—who a year later recorded woefully in his diary that Negrín was acting without consulting him and was always presenting him with accomplished facts[2] —made the following optimistic comment: "The new government has been received with general satisfaction. The people have heaved a sigh of relief. They expect energy, decision, the will to govern, the restoration of normal methods in the affairs of state, the crushing of indiscipline. Public anxiety . . . has been allayed by the belief that the government will soon put an end to the disorder in the rear. This is the most painful sore. The new premier has great confidence in his plans, in his authority. He affirms that the war will continue for a long time (another year!), and that he is preparing for this. Little known and still young, Negrín is intelligent, cultured, recognizes the problems and understands them. . . . One may agree or disagree with his personal views, but when I now speak to the head of the government I no longer have the impression that I am speaking to a corpse. After so many months this is a pleasant novelty for me."[3]

Despite the moderate complexion of the cabinet and the fact that the Communists held no more than the two seats they had occupied in the government of Largo Caballero, its composition was deceptive.

In the first place, although Julián Zugazagoitia, a Prietista, was made minister of the interior, the Communists not only retained all the pivotal positions in the police administration they had held previously,[4] but Lieutenant Colonel Antonio Ortega, a party member,[5] was named director general of security in place of Wenceslao Carrillo, a supporter of Largo Caballero. At the request of Negrín, Juan Simeón Vidarte, a Prietista and member of the Socialist party executive, took over the undersecretaryship of the interior. When urging him to accept the post, Negrín—according to Vidarte—made the following comment: "Look here, Vidarte, I made Zuga [Zugazagoitia] minister of the interior because Prieto asked me to. In reality, this is as though Prieto had two ministries. I know little about Zuga; he is not a friend of mine. He is Prieto's man. On the other hand, the Communists asked me to give the general direction of security to [Lieutenant] Colonel Ortega, who is an unconditional supporter of theirs. . . . Whom do I have in the administration? I am not offering you a post. I am asking of you a favor."[6] In his book, Zugazagoitia, who speaks of Ortega's "rapid evolution from moderate republicanism to enthusiastic Communist" refers to him as his "theoretical subordinate" and states that he did not appoint him to the position of director general of security.[7]

Second, although Indalecio Prieto held the defense ministry, the philo-Communist Julio Alvarez del Vayo kept his post as head of the general commissariat of war[8] that directed the political orientation of the armed forces, while Largo Caballero's executive order dismissing all political commissars whose appointment and rank had not been confirmed by 15 May was shelved, leaving the Communists entrenched in that vital body. It will be recalled that one of the Communist party's conditions for participating in the new government was that the general commissariat of war should enjoy autonomy in all matters relating to the appointment and political direction of the commissars.[9] According to Vidarte, when newsmen asked Negrín if any personal friend of Largo Caballero was going to join his administration, Negrín replied: "Of course, no one other than the chief commissar, Señor Alvarez del Vayo." Vidarte's comment: "Everyone knew . . . that no one at that time was more detested by Largo Caballero than his former minister of foreign affairs, whom he had flayed mercilessly in the cabinet. But Negrín combined the seriousness of a scientist with the sense of humor of a man of the world."[10]

Furthermore, Lieutenant Colonel Antonio Cordón, a Communist party member, whom Largo Caballero had removed from the technical secretariat of the undersecretaryship of war,[11] was reappointed to that post,[12] Captain Eleuterio Díaz Tendero, the philo-Communist, who had been dismissed from the highly sensitive information and control department,[13] was reinstated, and Miaja's eminently capable chief of staff, the enigmatic and politically adaptable Lieutenant Colonel Vicente Rojo, was promoted to the rank of general and made chief of the central general staff.[14] All these appointments were undoubtedly made in accordance with a prior agreement between Prieto and the Communists as a condition of his heading the defense ministry.[15]

Finally, although Alvarez del Vayo was replaced in the foreign ministry by former premier José Giral, a close friend of Azaña's, he left behind him a legacy of Communist functionaries in the ministry and in its various dependencies, including the foreign propaganda press agency, the Agencia Española, and the Foreign Press Bureau.[16]

In Catalonia, where the May events had resulted in the taking over of public order and defense by Valencia, the political victory of the Communists was consolidated by the formation of the Negrín government. The liberal republican, General Sebastián Pozas, head of the Civil Guard at the outbreak of the war, who had quietly entered the Communist party in October 1936,[17] when he was commander of the Army of the Center, and who, on 5 May, had been made military commander of Catalonia and of the Eastern Army in neighboring

Epilogue

Aragon, openly joined the PSUC and gave the Communists free rein. Furthermore, Lieutenant Colonel Emilio Torres, who was sympathetic toward the CNT and FAI and whom interior minister Angel Galarza had appointed police chief of Barcelona during the fighting in order to facilitate the passage of the assault guards through Catalonia,[18] was replaced on 8 June by former police chief of Madrid Lieutenant Colonel Ricardo Burillo, a Communist party member.[19]

Meanwhile, the *patrullas de control*, or patrols, the police squads created in the early days of the Revolution—whose attempted dissolution by the PSUC, as we have seen, had been one of the main causes of the political deadlock in Catalonia in March and April[20]—came under renewed assault.[21] They were dissolved on 4 June by a decree of the Esquerra councillor of the interior, Carlos Martí Feced,[22] who, since the taking over of public order by Valencia, had become a mere auxiliary of the newly appointed Communist director general of security, Lieutenant Colonel Ortega. Martí Feced, it will be recalled, was one of the four members of the provisional government formed during the May events. On 29 June, it was replaced by a new cabinet in which the CNT refused to participate at the last moment because of an alleged "maneuver" by President Companys.[23]

Hoping to foil any attempt to suppress the patrols, the CNT had argued unsuccessfully that they had remained neutral during the fighting in Barcelona.[24] Equally ineffectual was the gesture made by the patrols themselves after the fighting had ended, offering their services to Lieutenant Colonel Torres and to the Catalan government, a gesture that, although supported by Torres, was rebuffed by President Companys.[25] This was not surprising, for now that the central government had assumed control of public order Companys placed his hopes of political survival not in an accommodation with the CNT and FAI, but in the swift destruction of their armed power in the expectation that this alone would induce Valencia to restore to Catalonia her lost autonomy. Thus, while arguing that the central government should not have taken over the administration of public order, but, instead, should have provided the Generalitat with reinforcements,[26] he urged Valencia to proceed "rapidly" with the "cleaning up and disarming" of the frontier posts,[27] where, it will be recalled, Negrín's carabineers had begun to disarm the CNT and FAI even before the May events. But in the sequel Companys was disappointed, for in October 1937 the central government moved to Barcelona, shattering his hopes that the control of public order would soon be restored to Catalonia.

If the dissolution of the patrols was a heavy blow to the CNT and FAI, no less so was the loss of their power in countless towns and villages. On 15 May, the revolutionary committees—that had hitherto resisted the Generalitat's decree of 9 October 1936 providing for their replacement by municipal councils, in which the various organizations were to be seated in proportion to their representation in the cabinet—were declared illegal by the Catalan government. In fact, many of the committees were overturned by the newly arrived guards and carabineers even before they were outlawed in mid-May.

In succeeding weeks the story of Catalonia was one of mass arrests, of detentions in clandestine jails, of tortures, kidnappings, and assassinations, as well as of the destruction of agricultural and urban collectives. The spontaneous, undirected terror of the CNT and FAI in the heyday of the Revolution had now given way to the more sophisticated, centrally directed, and, hence, more fearful terror of the Communists. "A wave of blood and terror has swept over the communities of Catalonia," declared the national committee of the CNT in June 1937. "Our libertarian movement has kept silent . . . not out of cowardice, but out of discipline and a sense of responsibility. . . . With incomparable stoicism it has endured the assault on the collectives, on the constructive work of the proletariat."[28] On 1 July, the underground anarchist newspaper *Anarquía*, in its first issue, published in Barcelona, expressed the growing cleavage between the leadership of the libertarian movement and the rank and file. "In face of the serious situation confronting our organization, in face of the barbarous repression unleashed against us, in face of the assault on and destruction of our collectives and our revolutionary work, . . . we must sound a cry of alarm and urge the militant comrades [that is, the leaders] of the CNT and FAI, who optimistically believe that our revolution is advancing and that we are still a force to be feared and respected . . . that they should let the scales fall from their eyes. The repression in the rural areas is incredible. The hatred of the CNT and FAI has reached unsuspected heights. In an orgy of bloodletting, the assault guards, sent to maintain order, attack the villages and destroy everything, imprisoning and assassinating our comrades."[29]

While this repression was in progress, the POUM was being threatened with extinction. On 16 June, Lieutenant Colonel Burillo, the Communist police chief of Barcelona, acting on instructions from Lieutenant Colonel Ortega, the Communist director general of security, seized the POUM headquarters in Barcelona and other buildings of the party, arresting many of its leaders, its newspaper editors, and

Epilogue

a large number of foreign supporters on the ground of espionage on behalf of General Franco.[30]

Obeying secret orders received directly from the NKVD in Valencia[31]—Alexander Orlov's headquarters—Ortega withheld all knowledge of the impending coup from his immediate superior, interior minister Zugazagoitia.[32] As an additional precaution, so that the operation would not be thwarted, he dispatched to Ciudad Real, on a false alarm, the subdirector general of security, the moderate Socialist Gabriel Morón, whom Zugazagoitia had appointed "to keep me apprised of whatever might happen" in the police department because of his distrust of the director general.[33]

On 22 June, when the operation against the POUM had been consummated, *Las Noticias*, the Communist organ of the Catalan UGT, revealed the coup:

"A few days ago the police discovered in Barcelona an organization of enormous importance dedicated to espionage in various countries. . . . The most elementary caution compelled us . . . to remain silent with respect to this important police action, for otherwise we might have damaged the success of the entire operation. . . . But now we can give our readers some of the facts regarding this vast spy organization, whose best elements had infiltrated the POUM.

"The first step taken by the police was to arrest all the POUM leaders as well as a large number of foreigners of both sexes, who, it appears, had the closest contact with this espionage service. At present, the number of persons arrested is estimated at three hundred. . . . During the seizure of the party's buildings, documents of such great importance were found . . . that the culprits cannot in any way deny their guilt."

During the ensuing days and weeks, the repression against the POUM spread to other parts of Catalonia, to Valencia, and Madrid, and to its armed forces on the Aragon front.[34]

Nin, the party secretary and Stalin's most coveted prey,[35] was the prime target and the first to be arrested.[36] Taken to a secret prison near Madrid, he was subjected to horrendous torture in a vain attempt to extract a confession of espionage on behalf of General Franco, Hitler, and Mussolini, essential to a successful Moscow-style show trial in Spain.[37]

"What Stalin and his hirelings of the NKVD wanted," writes Julián Gorkin, a member at the time of the POUM executive and one of those arrested, "was not the assassination, pure and simple, of Nin and his principal comrades . . . , but our prosecution at a public trial, our conviction, and immediate execution, under the guise of republican legality—a trial on the model of the trials in Moscow and, later, of those in the so-called people's democracies. This appearance of legality was contained in the decree published on 23 June 1937 [a few days after the arrest of the POUM leaders], and its scope was both broad and precise enough to imprison, and even liquidate, all opponents of the Negrín government. . . . This decree had not received the approval of parliament and, furthermore, the Tribunals of Espionage and High Treason created by it were composed of three civilian and two military magistrates appointed by the government itself. Its dictatorial or, if one prefers, its executive character is therefore obvious. . . . But more serious of all was the retroactive character of the decree."[38]

Having failed to extract the required confession from Nin for a show trial in Spain, his tormentors may have decided that they had no alternative but to dispose of him. Julián Gorkin states that Enrique Castro, onetime member of the Communist party's central committee, assured him, after he had left the party, that "the personal executioner of Nin" had been his former comrade in the organization of the Fifth Regiment, Carlos Contreras (Vittorio Vidali), and that Orlov had selected him as "his immediate collaborator in the case of Nin."[39] But since Nin was internationally famous, his disappearance had to be explained. Hence, according to former politburo member Jesús Hernández, Contreras simulated a Nazi assault to "liberate" Nin from his secret place of captivity in Alcalá de Henares, the sham assault being executed by ten German members of the International Brigades, who carried him off, leaving behind incriminating documents purporting to show his connection with the Nazi secret police.[40] This alleged abduction of Nin by the Gestapo was the version universally adopted by the Communists to account for Nin's disappearance whenever the question was asked, "Where is Nin?"

But the exact form of Nin's death has never been established. Nor is it known for certain whether he was assassinated in Spain or shipped to Russia alive or dead. The moderate Socialist Vidarte, then undersecretary of the interior, relates in his memoirs that he and interior minister Zugazagoitia sent a special police agent to Madrid to investigate Nin's disappearance. The agent reported that Nin had been taken to a private home in Alcalá de Henares used as a "Communist checa," whence "screams and moans" had been heard, that one morning a large car picked up a crate and proceeded to Alicante, where it stopped alongside a Soviet ship, and that, in the agent's opinion, Nin left Spain alive.[41]

Forty years later, this version received some support, but by no means conclusive, from a certain Javier Jiménez, who, when interviewed by *Cambio 16*, the Madrid weekly, claimed that he had belonged to a special police unit in Madrid [a Brigada Especial] that was sent to Barcelona at the time of the coup against the POUM. He asserted not only that he had witnessed in Madrid the fabrication of documents with Nin's signature, designed to implicate the POUM in enemy espionage, but that, after the Civil War, he met the chaffeur who had driven him and other members of the unit to Barcelona and who had confessed that he had later taken Nin from Alcalá de Henares to Valencia, "where a Soviet ship was waiting."[42]

Whatever the fate of Nin, the Communists and their friends clung tenaciously to their version that he had been freed by a Nazi commando group. The Gestapo, they argued, could not afford to have such a valuable agent interrogated by the republican police regarding its activities in Spain.[43]

The NKVD chief, Alexander Orlov, who defected to the United States in 1938 and exposed many of the violent crimes of Stalin and the NKVD in other countries, remained silent on those committed in Spain. Nowhere in his books, articles, or testimony before the U.S. Senate subcommittee does he mention either the POUM or the disappearance of Andrés Nin. However, in private conversation many years after his defection, when Bertram D. Wolfe asked him pointblank, "Did you have a hand in the assassination of Nin?" Orlov replied that he did not, that he did not even know him, that his role in Spain had been "limited to counterespionage and guerrilla warfare in rebel territory"—his stock description of his activities—and that he had never been given a "murder job."[44] It was, of course, unlikely that he would incriminate himself.

Thirty years after his defection, in response to Stanley Payne's questionnaire, he denied any responsibility for the assassination of Nin and placed the entire blame on the Spanish Communists, avoiding any hint that the Kremlin, through its NKVD apparatus in Spain —of whose activities, as head operative from September 1936 to July 1938, he must of necessity be held responsible—had in any way been involved. "The leaders of the Spanish communist party," he stated, "had an axe to grind with the POUM," and "the disappearance of Nin was an act of political vengeance."

The Demise of the Revolution

The disappearance of Andrés Nin dealt a heavy moral blow to Negrín's administration, which had hoped to establish for itself a reputation for constitutional procedure in the eyes of the Western world. The premier's desk was piled high with telegrams and letters of protest from abroad.[45] Negrín was at first outraged by this stigma on his government only a month after its formation.[46] Nevertheless, to judge from the memoirs of the moderate Socialist Vidarte, who, it will be recalled, was undersecretary of the interior at the time of the events, his concern seems to have had more to do with the illegal nature of the repression rather than with the repression itself. "I believed at the time, and I still believe, after more than thirty years," he writes, "that there probably existed between Negrín and the Communists some kind of tacit understanding, whereby in return for their unconditional political support and for the shipment of arms . . . Negrín would permit them to carry out *within the law* the liquidation, ordered by Stalin, of a rival party that had taken up arms against the government."[47]

Jesús Hernández, who claims that he was unaware of the whereabouts of Nin and that he and José Díaz, the party secretary, opposed Orlov's operation on the grounds that it had been undertaken without the knowledge of interior minister Zugazagoitia,[48] confirms Negrín's indignation. "What have your people done with Nin?" Negrín asked him. "With obvious anger, Negrín told me that the interior minister had informed him of a whole series of abuses committed in Barcelona by the Soviet police, who behaved as though they were in their own country and didn't even trouble to notify the Spanish authorities, even as an act of courtesy, of the arrests of Spanish citizens, who were transferred from one place to another without judicial warrant, and were imprisoned in private prisons, totally beyond the control of the legal authorities. . . . I didn't know what to answer him. I could have told him that like he . . . I was also wondering where Nin was and that I detested Orlov and his gang of police. But I decided not to. I could see the storm descending on our party and resolved to defend it even though, in this case, the defense of the party meant implicitly defending a possible crime."[49]

The two cabinet meetings at which the disappearance of Nin was discussed were described by the minister of the interior as "almost savage."[50] "The Communist ministers," testifies Zugazagoitia—who, according to Hernández, wanted to know whether his jurisdiction as interior minister was to be "determined by the advice of certain Soviet 'technicians'"[51]—"defended their colleague [Lieutenant Colonel Ortega] with extraordinary passion. I stated that the director general could remain at his post, but in that case I would relinquish mine. Prieto, adopting a firm stand, reproached the Communists for the manner in which they conducted the debate and declared, in support of my position, that he would add his resignation to mine in the event Ortega were not replaced."[52]

"No one [in the cabinet] believed in our sincerity," writes Hernández, "when we stated that we did not know the whereabouts of Nin. We defended the presence of Soviet 'technicians' and 'advisers' as an expression of 'disinterested' help. . . . We emphasized once again how much the supply of arms from the USSR and the assistance we were receiving in the international arena from the Soviet Union meant to our cause. As the atmosphere remained hostile . . . I compromised by agreeing to the removal of Colonel Ortega—a scapegoat—for overstepping his functions and for not duly informing the minister."[53]

This was but a small concession, however, for the main objective of the Communists—the dissolution of the POUM—had been achieved. Most of the leaders of its executive committee were in jail, many of its less well-known militants had been imprisoned or shot, its press proscribed, its buildings occupied, and never again would it function effectively during the Civil War. True, a new executive committee was secretly formed that maintained contact with members in the rear and at the front as well as with sympathizers abroad. Also, underground editions of the party newspaper, La Batalla, were published,[54] but the new executive was arrested in April 1938 and, henceforth, what remained of the party apparatus functioned only spasmodically until the end of the Civil War.[55]

Negrín's indignation over the disappearance of Nin was fleeting. Only a month later, when talking to President Azaña, he doggedly supported the version that Nin had been abducted by the Gestapo. "He doesn't believe that it was the work of the Communists," Azaña commented in his diary on 22 July. "The Communists, of course, become indignant at the very idea. Negrín believes that Nin was abducted by . . . the Gestapo to prevent him from making revelations." "'Isn't that too novelistic?'" the disbelieving Azaña responded. "'No, sir,'" replied Negrín, who, to impress the president with the efficiency of the "formidable" Gestapo, proceeded to tell him of an attempt by the Nazi secret police to poison the Russian general staff in Madrid.[56]

During the trial of the POUM leaders in 1938, by one of the special tribunals created after their arrest the previous year, on charges of espionage and treason, Largo Caballero and Federica Montseny, as well as Julián Zugazagoitia and Manuel de Irujo, ministers of the interior and justice respectively at the time of the arrests, testified in their favor. The charges could not be proved, but the accused were sentenced to various terms of imprisonment for their participation in the May events.[57] "The trial," wrote Jesús Hernández, "was a crude comedy based on falsified documents and on statements extracted from wretched spies of Franco who were promised their lives—although afterward they were shot—provided that they declared they had maintained contact with leaders of the POUM. Magistrates and judges condemned, because they had to condemn, and because they were ordered to condemn. The 'evidence'—in whose documentary 'preparation' W. Roces [Wenceslao Roces, Hernandez's undersecretary of education][58] played a very active part—was so hollow and false that not one [of the POUM leaders] could be executed."[59]

Meanwhile, in various regions of the left camp the agrarian revolution was in sharp decline. Encouraged by the decree of 7 October 1936, issued by Communist minister of agriculture Vicente Uribe—giving legal status to expropriations carried out at the inception of the Revolution, but exempting from confiscation properties belonging to landowners who had not identified themselves with the military rebellion —many owners who had been forced to accept collectivization were now demanding the restitution of their land.[60] Furthermore, to the anguish of both anarchosyndicalists and left-wing Socialists, the Communists used the decree to encourage tenant farmers and sharecroppers, who before the war had been in conflict with the rural wage workers but had been swept up involuntarily by the collective farm movement, to recover their former parcels.

At the height of the offensive against the collective farms at the end of May 1937, left-wing Socialist Ricardo Zabalza, general secretary of the National Federation of Land Workers affiliated with the UGT, declared: "Our most fervent aim today is to guarantee the conquests of the Revolution . . . against which a world of enemies is rising up, namely, the reactionaries of yesterday and those who held land on lease because they were lackeys of the political bosses, whereas our members were either denied land or evicted from their wretched holdings. Today these reactionaries, protected by the famous decree of 7 October, are endeavoring to take by assault the collectivized estates with the object of dividing them up . . . and putting an end to the agrarian revolution."[61] A few weeks later, the general secretary of the CNT Peasants' Federation of Castile declared: "We have fought terrible battles with the Communists, especially with brigades and divisions under their control, which have assassinated our best peas-

Epilogue

ant militants and savagely destroyed our collective farms."⁶²

These attacks on the collectives damaged both rural economy and morale, for as the campaign reached its peak just before the summer harvest, the agricultural laborers abandoned their work in many places. The minister of agriculture then issued a decree promising help to the collectives to avoid "economic failure that might chill the faith of the land workers in the collective forms of cultivation they chose freely when they confiscated the land" and granting them legal status during the *current* agricultural year.⁶³

But no sooner had the crops been gathered than the government dissolved the anarchist-controlled Defense Council of Aragon that had been set up early in the war to control the Revolution in that part of Aragon occupied by the anti-Franco forces, predominantly libertarian, and appointed, as governor general of the region, José Ignacio Mantecón, a member of the Left Republican party, but a Communist supporter.⁶⁴ Using the Eleventh Division commanded by the Communist Enrique Líster, whom defense minister Prieto had previously dispatched to Aragon to carry out the dissolution of the council, Mantecón also broke up the collective farms.⁶⁵ Líster claimed after the war that Prieto, hating both anarchosyndicalists and Communists, hoped to "kill two birds with one stone" by getting the two factions to destroy each other.⁶⁶ But the truth is that the Communists required no prodding from Prieto to break the power of the CNT and FAI in Aragon.

Although the Communists endeavored to evade personal responsibility for the destruction of the collectives, José Silva, the Communist general secretary of the Institute of Agrarian Reform, acknowledged a few months later that "a very grave mistake" had been made. "Under cover of the order issued by the governor general," he wrote, "those persons who were discontented with the collectives—and who had good reason for being so, if the methods employed in forming them are taken into account—took them by assault, carrying away and dividing up the harvest and farm implements without respecting those collectives that had been formed without violence or pressure, that were prosperous, and were a model of organization, like the one in Candasmo. It is true that the governor's aim was to repair injustices . . . but the result was just the opposite from that intended. The measure only increased the confusion, and violence was exercised, but this time by the other side. As a result, labor in the fields was suspended almost entirely." To redress this situation the Communist party was later compelled to restore some of the collectives. "The recognition of the rights of the collectives," Silva added, "and the decision to return what had been unjustly taken away . . . brought things back to normal."[67]

But, in truth, the hatreds and resentments generated by these events were never dispelled, and the disillusionment among the anarchosyndicalist forces on the Aragon front contributed to its rapid collapse a few months later.

It should be stressed that the Communist decision to restore some of the dismantled collectives stemmed not only from the damage to rural economy and morale, but to the growing friction with Prieto, who, because of Azaña's political isolation and effeteness, was the principal hope of those liberal republicans and moderate Socialists who had not transferred their allegiance to the Communists. If, for his own ends, Prieto had supported the Communists against Largo Caballero, he soon made it clear that he was not their puppet, for he bluntly rejected an offer by the politburo to provide him "every day with suggestions, ideas, and views on military matters."[68] He also informed Gaykis, the Soviet ambassador who succeeded Rosenberg, that he would not support the fusion of the Socialist and Communist parties.[69] Furthermore, while Stalin hoped that a moderate course would induce Britain and France to raise the arms embargo and that the prolongation of the conflict would keep Germany away from Russia's borders, Prieto hoped that Anglo-French aid would counteract the mounting influence of Russia. "The Western democracies," he declared after the war, "fearful of communism, did not realize that this movement grew in Spain as a result of their own lack of assistance."[70] Increasingly pessimistic, Prieto, like President Azaña and Julián Besteiro, the right-wing Socialist, looked more and more to mediation to end the conflict. Many feelers were put out in 1937 and 1938, but General Franco, backed to the hilt by Germany and Italy and confident of ultimate victory, would consider nothing but unconditional surrender.

Within a few months of entering the defense ministry, Prieto, provoked by the proselytism and crescent power of the Communists in the armed forces, removed Alvarez del Vayo, the commissar general of war, and Francisco Antón, the inspector-commissar on the Madrid front,[71] who was secretary of the Madrid Communist party organization and General Miaja's principal mentor and activator.[72] He also ousted a number of other Communist or pro-Communist political commissars and high officers, including Alejandro García Val, the director general of military transportation, Eleuterio Díaz Tendero of

Epilogue

the information and control department, and Antonio Cordón, formerly technical secretary in the undersecretaryship of war, but now chief of staff of the Eastern Army. The last two officers, it will be recalled, had been removed by Caballero before being reappointed by Prieto after the May crisis. Furthermore, defying Soviet threats, Prieto discharged Major Gustavo Durán, the head of the Madrid section of the SIM—the military investigation service he had formed on the advice of the Russians—for naming hundreds of Communist agents.[73]

At this juncture the Communists halted their attacks on the collective farms. Although they did so partly for economic reasons, Prieto's hostility now impelled them to launch an all-out offensive against the moderate Socialist leader[74] and to seek a temporary accommodation with the CNT. For, much as the Communist party had relied for support on the segments of the rural and urban middle classes that were threatened with economic annihilation by the Revolution, it could not allow them to become too strong, lest with the political support of the moderate Socialists and republicans—now emboldened by the recoil of the Revolution—they should attempt to take the reins of government into their own hands. If they were to guide domestic and foreign policy, the Communists had to be supreme, and this was possible not only if they controlled the police and army but also skillfully balanced the various factions and class forces, exploiting to the full their mutual antagonisms and inherent self-interest.

Former politburo member Jesús Hernández writes:

In our political struggle, we could rely upon something the other organizations lacked: discipline, the concept of blind obedience, absolute submission to hierarchical control. . . . What did the others have in face of this granite monolith? A broken, divided, fragmented Socialist party, working in three different directions, with three representative figures: Prieto, Caballero, and Besteiro, who fought among themselves and to whom another was added shortly afterward: Negrín. We managed to exploit their suicidal antagonisms for our own ends. One day we supported one side against the other. The next day we reversed our position and supported the opposite side. And today, the next day, and every day we incited one side against the other so that they would destroy one another, a game we played in full view and not without success. Thus, to destroy Francisco Largo Caballero we relied principally on Negrín and, to a certain extent, on Prieto. To get rid of Prieto we utilized Negrín and other prominent Socialists, and had the war lasted we would not have hesitated to ally ourselves with the devil in order to exterminate Negrín if he had obstructed us. . . . Among the anarchosyndicalists the panorama was no better. . . . Although their ranks were tighter and more compact than those of the Socialists, we managed nevertheless to create a breach. We helped to deepen the schism—a product of evolution—that was developing in the CNT by drawing into government collaboration a large part of the an-

[464]

archist movement, which thereafter experienced a process of internal strife. . . . Nor did the republican parties . . . present a solid and homogeneous front. Cowed by the violent and disorderly character of the popular reaction to the [military] rebellion during the first days of the fighting, they allowed themselves, to a large degree, to be influenced and won over by our policy of order and discipline. Their value to us lay more in their name than in their effectiveness. For that reason we respected and defended them, but not without taking advantage of their good faith, using them like a Trojan horse when we had difficulty with other forces of the Popular Front.[75]

With every step up the ladder of power the Communists left fresh adversaries behind them. "When we broke with Caballero," Hernández continues, "we broke with the preponderant force of the Socialist party. . . . When we provoked the Caballero crisis . . . we made mortal enemies of more than a million men organized in the CNT. . . . The offensive against Prieto affronted the republican parties that saw in the Socialist leader . . . the brain that more than any other represented their republican policy. . . . If, during this period, a total collapse of our position did not occur, it was because all the forces that hated the Communists were incapable of forming a united front."[76]

Faced by Prieto's enmity toward them, a new shift in policy became necessary to maintain their balancing position in the scale of power. In a conciliatory gesture toward the leadership of the CNT, party secretary José Díaz declared that "those who say that we cannot talk of revolution because we are at war are totally mistaken." A few days later, on 4 October, "El Campesino," the Communist military commander on the central front, who had risen from the ranks of the militia, embraced his counterpart, Cipriano Mera, the anarchist commander of the CNT-FAI forces in that sector, at a public meeting in Madrid.[77] "This embrace," commented *Frente Rojo*, the Communist organ. "should be extended to all the workers of our Fatherland."[78]

At the same time, fearing that their opponents on the left might rally around Largo Caballero, who as secretary of the UGT executive had just negotiated a provisional alliance with the CNT, the Communists delivered a deathblow to the left Socialist leader. Acting in agreement with former supporters of Caballero and with the moderate Socialists—who, after the fall of his government, had seized *Adelante*, his mouthpiece in Valencia[79]—they formed a new executive on 1 October,[80] with González Peña, a former Prietista but now a Negrinista as president. In addition, Edmundo Domínguez was named vice-president, Rodríguez Vega, secretary, and Felipe Pretel, treasurer; all three were former adherents of Largo Caballero but now Communist supporters. On 19 October, Caballero denounced the Communist party at a mass meeting,[81] but was prevented from further activity by both his Socialist and Communist opponents and on 30 November was divested of his newspaper, *La Correspondencia de Valencia*, his last daily medium of communication.[82] The conflict over the two rival executives boiled on until January 1938, when it was settled by Léon Jouhaux, the French trade-union leader—then partial to the Communists—at the expense of Largo Caballero.[83]

Ignoring the fact that the Communists now controlled the UGT, the CNT, in defiance of some of the FAI leaders, started negotiations for a pact with the new executive and on 18 March 1938 signed a formal alliance.[84] By recognizing the authority of the state in such matters as nationalization and the regular army, the document was a complete negation of anarchist doctrine. Even the promise that the collective farms would be legalized implied submission to authority, a promise, however, that was not fulfilled, for the Communist-controlled ministry of agriculture never granted the collective farms permanent legal status. "The Communist party," wrote FAI leader Abad de Santillán after the war, who was then engaged in a bitter feud with members of the national committee of the CNT, "endeavored to lure the CNT leaders . . . in order to manipulate and exploit these rubber stamps for its policy of hegemony. The more the comrades of the national committee of the CNT heeded these advances, the more the peninsular committee of the FAI found itself at odds with the leadership of the CNT."[85]

Strengthened by their negotiations with the CNT, the Communists were ready for the coming showdown with Prieto. On 9 March, General Franco's forces had undertaken on the Aragon front their biggest offensive of the war. There was no organized resistance, and lack of combativity—a product of the internecine struggle—was widespread. The front crumbled, and the enemy reached the coast on 15 April, splitting the republican territory in two.

Toward the end of March, E. Labonne, the French ambassador, offered the cabinet sanctuary at the French embassy, and suggested that the fleet should sail to Toulon or Bizerta to prevent it from falling into the hands of General Franco. "This," Prieto commented tartly, "was the response France gave to our urgent request for matériel."[86] At a special meeting of the cabinet Negrín declared, according to interior minister Zugazagoitia, that he had rejected an offer by the French ambassador to initiate peace negotiations and that he had informed him of Spain's determination to fight on. The meeting was then continued under Azaña's chairmanship. He questioned the ad-

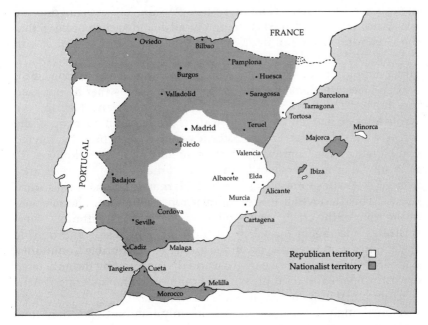

Division of Spain, 15 April 1938

visability of rejecting mediation, which might prove necessary within hours or days. Knowing that Prieto was as pessimistic as he, Azaña asked his advice, which inevitably reinforced his own conclusion that the war was lost.[87]

Meanwhile, the Communists, with the support of the CNT, had organized a demonstration in which assault guards and military forces participated. Cries of "Down with the treacherous ministers!" "Down with the minister of defense!" were heard by the assembled ministers.[88]

A few days later, on 29 March at a meeting of the cabinet during which Prieto, according to Negrín, "completely demoralized" his colleagues, the premier—once an ardent admirer and follower of Prieto —decided to remove him. Although Negrín affirmed that this decision was his own, Prieto asserted that the premier had "yielded to the demands of the Communist party."[89]

While the government crisis was still unresolved, Moscow instructed the Communist ministers, Hernández and Uribe, to withdraw from the cabinet. This tactic, Comintern delegate Togliatti explained to the politburo, was aimed at convincing "English and French opinion that the Communists are not interested in the conquest of power. . . . In this way we shall strengthen Anglo-French ties with the Soviets. If Hitler should decide on war he will have to wage it against the USSR and the Western democracies."[90] Hernández claims that he opposed the move. "The hatred and hostility for our party and Negrín," he wrote after he had left the party, "were shared unanimously by all the forces of the Popular Front. Negrín could govern only by relying completely on the Communist party's military and political power. To withdraw our ministers would have meant the death of the resistance policy."[91] A compromise was reached: Hernández alone would withdraw. "This [reduction in Communist representation]," he declared at the time of the crisis, while still a member of the politburo, "demonstrates once again the falsity of those persons inside and outside the country who have played on the existence of a terrible Communist danger, seeking to provoke distrust and division among the antifascist forces in Spain and to impress world opinion with blustering threats of Communist influence in the state machinery."[92]

Even though the Communists held only one portfolio, they now controlled more levers of command than hitherto. Premier Negrín—whom "El Campesino" and Hernández described, after they had both left the party, as the Communist party's "ambitious and docile tool"[93] and as "Moscow's man of confidence"[94]—took over the defense ministry, pursuing what Prieto called an "insensate policy of assuring the predominance of one party."[95] He elevated Antonio Cordón, whom Prieto had removed as chief of staff of the Eastern Army, to the undersecretaryship of war, promoted Nuñez Maza to the undersecretaryship of air, and appointed Pedro Prados to the post of Navy chief of staff; all three were Communist party members.[96] Furthermore, Díaz Tendero, ousted by Prieto from the vital information and control department, reappeared as head of the no less sensitive personnel section of the defense ministry, while Bibiano Fernández Ossorio y Tafall, who was undersecretary of the interior under General Sebastián Pozas at the outbreak of the Civil War, later director of the Left Republican organ *Política*, and now a fair-weather ally of the Communists, was made general commissar of war.[97] But more conspicuous than all these appointments was that of Hernández, who left the ministry of education to become chief political commissar of the Army of the Center, which represented 80 percent of the land forces.[98]

Although Julián Zugazagoitia, the moderate Socialist, was named secretary general of the defense ministry, unifying the undersecretary-ships of war and air, this post was purely decorative. In fact, according to a frank admission by Cordón, the undersecretary of war, Negrín reassured him "with a few pats on the shoulder" that the post was "in practice an honorary one with very slim possibilities for effective action."[99] He was right, of course, because the new undersecretaries, all of whom were Communists, obeyed only the mandate of the party. Moreover, 70 percent of the army command posts, Hernández claims, were in the party's hands.[100] "When I wish to learn something about the war," Zugazagoitia informed the Socialist executive in December 1938, "I have to buy a newspaper or ask a friend."[101] After the war he wrote, "Neither my presence in the general secretaryship nor the post itself made the slightest sense."[102]

As for the ministry of the interior, although Paulino Gómez, a moderate Socialist, headed this department, the Communists retained all their key positions in the police apparatus, including the post of director general of security, now occupied by Eduardo Cuevas de la Peña, a party member.[103] Through Soviet agents they also controlled the SIM[104] with its secret prisons and torture chambers for political opponents of the left and right.

The finance ministry went to Negrín's intimate, the Left Republican Francisco Méndez Aspe, who had been involved in the shipment to Moscow of Spanish gold reserves,[105] and who appointed Marcelino Fernández, a PSUC member, to head the carabineers,[106] the most powerful force of public order, characterized by its opponents as "Negrín's 100,000 sons." Furthermore, Alvarez del Vayo returned to the foreign ministry and, in addition to maintaining Communist control in the foreign propaganda press agency, the Agencia Española, and in the foreign press bureau, gave Negrín's close collaborator, Manuel Sánchez Arcos, a party member, the key post of undersecretaryship of propaganda.

The roles of the other ministers, including Basque nationalist Manuel de Irujo and Jaime Aiguadé of the Esquerra, were inconsequential. In any case, they resigned in August 1938 in protest at the central government's disregard of Catalan autonomy. No less trivial was the role of Segundo Blanco of the CNT, named minister of education as a sop to the libertarian movement, which was now so divided that some of its leaders, like FAI leader Abad de Santillán, favored a return to anarchist orthodoxy. Others, including former secretary of the CNT Horacio M. Prieto, convinced that *apoliticismo* was dead and libertarian communism only a distant goal, advocated the creation of a libertarian Socialist party that would participate in every organ of the state,[107] thus demonstrating anarchism's insoluble dilemma that to survive it must compete for power yet, by so doing, it must violate hallowed principles. If the anarchosyndicalists held only one portfolio, this was, according to a circular issued by the CNT, to "placate the bourgeois democracies," an illusion based on the hope that Britain and France might still raise the arms embargo.

From the time Juan Negrín formed his new government in April 1938, testifies "El Campesino," morale at the front and in the rear continued to decline. "The hatred of the Communists by the mass of the people reached such a point that during a meeting of the politburo one of the leaders had to declare: 'We cannot retreat. We must . . . stay in power at all costs, otherwise we shall be hunted like predatory animals through the streets.'"[108]

To reinforce their position, the Communists were compelled to rely more and more on their military and police power. At the fronts—where during Prieto's tenure of the defense ministry, they had, according to Zugazagoitia, assassinated Socialists who refused to join the party[109]—cajolery, coercion, and violence grew from day to day. "Thousands upon thousands of our comrades," said a report issued by the peninsular committee of the FAI in October 1938, "confess that they are more afraid of being assassinated [at the fronts] by the adversaries at their side than of being killed by the enemies they face."[110] And, in the rear, the dread of the SIM and secret police silenced all but the faintest criticism.

From now on Negrín, backed by Communist propaganda and Russian supplies, became the symbol of resistance. Russian aid, limited by logistics and by Stalin's resolve not to become too enmeshed in the conflict, was predicated on the belief that Britain and France would eventually be forced to intervene in defense of their own interests. "[Moscow] will try by every means to avoid being isolated, to force the Western democracies to fight Hitler, if war is the only course," Comintern adviser Stefanov told the Spanish politburo just before the fall of Prieto.[111]

In keeping with its resistance policy, the Negrín government attempted to conciliate foreign capital. On 27 April it decreed that the foreign hydroelectric enterprises, operated in Catalonia by the CNT under the name of Serveis Electrics Unificats de Catalunya, be dissolved[112] with the object of returning the plants to their former owners. This measure, commented the correspondent of the *New York Post* in Barcelona, "suggests that the government is taking drastic steps to conciliate big foreign capital and thereby the important financial interests which exert so much influence on the foreign policies of Britain and France."[113] Confident of Franco's ultimate victory, the companies involved ignored the gesture.

Simultaneously, government comptrollers (*interventores*) were appointed to decollectivize and nationalize certain Spanish enterprises —a policy that was promoted largely in the industrial region of Catalonia by the department of economy headed by the PSUC leader Estanislao Ruiz Ponsetti[114]—while others were returned to their original owners. Although comparatively few concerns were involved because many owners had been killed or had fled to nationalist territory at the outbreak of the Civil War, the Communist-controlled foreign press censorship that in the past had attempted to conceal the Revolution allowed foreign correspondents to make great play with the restitutions.

"If the loyalist republic ever were really 'Red', as its enemies call it," observed the correspondent of the *New York Post*, "the great work of handing back factories and mines to their original owners certainly shows that the label cannot now be properly applied. As a matter of fact, a great number of industrial properties were never collectivized and have continued to run under private management and ownership.

"Hundreds of others, which were taken over by soviets of workers, in the early days of the civil war, have been restored to the owners. The rest, a government official told me, also will be 'decollectivized' in the course of time. This official asserted that the Negrín government has become more conservative and capitalistic than the government existing before the Aragon offensive, and predicted that any future cabinet shifts would turn it even further to the right. What this official did not add was that the government in decollectivizing had a political motive. It demonstrated thereby, for the benefit of Britain, France, and the United States, that the loyalist government is not a 'Red' government."[115]

Although the actual number of restitutions may have been less than suggested, the mere threat of rolling back the economic conquests of the Revolution created doubts and anxieties in the libertarian movement. "We have rejected as a pernicious error or, worse still, as a dangerous maneuver, the tendency to sacrifice the most vital and precious conquests of our people for foreign aid, which of necessity is hypothetical," wrote *Solidaridad Obrera*.[116] "This would be tantamount to a vertical collapse of morale in our rear and, consequently, at the battle fronts. It would be equivalent to telling the combatants that they should renounce the most essential reasons for the struggle."[117]

In the hope of influencing the Western democracies, Negrín enunciated, on 1 May 1938, a thirteen-point program that included the promise of a Spain free of all foreign interference, with full civil and political rights and with freedom of religion. There was also an assurance that private property "legitimately acquired" and that "the property and legitimate interests of foreigners" who had not helped the military rebellion would be respected.

The genesis of the much-publicized thirteen-point program has historical interest. According to Louis Fischer, who handled Negrín's propaganda abroad,[118] it was inspired by Ivor Montagu, the British film intellectual and producer, whom he used to see in Alvarez del Vayo's antechamber waiting for permission from the defense department to take pictures at the front. "Once he said to me," Fischer relates in the American edition of *Men and Politics*, " 'You know, it seems to me that the Loyalist government ought to enunciate its war aims, a sort of Fourteen Points program like Woodrow Wilson's.' 'Wonderful idea,' I said, 'why had it never occurred to anybody?' I passed the idea on to del Vayo. . . . He talked to Negrín. Negrín said, 'Fine, write them.' Vayo drafted ten points and showed them to Negrín. Negrín said, 'We must have thirteen to show that we are not superstitious,' and he added three himself."[119] In the English edition, all reference to Ivor Montagu, who since 1929 had been a prominent member of the British Communist party,[120] was omitted, and the thirteen-point episode was "touched up," as Salvador Madariaga puts it, to adapt it to "English tastes."[121] "For some time," ran the English version, "the Loyalist leaders had considered the advisability of announcing their social peace aims. They hoped they would undermine morale in Franco territory and reinforce sympathy for Loyalist Spain in foreign countries. Del Vayo and Negrín drafted most of the war aims and they were finally approved at a solemn session of the Cabinet."[122]

But the thirteen-point program made no impression on the democratic powers. "Not a day passed until almost the end," wrote Alvarez del Vayo, "when we did not have fresh reasons to hope that the Western democracies would come to their senses and restore us our rights to buy from them. And always our hopes proved illusory."[123]

In spite of these disappointments, in spite of the immolation of Czechoslovakia by Britain and France in September 1938, in spite of the disastrous Ebro battle and the swift collapse of Catalonia without

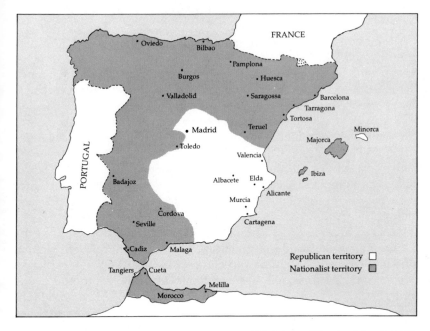

Division of Spain, March 1939

a struggle in February 1939, leaving only the central and southeastern parts of Spain to the Republic, Moscow—prior to negotiating its non-aggression pact with Hitler in a last but unsuccessful attempt to turn German military might against the West—instructed the Spanish Communists to continue the resistance policy. But the war was lost, and Stalin knew it. Nevertheless, the Spanish politburo declared on 23 February:

"The international situation has never been more unstable than it is today.

"Furthermore, the successes of the fascist invaders in Catalonia have increased their boldness, encouraging them to reveal still more clearly their plans of conquest, plunder, and war, and this in turn . . . increases the possibilities of direct and indirect aid for the Spanish people. . . . For all these reasons, we say that resistance is not only necessary but possible, and we affirm that, as on previous occasions when many persons believed that everything was lost . . . , our resistance can change the situation. It will permit new factors to develop, both in Spain and abroad, that will redound to our advantage and will open the prospect of victory."[124]

If the hopes of a European conflagration entertained by the Communists and other parties were disappointed, it was not because Britain and France were blind to the possible dangers of a Franco victory. If they refused to challenge Germany in Spain, it was because they hoped to avoid engaging the West until Germany had weakened herself in the East. Hence the policy of Britain and France throughout the war was determined not only by their hostility to the social revolution and subsequent Communist domination—of which they were fully apprised despite the efforts at concealment—but by the larger field of foreign politics. Hence no attempt at dissimulation, no attempt at curbing or even rolling back the Revolution, could have modified their policy.[125]

On 27 February, Great Britain and France officially recognized the Franco regime as the legal government of Spain. President Azaña, who had crossed the border into France after the Catalan debacle and had rejected Alvarez del Vayo's personal appeals to proceed to the central zone,[126] resigned on the day of recognition,[127] liberating himself at long last from his puppet role as constitutional cover, first, for the Revolution, and then for the incipient Communist dictatorship. Diego Martínez Barrio, the leader of Unión Republicana and speaker of the Cortes, who should have succeeded Azaña in accordance with the Constitution, also declined to return to Spain, as did other prominent republicans, Socialists, and anarchosyndicalists. Even General Vicente Rojo, the chief of the central general staff, who had enjoyed the confidence of the Communists, refused to return, convinced, according to Azaña's letter of resignation, that "the war was lost beyond recall."[128]

Enrique Líster, the Communist military leader, alleges that there were also prominent Communists who failed to return to Spain: Antonio Mije, Francisco Antón, and Luis Cabo Giorla, all members at that time of the politburo and the Madrid party organization, as well as Santiago Carrillo, the general secretary of the JSU, whose adherents in their immense majority were located in the central-southern zone. "In the airplane in which I left Toulouse," Líster alleges, "there were thirteen passengers despite the fact that there was room for thirty-three. . . . The point is that the aforementioned members of the politburo and of the executive commission of the JSU regarded the war as lost after the fall of Catalonia and behaved exactly like Azaña and Martínez Barrio."[129]

When the Communist leaders arrived in the central zone accompanied by Negrín and by members of his government as well as by Comintern delegates Togliatti and Stefanov, they found that the factions of the left had coalesced against them. Embittered by political injury and oppression, demoralized by the attacks on the Revolution, as were the left Socialists and the anarchosyndicalists, and exhausted by a protracted war that offered no hope of victory, they execrated the Negrín government—which the Socialist Luis Araquistáin described as the "most cynical and despotic" in Spanish history[130]—as much as they detested its resistance policy.

"Resist? What for? That is the universal question," wrote Zugazagoitia, the moderate Socialist. "The fall of Barcelona and the loss of Catalonia . . . have destroyed the hopes even of those who delude themselves the most: the Communists. The front-line troops see the relaxation of discipline and desertions increase alarmingly. Those who do not desert to the enemy leave the trenches and find their way home. . . . The persons who surround the premier are, like the premier himself, tied to his resistance policy: they are Communists."[131]

"Only men blinded by pride and arrogance," wrote Trifón Gómez, the moderate Socialist and head of the quartermaster corps, "could ignore the fact that everyone was hostile to them when they returned to the central-southern zone—everyone, that is, but the group of Communists who continued to manipulate Negrín. . . . It cannot be denied . . . that the conquest of Catalonia was a military walkover. In view of this, the policy of resistance advocated by the Negrín government lacked support among the people. . . . The truth is . . . that the government was a phantom. Not a single ministry functioned; the titular heads of the various departments had not the slightest desire to establish themselves; they were obsessed with the thought of assuring for themselves the means by which they could leave Spain."[132]

In this climate of dissolution, Negrín—at the behest of the politburo, which in turn obeyed the orders of Togliatti and Stefanov[133]—decreed the promotion of two prominent Communists, Antonio Cordón and Juan Modesto, to the rank of general, and a number of other leading Communist officers, including Enrique Líster and Francisco Galán, to the rank of colonel. In addition, he ordered the transfer or dismissal from their posts of various officers suspected of hostility to the party.[134] Fearing a Communist coup, Colonel Segismundo Casado, the commander of the Army of the Center who had been conspiring with Socialists, republican, and anarchosyndicalist leaders to overthrow Negrín, formed a National Council of Defense—comprising General Miaja, the Socialists Julián Besteiro and Wenceslao Carrillo, republicans Miguel San Andrés and José del Río, and anarchosyndicalists Eduardo Val and González Marín—in the hope of negotiating a surrender without reprisals.

Within hours, Negrín and his Communist entourage, including Togliatti, Stefanov, and La Pasionaria—all of whom had prudently avoided establishing themselves in Madrid and had kept close to an airport near the small town of Elda in the province of Alicante—escaped by plane. So swift was their departure that no directives were given to the Madrid party organization, which, aided by Communist military units, tried unsuccessfully to overthrow the defense council.

At meetings held in Moscow in the spring and summer of 1939, Líster claims that he accused the members of the politburo, who had returned to the central-southern zone, of defeatism. "That alone explains why they locked themselves up in Elda. . . . In one of those meetings . . . I said that I could never forget the painful impression I received on the morning of 6 March when, arriving at Elda from Cartagena . . . a few hours after Casado had rebelled, I found Dolores [La Pasionaria] and other party leaders preparing to leave by plane instead of studying what response they should give to the traitors of the Casado Junta."[135]

Jesús Hernández—who was in close touch with Negrín and Communist leaders during those dramatic hours and who claimed that Togliatti and Stefanov arrived in the central-southern zone with the "deliberate aim of putting an end to the resistance of the Republic"—held that Negrín's military measures were "clearly inspired by Moscow" and were "a cunning political provocation, an incitement to defiance and rebellion, the spark that was to ignite the rising."[136]

"The Casado group," said Comintern leader Dmitri Manuilsky in a discussion shortly after the war, at which Hernández was present, "fell into the trap . . . [and] the party was spared the responsibility for the final catastrophe. . . . Now that the Spanish masses are feeling the brutality of Franco's bloody repression, it is logical for them to think that it would have been better to have followed the advice of the Communists to resist to the death if necessary. . . . And they will turn in anger against the anarchists and Socialists, against the members of the junta of Casado. The maneuver of Ercoli [Togliatti's nom de guerre] has saved the political future and prestige of the Spanish Communists."[137]

Although Negrín had issued the military decrees at the behest of the politburo, his compliance did not spare him; for like others who have ceased to serve the purpose of the Kremlin he eventually became a scapegoat. Writing some years after the war, La Pasionaria, herself a member of the politburo, blamed Negrín personally for the decrees, charging that they were "counterproductive" and "caused profound indignation among the conspirators."[138] "Deep down within himself," she asserted earlier, "Negrín was hoping for a catastrophe that would free him from all government responsibility."[139]

With the flight of Negrín and his Communist entourage from Spain the policy of resistance had ended. On the National Council of Defense there now rested the historic responsibility of negotiating a settlement without reprisals. But in face of General Franco's insistence on unconditional surrender the efforts of the council aborted, and by the end of March the forces of the left were in full retreat.

On 1 April, General Franco declared that the war had ended.

Appendixes

Appendix I

On the question of the confiscation and control of property by the unions and also by the left-wing parties a great deal could be written based on left sources alone. But considerations of space do not permit more than a brief reference to some of these sources under each of the following heads:

RAILROADS. "The boards of directors disappeared," said one trade-union report, "and works councils were formed in which the working-class organizations were directly represented" (*CNT* [Madrid], 2 Oct. 1936). This control of the railroads by the working-class organizations is confirmed in the preamble of a government decree published in the *Gaceta de Madrid*, 16 Aug. 1936. See also *Avant*, 26 July 1936; *La Batalla* (Barcelona), 18 Aug. 1936; *Boletín de Información, CNT-FAI*, 26 Aug. 1936; *CNT* (Madrid), 5 Oct. 1936; *Cultura Proletaria*, 15 June 1940 (article by Gaston Leval); *El Día Gráfico*, 24 Sept. 1936; *Fragua Social*, 7 Apr. 1937; *Solidaridad Obrera* (Barcelona), 11, 19 Aug. 1936; *La Vanguardia*, 14 Oct. 1936; *Collectivizations*, 49–55; *De julio a julio* (article by Juan de Arroyo), 165–68; Gaston Leval, *Espagne libertaire, 1936–1939*, 277–78; Gaston Leval, *Né Franco né Stalin*, 97–111.

OTHER SECTIONS OF THE TRANSPORT INDUSTRY. According to Victor Zaragoza, secretary of the national committee of the CNT National Transport Federation, when interviewed by me, every important transport enterprise was appropriated by the labor unions. This excludes the Basque provinces, where there were fewer changes in the economic field (see, for example, G. L. Steer, *The Tree of Gernika*, 73). For the confiscation of some of the most important transport enterprises in Barcelona, Madrid, and Valencia, see *Boletín de Información, CNT-FAI*, 7 Aug. 1936, also article reproduced from this paper in *El Día Gráfico*, 18 Aug. 1936; *CNT* (Madrid), 7, 10 Aug. 1936; *La Noche*, 6 Aug. 1936; *Nosotros*, 8, 19 July 1937; *Política*, 8 Aug. 1936; *Solidaridad Obrera* (Barcelona), 1, 4 Aug., 13 Oct., 19 Nov., 17 Dec. 1936; *Tierra y Libertad* (Barcelona), 1 May 1937; *La Vanguardia*, 8 Oct. 1936; *Collectivizations*, 58–59; Leval, *Espagne libertaire, 1936–1939*, 266–75, Leval, *Né Franco né Stalin*, 111–22.

PUBLIC UTILITIES. According to Mariano Cardona Rosell, a member of the national committee of the CNT, every public utility enterprise in the left camp was taken over by the CNT and UGT (letter to me). Some of the most im-

Appendixes

portant were: Compañía Catalana de Gas y Electricidad, Compañía Hidro-eléctrica Española, Compañía Madrileña de Gas, Cooperativa Electra, Electra Valenciana, Elétrica Santillana, Empresa Concesionaria de las Aguas Subterráneas del Río Llobregat, Gas Lebon, Riegos y Fuerzas del Ebro, Saltos del Duero, Sociedad Anónima de Fuerzas Eléctricas, Sociedad General de Aguas de Barcelona, Unión Eléctrica Madrileña. For details on some of these enterprises, see *La Batalla* (Barcelona), 2, 23 Aug. 1936; *Boletín de Información, CNT-FAI*, 27 July 1937; *CNT* (Madrid), 31 Aug. 1936; *Luz y Fuerza*, Jan. 1938; *Nosotros*, 3 July 1937; *Solidaridad Obrera* (Barcelona), 13, 15 Aug. 1936, 10 Jan. 1937; Leval, *Espagne libertaire, 1936–1939*, 261–66; Leval, *Né Franco né Stalin*, 127–31.

MANUFACTURING, MINING, AND BANKING ENTERPRISES. See *Acracia*, 24 Oct. 1936; *La Batalla* (Barcelona), 22 Sept. 1936; *Boletín de Información, CNT-FAI*, 7 Aug., 30 Sept. 1936, also articles reproduced from this paper in *El Día Gráfico*, 5, 6, 14, 25 Aug. 1936; *Claridad*, 1 Mar. 1937 (speech by Vincente Uribe); *CNT* (Madrid), 23 Sept., 5–7 Oct. 1936; *CNT* (Paris), 26 Dec. 1947, 3 Dec. 1948, 20 Nov. 1949; *CNT-FAI-AIT Informationsdienst*, 15 Aug. 1936; *La Correspondencia de Valencia*, 2 Mar., 14 Aug. 1937; *Cultura Proletaria*, 25 Nov. 1939; *El Día Gráfico*, 6 Dec. 1936; *Diario Oficial de la Generalitat de Catalunya*, 28 Oct. 1936 (see preamble of the collectivization decree); *Documentos Históricos de España*, July 1938; *L'Espagne Antifasciste*, no. 8 (no date) and 21 Nov. 1936 (article by Christian Couderc); *España Libre* (Toulouse), 18 Sept. 1949; *Fragua Social*, as given in *Tierra y Libertad* (Barcelona), 13 Feb. 1937; *El Mercantil Valenciano*, 30 Aug. 1936, 11 May 1937 (statement by Belarmino Tomás); *Mundo Obrero* (Madrid), 20 Aug. 1936; *Nosotros*, 6, 14 July 1937, also article reproduced from this paper in *Boletín de Información, CNT-FAI*, 16 June 1937; *La Révolution Prolétarienne*, 25 Sept. 1936 (article by Jean Leunois); *El Socialista* (Madrid), 27 Aug. 1937; *Solidaridad Obrera* (Barcelona), 7, 18, 22 Aug., 4, 16, 19, 25, 29, 30 Sept., 21, 23 Oct., 18–21 Nov., 2, 5, 11, 15, 17, 19 Dec. 1936, 21, 28 Jan., 1, 24 Apr., 30 June, 15 Aug. (article by Cardona Rosell), 23 Oct. 1937; *Solidaridad Obrera* (Paris), 16 July 1949; *Spanish Revolution*, 5 Sept. 1936, 6 Aug. 1937; *Tierra y Libertad* (Barcelona), 30 Jan., 27 Mar., 24 July, 9, 16, 30 Oct., 13 Nov. 1937; *Treball*, 6 (speech by Angel Estivill), 13 Dec. 1936; *La Vanguardia*, 21 Apr. 1938 (interview with Vidal Rosell). See also José Díaz, *Tres años de lucha*, 350–66; H. E. Kaminski, *Ceux de Barcelone*, 223–27; Leval, *Espagne libertaire, 1936–1939*, 241–61; Gaston Leval, *Social Reconstruction in Spain*, 6–7, 10, 22–23, 32; Peter Merin, *Spain between Death and Birth*, 233–35; *Collectivisations*, 161, 170, 184, 189, 198, 201, 209. According to reliable information given to me by Antonio Villanueva, secretary at one time of the CNT metal workers' union of Valencia, the following firms were taken over by his union: Brunet, Davis, Mateu, Sanz, Torras, and Unión Naval de Levante.

URBAN REAL ESTATE. See, for example, *La Batalla* (Barcelona), 23 Sept. 1936; *Boletín de Información, CNT-FAI*, 29 Aug., 26 Sept., 7 Nov. 1936; *CNT* (Ma-

[480]

drid), 10 Aug. 1936; *El Día Gráfico*, 24 July, 29 Aug. 1936; *Mundo Obrero* (Madrid), 19–20 Nov., 2, 5, 17, 19 Dec. 1936, 20 Jan. 1937, 5 June 1938; *Tierra y Libertad* (Barcelona), 23 Jan. 1937 (article by Gaston Leval); decree of the minister of finance, published in the *Gaceta de Madrid*, 29 Sept. 1936, which confirms the appropriation of urban real estate by trade-union and political organizations; also statement to the press by the minister of finance, *El Pueblo*, 24 Dec. 1936; Vicente Sáenz, *España en sus gloriosas jornadas de julio y agosto de 1936*, 18; Lazarillo de Tormes (Benigno Bejarano), *España, cuña de la libertad*, 67.

MOTION-PICTURE THEATERS AND LEGITIMATE THEATERS. See *La Batalla* (Barcelona), 9 Aug. 1936; *Claridad*, 17 Aug. 1936; *CNT-AIT-FAI Informationsdienst*, 15 Aug. 1936; *La Humanitat*, 12 Sept. 1936; *Solidaridad Obrera* (Barcelona), 15 Aug., 19 Nov. 1936; *Tiempos Nuevos*, 1 Dec. 1936 (article by A. Souchy); *Ultima Hora*, 6 Aug. 1936; *La Veu de Catalunya*, 29 Oct. 1936; R. Louzon, *La contra revolución en España*, 34.

HOTELS, RESTAURANTS, BARS, AND DEPARTMENT STORES. See *Acracia*, 24 Oct. 1936; *La Batalla* (Barcelona), 27 Feb. 1937; *Boletín de Información, CNT-FAI*, as given in *El Día Gráfico*, 21 Aug., 25 Nov. 1936; *CNT* (Madrid), 7 Oct. 1936; *El Día Gráfico*, 24 July 1936; *Pravda*, 26 Sept. 1936 (article by Mikhail Koltzov); *Mundo Obrero* (Madrid), 2 Oct. 1936; *Política*, 15 Aug. 1936; *Solidaridad Obrera* (Barcelona), 1 Nov. 1936; *Spanish Revolution*, 6 Aug. 1937; *Tierra y Libertad* (Barcelona), 30 Oct. 1937; *Umbral*, no. 14, as given in *Documentos Históricas de España*, Mar. 1938; *La Vanguardia*, 24 Nov. 1937; Diego Abad de Santillán, *Por qué perdimos la guerra*, 80; Leval, *Social Reconstruction*, 32; Louzon, 34; *Collectivisations*, 27.

NEWSPAPERS AND PRINTING SHOPS. See *CNT* (Madrid), 24 July, 1 Sept., 7 Oct. 1936; *El Día Gráfico*, 28 July 1936; *Mundo Obrero* (Madrid), 21, 23 July, 27 Aug. 1936; *Treball*, 25 July 1936.

For additional information on the control by the labor unions of various branches of industry and trade, see Josep María Bricall, *Política econòmica de la Generalitat, 1936–1939*, Sam Dolgoff, *The Anarchist Collectives*, and Albert Pérez-Baró, *30 mesos de col·lectivisme a Catalunya*.

For the intervention by the ministry of industry and commerce in certain concerns in Madrid, see the *Gaceta de Madrid*, 27 July 1936; also *CNT* (Madrid), 3 Aug. 1936; *Mundo Obrero*, 1 Aug. 1936; *Política*, 18 Aug. 1936; and *Guerra y revolución en España, 1936–1939*, I, 269–71. It should be observed that the immense majority of these firms had previously been taken over by the labor unions. See, for example, Mikhail Koltzov in *Pravda*, 26 Sept. 1936.

Appendix II

For data on some of the agricultural collectives in different parts of the left camp, the following newspapers and periodicals published during and after

Appendixes

the Civil War may be consulted: *Acracia*, 19 July 1937 (Vallfogona, Castelló de Farfaña, Bellmunt de Urgel, La Portella, Os de Balaguer), 16, 17, 29, 30 Nov. 1937 (Belvis de Jarama, Alguaire, Serós, Mayals, Rosas de Llobregat), 16 Dec. 1937 (Palau de Anglesola); *La Batalla* (Barcelona), 26 Aug. 1936 (Raimut); *Boletín de Información, CNT-FAI*, 23 Sept. 1936 (Pont de Molins), 8 Oct. 1936 (Palafrugell, Caldas de Malavella), 24 Mar. 1937 (Cabra del Campo), 4, 17 Aug. 1937 (Candasnos, Peñarroya de Tastavins), 11 Feb. 1938 (Bujaraloz); *Castilla Libre*, 16 Apr. 1937 (Membrilla), as given in *Documentos Históricos de España*, Nov. 1937; *Claridad*, 14 Dec. 1936 (Guadasur), 16 Feb. 1937 (Badajoz); *CNT* (Madrid), 10, 17 Aug. 1936 (Puente de Arganda, Belvis de Jarama, Paracuellos de Jarama, Cobena, Villas Viejas), 1, 19, Sept. 1936 (Navilucillos, Utiel), 7–9 Oct. 1936 (collectives in the central region and Mestanza and Hellin), 19 June 1937 (Alcalá de Henares); *CNT* (Paris), 5, 12 Nov. 1938 (Madrid, García), 7, 28 Jan. 1949 (Hijar, Caspe, Angües, Fraga, Torrente de Cinca, Utillas, Peñalba, Farlete, Lécera, Aznara, La Fresnada, Mas de las Matas, Alarcón, Maella), 25 Dec. 1949 (Bot), 29 Jan. 1950 (Cerviá): *CNT* (Toulouse), 23 Nov. 1946 (Tivisa), 6 Sept. 1947 (Hospitalet de Llobregat), 17 Dec. 1950 (Villas Viejas); *Colectivismo*, 15 Aug. 1937 (Infantes), 15 Sept. 1937 (Iniesta), 15 Oct. 1937 (Castuera, Valdepeñas), 15 Dec. 1937 (Ibi), Jan.–Feb. 1938 (Marchamalo), 15 Mar. 1936 (Manises), 1 May 1936 (Los Estados de Santo Tomé), 1 June 1938 (Venta del Charco), 1 Aug. 1938 (Rafelguaraf), 1 Sept. 1938 (Villarubia de Santiago), 1 Dec. 1938 (Marchal); *La Correspondencia de Valencia*, 19 Oct. 1937 (Castuera); *Cultura Proletaria*, 2 Oct. 1937 (Peñarroya) 8, 29 Jan. 1938 (Perales de Tajuña, Hospitalet de Llobregat), 23 Apr. 1938 (Valencia province), 21, 28 Oct., 4, 11 Nov. 1939 (Calanda), 7, 21 Feb. 1948 (Farlete, Binéfar, Altamira, Fraga, Alcoriza, Monzón, Híjar, Alcañiz, Caspe), 28 Jan. 1950 (Ballobar); *Cultura y Acción*, 6 Aug. 1937 (Binéfar), 1 May 1937 (Alcañiz); *Documentos Históricos de España*, Dec. 1938 (Liria); *Fragua Social*, 17 June 1937 (Utiel), 28 Aug. 1937 (Cullera), 2 Dec. 1937 (Gramanet del Besós), 26 Feb. 1938 (Sueca); *Juventud Libre*, 31 Oct. 1936 (Utiel); *Le Libertaire*, 23 July 1948 (the Levante zone); *Mujeres Libres*, July 1937 (Calanda, Cabeza del Buey, Herrera del Castillo, Siruela); *Nosotros*, 19 Feb. 1937 (Simat de Valldigna), 24 June 1937 (Benaguacil), 1 Dec. 1937 (Madrid); *La Nouvelle Espagne Antifasciste*, 25 Nov. 1937 (Balsareny); *Orientaciones Nuevas*, 6 Feb. 1937 (Montmeló); *La Révolution Prolétarienne*, 10 Sept. 1937 (Segorbe); *Solidaridad Obrera* (Barcelona), 14 Aug. 1936 (Bujaraloz), 6 Oct. 1936 (La Figuera), 17, 19, 22, 28 Nov. 1936 (Valjunquera, Tarrassa, Premiá de Dalt, Martorell), 5, 11, 19, 27 Dec. 1936 (Serdanyola Ripollet, Villanueva y Geltrú, Sadurni de Noya, Rubi), 20 Jan. 1937 (Amposta), 26, 30 June 1937 (Oliete, Plá de Cabra), 10 Nov. 1937 (Lérida), 25 Dec. 1937 (Caravaca), 10 Dec. 1938 (Vilaboi); *Solidaridad Obrera* (Paris), 10 Feb. 1951 (Tamarite de Litera); *Tierra y Libertad* (Barcelona), 27 Aug. 1936 (Maella), 16 Jan. 1937 (Carcagente, Vallforguna de Balaguer, Pina de Ebro, Palafrugall), 13 Feb. 1937 (Llivia); *Umanità Nova*, 8 Jan. 1950 (Triana); *Umbral*, 24 July 1937 (Amposta); *Vida*, as given in *Solidaridad Obrera* (Barcelona), 22

Oct. 1937 (Beniopa, Oliva, Teresa, Tabernes de Valldigna, Benifairó, Simat). For additional data on rural collectives, see *Timón* (Barcelona), July 1938 (article by Agustín Souchy); Franz Borkenau, *The Spanish Cockpit*, 148–51; *Las colectividades campesinas, 1936–1939*; Sam Dolgoff, ed., *The Anarchist Collectives*; Gaston Leval, *Le communisme*, 60–66; Gaston Leval, *Espagne libertaire, 1936–39*, 83–256; Gaston Leval, *Né Franco né Stalin*, 143–300; Frank Mintz, *L'autogestion dans l'Espagne révolutionnaire*, 51–78, 98–111, and the latter's bibliography on collectivization published by Archives Internationales de Sociologie de la Coopération et Développement (supplément à *Communauté*, July–Dec. 1967); José Peirats, *Los anarquistas en la crisis política española*, 147–72; José Peirats, *La CNT en la revolución española*, I, 302–26, 331–53; Agustín Souchy, *Entre los campesinos de Aragón; Collectivisations*; also materials given in Appendix III.

Appendix III

Obviously no attempt has been made to cover in detail all aspects of the libertarian collectives. The interested reader should consult the following materials: *Boletín de Información, CNT-FAI*, 20 Feb. 1937 (Tabernes de Valldigna), 17 Aug. 1937 (Peñarroya de Tastavins); *CNT* (Madrid), 7 Oct. 1936 (Membrilla), 27 May 1937 (Torrevelilla); *CNT* (Paris), 24 Dec. 1948 (Binéfar), 27 Nov. 1949 (Santa Magdalena de Pulpis); *CNT* (Toulouse), 23 Aug. 1947 (Graus), 22 July 1951 (Ballobar); *Cultura y Acción*, 13 Mar. 1937 (Mosqueruela); *L'Espagne Antifasciste*, 21 Nov. 1936 (Alcoy, Enguerra, Játiva); *Fragua Social*, 6 Apr. 1937 (Bujaraloz), also article from this paper on Utiel, reproduced in *Boletín de Información, CNT-FAI*, 19 June 1937; *Juventud Libre*, 14 Nov. 1936 (Pedrilla); *Le Libertaire*, 15 July 1937, as given in *Spanish Revolution*, 6 Aug. 1937; *Mar y Tierra*, 15 Aug. 1937 (La Nucia); *Mujeres Libres*, July 1937 (Calanda); *Nosotros*, 24 Feb. 1937 (Beniopa); *Solidaridad Obrera* (Barcelona), 13, 19, 27 Nov. 1936 (Bujaraloz, Velilla de Ebro, Lécera, Farlete); *Solidaridad Obrera* (Mexico City), 17 May 1947 (Graus); *Solidaridad Obrera* (Paris), 24 Feb., 10 Mar. 1951 (Mas de las Matas), 7, 14, 21 Apr. 1951 (Graus), 23, 29 June 1951 (Alcolea de Cinca), 7, 14 July 1951 (Alcorisa); *Tierra y Libertad* (Barcelona), 17, 24 Sept. 1936 (Maella); 30 Jan. 1937 (Magdalena de Pulpis); *Tierra y Libertad* (Mexico City), 25 Jan. 1947 (Asco); 10 July 1947 (Ballobar); *Umanità Nova*, 25 Dec. 1950 (Santa Magdalena de Pulpis); Franz Borkenau, *The Spanish Cockpit*, 166–67; *Las colectividades campesinas, 1936–1939*; *Collectivisations*, 233–42; José Duque, "La situación de Aragón al comienzo de la guerra," 2–4; José Gabriel, *La vida y la muerte en Aragón*, 146; H. E. Kaminski, *Ceux de Barcelone*, 118–25; Aristide Lapeyre, *Le problème espagnol*, 18–20; Gaston Leval, *Espagne libertaire, 1936–39*, 85–236; Gaston Leval, *Né Franco né Stalin*, 143–300; Gaston Leval, *Social Reconstruction in Spain*, 12–13, 15, 17–18; José Peirats, *La CNT en la revolución española*, I, 319–26; Alardo Prats, *Vanguardia y retaguardia de Aragón*, 84–93; Agustín Souchy, *Entre los campesinos de Aragón*.

Notes

Chapter 1

1. See *Le contrat de travail dans la république espagnole*, 18.

2. *España*, 513. See also Edward E. Malefakis, *Agrarian Reform and Peasant Revolution in Spain*, 366–67; Antonio Ramos Oliveira, *Politics, Economics and Men of Modern Spain, 1808–1946*, 493; Richard A. H. Robinson, *The Origins of Franco's Spain*, 204–5.

3. *Discursos frente al parlamento*, 224.

4. "The socialist-controlled mixed juries [labor courts] caused trouble. The jury of Salamanca province permitted employment of UGT [socialist union] members only and forbade dismissals. Reapers were to be paid 12 pesetas for an eight-hour day, and since overtime was inevitable at harvest-time the daily wage rose to 19.65 pesetas, more than was earned by a skilled urban worker. With prices depressed, small holders simply could not pay these sums and joined the ranks of the unemployed laborers" (Robinson, 121).

5. For a brief account of the developments leading to the formation of the Popular Front, see Gabriel Jackson, *The Spanish Republic and the Civil War, 1931–1939*, 185–87; also chapter 7 of this volume.

6. *El Debate*, 6 Mar. 1936.

7. "In the two and one-half months between 1 May and the outbreak of the civil war on 18 July, the Ministry of Labor recorded 192 agricultural strikes, as many as during the whole of 1932 and almost half as many as during that entire year of trouble, 1933. The scale of the strikes was considerably greater than it had been previously" (Malefakis, 371).

8. Editorials in *El Obrero de la Tierra* protesting against the procrastination of the government can be found in the issues of 28 Mar., 11, 25 Apr. 1936. For the best study of the crisis in the countryside during the months before the Civil War, see Malefakis, 364–87, 375–78. This magisterial work, which won the American Historical Association's Adams prize as the best book on any aspect of European history to be published in 1970, provides the most thorough study in any language of land tenure, agrarian reform, and peasant revolution in Spain in the years before the Civil War.

9. Speech, reprinted in José Díaz, *Tres años de lucha*, 162.

10. Malefakis, who, as stated in note 8, has made the most thorough study of the agrarian crisis before the war, considers the figure of ninety villages excessive (369, n. 17).

11. César Falcón in *La Correspondance Internationale*, 9 May 1936. See also Pedro Checa, ibid.; E. Varga, ibid., 4 June 1936; the Spanish refugee periodical, *El Socialista* (Algiers), 16 Oct. 1944; *Times*, 15 Apr. 1936 (Madrid correspondent); Gerald Brenan, *The Spanish Labyrinth*, 312; José María Capo, *España desnuda*, 87–89; Horsfall Carter in *Listener*, 29 Apr. 1936; José Plá, *Historia de la segunda república española*, IV, 356–57; Ramos Oliveira, 539. The work by Capo acquires greater authority from the commendatory preface by

Marcelino Domingo, minister of education in the government formed after the February 1936 elections.

12. Paul Nizon in the *International Press Correspondence*, 1 Aug. 1936. Although published in August, this article was written before the outbreak of the Civil War.

13. Malefakis, 373–74, 383, and n. 69. See also Salvador de Madariaga, *Spain*, 452–53; speech in the Cortes by José María Cid, the right-wing Agrarian party deputy, giving his version of the situation in the countryside, *Diario de las Sesiones de Cortes*, 1 July 1936, 1743–53; Ricardo de la Cierva, *Historia de la guerra civil española*, 697.

14. Within the limits of this brief account, it is impossible to do more than give a rough idea of the magnitude of the strike wave; even to enumerate all the strikes would require many pages. The general picture given here is based on reports in the following Spanish newspapers: *El Adelanto* (Salamanca), *La Batalla* (Barcelona), *Claridad* (Madrid), *El Día Gráfico* (Barcelona), *Diario de Burgos* (Burgos), *La Libertad* (Madrid), *Mundo Obrero* (Madrid), *El Noticiero* (Saragossa), *Política* (Madrid), *El Socialista* (Madrid), *El Sol* (Madrid), *Solidaridad Obrera* (Barcelona), *Unión* (Seville).

15. *Gaceta de Madrid*, 1 Mar. 1936.

16. See, for example, the manifesto signed by their various associations, *El Sol*, 1 Mar. 1936; also Joaquín Arrarás, *Historia de la segunda república española*, IV, 79–80; *Dictamen de la comisión sobre ilegitimidad de poderes actuantes en 18 de julio de 1936*, 54–55; Robinson, 269. The liberal historian Jackson says: "Anarchist pistoleros occasionally forced employers to take on men who had never been their employees" (213).

17. *Rio Tinto Company Limited, Report of the Transactions at the Sixty-third Ordinary General Meeting*, 7.

18. *ABC* (Seville), 20 Jan. 1937.

19. For the best accounts of the stoppage, apart from the local press, and of the conflict between the Socialist and anarchosyndicalist unions, see Pierre Broué and Emile Témime, *La révolution et la guerre d'Espagne*, 79–80; Arrarás, *Historia*, IV, 327–29.

20. For information covering this period I am indebted to the following sources: Arrarás, *Historia*, IV, 441–67; Raymond Carr, *Spain, 1808–1939*, 626–36; José María Gil Robles, *No fué posible la paz*, 134–41; Jackson, 121–68; Alejandro Lerroux, *La pequeña historia*, 260–65; Madariaga, *Spain*, 421–43; Ramos Oliveira, 487–547; Robinson, 134–92; Hugh Thomas, *The Spanish Civil War* (rev. ed., 1965), 112–24.

21. Robinson, 135.

22. Quoted in ibid., 140.

23. Ibid., 141–42.

24. For accounts of the October rebellion, see materials cited in n. 20.

25. Clara Campoamor, *La révolution espagnole vue par une républicaine*, 71–72.

26. Jackson, 167.

27. See, for example, speech on 11 Apr. 1936 by the secretary of the Communist party, demanding the imprisonment and execution of Lerroux and Gil Robles, as reprinted in Díaz, 162.

28. Cierva, *Historia*, 693–94; Stanley Payne, *Falange*, 99–100.

29. Payne, *Falange*, 100; Robinson, 387, n. 97.

30. Vicente Palacio Atard, essay in *Aproximación historica de la guerra española, 1936–39*, 151; see also Stanley Payne, *Politics and the Military in Modern Spain*, 316.

31. In preparing this summary of events the newspapers mentioned in note 14, as well as the following materials, were consulted: Arrarás, *Historia*, IV, 66–67, 82–89, 114–15, 122–37, 186–89, 205–8, 228–30, 323–68, 371–73; Broué and Témime, 65–82; *Causa General*, 13–24; Cierva, *Historia*, 692–740, 792–95; Díaz, 172–73; José Díaz de Ville-

gas, *Guerra de liberación*, 45–48; Estado Mayor Central del Ejército, *Historia de la guerra de liberación, 1936–39*, I, 420–57; Gil Robles, *No fué posible la paz*, 630–707, 748–58, 761–65; *Guerra y revolución en España, 1936–1939*, I, 92–93, 102–3; Jackson, 196–232; Lerroux, *La pequeña historia*, 464–77; K. L. Maidanik, *Ispanskii proletariat y natsionalnerevoliutsionnoi voini, 1936–1937*, 64–66; Stanley Payne, *The Spanish Revolution*, 185–214; Plá, IV, 290–300, 311–23, 341–56, 375–83, 411–22; Indalecio Prieto, *Convulsiones de España*, I, 157–62, III, 133–34, 144; Ramos Oliveira, 539–41, 546–47; Robinson, 274–75, 392–93, n. 149; Carlos Seco Serrano, *Historia de España*, VI, 128–45; Thomas, 136–54, 170–77.

32. *The Politics of Modern Spain*, 168.

33. José Martín Blázquez, *I Helped to Build an Army*, 67.

34. "Peasants, Politics, and Civil War in Spain, 1931–1939," in Robert J. Bezucha, ed., *Modern European Social History*, 192–227.

35. Felipe Bertrán Güell, *Preparación y desarrollo del alzamiento nacional*, 116; see also Cierva, *Historia*, 763–64. The official history of the rising, Joaquín Arrarás, ed., *Historia de la cruzada española*, II, 467, reveals that a meeting of generals was held early in March "to prepare a defensive action should a situation of very grave danger for the country arise as was feared by the course of events." See also Arrarás, *Historia*, IV, 94–95; Manuel Goded (son of General Goded, leader of the revolt in Barcelona), *Un "faccioso" cien por cien*, 26.

36. Bertrán Güell, *Preparación*, 99–100.

37. Reported in *Manchester Guardian*, 4 Dec. 1937. See also reproduction of documents in the handwriting of Goicoechea, recording his interview with Mussolini on 31 March 1934, in *How Mussolini Provoked the Spanish Civil War*, 6–9.

38. *Memorias de la conspiración*, 34–41. A documented account of this meeting with the Italian government can be found in John F. Coverdale's excellent work, *Italian Intervention in the Spanish Civil War*, 50–54.

39. Lizarza, 40.

40. Essay in *Aproximación*, 73.

41. Ibid., 40–41. This is also the view of José María Gil Robles, the CEDA leader (see chapter 7, text to note 31).

42. Julio Romano, *Sanjurjo*, 188. For other conspiracies before and after the elections, see Cierva, *Historia*, 763–64. Because of his prestige and seniority, Sanjurjo was leader-designate of the military rebellion in July 1936, but was killed in a plane crash at the outbreak of the war when flying to Spain from Portugal, where he had been in exile. Leadership of the revolt was subsequently taken over by General Francisco Franco who, by decree of 29 September 1936, was named generalissimo of all the armed forces and head of state by the rebel Junta de Defensa Nacional set up in Burgos at the outbreak of the Civil War.

43. Quoted in Cierva, *Historia*, 740.

44. Arrarás, *Historia*, IV, 50–51, 56–61; Cierva, *Historia*, 639–41; Estado Mayor Central del Ejército, 420–22; *Guerra y revolución*, I, 81–82; Payne, *Politics*, 310–13; Robinson, 250–51, 384–85; Fernando de Valdesoto, *Francisco Franco*, 98–99.

45. Speech, 23 Feb. 1936, as reprinted in Díaz, 151.

46. Lizarza, 95–106. See also Cierva, *Historia*, 767. For the directives issued by Mola to the conspirators, see ibid., 769–85.

47. Ramos Oliveira, 544–45; Payne, *Politics*, 314; Robinson, 277; Thomas, 141.

48. *Politics*, 314–15. See also Cierva, *Historia*, 757–58.

49. Essay in *Aproximación*, 152–54.

50. *El Sol*, 19 Mar. 1936.

51. 19 Mar. 1936, as quoted in Cierva, *Historia*, 805.

52. For the best accounts of the conspiratorial activities in the army, see note 177, this chapter.

53. Because of the peculiarities of the electoral system, which favored large coalitions, the Popular Front won 258 seats in the Cortes, the center 62, and the right 152, although the number of votes cast was as follows: Popular Front, 4,206,156; center, 681,047; right, 3,783,601 (figures given by Madariaga, *Spain*, 445). While the figures given by various other sources differ, they nonetheless reveal that the popular vote was fairly equally divided between the Popular Front and the center-right. See, for example, Arrarás, *Historia* IV, 75–76; Payne, *Politics*, 311; Robinson, 248.

54. *La Libertad*, 16 Jan. 1936.

55. *Gaceta de Madrid*, 25 Apr. 1934.

56. Ibid., 24 Mar. 1935.

57. *Política del frente popular en agricultura*, 14. See also *Claridad*, 5, 26 Oct. 1935; *Democracia*, 22 Nov. 1935; *La reforma agraria en España*, 40–41; Robinson, 202–3.

58. *España*, 512. See also E. Allison Peers, *The Spanish Tragedy*, 145–46; Robinson, 161.

59. Robinson, 266–67. For Communist attacks on the church, demanding the end of subsidies and the expropriation of its wealth, see Díaz, 155, 163, 177, 191–92, 216.

60. Robinson, 266–67. See also Arrarás, *Historia*, IV, 222–26. After the outbreak of the Civil War, Barnés published a decree directing local authorities to take possession, in the name of the state, of all religious schools (*Gaceta de Madrid*, 28 July 1936).

61. For examples of this hostility, see Cierva, *Historia*, 758–59.

62. For a balanced account of these grievances by a liberal republican officer, see Colonel Jesús Pérez Salas, *Guerra en España, 1936–1939*, 22, 47–53, 85; see also Jackson, 66–67, 171; Madariaga, *Spain*, 489–90; Emilio Mola Vidal, *Obras completas*, 1043–1101; Payne, *Politics*, 266–76, 281, 284–85, 294, 300–304; Jorge Vigón Suerodíaz, *Milicia y política*, 287–96.

63. Speech in the Cortes, *Diario de las Sesiones de Cortes*, 3 Apr. 1936, 222.

64. José Manuel Liébana and G. Orizana, *El movimiento nacional*, 5.

65. Interview reported in *La Libertad*, 21 Feb. 1936.

66. *Diario de las Sesiones de Cortes*, 3 Apr. 1936, 223–24.

67. Ibid., 15 Apr. 1936, 288–89.

68. *Politics*, 318.

69. *Diario de las Sesiones de Cortes*, 15 Apr. 1936, 293, 297. An excellent account of Calvo Sotelo's policies is given in Robinson, to whose book I am indebted for bringing to my attention Calvo Sotelo's speech from which the above excerpts have been taken.

70. Robinson, 270–71, 394, n. 168.

71. Gil Robles, *No fué posible la paz*, 573–74, 623, n. 63. "Little by little," writes Cierva, "Gil Robles began to lose control of his most aggressive militants, who abandoned the ranks of the CEDA *en masse* to join Falange Española or the National Front [comprising the Alphonsine and Carlist monarchists]" (*Historia*, 741).

72. See text to nn. 22 and 23 this chapter.

73. See Robinson, 169, 173, 206, 208–12, 214, 244–45. I am greatly indebted to this superb chronological and analytical study of Gil Robles's policies during the 1933–39 period.

74. *Historia*, 740.

75. Robinson, 194, 226. In his memoirs, Gil Robles states that he turned down all suggestions by friends and collaborators that the CEDA should abandon its legal tactic (*No fué posible la paz*, 574).

76. José María de Fontana, *Los catalanes en la guerra de España*, 43. See also Gil Robles, *No fué posible la paz*, 623, n. 63, in which he mentions that the youth movement of the Derecha Regional Valenciana, one of the parties belonging to the CEDA, "agreed enthusiastically . . . to give their resolute support to those who were preparing the rising."

77. Cierva, *Historia*, 743–44.

78. *Diario de las Sesiones de Cortes*, 15 Apr. 1936, 300.

79. *No fué posible la paz*, 688, n. 25.

80. *Diario de las Sesiones de Cortes*, 19 May 1936, 696–97.

81. Quoted in Gil Robles, *No fué posible la paz*, 684.

82. *Historia*, 787.

83. Essay in Raymond Carr, ed., *The Republic and the Civil War in Spain*, 190.

84. *No fué posible la paz*, 684–85.

85. This assassination, which did much to unite the forces of the right, is discussed later in this chapter (see text to nn. 178–85).

86. Gil Robles, *No fué posible la paz*, 686, n. 23.

87. Ibid., 607, 787–89, 794, 797–99.

88. Ibid., 730.

89. Ibid., 798, n. 50. For further information on the transfer of 500,000 pesetas to General Mola, see Arrarás, ed., *Historia de la cruzada*, III, 456–57; Arrarás, *Historia*, III, 317.

90. Quoted by Marqués de Luca de Tena, *ABC* (Madrid), 1 May 1968; see also Cierva, *Historia*, 742–43.

91. Cierva, *Historia*, 741; see also Gil Robles, *No fué posible la paz*, 789.

92. Gil Robles, *No fué posible la paz*, 788.

93. Ibid., 789.

94. Agustín Calvet's political sympathies for Azaña are mentioned by Arrarás, *Historia*, IV, 325, who quotes from this article, and were confirmed to me by Pedro Voltes Bou, the director of the Instituto Municipal de Historia de Barcelona, to whom I am indebted for a reproduction of the entire article.

95. The belief of the leaders of the rebellion that after declaring martial law everything would be plain sailing is confirmed by Juan Antonio Ansaldo, who helped in the preparation of the insurrection (*Para que . . . ?*, 120). "Some of the leading officers responsible for the July rising," affirms Ricardo de la Cierva, "were fearful, even before the event, of the possibility of a long and bloody war, but the great majority hoped that victory would follow their coup almost immediately" ("The Nationalist Army in the Spanish Civil War," essay in Carr, ed., *The Republic and the Civil War in Spain*, 190).

96. Speech reported in *Solidaridad Obrera* (Barcelona), 22 Dec. 1936.

97. Ibid., 17 Jan. 1936.

98. Ibid., 2 Apr. 1936.

99. In his diary, on 4 Jan. 1933, Azaña, premier at the time, describes Casares Quiroga, who was interior minister, as "this good friend who is the best I have in the government" (Joaquín Arrarás, *Memorias íntimas de Azaña*, 109).

100. *La Libertad*, 16 Jan. 1936. In the matter of agriculture, the program promised: reduction of rents and taxes, suppression of usury, increase of agricultural credits, revaluation of agricultural produce, stimulation of exports, irrigation and afforestation, settlement of families on the land, and the repeal of the law of leases and the law providing for the return of their estates to landowners implicated in the Sanjurjo rising.

101. See his speeches, reported in *El Socialista* (Madrid), 2 May 1936; *La Libertad*, 26 May 1936; also quotations from Prieto in Arrarás, *Historia*, IV, 205–7.

102. *Historia de la guerra en España*, 4–5; see also Gabriel Morón, *Política de ayer y política de mañana*, 25.
103. *El Socialista* (Madrid), 14 Jan. 1936.
104. Malefakis, 254–55.
105. Ibid., 393.
106. Pp. 273–74.
107. For a critical account of the attempt to "Bolshevize" the Socialist movement and for the intraparty struggle among the three factions, headed by Julián Besteiro (right-wing), Indalecio Prieto (center), and Francisco Largo Caballero (left-wing), see Gabriel Mario de Coco, *Anti-Caballero*. See also Arrarás, *Historia*, IV, 139–41, 249–66; Robinson, 260–61, 271–72.
108. *Claridad*, 19 Mar. 1936.
109. See, for example, speech in Oviedo, *La Libertad*, 16 June 1936.
110. Robinson, 137. His position has not changed in 1936. See, for example, Gil Robles, *No fué posible la paz*, 657.
111. For a sympathetic biography of Besteiro, see Andrés Saborit, *Julián Besteiro*.
112. Interview given to Mikhail Koltzov (*Pravda*'s special correspondent) on 26 Aug. 1936, as published in *Novyi Mir*, Apr. 1938, 40. The interview was part of Koltzov's diary, which *Novyi Mir* serialized between April and September 1938 under the title "Ispanskii Dnevnik" (Spanish Diary). It was published in book form in 1957, fifteen years after his liquidation by Stalin (see chapter 2), as Volume 3 of *Izbrannye proizvedeniia* (Selected Works) and translated into Spanish by Ruedo Ibérico, Paris, in 1963, under the title *Diario de la guerra de España*. The diary is hereafter referred to as Koltzov, "Ispanskii Dnevnik," *Novyi Mir*.
113. *Mis recuerdos*, 145, 153.
114. See, for example, Zugazagoitia, 4; Prieto, *Convulsiones*, III, 158–59, 164; *Claridad*'s version of the incident (31 May 1936), as given in Fernando Díaz-Plaja, *La historia de España en sus documentos. El siglo XX. Dictadura . . . República 1923–36*, 870–72.
115. *Spain*, 455, 457.
116. See chapter 5, text to nn. 8 and 9.
117. See speech by Wenceslao Carrillo (a Largo Caballero Socialist), *La Correspondencia de Valencia*, 4 Sept. 1937.
118. See chapter 8, text to nn. 69–76.
119. *Claridad*, 19 Mar. 1936; *La Libertad*, 4 Apr. 1936.
120. Díaz, 165, 190, 194, 206.
121. *The Spanish Revolution*, 166–67. See also Largo Caballero's letter to José Bullejos, 20 Nov. 1939, as given in Largo Caballero, *¿Qué se puede hacer?*, 20–24.
122. See, for example, interview reported in *Claridad*, 7 Dec. 1935; speech, ibid., 11 Apr. 1936.
123. See article by José Díaz, general secretary of the Communist party, in *Correspondencia Internacional*, 17 Apr. 1936, as reprinted in Díaz, 133–39.
124. Ibid.
125. See chapter 6.
126. Speech on 11 Apr. 1926, as reprinted in Díaz, 165.
127. Speech in Cortes, *Diario de las Sesiones de Cortes*, 15 Apr. 1936, 311.
128. Article in *Correspondencia Internacional*, 17 Apr. 1936, as reprinted in Díaz, 133–39.
129. *Manuel*, 164.
130. Koltzov, "Ispanskii Dnevnik," *Novyi Mir*, Apr. 1938, 42.

131. José Duque, who became a member of the Central Committee of the Communist party in 1937, confirmed to me that in the months before the Civil War leading Communists were secretly hostile to Largo Caballero's policy.

132. See José Bullejos (a former secretary of the Communist party), *Europa entre dos guerras, 1918–1938*, 191–92.

133. *International Press Correspondence*, 9 May 1936.

134. *Claridad*, 9 Apr. 1936.

135. *El Socialista* (Madrid) 3 July 1936.

136. Ibid., 2 July 1936.

137. Article in *Correspondencia Internacional*, 17 Apr. 1936, reprinted in Díaz, 133–39.

138. *El Mercantil Valenciano*, 16 May 1936.

139. Eduardo Ortega Gasset, quoted in Gil Robles, *No fué posible la paz*, 450.

140. Zugazagoitia, 275.

141. See Arrarás, *Historia*, IV, 103–8, 175–78; Prieto's speech in the Cortes, *Diario de las Sesiones de Cortes*, 7 Apr. 1936, 242–50; Gil Robles, *No fué posible la paz*, 585, 592–96, 618; Arrarás, ed., *Historia de la cruzada*, II, 477, 488; Largo Caballero, *Mis recuerdos*, 155; Lerroux, *La pequeña historia*, 462; Joaquín Maurín, *Revolución y contrarrevolución en España* (epilogue, 1965), 237–38.

142. See Morón, 60–63.

143. See, for example, Gil Robles, *No fué posible la paz*, 450; Miguel Maura, *Así cayó Alfonso XIII*, 58, 153, 216–22.

144. *El Socialista* (Madrid), 2 May 1936.

145. As given in Arrarás, *Historia*, IV, 157.

146. Plá, IV, 384.

147. Maura, 222.

148. See statement issued by the executive, *El Socialista* (Madrid), 8 May 1936.

149. Payne, *The Spanish Revolution*, 195.

150. Speech in Mexico City, 21 Apr. 1940, as published in Indalecio Prieto, *Inauguración del círculo "Pablo Iglesias" de México*, 19. See also his statement in *El Mercantil Valenciano*, 16 May 1936.

151. *Obras completas*, Introduction, III, xxxi–ii.

152. *Yo fui ministro de Negrín*, 112.

153. *Mis recuerdos*, 115.

154. Speech on 24 Jan. 1947, as given in Saborit, *Julián Besteiro*, 364.

155. See n. 150, above.

156. *No fué posible la paz*, 617–19. See also Arrarás, *Historia*, IV, 274–76; Robinson, 263–64, 391, n. 137.

157. *Diario de las Sesiones de Cortes*, 19 May 1936, 690–94.

158. See for example, General Nuñez de Prado, as quoted by Diego Martínez Barrio in *Hoy*, 13 Apr. 1940; Major Aberri, ibid., 29 July 1939; Dolores Ibárruri (La Pasionaria), *El único camino*, 238, 252, 268; Largo Caballero, *Mis recuerdos*, 162–63; Prieto, *Convulsiones*, III, 143–44; Indalecio Prieto, *Palabras al viento*, 279–81; Zugazagoitia, 41.

159. Zugazagoitia, 23.

160. *El Sol* published six articles by Maura between 18 and 27 June.

161. Palacio Atard, essay in *Aproximación*, 152, Cierva, *Historia*, 807; Gil Robles, *No fué posible la paz*, 743–44.

162. Essay in *Aproximación*, 163–64. See also Cierva, *Historia*, 765, 807. As Verle B. Johnston observes, "In several cases assuming command necessitated the removal of superior officers of strong republican sympathies. This is one facet of the rebellion

which has not always been appreciated by students of the Civil War" (*Legions of Babel*, 20). Robinson, 376, n. 3, makes the following important point: "Conspirators were, in the main, *africanistas* removed from active commands in late February 1936; they had in most cases to get rid of Azañista garrison-commanders before 'pronouncing' against the government."

163. Azaña, *Obras*, Introduction, III, xxxii.

164. Zugazagoitia, 5–6.

165. Gil Robles, *No fué posible la paz*, 608.

166. Robinson, 288.

167. Díaz, 188 (speech, 1 June 1936); 199–200 (article in *Mundo Obrero* [Madrid], June 1936).

168. *Politics*, 330–31.

169. Reproduced in Manuel Aznar, *Historia militar de la guerra de España*, 31–32.

170. Ibid., 30.

171. Cierva, *Historia*, 785, 803; Payne, *Politics*, 334–35; Robinson, 288.

172. Payne, *Politics*, 332; Robinson, 288, 405, n. 274.

173. Robinson, 287–88.

174. As given in Cierva, *Historia*, 785. For the negative attitude of some officers toward the idea of a coup against the government, see ibid., 787; Palacio Atard, essay in *Aproximación*, 160–61, quoting General Queipo de Llano; Gil Robles, *No fué posible la paz*, 726–27; Antonio Olmedo Delgado and Lieutenant General José Cuesta Monereo, *General Queipo de Llano*, 85.

175. Pp. 735–816.

176. Ibid., 736–37.

177. Ibid., 437, n. 2. For other accounts of the conspiratorial activities of military leaders and their disagreements, see essay by Cierva, *Aproximación*, 72–79; Arrarás, *Historia*, IV, 295–322, 391–402; Jaime del Burgo, *Conspiración y guerra civil*, 521–52; Maximiano García Venero, *El General Fanjul*, 215–83; Gil Robles, *No fué posible la paz*, 709–87; *Guerra y revolución*, I, 96–102; Lizarza, 62–142; Payne, *Politics*, 314–40; Payne, *Falange*, 89–115; Robinson, 277–88; Seco Serrano, VI, 145–52; Thomas, 153–80; General Jorge Vigón, *General Mola*, 87–110.

178. Ramos Oliveira, 547. For accounts of the assassinations of Castillo and Calvo Sotelo, see Arrarás, *Historia*, IV, 345–68; Broué and Témime, 80–82; *Causa General*, 13–24; Cierva, *Historia*, 792–95; Estado Mayor Central del Ejército, 451–57; Gil Robles, *No fué posible la paz*, 746–56; Jackson, 229–30; Prieto, *Convulsiones*, I, 157–62, III, 133–34, 144; Robinson, 274–75; Seco Serrano, VI, 144–45; Thomas, 169–73; Zugazagoitia, 28–34.

179. *Historia*, 740.

180. Ibid., 792.

181. Article in *El Liberal*, 14 July 1936, quoted in Arrarás, *Historia*, IV, 362–63.

182. *El Sol*, 14 July 1936.

183. Zugazagoitia, 16–17.

184. As quoted in José Gutiérrez-Ravé, *Las cortes errantes del frente popular*, 99–100. "The accusation that the crime had been committed by the government's own agents," he writes, "was deleted from the official record at the request of the president of the Cortes, Diego Martínez Barrio, and did not appear in the official *Diario de las Sesiones de Cortes*" (ibid., 100).

185. Quoted in Arrarás, *Historia*, IV, 366; Zugazagoitia, 16.

186. See Díaz, 156, 165.

187. Indalecio Prieto in *Correo de Asturias*, 1 May 1943.

188. His announcement was not published at the time, but is quoted by Martínez Barrio in *Hoy*, 20 Apr. 1940.

189. Zugazagoitia, 40.

190. For corroborative testimony, see General José Asensio in *Nuestra España*, Nov. 1939, and Martín Blázquez, 112.

191. *El General Miaja*, 124–25.

192. When interviewed by me. It is noteworthy that Antonio López Fernández, General Miaja's secretary and admirer, states that the general did not approve of the manner in which the weapons were handed over (*Defensa de Madrid*, 64).

193. *Hoy*, 20 Apr. 1940.

194. César Falcón, *Madrid*, 60.

195. See, for example, Cierva, *Historia*, 608.

196. Campoamor, 42, 133, n. 1, confirms and supports Martínez Barrio's opposition to the distribution of arms. Clara Campoamor was a Radical party deputy until 1934 and mixed in Madrid political circles at the time of the rising (ibid., ii).

197. *Hoy*, 20 Apr. 1940.

198. *Correo de Asturias*, 1 May 1943.

199. *Hoy*, 27 Apr. 1940.

200. Quoted in Bertrán Güell, *Preparación*, 76; Rafael Fernández de Castro y Pedrera, *Vidas de soldados ilustres de la nueva España*, 190; and Joaquín Pérez Madrigal, *Augurios, estallido y episodios de la guerra civil*, 168; all three were supporters of the military rising.

201. Quoted in Gil Robles, *No fué posible la paz*, 791. Details of this conversation were given by Sánchez Román to someone who enjoyed Gil Robles's absolute confidence. Ibid.

202. This offer is confirmed by Ino Bernard, *Mola, mártir de España*, 77; José María Iribarren, *Mola*, 107; Carlos de la Válgoma, *Mola*, 406; Vigón, 115. However, it is not mentioned by Martínez Barrio.

203. According to Sánchez Román, quoted in Gil Robles, *No fué posible la paz*, 791.

204. Ibid.

205. *Hoy*, 27 Apr. 1940.

206. Ibid. García Venero reproduces a point-by-point program of conciliation, given to him years later by Ramón Feced, who became a member of Martínez Barrio's government, and drawn up by Sánchez Román for submission to the insurgent generals (*El General Fanjul*, 287–89). See also García Venero, *Historia de las internacionales en España*, III, 102–8.

207. The complete list of names, as given in the *Gaceta de Madrid*, 19 July 1936, was as follows: Diego Martínez Barrio, Manuel Blasco Garzón, Antonio Lara, Plácido Alvarez Buylla, Bernardo Giner de los Rios, Felipe Sánchez Román, Justino Azcárate, Ramón Feced, Enrique Ramos, Augusto Barcia, Marcelino Domingo, José Giral, Juan Lluhí y Vallesca, and José Miaja.

208. *Hoy*, 20 Apr. 1940. See also Marcelino Domingo, *España ante el mundo*, 231.

209. Zugazagoitia, 45.

210. Olmedo Delgado and Cuesta Monereo, 98–103. See also Thomas, 186–88.

211. Cierva, *Historia*, 767.

212. Cierva, essay in *Aproximación*, 78.

213. Cierva, *Historia*, 767.

214. See *Guerra y revolución*, I, 123–26; Olmedo Delgado and Cuesta Monereo, 138; Vigón, 185.

215. Olmedo Delgado and Cuesta Monereo, 137.
216. See also Liébana and Orizana, 175.
217. See also Francisco J. de Raymundo, *Cómo se inició el glorioso movimiento nacional en Valladolid y la gesta heroica del Alto del Léon*.
218. See, for example, Manuel Sánchez del Arco, *El sur de España en la reconquista de Madrid*, 24; J. Guzmán de Alfarache, *¡18 de julio!*, 68, 92, Angel Gollonet and José Morales, *Sangre y fuego, Malaga*, 24–25; Olmedo Delgado and Cuesta Monereo, 110–17.
219. See, for example, Liébana and Orizana, 144–45.
220. *Politics*, 278–79. For Miguel Maura's own account of the creation of the assault guard (which he achieved with Galarza's help) and of the problems of public order during his incumbency, as well as for his unqualified praise of Galarza as "an exemplary collaborator, discreet, capable, active, and loyal," see Maura, 265–76.
221. Zugazagoitia, 134.
222. IV, 381.
223. Time given by Barrio in *Hoy*, 27 Apr. 1940.
224. *El Noticiero*, 23 July 1936.
225. *Politics*, 334–35.
226. See decree, dated 29 Sept. 1936, as given in Fernando Díaz-Plaja, *La historia de España en sus documentos: La guerra, 1936–1939*, 249–50. For information on the initial disagreements among the rebel hierarchy over the terms of the decree, see Payne, *Falange*, 129–31; Payne, *Politics*, 369–73; Thomas, 365–66.
227. See Bolín, *Spain*, 10–52, for a fascinating account of this important event. It is noteworthy that according to Cierva the flight was financed by the notorious smuggler and tycoon, Juan March (*Historia*, 80). See also Gil Robles, *No fué posible la paz*, 780. In a statement issued by Gil Robles on 27 February 1942, he also claims to have had a hand in arranging the flight (published in *ABC* [Madrid], 1 May 1968). For accounts of the military insurrection in Spanish Morocco and in various parts of Spain, see Enrique Arques, *17 de julio. La epopeya de Africa*, 13–58, 89–95; Broué and Témime, 82–102; Victor de Frutos, *Los que NO perdieron la guerra*, 13–22; García Venero, *El General Fanjul*, 294–350; *Guerra y revolución*, I, 123–32, 138–75, 180–87; Arrarás, ed., *Historia de la cruzada*, II, 474–562, IV, 14–606, V, 15–560, VI, 15–436; Jackson, 232–46; César M. Lorenzo, *Les anarchistes espagnols et le pouvoir, 1868–1969*, 139–44; José Manuel Martínez Bande, *La invasión de Aragón y el desembarco en Mallorca*, 15–52; Olmedo Delgado and Cuesta Monereo, 98–138; Payne, *Politics*, 341–52; Luis Romero, *Tres días de julio*, 3–616; Seco Serrano, VI, 152–64; Thomas, 131–64, 186–89; Vigón, 111–211.
228. Quoted in Valdesoto, 115–17, n. 1.
229. *Guerra y revolución*, I, 121–22.
230. Martínez Barrio, *Hoy*, 27 Apr. 1940; Ibárruri, *El único camino*, 260.
231. See n. 207 for names of ministers.
232. 18 Jan. 1936.
233. 12 Oct. 1935.
234. 2 Apr. 1936.
235. Domingo, 233. According to Zugazagoitia, 45, Isaac Abeytua, the director of *Política*, organ of the Left Republican party, was strongly opposed to the government.
236. Eduardo de Guzmán, *Madrid, rojo y negro*, 37. See also Martínez Barrio, *Hoy*, 27 Apr. 1940; Manuél Blasco Garzón (a member of Martínez Barrio's government), in *España Republicana*, 6 Nov. 1947; Arturo Barea, *The Forging of a Rebel*, 510; *Guerra y revolución*, I, 122.
237. *Hoy*, 27 Apr. 1940. Sánchez Román, a member of the government, confirmed,

when interviewed by me, that Prieto urged Martínez Barrio to remain in office, contending that the street demonstrations did not warrant his resignation. This is corroborated by Largo Caballero in *Mis recuerdos*, 167.
238. Palacio Atard, essay in *Aproximación*, 50.

Chapter 2

1. José Giral in *La Vanguardia*, 19 July 1938. See also his speech reported in *La Voz Valenciana*, 10 Mar. 1937.
2. Speech reported in *Política*, 2 Nov. 1938. See also Manuel Azaña, *Obras Completas*, III, 487–88; *Guerra y revolución en España, 1936–1939*, I, 177; Indalecio Prieto, *Convulsiones de España*, III, 149.
3. *Gaceta de Madrid*, 7 Aug. 1936.
4. Azaña, *Obras*, IV, 862.
5. Information on the attitude and fate of the various garrisons can be found in the books listed in chapter 1, n. 227.
6. According to a meticulous study, based on primary sources, by Ricardo de la Cierva, *Historia de la guerra civil española*, 756–57, 760. See also Palacio Atard, essay in *Aproximación histórica de la guerra española, 1936–1939*, 41–42. Although Cierva cited these figures as representing the ideological division within the army (essay in Raymond Carr, ed., *The Republic and the Civil War in Spain*, 188), they were of necessity determined to a large degree by the territorial split, which Cierva himself does not entirely discount in his major work, *Historia*, 760–61.
7. *Nuestra guerra*, 275. Palacio Atard, a right-wing historian, puts the figure as high as 3,500. Palacio Atard, ed., *Cuadernos bibliográficos de la guerra de España, 1936–1939. Memorias y reportajes de testigos*, 1, 142.
8. *Freedom's Battle*, 122.
9. *Guerra en España, 1936–1939*, 259. See also Colonel Segismundo Casado, *National Review*, July 1939.
10. Essay in Carr, ed., *The Republic and the Civil War in Spain*, 190.
11. Essay in *Aproximación*, 41–42.
12. Salvador de Madariaga, *Spain*, 487.
13. An account of the attitude of the Civil Guard in the various provinces can be found in Arrarás, ed., *Historia de la cruzada española*. See also José Manuel Liébana and G. Orizana, *El movimiento nacional*.
14. According to a careful study by Cierva, *Historia*, 760.
15. See, for example, the account of Captain Reparaz of his escape together with a large body of civil guards from Jaen in Captain Reparaz y Tregallo de Souza, *Desde el cuartel general de Miaja, al santuario de la Virgen de la Cabeza*; report in *Solidaridad Obrera*, 18 Feb. 1937, of the attempt by forty civil guards to join General Franco's forces, and Julián Zugazagoitia, *Historia de la guerra en España*, 103.
16. According to *Mundo Obrero* (Madrid), 3 Nov. 1936.
17. *Gaceta de Madrid*, 21 Aug. 1936.
18. This corps, according to information given to me by José Muñoz López, top-ranking official in the SIM (Military Investigation Service) in the later part of the war, ceased to function entirely at the outbreak of the rebellion and had to be recreated, only three hundred of its three thousand members remaining loyal to the government.
19. Figure given by Cierva, *Historia*, 757.

20. Some of the provincial capitals where the assault guards supported the rising were Burgos, Huesca, Saragossa, Valladolid, Cáceres, Granada, León, Logroño, Pamplona, Salamanca (Liébana and Orizana, 209–10, 154, 201–2, 192, 216, 193 respectively), Oviedo (Oscar Pérez Solis, *Sitio y defensa de Oviedo*, 24; Germiniano Carrascal, *Asturias*, 52), and Teruel (*Historia de la cruzada*, IV, 238).

21. For frank accounts of the absolute impotence of the remnants of the government police corps in the first days of the war, see speech by the Socialist politician Angel Galarza (*La Correspondencia de Valencia*, 5 Aug. 1937), who became minister of the interior in September 1936; speech by Juan García Oliver, the anarchist leader, who was made minister of justice in November 1936 (*Fragua Social*, 1 June 1937). See also Jesús de Galíndez (a friend of the Republic), *Los vascos en el Madrid sitiado*, 15–19, and the preamble to the minister of the interior's decree of 26 Dec. 1936 in *Gaceta de la República*, 27 Dec. 1936.

22. *Freedom's Battle*, 261.

23. Ibid., 224.

24. Dolores Ibárruri, *Speeches and Articles, 1936–38*, 214. "The republican state," writes Fernando Claudín, a Communist at the time, "collapsed like a house of cards" (*La crisis del movimiento comunista*, 179).

25. Zugazagoitia, 47.

26. Angel Ossorio y Gallardo, *Vida y sacrificio de Companys*, 179, also 169. Should further corroborative testimony from the republican camp on the collapse of the state still be needed, see Manuel Azaña, *Madrid* (speech of 13 Nov. 1937), 7–8; *Política*, 16 July 1938 (editorial); *La Correspondencia de Valencia*, 5 Aug. 1937 (speech by Angel Galarza); *El Poble Català*, 2 Feb. 1940 (article by Major Josep Guarner).

27. Speech reported by *El Dia Gráfico*, 2 Dec. 1937.

28. *Treball*, 22 July 1936. See *La Humanitat*, 6 Aug. 1936, for the control of the entire Catalan French border from Bausén to Port-Bou by the working-class militia.

29. M. Sterling (Mark Sharron) in *Modern Monthly*, Dec. 1936. See also Walter Duranty in the *New York Times*, 17 Sept. 1936; R. Louzon in *La Révolution Prolétarienne*, 10 Aug. 1936; Alvarez del Vayo, *Freedom's Battle*, 164; H. E. Kaminski, *Ceux de Barcelone*, 11; John Langdon-Davies, *Behind the Spanish Barricades*, 90–91; Pérez Salas, 122.

30. Bruno Alonso, *La flota republicana y la guerra civil de España*, 25.

31. Zugazagoitia, 157. For the lack of discipline in the republican fleet, see article by N. Kuznetsov, Soviet naval attaché and adviser to Antonio Ruiz, chief of the Cartagena Naval Base, in *Pod znamenem ispanskoi respubliki, 1936–1939*, 198. See also Admiral Francisco Moreno, chief of General Franco's fleet during the Civil War, for reference to the assassination of officers and the ineffectualness of the republican fleet, *La guerra en el mar*, 69–70, 83–84 and passim. Stanley G. Payne, *Politics and the Military in Modern Spain*, 359, 513–14, n. 78, also offers valuabte information.

32. An exception must be made of the Basque provinces, where events took a less revolutionary course. See Manuel de Irujo, "La guerra civil en Euzkadi antes del estatuto," 23–25, 45–46, 50–52, 64–65, and report to the central government by José Antonio Aguirre, premier of the autonomous Basque government, 2–4, 7–8, 10–11, 13–15, 17–18, 22; José María Arenillas, *Euzkadi, la cuestión nacional y la revolución socialista*; A. de Lizarra, *Los vascos y la república española*, 58–59 and passim.

33. Juan López, speech published in *CNT* (Madrid), 21 Sept. 1936. See also his article in *Cultura Proletaria*, 8 Jan. 1938, and speech reported in *Fragua Social*, 29 May 1937.

34. *Spartacus*, Sept.–Oct. 1938.

35. *La revolución en los ayuntamientos*, 16–17.

36. *Boletín de Información, CNT-FAI*, as given in *El Día Gráfico*, 16 Aug. 1936.

37. *Politics, Economics and Men of Modern Spain, 1808–1946*, 595. See also speeches by the Socialist politician, Angel Galarza, who became minister of the interior in September 1936, *La Correspondencia de Valencia*, 2 Feb. 1937, 5 Aug. 1937, and R. Louzon in *La Révolution Prolétarienne*, 10 Aug. 1936; César M. Lorenzo, *Les anarchistes espagnols et le pouvoir, 1868–1969*, 182–204, Carlos M. Rama, *La crisis española del siglo XX*, 294.

38. Speech reported in *Fragua Social*, 1 June 1937.

39. *The Forging of a Rebel*, 536, see also 545–47. For an account by a republican Cortes deputy of the collapse of the administration of justice in the region of Catalonia, see Mariano Rubió i Tudurí, *La justicia en Cataluña*, 13.

40. For the names of those assassinated, see *Causa General*, 352–54; also Francisco Lacruz, *El alzamiento, la revolución y el terror en Barcelona*, 159.

41. For the destruction in November 1936 of the principal judicial records in Madrid by the anarchist leader, Juan García Oliver, then minister of justice, see deposition by Luis Palud Clausó, as given in *Causa General*, 363–65. For the burning of judicial records in Barcelona and Castellón respectively, see Rubió i Tudurí, 13, and *Datos complementarios para la historia de España*, 237.

42. *Gaceta de Madrid*, 7 Oct. 1936.

43. *Convulsiones*, II, 314–16.

44. Galíndez, 10. For the freeing of the convicts from the San Miguel de los Reyes Penitentiary, see chapter 23, text to nn. 3 and 4, also Julián Gorkin, *Caníbales políticos*, 120, for the release of prisoners from the Model Prison, Madrid.

45. *Spain*, 496.

46. See, for example, the memorandum presented to the Largo Caballero government by Manuel de Irujo, Basque Nationalist minister, as reproduced in Lizarra, 200–204.

47. 15 Aug. 1936.

48. *Ruta*, 14 Nov. 1936.

49. *Tierra y Libertad* (Barcelona), 13 Aug. 1936.

50. 29 July 1936. For confirmatory testimony by nonanarchist, but prorepublican sources, on the destruction of ecclesiastical property, see Ramos Oliveira, 571; essay by Lawrence Fernsworth in Frank Hanighen, ed., *Nothing but Danger*, 13–47.

51. Cardenal Isidro Gomá y Tomás, *Pastorales de la guerra de España*, 169.

52. For confirmation by a prorepublican source of the imprisonment and killing of thousands of members of the priesthood and religious orders, see memorandum presented to the Largo Caballero government by Manuel de Irujo, Basque Nationalist minister, as reproduced in Lizarra, 200–204. Irujo also stated that in the Basque provinces nobody attacked the church or interfered with religious worship because, in contrast with the rest of the left camp, the clergy in those provinces sympathized with democratic and republican institutions. The most reliable study of the assassination of members of the priesthood and religious orders, the result of many years of diligent research, can be found in Antonio Montero's *Historia de la persecución religiosa en España, 1936–1939*, 762–883, who lists the names, places, and dates of assassination of 6,832 religious personnel.

53. For criticism of these republicans by Fernando Valera, a Cortes deputy and prominent member of Unión Republicana, see speech, reported in *El Pueblo*, 27 Jan. 1937. See also article by Juan J. Domenichina, a leading intellectual of the Republican Left party, in *Hoy*, 28 Dec. 1940.

54. *Obras*, IV, 624.

55. *International Law and Diplomacy in the Spanish Civil Strife*, 157.
56. *Los sucesos de España vistos por un diplomático*, 338.
57. *Freedom's Battle*, 240.
58. *Diplomat im roten Madrid*, 59.
59. Federica Montseny in *La Revista Blanca*, 30 July 1936.
60. Diego Abad de Santillán, *La revolución y la guerra en España*, 176.
61. Galíndez, 9–10. It may never be possible—to judge from the conflicting studies made by Hugh Thomas, *The Spanish Civil War* (1965), 218–37, 789–90, and Gabriel Jackson, *The Spanish Republic and the Civil War, 1931–1939*, 526–40, on the basis of the meager evidence available even forty years later—to provide accurate figures on the behind-the-battlelines assassinations. As Thomas points out (789) rebel or Nationalist estimates of the number of assassinations in the Popular Front zone ran initially as high as three or four hundred thousand. A figure of "more than three hundred thousand laymen" assassinated is given by the Spanish bishops in their collective letter, dated 1 July 1937 (Gomá y Tomás, 169). But these estimates were subsequently revised downward to about 60,000. On the other hand, *Causa General*, 390, which was first published by the Ministry of Justice in 1943 and contains a mass of evidence concerning executions in the left camp, gave the number of those "duly investigated" as 85,940. In contrast, Jackson, 533, arrives at a "most tentative estimate" of 20,000 deaths by assassination in the Popular Front zone, a low figure if one takes into account the 6,832 religious personnel assassinated (see n. 52).

Accurate estimates are likewise unavailable for the number of wartime killings in Nationalist Spain. The figure of 750,000 executions named by the Spanish republican writer, Ramón Sender, for the whole of Nationalist Spain to mid-1938 (Thomas, 223) and that of 150,000 for the military territory of the Second Organic Division given by Antonio Bahamonde, former propaganda chief to General Queipo de Llano, commander of the division, comprising the provinces of Badajoz, Cadiz, Cordova, Granada, Huelva, Malaga, and Seville (*Memoirs of a Spanish Nationalist*, 90) appear definitely exaggerated to Thomas, 223, who considers that Nationalist assassinations "are unlikely to have numbered more than 50,000" (789). On the other hand, Jackson, 535, citing estimates given to him by a notary and former member of the Catholic CEDA, names figures of 47,000 for the province of Seville alone and 32,000 and 26,000 respectively for the provinces of Cordova and Granada. What appear to be more sober estimates for the number of killings in some of the provinces controlled by the Nationalist and Popular Front forces are given by a Basque priest, using the pseudonym of Juan de Iturralde, in *El catolicismo y la cruzada de Franco*, 96–155. For the severity of the repression in Burgos, the seat of the Nationalist government, see Antonio Ruiz Vilaplana (dean and president of the College of Judicial Commissioners until he fled abroad in 1938), *Burgos Justice*, 72–77, 84–85, 92–95. For the repression in the province of Granada, see Ian Gibson, *La represión nacionalista de Granada en 1936 y la muerte de Federico García Lorca*, 50–59, and Gerald Brenan, *The Face of Spain*, 131–60. A chapter on the gruesome nature and extent of the repression in the Nationalist camp can be found in Payne, *Politics*, 409–20, who originally supported Jackson's contention (as opposed to Thomas's view) that during the wartime period Nationalist executions exceeded those carried out by the left. However, in a later work (*The Spanish Revolution*, 225) he states: "Though the Red Terror may have taken more lives than the Nationalist repression while the war lasted, the victors were subsequently able to complete the task at their leisure."

62. *La velada en Benicarló*, 96. This book is in the form of a dialogue. Garcés, a former

minister, who makes the above statement, expresses ideas commonly attributed to Manuel Azaña.

63. The same, of course, is true of the Government of the Generalitat in the semiautonomous region of Catalonia, which, in the words of Angel Ossorio y Gallardo, *Vida y sacrificio de Companys*, 172, had become a "purely nominal organ," the real power in the region having been assumed by the Central Antifascist Militia Committee.

64. Confirmation of this was given to the author by several trade-union leaders.

65. Barea, 660.

66. See, for example, *Boletín de Información, CNT-FAI*, 25 Aug. 1936; *Solidaridad Obrera* (Barcelona), 31 July 1938.

67. See, for example, Horacio Prieto, *Palabras al viento*, 281, and his article in *Correo de Asturias*, 15 Aug. 1942; Zugazagoitia, 47; Alvarez del Vayo, *Freedom's Battle*, 262; César Falcón, *Madrid*, 122; Pérez Salas, 113; Major Josep Guarner in *El Poble Català*, 2 Feb. 1940.

68. *Half of Spain Died*, 121.

69. Speech, 9 May 1937, José Díaz, *Tres años de lucha*, 428.

70. *Treball*, 9 Apr. 1937. See also Antonio Mije (member of the politburo), *Por una potente industria de guerra*, 3; Federico Melchor (member of the Executive Committee of the JSU, the Communist-run Unified Socialist Youth Federation), *Organicemos la producción*, 4.

71. *Pravda*, 26 Sept. 1936.

72. See the preamble of a decree published in the official *Gaceta de la República* (formerly *Gaceta de Madrid*), 22 Oct. 1937. For earlier references to the destruction of property records, see speech by the undersecretary of finance, Jerónimo Bugeda, as reported in *El Día Gráfico*, 9 Feb. 1937; article by Federica Montseny in *Tierra y Libertad* (Barcelona), 29 Oct. 1936; report of the Committee of War of the Iron Column, *Nosotros*, 16 Feb. 1937; *Solidaridad Obrera* (Barcelona), 13 Aug. 1936 (article on Pina).

73. Report to the central committee of the Communist party, 5–8 Mar. 1937, in Díaz, 351.

74. *Tribuna*, Oct. 1948.

75. Franz Borkenau, *The Spanish Cockpit*, 148.

76. For some of the institute's reports listing confiscated properties, see *Claridad*, 12, 14 Oct. 1936; *CNT* (Madrid), 15, 18, 19 Aug. 1936; *Mundo Obrero* (Madrid), 8 Aug. 1936; *Política*, 11, 14, 23, 27, 28, 30 Aug.; 1, 16, 17, 23–25, 27 Sept.; 10, 15, 28 Oct. 1936; *El Socialista* (Madrid), 29 Aug., 29 Sept. 1936. For data on the collectivization of landed property, see Appendix II.

77. *Boletín de Información, CNT-FAI*, 25 Aug. 1936.

78. Statement issued by the Barcelona Traction, Light, and Power Company, Limited, on 3 Sept. 1936; see also statement issued on 16 Nov. 1936.

79. *Obras*, III, 497.

Chapter 3

1. These confiscations, to be sure, were often carried out without the approval of the national leaders of the UGT. For criticisms by Pascual Tomás, its vice-secretary, of the confiscation of small property by local UGT unions, see *La Correspondencia de Valencia*, 21 Dec. 1936; *Adelante* (Valencia), 13 Feb. 1937; *Spartacus*, July–Aug. 1938.

2. See *Claridad*, 27 Aug. 1936; *CNT* (Madrid), 7 Oct. 1936.

3. See speech by the local Communist party trade-union secretary, reported in *Frente*

Rojo, 30 Mar. 1937. In a letter to the author, Antonio Villaneuva, a member of the Valencia CNT, stated that the premises and equipment of nearly all the printers, cabinetmakers, tailors, dressmakers, barbers, beauticians, bootmakers, and other leather goods producers were taken over by the unions of that city. For the collectivizations of the bakeries, confectioneries, hotels, cafés, and bars in Valencia, see *Nosotros*, 27 Nov., 3 Dec. 1937.

4. The revolutionary developments in this region are dealt with in chapters 27 and 28.

5. See the anarchosyndicalist organ, *Solidaridad Obrera* (Barcelona), 19 Dec. 1936; also speech by Federico Melchor, a Communist, as reprinted in Melchor, *Organicemos la producción*, 4–5

6. *Solidaridad Obrera* (Barcelona), 3, 4 Dec. 1936.

7. Ibid., 29 Dec. 1936.

8. Ibid., 7 Oct. 1936.

9. See account in *Tierra y Libertad*, 21 Aug. 1937.

10. Ibid.

11. *Solidaridad Obrera* (Barcelona), 15 Dec. 1936.

12. See, for example, *CNT* (Madrid), 10 Aug. 1936 (Madrid province); *Tierra y Libertad* (Barcelona), 23 Jan. 1937 (Carcagente); *Orientaciones Nuevas*, 6 Feb. 1937 (Montmeló).

13. See articles on the CLUEA (Consejo Levantino Unificado de la Exportación Agrícola) in *Fragua Social*, 31 Jan. 1937; *Nosotros*, 19 Apr. 1937; also Manuel Villar, *España en la ruta de la libertad*, 51. Although the UGT was represented in the CLUEA, the CNT was the dominant influence.

14. For examples not already given in this chapter, the reader is referred to the following publications: *Acracia*, 24 Oct. 1936, 17 Nov., 3 Dec. 1937; *La Batalla* (Barcelona), 3 Oct. 1936; *Boletín de Información, CNT-FAI*, 14, 17, 23 Sept., 8 Oct., 7 Nov. 1936; *CNT* (Madrid), 10 Aug., 19, 23 Sept., 7, 8, 16 Oct. 1936; *Cultura Proletaria*, 8 Jan. 1938; *El Día Gráfico*, 4 Sept., 25 Nov. 1936; *España Libre* (Toulouse), 18 Sept. 1949 (article by A. Costales); *Ideas*, 7 Jan. 1937; *Nosotros*, 15 Feb., 15 Nov. 1937; *El Noticiero Universal*, 11 Sept. 1936; *La Nouvelle Espagne Antifasciste*, 2 Dec. 1937; *Orientaciones Nuevas*, 30 Jan., 6 Feb. 1937; *La Révolution Prolétarienne*, 25 June 1937 (article by R. Louzon); *Solidaridad Obrera* (Barcelona), 13 Aug., 24 Sept., 18–20, 22 Nov., 2, 5, 11, 15, 17, 19, 25, 27 Dec. 1936; 20 Jan., 23 Apr., 30 June, 3 Aug. (article by Mariano Cardona Rosell) 1937; *Solidaridad Obrera* (Paris), 10 Feb. 1951 (article by Gaston Leval); *Tierra y Libertad* (Barcelona), 23 Jan. (article by Gaston Leval), 27 Feb., 17 Apr., 25 Dec. 1937; 15 Jan. 1938; *Umbral*, 24 July 1937; Gaston Leval, *L'indispensable révolution*, 192; Gaston Leval, *Né Franco né Stalin*, 131–42 and passim; Gaston Leval, *Social Reconstruction in Spain*, 10–11; *Collectivisations*, 27, 187, 204–5. See also chapter 4 and Appendix III.

15. 4 Feb. 1937.

16. *Solidaridad Obrera*, (Barcelona) 1 Sept. 1937; see also *Las Noticias*, 1 July 1937.

17. *Solidaridad Obrera* (Barcelona), 1 Sept. 1937.

18. Ibid., 2 Oct. 1937

19. Ibid., 24 Dec. 1936; see also *Boletín de Información, CNT-FAI*, 25 Dec. 1936; Aristide Lapeyre, *Le problème espagnol*, 22–23.

20. *Boletín de Información, CNT-FAI*, 10 Apr. 1937; see also *CNT* (Paris), 17 July 1949.

21. *Tierra y Libertad*, 23 Jan. 1937; see also *Solidaridad Obrera* (Barcelona), 20 Jan. 1937.

22. *Solidaridad Obrera* (Barcelona), 23 Nov. 1938; *Ultima Hora*, 28 Sept. 1936; Aristide Lapeyre, 22; *Collectivisations*, 139–47.

23. For this information I am indebted to Antonio Villanueva, a member of the Valen-

cia CNT. For details of the collectivized clothing industry in that city, see *Nosotros*, 21 Oct. 1937.

24. *Solidaridad Obrera* (Barcelona), 20 Oct. 1936.

25. *CNT* (Madrid), 23 Sept. 1936; Leval, *L'indispensable révolution*, 192–93; Leval, *Social Reconstruction*, 23.

26. Leval, *Social Reconstruction*, 32.

27. *Boletín de Información, CNT-FAI*, 18 Aug. 1937.

28. Ibid., 15 Jan. 1937.

29. Ibid., 17 Sept. 1936; *Dialética*, Feb. 1938; José Peirats, *La CNT en la revolución española*, I, 174–75.

30. According to Mariano Cardona Rosell, member of the national committee of the CNT, in a letter to me.

31. See *Tierra y Libertad* (Barcelona), 23 Jan. 1937 (article by Gaston Leval).

32. Leval, *L'indispensable révolution*, 192; Leval, *Social Reconstruction*, 11.

33. Speech by Tomás Cano Ruiz at the closing session of the November 1936 congress of the Valencia CNT, quoted in *Fragua Social*, 17 Nov. 1936.

34. *Solidaridad Obrera* (Barcelona), 7 Apr. 1937. See also ibid., 4 Oct. 1936, 4 Feb. 1937.

35. The opposition of countless small businessmen to the collectivization movement in Catalonia was frankly admitted in an official report of the CNT; see report of the Junta del Control del Comité Económico, as given in *Memoria del congreso extraordinario de la confederación regional del trabajo de Cataluña celebrado en Barcelona los días 25 de febrero al 3 de marzo de 1937*, 363–65.

36. *Solidaridad Obrera* (Barcelona), 9 Sept. 1936.

37. 29 Aug. 1936. See also ibid., 8 Aug., 3 Sept., 8 Oct. 1936; statement issued by the regional committee of the Catalan CNT and by the peninsular commitee of the FAI, as given in *El Día Gráfico*, 26 Aug. 1936.

Chapter 4

1. *Agrarian Reform and Peasant Revolution in Spain*, 386, n. 75. Malefakis also points out that where the military rebellion was successful, the settlers placed by the Republic were for the most part ousted from their holdings: "The official Nationalist position distinguished between settlements made under the Popular Front, which were immediately undone on the grounds that they were illegitimate, and the lesser settlements made earlier, the legitimacy of which was accepted until 1941, when the entire legacy of the IRA was liquidated. In some areas, however, particularly those under the control of General Queipo de Llano, the yunteros, who had received temporary grants of land in the spring of 1936 were also allowed to remain on their holdings until the end of the war" (ibid., 386, n. 76).

2. See, for example, J. Valero, in *Fragua Social*, 23 July 1937.

3. 16 Jan. 1937.

4. *Tiempos Nuevos*, Sept. 1938.

5. *La revolución y la guerra en España*, 107–8. See also *Solidaridad Obrera* (Barcelona), 4 Sept. 1936; *Frente Libertario*, 7 June 1937.

6. See, for example, "Como trabajan nuestros técnicos," *Colectivismo*, 15 Nov. 1937; also statement by a local secretary of the National Federation of Land Workers, in *Adelante* (Valencia), 16 June 1937.

7. *Adelante* (Valencia), 1 Apr. 1937.

8. *El Obrero de la Tierra*, 30 Aug. 1936, as reprinted in *Adelante* (Valencia), 21 July 1937.

In December 1936, however, the national committee of the federation resolved that each of its members who were opposed to the collectivization of the large estates would receive a proportionate piece of land (quoted in *Por la revolución agraria*, 8).

9. *Juventud Libre*, 3 July 1937. See also speech by Juan J. Domenech, *Solidaridad Obrera* (Barcelona), 7 Jan. 1937; report from Barbastro signed by Cosme Sampériz, ibid., 1 Sept. 1936; article by Gaston Leval on Carcagente, *Tierra y Libertad* (Barcelona), 16 Jan. 1937.

10. See *CNT* (Madrid), 5 Apr. 1937 (CNT Peasant Congress of Castile); *Fragua Social*, 15 Nov. 1936 (8th Session of the Congress of the Valencia CNT); *Solidaridad Obrera* (Barcelona), 8 Sept. 1936 (Congress of the CNT Peasants' Union of Catalonia); *Adelante* (Valencia), 10 Mar. 1937 (resolution approved by the provincial congress of the UGT Land Workers of Valencia); *Claridad*, 16 Dec. 1936 (editorial, part of which is quoted in chapter 17, text to n. 15); *La Correspondencia de Valencia*, 21 Dec. 1936 (speech by Pascual Tomás, vice-secretary of the UGT); resolution and manifesto of the National Federation of Land Workers, December 1936, as reprinted in *Por la revolución agraria*, 5–13, 29–33, see also 38–39.

11. *Verdad*, 8 Jan. 1937.

12. See *CNT* (Madrid), 5 Apr. 1937 (CNT Peasant Congress of Castile); *Cultura y Acción*, 18 Feb. 1937 (Congress of Agricultural Collectives of Aragon); *Fragua Social*, 15 Nov. 1936 (8th Session of the Congress of the Valencia CNT); *Solidaridad Obrera* (Barcelona), 8 Sept. 1936 (Congress of CNT Peasants' Union of Catalonia); *Adelante* (Valencia), 10 Mar. 1937 (provincial congress of the UGT Land Workers of Valencia); *Claridad*, 25 Oct. 1936 (provincial congress of the UGT Land Workers of Granada); resolution and manifesto of the National Federation of Land Workers, December 1936, as reprinted in *Por la revolución agraria*, 5–13, 29–33.

13. See, for example, what happened in the village of Guadasur, which was controlled by the UGT and CNT, *Claridad*, 14 Dec. 1936; also resolution approved by the delegates of twenty-one villages controlled by the CNT in Aragon, as given in *Solidaridad Obrera* (Barcelona), 26 Aug. 1936. Of the village of Calanda, Gaston Leval, the well-known foreign anarchist, wrote: "The individualists were allowed a minimum of freedom. They could possess land because that is what they desired, but they could not trade with the fruit of their labor. They could not speculate and compete disloyally with the young collective" (*Cultura Proletaria*, 4 Nov. 1939). It is not undeserving of notice that after the formation early in 1937 of the National Peasants' Federation affiliated with the CNT, this organization became, at least theoretically, the sole distributor of the agricultural produce of the individual cultivators and collective farms that came under its jurisdiction (see *Estatutos de la federación nacional de campesinos*, 13).

14. See *Adelante* (Valencia), 21 Apr. 1937; also article by Ricardo Zabalza, general secretary of the National Federation of Land Workers, published in *CNT* (Madrid), 26 May 1937.

15. Isaac Puente, *Finalidad de la CNT*, 3. See also resolution on libertarian communism approved at the Extraordinary Congress of the CNT, as given in *Solidaridad Obrera* (Barcelona), 12 May 1936.

16. Puente, *Finalidad de la CNT*, 4. See also ibid., 24–26, and *La Revista Blanca*, 25 Jan. 1937.

17. Puente, *Finalidad de la CNT*, 4.

18. Federico Urales, *La anarquía al alcance de todos*, 29.

19. Isaac Puente in *Tierra y Libertad* (Barcelona), supplement, Aug. 1932, as reprinted in Puente, *Propaganda*, 101.

20. *Die Soziale Revolution*, no. 3, Jan. 1937. "The men and women who stormed the convents [in Barcelona] burned everything they found inside, including money. How well I remember that rugged worker who proudly showed me the corner of a burned thousand peseta bill" (Federica Montseny, "19 de Julio Catalán," *Fragua Social*, 19 July 1937, as reprinted in *De julio a julio*, 22).

21. Agustín Souchy in *Tierra y Libertad* (Barcelona), 6 Aug. 1938.

22. H. E. Kaminski, *Ceux de Barcelone*, 118–21.

23. Ibid., 121–22.

24. Franz Borkenau, *The Spanish Cockpit*, 166–67.

25. *Tierra y Libertad* (Barcelona), 30 Jan. 1937.

26. Agustín Souchy, *Entre los campesinos de Aragón*, 73.

27. 13 July 1934, 8 June 1934, respectively.

28. Alardo Prats, *Vanguardia y retaguardia de Aragon*, 85–93.

29. *Collectivisations*, 239–40.

30. *Entre los campesinos de Aragón*, 92.

31. Ibid., 84–85.

32. Ibid., 45–47.

33. 24 Sept. 1936.

34. *Entre los campesinos de Aragón*, 66.

35. Quoted in Diego Abad de Santillán, *Timón* (Barcelona), Aug. 1938.

36. Quoted in Diego Abad de Santillán, *La bancarrota del sistema económico y político del capitalismo*, 53.

37. *Bog i gosudarstvo*, 16.

38. 5 June 1936.

39. 5 Aug. 1936. See also *Solidaridad Obrera* (Barcelona), 15 Aug. 1936.

40. Souchy, *Entre los campesinos de Aragón*, 87–88.

41. Report from Albalate de Cinca in *Solidaridad Obrera* (Barcelona), 26 Aug. 1936.

42. *Cultura y Acción*, 18 Feb. 1937.

43. Paraphrase by *Solidaridad Obrera* (Barcelona), 9 Sept. 1936, of a passage in a speech by Ramón Porté, delegate for Tarragona province and member of the regional committee of the Catalan CNT. He drew attention in this passage to similar warnings by previous speakers.

44. See, for example, *Castilla Libre*, 30 Mar. 1937; *CNT* (Madrid), 10 Aug. 1936; *Cultura y Acción*, as given in *Boletín de Información, CNT-FAI*, 4 Aug. 1937; *Nosotros*, 24 June 1937; *Solidaridad Obrera* (Barcelona), 19 Dec. 1936, 13 May 1937; *Tierra y Libertad* (Barcelona), 16 Jan. 1937; *Timón* (Barcelona), July 1938 (article by Souchy).

45. *Juventud Libre*, 10 July 1937. See also ibid., 14 Nov. 1936 (article on Pedralba).

46. *Solidaridad Obrera* (Barcelona), 19 Nov. 1936. See also article on Calanda in *Mujeres Libres*, July 1937.

47. This is the figure given by the anarchosyndicalist leader, Diego Abad de Santillán, *Por qué perdimos la guerra*, 94. It was confirmed to the author by José Duque and José Almudí, the two Communist members of the Defense Council of Aragon, the principal administrative organ in the region during the early months of the Revolution. See also Prats (a Socialist), 81, who says that 70 percent of the land was collectivized.

48. Figure given by César Martinez Lorenzo, *Les anarchistes espagnols et le pouvoir, 1868–1969*, 152, n. 17; José Peirats, *Los anarquistas en la crisis política española*, 300; Prats, 81.

49. It is noteworthy that the anarchists did not refer to the foremost men of their movement as leaders because this term implied authority and control. Instead, they

used the words, "representatives," "delegates," "militants." Still, as these men possessed the qualities of leadership in their ability to guide and influence the members of the CNT and FAI, and, indeed, were leaders by almost every test that distinguishes the leadership of a movement from the rank and file, I prefer to use this term.

50. *CNT* (Madrid), 6 Oct. 1936.

51. *Solidaridad Obrera* (Barcelona), 27 Nov. 1936.

52. *Fragua Social*, 6 Apr. 1937.

53. See text to nn. 12 and 13, this chapter. In the village of Gelsa, for instance, a proclamation was issued as soon as the revolutionary regime was instituted, stating that "those persons who do not deposit food and clothing of all kinds [in the communal warehouse], but keep them to enrich themselves, will suffer the maximum penalty" (*Solidaridad Obrera* [Barcelona], 16 Aug. 1936).

54. See resolution approved at the Congress of Agricultural Collectives of Aragon, as given in *Cultura y Acción*, 18 Feb. 1937; also preface by Agustín Souchy to *Collectivisations*, 20, and *Frente Libertario*, 25 Dec. 1937.

55. See statement by the councillor of agriculture of the Catalan government, *El Día Gráfico*, 3 Jan. 1937; also notice issued by the Peasant Federation of Valencia province, *Verdad*, 21 Jan. 1937.

56. An interesting example was the collective of Prat de Llobregat. According to an account in *Tierra y Libertad* (Barcelona), the FAI organ, 2 July 1938, it was set up in October 1936 by one thousand farm laborers, tenant farmers, and peasant owners who had agreed "almost unanimously" to the collective cultivation of the soil. But no sooner had the political situation changed to the disadvantage of the CNT and FAI than the tenant farmers and peasant owners demanded the restoration of their properties, the original collective, according to this account, being reduced to a quarter of its former size.

57. *Timón* (Barcelona), July 1938

58. See, for example, *Cultura y Acción*, 6 Aug. 1937; *Juventud Libre*, 10 July 1937 (statement by Criado, general secretary of the CNT Peasants' Federation of Castile); *Solidaridad Obrera* (Barcelona), 11 July 1937; also Abad de Santillán, *La revolución*, 103, and Gaston Leval, *Social Reconstruction in Spain*, 13.

59. Article in *Estudios*, quoted in Henri Rabasseire, *Espagne: creuset politique*, 130. See also *Frente Libertario*, the CNT newspaper, 25 Dec. 1937.

60. 10 Sept. 1936.

61. Article in *Llibertat*, 29 Sept. 1936, as reprinted in Juan Peiró, *Perill a la reraguarda*, 102–3; see also ibid., 107–10, 158–59, and Joaquín Ascaso (the anarchist president of the Defense Council of Aragon) in *Cultura y Acción*, 28 July 1937.

62. *Il Risveglio Anarchico*, 30 Nov. 1929.

63. *Unmanità Nova*, 14 Oct. 1922, as given in Luis Fabbri, *Vida y pensamiento de Malatesta*, 220.

64. *Gosudarstvennost i anarkhiia* (State and Anarchy), 234–35.

65. "A Contribution to the History of the Question of Dictatorship," *Communist International*, no. 14, 6 Nov. 1920, in *Collected Works*, XXXI, 326 (4th Russian edition), as quoted by Bertram Wolfe, *Khrushchev and Stalin's Ghost*, 9.

66. "Marxism and the Russian Revolution," in Milorad M. Drachkovitch, ed., *Fifty Years of Communism in Russia*, 32.

67. Lorenzo, 73–74. The author of this work is the son of Horacio M. Prieto, secretary in 1936 of the CNT National Committee, who both before and during the Civil War had serious differences with the FAI. Although Lorenzo—who does not reveal his relation-

ship to Prieto—makes a special effort to defend his father's attitudes, the book is nonetheless an extraordinarily valuable contribution to the history of the Spanish libertarian movement.

Chapter 5

1. From a radio address reported in *Solidaridad Obrera* (Barcelona), 20 Sept. 1936.

2. Clara Campoamor, *La révolution espagnole vue par une républicaine*, 103.

3. John Langdon-Davies, *Behind the Spanish Barricades*, 123–24. See also Louis Fischer, *Men and Politics*, 353; Jesús de Galíndez, *Los vascos en el Madrid sitiado*, 22; Frank Jellinek, *The Civil War in Spain*, 380; H. E. Kaminski, *Ceux de Barcelone*, 30–31; Megan Laird in *Atlantic Monthly*, Nov. 1936; E. Puig Mora, *La tragedia roja en Barcelona*, 52; *CNT* (Madrid), 28 May 1937 (article by J. García Pradas); *Solidaridad Obrera* (Barcelona), 11 Aug. 1936 (article by Sixto).

4. Federica Montseny in *La Revista Blanca*, 30 July 1936.

5. See chapter 2, text to n. 54.

6. *Mis Memorias*, 226.

7. Speech reported in *Política*, 6 Dec. 1938. See also ibid., 13 Jan. 1937. For criticism of the laissez-faire attitude of the republican parties by a republican officer, see Jesús Pérez Salas, *Guerra en España, 1936–1939*, 135.

8. This figure is given by Manuel Delicado, a member of the central committee, as the 18 July 1936 membership (*La Correspondencia Internacional*, 23 July 1939). However, some twenty-five years later, Dolores Ibárruri (La Pasionaria), then secretary, in Moscow, of the Spanish Communist party in exile, claimed that the membership had risen from thirty thousand in January to more than one hundred thousand in July 1936 (*El único camino*, 375). This figure is likewise given in the official Communist history, *Guerra y revolución en España, 1936–1939*, I, 87 (published in Moscow in 1967 and in whose preparation La Pasionaria had a leading hand), which also claims that because of the number of its members "the Communist party was already at that time [July 1936] the strongest party of Spanish democracy." On the basis of my own research I am inclined to accept the lower figure of forty thousand as being closer to the true membership in July.

9. See report to the central committee in March 1937, by José Díaz, general secretary of the party, in Díaz, *Tres años de lucha*, 390.

10. Antonio Ramos Oliveira, *Politics, Economics and Men of Modern Spain, 1808–1946*, 599.

11. See, for example, Julio Mateu, general secretary of the Communist-run Peasant Federation of Valencia province, text to n. 23, this chapter.

12. For information on this party, see pp. 130, 376–78.

13. 27 July 1936.

14. This hostility of a large part of the small bourgeoisie to the Revolution was acknowledged in an official report of the CNT: see report of the Junta del Control del Comité Económico, as given in *Memoria del congreso extraordinario de la confederación regional del trabajo de Cataluña celebrado en Barcelona los días 25 de febrero al 3 de marzo de 1937*, 363–65.

15. 8 Aug. 1936. For other Communist statements and articles in the first months of the war in defense of the urban middle classes, see *Mundo Obrero* (Madrid), 5, 13–15, 20, 31 Aug., 16 Sept. 1936; *Treball*, 17 Aug., 22 Sept., 22 Dec. (speech by Sesé) 1936; Díaz, 273, 311, 331. The following lines, taken from an article by a former foreign Communist, who served in the International Brigades in Spain, are worth quoting: "In

Murcia and elsewhere I saw that our placards and leaflets appealed for shopkeepers' membership with the promise of absolute support of private property" (Henry Scott Beattie in *Canadian Forum*, April, 1938).

16. This figure is given by Antonio Mije, a member of the politburo of the Communist party, *Frente Rojo*, 21 Oct. 1937; see also Miguel Ferrer, secretary-general of the Communist-controlled UGT of Catalonia, in *La Vanguardia*, 9 Apr. 1938.

17. 25 Apr. 1937.

18. Lenin, *Sochineniia* (Moscow, 1950), XXIX, 133, as quoted by Ivo J. Lederer, "Soviet Foreign Policy," in Milorad M. Drachkovitch, ed., *Fifty Years of Communism in Russia*, 177.

19. Speech reported in *Política*, 19 Apr. 1937.

20. Article in *Amanecer Rojo*, reprinted in *Verdad*, 2 Dec. 1936.

21. *Verdad*, 8 Dec. 1936.

22. Ibid., 1 Dec. 1936. For other speeches by Communist leaders in support of the small and middle peasant, see *El Mercantil Valenciano*, 24 Jan. 1937 (Uribe); *Treball*, 20 Oct. 1936 (Comorera), 7 Feb. 1937 (Colomer); Segis Alvarez, *La juventud y los campesinos*; Díaz, 272, 309–11, 326–27; *El partido comunista por la libertad y la independencia de España*, 181–91.

23. Julio Mateu, general secretary of the federation, *La obra de la federación campesina*, 7.

24. *Claridad*, 14 Dec. 1936. See also article by Santiago Bosca in the left-wing Socialist *Adelante* (Valencia), as given in *CNT* (Madrid), 15 May 1937, and letter from the Valencia secretariat of the Federation of Land Workers (Socialist) to the Peasant Federation, published in *Fragua Social*, 12 Aug. 1937. For a strong attack by an anarchosyndicalist on the well-to-do farmers who entered the Peasant Federation, see *Nosotros*, 5 June 1937.

25. Mateu, 9–10.

26. *Mundo Obrero* (Madrid), 30 July 1936.

Chapter 6

1. Executive Committee of the Communist International. *XIII Plenum IKKI. Stenografichleskii otchet* (Thirteenth Plenum of the Executive Committee of the Communist International; Stenographic Report), 531. See also "The Struggle against Fascism, the Struggle for Power, for the Workers and Peasants' Republic in Spain," *Communist International*, 5 Dec. 1934.

2. *Stalin*, 415.

3. 4 Mar. 1933.

4. Speech at the Fourth Session of the Central Executive Committee of the Soviet Union, as reported by *Izvestiia*, 29 Dec. 1933.

5. 12 Oct. 1934.

6. Speech at the Seventh Congress of the Soviets of the USSR, reported by *Izvestiia*, 29 Jan. 1935.

7. André Géraud (Pertinax), *The Gravediggers of France*, 244–45, 342–43; Geneviève Tabouis, *Blackmail or War*, 90.

8. Tabouis, *Blackmail*, 91–93; Winston Churchill, *The Gathering Storm*, 134–35; Louis Fischer, *Russia's Road from Peace to War*, 264–65; Henri de Kerillis, *Français! Voici la guerre*, 111–12. For a well-documented account of the French Communist party's opposition to the defense program before the signing of the Franco-Soviet pact, see Maurice Ceyrat, *La trahison permanente*, 26–41. After the conclusion of the treaty, Stalin gave public ap-

proval to the program (see official communiqué as published in *Le Temps*, 17 May 1935), and sometime afterward the French Communist party executed a turnabout.

9. Max Beloff, *The Foreign Policy of Soviet Russia, 1929–1941*, I, 157; Churchill, *Gathering Storm*, 135; Fischer, *Russia's Road*, 265; Paul Reynaud, *La France a sauvé l'Europe*, I, 115ff. In his book *De la place de la Concorde au cours de l'Intendance*, Fabry, minister of war at the time of the signing of the Franco-Soviet pact, reveals that both he and Gastón Laval, the prime minister, were opposed to the idea of a military convention (quoted by Paul Reynaud in his testimony before the Parliamentary Commission of Inquiry set up in 1947 to investigate the events that took place in France between 1933 and 1945, *Les événements survenus en France de 1933 à 1945*, 89–90).

10. See Beloff, I, 160; Kerillis, 117; Charles A. Micaud, *The French Right and Nazi Germany, 1933–1939*, 68; Geneviève Tabouis, *Ils l'ont appelée Cassandre*, 244–45.

11. U.S. Department of State, *Documents on German Foreign Policy, 1918–1945*, III, 67.

12. *L'Humanité*, 17 May 1935. See also ibid., 16 May 1935, article, by M. Magnien.

13. *The Time for Decision*, 321.

14. *Ambassador Dodd's Diary, 1933–1938*, 241.

15. *Daily Mail*, 28 Nov. 1933. See also Micaud, 71–74.

16. Quoted in Marquess of Londonderry, *Wings of Destiny*, 171.

17. *Combat*, Nov. 1938. See also excerpt from article by Léon Bailby, *Le Jour*, 24 Sept. 1936, quoted in chapter 7, text to n. 6.

18. Quoted in Londonderry, 187.

19. P. 55.

20. See Beloff, I, 188–89; Fischer, *Russia's Road*, 265; Arthur Koestler, *The Invisible Writing*, 313–14.

21. David T. Cattell, *Communism and the Spanish Civil War*, 29–31; Ricardo de la Cierva, article in *Aproximación historica a la guerra española, 1936–1939*, 61–64.

22. *International Press Correspondence*, 19 Sept. 1935.

23. *Times* (London), 7 Feb. 1935.

24. Churchill, *Arms and the Covenant*, 249. See also Churchill, *Gathering Storm*, 137–41.

25. Beloff, I, 133–34.

26. See Churchill, *Gathering Storm*, 189.

27. *International Press Correspondence*, 19 Sept. 1935.

28. Ibid.

29. Cattell, *Communism*, 30.

Chapter 7

1. U.S. Department of State, *Documents on German Foreign Policy, 1918–1945*, III, 1–2 (hereafter cited by title). See also the official (pro-Franco) Joaquín Arrarás, ed., *Historia de la cruzada española*, III, 127. For the most carefully documented and scholarly work on this subject, see Angel Viñas, *La Alemania nazi y el 18 de julio*.

2. See Werner Beumelburg, *Kampf um Spanien*, 22–29; Wulf Bley, *Das Buch der Spanienflieger*, 23–27, 31–32; Max Graf Hoyos, *Pedros y Pablos*, 15–22; Otto Schempp, *Das autoritäre Spanien*, 69–71; Rudolf Stache, *Armee mit geheimen Auftrag*, 10–26; Hannes Trautloft, *Als Jagdflieger in Spanien*, 29; official account of German intervention published in the German press (as reported in the *Daily Telegraph*, 31 May 1939); special number of *Die Wehrmacht* entitled *Wir Kämpften in Spanien*, issued in May 1939 by the German High Command. According to the above-mentioned official account published in the German press, the first armored car detachment was sent out in October 1936. It

consisted of staff, two companies, and a transport company, and, in addition to taking part in the fighting, formed a school of instruction for Spaniards in the use of armored cars, guns, and flamethrowers. In November, according to the same account, a complete air force corps arrived in Spain, composed of combat, pursuit, and reconnaissance planes, as well as intelligence and antiaircraft detachments. In an article published in the special number of *Die Wehrmacht*, mentioned above, General Sperrle stated that 6,500 German "volunteers" reached Spain at the beginning of November 1936.

3. International Military Tribunal. *The Trial of German Major War Criminals*, Part IX, 93.

4. See memorandum by the acting state secretary of the German foreign office, Hans Heinrich Dieckhoff, as reprinted in *Documents on German Foreign Policy, 1918–1945*, III, 155–56; also ibid., 168, 222, 230, 265, 391–92, and Ernst von Weizsäcker, *Memoirs of Ernst von Weizsäcker*, 113–14.

5. *Documents on German Foreign Policy, 1918–1945*, III, 279. See also excerpt of a report by the German ambassador in Rome to the Wilhelmstrasse, dated 18 December 1936, on the interests of Germany and Italy in the Spanish conflict (text to n. 35, this chapter).

6. Léon Bailby in *Le Jour*, 24 Sept. 1936. See also Pierre Bernus in *Journal des Débats*, 15 Aug. 1936; Pierre Gaxotte in *Candide*, 27 Aug. 1936; Pierre Dominique in *La République*, 8, 9 Oct. 1936.

7. The nonintervention system is extensively studied by Norman J. Padelford, *International Law and Diplomacy in the Spanish Civil Strife*. For violations of the Non-Intervention Agreement, see David T. Cattell, *Soviet Diplomacy and the Spanish Civil War*; also Dante A. Puzzo, *Spain and the Great Powers, 1936–1941*.

8. *Daily Worker*, 9 Sept. 1936. For further evidence of Soviet fears, see Cattell, *Soviet Diplomacy*, 15–16.

9. See, for example, Joaquín Arrarás, *Historia de la segunda república española*, IV, 266–70; Manuel Aznar, *Historia Militar de la guerra de España*, 25–30; *Exposure of the Secret Plan to Establish a Soviet in Spain*.

10. *No fué posible la paz*, 705–6.

11. *El mito de la cruzada de Franco*, 247–58.

12. *Historia de la guerra civil española*, I, 709. See also Cierva, *Los documentos de la primavera trágica*, 428.

13. *Historia*, 713–20.

14. José Díaz, speech, 11 Apr. 1936, as reprinted in Díaz, *Tres años de lucha*, 165.

15. José Díaz, speech in Cortes, *Diario de las Sesiones de Cortes*, 15 Apr. 1936, 311.

16. Díaz, speech, 5 Apr. 1936, as reprinted in Díaz, 155.

17. Article in *La Correspondencia Internacional*, 17 Apr. 1936, as reprinted in Díaz, 133–39; see also article in *Mundo Obrero* (Madrid), 1 May 1936, in Díaz, 184–85.

18. Díaz, speech, 1 June 1936, as reprinted in Díaz, 188; article in *Mundo Obrero* (Madrid), June 1936, as reprinted in Díaz, 199.

19. Díaz, speech, 5 July 1936, as reprinted in Díaz, 215.

20. See chapter 1.

21. See *Mundo Obrero* (Madrid), 6, 8–11, 13, 15–17 July 1936; also José Bullejos (a former secretary of the Communist party), *Europa entre dos guerras, 1918–1938*, 189–90.

22. See, for example, General Francesco Belforte, *La guerra civile in Spagna*, III, 28; Guido Mattioli, *L'aviazione legionari in Spagna*, 22–28; *Le Forze Armate* (official organ of the Italian War Office), 8 June 1939. According to the latter publication, Italian warships assisted General Franco's forces in the defense of Majorca and the occupation of the neighboring island of Ibiza in September 1936. With regard to Italian ground forces, the first contingent of black shirts, numbering three thousand, did not leave Italy until 18

December 1936 (see telegrams from the German ambassador in Rome to the Wilhelmstrasse, as given in *Documents on Germany Foreign Policy, 1918–1945*, III, 169, 173. The first shipment of Italian artillery, antiaircraft guns, and armored cars, however, reached Spain toward the end of September (Aznar, 316). The entire question of Italian aid to General Franco is covered most thoroughly in John F. Coverdale, *Italian Intervention in the Spanish Civil War.*

23. See chapter 1, text to nn. 37–41.

24. *Memorias de la conspiración*, 41.

25. See chapter 1, text to n. 227.

26. See chapter 1, n. 42.

27. *Fu la Spagna*, 63.

28. Bolín, *Spain*, 53, 159–72. For a copy of the document signed by General Franco, see photograph, ibid., between pp. 38–39.

29. See chapter 1, text to nn. 37–41.

30. *No fué posible la paz*, 713.

31. III, 126. For the best account of Mussolini's initial hesitancy to enter the Spanish conflict, see Coverdale, 66–84.

32. *Triumph of Treason*, 340–41.

33. U.S. Department of State, *Foreign Relations of the United States*, II, 467.

34. *Documents on German Foreign Policy, 1918–1945*, III, 170–73. The motives for Italian intervention are discussed in Coverdale, 74–84.

35. Krivitsky's claim that Stalin's underlying goal was to reach an understanding with Germany was made four months before the signing of the Soviet-German nonaggression pact of 23 August 1939. See his articles in the *Saturday Evening Post*, 22 and 29 Apr. 1939.

36. *In Stalin's Secret Service*, 80–81.

37. See, for example, the *New Masses*, 9 May 1939, and the reply to these accusations by the *Saturday Evening Post*, 24 June 1939.

38. *Sotsialisticheskii Vestnik*, 18, 31 Mar.; 15, 29 Apr. 1938; *Saturday Evening Post*, 15, 22, 29 Apr., 17, 24 June, 4 Nov. 1939; Krivitsky.

39. For the best accounts of the Krivitsky affair, see Paul Wohl in the *Commonwealth*, 28 Feb. 1941, and Flora Lewis in the *Washington Post*, 13 Feb. 1966. Krivitsky's fear of assassination is described by Victor Serge (who knew him personally) in *Mémoires d'un révolutionnaire*, 374.

40. *Sotsialisticheskii Vestnik*, 25 Feb. 1941. Nicolaevsky's testimony is bolstered by the fact that he knew Krivitsky intimately. See also Paul Wohl (who also knew him intimately) in the *Commonwealth*, 29 Feb. 1941.

41. *The Spanish Civil War*, 1st ed. (1961), 263, n. 1. I am indebted to John Amsden for giving me a copy of his unpublished manuscript, "Krivitsky," in which he critically discusses the attitudes of various Spanish Civil War historians (including Thomas) toward Krivitsky. The copy of the manuscript has been deposited with the Hoover Institution, Stanford.

42. *The Spanish Civil War*, rev. ed. (1965), 337, n. 1.

43. Article, *Saturday Evening Post*, 29 Apr. 1939; see also Krivitsky, 21. Krivitsky first referred publicly to Stalin's desire for a pact with Hitler in March 1938 (see quotation at the end of the next note).

44. *The Communist Party of the Soviet Union*, 485, n. 2. Schapiro expresses his indebtedness to John Erickson of St. Andrews University for a copy of the document. I, too, am most grateful to Professor Erickson for giving me the reference to this document

and to other important papers relating to Kandelaki's overtures, dated 6, 17, 19, and 20 Feb. 1937, namely, *Kandelaki Mission* Auswärtiges Amt. Film Serial 1907 H/429294–324 (National Archives, Washington D.C.), and for bringing to my attention his imposing work, *The Soviet High Command*, published in 1962, in which he discusses the secret negotiations and Kandelaki's role therein (396–97, 432, 453, 458, 464, 731, n. 79). Why these important papers were left out of the official *Documents on German Foreign Policy, 1918–1945*, Series D. Vol. III, where they strictly belong, has not been satisfactorily explained. Were they inadvertently omitted or were they considered too embarrassing to the Soviet government at the time the selection was made? The reason given to me by one authority regarding the document of 11 February, to which Leonard Schapiro refers (that "it was deleted—or missed—from the collections," because "no one had paid much attention to it since it came generally under 'trade discussions.' And, in any event, who would know the name Kandelaki?") is far from satisfactory inasmuch as Vols. IV and V, Series C, of *Documents on German Foreign Policy, 1918–1945*, contain numerous documents referring to Kandelaki and his trade negotiations with the Germans between 9 April 1935 and 6 May 1936. Some of these reveal the Soviet desire for improved political relations between the two countries (Vol. IV, 28–29, 453–54, 783–84, 870–71, 967–72; Vol. V, 488–91, 512, 571–73), but they are far less important than the documents that somehow escaped publication. The claim that Stalin was putting out feelers for a political agreement with Germany as early as 1936–37 was not acceptable to some historians even in the early 1950s, including this writer. "Many books published by émigrés from the USSR contain sensational stories about secret German-Soviet relations, especially in the nineteen-thirties," Edward Hallett Carr wrote in 1951, "but these frequently contradict one another and are still unsubstantiated by serious evidence" (*German-Soviet Relations between the Two World Wars, 1919–1939*, 141). It is therefore interesting to recall what the well-informed Krivitsky had written as far back as March 1938, but to which little attention was paid at the time. "In the fall of 1935 . . . ," he wrote, "it seemed to Stalin that a favorable moment was approaching for successful negotiations. Stalin's optimism can be explained by the fact that at that time Germany had extended new credits on favorable terms to the Soviet Union. And right away one could hear in the Politburo the much-flaunted phrase of Stalin: 'Well, how can we expect Hitler to wage war against us if he gives us all these credits?' . . . That credits have been decided upon is a fact, but the rest of the matter remains unchanged. Nevertheless, Stalin is confident and will not give up. In the fall of 1936, it again seems to Stalin that Hitler will agree to negotiate. During the Politburo meeting all the preliminary data is carefully examined. . . . The work of preparing for the talks is given to the Soviet trade representative Kandelaki and to a resident [in Berlin] of the People's Commissariat of Internal Affairs. . . . In the spring of 1937, Kandelaki goes to Moscow together with the aforementioned resident of the PCIA. When they arrive there the mood in the Politburo is elevated; everybody is talking about the forthcoming great events that will change the course of our foreign policy by 180 degrees. . . . In Europe, a colossal game is being played by Hitler and Stalin. It is impossible to say at this time who in the end will deceive whom" (*Sotsialisticheskii Vestnik*, 31 Mar. 1938).

45. *Soy del quinto regimiento*, 235–36.

46. *Documents on German Foreign Policy, 1918–1945*, III, 89.

47. Ibid., 100.

48. *The Last Days of Madrid*, 51.

49. *Así fué la defensa de Madrid*, 213.

50. See Manuilsky's report to the Eighteenth Congress of the Communist Party of the

Soviet Union on 10 March 1939, as given in *The Land of Socialism Today and Tomorrow*, 57–100.

51. *Brigate internazionali in Spagna*, 30.

52. See chapter 21, text to nn. 82 and 83.

53. *Las brigadas internacionales*, 49.

54. Krivitisky, 80, also 85.

55. As given in *Acción Socialista*, 1 Feb. 1952. For Hernández's expulsion from the party in 1944, see his book, *En el país de la gran mentira*, 215–27.

56. See, for example, speeches at the Radical party congress, reported in *L'Ere Nouvelle*, 25 Oct. 1936.

57. See, for example, the *Daily Herald*, 10 Oct. 1936.

58. R. Palme Dutt in *Labour Monthly*, Aug. 1936.

59. For an excellent account of the Soviet dilemma, see Fernando Claudín (a Communist for thirty years), *La crisis del movimiento comunista*, 180–81.

60. David T. Cattell, *Communism and the Spanish Civil War*, 58.

61. *L'Humanité*, 4 Aug. 1936; *Communist International*, Oct. 1936; *International Press Correspondence*, 8 Aug. 1936; *Daily Worker*, 5 Aug. 1936.

62. *L'Humanité*, 3 Aug. 1936.

63. Ibid. See also statement to the foreign press representatives in Madrid by Jesús Hernández, as given in *Mundo Obrero* (Madrid), 8 Aug. 1936.

64. *International Press Correspondence*, 8 Aug. 1936.

65. Franz Borkenau, *The Spanish Cockpit*, 110.

66. *Mundo Obrero* (Madrid), 18 Aug. 1936; *International Press Correspondence*, 29 Aug. 1936. Despite the above quotations, which appeared in the text or footnotes of my work, *The Grand Camouflage*, 101–3, demonstrating that the Communists attempted to minimize or conceal from the outside world the depth of the social revolution that had swept the country, Herbert R. Southworth ridicules my thesis that there was an attempt at concealment (*El mito*, 155).

Chapter 8

1. Frank E. Manuel, *The Politics of Modern Spain*, 164.

2. José Díaz, *Tres años de lucha*, 352.

3. André Marty, *En Espagne . . . où se joue le destin de l'Europe*, 34.

4. Reported in *Mundo Obrero* (Madrid), 9 Sept. 1936.

5. Letter to me. Other prominent left-wing Socialists simply ignored my written requests for information on this matter.

6. Report from London, *La Humanitat*, 13 Aug. 1936.

7. "While it is not mandatory under international law for other governments to allow an established, friendly government seeking to suppress a rebellion to purchase arms and supplies in their markets, it is generally acceded to in practice" (Dante A. Puzzo, *Spain and the Great Powers, 1936–1941*, 149–50). On the other hand, Julio Alvarez del Vayo, the pro-Communist foreign minister in the government that succeeded Giral's cabinet in September 1936, wrote: "Juridically there was no possible defense for Non-Intervention. To refuse a legitimate government, with whom the United Kingdom and France were maintaining normal diplomatic relations, their indisputable right to acquire the material necessary to subdue the revolt of a few rebel generals was the very extreme of arbitrary conduct" (*Freedom's Battle*, 44).

8. *Guerra y revolución en España, 1936–1939*, I, 265.

9. *The Invisible Writing*, 372.

10. "Ispanskii Dnevnik," *Novyi Mir*, Apr. 1938, 41–42. For information on "Ispanskii Dnevnik" (Koltzov's diary), see chapter 4, no. 112.

11. Clara Campoamor, *La révolution espagnole vue par une républicaine*, 143–46; cf. Henri Rabasseire, *Espagne: creuset politique*, 98. See also Pierre Broué and Emile Témime, *La révolution et la guerre d'Espagne*, 180–81, and Fernando Claudín, *La crisis del movimiento comunista*, 610, who gives credence to this version.

12. *Guerra y revolución*, II, 45–46.

13. "Ispanskii Dnevnik," *Novyi Mir*, Apr. 1938, 39–40.

14. *La guerre d'Espagne*, 146.

15. "Ispanskii Dnevnik," *Novyi Mir*, Apr. 1938, 40.

16. 4 Sept. 1936.

17. See chapter 9, text to nn. 2–12.

18. The condition that he would not form a government unless the Communists shared the responsibilities of office is corroborated by a variety of sources: Alvarez del Vayo, *Freedom's Battle*, 212; Jesús Hernández, *Yo fui un ministro de Stalin*, 47; *Guerra y revolución*, II, 47; *Historia del partido comunista de España*, 139. The last two volumes are official histories of the Civil War and Spanish Communist party written by commissions presided over by La Pasionaria.

19. "Ispanskii Dnevnik," *Novyi Mir*, Apr. 1938, 46–47.

20. *Madrid*, 159.

21. *Yo fui un ministro de Stalin*, 47.

22. As given in the official *Gaceta de Madrid*, 5 Sept. 1936.

23. Ibid., 16 Sept. 1936.

24. Ibid., 26 Sept. 1936.

25. *Why Spain Fights On*, 37. See also excerpt from article by Marcel Rosenberg (Soviet ambassador to Spain until April 1937) in the *Journal de Moscou*, as quoted by *Le Temps*, 1 May 1937.

26. Jesús de Galíndez, *Las vascos en el Madrid sitiado*, 19.

27. This passage is on p. 68 of the report (see Bibliography, part II).

28. Actually, the only Catholic was Manuel de Irujo, a member of the Basque Nationalist party, as indicated above in the list of cabinet members.

29. *Guerra y revolución*, II, 49.

30. *The Spanish Revolution*, 235.

31. See chapter 5, no. 8.

32. Díaz, 390.

33. *Politics, Economics and Men of Modern Spain, 1808–1946*, 599.

34. *Nation*, 7 Aug. 1937.

35. Arturo Barea, *The Forging of a Rebel*, 706.

36. F. Ferrándiz Alborz, *La bestia contra España*, 95.

37. See, for example, *Política*, 24 Nov., 1 Dec. 1936.

38. Claudín, 186.

39. Henry Buckley, *Life and Death of the Spanish Republic*, 402.

40. 6 Nov. 1936.

41. Speech, *La Voz Valenciana*, 10 Mar. 1937.

42. Speech, 21 Apr. 1940, as given in Prieto, *Inauguración del círculo "Pablo Iglesias" de México*, 13. See also article by Juan López, *CNT* (Madrid), 19 June 1937.

43. *Yo, comunista en Rusia*, 29.

44. *The Spanish Labyrinth*, 326.

45. See text to nn. 77–80, this chapter.

46. *Les anarchistes espagnoles et le pouvoir, 1868–1969*, 96–97, n. 78.

47. Ibid., 210–11.

48. Ibid., 211–12.

49. Ibid., 236–37. For information about the author of this important book, see chapter 4, n. 67.

50. Carlos de Baráibar, *Vía Libre*, 5 Aug. 1939. See also excerpt from his article in *Timon* (Buenos Aires), June 1940, as quoted in chapter 25, text to n. 81, and excerpt from article by the left Socialist leader, Rodolfo Llopis, as quoted in chapter 24, text to n. 40.

51. Barea, 579.

52. For an account by a left-wing Socialist of how the Socialist party in the provincial capital of Alicante, where it was the strongest political organization, had failed to compete successfully with the Communists and anarchists for the control of leading positions, see Ferrándiz Alborz, 64–65.

53. Report to the Labor and Socialist International dated 23 May 1939, published in special issue of *Independent News* [June 1939?].

54. *Política de ayer y política de mañana*, 79, 88.

55. *Yo fui un ministro de Stalin*, 135.

56. See his letter to José Bullejos, 20 Nov. 1939, as given in Francisco Largo Caballero, *¿Qué se puede hacer?*, 20–24. See also chapter 1, text to nn. 119–21.

57. For reference to this by Largo Caballero, see his speech as given in Francisco Largo Caballero, *La UGT y la guerra*, 32. For detailed information on the PSUC, see chapter 27, text to nn. 53–56.

58. See Largo Caballero, *La UGT y la guerra*, 32, also *Adelante*, Largo Caballero's organ in Valencia, 8 Apr. 1937.

59. For complaints in the left-wing Socialist press regarding some of these methods, such as flattery, offers of material gain, and coercion, see article in the *Boletín de la Unión de Trabajadores*, as given in *Claridad*, 11 Mar. 1937; also article by S. Esteve Gregori in *Adelante* (Valencia), 27 Mar. 1937.

60. See chapter 9, text to nn. 2–12.

61. See report by Wenceslao Carrillo to the Labor and Socialist International, 23 May 1939, in which the Communist sympathies of Domínguez, Rosal, and Pretel are mentioned, as published in special issue of *Independent News* [June 1939?]. For Rosal's criticism of Largo Caballero's "anti-Communist" and "anti-Soviet" position in 1937, which he ascribes largely to the influence of "Caballero's eminence grise, Luis Araquistáin," see his book, *Historia de la UGT de España, 1901–1939*, II, 621–31.

62. See article by left Socialist leader, Rodolfo Llopis, *Tribuna*, Mar. 1949, and Julian Zugazagoitia, *Historia de la guerra en España*, 170.

63. Francisco Montiel, *Por qué he ingresado en el partido comunista*, 4.

64. Juventudes Socialistas Unificadas.

65. See José Díaz in *International Press Correspondence*, 9 May 1936; Segis Alvarez, *Nuestra organización y nuestros cuadros*, 7; *Mundo Obrero* (Madrid), 2 Apr. 1936, as given in Ricardo de Cierva, *Los documentos de la primavera trágica*, 459–61; also *Mundo Obrero* (Madrid), 6 Apr. 1936.

66. *En marcha hacia la victoria*, 13.

67. See his speech, *Frente Rojo*, 2 Apr. 1937.

68. *El comunismo y la guerra de España*, 9. According to Amaro del Rosal, former Caballerista and member of the UGT executive committee, who supported the Communists during and after the war, Caballero was frequently visited in jail after the 1934 rebellion

by delegates of the Comintern, including Codovila, "who were always accompanied by Araquistáin and Alvarez del Vayo" (*Historia de la UGT*, II, 622).

69. See Santiago Carrillo's tribute to Largo Caballero for his help in effecting the fusion (speech, reported in *Mundo Obrero* [Madrid], 6 Apr. 1936).

70. Passages from this statement are quoted by Carlos Hernández Zancajo, *Tercera etapa de octubre*, 9–11.

71. See Luis Romero Solano, *Vísperas de la guerra de España*, 77. Romero Solano represent Estremadura on the national committee of the Socialist Youth Federation.

72. The estimate of Antonio Escribano, organizational secretary of the JSU in Alicante province, in a letter to me. It will be recalled, however, that Santiago Carrillo, the general secretary of the JSU, gives forty thousand as the figure for the *combined* membership at the time of the fusion, but the ratio of three to fifty may be fairly accurate. The Communist writer, Evgenii S. Varga, in his book *Ispaniia v revoluitsii*, 117, gives the number of young Communists alone as fifty-one thousand, obviously an exaggerated figure.

73. See, for example, his article in *Claridad*, 13 May 1936; speech in Saragossa, reported in ibid., 1 June 1936.

74. For example, Alfredo Cabello, José Cazorla, José Laín, Federico Melchor, and Serrano Poncela. The Spanish Communist refugee periodical *España Popular* of 15 June 1940 gives the date of José Cazorla's entry into the Communist party as 7 November 1936. According to Enrique Castro, onetime commander in chief of the Communist Fifth Regiment and former member of the party's central committee, both Santiago Carrillo and José Cazorla joined the party on 6 November 1936 (*Hombres made in Moscú*, 439). For Santiago Carrillo's defense of their action, see Carrillo, *La juventud, factor de la victoria*, 14.

75. According to Pedro Checa, a member of the central committee, in a speech in March 1937 (*A un gran partido, una gran organización*, 23).

76. *Timón* (Buenos Aires), June 1940.

77. *Hombres*, 374.

78. *La gran estafa*, 307.

79. Ibid., 309–10.

80. For the information on Togliatti, I am grateful to a number of Spanist Communist refugees, whom I met in Mexico in 1939 and 1940.

81. U.S. Congress, Senate, Committee on the Judiciary, *Scope of Soviet Activity in the United States*, 3446.

82. From an unpublished commentary on Verle B. Johnston's "The International Brigades in the Spanish Civil War, 1936–1939" (Hoover Institution archives). For other biographical details on Togliatti, see Marcella and Maurizio Ferrara, *Conversando con Togliatti*; prologue by Adolfo Sánchez Vázquez in Palmiro Togliatti, *Escritos políticos*, 9–16; Hugh Thomas, *The Spanish Civil War* (1965), index, 904.

83. As given in *Nuestra lucha por la unidad*, 34. See also Santiago Carrillo, *Somos la organización de la juventud*, 6–9.

84. Carrillo, *En marcha*, 9.

85. Letter to me, written after the war.

86. The letters were published in *La Correspondencia de Valencia*, 31 Mar., 1 Apr. 1937, respectively. See also statement by José Gregori Martínez in *Adelante* (Valencia) as given in *La Correspondencia de Valencia*, 9 Apr. 1937.

Chapter 9

1. For the composition of the government, see chapter 8, text to n. 22.

2. See, for example, Francisco Largo Caballero, *Mis recuerdos*, 212; Luis Araquistáin, *El comunismo y la guerre de España*, 8, and his letter to Diego Martínez Barrio, as given in *Vía Libre*, 15 May 1939; also Carlos de Baráibar in *Timón* (Buenos Aires), June 1940; Wenceslao Carrillo in ibid., Nov. 1939; Indalecio Prieto in *Correo de Asturias*, 10 July 1943.

3. See *Claridad*, 15 Mar. 1939; also report of Wenceslao Carrillo to the Labor and Socialist International, 23 May 1939, as given in special issue of *Independent News* [June 1939?].

4. See his articles in *Claridad*, 5 Oct., 9 Nov. 1935; also *Times*, 2 Mar. 1936 (dispatch from Madrid); speech reported in *Verdad*, 13 Aug. 1937, showing his position prior to the war.

5. See chapter 8, text to n. 68.

6. See his articles in *Frente Rojo*, 19 June 1937, and speech, *Verdad*, 13 Aug. 1937; also Dolores Ibárruri's reference to him in her speech at the plenary session of the central committee of the Communist party, 17 June 1937 (*Frente Rojo*, 21 June 1937).

7. Julio Alvarez del Vayo, *The Last Optimist*, 323.

8. Ibid., 228

9. Quoted in Enrique Castro, *Hombres made in Moscú*, 659. See also chapter 21, text to n. 29, and chapter 25, text to nn. 97–102.

10. Castro, *Hombres*, 553.

11. Article in *Socialist Review*, Sept. 1937.

12. See letter by Simone in *Tiempo*, 27 Aug. 1943; also Claud Cockburn (alias Frank Pitcairn, reporter for the Communist London *Daily Worker* during the Civil War), *A Discord of Trumpets*, 305–9, and *Crossing the Line*, 26–28; Arthur Koestler, *The Invisible Writing*, 400–401, 409. After World War II Simone became editor of the Czech Communist newspaper *Rude Pravo* during the Stalinist-controlled regime of Klement Gottwald and was placed on trial and hanged in 1952 with ten other prominent Communists, mostly Jews, including Rudolf Slansky, former secretary general of the Czech Communist party and premier, after "confessing" to crimes of "sabotage, treason, and espionage" (see Arthur G. London, a Communist and former vice-minister of foreign affairs, who, with two other leading Communists, was sentenced during the same trial to life imprisonment, *L'aveu*, 277–324). Sixteen years later, in 1968, Simone and all the other convicted men were "rehabilitated" (ibid., 324).

13. Because of his services to the Communist cause, some Spaniards have concluded that at the beginning of the war he was a member of the left wing of the Socialist party. This is untrue. See, for example, Julián Zugazagoitia (a moderate Socialist), *Historia de la guerra en España*, 138, who shows that he was a follower of Prieto's.

14. See, for example, Luis Araquistáin (letter to Martínez Barrio, as given in *Vía Libre*, 15 May 1939; *El comunismo*, 14, 17); Carlos de Baráibar (*Timón* [Buenos Aires], June 1940); Wenceslao Carrillo (speech in May 1946, as given in *Segundo congreso del partido socialista obrero español en el exilio*, 95–107; Carrillo, *El último episodio de la guerra civil española*, 10); Gabriel Morón, *Política de ayer y política de mañana*, 108–9; Indalecio Prieto (*Cómo y por qué salí del ministerio de defensa nacional*, prologues to the Mexican and French editions, 12, 25; Prieto, *Convulsiones de España*, II, 141, III, 219; *Epistolario, Prieto y Negrín*, 17, 99–100; article in *Correo de Asturias*, 10 July 1943; article in *El Socialista* [Paris], 9 Nov. 1950; interview given by Prieto to the United Press, reported in *El Universal*,

30 July 1939); Zugazagoitia, 408, 464, 535. But see also the testimony of Segismundo Casado, *The Last Days of Madrid*, 101, 281, and Jesús Pérez Salas, *Guerra en España, 1936–1939*, 141, 162, as well as editorials in *Política*, 16, 20 Mar. 1939. For confirmation by two former leading Communists that Negrín was controlled by the party, see Castro, *Hombres*, 660; Valentín González (El Campesino), article in *Solidaridad Obrera* (Paris), 11 Mar. 1951, who describes Negrín as the Communists' "ambitious and docile tool."

15. Information given to me by Vittorio Vidali, known in Spain as Carlos Contreras, one of the principal organizers of the regiment.

16. See *Claridad*, 15 Mar. 1939; also report of Wenceslao Carrillo to the Labor and Socialist International, 23 May 1939, as given in the special issue of *Independent News* [June 1939?].

17. See Angel Garlarza in *El Socialista Español*, 2 Dec. 1946.

18. *My Mission to Spain*, 358.

19. See also the American historian Dante A. Puzzo, *Spain and the Great Powers, 1936–1941*, 186, 267, n. 48, whose authority for Negrín's alleged independence of the Communists is no other than Alvarez del Vayo.

20. *The Tragedy of Manuel Azaña and the Fate of the Spanish Republic*, 182.

21. *Half of Spain Died*, 225–26.

22. *The Spanish Civil War*, 556 and n. 1.

23. According to Pablo de Azcárate's son, Manuel, today (1978) one of the leaders of the Spanish Communist party, Negrín was "perhaps the political figure who exercised the greatest influence" upon his father (see his preface to Pablo de Azcárate, *Mi embajada en Londres durante la guerra civil española*, 17).

24. See *Españoles de mi tiempo*, 414.

25. *In Stalin's Secret Service*, 96–97. See chapter 7, text to nn. 38–43, for information on Krivitsky.

26. Ibid., 99–100.

27. *Epistolario, Prieto y Negrín*, 104. In this postwar exchange of correspondence Negrín does not deny Prieto's allegation regarding Louis Fischer.

28. *Nation*, 13 Jan. 1940.

29. *The Last Optimist*, 291. He adds on p. 292: "[A point that] Negrín considered essential to the maintenance of good relations with the Russians was a clear understanding that he would not tolerate, from anyone, even the suggestion of intervention in the affairs of the republican government or in the internal policy of Spain."

30. *El oro español en la guerra civil*, 212–13, n. 69, 226, 235, 261, 278, 281. This remarkable six-hundred page volume, published in November 1976 and based largely on classified documents found in the Bank of Spain and the Ministry of Finance in 1973, is by far the most important work published to date on the mobilization of the Spanish gold reserves and on other aspects of republican finances during the Civil War.

Although published by the finance ministry's Instituto de Estudios Fiscales, all but a dozen copies were seized by the foreign affairs ministry and its distribution was forbidden. Up to this day (February 1978) no explanation has been given, but it is believed that the ministry feared that the book might jeopardize the negotiations then in progress for the resumption of diplomatic relations between Spain and the USSR (see article by David Wingeate Pike in *World Affairs Report*, Mar. 1977). Meanwhile, Professor Viñas has completed another book, based on the solid research and documentation of the first, but enriched by new material and discussion. As this second work (to be published by Ediciones Grijalbo of Barcelona) will not appear until the fall of 1978, I am grateful to him for allowing me to read several chapters ahead of time. I am also indebted to him for suggestions regarding my treatment of the gold question, several of which I have incorporated in this chapter.

31. *El oro español*, 212–13, n. 69. In a new work (see n. 30) and in a letter to me Viñas contends that Stashevsky's role has been overestimated.

32. Krivitsky, 99–100.

33. Orlov gives 13 August 1938 as the date he received political asylum in the United States, one month after leaving Spain (Orlov, *The Secret History of Stalin's Crimes*, xv). In *The Legacy of Alexander Orlov*, prepared by the U.S. Senate Subcommittee on Internal Security after Orlov's death in the United States on 10 April 1973, which contains a photograph of Orlov, his name at birth is given as Leon Lazarevich Feldbin and his party name as Lev Lazarevich Nikol'skiy (pp. 3–4). Orlov informed the subcommittee on 28 September 1955 that he was sent by the politburo to Spain in September 1936 (p. 16). "I had arrived in Madrid on September 16, 1936, about two months after the outbreak of the Spanish Civil War," he wrote in 1966, "to head a large Soviet mission in intelligence and of military experts. As a general in the Intelligence Service (NKVD), I was chief Soviet adviser to the republican government on intelligence, counterintelligence and guerrilla warfare, a post I was to hold for nearly two years" (*Reader's Digest*, Nov. 1966).

34. *Reader's Digest*, Nov. 1966. Viñas, *El oro español*, 190, states that Negrín was the "driving force" in the decision to send the gold to Russia.

35. Viñas, *El oro español*, 76, gives the weight of the gold actually sent to Russia as 510 metric tons.

36. Marcelino Pascua, "Oro español en Moscú," *Cuadernos para el Diálogo*, June–July 1970.

37. Ibid.

38. Viñas, *El oro español*, 140.

39. The text of the decree is reproduced in *Causa General*, Anexo XIII. See also Viñas, *El oro español*, 133–34.

40. Viñas, *El oro español*, 146–47, states that the ten thousand cases of gold were transported by rail between 15 and 21 September and gives the exact times of departure of the trains.

41. Viñas, *El oro español*, 139, 137.

42. Ibid., 129.

43. Ibid., 76.

44. For a detailed account of the shipments to France and other related information, see ibid., 47–89.

45. For a list of the principal recipients of funds, together with the sums they received, see ibid., 87; see also 121–23 for additional information.

46. Quoted in ibid., 84–85.

47. Quoted in ibid., 99.

48. Ibid., 101–5.

49. Ibid., 105–21.

50. Ibid., 35. For some of the provisions of this law, see ibid., 33–34. In order to circumvent the law, both the Giral and Largo Caballero cabinets approved certain confidential decrees relating to the export of gold and allocation of foreign exchange, although after the gold shipments to France had already begun (ibid., 38–39). See also 553–57, for the confidential decree of 29 April 1938, by which the gold sales were made legal. It was approved long after the gold reserves in their entirety had been shipped abroad, leaving the paper currency in circulation without any gold backing. According

to Viñas, no republican leader ever acknowledged the existence of this decree (article in *Historia 16*, Mar. 1977).

51. *The Last Optimist*, 284.

52. Viñas, *El oro español*, 227. In the opinion of this eminently objective scholar, who recognizes the political disadvantages of shipping the bulk of the gold reserves to Russia, they could not have been sent to any other country and mobilized as effectively for the war effort (ibid., 182–87). See also Mariano Ansó, *Yo fui ministro de Negrín*, 309–11. In his article, "Oro español en Moscú," Marcelino Pascua, the former Spanish ambassador to Moscow, discusses the reasons why it was considered impractical or unwise to ship the gold to England, France, Switzerland, the United States, or Mexico (*Cuadernos al Diálogo*, June–July 1970).

53. For the secrecy that surrounded the bank's operations and its failure to publish any records of the accounts held by the republican government, see Viñas, 362. For additional information relating to this bank, see ibid., 81, 227–29, 460–61.

54. U.S. Congress, Senate, Committee on the Judiciary, *Scope of Soviet Activity in the United States*, 3430.

55. According to Viñas, *El oro español*, 147–50, 1,998 cases went to France and 202 were sent to the Ministry of Finance in Valencia.

56. Luis Bolín, *Spain: The Vital Years*, 375–82, reproduces the official eight-page receipt in its French version.

57. The figures of $518 million and 460.52 metric tons are given by Viñas, *El oro español*, 207–10.

58. Ansó, 313–30. The Spanish edition of Luis Bolín's book, *España! Los años vitales*, contains copies of several documents turned over to the Franco government that are not in the English edition.

59. Ansó, 325–29. In a letter to me, Viñas claims that Ansó's version regarding the units of the Spanish fleet is incorrect. "They had been embargoed," he writes, "in Odessa in order to secure payment of certain sums owing to Soviet commercial agencies. The Soviet authorities had tried to acquire them or lease them. Finally, in February 1939 [one month before the end of the war] the republican government decided to accept a Russian offer to buy them." In the manuscript of his new work (see n. 30, above), Viñas refers to only five vessels, not to "numerous units," as does Ansó.

60. *Reader's Digest*, Nov. 1966.

61. U.S. Congress, Senate, *Scope of Soviet Activity*, 3431–32.

62. *The Last Optimist*, 285–86.

63. *Reader's Digest*, Nov. 1966.

64. U.S. Congress, Senate, *Scope of Soviet Activity*, 3431–32.

65. See article by N. Kuznetsov, Soviet naval attaché and adviser to Antonio Ruiz, chief of the Cartagena Naval Base, in *Pod znamenen ispanskoi respubliki, 1936–1939*, 241–44. The number of Soviet vessels is confirmed by Marcelino Pascua, "Oro español en Moscú," *Cuadernos para el Diálogo*, June–July 1970.

66. Krivitsky, 112–13.

67. "Oro español en Moscú," *Cuadernos para el Diálogo*, June–July 1970.

68. See Viñas, *El oro español*, Table 19 (between pp. 244–45), for a detailed account of the melting and refining, based on official Soviet figures that he found in the Bank of Spain, of varying amounts of gold that were sold in accordance with fifteen orders received from the Spanish treasury.

69. Unpublished manuscript, chapter VI, n. 66 and text; chapter VIII, n. 6 (see n. 30, above). In a letter to me, Viñas states: "The matter of the four bank employees has

given rise to many accusations, but it appears that their stay in Moscow was due to the fact that the republican authorities themselves did not want them to return."

70. *El oro español*, 197, n. 57.

71. Unpublished manuscript, chapter VIII, n. 6 (see n. 30, above). For Indalecio Prieto's account, see *Cómo y por qué salí del ministerio de defensa nacional* (preface to the Mexican edition), 16.

72. Pp. 217, 313. Prieto says: "The high-ranking Soviet officials who participated in the matter [of the Spanish gold] disappeared from the scene: finance minister Grinko; the director of the Gosbank [State Bank] Marguliz; the subdirector Cagan; the representative [in the State Bank] of the finance ministry, Ivanovsky; the new director of the State Bank, Martinson. All lost their jobs, several went to prison, and Grinko was shot."—*Cómo y por qué salí del ministerio de defensa nacional* (preface to the Mexican edition), 16.

73. Viñas, *El oro español*, 229–56. See also chapter VII and VIII of Viñas's manuscript (n. 30, above).

74. Unpublished manuscript, chapter VIII and IX (see n. 30, above).

75. *Convulsiones*, II, 146–47.

76. Ansó, 328; Alvarez del Vayo, *The Last Optimist*, 284.

77. See n. 39, above, and text.

78. Prieto later claimed that not until 1954, several years after Largo Caballero's death, when the latter's memoirs, *Mis recuerdos*, were published, did he learn that Largo Caballero was aware of and approved the shipment to Russia (*Convulsiones*, III, 221, article dated 5 Dec. 1956).

79. *Cómo y por qué salí del ministerio de defensa nacional* (preface to the Mexican edition), Apr. 1940, 15. Nevertheless, Marcelino Pascua claims that Negrín told him that Prieto's presence in Cartagena was the result of a prior agreement between the two men (article in *Cuadernos del Diálogo*, June–July 1970). Viñas, in his new work, chapter VI, text to n. 9 (see n. 30, above), expresses his doubts regarding Prieto's professed ignorance.

80. *Convulsiones*, II, 124, article dated 6 Feb. 1957.

81. U.S. Congress, Senate, *Scope of Soviet Activity*, 3433. My italics. See also article by Orlov in *Reader's Digest*, Nov. 1966.

82. *The Last Optimist*, 284.

83. Ibid., 283. My italics.

84. *Convulsiones*, II, 124–25, article dated 6 Feb. 1957.

85. Ibid., 131–33, article dated 19 Nov. 1958.

86. Ansó, 312.

87. Article by N. Kuznetsov in *Pod znamenen*, 241–44. This evidence disposes of Marcelino Pascua's claim that it was decided that the four Soviet vessels should leave Cartagena at night and sail to Odessa unescorted so as not to arouse the suspicion of the enemy (article in *Cuadernos para el Diálogo*, June–July 1970).

88. *The Last Optimist*, 285. Marcelino Pascua claims that Negrín told him repeatedly that Azaña had never objected to the gold shipment to the USSR (article in *Cuadernos para el Diálogo*, June–July 1970).

89. *Convulsiones*, II, 133, article dated Nov. 1958.

90. Article in *Cuadernos para el Diálogo*, June–July 1970.

91. *Mis recuerdos*, 203–4.

92. U.S. Congress, Senate, *Scope of Soviet Activity*, 3431, 3433–34.

93. Article in *Life*, 27 Apr. 1953.

94. Casado, 52.

95. Ibid., 54.

96. *El comunismo*, 24–25.

97. Ibid., 26.

98. Louis Fischer claims that at no time were there more than 700 Soviet Russians in Spain (*Men and Politics*, 498). Krivitsky, 95, on the other hand, places the igure at under 2,000. For a list of more than 360 Soviet participants, both civilian and military, gleaned from published sources, see José Luis Alcofar Massaes, *Los asesores soviéticos en la guerra civil española*, 153–62.

99. Ignacio Hidalgo de Cisneros, the Spanish chief of the air force, when interviewed by me after the war, stated that Soviet pilots were relieved every few months and that altogether one thousand flew in Spain during the war. The German pilots were also relieved frequently to gain experience, according to Hermann Goering, Hitler's Air Force chief (see chapter 7).

100. *Cómo y por qué salí del ministerio de defensa national* (prologue to the French edition), 24–25. See also excerpt from Largo Caballero's unpublished memoirs, quoted in chapter 21, text to n. 43.

101. Pp. 126–27.

102. 4 Oct. 1936.

103. Quoted by Julián Gorkin in *Workers' Age*, 31 May 1939.

104. Excerpts from his statement, which was made on 4 December 1936, were given to me by the delegation itself when I was representing the United Press in Valencia and were approved for transmission to the United Press office in London by the foreign press censorship. They were not published in any of the newspapers I consulted (see Bibliography: "Burnet Bolloten. Dispatch from Valencia to the United Press").

105. *Manchester Guardian*, 25 Nov. 1936. See also his statement to the Duchess of Atholl and other women members of Parliament as given in *Claridad*, 22 Apr. 1937.

106. *Discurso del presidente del consejo de ministros, Francisco Largo Caballero, el 1° de febrero de 1937*, 9, as given in Carlos M. Rama, *La crisis española del siglo XX*, 260.

107. *Política*, 5 Sept. 1936.

108. 1 Oct. 1936.

109. The Left Republican party was not the only liberal party that attempted to conceal the changes in the economic, social, and political life of the left camp. See, for example, radio address to world opinion by Diego Martínez Barrio, vice-president of the Republic and leader of the Republican Union party, as reported in *Política*, 2 Aug. 1936.

110. *Política*, 2 Dec. 1936.

111. Article in *Left News*, Jan. 1943.

112. *Españoles de mi tiempo*, 407–14.

113. *Mis recuerdos*, 187.

114. *Palabras al viento*, 282.

115. Sedwick, 174–75.

116. III, xxxiii.

117. *Freedom's Battle*, 214.

118. *Obras*, III, 558.

119. *Mis recuerdos*, 187.

120. *Memorias, 2*, 457.

121. *Así cayó Alfonso XIII*, 167, also 230.

122. Sedwick, 169.

123. The full text of the letter in French—the language of diplomacy—is in Ma-

dariaga, *Spain*, 672–74. It was first published in English, however, together with a facsimile of the first and last pages, in an article by Luis Araquistáin that appeared shortly after the war in the *New York Times* of 4 June 1939. The letter is reproduced in Russian, together with a Spanish translation, in the official Spanish Communist history of the Civil War, *Guerra y revolución en España, 1936–1939*, II, 100–102.

124. For a photostatic copy of the reply (in French), see *Guerra y revolución*, II, between pp. 102–3.

Chapter 10

1. See chapter 8, n. 7.

2. J. V. Stalin, *Sochineniia*, VII, 14. I am indebted to Isaac Deutscher for having brought this passage to my attention in his work on Stalin.

3. *The Spanish Civil War* (1965), 284.

4. Quoted by Iain Macleod (his biographer), *Neville Chamberlain*, 273.

5. U.S. Department of State, *Foreign Relations of the United States*, II, 575.

6. 29 Nov. 1936.

7. See the proposal made to Germany in December 1936 by Anthony Eden, British foreign secretary, as outlined in a communication from Joachim von Ribbentrop, German ambassador in Great Britain, to the Wilhelmstrasse (U.S. Department of State, *Documents on German Foreign Policy, 1918–1945*, III, 158–59).

8. Pertinax (André Géraud) in prologue to E. N. Dzelepy, *The Spanish Plot*, vii. See also Maurice Pujo in *L'Action Française*, 25 July 1936; Vicent Auriol, quoted by Indalecio Prieto in *España Republicana*, 17 July 1948; Fenner Brockway, *Workers' Front*, 159–60; Pierre Lazareff, *Deadline*, 134; Thomas, 331; Alexander Werth, *Which Way France?*, 397.

9. See, for example, David T. Cattell, *Soviet Diplomacy and the Spanish Civil War*, 10–11, 14.

10. See report by the U.S. chargé d'affaires in Paris to the secretary of state on 20 August 1936 stating that, according to Audré Blumel, Léon Blum's chef de cabinet, "the British government at first had been rather lukewarm in its support of the French initiative for a non-intervention pact" (U.S. Department of State, *Foreign Relations of the United States*, II, 503).

11. According to Louis Lévy, an intimate of Léon Blum, *Vérités sur la France*, 114.

12. See his testimony before the Parliamentary Commission of Inquiry set up in 1947 to investigate the events that took place in France between 1933 and 1945, as given in *Les événements survenus en France de 1933 à 1945*, I, 216–17. At the Radical party congress held in October 1936 a resolution was approved commending the government for having "averted a grave international peril" by proposing the Non-Intervention Agreement (see *L'Ere Nouvelle*, 24 Oct. 1936).

Researchers seeking a comprehensive picture of the attitudes of the different political parties and factions in France during the Spanish Civil War, as seen through the French press, will find David Wingeate Pike's meticulous *Les français et la guerre d'Espagne, 1936–1939*, invaluable. Pike's vast array of quoted material, based on the study of thousands of newspaper and magazine issues, will spare students and historians an endless amount of drudgery. See also his earlier studies *Conjecture, Propaganda, and Deceit and the Spanish Civil War* and *La crise espagnole de 1936 vue par la presse française*.

13. See chapter 7, text to n. 6.

14. See chapter 6, nn. 9 and 10. "The foreign policy of the Popular Front was weakened by the fact that the Franco-Soviet Pact, which should have been its solid

basis, was really accepted only by the Communist deputies, by a small part of the Socialist party, and by barely half the radicals. Were not the arguments of Léon Blum himself, in his articles in the *Populaire*, perhaps the most difficult to dismiss by those who wished to see the pact ratified? His policy was one of weakness. His personal views on collective security—'Fundamentally, can we logically be expected to run the risk of a war now in order to avoid another later on?'—were floating around more than ever'' (Geneviève Tabouis, *Ils l'ont appelée Cassandre*, 297).

15. 6 July 1936.

16. 20 Dec. 1936.

17. *Observer*, 1 Nov. 1936.

18. Letter dated 6 Feb. 1937, quoted in *Mission to Moscow*, 57–60. See also letter dated 19 Feb. 1937, ibid., 77–79.

19. In a frank account published after the Civil War of Italian assistance to General Franco, *Le Forze Armate*, the official organ of the Italian war office, revealed (8 June 1939) that between mid-December 1936 and mid-April 1937 the navy had transported 100,000 men to Spain in addition to 4,370 motor vehicles, 40,000 tons of war material, and 750 heavy guns. The journal also revealed that units of the Italian fleet had been employed in the early stages of the war not only in escorting Italian transports from Italian to Spanish ports but in naval operations against the republican fleet and coast as well as against ships bringing cargoes to republican ports, many of which had been sunk. For an equally frank account of German intervention in the early part of the war, see the special number of *Die Wehrmacht* entitled *Wir Kämpften in Spanien*, issued in May 1939 by the German High Command.

20. See chapter 6, n. 9.

21. See reference in the *Daily Herald*, 13 Jan. 1937, to the Labor party's appeal to the labor movement to "establish unity within its own ranks and not by association with organizations in conflict with the aims of the party."

22. For further information on "Pedro," see chapter 27, text to nn. 61–66.

23. According to Miguel Serra Pamies, a member of the central committee, when interviewed by me in 1940.

24. *El Día Gráfico*, 31 Jan. 1937.

25. *Treball*, 2 Feb. 1937.

26. For this information I am grateful to the PSUC leader mentioned in n. 23, above.

27. See Salvador de Madariaga's comments, chapter 9, text to n. 112.

28. *Mi embajada en Londres durante la guerra civil española*, 73. For the full text of the note, see ibid., 266–68.

29. *Yo fui un ministro de Stalin*, 75.

30. See, for example, *Daily Telegraph* and *Le Temps*, 11 Jan. 1937.

31. *Yo fui un ministro de Stalin*, 75–76.

32. *Convulsiones de España*, II, 92.

33. See *Times*, 12 Apr. 1937.

34. *El Adelanto*, 17 Mar. 1937.

35. Ibid.

36. *Freedom's Battle*, 235.

37. For the British and French replies, see the *Times*, 22 Apr. 1937. "Contrary to the calculations of the Kremlin 'strategists,'" writes Jesús Hernández, former politburo member, "neither France nor England nibbled at the bait" (*Yo fui un ministro de Stalin*, 76).

38. "When, after Munich, it became clear that the British government had decided to

follow very closely the policy of friendship with Rome which had already been initiated with the Anglo-Italian Agreement of the previous April," Alvarez del Vayo writes (*Freedom's Battle*, 255), "the Spanish government—in spite of its tremendous opposition to Italian intervention in Spain—did not hesitate to inform the British government categorically that if the latter would put an end to this intervention the victory and consolidation of the Republic in Spain would afford no obstacle whatever to a policy of collaboration with Italy in the Mediterranean. They even went as far as to declare that they would themselves be willing to collaborate with Italy on the basis of natural respect for the integrity and political independence of either state. This declaration, which I communicated personally to M. Fouques Duparc, the French chargé d'affaires in Barcelona, was also ignored by the British government."

39. Ibid., 238–39.

40. Quoted in Hernández, *Yo fui un ministro de Stalin*, 159.

41. *Frente Rojo*, 30 Mar. 1938, as reprinted in José Díaz, *Tres años de lucha*, 559.

42. Address in May 1939 before the Council of Foreign Relations in New York, quoted in Alvarez del Vayo, *Freedom's Battle*, 76.

43. See chapter 7.

44. International Military Tribunal, *The Trial of German Major War Criminals*, Part X, 181.

45. U.S. Department of State, *Nazi-Soviet Relations, 1939–1941*.

46. *Handbook of Intelligence and Guerrilla Warfare*, 20–23. Enrique Líster, commander of the Communist-controlled Fifth Regiment, also affirms that the Russians sent their best weapons to Spain (*Nuestra guerra*, 75–76).

47. *Saturday Evening Post*, 29 Apr. 1939.

48. *Mundo Obrero* (Madrid), 26 Feb. 1939.

49. *El último episodio de la guerra civil española*, 5–6.

50. *Freedom's Battle*, 66.

51. See chapter 6, text to nn. 23–26.

52. *Moscow, Tokyo, London*, 237–41.

53. For example, E. H. Carr and A. J. P. Taylor.

54. *Documents and Materials Relating to the Eve of the Second World War*, II, 183–89. Referring to Sir Horace Wilson's proposals, the Oxford historian, A. J. P. Taylor, writes: "Wilson produced a memorandum on 10 Downing Street notepaper, which, not surprisingly, has disappeared from the British records. This proposed an Anglo-German treaty of non-aggression and non-interference. . . . A pact of this kind 'would enable Britain to rid herself of her commitments vis-à-vis Poland.' . . . [It] is inconceivable that these proposals were made without Chamberlain's knowledge or approval" (*The Origins of the Second World War*, 244–45).

55. Taylor, 163.

56. See chapter 6. For the Russian view that Anglo-French diplomacy, even after the Nazi invasion of Poland and the formal declaration of war by Great Britain and France against Germany in September 1939, still aimed at pushing Germany and the Soviet Union into conflict, see Ivan Maisky (Soviet ambassador to the United Kingdom from 1932 to 1943), *Memoirs of a Soviet Ambassador*, 10–15. Obviously, of course, *in the long run* Britain and France could no more have desired Germany to obtain a complete mastery over the greater part of Europe than they could Russia. They wished for the domination of neither, as German leaders were supremely conscious. Hence, if, after the occupation of Poland, Germany invaded Belgium, France, and the Netherlands, before attacking the Soviet Union, this was because the subjection of western Europe and the con-

trol of its coastline were, in the German mind, indispensable prerequisites for war on the Soviet Union; for although Britain and France encouraged German ambitions in eastern Europe, Germany could not feel certain that once she was involved in an exhausting struggle on Soviet soil, these powers would not attempt, with the help of allies, to restore the balance in their favor. Undoubtedly the conviction that Germany would not attack Russia before assailing the West lay at the root of some of the opposition in Britain and France to the policy of giving Germany a free hand in eastern Europe. See, for example, Henri de Kerillis (right-wing French deputy), *Français, voici la guerre!*, 147–48.

57. See chapter 7, text to nn. 59–66.

58. As given in *Acción Socialista*, 15 Jan. 1952. For Hernández's expulsion from the party in 1944, see his book, *En el pais de la gran mentira*, 215–27.

59. *Solidaridad Obrera* (Paris), 11 Mar. 1951. After the close of the Civil War, El Campesino took refuge in Russia, whence he escaped ten years later completely disillusioned. See his book *La vie et la mort en U.R.S.S., 1939–1949*.

Chapter 11

1. See chapter 2.

2. See, for example, *Tierra y Libertad* (Barcelona), the FAI organ, 29 Oct. 1938; Horacio M. Prieto, secretary in 1936 of the national committee of the CNT, *Marxismo y socialismo libertario*, 62–64.

3. See chapter 4, text to nn. 15 and 16.

4. *Les anarchistes espagnols et le pouvoir, 1868–1969*, 66–68. For information about the author of this valuable book, see chapter 4, n. 67.

5. *Espoir*, 3 Apr. 1977.

6. See anarchosyndicalist *Memoria del congreso extraordinario celebrado en Madrid los días 11 al 16 de junio de 1931*, 38.

7. See, for example, *Solidaridad Obrera* (Barcelona), 18 Apr., 8 May 1937. It is noteworthy that in his review of the Mexican edition of my book *The Grand Camouflage* (*La revolución española*), Diego Abad de Santillán, the CNT-FAI leader, objected to my use of the word "domination" (*Reconstruir*, Jan.–Feb. 1965).

8. For example, Victor Zaragoza, secretary of the national committee of the CNT National Transport Federation, when interviewed by me in Mexico in 1940.

9. *Los anarquistas en la crisis política española*, 276–77.

10. See, for example, Lorenzo, 68–70, 79, 93.

11. See, for example, letter of Luis Araquistáin, published in *Left News*, Dec. 1942, on the opposition of Juan Negrín to anarchosyndicalist participation in the government.

12. The political developments in Catalonia are dealt with in chapters 27 and 28.

13. Diego Abad de Santillán, *La bancarrota del sistema económico y político del capitalismo*, 55.

14. 3 July 1936.

15. *Gosudarstvennost i anarkhiia* (State and Anarchy), 234.

16. Article in *L'Adunata dei Refrattari*, 12 Mar. 1932.

17. *Tierra y Libertad* (Barcelona), 15 Sept. 1933.

18. Ibid., 27 Oct. 1933.

19. Germinal Esgleas in *La Revista Blanca*, 18 Jan. 1935.

20. José Bonet in *Tierra y Libertad* (Barcelona), 22 Sept. 1933.

21. Isaac Puente in *CNT* (Madrid), 19 June 1933, as reproduced in Puente, *Propaganda*, 129–30.

22. See, for example, Germinal Esgleas in *La Revista Blanca*, 18 Jan. 1935.

23. 27 Oct. 1933.

24. *CNT* (Madrid), 24 Oct. 1933, as reproduced in Puente, *Propaganda*, 126.

25. 10 Nov. 1933.

26. See Solidaridad Obrera (Barcelona), 17 Jan., 2 Apr. 1936.

27. See speech by Juan López in *Fragua Social*, 16 Feb. 1937; also Federica Montseny, *María Silva*, 28; Ricardo Sanz, *El sindicalismo y la política*, 262–63.

28. Diego Abad de Santillán, the CNT-FAI leader, makes this point clear in both *Por qué perdimos la guerra*, 36–37, and *La revolución y la guerra en España*, 30. In the former he also states that the right "endeavored by every means to encourage us to abstain from voting, as in the case of Cádiz . . . , where [it] offered us half a million pesetas to carry on our usual antielectoral propaganda."

Chapter 12

1. *The Spanish Labyrinth*, 224.

2. Quoted in Helmut Ruediger, *Ensayo crítico sobre la revolución española*, 25. During the Civil War Ruediger was representative in Spain of the International Workingmen's Association, with which the CNT was affiliated.

3. *The Spanish Labyrinth*, 258–59. See also César M. Lorenzo, *Les anarchistes espagnols et le pouvoir, 1868–1969*, 76–77; S. Cánovas Cervantes, *Durruti y Ascaso*, 15; José Peirats, *La CNT en la revolución española*, I, 35–36; Richard A. H. Robinson, *The Origins of Franco's Spain*, 120–21.

4. Jacinto Toryho, a prominent CNT-FAI member, in *Vía Libre*, 19 May 1940.

5. See, for example, Rudolf Rocker, *Anarcho-Syndicalism*, 116.

6. "Declaración de principios de la Asociación Internacional de Trabajadores," as reproduced in *Internacional*, May 1938.

7. In *Solidaridad Obrera* (Barcelona), 15 Apr. 1932, as given in Puente, *Propaganda*, 132.

8. See chapter 1, text to nn. 103–6.

9. See chapter 1, text to nn. 107–8.

10. Speech published in *Claridad*, 11 Apr. 1936.

11. *Solidaridad Obrera* (Barcelona), 24 Apr. 1936.

12. Ibid., 7 June 1936.

13. See, for example, *Claridad*, 7, 9 July 1936.

14. Frank E. Manuel, *The Politics of Modern Spain*, 167.

15. 3 June 1936.

16. For some idea of these, see the following materials: speeches by Pascual Tomás, vice-secretary of the UGT, as reported in *La Correspondencia de Valencia*, 21 Dec. 1936, 17 Feb. 1937; *CNT* (Madrid), 26 Feb., 3 Mar. 1937; *Claridad*, 13 Apr. 1937; document signed by the national committee of the CNT and the executive committee of the UGT, dated 26 Nov. 1936, as given in Peirats, *La CNT*, I, 252–53; excerpts from speeches of delegates at a meeting of the CNT unions of the central region, as given in *CNT* (Madrid), 8 Oct. 1936.

17. 25 Oct. 1936.

18. Lorenzo, 222; also *Claridad*, 27 Oct. 1936.

19. 28 Oct. 1936.

20. I realize that some persons may not accept the whole of this statement, but it has not been made without very careful research. The total number of persons in the anti-Franco camp belonging to each federation may have been between 1.5 million and 1.75 million, but no figures on the wartime membership can be given with any degree of exactitude. Estimates above and below these figures by sources siding with one organization or the other have been made, but as there is no way of checking their accuracy nothing would be gained by burdening the text with them.

21. Lorenzo, 222.

22. Ibid.

23. 5 Sept. 1936.

24. Lorenzo, 222–23.

25. Ibid.

26. Ibid., 224.

27. Ibid.

28. *El anarquismo español en la lucha política*, 7.

29. See resolution published in *CNT* (Madrid), 17 Sept. 1936.

30. From an unpublished work by Lazarillo de Tormes (Benigno Bejarano), "Les morts ne vous pardonnent pas," 69.

31. Lorenzo, 249.

32. *Internacional*, July–Aug. 1938.

33. See resolution published in *CNT* (Madrid), 17 Sept. 1936.

34. 25 Sept. 1936.

35. Lorenzo, 227–28.

36. For some of the most interesting editorials in the anarchosyndicalist press, see *CNT* (Madrid), 19 Sept., 6 Oct. 1936; *Solidaridad Obrera* (Barcelona), 30 Sept., 2, 4 Oct. 1936.

37. For the attitude of the republicans and Communists, see, for example, *El Mercantil Valenciano*, 8 Oct. 1936 (speech by Angel Moliner, Cortes deputy representing the Left Republican party); *Treball*, 1 Oct. 1936; *Verdad*, 22 Sept. 1936.

38. 30 Sept. 1936.

39. 31 Oct. 1936.

40. Letter to me.

41. Lorenzo, 228–29.

42. *El anarquismo español en la lucha política*, 6; also 7.

43. 23 Oct. 1936.

44. See *CNT* (Madrid), 30 Oct. 1936, and Largo Caballero's statement to the correspondent of the *Daily Express*, published in *Claridad*, 29 Oct. 1936.

45. The new appointments and the shifts they entailed are given in the *Gaceta de Madrid*, 5 Nov. 1936.

46. Lazarillo de Tormes (Benigno Bejarano), *España, cuña de la libertad*, 83.

47. See *Claridad*, 25 Oct. 1936. "The grave problems created by the encirclement of Madrid and the urgent necessity of avoiding internal disorders had decided Caballero to bring the CNT into the government, thereby forming a bloc of all the antifascist forces of the country" (Julio Alvarez del Vayo, *Freedom's Battle*, 215).

48. Francisco Largo Caballero, *Mis recuerdos*, 187.

49. *Freedom's Battle*, 216.

50. See chapter 9, text to nn. 113–16.

51. *Mis recuerdos*, 188.

52. *Freedom's Battle*, 215–16.

53. *Obras completas*, IV, 592.

54. *La república y la guerra*, 418–19.
55. Julián Zugazagoitia, *Historia de la guerra en España*, 181.
56. See chapter 23.
57. Alvarez del Vayo's version of this incident is in *Freedom's Battle*, 217–18.
58. *De mi vida*, 324–25.
59. Ibid., 325–26.
60. *Guerra, exilio y cárcel de un anarcosindicalista*, 74–77.
61. As César M. Lorenzo points out, "All the directive organs of the political and trade-union organizations left Madrid about the same time, 7 November, the day of the government's departure" (255, n. 2).
62. Ibid., 254–55.
63. See resolution approved by the regional congress of the Catalan CNT in April 1937, as given in article by P. Bernaud (Bernardo Pou), *Universo*, 1 May 1948, in which this fact is mentioned; also report of Mariano Vázquez (secretary of the national committee of the CNT from 19 November 1936), to the Extraordinary Congress of the AIT, as reproduced in *L'Espagne Nouvelle*, 15 Mar. 1939, and J. Capdevila in *Solidaridad Obrera* (Paris), 7 Apr. 1951.
64. 4 Nov. 1936.
65. See manifesto issued by the Regional Federation of Anarchist Groups of Catalonia, as given in *Tierra y Libertad* (Barcelona), 19 Dec. 1936. A manifesto issued by the Federation of Anarchist Groups of the Central Region affirmed that in spite of the CNT's entry into the government, "there is not the slightest contradiction with our doctrines" (as given in *Cultura Proletaria*, 20 Mar. 1937). See also speech by Juan López (CNT minister of commerce), *Solidaridad Obrera* (Barcelona), 11 Feb. 1937; *Tierra y Libertad* (Barcelona), 22 May, 30 Oct. 1937, and the manifesto of the peninsular committee of the FAI, addressed to the international libertarian movement, as reproduced in *Cultura Proletaria*, 23 Oct. 1937.
66. *Internacional*, Oct. 1938.
67. José Peirats, *Los anarquistas en la crisis política española*, 216.
68. As given in *Fragua Social*, 8 June 1937.
69. For a detailed account of the leading role played by Horacio Prieto in the selection of the CNT-FAI representatives, see Lorenzo (his son), 232–34.
70. *Inquiétudes*, special number, July 1947.
71. Speech in Barcelona, *Solidaridad Obrera*, 5 Jan. 1937. See also her speech reported in *Fragua Social*, 8 June 1937.
72. Letter to me after the war.
73. Reported in *Boletín de Información*, *CNT-FAI*, 23 Dec. 1936.
74. *Internacional*, June 1938. See also resolution approved by the regional congress of the Catalan CNT in April 1937, as given in article by P. Bernard (Bernardo Pou) in *Universo*, 1 May 1948.
75. Speech reported in *Le Libertaire*, 24 June 1937.
76. Speech reported in *Fragua Social*, 29 May 1937.
77. Lorenzo, 235.

Chapter 13

1. See chapter 2.
2. See, for example, *Los soviets en España*.
3. 9 Sept. 1936. See also *Verdad*, 30 Dec. 1936.

4. 20 Dec. 1936. The text given here is a retranslation from the anarchosyndicalist German-language periodical *Die Soziale Revolution* (Barcelona), no. 5–6, Feb. 1937. The Spanish text was unavailable.

5. Letter to me.

6. Article in *Política*, 23 Feb. 1937.

7. Solano Palacio in *Tiempos Nuevos*, 28 Sept. 1938.

8. See speech by Juan López, CNT minister of commerce, reported in *Fragua Social*, 29 May 1937.

9. See *Gaceta de la República*, 25 Dec. 1936, 7 Jan. 1937.

10. Ibid., 26 Dec. 1936. None of these decrees, it should be noted, applied to the semiautonomous region of Catalonia, where events took a different course, as will be seen in chapters 27 and 28.

11. See chapter 9, text to n. 103.

12. For attacks by the Communists on the committees for levying taxes and requisitioning harvests, see *Verdad*, 1, 8, 30 Dec. 1936, 12 Jan. 1937 (speech by Juan José Escrich); *Frente Rojo*, 31 Mar. 1937.

13. 19 Feb. 1937. See also speech by Largo Caballero at the session of the Cortes held on 1 February 1937, as reported in *El Día Gráfico*, 2 Feb. 1937. For other criticisms of the committees by moderate as well as by left-wing Socialists, see *Claridad*, 16 Feb. 1937 (article by Leoncio Pérez); *La Correspondencia de Valencia*, 30 Nov. 1936 (speech by Molina Conejero), 1 Feb. 1937 (speech by Jerónimo Bugeda), 2 Feb. 1937 (speech by Angel Galarza), 16 Feb. 1937 (speech by Rodolfo Llopis); *El Socialista* (Madrid), 2, 10, 11 Mar. 1937 (editorial articles); *Verdad*, 9 Jan. 1937 (speech by Juan Tundidor).

14. 25 Dec. 1936.

15. Speech reported by *Solidaridad Obrera* (Barcelona), 29 Nov. 1936.

16. 30 Mar. 1937.

17. *Verdad*, 26 Jan. 1937.

Chapter 14

1. See chapter 2.

2. Speech reported in *La Correspondencia de Valencia*, 5 Aug. 1937.

3. 18 Sept. 1936.

4. *The Forging of a Rebel*, 536. For testimony by opponents of the military rebellion on the excesses committed by the left during this early period of revolutionary terror, see speech by Wenceslao Carrillo, *La Correspondencia de Valencia*, 4 Aug. 1937; Juan José Domenichina in *Hoy*, 30 Nov. 1940; Jesús de Galíndez, *Los vascos en el Madrid sitiado*, 15–19, 42–43, 67–69; Miguel Peydro in *Correo de Asturias*, 25 Jan. 1941; Indalecio Prieto in ibid., 15 Aug. 1942; Sánchez Roca, interview published in *Solidaridad Obrera* (Barcelona), 17 Sept. 1937; Julián Zugazagoitia, *Historia de la guerra en España*, 111–12.

5. *Gaceta de Madrid*, 31 Aug. 1936.

6. See chapter 2.

7. Speech reported in *La Correspondencia de Valencia*, 5 Aug. 1937.

8. Ramón Salas Larrazábal gives a figure of 15,251 (article in *Aproximación histórica de la guerra española, 1936–1939*, 100). Ricardo de Cierva (*Historia de la guerra civil española*, I, 760) provides the following breakdown: 700 officers, 1,090 noncommissioned officers, and 13,000 men, a total of 14,790, of which 8,750 were in the left camp on 20 July 1936. Diego Abad de Santillán (*Por qué perdimos la guerra*, 236) names a total figure of 15,600.

9. James Minifie in the *New York Herald Tribune* (dispatch from Valencia), 28 Apr. 1937.

See also Henry Buckley, *Life and Death of the Spanish Republic*, 311. Negrín himself estimated in mid-November 1936 that the force would soon number thirty thousand (*Gaceta de la República*, 8 Nov. 1936).

10. Buckley, 311.

11. Reported in *Verdad*, 27 Dec. 1936.

12. See, for example, speech by Fidel Miró, reported in *Ruta*, 18 Feb. 1937.

13. 28 Apr. 1937.

14. *Gaceta de Madrid*, 17 Sept. 1936.

15. Ibid.

16. See speech by Angel Galarza, reported in *La Correspondencia de Valencia*, 5 Aug. 1937. The decree did not apply to Catalonia. The reconstruction of the regular police corps in that region is dealt with in chapter 27.

17. Resolution approved at the Congress of the Valencia CNT in November 1936, *Fragua Social*, 18 Nov. 1936. See also *Frente Libertario*, 10 Apr. 1937.

18. For protests against the disarming and arrest of anarchosyndicalists and the occupation of villages by the police, see speech by Tomás Cano Ruiz at the closing session of the Congress of the Valencia CNT, reported in *Fragua Social*, 7 Nov. 1936; manifesto issued by the CNT of the central region, published in *El Día Gráfico*, 23 Dec. 1936; *Fragua Social*, 23 Apr. 1937; *Nosotros*, 13 Mar., 5, 7, 8, 10 Apr. 1937. See also *Memoria del pleno regional de grupos anarquistas de Levante celebrado en Alicante, durante los días 11, 12, 13, 14 y 15 del mes de abril de 1937*, 128–31, 133; *Actas del congreso regional de sindicatos de Levante celebrado en Alicante, en el Teatro Verano, los días 15, 16, 17, 18 y 19 de julio de 1937*, 199–205.

19. See, for example, instructions published in *La Correspondencia de Valencia*, 15 Feb. 1937; also *Gaceta de la República*, 13 Mar. 1937.

20. See chapter 2.

21. *Gaceta de Madrid*, 24, 26 Aug. 1936; see also ibid., 7 Oct. 1936.

22. See speech by García Oliver, CNT-FAI minister of justice in the Largo Caballero government, reported in *Fragua Social*, 1 June 1937.

23. See, for example, *Frente Libertario*, 10 Mar. 1937; also General José Asensio on Margarita Nelken, as quoted by Julián Gorkin, *Caníbales políticos*, 218; interview given to *CNT* (Madrid) by Wenceslao Carrillo, director general of security from December 1936 to May 1937, as reported in *La Correspondencia de Valencia*, 11 Aug. 1937; Jesús Pérez Salas, *Guerra en España, 1936–1939*, 160.

24. For this information I am grateful to José Muñoz López, a member of the secret police and later a high-ranking official of the SIM (Military Investigation Service). At the end of April 1937, Juan Galán was made inspector of the armed forces under the control of the ministry of the interior (see *Gaceta de la Repúbilica*, 30 Apr. 1937).

25. For this information I am likewise indebted to José Muñoz López.

26. Because the Soviet secret police was variously referred to in the 1930s as the GPU, OGPU, or NKVD, the following information taken from the *McGraw-Hill Encyclopedia of Russia and the Soviet Union*, 502, should clarify the matter. By a decree of February 1922, a State Political Administration (GPU) was established in the People's Commissariat of Internal Affairs (NKVD). In 1923 the GPU was taken out of the NKVD and transformed into a Unified State Political Administration (OGPU) attached to the Sovnarkom (Council of People's Commissars). In 1934 a new reorganization took place. By a decree of 10 July, the functions of the OGPU were transferred to the NKVD. Nevertheless, long after 10 July 1934, the Soviet secret police was still commonly referred to as the GPU, or OGPU, probably, in many instances, through force of habit.

27. *In Stalin's Secret Service*, 82.
28. See chapter 7, text to nn. 37–40.
29. P. 4. His full party name is given as Lev Lazarevich Nikol'skiy.
30. See chapter 9, n. 33.
31. Article in the *Reader's Digest*, Nov. 1966.
32. *Men and Politics*, 361.
33. I am grateful to Payne for having furnished me with a copy of the reply signed by Orlov. The copy is in the archives of the Hoover Institution, Stanford.
34. Orlov also asserted in reply to Payne's questionnaire that Krivitsky "had never been chief of intelligence in all of Europe." This is true, but then Krivitsky claimed only that he was "chief of Soviet military intelligence in western Europe." It is noteworthy that when Benjamin Mandel, director of research for the U.S. Senate Subcommittee, referred (on 28 September 1955) to Krivitsky as a "ranking NKVD official" Orlov did not contradict him (U.S. Congress, Senate, Committee on the Judiciary, *The Legacy of Alexander Orlov*, 29).
35. David T. Cattell observes: "It may be true that the communists instigated the terror and took an active lead in it, but in their activities they received the cooperation and assistance of the socialist and republican groups " (*Communism and the Spanish Civil War*, 134–35). It would have been more accurate had he said "of *some* socialist and republican groups."
36. My italics.
37. See, for example, Orlov, "Answers to the Questionnaire of Professor Stanley G. Payne"; article in *Reader's Digest*, Nov. 1966; *The Secret History of Stalin's Crimes*, p. x.
38. *Men and Politics*, 361.
39. See n. 26 of this chapter.
40. Krivitsky, 102. See also ibid., 106–7, quoted, p. 291. The tale of arrests without judicial warrant, of detentions in clandestine jails, of tortures, kidnappings, and assassinations by the NKVD and the Communist-controlled Spanish secret police is amply confirmed by left-wing sources; see, for example, AIT, *Boletín de Información*, Service d'Information Français de l'AIT, Special Edition, 11 May 1937, p. 4 (mimeographed), cited in Cattell, *Communism*, 133, 237, n. 3; CNT (Madrid), 17 Apr. 1937 (statement by Melchor Rodríguez); *La Correspondencia de Valencia*, 24 Feb. 1937 (open letter of the provincial secretariat of the Valencia UGT); *Cultura Proletaria*, 25 Sept., 18 Dec. 1937; *L'Espagne Nouvelle*, 17 Sept. 1937 (article by Ethel MacDonald); *Fragua Social*, 16, 17 Apr. 1937; *Frente Libertario*, 9 Apr. 1937; *Independent News*, 7 Nov., 4 Dec. 1937; *Modern Monthly*, Sept. 1937 (article by Anita Brenner); *La Révolution Prolétarienne*, July 1947 (article by Jordi Arquer); *El Socialista* (Madrid), 20 Apr. 1937; *Solidaridad Obrera* (Barcelona), 25 Apr. 1937; *Workers' Age*, 22 Feb. 1937 (article by George Kopp), 15 Jan. 1938 (excerpt from report by John McGovern); Abad de Santillán, *Por qué perdimos la guerra*, 183, 185–90; *L'assassinat de Andrés Nin*, 18–19; Franz Borkenau, *The Spanish Cockpit*, 239–40; Fenner Brockway, *Workers' Front*, 123–24; "El Campesino" (Valentín González), *La vie et la mort en U.R.S.S., 1939–1949*, 206; Louis Fischer, *Russia's Road from Peace to War*, 284; Gorkin, *Caníbales políticos*, 133, 176–79, 184, 227–40, and *El proceso de Moscú en Barcelona*, 53–56, 61, 106–266; Krivitsky, 72–73; Katia Landau, *Le stalinisme en Espagne*, 14–17, 24, 27, 33–34, 45–48; John McGovern, *Terror in Spain*, 5, 9; Gabriel Morón, *Política de ayer y política de mañana*, 99; G. Munis, *Jalones de derrota*, 388–90; José Peirats, *Los anarquistas en la crisis política española* 265–73. See also letter, dated 26 January 1939, from George Kopp, a former commander of the Partido Obrero de Unificación Marxista (Workers' Party of Marxist Unification) militia, to Harry Milton, also a former combatant in the

POUM militia, that he personally had been in "17 secret GPU [NKVD] prisons." I am indebted to Harry Milton for a copy of this letter, which has been deposited with the Hoover Institution, Stanford (Bolloten Collection).

Chapter 15

1. The full text of the decree, which appeared in the official *Gaceta de Madrid* on 2 Aug. 1936, is given in *Guerra y revolución en España, 1936–1939*, I, 270.

2. For the intervention by the ministry of industry and commerce in industrial concerns in Madrid both before and after the publication of the decree of 2 August, see *Gaceta de Madrid*, 27 July 1936; *CNT* (Madrid), 3 Aug. 1936; *Mundo Obrero* (Madrid), 1 Aug. 1936; *Política*, 18 Aug. 1936.

3. *Guerra y revolución*, I, 271.

4. See statement issued by the executive committee of the UGT metallurgical federation, *La Correspondencia de Valencia*, 2 Mar. 1937.

5. See, for example, *Verdad*, 8 Dec. 1936 (speech by José Díaz), 17 Dec. 1936 (Communist party manifesto), 23 Dec. 1936 (editorial); speech by José Díaz on 8 Feb. 1937, as given in *Tres años de lucha* 325; *Frente Rojo*, 27 Feb. 1937 (editorial), 19 Mar. 1937 (manifesto of the central committee of the Communist party).

6. Diego Abad de Santillán, *After the Revolution*, 122. See also *Boletín de Información, CNT-FAI*, 21 June 1937; speech by Juan López in *Fragua Social*, 6 Oct. 1936; *Solidaridad Obrera* (Barcelona), 25 Sept. 1936 (interview with España Industrial); manifesto of the Communist party, as given in *Verdad*, 17 Dec. 1936; report of Helmut Ruediger, representative in Spain of the International Workingmen's Association, with which the CNT was affiliated, *Informe para el congreso extraordinario de la AIT, el día 6 de diciembre de 1937*; Albert Pérez-Baró, *30 mesos de collectivisme a Catalunya*, 43.

7. See joint statement issued by the national committees of the CNT and UGT textile federations, as given in *Claridad*, 3 Mar. 1937; *Tierra y Libertad* (Barcelona), 2 Jan. 1937; speech by Jesús Hernández in May 1937, as given in Hernández, *El partido comunista antes, durante y después de la crisis del gobierno Largo Caballero*, 41; speech by Antonio Mije, as given in Mije, *Por una potente industria de guerra*, 4.

8. *Men and Politics*, 421.

9. See statement by the secretary of the national committee of the CNT at the Extraordinary Congress of the Catalan CNT in *Memoria del congreso extraordinario de la confederación regional del trabajo de Cataluña celebrado en Barcelona los días 25 de febrero al 3 de marzo de 1937*, 197. "If nationalization were carried out in Spain, as the Socialists and Communists desire," said *Nosotros*, the anarchist newspaper (9 Mar. 1937), "we should be on the way to a dictatorship, because by nationalizing everything the government would become the master, the chief, the absolute boss of everyone and everything." See also Juan Negre, *¿Qué es el colectivismo anarquista?* 5.

10. See, for example, *Tierra y Libertad* (Barcelona), 26 Dec. 1936 ("Posición de la FAI" and article by Gaston Leval), 30 Jan. 1937 ("Se impone la socialización" and "Hacia nuevas realizaciones"), 6 Feb. 1937; also *Boletín de Información, CNT-FAI*, 23 Dec. 1936; Mariano Cardona Rosell, *Aspectos económicos de nuestra revolución*, 3, 6; *Collectivisations*, 13–16.

11. For data from anarchosyndicalist sources on the development of these tendencies, see *Boletín de Información, CNT-FAI*, 21 June 1937 (speech by C. Bassols); *Cultura y Acción*, 24 July 1937 (article by Máximo Llorca); *Regeneración*, 15 Mar. 1938 (article by H. N. Ruiz); *Solidaridad Obrera* (Barcelona), 24 Apr. 1937 (speech by Playan); *Tierra y Liber-*

tad (Barcelona), 1 May 1937 (article by Juan P. Fábregas); César M. Lorenzo, *Les anarchistes espagnols et le pouvoir, 1868–1969*, 246–47.

12. See chapter 3 for these and other examples; also *Documentos Históricos de España*, Mar. 1938; *Tierra y Libertad* (Barcelona), 9, 16 Oct., 13 Nov. 1937.

13. See, for example, *Las Noticias*, 14 Apr. 1937 (speech by Riera); *Solidaridad Obrera* (Barcelona), 24 Apr. 1937 (speech by Playan); also *Tiempos Nuevos*, Sept., Oct. 1937.

14. See speeches by Pascual Tomás, the left-wing Socialist and vice-secretary of the UGT, in *La Correspondencia de Valencia*, 21 Dec. 1936, 11 Jan., 17 Feb., 9 Apr. 1937, and other references by him to nationalization in *Adelante* (Valencia), 13 Feb. 1937, and *Claridad*, 6 Apr. 1937.

15. See chapter 3, n. 1.

16. Reply to questionnaire sent to Cardona Rosell by me.

17. Because of their contempt for money, the libertarians never attempted to organize the bank employees and gave the UGT free rein, much to their regret during the Civil War.

18. See chapter 8, n. 61.

19. See his statements published in *La Correspondencia de Valencia*, 6 Jan. 1937, and in *El Día Gráfico*, 9 Feb. 1937; also his decree on state intervention in industrial enterprises, as given in *Gaceta de la República*, 24 Feb. 1937, and his order of 2 Mar. 1937, ibid., 7 Mar. 1937.

20. Peiró, *Mi gestion en el ministerio de industria*, as given in *Guerra y revolución*, II, 276.

21. *Guerra y revolución*, II, 276.

22. *Los anarquistas en la crisis política española*, 263–64. For the difficulty the CNT encountered in obtaining funds from the government for its collectivized enterprises, see also Juan López, "Evolución del sindicalismo español," in *Comunidad Ibérica*, Nov.–Dec. 1964, 32, quoted in Lorenzo, 244, n. 11; prologue to speech by Peiró (*De la fábrica de vidrio de Mataró al ministerio de industria*), quoted in Lorenzo, 257, n. 6.

23. Report to the central committee of the Communist party in March 1937, reprinted in Díaz, 353.

Chapter 16

1. Speech reported in *Frente Rojo*, 30 Mar. 1937.

2. Speech in January 1937, as published in Melchor, *Organicemos la producción*, 6–8.

3. Speech reported in *Mundo Obrero* (Madrid), 18 May 1938.

4. Carrillo, *En marcha hacia la victoria*, 10.

5. *El frente de la producción, una industria grande para ganar la guerra*, 13, quoted in David T. Cattell, *Communism and the Spanish Civil War*, 62.

6. Open letter to Carrillo published in *La Correspondencia de Valencia*, 1 Apr. 1937.

7. Letter published in *Juventud Libre*, 1 May 1937. See also article by Federico Fernández López in *Adelante* (Valencia), 28 May 1937.

8. Letter to me.

9. See, for example, speech by Juan López, 7 Feb. 1937, reprinted in López, *Concepto del federalismo en la guerra y en la revolución*, 3–4.

10. *CNT* (Madrid), 19 June 1937.

11. 19 Jan. 1937.

12. 2 Feb. 1937. See also *Juventud Libre*, 6 Feb. 1937; *Solidaridad Obrera* (Barcelona), 9 Feb. 1937; *Tierra y Libertad* (Barcelona), 23 Jan. 1937.

13. See speech by La Pasionaria, chapter 5.

14. 3 Feb. 1937. See also *Mundo Obrero* (Madrid), 5 Feb. 1937.

15. Díaz, *Tres años de lucha*, 349–52. See also his speech at the plenary session of the central committee of the PSUC, reported in *Treball*, 9 Feb. 1936.

16. 10 Apr. 1937.

17. Speech at a meeting of the Libertarian Youth, reported, *CNT* (Madrid), 4 May 1937.

18. 22 May 1937. For other attacks in the libertarian press accusing the Communists of trying to return to the Republic of 1931, see *Juventud Libre*, 9 May 1937; *Ruta*, 1, 17 Apr. 1937.

Chapter 17

1. *Gaceta de Madrid*, 8 Oct. 1936.

2. 10 Oct. 1936.

3. One hectare is equivalent to approximately two and a half acres.

4. 20 Mar. 1937.

5. Article in *CNT* (Madrid), 26 May 1937.

6. *Tribuna*, Oct. 1948.

7. 12 Oct. 1936.

8. *Por la revolución agraria*, 44.

9. Speech, *Juventud Libre*, 24 July 1937. See also article in *Castilla Libre*, 30 Mar. 1937, quoting a member of the provincial committee of the CNT of Ciudad Libre (formerly Ciudad Real) as saying that a delegate of the minister of agriculture in that province had demanded the return of their land to persons who were not fascists; and letter sent to the minister of agriculture by Ricardo Zabalza, general secretary of the National Federation of Land Workers (published in *Adelante* [Valencia], 29 May 1937), complaining that a delegate of the Institute of Agrarian Reform had ordered the restoration of a large estate to its original owner in the village of Garvayuela, Badajoz.

10. See chapter 5.

11. *Claridad*, 14 Dec. 1936.

12. For indications of the hostility created among left-wing Socialists, see replies of various provincial secretaries of the National Federation of Land Workers to questions posed by the Socialist newspaper, *Adelante* (Valencia), regarding Communist policy in the countryside, as given in *Adelante*, 17, 20 June 1937, and *CNT* (Madrid), 14, 21 June 1937. See also *Colectivismo*, 1 May 1938 (article by A. Fernández Ballesteros).

13. See, for example, speech by minister of agriculture Vicente Uribe, reported in *Verdad*, 8 Dec. 1936.

14. See chapter 4, text to n. 11.

15. 16 Dec. 1936.

16. Speech at the National Conference of the Unified Socialist Youth Federation in January 1937 (Carrillo, *En marcha hacia la victoria*, 41).

17. *Adelante* (Valencia), 3 July 1937.

18. Ibid. See also *Por la revolución agraria*, 42–43, and statement by Ramón Arcos Arnau, provincial secretary of the Madrid section of the Federation of Land Workers, as given in *CNT* (Madrid), 14 June 1937.

19. *Por la revolución agraria*, 42–43. See also *Adelante*, 17 June 1937 (reply by Jesús Pérez Salas to questions posed by the newspaper regarding Communist policy in the

countryside); *Colectivismo*, 15 Sept. 1937; Jan.–Feb. 1938; 1 May 1938 (article by A. Fernández Ballesteros).

20. Interview given to *Adelante* (Valencia), reprinted in *Solidaridad Obrera*, 28 May 1937. See also his letter to minister of agriculture, *Adelante* (Valencia), 29 May 1937, and articles by José España in *Cultura y Acción*, 5 June 1937, and in *Nosotros*, 3 June 1937.

21. See chapter 12, text to n. 62.

22. *Castilla Libre*, 10 Apr. 1937. See also Zabalza's letter to the minister of agriculture, *Adelante* (Valencia), 29 May 1937.

23. *Castilla libre*, 10 Apr. 1937. See also *Castilla Libre*, 31 Mar. 1937 (article by Isabelo Romero); *CNT* (Madrid), 26 Mar., 29 May 1937; *Frente Libertario*, 20 Mar., 6 Apr. 1937; *Spanish Revolution* (Barcelona), 2 July 1937.

24. Interview given to *Juventud Libre*, 10 July 1937. See also *Acracia*, 19 Mar. 1937 (article by M. Salas); *CNT* (Madrid), 29 May 1937; José Peirats, *La CNT en la revolución española*, I, 320, 323.

25. Anibal Ponce, *Examen de la España actual*, 75, says there were nearly fifty; José María Capo, *España desnuda*, 88, puts the number at thirty-five. See also *Claridad*, 7, 9 Apr. 1936.

26. Cordova Iturburu, *España bajo el comando del pueblo*, 154.

27. *Gaceta de la República*, 9 June 1937.

28. 11 June 1937.

29. See, for example, interview given to *Juventud Libre*, 10 July 1937, by the general secretary of the CNT Peasants' Federation of Castile; report on the Madrid Congress of the Libertarian Youth, ibid., 31 July 1937; *Castilla Libre*, 30 Mar. 1937 (article on Ciudad Libre); *Fragua Social*, 21 Oct. 1937; Juan López, "Evolución del sindicalismo español," in *Comunidad Ibérica*, Nov.–Dec. 1964, quoted in César M. Lorenzo, *Les anarchistes espagnols et le pouvoir, 1868–1969*, 244, n. 11.

30. Letters to me.

31. See the composition of the department, as given in the decree of 30 January 1937 (*Gaceta de la República*, 2 Feb. 1937).

32. My italics.

33. 11 June 1937.

34. Reprinted in *Alianza CNT-UGT*, 131–41.

35. 3 Oct. 1938.

36. See chapter 29.

37. *Solidaridad Obrera* (Barcelona), 2 Nov. 1936. See also "De julio a julio," *Fragua Social*, 19 July 1937, as reprinted in *De julio a julio*, 9–18.

38. In this context cantonalism implies a libertarian system of administration based on the division of the national territory into small, independent administrative units or cantons without a central governing body.

39. The Syndicalist party was a small splinter party formed by Angel Pestaña, a leading member of the CNT, who in opposition to the FAI, had sought unsuccessfully before the war to bring the CNT into the field of political and parliamentary activity. Angel Pestaña was the party's only representative in the Cortes in 1936. Its role during the Civil War was insignificant, particularly after Pestaña's death in 1937.

40. Lorenzo, 149–50.

41. Ibid., 150–51.

42. *El Día Gráfico*, 9 Dec. 1936.

43. For collectivization in Aragon at the beginning of the war, see chapter 4, text to nn. 48–59; also José Duque, "La situación en Aragón al comienzo de la guerra."

44. See, for example, *Frente Rojo*, 4 Aug. 1937; *Verdad*, 5 Aug. 1937; *Fragua Social*'s comments, 5 Aug. 1937; Duque, 30–43; José Peirats, *Los anarquistas en la crisis política española*, 291–94.

45. Líster, *Nuestra guerra*, 151–55.

46. Ibid., 152; see also Ricardo Sanz, *Los que fuimos a Madrid*, 154.

47. *Nuestra guerra*, 155.

48. 12 Aug. 1937.

49. See the Spanish Communist refugee periodical, *España Popular*, 23 Jan. 1948; also Peirats, *Los anarquistas*, 294.

50. *Nuestra guerra*, 160.

51. Sanz, *Los que fuimos a Madrid*, 157.

52. *Fragua Social*, 23 Oct. 1937. Accounts by other libertarian sources of the dissolution of the Defense Council and the repression that followed can be found in *Acción Libertaria*, 22 Sept. 1937; *Cultura Proletaria*, 17 Jan. 1948 (article by Miguel Jiménez); *Documentos Históricos de España*, May 1939 (summary of a report by the Aragon CNT to the central government); *L'Espagne Nouvelle*, 1, 29 Oct. 1937; *Frente Libertario*, 27 Aug. 1937; *Juventud Libre*, 4 Sept. 1937; *Spanish Labor Bulletin*, 3 Feb. 1938; *Spanish Revolution* (New York), 22 Oct. 1937, 28 Feb. 1938; Peirats, *Los anarquistas*, 283–302; Alardo Prats, *Vanguardia y retaguardia de Aragón*, 157–58.

53. Conversation with me.

54. Interviewed by me after the war.

55. *La revolución popular en el campo*, 17.

56. *Los anarquistas*, 301.

57. Silva, 17–18

58. *Los anarquistas*, 300–301.

59. Ibid., 301–2.

60. See, for example, *Frente Rojo*, 27 Jan. 1938.

Chapter 18

1. Chapter 2.

2. *Obras completas*, III, 487–88.

3. See José Martín Blázquez (an officer in the war ministry), *I Helped to Build an Army*, 189; Jesús Pérez Salas, *Guerra en España, 1936–1939*, 115.

4. Pérez Salas, 259. See also L. Romero Solano, *Vísperas de la guerra de España*, 380.

5. *Gaceta de Madrid*, 28 July 1936.

6. Ibid., 3 Aug. 1936.

7. Ibid., 18 Aug. 1936.

8. Azaña, *Obras*, III, 488.

9. See chapter 22.

10. Information given to me by Giral, who also stated that Largo Caballero had a "violent temper" and "put up a terrible opposition to the formation of the volunteer army." For Azaña's testimony, see *Obras*, IV, 862.

11. 20 Aug. 1936.

12. According to Giral, when interviewed by me.

13. See chapter 8.

14. 21 Aug. 1936.

15. *Gaceta de Madrid*, 27 Aug. 1936.

16. See *Política*, 19 Aug. 1936.

17. "Ispanskii Dnevnik," *Novyi Mir*, Apr. 1938, 41–42.

18. *Obras*, III, 488–89.

19. H. E. Kaminski, *Ceux de Barcelone*, 244.

20. *Historia militar de la guerra de España*, 601–2. See also ibid., 106. For materials on the matter of discipline, see, for example, Pérez Salas, 145; verbatim report of a meeting of political and military leaders on the Aragon front in September 1936; speech by Enrique Líster, quoted in *Mundo Obrero* (Madrid), 12 Oct. 1936; for a frank account of the behavior of the Socialist militia on the Toledo front, see Romero Solano (former Socialist deputy for Cáceres), 308–10.

21. Pérez Salas, 131–32. See, also César M. Lorenzo, *Les anarchistes espagnols et le pouvoir, 1868–1969*, 247.

22. Miguel González Inestal in *Internaciónal*, July–Aug. 1938.

23. *The Forging of a Rebel*, 536–37.

24. This typically Spanish insult is what Major Aberri implies.

25. *Hoy*, 12 Aug. 1939.

26. Martín Blázquez, 143.

27. *Freedom's Battle*, 28. See also Romero Solano, 308, and speech by Rodolfo Llopis reported in *La Correspondencia de Valencia*, 13 Aug. 1937.

28. See decree published in the *Gaceta de Madrid*, 3 Aug. 1936, and subsequent amendments, ibid., 20 Sept., 4 Oct. 1936.

29. See, for example, Martín Blázquez, 131–34, whose testimony was amply confirmed to me by Alejandro García Val, who became director of road transport later in the war.

30. See Carreño España on the Madrid transport problem, as recorded in the minutes of the Madrid Defense Council (*Actas de la junta de defensa de Madrid*, 456).

31. See, for example, Manuel Azaña, *La velada en Benicarló*, 107.

32. When interviewed by me.

33. This is confirmed by German diplomats in General Franco's territory. See Hans Hermann Voelckers's and Lieutenant General Wilhelm Faupel's communications to the German Foreign Ministry, as given in U.S. Department of State, *Documents on German Foreign Policy, 1918–1945*, III, 137–39, 159–62. The Carlist (monarchist) and Falangist (fascist) militia units, which in the early months of the war were not subordinate to the regular army, suffered from some of the defects that afflicted the left-wing militia. According to Ramón Serrano Suñer, foreign minister and member of the Falange, they were "not always sufficiently disciplined" (*Entre Hendaya y Gibraltar*, 43).

34. See chapter 7.

35. Although Russian bombers reached Spain in October, the first combat planes did not arrive until 2 November (see chapter 7).

36. For accounts by eyewitnesses in the anti-Franco camp of the siege of the Alcázar of Toledo, see Louis Fischer, *Men and Politics*, 359–62, 365–69; Luis Quintanilla, *Los rehenes del Alcázar de Toledo*; article by Clara Candiani in *La Dépêche de Toulouse*, 3 Oct. 1936.

37. At a meeting of political and military leaders on the Aragon front in September 1936 (see verbatim report in Bibliography).

Chapter 19

1. 22 June 1934.

2. 22 Aug. 1936.

3. *Fragua Social*, 18 Nov. 1936.

4. For further details see the anarchist *Nosotros*, 16 Feb., 12, 13, 15–17 Mar. 1937, the CNT papers, *Fragua Social*, 8 Sept., 14, 18 Nov. 1936, and *Solidaridad Obrera* (Barcelona), 24 Sept. 1936, also Lazarillo del Tormes (Benigno Bejarano), *España, tumba del fascismo*, 82.

5. On the Madrid front the group consisted of twenty men (Eduardo de Guzman, *Madrid, rojo y negro*, 78).

6. On the Madrid front there were also battalions composed of a certain number of centuries (ibid.).

7. See, for example, resolution passed at the regional congress of the Valencia CNT establishing a uniform structure for the CNT-FAI columns formed in that region (*Fragua Social*, 18 Nov. 1936).

8. Ibid.

9. Ibid. See also statement by Buenaventura Durruti in *CNT* (Madrid), 6 Oct. 1936.

10. *Boletín de Información, CNT-FAI*, as given in *Spanish Revolution* (New York), 8 Jan. 1936.

11. *Fragua Social*, 8 Sept. 1936. See also Cipriano Mera, *Guerra, exilio y cárcel de un anarcosindicalista*, 108.

12. 7 Aug. 1936.

13. *Fragua Social*, 21 Nov. 1936. For other appeals for discipline, see ibid., 17 Nov. 1936 (speech by Juan Peiró), 24 Nov. 1936 (article by Claro J. Sendón); *Solidaridad Obrera* (Barcelona), 1 Oct. 1936 (article by Jaime Balius), 3 Oct. 1936 (editorial note), 27 Oct. 1936 (article by Luka-Zaga), 5 Dec. 1936 (speech by García Oliver); *CNT* (Madrid), 3 Oct. 1936 (editorial), 5 Oct. 1936 (report by the CNT of the central region), 8 Oct. 1936 (speech by Federica Montseny).

14. *España Libre* (Toulouse), 11 Sept. 1949. Durruti's death on the Madrid front, where he transferred his column when the fall of Madrid appeared imminent, remains a mystery to this day. Even the anarchosyndicalists themselves cannot agree as to whether he was killed by an enemy bullet or by one of his own men. See, for example, Federica Montseny, ibid., 21 Nov. 1976. Mera, 90–92, is positive he was killed by an enemy bullet.

15. A. G. Gilabert in *Tierra y Libertad* (Barcelona), 12 Dec. 1936.

16. Published in *CNT* (Madrid), 3 Oct. 1936.

17. *Frente Libertario*, 20 Oct. 1936.

18. *Ruta*, 28 Nov. 1936.

Chapter 20

1. That it did exist is proved by the following extract from an article in a Communist military paper: "There are still cases, though not as frequent as before, of comrades who have no sense of responsibility, who abandon their posts in order to roam around the town, and we know that the result of such excursions is the purchase of liquor" (*Pasaremos*, 31 Dec. 1936).

2. 22 July 1936.

3. Leader, after World War II, of the Trieste Communist party, and, in later years, Italian Communist senator.

4. See, for example, *Política*, organ of the Left Republican party, 30 July 1936.

5. Anna Louise Strong (associate editor at that time of the *Moscow Daily News*), *Spain in Arms*, 41–43. For further information on the regiment from Communist sources, see *Guerra y revolución en España, 1936–1939*, I, 298–306; Enrique Líster (who succeeded En-

rique Castro as its commander in chief in September 1936), *Nuestra guerra*, 61–73; Juan Modesto, *Soy del quinto regimiento*, 54–56.

6. Carlos Contreras, speech reported in *Mundo Obrero* (Madrid), 21 Dec. 1936; see also José Díaz, *Tres años de lucha*, 297 (speech, 27 Jan. 1937).

7. Simone Téry, *Front de la liberté*, 182.

8. *Nuestra guerra*, 62.

9. *Historia del ejército popular de la república*, I, 1147–48.

10. Quoted in Jesús Hernández, *Negro y rojo*, 332.

11. Ralph Bates (assistant commissar of the Fifteenth International Brigade) in *New Republic*, 20 Oct. 1937.

12. At the outbreak of the conflict, Barceló was aide-de-camp to Casares Quiroga, the Left Republican premier and war minister (see José Martín Blázquez, *I Helped to Build an Army*, 121). Although he figured publicly as a member of the Left Republican party (see his speech in *La Libertad*, 11 Aug. 1936), his real allegiance was to the Communist party, of which he had actually been a member, according to a Spanish Communist refugee newspaper (*España Popular*, 11 Mar. 1940) since 1935. This paper erroneously refers to him as Eduardo instead of Luis Barceló, but there is no mistaking his identity.

13. See notices issued by the Inspección General de Milicias published in *Claridad*, 19, 25 Aug .1936.

14. See, for example, Jesús Pérez Salas, *Guerra en España, 1936–1939*, 146.

15. Martín Blázquez, 205. See also Pierre Broué and Emile Témime, *La révolution et la guerre d'Espagne*, 212–13, both opponents of the party.

16. According to information given to me by Carlos Contreras (Vittorio Vidali).

17. *The Last Days of Madrid*, 51.

18. Speech reported in *Pasaremos*, 31 Jan. 1937.

19. *Nuestra guerra*, 75.

20. Letter to me. For complaints by the CNT that its units on the Madrid front were being discriminated against in the distribution of arms, see, for example, *Frente Libertario*, 24, 27 Oct. 1936.

21. According to information given to me by Carlos Contreras (Vittorio Vidali).

22. Quoted in Hernández, *Negro y rojo*, 331. See also Díaz, 297 (speech, 27 Jan. 1937); Líster, *Nuestra guerra*, 62; Pasionaria, speech reported in *Frente Rojo*, 20 Feb. 1937.

23. 6 Feb. 1937. See also "El Campesino" (former Communist), *La vie et la mort en U.R.S.S, 1939–1949*, 12.

Chapter 21

1. See chapter 18.

2. See, for example, *Mundo Obrero* (Madrid), 17 Sept. 1936.

3. See *Gaceta de Madrid*, 29, 30 Sept., 16, 30 Oct. 1936.

4. *Men and Politics*, 354.

5. See editorials and speeches published in *Mundo Obrero*, *Verdad*, and *Milicia Popular* of the period.

6. See *Milicia Popular*, 17, 19, 28 Dec. 1936; also *Volunteer for Liberty*, 1 June 1937, which gives an account of the disbanding of the Fifth Regiment.

7. So called because they were composed of infantry, cavalry, artillery, and basic services (see Enrique Líster, *Nuestra guerra*, 75; José Martín Blázquez, *I Helped to Build an Army*, 293; Colonel Segismundo Casado in *National Review*, July 1939, who, according

to his book, *The Last Days of Madrid*, 52, helped to organize the brigades). The word "mixed" was also appropriate in another sense because, in addition to the old militia volunteers, the brigades consisted of recruits, professional army officers, members of the police corps, and *carabineros* (excise and customs officials).

8. Louis Fischer, *Men and Politics*, 383, gives the name of this officer as "Fritz"—a pseudonym. His real name was P. Batov, and he joined Líster's First Brigade in October 1936 before helping to organize the International Brigades (*Pod znamenem ispanskoi respubliki, 1936–1939*, 281–84 (see no. 111, this chapter, for information on this book). Batov was succeeded briefly by K. A. Meretskov, in later years a marshall and Red Army chief of staff (see text to nn. 211 and 212, this chapter).

9. See *Milicia Popular*, 17 Oct. 1936; Líster, *Nuestra guerra*, 74.

10. See chapter 20, n. 3.

11. Information given to me after the war by Contreras.

12. Letter to me.

13. *Nuestra guerra*, 74–75.

14. A few weeks later Cordón was made head of the technical secretariat of the undersecretaryship of war, which controlled the personnel, matériel, army pay, audit, coordination, court-martial, engineering, and supply departments as well as the war experiments committee. See Martín Blázquez (one of two technical secretaries who assisted Cordón), 279; also *Diario Oficial del Ministerio de la Guerra*, 2 Nov. 1936. Cordón's membership in the Communist party is confirmed by the official Communist history of the Civil War, *Guerra y revolución en España, 1936–1939*, I, 300. See also Cordón's book, *Trayectoria*, 289, 297, for García Val's and his own Communist party membership.

15. This department examined the antecedents of every man before he could enter the army (see Martín Blázquez, 121; Casado, 49–50).

16. *Guerra y revolución*, I, 66. See also *Aproximación histórica de la guerra española, 1936–1939*, article by Ramón Salas Larrazábal, 104–5; Ricardo de Cierva, *Historia de la guerra civil española*, 758.

17. He was appointed to this post when Largo Caballero became war minister (*Diario Oficial del Ministerio de la Guerra*, 5 Sept. 1936). His adjutant was Alejandro García Val, the Communist party member mentioned above, who, in accordance with the procedure governing such appointments, was nominated by Largo Caballero on the proposal of the chief of the general staff.

18. For this information I am indebted to Communists as well as non-Communists. For further details regarding these officers, see Enrique Castro, *Hombres made in Moscú*, 553–54, Cordón, 273, 288, 296, and Martín Blázquez, 320.

19. See circular order signed by Largo Caballero, *Gaceta de Madrid*, 16 Oct. 1936. The Communists later claimed that, on repeated occasions, they had urged the war minister to establish the commissariat (see, for example, Francisco Antón in *Nuestra Bandera*, Jan.–Feb. 1938).

20. *Mundo Obrero* (Madrid), 26 Apr. 1937. See also *Informaciones*, 8 Aug. 1936; *Claridad*, 15 Oct. 1936.

21. See, for example, José Díaz's speech, 22 Oct. 1936, as reprinted in Díaz, *Tres años de lucha*, 255.

22. See circular orders signed by Largo Caballero, *Diario Oficial del Ministerio de la Guerra*, 16 Oct. 1937; also regulations issued by the general commissariat of war, published in *Claridad*, 5 Nov. 1936.

23. "The political commissar must make his men understand the necessity of a conscious and iron discipline," ran one of the regulations issued by the general commis-

sariat of war. "By constant work he must ensure this discipline as well as obedience to the officers" (published in *Claridad*, 5 Nov. 1936).

24. "The political commissar," said the organ of the CNT Defense Committee of Madrid, "must at every moment analyze the psychological condition of his troops, so as to harangue them in moments of moral depression" (*Frente Libertario*, 20 Feb. 1937).

25. *Verdad*, 27 Jan. 1937.

26. Ibid.

27. *Frente Rojo*, 17 Apr. 1937.

28. The other three subcommissariats were held by Crescenciano Bilbao, a moderate or Prieto Socialist, Angel Pestaña, the leader of the Syndicalist party, and Angel G. Gil Roldán, a CNT member (see *Diario Oficial del Ministerio de la Guerra*, 16 Oct. 1936).

29. See Carlos de Baráibar (left Socialist leader) in *Timón* (Buenos Aires), June 1940; Enrique Castro (first commander in chief of the Communist Fifth Regiment and a former member of the central committee of the Communist party), *Hombres*, 553–58. For other references to Alvarez del Vayo's pro-Communist activities as commissar general, see Wenceslao Carrillo (left Socialist leader), *Timón* (Buenos Aires), Nov. 1939; Luis Araquistáin (left Socialist leader), *El comunismo y le guerra de España*, 8; Francisco Largo Caballero, *Mis recuerdos*, 212; Francisco Largo Caballero, *La UGT y la guerra*, 10–11; Indalecio Prieto (moderate Socialist leader) in *Correo de Asturias*, 10 July 1943; Casado, 57; also for Communist praise of his work in the commissariat, see *Frento Rojo*, 16 Apr., 19 May 1937, and *Pasaremos*, 8 May 1937.

30. See *Nuestra lucha por la unidad*, 35; also Pedro Checa, *A un gran partido, una gran organización*, 23.

31. This was only a small party, formed by dissident members of the CNT, and had no influence on the course of events. See chapter 17, n. 39.

32. See chapter 25.

33. Conversation with me after the war.

34. See Carlos de Baráibar in *Timón* (Buenos Aires), June 1940.

35. Pablo Clavego, *Algunas normas para el trabajo de los comisarios políticos* (Communist party handbook on the commissar's functions), 24.

36. From speech by Antonio Mije, member of the politburo, reported in *Mundo Obrero* (Madrid), 9 Sept. 1936.

37. *Acción Socialista*, 15 Mar. 1952.

38. *Correo de Asturias*, 10 July 1943. See also Indalecio Prieto, *Inauguración del círculo "Pablo Iglesias" de México*, 22.

39. *Guerra en España, 1936–1939*, 144. See also Casado, 57.

40. *Gaceta de Madrid*, 7 Oct. 1936.

41. *El comunismo*, 24. For further information on Gorev, see text to nn. 162–81 and 199–202, this chapter.

42. *National Review*, July 1939. See also Casado, 53–54.

43. Quoted from Largo Caballero's unpublished memoirs by Luis Araquistáin, *El comunismo*, 25.

44. Article in *Argentina Libre* (Buenos Aires), 13 Mar. 1941, as given in Pablo de Azcárate, *Mi embajada en Londres durante la guerra civil española*, 313–14.

45. *The Forging of a Rebel*, 585. See also ibid., 604.

46. Chapters 2, 9, and 14.

47. P. 237.

48. P. 162.

49. Bolloten, 272–73; also quoted in chapter 24 of this book.

50. See chapter 8.

51. *Milicia Popular*, 6 Sept. 1936.

52. Enrique Castro (commander in chief of the Fifth Regiment) in *Mundo Obrero* (Madrid), 10 Sept. 1936; see also ibid., 8 Sept. 1936.

53. Ibid.; see also letter to Asensio from Alejandro García Val on behalf of the Fifth Regiment, notifying him of its decision to make him an honorary commander, published in Asensio, *El General Asensio*, 105.

54. So said Alejandro García Val (see n. 14, above) when interviewed by me after the war. García Val, an officer in the Fifth Regiment (see previous footnote), it will be recalled, later became a member of the operations section of the general staff.

55. See César Falcón, *Madrid*, 177.

56. Casado, 75–76.

57. *El Socialista* (Madrid), 12 Mar. 1939. See also Bruno Alonso, *La flota republicana y le guerra civil de España*, 89–90.

58. See, for example, Martín Blázquez, 264, 280, 291; also the Communist Antonio Cordón, 282–84, who, although a vehement opponent of Asensio's, credits him with considerable ability as well as with many practical accomplishments in building the Popular Army; and the pro-Communist Amaro del Rosal, *Historia de la U.G.T. de España*, 616, who describes Asensio as "a great military man."

59. See, for example, Julián Zugazagoitia, *Historia de la guerra en España*, 141–43, 152–53; Martín Blázquez, 263.

60. Fischer, *Men and Politics*, 372–74.

61. *Freedom's Battle*, 126.

62. Ibid.

63. As given in Asensio, 107.

64. *Mis recuerdos*, 192.

65. Casado, 51. For Casado's reinstatement by Largo Caballero, see ibid., 63.

66. According to Enrique Castro, a former member of the central committee, in a letter to me. See also his book, *Hombres*, 553–54.

67. For information regarding this diary, see chapter 1, n. 112. For biographical data on Koltzov, see chapter 8, text to n. 9, and this chapter, text to nn. 184–90.

68. "Ispanskii Dnevnik," *Novyi Mir*, Apr. 1938, 123–24.

69. Prieto, *De mi vida*, 324–25; Zugazagoitia, 162; *Guerra y revolución*, II, 141–42.

70. As quoted in *Guerra y revolución*, II, 161.

71. Ibid.

72. Antonio López Fernández, *Defensa de Madrid*, 88.

73. *Así fué la defensa de Madrid*, 48. Rojo discusses what might have happened if the mistake had not been discovered early enough. See also Cordón, 278–97, for an interesting account of this incident.

74. *Así fué la defensa de Madrid*, 48.

75. For the full text of the instructions, see ibid., 247; also *Guerra y revolución*, II, 148–49; López Fernández, 85–87. Rojo (*Así fué la defensa de Madrid*, 47–48) analyzes certain contradictions in the instructions.

76. For some idea of the disorganization on the central front, see Rojo, *Así fué la defensa de Madrid*, 23–24, 36–37; also Rojo, *España heroica*, 47–51.

77. Zugazagoitia, 181.

78. *España heroica*, 47.

79. Zugazagoitia, 181.

80. When interviewed by me after the war.

81. "Ispanskii Dnevnik," *Novyi Mir*, May 1938, 56.

82. Vincent Brome, *The International Brigades*, 77–78. See also Andreu Castells, *Las brigadas internacionales de la guerra de España*, 102.

83. *The Spanish Civil War* (1965), 412–13.

84. *The Struggle for Madrid*, 144. The saga of the International Brigades lies of necessity beyond the scope of this work. Hundreds of books and articles have been written on the subject, among which Vincent Brome's *The International Brigades* and Verle B. Johnston's *Legions of Babel* are recommended. The latter was badly mutilated by the editors through the elimination of a significant amount of amplifying and qualifying material, but fortunately a copy of the original typescript has been deposited with the Hoover Institution on War, Revolution, and Peace, Stanford. These two works, which contain much valuable information on the brigades, have extensive bibliographies, as do Colodny's *The Struggle for Madrid* and Thomas's *The Spanish Civil War* (1965). The exact date of the Eleventh International Brigade's entry into action is still uncertain. Brome (80), Colodny (66–67), Thomas (412–13), and Vittorio Vidali, *Spagna lunga battaglia* (203) state that it first came under fire on the evening of 8 November—a date also given by the official Spanish Communist history of the Civil War (*Guerra y revolución*, II, 168), but Johnston (168, n. 23) adduces evidence (including that of Luigi Longo, political commissar of the Twelfth International Brigade), that puts the date as 9 November. To add to the discrepancy, Vicente Rojo, Miaja's chief of staff, states categorically that the Eleventh Brigade did not go into battle until 10 November (*Así fué la defensa de Madrid*, 222). For differing opinions regarding the highly controversial subject as to whether or not the brigades saved Madrid, see, for example, *Guerra y revolución*, II, 170–71, Rojo, *Así fué la defensa de Madrid*, 84, which agree that they did not, also Verle Johnston, *Legions of Babel*, 56, 171, n. 40, who cites Louis Fischer, Gustav Regler, and Julián Zugazagoitia, on the one hand, as saying that the brigades "did save Madrid," and Pietro Nenni, Dolores Ibárruri, and Tom Wintringham, on the other, who "agree that the brigades were only one of several important factors."

85. See text of official letter Rojo received from General Miaja, dated 6 November, notifying him of his appointment by Largo Caballero (as given in Rojo, *Así fué la defensa de Madrid*, 248).

86. Ibid.

87. López Fernández, 105.

88. Cecil D. Eby, *The Siege of Alcázar*, 144.

89. *Historia del ejército popular de la república*, I, 574–75.

90. "Ispanskii Dnevnik," *Novyi Mir*, May 1938, 86. For Rojo's extraordinary ability and capacity for work and for his vital role in the defense of Madrid, see the right-wing historian Salas Larrazábal, I, 574–75, 642.

91. "Ispanskii Dnevnik," *Novyi Mir*, June 1938, 33–34. Some of the major problems that confronted Rojo are given in his work, *Así fué la defensa de Madrid*, 59–60.

92. "Ispanskii Dnevnik," *Novyi Mir*, June 1938, 54–55.

93. *Give Me Combat*, 269.

94. *Causa general*, 289–90.

95. In a letter to me.

96. *Mis recuerdos*, 213–14. See also José María Gil Robles, *No fué posible la paz*, 708.

97. See, for example, the pro-Franco historian, Manuel Aznar, *Historia militar de la guerra de España*, 200, and Salas Larrazábal, I, 574–75, quoted earlier in this chapter.

98. Testimony given to me by Carlos Contreras (Vittorio Vidali), chief political commissar of the Fifth Regiment. Koltzov, on the other hand, says that Rojo "placed him-

self immediately at the disposal of the government" ("Ispanskii Dnevnik," *Novyi Mir*, June 1938, 34).

99. See, for example, Lázaro Somoza Silva, *El General Miaja*, 122–23.

100. Chapter 1.

101. Evidence of Luis Fernández Castañeda, a subordinate at the time of Miaja, as quoted by Maximiano García Venero, *El General Fanjul*, 289–90.

102. Chapter 1.

103. I am obliged to Giral for this information.

104. This information was given to me by General Sebastián Pozas, who was well acquainted with the incident.

105. *The Owl of Minerva*, 283.

106. *International Press Correspondence*, 17 May 1938.

107. Zugazagoitia, 197.

108. Casado, 63–64. See also Castro, *Hombres*, 452–53.

109. *España Popular*, 9 Nov. 1940. See also Cordón, 288 and 278–79, for this Communist officer's account of Miaja's undistinguished career.

110. *Eve of War, 1933–41*, 146, 235.

111. *Pod znamenem*, 152. This important book, which contains articles written by some of the principal Soviet officers who served in Spain during the war and who survived Stalin's purges, was published in Moscow in 1965 and translated into Spanish under the title *Bajo la bandera de la España republicana*. I am greatly indebted to Hilja Kukk of the Hoover Institution, Stanford, for translating portions of the Russian text, for her invaluable biographical research on Soviet officers and civilian personnel who served in Spain, and for her work in translating excerpts from many Soviet sources.

112. *Hombres*, 452.

113. *The Education of a Correspondent*, 143–44.

114. *Mis recuerdos*, 213.

115. See Martínez Cartón, member of the central committee of the Communist party, in *International Press Correspondence*, 17 May 1938; also Edmundo Domínguez (*Los vencedores de Negrín*, 203), who likewise confirms the guiding role of Antón. Domínguez, a left-wing Socialist and secretary of the UGT National Federation of Building Workers in July 1936, followed Communist policy during the war, finally becoming inspector-commissar of the central front.

116. *Men and Politics*, 593. It is noteworthy that Salas Larrazábal (I, 576), whose meticulously documented four-volume history of the People's Army deserves the highest praise, credits Miaja with greater intelligence, political independence, and military ability than reflected in these pages. My own knowledge of Miaja gleaned through considerable research prevents me from subscribing to this assessment, least of all to the view that Miaja was a "great chief."

117. 6 Feb. 1937, article by Hugh Slater. See also speech by Jesús Hernández, Communist minister of education (28 May 1937), referring to Largo Caballero's hostility to Miaja because he was "impregnated with Communist policy" (Jesús Hernández, *El partido comunista antes, durante y después de la crisis del gobierno Largo Caballero*, 24).

118. *Obras completas*, IV, 589.

119. *Así fué la defensa de Madrid*, 33.

120. Speech in Madrid, 11 Nov. 1936, as given in Díaz, 261.

121. 10 Nov. 1936.

122. Although Frade figured in the list as a Socialist, he was actually a Communist. This was confirmed to me by several Socialists. See also Barea, 579; Colodny, 51, 173, n. 49.

123. Carrillo joined the Communist party on 6 November 1936, according to Castro, *Hombres*, 439.

124. Although officially representing the UGT, the Socialist labor federation, Yagüe's membership in the Communist party was common knowledge.

125. *Así fué la defensa de Madrid*, 150.

126. Ibid., 31.

127. See *Pod znamenem*, published in Moscow in 1966 (articles by Marshals Voronov and Malinovsky, 95, 166–67, 183); Marshal Kirill A. Meretskov, *Na sluzhbe narodu*, 144. Meretskov also states that Rojo's outlook "was considerably more to the left than Miaja's."

128. *Guerra y revolución*, II, 152.

129. *The Siege of the Alcázar*, 148. See also document signed by Moscardó in *Causa general*, Annex X, 313–34.

130. When questioned by me after the war.

131. "Ispanskii Dnevik," *Novyi Mir*, June 1938, 35.

132. Pérez Salas, 147, 152, 169–70, 185. It is worth mentioning that Largo Caballero refers to Rojo's support of the Communists and even claims, though without supporting evidence, that he was a Communist (*Mis recuerdos*, 195, 214).

133. For example, Thomas, 460.

134. See Castro, *Hombres*, 317–18, 554.

135. Martín Blázquez, 283. See also Aznar, 428; Francisco Casares, *Azaña y ellos*, 256.

136. *Hombres*, 554.

137. Ibid., 318.

138. Quoted in Tsvetan Kristanov, *Za svobodu Ispanii*, 335.

139. *In Stalin's Secret Service*, 97.

140. For example, Pierre Broué and Emile Témime, *La révolution et la guerre d'Espagne*, 354, n. 21; Colodny, 62, 179–80, n. 101; Ypsilon (pseud. Julian Gumperz and Robert Rindl), *Pattern for World Revolution*, 422.

141. When questioned by me after the war.

142. Zugazagoitia, 198.

143. *Der spanische Krieg*, 69.

144. *Two Wars and More to Come*, 210.

145. Krivitsky, 97–98.

146. Statement to me after the war.

147. Johnston, 57.

148. When questioned by me after the war.

149. *Men and Politics*, 401.

150. *Así fué la defensa de Madrid*, 215.

151. P. 55.

152. Rojo gives the full text of his letter on pp. 253–55, with comments on p. 223.

153. *Nuestra guerra* and *El único camino*.

154. *Guerra y revolución*, II, 169.

155. *Guerra y revolución*, II, 169. On the other hand, Carlos Contreras (Vittorio Vidali), the Italian Communist and chief political commissar of the Fifth Regiment, refers favorably to Kléber twice in *Spagna lunga battaglia* (203, 304).

156. *The Spanish Cockpit*, 274–75.

157. For example, Brome, 143; David T. Cattell, *Communism and the Spanish Civil War*, 130–31; Thomas, 455.

158. *The Spanish Cockpit*, 275. For a critical analysis of Borkenau's version see Colodny, 215–16.

159. Verbal evidence from Carlos Contreras, from the British Communist, journalist, and writer Claud Cockburn (alias Frank Pitcairn), and from Gabriel García Maroto of the general commissariat of war when interviewed by me after the war.

160. When questioned by me after the war. Rojo himself refers to Kléber's dismissal, but does not state why or by whom he was dismissed (*Así fué la defensa de Madrid*, 223).

161. Fischer, *Men and Politics*, 405.

162. See Stanley Weintraub, *The Last Great Cause*, 235; also Fischer, *Men and Politics*, 412, 427.

163. *Men and Politics*, 395, 398. Fischer reaffirmed this view in 1969, twenty-eight years later (*Russia's Road from Peace to War*, 278).

164. Personal conversation.

165. It is noteworthy that Gorev's tank commander, General Pavlov, who apparently was not liquidated until 1941 (see n. 208, this chapter), is referred to several times in the diary under the Spanish pseudonym of "Del Pablo" ("Ispanskii Dnevnik," *Novyi Mir*, June 1938, 53, 78–79, 87), but there is no reference to Gorev even under an assumed named. When published in book form in 1957, after Stalin's death, as Volume 3 of *Isbrannye proizvedeniia* (Selected Works), the diary still contained no reference to Gorev, but then it was not until the 1960s that Soviet works revealed the true names of many Soviet officers who had served in Spain. For Gorev's liquidation during the purges, see text to nn. 199–202, this chapter.

166. See pp. 274–75, 281.

167. *Eve of War, 1933–41*, 146. For other accounts of Gorev, see Barea, 628–30; Castro, *Hombres*, 453–54; Fischer, *Men and Politics*, 363, 395, 398.

168. *Así fué la defensa de Madrid*, 31, 214–15. According to Rojo, Gorev was a colonel, but was promoted to the rank of general before leaving Spain (ibid., 214). However, two Soviet officers (N. Voronov, who reached Madrid in October 1936, and Rodion Malinovsky, who arrived in December 1936 or January 1937) refer to Gorev as a brigadier general at the time of their arrival (*Pod znamenem*, 72, 146).

169. For example, Broué and Témime, 346, n. 8; Colodny, 165; Gabriel Jackson, *The Spanish Republic and the Civil War, 1931–1939*, 319.

170. *Bortsy Latvii v Ispanii, 1936–1939*, 516; Ehrenburg, *Eve of War, 1933–41*, 152, 176; Alexander Orlov, *The Secret History of Stalin's Crimes*, 235. It is strange indeed that the unusually well-informed Koltzov, in a conversation with Louis Fischer in Madrid at the end of October 1936, did not identify Ian K. Berzin, the top Soviet military adviser correctly. "One evening," writes Fischer, "Mikhail Koltzov took me to dinner in the special Soviet restaurant in Madrid's elegant Palace Hotel. It was unusually full. Soviet military personnel had arrived—all dressed in ill-fitting, Moscow-made blue serge suits. 'Who,' Koltzov asked, 'is the top officer here? Guess.' I indicated a tall, gaunt man with a thick mat of gray hair. 'No,' Koltzov corrected, 'that's General Jan [Ian] Berzin. The commanding general is this one,' and he nodded in the direction of a shorter person with a ruddy, kindly face and silver hair. I subsequently met him, General 'Grishin,' in the headquarters of the Spanish General Staff" (*Russia's Road*, 277–78).

171. *Pod znamenem* 145–46 (article by Marshal Malinovsky, in which he mentions Gorev's dual capacity); ibid., 74–75 (photographs of Gorev and Berzin, captioned "Soviet military attaché in Spain" and "Principal military adviser" respectively; Nikolai G. Kuznetsov (Soviet naval attaché and adviser to the Spanish Republican Fleet in

1936–37), *Na dalekom meridiane*, 232, and *Bortsy Latvii v Ispanii, 1936–1939*, 407. Actually, Krivitsky (96), the Soviet defector, had revealed as far back as 1939 that Ian Berzin was the top military adviser in Spain, but the Communist offensive denouncing him as an imposter undermined his evidence at the time.

172. See Castro, *Hombres*, 456–58, Castro, *J'ai perdu la foi à Moscou*, 124; Carlo Penchienati (commander of the Garibaldi Brigade), *Brigate internazionali in Spagne*, 34; *Pod znamenem*, 146.

173. *Pod znamenem*, article by Marshal Malinovsky, 161.

174. Ibid., article by Voronov, 74.

175. Ibid., article by Major General of Aviation G. Prokofiev, 537. For additional information on Smushkevich and his successor, E. S. Ptukhin, see Dmitrii Ia. Zilmanovich, *Na orbite bolshoi zhizni*, 174, 178, 262, 282–83.

176. These were the reasons they both gave me after the war. The same reasons for his joining the party are also given by Hidalgo de Cisneros in his *Memorias*, II, 315, 317.

177. *Nuestra guerra*, 100.

178. *Pod znamenem*, 537.

179. Zilmanovich, 178.

180. Ehrenburg, *Eve of War, 1933–41*, 152; *Who Was Who in the USSR*, 512.

181. Nikita Khrushchev, *Speech at a Session of the 20th Congress of the Communist Party of the Soviet Union on February 25, 1956*, 31.

182. *Eve of War, 1933–41*, 152.

183. *Russia's Road*, 300.

184. Ehrenburg, *Eve of War, 1933–41*, 166, 290, 202.

185. P. 290.

186. P. 597.

187. II, 484.

188. *Men and Politics*, 494–95.

189. Ibid., 302.

190. *A Discord of Trumpets*, 304–5.

191. P. 67. According to the same source, he was posthumously rehabilitated.

192. *Eve of War, 1933–41*, 176, 190.

193. I am indebted to Robert Conquest's *The Great Terror*, 231, for bringing this issue of *Komsomolskaya Pravda* to my attention. In an article by S. Goliakov and V. Ponizovskii, the writers say simply, "Today we observe the seventy-fourth birthday of Ian K. Berzin, whose life was ended twenty-seven years ago [1937] by Beria's hirelings."

194. P. 410.

195. Krivitsky, 114.

196. Although the functions of the OGPU were transferred to the NKVD in 1934, the NKVD was for some time still commonly referred to as the OGPU or GPU (see chapter 14, n. 26).

197. Krivitsky, 96–97, 106–7.

198. Ibid., 113–14.

199. *Eve of War, 1933–41*, 190.

200. Fischer, *Men and Politics*, 392.

201. Kuznetsov, 32.

202. *The Secret History of Stalin's Crimes*, 235–36.

203. *Bolshaia sovietskaia entsiklopediia*, 2d ed., vol. 9, published in 1951.

204. *Prominent Personalities in the USSR*, 341.

205. Pp. 512, 520, 466.

206. *The Aim of a Lifetime*, 79.

207. Thomas, 777, states that "he vanished in 1941 due to reasons connected with foolishness over Red Army equipment." There is no mention of Kulik in the otherwise highly informative *Who Was Who in the USSR* published in 1972. Castro (*Hombres*, 458) says that Kulik was "rewarded with the rank of marshal" after his return from Spain.

208. Thomas, 777, says he was "shot by Stalin in 1941 when he had lost his army during the first week of the German advance," but cites no source. Pavlov is not included in *Who Was Who in the USSR* published in 1972.

209. *Eve of War, 1933–41*, 176. Ehrenburg does not give the date of Pavlov's death.

210. *Pod znamenem*, 275, 313, 446–47, 483, 485, 503.

211. *Who Was Who in the USSR*, 365; *Prominent Personalities in the USSR*, 403.

212. See his memoirs, *Na sluzhbe narodu*, 130, 136, 141, 143, 166. See also P. Ia. Egorov, *Marshal Meretskov*, 40–52.

213. *Eve of War, 1933–41*, 154. See also *Guerra y revolución*, II, 174, and n. 2.

214. Regler gives the name of Maximovich as the leader of the Russian delegation. This may have been a pseudonym as I have not found any reference to a Maximovich in Spain in February 1937. There was a General Maximov, who succeeded Shtern (Grigorovich) as the highest Soviet adviser (see Fischer, *Men and Politics*, 543), but that was not until 1938.

215. *The Owl of Minerva*, 294–95.

216. Ibid., 292–93.

217. Generalnyi Shtab RKKA, *Upravlenie voiskami i rabota shtabov v ispanskoi respublikanskoi armii*, 125.

218. Essay by Julián Gorkin in Jeane J. Kirkpatrick, ed., *The Strategy of Deception*, 196.

219. See chapter 9, n. 123.

220. A photostatic copy of the original letter in French is reproduced in *Guerra y revolución*, II, between pp. 102–3.

221. Letter of 21 December 1936.

222. See quotation from his unpublished memoirs in this chapter, text to n. 43.

223. *Actas de la junta de defensa de Madrid*, 422–23.

224. When interviewed by me after the war.

225. Chapter 9, text to n. 96.

226. See text to n. 43, this chapter.

227. *The Last Days of Madrid*, 54. See also ibid., 55–57; Casado's article in the *National Review*, July 1939, quoted p. 265; and Largo Caballero, *Mis recuerdos*, 206.

228. See chapter 20, text to n. 20. Alejandro García Val, Communist party member who was made chief of the transport section of the general staff in November 1936, told me after the war that when Russian trucks reached Spain he organized with the aid of party members and sympathizers in the UGT the first three militarized motor transport battalions composed of six hundred vehicles and three thousand men.

229. For non-Communist praise of Spanish Communist units, see, for example, *Política* (organ of the Left Republican party), 11 Nov.1936, and Colonel Segismundo Casado (whom no one can accuse of being partial to the Communists), *The Last Days of Madrid*, 96, who says that there were "plenty of communist units which distinguished themselves by their impetuous fighting."

230. See, for example, Diego Abad de Santillán, *La revolución y la guerra en España*, 131–32.

231. See also Pérez Salas, 128, Zugazagoitia, 195, and Guzmán, *Madrid, rojo y negro* (director of the FAI organ in Madrid, *Castilla Libre*), 164, 200, who praises the courage,

intelligence, discipline, and military skill of the International Brigades and gives full credit to the example they set to the anarchosyndicalist militia on the Madrid front: "[Our men]," he commented, "observe them, and, with that wonderful power of adaptation the Spanish people possesses, they imitate them without losing any time."

232. 25 Nov. 1936.

233. *Politics, Economics and Men of Modern Spain, 1808–1946*, 599.

234. See text to nn. 172 and 207, this chapter.

235. *Yo fui un ministro de Stalin*, 80.

236. *Hombres*, 457.

237. *Who Was Who in the USSR*, 365.

238. *Pod znamenem*, 151.

239. See, for example, the official (Franco) history of the Civil War, *Historia de la cruzada española*, IV, 381, 391; *Política*, 23 Oct. 1936. When interviewed by me after the war, Captain Aniceto Carbajal, son-in-law of Pozas, stated that a few days after the February elections, when General Franco was still chief of the general staff, he tried through his intermediacy to purchase Pozas's support for a "National Government" by offering him a sum of money deposited in a Swiss bank.

240. See speech by Jerónimo Bujeda, *El Socialista* (Madrid), 19 July 1937.

241. Louis Fischer, who was in a position to know, stated in 1937 that he was a member of the party (*Why Spain Fights On*, 39).

242. See Pérez Salas, 141–42; Zugazagoitia, 406.

243. According to Alejandro García Val, Communist member of the general staff, when interviewed by me after the war.

244. Pérez Salas, 146–47.

245. *La flota republicana y la guerra civil de España*, 38.

246. Martín Blázquez, 241.

247. Quoted in Julián Gorkin, *Caníbales políticos*, 217. In an article in *Francisco Largo Caballero, 1869–1946*, 74, Federica Montseny, a cabinet colleague, refers to his "unipersonal" conception of power.

248. An employee in the war ministry who was in intimate contact with José María Aguirre, Largo Caballero's politicomilitary secretary, informed me that the relations between the Russian officers and Largo Caballero became very bad after December 1936 and that the Russians were particularly concerned about the political orientation of the army.

249. *El comunismo*, 10.

250. *Hoy*, 5 Dec. 1942.

251. *Eve of War, 1933–41*, 190.

252. *Obras*, IV, 701.

253. Ibid., 711.

254. My own personal judgment during a luncheon interview in March 1937, arranged for me by Mirova, the Tass news agency representative, herself a later victim, as has been noted, of Stalin's purges.

255. Speech in the *Centro Republicano Español* (Mexico City), 29 Mar. 1946, as given in *Adelante* (Mexico City), 1 Apr. 1946.

256. See chapter 18, text to nn. 10–11, and this chapter, text to n. 4.

Chapter 22

1. 27 Oct. 1936.

2. Speech, reported by *Fragua Social*, 18 Oct. 1936.

3. 11 Feb. 1937.

4. As given in *Solidaridad Obrera* (Barcelona), 12 May 1936.

5. See chapter 18, text to nn. 6–9.

6. 5 Aug. 1936.

7. Speech reported in *CNT* (Madrid), 12 Sept. 1936.

8. Speech in January 1937 reprinted in *En marcha hacia la victoria*, 51.

9. Resolution approved at a plenary meeting of representatives of the regional committees of the CNT, as given in *CNT* (Madrid), 17 Sept. 1936.

10. "We failed to transform as rapidly as we should have done the spontaneous columns of the first days into regularly organized units. Positions were lost by us and taken by the Communists" (Mariano Vázquez, secretary of the national committee of the CNT speaking at an AIT congress, reported in supplement of *Espagne Nouvelle*, 15 Mar. 1939).

11. *Internacional*, June 1938.

12. Speech at Valencia CNT congress, November 1936, reported by *Fragua Social*, 17 Nov. 1936.

13. Ibid.

14. Indeed, this was the opinion given to me by Gabriel García Maroto, a friend of Alvarez del Vayo, who became a member of the new body.

15. *Gaceta de la República*, 10 Nov. 1936.

16. Ibid.

17. In a demonstration held on 14 February 1937 (see chapter 25, text to n. 39), the Communists in a ten-point petition presented to Largo Caballero demanded inter alia that the Higher War Council should be allowed to fulfill "the mission for which it was created," and two weeks later their organ, *Frente Rojo*, urged that it "should meet methodically and as often as necessary for discussing and reaching agreement upon all questions of the war," among which it included "the appointment and control of officers and the cleansing of the army of all hostile and incapable elements" (quoted in *Mundo Obrero* [Madrid], 2 Mar. 1937).

18. *Fragua Social*, 19 Nov. 1936.

19. Guzmán, *Madrid, rojo y negro*, 200.

20. *Fragua Social*, 14 Nov. 1936.

21. "Unpublished Article by a Regular Army Corporal."

22. *Mi desembarco en Mallorca*, 113–14.

23. *Solidaridad Obrera* (Barcelona), 1 Dec. 1936.

24. *CNT* (Madrid), 20 Sept. 1937. See also his proclamation to the anarchosyndicalist militia on the Madrid front, published in *Castilla Libre*, 17 Feb. 1937, and his book, *Guerra, exilio y cárcel de un anarcosindicalista*, 109–11, 113, 116.

25. 14 Jan. 1937.

26. Guzmán, *Madrid, rojo y negro*, 200.

27. *CNT* (Madrid), 23 Feb. 1937.

28. *Mundo Obrero* (Madrid), as given in *Fragua Social*, 26 Sept. 1937.

29. *Bulletin de la Généralité de la Catalogne* (issued by the Propaganda Department of the Catalan government), 30 Mar. 1937, as quoted in *Le Libertaire*, 8 Apr. 1937. See also Maxim Llorca in *Ideas*, 29 Apr. 1937.

30. See speech by Mariano Vázquez, secretary of the national committee of the CNT, published in *Memoria del congreso extraordinario de la confederación regional del trabajo de Cataluña celebrado en Barcelona los días 25 de febrero al 3 de marzo de 1937*, 178–85.

31. *Fragua Social*, 1 June 1937.

32. Testimony by García Oliver, in reply to a questionnaire sent to him by me after the

war through the German anarchist Agustín Souchy. That the anarchosyndicalists were in a minority was emphasized by Mariano Vázquez, secretary of the national committee of the CNT, in a speech published in *Memoria del congreso extraordinario de la confederación regional del trabajo de Cataluña celebrado en Barcelona los días 25 de febrero al 3 de marzo de 1937*, 178–85.

33. Reply to questionnaire. See previous footnote.

34. *I Helped to Build an Army*, 299. In his book, Cordón, a Communist, also speaks highly of García Oliver's work in the officers' training schools (*Trayectoria*, 282).

35. See, for example, *CNT* (Madrid), 28 Apr. 1937.

36. Ibid., 10 Apr. 1937.

37. As given in J. García Pradas, *Antifascismo proletario*, 46.

38. Máximo Llorca, in *Ideas*, 29 Apr. 1937.

39. *La tragedia del norte*, 135.

40. *CNT* (Madrid), 1 Mar. 1937.

41. *Cipriano Mera, revolucionario*, 60.

42. For information regarding the mixed brigades, see chapter 21, n. 7.

43. Two republican officers confirm this: Martín Blázquez, 295, and Segismundo Casado (article in *National Review*, July 1939), who, while criticizing the mixed brigades on technical grounds, says: "[The government] committed the very serious initial mistake of accepting the opinion of the 'friendly Russian advisers.'" In his book, Casado, who was appointed to organize the first brigades, writes: "One Russian general and two Russian colonels were chosen to help me in this mission by order of the minister [Largo Caballero]" (*The Last Days of Madrid*, 52).

44. Martín Blázquez, 297.

45. A short account of the military reasons for the creation of mixed brigades is given by Martín Blázquez, 293–95. For a criticism on technical grounds, see Colonel Segismundo Casado in *National Review*, July 1939.

46. *Elementos distinados al pleno de la AIT del 11 junio de 1937 en vista de la discusión sobre la situación española*, as given in *Guerra y revolución en España, 1936–1939*, III, 63, n. 1.

47. In letters to me.

48. See chapter 21, text to nn. 211–12.

49. Bolloten Collection, Archives, Hoover Institution on War, Revolution, and Peace, Stanford.

50. Although officially the organ of the Valencia FAI and unofficially the organ of the Valencia Libertarian Youth, *Nosotros* was also the mouthpiece of the Iron Column by virtue of the help these two organizations received in money and men from the column (see César M. Lorenzo, *Les anarchistes espagnols et le pouvoir, 1868–1969*, 187).

51. 11 Feb. 1937.

Chapter 23

1. *Fragua Social*, 14 Nov. 1936.

2. Ibid.

3. This was the figure given by an Iron Column delegate at a CNT congress, reported in ibid.; see also José Martín Blázquez, *I Helped to Build an Army*, 296.

4. *Nosotros*, 16 Feb. 1937.

5. This was admitted to me by a Valencia anarchosyndicalist who had been in close contact with members of the column.

6. In a letter to the author, Federica Montseny, who was a member of the national

committee of the CNT, emphasizes this friction and states that the Valencia CNT demanded that the column should purge itself of the malefactors in its ranks.

7. This information was given to me by a well-informed member of the Valencia CNT.

8. "During our stay in Valencia," ran a manifesto issued by the column, "we noticed that, whereas our negotiations for the purchase of arms had failed, because of the lack of hard cash, in many shops there was a large quantity of gold and other precious metals, and it was this consideration that induced us to seize the gold, silver, and platinum in several jewelers' shops" (as given in *Cultura Proletaria*, 7 Nov. 1936).

9. See chapter 22, text to nn. 18 and 19.

10. Martín Blázquez, 296.

11. Report to the general commissariat of war, dated 18 February 1937 (Bolloten Collection, Archives, Hoover Institution on War, Revolution, and Peace, Stanford).

12. This was confirmed to me by Rodolfo Llopis, Largo Caballero's undersecretary in the premiership in his reply to questionnaire. See also Francisco Largo Caballero, *La UGT y la guerra*, 10–11.

13. See statement published in *Nosotros*, 2 Jan. 1937.

14. *Nosotros*, 16 Feb. 1937.

15. *Diario Oficial del Ministerio de la Guerra*, as given in *La Correspondencia de Valencia*, 3 Mar. 1937.

16. Martín Blázquez, 323.

17. Ibid.

18. *El Pueblo*, 13 Mar. 1937. For an account of the events by the national committee of the CNT, see *Boletín de Información y Orientación Orgánica del Comité Peninsular de la Federación Anarquista Ibérica*, 1 May 1937. Although neither of these reports mentioned the role of the Iron Column in the events, its members were, as everyone knew at the time, among the principal participants.

19. 23 Mar. 1937.

20. Issued 6 Mar. 1937; published in *Nosotros*, 9 Mar. 1937.

21. *Frente Rojo*, 19 Mar. 1937.

22. See 12–13, 15–17 Mar. 1937. For information on *Nosotros*, see chapter 22, n. 50.

23. In Spanish the second person singular is used for familiar address.

24. See *Nosotros*, 24 Mar. 1937.

25. Ibid., 27 Mar. 1937.

Chapter 24

1. Bolloten Collection, Archives, Hoover Institution on War, Revolution, and Peace, Stanford.

2. I, 803–57.

3. Pp. 139–242.

4. See Antonio Cordón, *Trayectoria*, 284, 292–93, 295, who holds General Asensio responsible for the appointment.

5. The text of the indictment against Villalba is reproduced in José Manuel Martínez Bande, *La campaña de Andalucía*, 218–24.

6. *La Vanguardia*, 3 Nov. 1938. At the outbreak of the Civil War, Colonel Villalba was commander of the Barbastro garrison in Aragon. His failure to join the military revolt was a heavy blow to Emilio Mola, the organizer of the conspiracy on the Peninsula, for it gave the CNT-FAI militia in the adjoining region of Catalonia sufficient time to occupy a large part of Aragon. Mola later accused Villalba of having demanded 100,000

pesetas as his price for bringing his troops into the conspiracy (speech, Jan. 1937, in Mola, *Obras completas*, 1188), but although Iribarren, Mola's secretary, mentions this (Stanley G. Payne, *Politics and the Military in Modern Spain*, 508, n. 59), it is not, to my knowledge, corroborated by any other source. For further information on Villalba, see Cordón, 290–95, and Lieutenant Colonel Vicente Guarner, *Cataluña en la guerra de España, 1936–39*, 169–72.

7. See editorials and speeches published in *Mundo Obrero*, *Verdad*, and *Milicia Popular* of the period.

8. "Ispanskii Dnevnik," *Novyi Mir*, June 1938, 71.

9. *Na sluzhbe narodu*, 134.

10. Cordón, 258.

11. Cordón, 258.

12. "Ispanskii Dnevnik," *Novyi Mir*, June 1938, 71.

13. *Gaceta de Madrid*, 30 Sept. 1937.

14. See article in *Claridad*, Largo Caballero's newspaper, 20 Aug. 1936, quoted in chapter 18, text to n. 11.

15. Quoted in D. and A. Prudhommeaux, *Catalogne Libertaire, 1936–1937*, 19–20. See also statements by the delegates of Puertollano and the Madrid Printers' Union at the CNT Plenum of the Central Region reported in *CNT* (Madrid), 5 Oct. 1936.

16. Quoted by Máximo de Dios at a meeting of the Madrid Defense Council on 19 February 1937 (*Actas de la junta de defensa de Madrid*).

17. *Gaceta de Madrid*, 30 Oct. 1936.

18. *La Correspondencia de Valencia*, 11 Feb. 1937.

19. *Gaceta de la República*, 21 Feb. 1937. See also Jesús Hernández's statement to the press, published in *CNT* (Madrid), 17 Feb. 1937.

20. Notice published in *Cultura y Acción*, 3 Mar. 1937.

21. *Diario Oficial del Ministerio de la Guerra*, 9 Mar. 1937.

22. *Fragua Social*, 16 Mar. 1937.

23. 21 Apr. 1937.

24. See, for example, Communist party statement issued after the fall of Malaga, *Frente Rojo*, 10 Feb. 1937; also ibid., 12 Feb. 1937.

25. *Hombres made in Moscú*, 489.

26. *Mis recuerdos*, 192–93.

27. Ibid., 193; Baráibar, articles in *Timón* (Buenos Aires), June 1940, and *España Libre* (New York), 1 Jan. 1942; Wenceslao Carrillo, open letter to Indalecio Prieto, published in *Mundo*, Aug. 1943. See also the former Caballerista and pro-Communist, Amaro del Rosal, *Historia de la U.G.T. de España*, 636, who ignores the reason for Rosenberg's visit and blames the entire episode on Largo Caballero's changed "political line."

28. *Hoy*, 5 Dec. 1942.

29. *Mis recuerdos*, 193.

30. *Historia de la U.G.T.*, 616.

31. Cordón, 296. See also ibid., 284, 292–93, 295, for his hostility to Asensio.

32. Chapter 9, n. 123.

33. A photostatic copy of his reply, in French, is reproduced in *Guerra y revolución en España, 1936–1939*, II, between pp. 102–3.

34. *El comunismo y la guerra de España*, 27–28. See also Largo Caballero, *Mis recuerdos*, 225–26. Amaro del Rosal, a former Caballerista, writes: "The slogan of unification—of unity—was promoted before the war and in its early stage by Caballero and by the whole Caballero group, of which Araquistáin was the spiritual director" (*Historia de la UGT*, II, 629–31).

35. See *Claridad*, 19 Mar. 1936; *La Libertad*, 4 Apr. 1936.
36. Chapter 29.
37. As published in *Claridad*, 12 Mar. 1936.
38. Speech in Madrid, 17 Oct. 1937, as reprinted in Francisco Largo Caballero, *La UGT y la guerra*, 41.
39. See chapter 8, text to nn. 62 and 63.
40. *Tribuna*, Mar. 1949. See also Rodolfo Llopis's speech, reported in *La Correspondencia de Valencia*, 13 Aug. 1937.
41. See article by Ginés Ganga in *Hoy*, 12 Dec. 1942; also Largo Caballero's speech in Madrid, Oct. 1937, as given in Largo Caballero, *La UGT y la guerra*, 5, and Largo Caballero, *Mis recuerdos*, 225.
42. *Mis recuerdos*, 223–26. See also Araquistáin, *El comunismo*, 28.
43. Personal recollection.
44. *Hombres*, 489–90.
45. Ibid., 490.
46. Speech in Madrid, Oct. 1937, as given in Largo Caballero, *La UGT y la guerra*, 5–6.

Chapter 25

1. 16 Feb. 1937.
2. *Freedom's Battle*, 126.
3. Ibid.
4. 21 Feb. 1937.
5. *Gaceta de la República*, 21 Feb. 1937.
6. For attacks in CNT-FAI newspapers, see *Castilla Libre*, 19 Feb. 1937; *CNT* (Madrid), 17 Feb. 1937; *Fragua Social*, 23 Feb. 1937; *Frente Libertario*, 16 Feb. 1937; *Solidaridad Obrera*, 20, 25, 27 Feb. 1937.
7. José Martín Blázquez, *I Helped to Build an Army*, 217.
8. *Gaceta de la República*, 21 Feb. 1937.
9. For the importance of this post, see chapter 21, n. 14.
10. *Gaceta de la República*, 23 Feb. 1937.
11. That he was a sympathizer was confirmed to me by Alejandro García Val, himself a Communist party member and adjutant of Major Manuel Estrada, the former chief of the general staff.
12. See chapter 21, text to n. 16.
13. *Gaceta de la República*, 21 Feb. 1937.
14. Martín Blázquez, 320. Cordón, *Trayectoria*, 296, affirms that the dismissals were a "form of reprisal" against the Communist party by Largo Caballero, "undoubtedly on the advice of the general."
15. Martín Blázquez, 121; Segismundo Casado, *The Last Days of Madrid*, 49–50.
16. Personal interview after the war. See Jesús Pérez Salas, *Guerra en España, 1936–1939*, 147, who confirms Díaz Tendero's pro-Communist activities later in the war. However, Cordón, 288, stresses the fact that he was not a Communist, by which he no doubt means a member of the party.
17. *The Spanish Revolution*, 321
18. Letter to me after the war.
19. These were, according to the *Gaceta de la República*, 23 Feb. 1937: José Díaz Alor, Luis Barrero Hernando, Mariano Muñoz Sánchez, Carlos Hernández Zancajo, Manuel Arias Fernández, and Julio de Mora Martínez.

20. Specific reference was made to the general commissar (Alvarez del Vayo), the secretary general (Felipe Pretel), both secret Communist supporters, and to the subcommissars of war, the chief of whom was Antonio Mije, a member of the politburo of the Communist party.

21. See circular order published in the *Gaceta de la República*, 23 Feb. 1937.

22. See *Frente Rojo*, 24 Feb. 1937.

23. This information was given to me after the war by Carlos Contreras (Vittorio Vidali), chief political commissar of the Fifth Regiment, who was well acquainted with Díaz Tendero.

24. Letter to me after the war.

25. Ibid.

26. *Adelante* (Valencia), 24 Feb. 1937.

27. Ibid.

28. 25 Feb. 1937.

29. *La Correspondencia de Valencia*, 2 Mar. 1937.

30. 25 Feb. 1937.

31. See *Claridad*, 28 Feb. 1937.

32. Ibid.

33. See *Memoria del congreso extraordinario de la confederación regional del trabajo de Cataluña celebrado en Barcelona los días 25 de febrero al 3 de marzo de 1937*.

34. Report to the AIT, dated 8 May 1937.

35. The text of the indictment is given in his book, *El General Asensio*, 29–62. This book in defense of his position was written in jail.

36. See his letters to Asensio, ibid., 110–11.

37. As an example of Largo Caballero's concern for foreign opinion because of Communist influence in the army, see his speech, Oct. 1937, *La UGT y la guerra*, 16.

38. Ibid., 5.

39. *Adelante* (Valencia), 13 Feb. 1937. See also Largo Caballero's statement on compulsory military service issued a few days before the demonstration, chapter 24, text to n. 18.

40. *Claridad*, 27 Feb. 1937.

41. Hernández, *El partido comunista antes, durante y después de la crisis del gobierno Largo Caballero*, 11.

42. See, for example, *Mundo Obrero* (Madrid), 1 Mar. 1937.

43. *El Día Gráfico*, 28 Feb. 1937.

44. *Guerra y revolución en España, 1936–1939*, I, II, III.

45. Orlov, "Answers to the Questionnaire of Professor Stanley G. Payne," 15–16.

46. *Yo fui un ministro de Stalin*, 66–71.

47. Orlov, "Answers to the Questionnaire of Professor Stanley G. Payne," 15–16. "Those familiar with Stalin's policy of manipulating the foreign communist parties (always through the machinery of the Comintern)," Orlov writes, "will recognize at once the absurdity of Hernández' assertion that two Soviet diplomats—Gaikis and I—were present at a Politburo meeting of the Spanish Communist Party." Hernández, it will be recalled, makes a special point of mentioning that they were attending such a meeting "for the first time."

48. *Yo fui un ministro de Stalin*, 90.

49. U.S. Congress, Senate, Committee on the Judiciary, *The Legacy of Alexander Orlov*.

50. This description was confirmed to me by Bertram D. Wolfe and his wife Ella, who became well acquainted with him some years after his defection to the United States.

51. *Men and Politics*, 361.
52. The anti-Stalinist POUM, the Partido Obrero de Unificación Marxista, is dealt with in chapter 27.
53. *El proceso de Moscú en Barcelona*, 173.
54. According to my correspondence with Gorkin.
55. *Yo fui un ministro de Stalin*, 59, 90. The former Communist Eudocio Ravines, who worked on the editorial staff of *Frente Rojo*, refers frequently in his book to a Colonel Bielov of the NKVD, whom he knew personally, but does not mention Orlov (*La gran estafa*, 338, 340, 346, 349, 358, 374–78).
56. Orlov, article, *Reader's Digest*, Nov. 1966.
57. *Yo fui un ministro de Stalin*, 66, 69, 90–98, 109–13.
58. *The Last Optimist*, 285–86, quoted in chapter 9, text to n. 61.
59. *Yo fui un ministro de Stalin*, 90–94.
60. Marcella Ferrara and Maurizio Ferrara, *Conversando con Togliatti*, 261.
61. Orlov, "Answers to the Questionnaire of Professor Stanley G. Payne," 16.
62. Palmiro Togliatti, *Escritos políticos*, prologue by Adolfo Sánchez Vázquez, 11.
63. *Yo fui un ministro de Stalin*, 33–36, 49, 79–84.
64. *El proceso de Moscú en Barcelona*, 79–80, n. 7.
65. *Yo fui un ministro de Stalin*, 66.
66. Date given in José Díaz, *Tres años de lucha*, 341.
67. *Yo fui un ministro de Stalin*, 73.
68. See his speech in Hernández, *Todo dentro del frente popular*.
69. *Yo fui un ministro de Stalin*, 73.
70. Ibid., 85.
71. Chapter 21, text to n. 66.
72. For this information I am indebted to the staff of the Febus news agency, which was in daily contact with persons having close relations with members of the government and the Higher War Council.
73. See his speech of 28 May 1937 in Hernández, *El partido comunista*, 24.
74. 2 Mar. 1937.
75. *Hombres Made in Moscú*, 489.
76. Largo Caballero, *Mis recuerdos*, 195.
77. For cancellation of the appointment, see *Gaceta de la República*, 16 Mar. 1937; Largo Caballero, *Mis recuerdos*, 195; Vicente Rojo, *Así fué la defensa de Madrid*, 216.
78. For a war ministry announcement paying tribute to Martínez Cabrera, see *El Mercantil Valenciano*, 16 Mar. 1937. Although Largo Caballero says that he did not fill the vacancy (*Mis recuerdos*, 195), there is evidence that Martínez Cabrera was replaced, at least provisionally, by Colonel Alvarez Coque, a republican (see article by Vicente Guarner, *España Nueva*, 18 Mar. 1950; also Ramón Salas Larrazábal, *Historia del ejercito popular de la república*, I, 1075–76). Rojo was made chief of the central general staff after the fall of Largo Caballero in May 1937 (see *Guerra y revolución*, III, 88).
79. *Mis recuerdos*, 195.
80. Article in *Timón* (Buenos Aires), June 1940.
81. Ibid.
82. *Vía Libre*, 5 Aug. 1939.
83. Article in *Timón* (Buenos Aires), June 1940.
84. Ibid.
85. *Vía Libre*, 5 Aug. 1939.
86. *Mis recuerdos*, 209.

87. Speech reported in *Fragua Social*, 7 July 1937.

88. *El Socialista* (Madrid), 25 Feb. 1937.

89. Article in *Timón* (Buenos Aires), June 1940.

90. 28 June 1937.

91. For this information I am indebted to a member of the staff of José María Aguirre, Largo Caballero's politicomilitary secretary.

92. Article in *Timón* (Buenos Aires), June 1940.

93. Ibid.

94. *Frente Rojo*, 29 Mar. 1937.

95. See letter sent by *Claridad*, at that time still a Largo Caballero Socialist organ, to Francisco Antón, the secretary of the Madrid Communist party organization and inspector-commissar of the central front, charging that the Madrid section of the commissariat of war, which he controlled, was obstructing the distribution of that paper at the front (published in *Claridad*, 1 Mar. 1937). See also *Frente Libertario*, 20 Feb. 1937, complaining that the CNT-FAI newspapers were not reaching the front regularly owing to sabotage.

96. At the beginning of March, Pascual Tomás, supporter of Largo Caballero and vice-secretary of the UGT, declared that political commissars who tried to make converts, "often using methods in opposition to all sense of decency," should not be allowed to remain in their positions a moment longer (*La Correspondencia de Valencia*, 3 Mar. 1937). See also interviews with Tomás published in *El Pueblo*, 16 Feb. 1937; *Claridad*, 16 Feb. 1937, and his article, ibid., 6 Apr. 1937. Even Antonio Mije, Communist head of the subcommissariat of organization, admitted in April 1937 that there had been some "overstepping of powers" by commissars (see *Frente Rojo*, 15 Apr. 1937).

97. See chapter 21, text to n. 27.

98. *Gaceta de la República*, 26 Nov. 1936.

99. For this information I am grateful to Gabriel García Maroto, head of the subcommissariat of propaganda.

100. *Mis recuerdos*, 212; see also Largo Caballero, *La UGT y la guerra*, 10–11.

101. *Freedom's Battle*, 127.

102. *Give Me Combat*, 179–82.

103. For Alvarez del Vayo's own account of this incident, see *Freedom's Battle*, 219–20; for Prieto's, see Prieto, *Convulsiones en España*, II, 141.

104. *Correo de Asturias*, 10 July 1943.

105. Some idea of the extent to which Largo Caballero's concern for Spain's position in the League of Nations influenced his behavior was given in text to nn. 37 and 38, this chapter.

106. *Gaceta de la República*, 17 Apr. 1937.

107. 16 Apr. 1937.

108. 17 Apr. 1937.

109. *Frente Rojo*, 17 Apr. 1937. For criticism of the order in *Mundo Obrero*, the Madrid Communist organ, see, for example, issues for 24, 29 Apr. 1937.

110. 20 Apr. 1937.

111. 20 Apr. 1937 (*Frente Rojo* was an evening paper).

112. 22 Apr. 1937. For charges by *Adelante* that Francisco Antón, inspector-commissar of the central front and secretary of the Madrid Communist party organization, had replaced Socialist by Communist commissars, see issues 23–25 Apr. 1937. For *Frente Rojo*'s replies, see issues of 23, 24 Apr. 1937.

113. 25 Dec. 1936. See also *CNT* (Madrid), 25 Feb. 1937.

114. 22 Apr. 1937. For other articles approving the war minister's order, see issues of 23, 26, 27 Apr. 1937; also *Fragua Social*, 27 Apr. 1937.

115. See, for example, report by José Díaz to the central committee of the Communist party, 8 Mar. 1937, as reprinted in Díaz, 363–64; speech by Francisco Antón, *Mundo Obrero* (Madrid), 18 Mar. 1937; manifesto of the central committee of the Communist party, *Frente Rojo*, 19 Mar. 1937; editorials, ibid., 23, 31 Mar., 8, 13 Apr., 18 May 1937.

116. *Gaceta de la República*, 17 Feb. 1937. Cordón (259) asserts that Largo Caballero "hindered in every way he could the rapid promotion of the militia to command positions."

117. On 27 January 1937, at a public meeting held to celebrate the formal dissolution of the Fifth Regiment, José Díaz had declared that the posts of generals and other officers whose hearts were not in the war "should be occupied by the new talents discovered in the Fifth Regiment" (speech reprinted in Díaz, 297). Although, after the publication of the decree of 16 February, the Communists frequently referred to the question of promotions and implicitly criticized Largo Caballero's policy (see, for example, José Díaz's report to the central committee of the Communist party, 8 Mar. 1937, ibid., 367, the resolution of the central committee, *Mundo Obrero* [Madrid], 7 Apr. 1937, also *Frente Rojo*, 21 Apr. 1937), there was no open criticism of the decree itself until January 1938 (ibid., 5 Jan. 1938), when the provision restricting the promotion of militia leaders was annulled (*Gaceta de la República*, 5 Jan. 1938). For sharp criticism of the decree in the official Communist history of the Civil War, see *Guerra y revolución*, III, 62–63.

118. *Guerra y revolución*, III, 63.

119. Quoted in *Castilla Libre*, 31 Mar. 1937. For *Frente Rojo*'s reply to an attack on Uribe by *Adelante* (Valencia), see issue for 21 Apr. 1937. For all details regarding Hernández and Uribe not contained in the above newspapers I am indebted to members of the staff of the Febus news agency.

120. 22 Apr. 1937.

121. 22 Apr. 1937.

122. 23 Apr. 1937.

Chapter 26

1. For the factional strife within the Socialist party before and during the Civil War, see chapter 1, text to nn. 101–15, and chapter 8, nn. 15, 53–54.

2. *El Socialista* (Madrid), 3 July 1936.

3. See chapter 8, text to nn. 64–76.

4. *El Socialista* (Madrid), 2 July 1936.

5. Article in *Correspondencia Internacional*, 17 Apr. 1936, reprinted in José Díaz, *Tres años de lucha*, 133–39.

6. See chapter 1, text to nn. 138–54.

7. 15 Apr. 1936, pp. 3, 6.

8. Chapter 1, text to nn. 125–33.

9. See Gabriel Morón, *Política de ayer y política de mañana*, 106–7.

10. See Constancia de la Mora (Hidalgo de Cisneros's wife), *In Place of Splendor*, 179–80, 195.

11. Chapter 21, text to n. 176.

12. Statement to me when interviewed after the war.

13. This was well known in Communist circles and was confirmed to me by José Duque, a member during the war of the central committee of the Communist party.

14. Nenni, *La guerre d'Espagne*, 67, n. 2. At a meeting of the executive committee of the Socialist party in the summer of 1937, Prieto is said to have come out flatly in favor of fusion on the ground that the only help the government could hope to receive was from Russia (Morón, 107; Alvarez del Vayo, *Freedom's Battle*, 67).

15. *El Socialista* (Paris), 9 Nov. 1950.

16. See chapter 1, text to nn. 148 and 149.

17. José María Gil Robles, *No fué posible la paz*, 657.

18. Statement to me when interviewed after the war.

19. His attitude is reflected in the editorials of *Informaciones*, his mouthpiece, and of *El Socialista* (Madrid), the organ of the Socialist party executive. See, for example, *Informaciones*, 5 Aug. 1936, and *El Socialista*, 2, 10, 11 Mar. 1937. The director of the latter, Julián Zugazagoitia, was Prieto's man of confidence.

20. See also Indalecio Prieto, *Convulsiones de España*, III, 163–64.

21. See chapter 10, text to nn. 1–3.

22. Speech in Mexico City, 21 Apr. 1940, as published in *Inauguración del círculo "Pablo Iglesias" de México*, 13.

23. See, for example, articles published on 14 Jan., 20, 25 Feb., 6 Mar., 22, 23, 25 Apr., 15 May 1937; also circular letter of the executive committee, *El Socialista*, 28 Mar. 1937.

24. Ravines, *La gran estafa*, 311. Ravines worked on the editorial staff of *Frente Rojo*, the Communist organ in Valencia (ibid., 309).

25. *Frente Rojo*, 29 Mar. 1937.

26. See announcement published in *Frente Rojo*, 26 Apr. 1937.

27. See speeches by Ramón Lamoneda, reported in *El Socialista*, 16 July 1937; *Adelante* (Valencia), 3 Aug. 1937.

Chapter 27

1. See chapter 29, text to n. 5.

2. For as objective and detailed an account as one might hope for of the respective roles played by the assault and civil guards, and by the CNT and FAI, in the defeat of the military rebellion in Barcelona on 19 and 20 July, see Frederic Escofet, *Al servei de Catalunya i de la república*. Major Escofet was general commissioner of public order in Catalonia at the time of the insurrection. See also Lieutenant Colonel Vicente Guarner, *Cataluña en la guerra de España, 1936–39*, 103–32. Guarner was "jefe superior" of public order in Catalonia when the military rebellion took place.

3. See chapters 2 and 3 for material on the economic revolution in Catalonia.

4. Article in *Vu*, 29 Aug. 1936.

5. See chapter 2, text to nn. 27–29.

6. See chapter 11.

7. According to Pérez Farràs, the commander of the corps, it comprised four hundred men in October 1934 (*Full Català*, Oct. 1942). Since that date it had not increased in size.

8. As quoted by García Oliver in article, "El Comité Central de las Milicias Antifascistas de Cataluña," published in *De julio a julio*, 194–95.

9. Escofet, 406–7.

10. Ossorio y Galardo, *Vida y sacrificio de Companys*, 170–71, and Carles Pi Sunyer, *La república y la guerra*, 391–92.

11. Article in *De julio a julio*, 193–94.

12. *Por qué perdimos la guerra*, 53.

13. 17 June 1933.

14. *La Continental Obrera*, Feb. 1935.

15. Article in *De julio a julio*, 195.

16. Reported in *La Publicitat*, 17 Oct. 1936. See also his statement in *El Liberal*, as given in *Ultima Hora*, 1 Sept. 1936.

17. *La revolución y la guerra en España*, 148. See also statement by Sebastián Clara, former director of *Solidaridad Obrera*, as given in *Las Noticias*, 22 Aug. 1936.

18. See, for example, *La Publicitat*, 26 July 1936; *La Humanitat*, 1 Aug. 1936; *Treball*, 26 Aug. 1936.

19. *Vida*, 189. See also Lluhi Vallescà, *Lluis Companys Jover*, 58; *España Republicana*, 25 Oct. 1941. This humanitarian conduct did not help Companys when in 1940, after the German occupation of France, he was turned over to General Franco and executed (see, for example, Domènec de Bellmunt, *Lluis Companys*, 136–49; Indalecio Prieto, "Homenaje a Luis Companys," *España Libre*, 12 Dec. 1943). Many lives were saved in Barcelona by other republicans; see, for example, Pi Sunyer, 402–3, and Ramon Salas Larrazábal, *Historia del ejército popular de la república*, I, 1022, on Escofet, the general commissioner of public order.

20. See sources cited in n. 18.

21. See, for example, speeches by Juan Casanovas, first councillor (prime minister) in the Catalan government as given in *La Humanitat*, 29 July 1936; *El Día Gráfico*, 19 Aug., 15 Sept. 1936; Ventura Gassol, councillor of culture, as given in *La Humanitat*, 30 July 1936; Carles Pi y Sunyer, mayor of Barcelona, as given in *Ultima Hora*, 22 Aug. 1936.

22. See, for example, 30 July, 11, 13 Aug. 1936; also 26 Aug. 1936, as quoted by *La Batalla* (Barcelona), 27 Aug. 1936; and 24 Sept. 1936, as quoted by *El Noticiero Universal*, 24 Sept. 1936.

23. *La Revista Blanca*, 30 July 1936.

24. *La revolución*, 43. See also his article in *Timón* (Barcelona), Aug. 1938.

25. Article in *De julio a julio*, 195–96.

26. See *Solidaridad Obrera* (Barcelona), 16 Aug. 1936, 19 July 1938; *Tierra y Libertad* (Barcelona), 2 Apr. 1937; Federica Montseny in *Boletín de Información, CNT-FAI*, 22 July 1938.

27. See chapter 4, text to nn. 41–67.

28. Escofet, 405.

29. *Internacional*, July–Aug. 1938. Ruediger was also director of the German-language papers, *CNT-FAI-AIT Informationsdienst* and *Die Soziale Revolution*, both published in Barcelona.

30. For the names of the committee members and the organizations they represented, see *Solidaridad Obrera* (Barcelona), 21 July 1936.

31. Article in *De julio a julio*, 195–96.

32. *Vida*, 171.

33. *Por qué perdimos la guerra*, 69.

34. *Tiempos Nuevos*, May–June 1937.

35. On 23 July it issued a decree empowering it to intervene in the operations of the private banks (*Butlletí Oficial de la Generalitat de Catalunya*, 25 July 1936), and a month later, by the terms of a decree dated 27 August 1936 (*Ultima Hora*, 28 Aug. 1936), it assumed control of the branches of the Bank of Spain.

36. *Butlletí Oficial de la Generalitat de Catalunya*. Its name was changed to *Diari Oficial* on 26 August 1936.

37. Ibid., 24 July 1936.
38. Ibid., 26 July 1936.
39. Ibid., 31 July 1936.
40. Ibid., 7 Aug. 1936.
41. Ibid., 11 Aug. 1936.
42. Ibid., 31 July, 6, 7, 12, 16, 18 Aug. 1936, and in *Diari Oficial* (see n. 36, above), 26, 29 Aug. 1936.
43. For appointments of comptrollers or *interventores* by the Generalitat government, see *Butlletí Oficial*, 12, 13, 16, 17, 25 Aug. 1936, and *Diari Oficial*, 26, 28, 30, 31 Aug. 1936.
44. *Boletín de Información, CNT-FAI*, as given in *Las Noticias*, 11 Aug. 1936.
45. For the collectivization of small business enterprises in Catalonia, see chapter 3.
46. 10 Sept. 1936. See also quotation from Juan Peiró, *Perill a la reraguarda*, 102–3, as given in chapter 4, text to n. 61.
47. 29 Aug. 1936. For a more complete quotation from this article, see chapter 3, text to n. 37.
48. 8 Aug. 1936. A more complete quotation from this article can be found in chapter 5, text to n. 15.
49. *Treball*, 10 Sept. 1936.
50. See chapter 5, text to nn. 16–17.
51. See Largo Caballero, *La UGT y la guerra*, 32; also *Adelante*, Largo Caballero's organ in Valencia, 8 Apr. 1937.
52. *Solidaridad Obrera* (Barcelona), 8 Apr. 1937.
53. See Ralph Bates, *Daily Worker*, 12 Dec. 1936.
54. *Treball*, 27 July 1937.
55. See Joan Gilabert in *Butlletí del Partit Socialista Català*, 31 Mar. 1943; also Victor Alba, *El marxismo en España, 1919–1939*, I, 393.
56. For this information, I am grateful to Miguel Serra Pamies, a member of the PSUC's central committee, who, as secretary of the Socialist Union, participated in the negotiations.
57. *Cataluña, en pie de guerra*, 15.
58. *Ideas*, 24 June 1937.
59. Comorera, *Informe presentado en la primera conferencia nacional del partido socialista unificado de Cataluña*, 30.
60. Colomer, *Informe presentat a la primera conferencia nacional del partit socialista unificat de Catalunya I.C.*, 30.
61. Evidence from Serra Pamies, a member of the PSUC's central committee, in conversation with me after the war.
62. See Pedro Checa (a member of the central committee of the Spanish Communist party), *A un gran partido, una gran organización*, 23.
63. Information given to me by Serra Pamies, see n. 61.
64. Article by Felipe Matas in *Nuestra Bandera*, 31 Dec. 1943. Some years later Comorera died in prison in Spain, where, according to Victor Alba, "he had returned, when his comrades of the PSUC in exile, removed him from the leadership; he hoped to link up with the clandestine cadres of the party, although what he found there was a denunciation to the Spanish police by his own 'friends,' and an open letter from his daughter accusing him of being a traitor" (*El marxismo en España, 1919–1939*, II, 496–97).
65. Testimony of Serra Pamies (see n. 61).
66. See Julián Gorkin, *Caníbales políticos*, 81–83, and *El proceso de Moscú en Barcelona*, 51, in both of which Gorkin gives what appears to be a reliable account of Pedro's

authority over the Soviet consul general. Lieutenant Colonel Vicente Guarner, 258, alleges that NKVD chief Alexander Orlov delegated to Gerö the creation of a Soviet-style secret police organization in Barcelona and that Gerö "put an end to Antonov-Ovseenko by sending him to his death in Moscow."

67. *Por qué perdimos la guerra*, 116.

68. Alba, *El marxismo*, I, 392.

69. At the outbreak of the Civil War, Maurín was imprisoned in insurgent territory and was released some years later. After his death in the United States in 1975, his documents were acquired by the Hoover Institution, Stanford.

70. See, for example, *La Batalla* (Barcelona), 24 Dec. 1936; ibid., 24, 27 Apr. 1937 (articles by Gorkin). For Nin's break with Trotsky in 1934, see Gorkin, *El proceso de Moscú en Barcelona*, 38.

71. In this they were joined by Mikhail Koltzov, *Pravda*'s special correspondent in Spain. See, for example, his article in *La Humanité*, as given in *La Batalla* (Barcelona), 27 Jan. 1937.

72. See, for example, Léon Trotsky, *La révolution espagnole, 1930–36*, 273–307; Trotsky, *Escritos sobre España*, 123–32; article in *Unser Wort*, mid-February 1936; and English translation in *New Militant*, 15 Feb. 1936; also *Unser Wort*, early May 1936.

73. Mid-August 1937. In a letter to me in 1948, Manuel Grandizo Munis (known as G. Munis) informed me that he founded the Spanish section of the Fourth International in November 1936 and that POUM expelled from the party those members who were sympathetic to the ideas of the Bolshevik Leninists. In a letter to Trotsky, dated 11 October 1937, Harry Milton, himself a Trotskyist at the time, who fought with the POUM militia on the Aragon front, stated that Moulin, "the leading comrade of our group," had been expelled from the POUM at the beginning of the year. Harry Milton, "Copies of correspondence with Leon Trotsky and George Kopp." I am grateful to Harry Milton for these copies. Paul Thalmann, another Trotskyist and onetime secretary of the Communist youth in Switzerland, who fought with the POUM militia, alleges in an interview published in a recent work: "There was strong right wing in the POUM that made short work of the Trotskyists; they also shot some—this, one should also know" (Clara Thalmann and Paul Thalmann, *Revolution für die Freiheit*, 380).

74. *Civil War in Spain*, 68–70.

75. *Unser Wort*, early December 1936.

76. *La Batalla* (Barcelona), 24 Oct. 1936. For differences of opinion within the POUM itself as to the advisability of entering the government, see Alba, *El marxismo*, 320–24.

77. The FOUS was formed on 1 May 1936. It was made up of the local trade-union federations of Lérida, Tarragona, and Gerona (which had been expelled from the CNT for eluding anarchist influence) and a number of autonomous unions (see Pedro Bonet, its first assistant secretary, in *La Batalla* [Paris], Feb.–Mar. 1972, Mar. 1976).

78. Walter Held, *Die spanische Revolution*, 15; see also Léon Trotsky, *Leçon d'Espagne*, 67–68, and his letter of 10 Mar. 1939 to Daniel Guérin, in the *New International*, May 1939, charging that the POUM "refrained from penetrating into the midst of the [CNT] in order not to disturb relations with the summits of this organization." For one of the most trenchant attacks by a Trotskyist on the entire policy of the POUM leadership during the Civil War, see Felix Morrow, *Revolution and Counter-Revolution in Spain*, 40–102.

79. *La Batalla* (Barcelona), 15 Oct. 1936.

80. H. E. Kaminski, *Ceux de Barcelone*, 167.

81. See *La Batalla* (Barcelona), 18 Oct., 25 Nov., 13, 19, 22 Dec. 1936; 16, 22 Jan., 5 Feb. 1937.

82. 27 Jan. 1937.

83. See *La Batalla*, quoted by Alba, *El marxismo*, I, 316.

84. Ibid., 317.

85. Manuel Grandizo Munis, *Jalones de derrota*, 286.

86. See Alba, *Historia de la segunda república española*, 255; *El marxismo*, I, 317.

87. 25 Jan. 1937.

88. 27 Jan. 1937.

89. Until his arrest in rebel territory at the outbreak of the Civil War, Joaquín Maurin, the party secretary, had been director of *La Batalla*.

90. 15 Sept. 1936.

91. *En marcha hacia la victora*, 11.

92. According to Juan Comorera, PSUC secretary, in speech, reported in *Treball*, 22 Dec. 1936.

93. Reported in *Solidaridad Obrera* (Barcelona), 9 Dec. 1936.

94. Ibid., 10 Dec. 1936.

95. See n. 22, this chapter. Until December 1936 one looks in vain in the Esquerra newspapers, *La Humanitat* and *Ultima Hora*, for anything even remotely approaching the aggressiveness of the PSUC.

96. 11 Dec. 1936.

97. *Treball*, 13 Dec. 1936.

98. Ibid., 22 Dec. 1936.

99. Article by N. Molins y Fábrega, *La Batalla*, 16 Dec. 1936.

100. Ibid., 13 Dec. 1936.

101. See n. 77, this chapter, for reference to the FOUS, the POUM's trade-union organization before the Civil War, which was made up partially of unions that had been expelled from the CNT for eluding anarchist influence.

102. *La Batalla* (Barcelona), 18 Dec. 1936.

103. Rudolf Rocker, *Extranjeros en España*, 91. This allegation was also made by another foreign anarchist (see *Vanguard*, June 1937), but I have found no confirmation by Spanish anarchist leaders of any *direct* threat. However, David T. Cattell says: "Soviet aid was used to discriminate against the revolutionaries in Catalonia in several ways. There is good circumstantial evidence that the Soviet Union set these conditions for aiding Catalonia: that the dissident Communist POUM should not be allowed to participate any longer in the Catalonia Generalitat, and that the Catalonian government should submit to the over-all program set down by the central government" (*Communism and the Spanish Civil War*, 109).

104. See list of central committee members elected at the beginning of March 1937, as given in Checa, *A un gran partido*, 23.

105. 17 Dec. 1936.

106. *La Batalla* (Barcelona), 18 Dec. 1936.

107. Ibid., 20 Dec. 1936.

108. See *Ultima Hora*, 28 Dec. 1936; *La Humanitat*, 29 Dec. 1936.

109. *La Humanitat*, 29 Dec. 1936.

110. 30 Dec. 1936. See also *Solidaridad Obrera* (Barcelona), 29 Dec. 1936.

111. For this information I am indebted to Felipe Ubach, an aide in the premier's office, when interviewed by me after the war.

112. *Boletín de Información, CNT-FAI*, 26 Mar. 1937.

113. *Solidaridad Obrera* (Barcelona), 6 Feb. 1937.

114. *Treball*, 18 Mar. 1937.

115. *Tiempos Nuevos*, Feb. 1937.
116. *España Popular*, 30 May 1940.
117. For a PSUC reference to its influence over the CADCI, see Colomer, 15.
118. See chapter 3, text to nn. 6–14.
119. *Treball*, 22 Dec. 1936.
120. *Solidaridad Obrera* (Barcelona), 21 Apr. 1937.
121. *La Batalla* (Barcelona), 23 Apr. 1937.
122. For a glowing tribute to Aiguadé by the Spanish Communists after the war, see *España Popular*, 7 Dec. 1946.
123. *Treball*, 1 Jan. 1937.
124. 28 Jan. 1937.
125. See *Diari Oficial*, 4 Mar. 1937, as given in *El Día Gráfico*, 5 Mar. 1937.
126. In announcing the approval of the decrees, which had been heatedly debated during five cabinet sessions, Premier Tarradellas stated, according to *Treball*, the PSUC organ, that they had been "carefully studied and approved by all the councillors and their respective organizations" (2 Mar. 1937). On the other hand, *La Batalla*, the POUM organ (3 Mar. 1937) reported Tarradellas as saying that there had been agreement among all the cabinet members "on the majority of the provisions in the decrees," which was another way of saying that there had been disagreement on some.
127. *La Batalla*, 3 Mar. 1937.
128. 4 Mar. 1937.
129. Statement to the press by Tarradellas, *Treball*, 17 Mar. 1937.
130. Ibid.
131. *El Día Gráfico*, 1 Nov. 1936; also communiqué issued by the defense council published in ibid., 3 Nov. 1936.
132. See chapter 24, text to n. 15.
133. José del Barrio in *Treball*, 3 Feb. 1937.
134. *Solidaridad Obrera* (Barcelona), 13 Feb. 1937.
135. *La Batalla* (Barcelona), 21 Feb. 1937.
136. *El Día Gráfico*, 2 Mar. 1937.
137. *Treball*, 5 Mar. 1937.
138. 6 Mar. 1937.
139. Little information relating to the accords was ever published and then only in general terms. See, for example, *El Día Gráfico*, 4 Mar. 1937; *La Batalla* (Barcelona), 5 Mar. 1937; *Ultima Hora*, 5 Mar. 1937. Salas Larrazábal, I, 1042–45, however, sheds some light on this matter, but, despite his diligent research, was unable to find any official order merging the Catalan militia with the Popular Army.
140. See *Treball*, 20 Mar. 1937. The dates were set as follows: 1934–36 classes, 22, 23, 25, 27, 30 March; 1932–33 classes, 5 April.
141. The article appeared under Enrique Adroher's pen name of "Gironella."
142. *El Día Gráfico*, 19 Mar. 1937; see also ibid., 4 Mar. 1937.
143. Letter to me, dated 24 June 1946. See file, "Los Amigos de Durruti," Bolloten Collection, Archives, Hoover Institution on War, Revolution, and Peace, Stanford.
144. *The Civil War in Spain*, 541.
145. *Unser Wort*, early May 1939. For material dealing with the creation and activity of the Friends of Durruti, see file, "Los Amigos de Durruti," containing letters from Balius to me, written after the war, and photostatic copy of Jordi Arquer's typewritten data on the organization, based primarily on interviews with Balius and other members, Bolloten Collection, Hoover Institution, Stanford. See also Thalmann and Thalmann, 190,

for information on Balius and the Friends of Durruti. The authors were both Trotskyists and active in Barcelona during the Civil War.

146. Although Isgleas resigned on 23 March, the crisis was not officially disclosed until 26 March. For the call-up dates, see n. 140, above.

147. FAI manifesto published in *Tierra y Libertad* (Barcelona), 3 Apr. 1937.

148. *Treball*, 30 Mar. 1937.

149. Comorera, speech at public meeting, *Treball*, 9 Apr. 1937; see also Tarradellas, statement to the press, ibid., 3 Apr. 1937; Sesé, secretary of the Catalan UGT, statement to *El Noticiero Universal*, as given in *La Publicitat*, 3 Apr. 1937.

150. *Solidaridad Obrera* (Barcelona), 4 Apr. 1937.

151. *Treball*, 28 Mar. 1937.

152. Ibid., 8 Apr. 1937.

153. 8 Apr. 1937.

154. Speech 9 Apr. 1937, published in *La Batalla* (Barcelona), 11 Apr. 1937.

155. Luis Companys, "Notes and Documents on the Fighting in Barcelona, 3–7 May 1937." A copy of this invaluable material came into my possession during the war through the courtesy of Ricardo del Rio, the head of the Febus news agency in Valencia (Bolloten Collection, Archives, Hoover Institution, Stanford). The authenticity of this material, which I have used frequently in the next chapter, was confirmed to me by several knowledgeable Spaniards, including Felipe Ubach, an aide to Premier Tarradellas, who claims that he saw and read a copy in the possession of the premier. Furthermore, Angel Ossorio y Gallardo, the republican jurist, obviously had a copy of the same material to judge from the short excerpts quoted in his biography of Companys, *Vida*, 177–78.

156. *La Batalla* (Barcelona), 17 Apr. 1937.

157. Ibid., 18 Apr. 1937.

158. *El Día Gráfico*, 25 Apr. 1937; *Treball*, 25 Apr. 1937.

159. *Treball*, 27 Apr. 1937.

160. 27 Apr. 1937

161. 27 Apr. 1937.

162. *Treball*, 27 Apr. 1937.

163. Ibid., 28 Apr. 1937.

164. *Solidaridad Obrera* (Barcelona), 28 Apr. 1937; see also ibid., 29 Apr. 1937.

165. Article by Juan Andrade, *La Batalla* (Barcelona), 28 Apr. 1937.

166. *Solidaridad Obrera* (Barcelona), 29 Apr. 1937 (editorial and statement issued by secretary of the councillor of internal security); *El Día Gráfico*, 1 May 1937.

167. *El Día Gráfico*, 1 May 1937.

168. *Gaceta de la República*, 16 Apr. 1937.

169. *La Vanguardia*, 28 Apr. 1937; *La Humanitat*, 28 Apr. 1937; *Diari de Barcelona*, 29 Apr. 1937.

170. *La Publicitat*, 30 Apr. 1937.

171. Agustín Souchy [Bauer], *La verdad sobre los sucesos en la retaguardia leal*, 11; George Orwell, *Homage to Catalonia*, 160.

172. *La Batalla* (Barcelona), 1 May 1937.

173. Ibid.

Chapter 28

1. *Solidaridad Obrera* (Barcelona), 29 Jan. 1937.
2. Ibid., 4 May 1937.
3. Speech, *Treball*, 2 June 1937.
4. Luis Companys, "Notes and Documents on the Fighting in Barcelona, 3–7 May 1937," see chapter 27, n. 155.
5. *Por qué perdimos la guerra*, 133.
6. *Solidaridad Obrera* (Barcelona), 4 May 1937; Manuel Cruells, *Mayo sangriento*, 48. Cruells was a staff reporter in May 1937 on the *Diari de Barcelona*.
7. The official Communist history of the Civil War claims that Aiguadé was given authority to occupy the telephone exchange during a meeting of the Generalitat government "despite anarchist opposition" (*Guerra y revolución en España, 1936–1939*, III, 72). On the other hand, the CNT claimed that everyone in the government agreed that "Aiguadé had overstepped his authority" (report on the May events by the national committee of the CNT, *Cultura Proletaria*, 19 June 1937). See also *Boletín de Información* (CNT national committee), 24 June 1937; *Solidaridad Obrera*, 12 May 1937 (report by regional committees of the CNT, FAI, and Libertarian Youth). Furthermore, President Azaña states, apparently on the evidence of Tarradellas, that Aiguadé did not inform the other councillors of his decision (*Obras completas*, IV, 576).
8. See chapter 9, text to n. 113.
9. Azaña, *Obras*, IV, 576.
10. Ibid., IV, 577.
11. CNT national committee report, *Cultura Proletaria*, 19 June 1937.
12. *La CNT en la revolución española*, II, 192. Felipe Ubach, an aide to Premier Tarradellas, told me after the war that the premier was opposed to the raid on the *telefónica*, but nevertheless sided with Companys during the cabinet debate out of loyalty to the president.
13. Cruells, 55–56.
14. *Cultura Proletaria*, 12 June 1937.
15. *Homage to Catalonia*, 169.
16. *La Batalla* (Barcelona), 4 May 1937.
17. After the cessation of hostilities the CNT defense committee in Sans released four hundred national republican guards, whom it had arrested at the inception of the fighting (see *Solidaridad Obrera* [Barcelona], 9 May 1937).
18. *La revolución y la guerra en España*, 144. President Azaña records: "All the working-class suburbs were in the hands of the rebels. The Generalitat, the departments of the interior and finance, etcetera, etcetera, were besieged" (*Obras*, IV, 579).
19. Interview, *Fragua Social*, 15 May 1937.
20. Evidence from Cándido Bolívar, when interviewed by me after the war.
21. CNT national committee report, *Cultura Proletaria*, 19 June 1937.
22. *Obras*, IV, 577–78. Jaume Miravittles, a member of the Esquerra, who accompanied Tarradellas on his hazardous trip through Barcelona to the parliament building to see Azaña writes: "The interview with Azaña was painful. We found a man physically and morally destroyed" (*Episodis de la guerra civil espanyola*, 148).
23. *Obras*, IV, 578.
24. *Caníbales políticos*, 69–70.
25. Companys, "Notes and Documents." The date of the telephone conversation is given erroneously as Tuesday, 7 May, instead of Tuesday, 4 May.

26. Orwell, 174–75.

27. No attempt is made in this chapter to provide a detailed account of the street fighting. Firsthand reports can be found in the following: *La Batalla* (Barcelona), *Boletín de Información, CNT-FAI, Catalunya, El Día Gráfico, Las Noticias, El Noticiero Universal, La Publicitat, Solidaridad Obrera* (Barcelona), *Treball, Ultima Hora, La Vanguardia* (all of which were published almost every day during the events); Abad de Santillán, *Por qué perdimos la guerra*; Cruells; Marcel Ollivier, *Les journées sanglantes de Barcelone*; Orwell; Agustín Souchy [Bauer], *La verdad sobre los sucesos en la retaguardia leal.*

28. Interview, *Fragua Social*, 15 May 1937.

29. *La revolución*, 147.

30. As given in Rudolf Rocker, *Extranjeros en España*, 130; see also Souchy, *La verdad*, 19.

31. See *Caníbales políticos*, 70.

32. Statement made to Charles Orr, editor of the *Spanish Revolution*, English-language bulletin of the POUM (quoted in Felix Morrow, *Revolution and Counter-Revolution in Spain*, 100).

33. Orwell, 208.

34. 4 May 1937.

35. CNT national committee report, *Cultura Proletaria*, 19 June 1937.

36. Ibid.

37. Ibid.

38. Both Carlos Hernández Zancajo and Mariano Muñoz Sánchez, it may be recalled, were appointed by Largo Caballero in February 1937 to scrutinize the work of officers and commissars of every rank (see chapter 25, text to nn. 19 and 20).

39. Companys, "Notes and Documents."

40. Ibid. Under the provisions of the statute, Madrid was empowered to take control of internal order in Catalonia if the interests of the state were threatened.

41. Ibid.

42. A copy of this document was loaned to me by Jordi Arquer, to whom I am indebted for much scrupulous research. A typewritten copy is deposited in the Bolloten Collection, Hoover Institution, Stanford. The Spanish Communists were obviously unaware of the existence of this document when they published a glowing tribute to Aiguadé in their refugee newspaper, *España Popular*, on 7 Dec. 1946.

43. Prieto, *Palabras al viento*, 203.

44. Statement to me by Cisneros, when interviewed after the war.

45. Information given to me by Constancia de la Mora, the wife of air force chief Hidalgo de Cisneros. The messages were read by her in the navy and air ministry and are probably those referred to in n. 103, below.

46. *Obras*, IV, 580.

47. *La Vanguardia*, 5 May 1937.

48. *La verdad*, 19.

49. 4 May 1937.

50. National committee report, *Cultura Proletaria*, 19 June 1937.

51. Ibid.

52. *Solidaridad Obrera* (Barcelona), 5 May 1937.

53. Ibid.

54. *Cultura Proletaria*, 12 June 1937.

55. *Ensayo crítico sobre la revolución española*, 23–24.

56. National committee report, *Cultura Proletaria*, 19 June 1937.

57. *La Voz Valenciana*, 5 May 1937.

58. Companys, "Notes and Documents."

59. Statement issued by national committee of the CNT, published in *Fragua Social*, 7 May 1937.

60. *Fragua Social*, 15 May 1937.

61. For an account by the Trotskyists, Clara and Paul Thalmann, both members of the Bolshevik Leninists, of the efforts by Moulin, one of their most active militants, to influence Jaime Balius, the vice-secretary of the Friends of Durruti, "in all-night discussions," to abandon his "innate anarchist mistrust of the Marxists" and to collaborate with the Trotskyists, see *Revolution für die Freiheit*, 189–90.

62. As given in Morrow, *Revolution*, 82; see also Orwell, 207.

63. As reproduced in *La Batalla* (Barcelona), 6 May 1937. See also Fenner Brockway, *Truth about Barcelona*, 10; Morrow, *Revolution*, 82; G. Munis, *Jalones de derrota*, 305; Orwell, 207.

64. 6 May 1937. See also *Treball*, 6 May 1937, for the PSUC's criticism of *La Batalla*.

65. There is no record in any of the newspapers of the period of any appeal over the radio by POUM leaders for a cease-fire.

66. See text to n. 34, above.

67. 19 May 1937.

68. This appears to be a reference to the conference held on the night of 3 May (see text to n. 24).

69. *Revolution*, 94, and footnote.

70. *Vanguard*, Feb. 1939.

71. *IV International*, 1 June 1937.

72. *Service d'Information et de Presse por la Quatrième Internationale*, June 1937.

73. *Unser Wort*, mid-March 1939.

74. Speech on 9 May 1937, as given in Díaz, *Tres años de lucha*, 432. This speech is quoted more fully at the beginning of chapter 29.

75. 9 May 1937.

76. 10 May 1937. See also his article in *Labour Monthly*, Aug. 1937.

77. *International Press Correspondence*, 11 Nov. 1937.

78. *My Mission to Spain*, 356.

79. Editorial, reviewing events, 14 May 1937.

80. 6 May 1937.

81. According to Companys, the news that the government had taken over public order was received at 12:30 P.M. ("Notes and Documents").

82. National committee report, *Cultura Proletaria*, 19 June 1937.

83. 21 May 1937, as given in Souchy, *La verdad*, 59.

84. *La Correspondencia de Valencia* (evening newspaper), 5 May 1937.

85. *El Día Gráfico*, 15 June 1937.

86. *La Vanguardia*, 6 May 1937.

87. According to Miguel Serra Pamies, a member of the PSUC's central committee and councillor in the Generalitat government after the May events (personal interview after the war, when he had ceased to be a member of the party).

88. Within a few days after the fighting had ended and the region had been occupied by twelve thousand assault guards, Companys expressed the hope in an interview given to *Ce Soir* (Paris) that the administration of public order would be returned to the region (as given in *Hoja Oficial del Lunes*, 17 May 1937).

89. *La revolución*, 148–50.

90. *Solidaridad Obrera* (Barcelona), 6 May 1937.
91. He was replaced by Rafael Vidiella, the PSUC-UGT leader.
92. *Cultura Proletaria*, 19 June 1937.
93. *Frente Rojo*, 6 May 1938. See also speech by Rafael Vidiella, ibid., 4 June 1938.
94. *La Verdad*, 30–31.
95. *El Noticiero Universal*, 6 May 1937.
96. *El Día Gráfico*, 6 May 1937.
97. Azaña, *Obras*, IV, 580–81.
98, Ibid., 585, 587.
99. Ibid., 581.
100. See chapter 9, text to n. 114.
101. See his remarks to Largo Caballero, chapter 9, text to n. 119.
102. According to information given to me by Cisneros.
103. *Obras*, IV, 581. The tapes of the frequent messages exchanged between Prieto and Azaña during the fighting have been preserved by the Servicio Histórico Militar of Madrid. Ramón Salas Larrazábal, *Historia del ejército popular de la república*, I, 1027, states that from a reading of the tapes Azaña appears "fearful, cowardly, and supplicatory." This appriasal I have been able to verify thanks to the courtesy of José Clavería Prenafeta of the Servicio Histórico Militar, who provided me with a microfilm copy. The tapes are published, in part, by Colonel José Manuel Martínez Bande, *La invasión de Aragón y el desembarco en Mallorca*, 282–92. My copy is with the Bolloten Collection, Archives, Hoover Institution, Stanford.
104. *Obras*, IV, 584.
105. Ibid., 585.
106. *Historia de la guerra en España*, 255–56.
107. *Obras*, IV, 585–88.
108. *La verdad*, 24.
109. As given in Cruells, 70.
110. This was confirmed to me by Jaime Balius, vice-secretary of the Friends of Durruti (see his letter dated 24 June 1946 in file "Amigos of Durruti," Bolloten Collection, Archives, Hoover Institution, Stanford).
111. *Solidaridad Obrera* (Barcelona), 6 May 1937.
112. Morrow, *Revolution*, 95.
113. Orwell, 183–84.
114. *El Noticiero Universal*, 6 May 1937.
115. *El Día Gráfico*, 6 May 1937.
116. *El Noticiero Universal*, 6 May 1937.
117. *Solidaridad Obrera* (Barcelona), 6 May 1937.
118. *El Noticiero Universal*, 6 May 1937.
119. *Cultura Proletaria*, 19 June 1937.
120. *La Batalla* (Barcelona), 13 May 1937.
121. See chapter 27, n. 155. The date of the document is given erroneously as Tuesday, 7 May, but it is obvious from internal evidence that the date should have been Thursday, 6 May.
122. See *La Publicitat*, 8 May 1937. Torres was regarded as being friendly to the CNT and FAI (Abad de Santillán, *Por qué perdimos la guerra*, 136; Victor Alba, *El marxismo en España, 1919–1939*, II, 448; R. Louzon, *La contra-revolución en España*, 123, n. 6; Salas Larrazábal, I, 1039–40). At all events, he was replaced a few weeks later, after the fall of the Largo Caballero government, by Lieutenant Colonel Ricardo Burillo, a Communist party member and former police chief of Madrid.

123. The appointments made by Galarza, published in the *Gaceta de la República*, 11 May 1937, were as follows: José Echevarría Novoa, delegate of public order; Emilio Torres Iglesias, police chief of Barcelona; José María Díaz de Ceballos, general commissioner of security (as given in *Solidaridad Obrera* [Barcelona], 12 May 1937).

124. *Cultura Proletaria*, 19 June 1937.

125. *Solidaridad Obrera* (Barcelona), 16 May 1937; *Treball*, 14 May 1937; also Companys, "Notes and Documents," and Cruells, 89.

126. 16 May 1937.

127. *Solidaridad Obrera* (Barcelona), 7 May 1937.

128. Barcelona correspondent, *Times*, 12 May 1937. *Solidaridad Obrera* (Barcelona), 9 May 1937, reported that five thousand assault guards arrived on the evening of 7 May.

Chapter 29

1. Reprinted in Díaz, *Tres años de lucha*, 431–33. See also *Frente Rojo*, 10, 11, 13 May 1937; *Treball*, 15 May 1937.

2. See chapter 26.

3. *Guerra y revolución en España, 1936–1939*, III, 79.

4. Azaña, *Obras completas*, IV, 587–88.

5. Ibid., 591–92.

6. Ibid., 585.

7. Ibid., 588–89.

8. Ibid., 592–93.

9. See chapter 25, text to nn. 106–14.

10. *Obras*, IV, 595–96.

11. See his speech in October 1937, giving his account of this episode, reprinted in Largo Caballero, *La UGT y la guerra*, 8; also Juan Peiró (CNT minister of industry at the time), *Problemas y cintarazos*, 201–2.

12. Largo Caballero, *La UGT y la guerra*, 8.

13. *Yo fuí un ministro de Stalin*, 85.

14. *Adelante* (Mexico City), 1 Apr. 1946.

15. *Historia de la guerra en España*, 274.

16. *Adelante* (Mexico City), 1 Apr. 1946. See also Indalecio Prieto, *Convulsiones de España*, II, 94.

17. *Mundo Obrero* (Paris), 25 Sept. 1947. See chapter 1, text to nn. 148–52.

18. *Política de ayer y política de mañana*, 85.

19. *Obras*, IV, 595.

20. Ibid.

21. Ibid., 596. See also ibid., 613–14, 616–17. For the Communist view of the project, see *Guerra y revolución*, III, 80 and n. 3.

22. See chapter 24, text to nn. 24–29; chapter 25, text to nn. 1–5 and 71–79. That the offensive was planned by Asensio and Martínez Cabrera is confirmed by Ramón Salas Larrazábal, *Historia del ejército popular de la república*, I, 1076, who states that Alvarez Coque, who succeeded Martínez Cabrera as provisional head of the general staff, "inherited" the plans of these two generals relating to the operation.

23. *Obras*, IV, 589.

24. Salas Larrazábal, I, 1082–83.

25. *El comunismo y la guerra de España*, 13.

26. Salas Larrazábal, I, 1077–78.

27. For a scrupulously documented account of the precise units to be used in the operation, for the delays in its execution, and for an objective appraisal of its chances of success, see ibid., 1075–83.

28. See Miaja's communication, dated 1 May 1937, to Largo Caballero (Library of Congress); Azaña, *Obras*, IV, 590–91; Segismundo Casado, *The Last Days of Madrid*, 71–72; Francisco Largo Caballero, *Mis recuerdos*, 215; Salas Larrazábal, I, 1078–80.

29. *El comunismo*, 13. See also Largo Caballero, *Mis recuerdos*, 215.

30. Casado, 72–73.

31. *Mis recuerdos*, 214–15.

32. *Yo fui un ministro de Stalin*, 79–85.

33. *Obras*, IV, 595.

34. Ibid., 596–97.

35. *Mis recuerdos*, 219.

36. *Obras*, IV, 597.

37. *El comunismo*, 14.

38. *Mis recuerdos*, 219.

39. *El Mercantil Valenciano*, 22 July 1937.

40. *El comunismo*, 14.

41. *Todos fuimos culpables*, 656.

42. Morón, 60–63.

43. *Mis recuerdos*, 220.

44. *Obras*, IV, 598.

45. Ibid.

46. See, for example, ibid., 598, quoting Martínez Barrio; Largo Caballero, *Mis recuerdos*, 219–22.

47. *Obras*, IV, 598.

48. Ibid., 600–601.

49. See document issued by the party's central committee, published in *El Mercantil Valenciano*, 16 May 1937.

50. See point 6 of its declaration, published in *El Socialista* (Madrid), 18 May 1937.

51. Article in *España Popular*, 11 Mar. 1940.

52. *Claridad*, 15 May 1937.

53. *Obras*, IV, 602.

54. Letter to José Bullejos, 20 Nov. 1939, published in *¿Qué se puede hacer?*, 20–24.

55. *Mis recuerdos*, 222–23.

56. *Frente Libertario*, 17 May 1937.

57. *Fragua Social*, 16 May 1937.

58. *Solidaridad Obrera* (Barcelona), 16 May 1937.

59. *Fragua Social*, 16 May 1937.

60. See his plan, as given in *La Correspondencia de Valencia*, 17 May 1937.

61. *Fragua Social*, 18 May 1937.

62. See his plan, as given in the evening newspaper, *La Correspondencia de Valencia*, 17 May 1937.

63. See letter published in the evening newspaper, *Frente Rojo*, 17 May 1937.

64. See letter to Largo Caballero published in *El Socialista* (Madrid), 18 May 1937.

65. Reply to Largo Caballero, as given in the evening newspaper, *Frente Rojo*, 17 May 1937.

66. Azaña, *Obras*, IV, 602.

67. See report from Valencia by the Febus news agency, "Una referencia de la reunión

celebrada en la Presidencia de la República," published in *Mundo Obrero* (Madrid), 17 May 1937.

68. *Obras*, IV, 602.

69. *Convulsiones*, II, 94.

70. Vidarte, 663.

71. *Obras*, IV, 603. See also Zugazagoitia, 274.

72. See chapter 26, text to nn. 9–14.

73. *Convulsiones*, III, 219–21, article entitled, "Un hombre singular." The peculiarities attributed to Negrín by Prieto were common knowledge among those who knew him and were confirmed to me by several reliable sources. See also Carles Pi Sunyer, *La república y la guerra*, 474; Zugazagoitia, 336; and Frank Sedwick, *The Tragedy of Manuel Azaña and the Fate of the Spanish Republic*, 183, who describes Negrín as a "tactless, indecorous, disorganized, and unscrupulous man, whom even his friends admit to have been a kind of Rasputin-of-the-stomach-and-sex in his personal life."

74. *In Stalin's Secret Service*, 100–101.

75. Personal interview. It will be recalled that in March 1937 Togliatti, according to Hernández, had also favored Negrín as Largo Caballero's successor (*Yo fui un ministro de Stalin*, 71).

76. Krivitsky, 100–101. See also Madariaga, *Spain*, 515.

77. For reference to Negrín's subservience to the Communists during the latter part of the war, see chapter 9, text to nn. 13–24.

78. *Spain*, 521.

79. *Yo fui un ministro de Stalin*, 86–88.

80. *Mis recuerdos*, 226.

81. See chapter 10, n. 59.

82. *Solidaridad Obrera* (Paris), 11 Mar. 1951.

Chapter 30

1. As given in the *Gaceta de la República*, 18 May 1937.

2. *Obras completas*, IV, 877, 880–83.

3. Ibid., IV, 603.

4. See chapter 14, text to nn. 23–25.

5. See, for example, Azaña, quoting Prieto, *Obras*, IV, 638; Jesús Hernández, *Yo fui un ministro de Stalin*, 89, 98; Gabriel Morón, *Política de ayer y política de mañana*, quoting Zugazagoitia, 95.

6. *Todos fuimos culpables*, 670.

7. *Historia de la guerra en España*, 292–93.

8. See, for example, Azaña, quoting Prieto, *Obras*, IV, 638.

9. See chapter 29, text to n. 49.

10. Vidarte, 672.

11. See chapter 25, text to nn. 9 and 10.

12. *Diario Oficial del Ministerio de Defensa*, no. 127, as given in Ramón Salas Larrazábal, *Historia del ejército popular de la república*, II, 1206, n. 1. Cordón was later made chief of staff of the Eastern Army in Aragon.

13. Chapter 25, text to nn. 12–14.

14. *Gaceta de la República*, 21 May 1937.

15. See chapter 29, text to n. 51.

16. See chapter 9, text to n. 12.

17. Chapter 21, text to nn. 234–42.

18. Chapter 28, text to n. 122.

19. *Gaceta de la República*, 8 June 1937.

20. Chapter 27.

21. *Treball*, 12, 13, 16, 19–22 May 1937.

22. *Diari Oficial de la Generalitat de Catalunya*, 5 June 1937, as given in *Las Noticias*, 6 June 1937. For the disarming of the patrols, see *El Día Gráfico*, 10, 18, 29 June 1937; *Las Noticias*, 9 June 1937; *Tierra y Libertad* (Barcelona), 12 June 1937.

23. See statement issued by the regional committee of the CNT, *Boletín de Información, CNT-FAI*, 30 June 1937; also letter addressed to Companys by the CNT, *El Día Gráfico*, 1 July 1937. For an account of the government crisis by a member of the new cabinet, see Carles Pi Sunyer, *La república y la guerra*, 445–47.

24. See *Boletín de Información, CNT-FAI*, 6 May 1937; *Solidaridad Obrera* (Barcelona), 13, 14, 18, 19, 21, 22 May 1937; also statement by the secretary general of the patrols published in *La Batalla* (Barcelona), 13 May 1937.

25. Luis Companys, "Notes and Documents on the Fighting in Barcelona, 3–7 May 1937."

26. Ibid.

27. Ibid.

28. *Fragua Social*, 12 June 1937.

29. In September 1937 the CNT national committee stated that there were thousands of "proven antifascists and revolutionaries" in jail (ibid., 21 Sept. 1937).

30. *Las Noticias*, 22 June 1937; Julián Gorkin, *El proceso de Moscú en Barcelona*, 106–40, 220–21; Hernández, *Yo fuí un ministro de Stalin*, 98; Katia Landau, *Le stalinisme en Espagne*, 14–16, 47; G. Munis, *Jalones de derrota*, 389–90; Andrés Suárez, *El proceso contra el POUM*, 83–84.

31. Gorkin, *El proceso*, 98; Hernández, *Yo fuí un ministro de Stalin*, 90–91, 98; Morón, 98; Indalecio Prieto, *Convulsiones de España*, II, 117.

32. Victor Alba, *Dos revolucionarios* (memorandum of Olga Nin), 490; Gorkin, *El proceso*, 98, 162; Hernández, *Yo fuí un ministro de Stalin*, 90–91; Morón, 96–98; Suárez, 102–4; Zugazagoitia, 278. Orlov, however, in reply to Payne's questionnaire, says that Zugazagoitia "signed a warrant for the death of Andrés Nin and the other members of the central committee of the POUM." This, of course, was totally untrue (see Orlov, "Answers to the Questionnaire of Professor Stanley G. Payne").

33. Morón, 95–98, in which Morón describes the maneuver to remove him from Valencia while the Communist coup was in progress.

34. Victor Alba, *El marxismo en España, 1919–1939*, II, 521–29; Suárez, 87–99.

35. Hernández, *Yo fuí un ministro de Stalin*, 111.

36. Gorkin, *El proceso*, 108.

37. Ibid., 157, 171–73; Hernández, *Yo fuí un ministro de Stalin*, 124–26.

38. *El proceso*, 157–58.

39. Ibid., 15, 168 and n. For a profile of Contreras, see Julián Gorkin, *L'assassinat de Trotsky*, 267–73.

40. *Yo fuí un ministro de Stalin*, 126.

41. Vidarte, 728–29.

42. *Cambio 16*, Oct. 1977. I am indebted to Professor Stanley Payne for bringing this article to my attention.

43. See, for example, Azaña (quoting Negrín), *Obras*, IV, 692; Zugazagoitia (quoting Ortega), 278–79, also 280–81.

44. Conversation with Wolfe.

45. Hernández, *Yo fuí un ministro de Stalin*, 119.

46. Information I gathered in Valencia toward the end of June 1937.

47. Vidarte, 731.

48. *Yo fuí un ministro de Stalin*, 91, 97, 101.

49. Ibid., 109.

50. Zugazagoitia, 281.

51. *Yo fuí un ministro de Stalin*, 112.

52. Zugazagoitia, 281.

53. *Yo fuí un ministro de Stalin*, 113.

54. The first number of the underground edition of *La Batalla* was published on 10 July 1937. A copy is in the Bolloten Collection, Archives, Hoover Institution on War, Revolution, and Peace, Stanford.

55. Wilebaldo Solano, the secretary general of the POUM's youth organization, the JCI, and a member of the second executive committee of the party, points out in a document prepared by him relating to the organization's clandestine activity: "The majority of historians speak of the 'liquidation of the POUM,' when referring to the police coup of 16 June 1937. In general, they refer to the disappearance of the POUM as a result of the repression as though it were an established fact. This is absolutely false and must be refuted. The POUM continued its activity in clandestinity, although under very difficult conditions" ("Notas sobre el POUM en la Revolución de 1936." A copy of this document, dated March 1973, is in the Bolloten Collection, Hoover Institution, Stanford).

56. *Obras*, IV, 692. See also Zugazagoitia, 281, who says that Negrín tried to convince him that "everything was possible." However, many years later, Negrín, when asked by Vidarte what he thought about the Nin case, replied, "I believe the Communists killed him" (Vidarte, 729).

57. The indictment and sentence can be found in Suárez, 195–209. Julián Gorkin points out an interesting fact: The Communist press, he writes, that had been "howling for death" did not publish the sentence nor did the press censorship allow the other newspapers to do so (*El proceso*, 265). Two leaders of the small group of Bolshevik Leninists, Munis and Carlini, were also arrested in 1937. They were still awaiting trial in Barcelona in January 1939 when Catalonia fell to General Franco. They managed to escape to France, as did the POUM leaders.

58. For further information on Roces, see Eduardo Comín Colomer, *Historia secreta de la segunda república*, 589–90.

59. *Yo fuí un ministro de Stalin*, 127. For the best source material on the repression and trial of the POUM, see Alba, *El marxismo; Autour de procès du P.O.U.M.*, Gorkin (the POUM leader and one of the accused), *Caníbales políticos* and *El proceso*; Landau; John McGovern, *Terror in Spain*; George Orwell, *Homage to Catalonia*; Wilebaldo Solano, *The Spanish Revolution*; Suárez; also articles by Jordi Arquer in *Enllà*, June 1945, and *La Révolution Prolétarienne*, July 1947. For the Communist case against the POUM (in addition to the indictment that can be found in Suárez, 195–209), see Georges Soria (correspondent in Spain of *L'Humanité*), *Trotskyism in the Service of Franco*, and Max Rieger, *Espionnage en Espagne*. The latter was translated into several languages and was widely distributed. Its author was unknown and never identified, but an attempt was made to dignify the book by the inclusion of a preface by José Bergamin, the well-known dissident Catholic intellectual, who said: "The Spanish Trotskyist organization of the POUM has been revealed, through the [treasonable events] of May 1937, as a very efficient tool of the fascists within republican territory" (p. 11).

60. The brief account that follows on the agricultural developments in regions other than Catalonia is based on material in Chapter 17.

61. Interview given to *Adelante* (Valencia), reprinted in *Solidaridad Obrera* (Barcelona), 28 May 1937. The quotation is given at greater length in chapter 17.

62. Interview given to *Juventud Libre*, 10 July 1937.

63. *Gaceta de la República*, 9 June 1937. For more information on the decree, see chapter 17.

64. See chapter 17.

65. Chapter 17. For the secrecy with which the operation against the Council of Aragon was carried out, see Antonio Cordón, *Trayectoria*, 350–52.

66. *Nuestra guerra*, 156.

67. *La revolución popular en el campo*, 17–18, quoted at a greater length in chapter 17.

68. Indalecio Prieto, *Cómo y por qué salí del ministerio de defensa nacional*, 37.

69. Article in *El Socialista* (Paris), 9 Nov. 1950.

70. Speech in Mexico City, 21 Apr. 1940, as given in *Inauguración del círculo "Pablo Iglesias" de Mexico*, 13.

71. Hernández, *Yo fui un ministro de Stalin*, 160.

72. See chapter 21, n. 115.

73. For Prieto's account of this episode, see *Cómo y por qué salí del ministerio de defensa nacional*, 76–79. See also Hernández, *Yo fui un ministro de Stalin*, 122. Orlov states that Prieto at first resisted his "insistent requests" that he let him organize a military intelligence service. "The answer he gave almost knocked me down. 'I am afraid,' he said with a roguish smile, 'that having the intelligence apparatus in your hands, you will come one day, arrest me and the other members of the government, and install our Spanish communists in power.'" Orlov then offered to supply "only advisers who would provide the know-how," which, he says, "seemed to satisfy" Prieto (Orlov, "Answers to the Questionnaire of Professor S. G. Payne," 19–20).

74. Hernández, *Yo fui un ministro de Stalin*, 128–32.

75. Ibid., 135–36.

76. Ibid., 140.

77. See *CNT* (Madrid, evening paper), 4 Oct. 1937.

78. 5 Oct. 1937.

79. Largo Caballero, *Mis recuerdos*, 231–32.

80. Ibid. For an account by a former Caballero supporter of the UGT crisis, see Amaro del Rosal, *Historia de la UGT de España*, II, 645–80.

81. See his speech as given in Largo Caballero, *La UGT y la guerra*.

82. Largo Caballero, *Mis recuerdos*, 231–32.

83. Ibid., 233–34.

84. See *Alianza CNT-UGT* for terms of the alliance.

85. *Por qué perdimos la guerra*, 180.

86. *Epistolario, Prieto y Negrín*, 107.

87. Zugazagoitia, 371–76.

88. *Epistolario, Prieto y Negrín*, 105; Hernández, *Yo fui un ministro de Stalin*, 161.

89. *Epistolario, Prieto y Negrín*, 23, 16.

90. Quoted in Hernández, *Yo fui un ministro de Stalin*, 166–67.

91. Ibid., 165–66.

92. Statement to the press, *La Vanguardia*, 9 Apr. 1938.

93. *Solidaridad Obrera* (Paris), 11 May 1951.

94. *Yo fui un ministro de Stalin*, 157.

95. *Epistolario, Prieto y Negrín*, 17.

96. Ibid., 29–30, 33, 99–100. See also Cordón, 389, for his appointment by Negrín.

97. For Ossorio y Tafall's support of the Communists see, for example, the anarcho-syndicalist historian José Peirats, *La CNT en la revolución española*, III, 227; also Manuel Tagüeña (former Communist and commander of the Fifteenth Army Corps), *Testimonio de dos guerras*, 309. At the time of the Casado coup in March 1939, however, he offered his "unconditional adherence" to the National Defense Council, which overthrew Negrín (see *Adelante* [Alicante], 7 Mar. 1939).

98. *Epistolario, Prieto y Negrín*, 99.

99. Cordón, 395. See also *Epistolario, Prieto y Negrín*, 99; Jesús Pérez Salas, *Guerra en España, 1936–1939*, 194–95; Zugazagoitia, 408, 417, 423–24.

100. *Yo fui un minstro de Stalin*, 144. The anarchosyndicalist Peirats claims that by mid-1938, 80–90 percent of the command posts were in Communist hands (*La CNT en la revolución española*, III, 223).

101. Quoted in *Epistolario, Prieto y Negrín*, 101.

102. Zugazagoitia, 423–24.

103. *Epistolario, Prieto y Negrín*, 100.

104. Hernández, *Yo fui un ministro de Stalin*, 180; Peirats, *Los anarquistas en la crisis política española*, 269–73. See 464 and n. 73, 469–70, 574. For an account of the growing importance and abuses by the SIM in 1938, see the moderate republican, Pi Sunyer, 479–80, 519–20.

105. See chapter 9, text to n. 64.

106. *Epistolario, Prieto y Negrín*, 100.

107. See article in *Timón* (Barcelona) as given in Horacio M. Prieto, *El anarquismo español en la lucha política*, 28–35.

108. *Comunista en España y antistalinista en la U.R.S.S.*, 72.

109. Quoted in Prieto, *Cómo y por qué salí del ministerio de defensa nacional*, 48.

110. As given in Peirats, *La CNT en la revolución española*, III, 251.

111. Quoted in Hernández, *Yo fui un ministro de Stalin*, 159.

112. *Gaceta de la República*, 28 Apr. 1938.

113. 16 June 1938.

114. See Josep María Bricall, *Política econòmica de la Generalitat, 1936–1939*, 346.

115. 15 June 1938.

116. 1 Oct. 1938.

117. 28 Nov. 1938.

118. Chapter 9, text to n.27.

119. Pp. 491–92.

120. See interview with Ivor Montagu in *Screen*, Autumn 1972.

121. *Spain*, 541.

122. *Men and Politics*, 465 (English edition).

123. *Freedom's Battle*, 66.

124. *Mundo Obrero* (Madrid), 28 Feb. 1939. This quotation is given at greater length in chapter 10.

125. For a more detailed account of the policies of Britain and France and of the general European situation, see chapters 6, 7, and 10.

126. Julio Alvarez del Vayo, *Give Me Combat*, 171.

127. A photographic reproduction of his letter of resignation, dated 27 February 1939, can be found in Eduardo Comín Colomer, *La república en el exilio*, between pp. 152–53.

128. Ibid.

129. Líster, ¡Basta!, 117. The reader should be alerted to the fact that this book was written in 1971, when Líster was trying to wrest control of the party from Santiago Carrillo, then general secretary, and from La Pasionaria, its president.

130. In a letter to Martínez Barrio, 4 Apr. 1939, as given in Andrés Saborit, Julián Besteiro, 398.

131. Zugazagoitia, 534–35.

132. Quoted in Epistolario, Prieto y Negrín, 117–18. Former politburo member Hernández describes the Negrín government as "a mute, paralytic phantom that neither governed nor spoke and that lacked the machinery of government and a fixed place of residence" (Yo fui un ministro de Stalin, 183–84).

133. Hernández, Yo fui un ministro de Stalin, 187.

134. For some of the promotions, transfers, and dismissals, see Hernández, Yo fui un ministro de Stalin, 187; Dolores Ibárruri (La Pasionaria), El único camino, 433; Tagüeña, 307; Trifón Gómez, quoted in Epistolario, Prieto y Negrín, 119–20; also Salas Larrazábal, who reproduces the Diario Oficial del Ministerio de Defensa Nacional, 1, 3 Mar. 1939, which published the decrees and orders relating to these changes, IV, 3399–3408.

135. ¡Basta!, 117–18. See n. 129.

136. Yo fui un ministro de Stalin, 183, 187.

137. Quoted in ibid., 256.

138. Ibárruri, El único camino, 445.

139. Ibid., 433.

Bibliography

I. Books and Pamphlets

Over three thousand books and pamphlets have been consulted, but because considerations of space do not permit a complete bibliographical listing, only those sources are given that have been cited in the text or in the notes, or that have been most helpful to the author. Books and pamphlets published before the Spanish Civil War are not included unless they have been cited in this work. All publications marked with an asterisk are in private possession, but photographic reproductions, either of the entire publication or of the pages referred to in the present work, are in the archives of the Hoover Institution. All other books and pamphlets listed are in one or more of the libraries specified at the beginning of this volume.

A Boss for Spain. Madrid: SIE, 1964.

Abad de Santillán, Diego. *After the Revolution.* New York: Greenberg, 1937.

———. *Los anarquistas y la reacción contemporánea.* Mexico City: Ediciones del Grupo Cultural "Ricardo Flores Magon," 1925.

———. *La bancarrota del sistema económico y político del capitalismo.* Buenos Aires: Nervio, 1932.

———. *Contribución a la historia del movimiento obrero español.* Puebla, Mexico: Cajica, 1965.

———. *El organismo económico de la revolución: Cómo vivimos y cómo podríamos vivir en España.* Barcelona: Tierra y Libertad, 1938.

———. *Por qué perdimos la guerra.* Buenos Aires: Imán, 1940.

———. *La revolución y la guerra en España.* Havana: "El Libro," 1938.

Acedo Colunga, General Felipe. *José Calvo Sotelo.* Barcelona: AHR, 1957.

La agresión italiana: Documentos ocupados a las unidades italianas en la acción de Guadalajara. Valencia: Ministerio de Estado, 1937.

Aguado, Emiliano. *Don Manuel Azaña Díaz.* Barcelona: Nauta, 1972.

Aiguader, Jaime. *Cataluña y la revolucion.* Madrid: Zevs, 1932.

Aláiz, Felipe. *Indalecio Prieto: Padrino de Negrín y campeón anticomunista.* Toulouse: "Páginas Libres," n.d.

Alba, Luz de. *19 de julio.* Montevideo: Esfuerzo, 1937.

Alba, Victor. *Dos revolucionarios: Joaquín Maurín, Andreu Nin.* Madrid: Seminarios y Ediciones, 1975.

———. *Historia de la segunda república española.* Mexico City: Libro Mex, 1960.

Bibliography

————. *El marxismo en España, 1919–1939*. Historia del B.O.C. y del P.O.U.M. Vols. I, II. Mexico City: Costa-Amic, 1973.

Albert Despujol, Carlos de. *La gran tragedia de España, 1931–1939*. Madrid: Sánchez de Ocaña, 1940.

Alcofar Nassaes, José Luis. *Los asesores sovieticos en la guerra civil española*. Preface by Wilfredo Espina. Madrid: Dopesa, 1971.

Aldana, B. F. *Como fué la guerra en Aragón*. Barcelona: Ediciones "Como Fué," 1937.

Algarra Rafegas, Commandant Antonio. *El asedio de Huesca*. Saragossa: Talleres Editoriales "El Noticiero," 1941.

Alianza CNT-UGT. Barcelona: Tierra y Libertad, 1938.

Alonso, Bruno. *La flota republicana y la guerra civil de España*. Mexico City: Imprenta Grafos, 1944.

Alvarez, Basilio. *España en el crisol*. Buenos Aires: Colección Claridad, 1937.

Alvarez, Segis. *La juventud y los campesinos: Conferencia Nacional de Juventudes, enero de 1937*. Valencia: JSU de España, 1937.

————. *Nuestra organización y nuestros cuadros*. Valencia: JSU de España, 1937.

Alvarez del Vayo, Julio. *Deux discours prononcés à la 101me session de la Societé des Nations*. Paris: Services d'Information du Rassemblement Universel pour la Paix, 1938.

————. *L'Espagne accuse*. Paris: Comité Franco-Espagnol, 1936.

————. *Freedom's Battle*. New York: Knopf, 1940.

————. *Give Me Combat*. Boston: Little, Brown, 1973.

————. *The Last Optimist*. New York: Viking Press, 1950.

————. *Speech at the Council of the League of Nations, May, 1938*. London: Union of Democratic Control, 1938.

Amsden, Jon. *Convenios colectivos y lucha de clases en España*. Paris: Ruedo Ibèrico, 1974.

Anarcosindicalismo: Antecedentes, Declaración de principios. Finalidades y tácticas. Toulouse: Espoir, 1947.

Andrade, Juan. *Algunas "Notas Políticas" de la revolución Española, 1936–1937*. Paris: La Batalla, 1969.

Un año de las brigadas internacionales. Madrid: Ediciones del Comisariado de las Brigadas Internacionales, [1937?].

Ansaldo, Juan Antonio. *¿Para qué . . . ? De Alfonso XIII a Juan III*. Buenos Aires: Vasca Ekin, S.R.L., 1951.

Ansó, Mariano. *Yo fui ministro de Negrín*. Barcelona: Planeta, 1976.

Aproximación histórica de la guerra española, 1936–1939. Madrid: Universidad de Madrid, 1970.

Araceli, Gabriel. *Valencia 1936*. Saragossa: Talleres Editoriales de "El Noticiero," 1939.

*Araquistáin, Luis. *El comunismo y la guerra de España*. Carmaux (Tarn): 1939.

————. *Mis tratos con los comunistas*. Ediciones de la Secretaría de Propaganda del P.S.O.E. en Francia, n.d.

————. *La verdad sobre la intervención y la no-intervención en España*. Madrid: n.p.

Arques, Enrique. *17 de julio: La epopeya de Africa*. Madrid: Reus, 1948.

Arrabal, Juan. *José María Gil Robles*. Avila: Senén Martín Díaz, 1935.

Arraras, Joaquín. *Historia de la cruzada española*. 12 vols. Madrid: Ediciones Españolas, 1940.

————. *Historia de la segunda república española*. Vols. I, II, III, IV. Madrid: Editora Nacional, 1964 and 1968.

————. *Memorias íntimas de Azaña*. Madrid: Ediciones Españolas, 1939.

————. *El sitio del Alcázar de Toledo*. Saragossa: Editorial Heraldo de Aragón, 1937.

Asedio de Huesca. Huesca: Ayuntamiento de Huesca, [1938?].

Asensio, General. *El General Asensio: Su lealtad a la república*. Barcelona: Artes Gráficas CNT, [1938?].

L'assassinat de Andrés Nin. Paris: Spartacus, 1939.

Autour du procès du P.O.U.M., Paris: Independent News, 1938.

Avilés, Gabriel. *Tribunales rojos: Vistos por un abogado defensor*. Barcelona: Destino, 1939.

Azaña, Manuel. *Madrid*. London: Friends of Spain, 1937.

————. *Obras completas*, ed. Juan Marichal. Vols. III, IV. Mexico City: Oasis, 1967, 1968.

————. *Speech by His Excellency the President of the Spanish Republic, January 21, 1937*. London: Press Department of the Spanish Embassy in London, [1937?].

————. *La velada en Benicarló*. Buenos Aires: Editorial Losada, 1939.

————. *A Year of War in Spain*. London: Friends of Spain, 1937.

Azaretto, Manuel. *Las pendientes resbaladizas: Los anarquistas en España*. Preface by José A. Barrionuevo. Montevideo: "Germinal," 1939.

Azcárate, Pablo de. *Mi embajada en Londres durante la guerra civil española*. Barcelona: Ariel, 1976.

Aznar, Manuel. *Historia militar de la guerra de España*. Madrid: "Idea," 1940.

Bahamonde y Sánchez de Castro, Antonio. *Un año con Queipo de Llano*. Mexico City: "Nuestro Tiempo," 1938.

Bajo la bandera de la España republicana. Moscow: Progreso, n.d.

Bakunin, M. A. *Bog i gosudarstvo*. New York: Union of Russian Workers of the City of New York, 1918.

————. *Gosudarstvennost i anarkhiia*. Petersburg-Moscow: Gosudarstvennoe Izdanie, 1922.

Balbontin, José Antonio. *La España de mi experiencia*. Mexico City: Colección Aquelarre, 1952.

Barea, Arturo. *The Forging of a Rebel*. New York: Reynal Hitchcock, 1946.

Battaglione Garibaldi. Paris: Edizioni di Coltura Sociale, 1937.

Bayo, Captain Alberto. *Mi desembarco en Mallorca: De la guerra civil española*. Guadalajara, Mexico: Imprenta Gráfica, 1944.

Bibliography

Bécarud, Jean. *La segunda república española*. Madrid: Taurus Ediciones, 1967.
————, and Lapouge, Gilles. *Anarchistes d'Espagne*. Paris: André Balland, 1970.
Belforte, General Francesco. *La guerra civile in Spagna. I, La disintegrazione dello stato*. Milan: Istitúto per gli studi di politica internazionale, 1938.
————. *La guerra civile in Spagna. II, Gli interventi stranieri nella Spagna rossa*. Milan: Istitúto per gli studi di politica internazionale, 1939.
————. *La guerra civile in Spagna. III, La campagna dei volontari italiani*. Milan: Istitúto per gli studi di politica internazionale, 1939.
————. *La guerra civile in Spagna. IV, La camapgna dei volontari italiani e la vittoria di Franco*. Milan: Istituto per gli studi di politica internazionale, 1939.
Bellmunt, Domènec de. *Lluis Companys*. Toulouse: Edicions "Foc Nou," 1945.
Beloff, Max. *The Foreign Policy of Soviet Russia, 1929–1941*. 2 vols. London-New York-Toronto: Oxford University Press, 1947.
Bernard, Ino. *Mola, martir de España*. Granada: Editorial y Librería Prieto, 1938.
Bertrán Güell, Felipe. *Caudillo, profetas y soldados*. Madrid-Barcelona: Editorial Juventud, 1939.
————. *Preparación y desarrollo del alzamiento nacional*. Valladolid: Santarén, 1938.
Bessie, Alvah. *Men in Battle*. New York: Charles Scribner's Sons, 1939.
Besteiro, Julián. *Marxismo y antimarxismo*. Mexico City: Pablo Iglesias, 1966.
Beumelburg, Werner. *Kampf um Spanien: Die Geschichte der Legion Condor*. Oldenburg-Berlin: Gerhard Stalling, 1939.
Bezucha, Robert J., ed. *Modern European Social History*. Boston: Heath, 1972.
Bilainkin, George. *Ivan Mikhailovitch Maisky: Ten Years Ambassador*. London: Allen & Unwin, 1944.
Bley, Wulf. *Das Buch der Spanienflieger*. Leipzig: Hase & Koehler, 1939.
Bolín, Luis. *España: Los años vitales*. Madrid: Espasa Calpe, 1967.
————. *Spain: The Vital Years*. London: Cassell, 1967. (English version of above.)
Bollati, Ambrogio, and Bono, Giulio del. *La guerra di Spagna*. Torino: Giulio Einaudi, 1937.
Bolloten, Burnett. *The Grand Camouflage: The Spanish Civil War and Revolution, 1936–39*. New York: Praeger, 1961 and 1968. Introduction to the Second Printing by H. R. Trevor-Roper.
Bolshaia sovetskaia entsiklopediia. Moscow: [1st ed. 1926–47; 2d ed. 1950–60; 3d ed. 1970–].
Borkenau, Franz. *The Spanish Cockpit*. London: Faber and Faber, 1937.
Borras, T. *Checas de Madrid*. Madrid: Escelicer, 1940.
Bortsy Latvii v Ispanii, 1936–1939: Vospominaniia i dokumenty. Riga: Institut Istori Partii pri Tsk KP Latvii. Filial Instituta Marksizma-Leninizma pri Tsk. KPSS., 1970.
Bowers, Claude. *My Mission to Spain*. New York: Simon and Schuster, 1954.

Bibliography

Brademas, John. *Anarchosyndicalismo y revolución en España, 1930–1937*. Barcelona: Ariel, 1974.

Bravo Morata, Federico. *Historia de Madrid*. Vol. III. Madrid: Fenecia, 1968.

Brenan, Gerald. *The Face of Spain*. New York: Pellegrini & Cudahy, 1951.

———. *The Spanish Labyrinth*. London: Cambridge University Press, 1943.

Bricall, Joseph M. *L'expérience catalane d'autogestion ouvrière durant la guerre civile, 1936–1939*. Paris: I.S.E.A., 1972.

———. *Política económica de la Generalitat, 1936–1939*. Barcelona: Edicions 62, 1970.

La brigada del amanecer. Valladolid: Santarén, n.d.

Brockway, Fenner. *Truth about Barcelona*. London: Independent Labour Party, 1937.

———. *Workers' Front*. London: Secker and Warburg, 1938.

Brome, Vincent. *The International Brigades*. London: Heinemann, 1965.

Broué, Pierre, and Témime, Emile. *La révolution et la guerre d'Espagne*. Paris: Les Editions de Minuit, 1961.

Buckley, Henry. *Life and Death of the Spanish Republic*. London: Hamish Hamilton, 1940.

Bullejos, José. *La comintern en España: Recuerdos de mi vida*. Mexico City: Impresiones Modernas, 1972.

———. *España en la segunda república*. Mexico City: Impresiones Modernas, 1967.

———. *Europa entre dos guerras, 1918–1938*. Mexico City: Castilla, 1945.

Burgo, Jaime del. *Conspiración y guerra civil*. Madrid: Alfaquara, 1970.

Cabo Giorla, Luis. *Primera conferencia nacional del P.S.U.C.* [Valencia?]: Ediciones del Departamento de Agitación y Propaganda del PSUC, 1937.

El camino de la victoria. Valencia: Gráficas Genovés, [1936?].

"El Campesino," General. *La vie et la mort en U.R.S.S., 1939–1949*. Paris: Librairie Plon, 1950.

———. *Comunista en España y antistalinista en la U.R.S.S.* Mexico City: Guarania, 1952.

Campoamor, Clara. *La révolution espagnole vue par une républicaine*. Paris: Plon, 1937.

Cánovas Cervantes, S. *Apuntes históricos de "Solidaridad Obrera."* Barcelona: Ediciones C.R.T., n.d.

———. *De Franco a Negrín pasando por el partido comunista: Historia de la revolución española*. Toulouse: Colección "Páginas Libres," n.d.

———. *Durruti y Ascaso: La CNT y la revolución de julio*. Toulouse: Ediciones "Páginas Libres," n.d.

Cantalupo, Roberto. *Fu la Spagna*. Ambasciáta presso Franco. Fabbráio-Aprile 1937. Milan: Arnolde Mondadori, 1948.

Cantarero del Castillo, Manuel. *Tragedia del socialismo español*. Barcelona: Dopesa, 1971.

Capo, José María. *España desnuda*. Havana: Publicaciones España, 1938.

Bibliography

Cardona Rosell, Mariano. *Aspectos económicos de nuestra revolución*. Barcelona: Oficinas de Propaganda CNT-FAI, 1937.

Carr, Edward Hallet. *German-Soviet Relations between the Two World Wars, 1919-1939*. Baltimore: The Johns Hopkins Press, 1951.

Carr, Raymond, ed., *The Republic and the Civil War in Spain*. London: Macmillan, 1971.

————. *Spain, 1808-1939*. Oxford: Oxford University Press, 1966.

Carrascal, Geminiano. *Asturias: 18 julio 1936-21 octubre 1937*. Valladolid: Casa Martín, 1938.

Carrillo, Santiago. *En marcha hacia la victoria*. Conferencia nacional de juventudes. [Valencia?], 1937.

————. *La juventud, factor de la victoria*. Valencia: Partido Comunista de España, 1937.

————. *Somos la organización de la juventud*. Madrid: n.p., n.d.

Carrillo, Wenceslao. *El último episodio de la guerra civil española*. Toulouse: La Secretaría de Publicaciones de la J.S.E. en Francia, 1945.

Carrión, Pascual. *Los latifundios en España*. Madrid: Gráficas Reunidas, 1932.

Casado, Colonel Segismundo. *The Last Days of Madrid*. London: Peter Davies, 1939.

Casares, Francisco. *Azaña y ellos*. Granada: Librería Prieto, 1938.

Castells, Andreu. *Las brigadas internacionales de la guerra de España*. Barcelona: Ariel, 1974.

Castro, Enrique. *Balance y perspectivas de nuestra guerra*. Barcelona: Partido Comunista de España, Comisión Nacional de Agit-Prop, 1937.

————. *Hombres made in Moscú*. Mexico City: Publications Mañana, 1960.

————. *J'ai perdu la foi à Moscou*. Paris: Gallimard, 1950.

Cattell, David T. *Communism and the Spanish Civil War*. Berkeley: University of California Press, 1955.

————. *Soviet Diplomacy and the Spanish Civil War*. Berkeley: University of California Press, 1957.

Ceyrat, Maurice. *La trahison permanente. Parti communiste et politique russe*. Paris: Spartacus, 1948.

Checa, Pedro. *A un gran partido, una gran organización*. [Valencia?]: Partido Comunista de España, Comisión Nacional de Agit-Prop, 1937.

————. *Qué es y cómo funciona el partido comunista*. Valencia: Partido Comunista de España, n.d.

————. *Tareas de organización y trabajo práctico del partido*. Madrid-Barcelona: Partido Comunista de España, 1938.

Churchill, Winston. *Arms and the Covenant*. London: George G. Harrap and Co., 1938.

————. *The Gathering Storm*. Boston: Houghton Mifflin, 1948.

Ciano, Count. *The Ciano Diaries, 1939-1943*. Garden City: Garden City Publishing Co., 1947.

Cierva y de Hoces, Ricardo de. *Cien libros básicos sobre la guerra de España*. Madrid: Publicaciones Españolas, 1966.

Bibliography

————. *Los documentos de la primavera trágica: Análisis documental de los antecedentes immediatos del 18 de julio de 1936.* Madrid: Ministerio de Información y Turismo, Secretaría General Técnica, 1967.

————. *Historia de la guerra civil española.* Vol. I. Madrid: San Martín, 1969.

————. *Historia ilustrada de la guerra civil española.* Vols. I, II. Barcelona: Danae, 1971.

————. *Leyenda y tragedia de las brigadas internacionales.* Madrid: Prensa Española, 1973.

Claudín, Fernando, *La crisis del movimiento comunista.* Vol. I, *De la kominform al komintern.* Preface by Jorge Semprún. Paris: Ruedo Ibérico, 1970.

Clavego, Pablo. *Algunas normas para el trabajo de los comisarios políticos.* Madrid: Europa América, [1937?].

Cockburn, Claud. *Crossing the Line.* London: Macgibbon and Kee, 1958.

————. *A Discord of Trumpets.* New York: Simon and Schuster, 1956.

Las colectividades campesinas, 1936–1939. Barcelona: Tusquets, 1977.

Collectivisations. See p. 603, below.

Colodny, Robert Garland. *The Struggle for Madrid: The Central Epic of the Spanish Conflict, 1936–37.* New York: Paine-Whitman, 1958.

Colomer, Victor. *Informe presentat a la primera conferencia nacional del partit socialista unificat de catalunya I.C.* Barcelona: Ediciones del Secretariat d'Agitacio i Propaganda del P.S.U., [Barcelona?] 1937.

Colton, Joel. *Léon Blum: Humanist in Politics.* New York: Knopf, 1966.

Comarcal de Utrillas (Teruel): En lucha por la libertad, contra el facismo, 1936–1939. Ediciones "Cultura y Acción." No publisher indicated, [1972?].

Comarcal de Valderrobres (Teruel): Sus luchas sociales y revolucionarias. "Cultura y Acción." No publisher indicated, [1972?].

Comín Colomer, Eduardo. *Historia del anarquismo español.* Vols. I, II. Barcelona: AHR, 1956.

————. *Historia del partido comunista de España.* Vols. I, II, III. Madrid: Editora Nacional, 1965.

————. *Historia de la primera república.* Barcelona: AHR, 1956.

————. *Historia secreta de la segunda república.* Barcelona: AHR, 1959.

————. *La república en el exilio.* Barcelona: AHR, 1957.

Comorera, Juan. *Cataluña, en pie de guerra: Discurso pronunciado en el pleno ampliado del C. C. del partido comunista de España.* [Valencia?]: Ediciones del Partido Comunista de España, 1937.

————. *Informe presentado a la primera conferencia nacional del partido socialista unificado de Catalunya I. C. por su secretario general.* [Barcelona?]: Ediciones del Secretariado de Agitación y Propaganda del P.S.U., [1937?].

Conquest, Robert. *The Great Terror.* New York: Macmillan, 1968.

Le contrat de travail dans la république espagnole. Madrid: Ministère du Travail et de Prévoyance, Gráficas Reunidas, 1937.

Contreras, Carlos J. *Nuestro gran ejército popular.* Barcelona: Partido Comunista de España, Comisión Nacional de Agit-Prop, 1937.

————. *La quinta columna.* Valencia: Partido Comunista de España, [1937?].

Bibliography

Cordón, Antonio. *Trayectoria*. Paris: Ebro, 1971.

Cot, Pierre. *Triumph of Treason*. New York: Ziff-Davis, 1944.

Coverdale, John F. *Italian Intervention in the Spanish Civil War*. Princeton: Princeton University Press, 1975.

Cruells, Manuel. *Mayo sangriento: Barcelona, 1937*. Barcelona: Editorial Juventud, 1970.

Dahms, Helmut Günther. *Der spanische Burgerkrieg, 1936–1939*. Tubingen: Rainer Wunderlich, 1962.

Dashar, M. *The Revolutionary Movement in Spain*. New York: Libertarian Publishing Society, n.d.

Datos complementarios para la historia de España: Guerra de liberación, 1936–1939. Madrid: 1945. (In University of California Library, Los Angeles.)

Davies, Joseph E. *Mission to Moscow*. New York: Simon and Schuster, 1941.

Decret de collectivizacions. Barcelona: Conselleria d'Economia, Generalitat de Catalunya, 1936.

Decret sobre la collectivització i control de la industria i el comerç a Catalunya. Barcelona: Conselleria d'Economia, Catalunya, Industries Grafiques Seiz i Barral Germans, 1936.

De julio a julio: Un año de lucha. Barcelona: Tierra y Libertad, 1937.

Delperrie de Bayac, Jacques. *Les brigades internationales*. Paris: Fayard, 1968.

Deutscher, Isaac. *Stalin: A Political Biography*. New York and London: Oxford University Press, 1949.

Díaz, José. *Tres años de lucha*. Paris: Librairie du Globe, 1969.

Díaz del Moral, Juan. *Historia de las agitaciones campesinas andaluzas*. Madrid: Alianza, 1967.

Díaz de Villegas, General José. *Guerra de liberación*. Barcelona: Editorial AHR, 1958.

———. *La guerra revolucionaria*. Madrid: Europa, 1963.

Dictamen de la comisión sobre ilegitimidad de poderes en 18 de julio de 1936. Madrid: Editora Nacional, 1939.

Diego Sevilla, Andrés. *Historia política de la zona roja*. Madrid: Rialp, S.A., 1963.

Dirksen, Herbert von. *Moscow, Tokyo, London: Twenty Years of German Foreign Policy*. London: Hutchinson, 1951.

Dodd, William E., *Ambassador Dodd's Diary 1933–1938*. New York: Harcourt Brace, 1941.

Dolgoff, Sam, ed. *The Anarchist Collectives*. New York: Free Life Editions, 1974.

Domènec de Bellmunt, *Lluis Companys*. Toulouse: "Foc Nou," 1945.

Domingo, Marcelino. *España ante el mundo*. Mexico City: "Mexico Nuevo," 1937.

Domínguez, Edmundo. *Los vencedores de Negrín*. Mexico City: Nuestro Pueblo, 1940.

Drachkovitch, Milorad M. *See* Lazitch, Branko.

Bibliography

————, ed. *Fifty Years of Communism in Russia*. Hoover Institution Publications. University Park: Pennsylvania State University Press, 1967.

Dzelepy, E. N. *The Spanish Plot*. London: King, 1937.

Eby, Cecil D. *The Siege of the Alcázar*. New York: Random House, 1965.

Egorov, P. Ia. *Marshal Meretskov*. Moscow: Voennoe Izd., 1974.

Ehrenburg, Ilya. *Corresponsal en España*. Buenos Aires: Tiempo Contemporáneo, 1968.

————. *Eve of War, 1933–41*. London: Macgibbon, 1963.

Epistolario, Prieto y Negrín. Paris: Imprimerie Nouvelle, 1939.

Epopée d'Espagne: Brigades internationales, 1936–1939. Paris: L'Amicale des Anciens Volontaires français en Espagne Républicaine: Paris, 1957.

Erickson, John. *The Soviet High Command: A Military-Political History, 1918–1945*. [London]: St. Martin's Press, 1962.

Escofet, Frederic. *Al servei de Catalunya i de la república: La victoria (19 de julio 1936)*. Paris: Ediciones catalanes de Paris, 1973.

España, su lucha y sus ideales: Documentos de Ossorio y Gallardo, Federica Montseny, Juan P. Fábregas, F. Martí Ibañez, García Oliver, H. Noja Ruiz. Buenos Aires: Acento, 1937.

Estado Mayor Central del Ejército. *Historia de la guerra de liberación, 1936–39*. Vol. I. Madrid: Servicio Histórico Militar, 1945.

Estatutos de la federación nacional de campesinos. Valencia: n.p., 1937.

Esteban-Infantes, General Emilio. *General Sanjurjo*. Barcelona: AHR, 1957.

Exposure of the Secret Plan to Establish a Soviet in Spain. London: Friends of National Spain, n.d.

Fabbri, Luis. *¿Que es la anarquia?* Toulouse: "Tiempos Nuevos," n.d.

————. *Vida y pensamiento de Malatesta*. Barcelona: Tierra y Libertad, 1938.

Fábregas, Juan P. *Los factores económicos de la revolución española*. Barcelona: Oficinas de Propaganda CNT-FAI, 1937.

Falcón, César. *Madrid*. Madrid-Barcelona: Nuestro Pueblo, 1938.

Falsifiers of History. Moscow: Foreign Languages Publishing House, 1948.

Fernández Almagro, Melchor. *Catalanismo y república española*. Madrid: Espasa-Calpe, 1932.

————. *Historia de la república española, 1931–36*. Madrid: Editorial Biblioteca Nueva, 1940.

Fernández Arias, Adelardo. *Gil Robles: ¡La esperanza de España!* Madrid: Comentarios del Momento, 1936.

Fernández de Castro y Pedrera, Rafael. *Hacia las rutas de una nueva España*. Melilla: Artes Gráficas Postal Exprés, 1940.

————. *Vidas de soldados ilustres de la nueva España: Franco, Mola, Varela*. Melilla: Artes Gráficas Postal Exprés, 1937.

Ferrándiz Alborz, F. *La bestia contra España*. Montevideo: n.p., 1951.

Ferrara, Marcella, and Ferrara, Maurizio. *Conversando con Togliatti*. Rome: Edizioni de Cultura Sociale, 1954.

Fischer, Louis. *Men and Politics*. London: Cape, 1941.

Bibliography

_____. *Men and Politics.* New York: Duell, Sloan and Pierce, 1941.

_____. *Russia's Road from Peace to War: Soviet Foreign Relations, 1917–1941.* New York: Harper, 1969.

_____. *Why Spain Fights On.* London: Union of Democratic Control, [1937?].

Fontana, José María. *Los catalanes en la guerra de España.* Madrid: Samarán, 1951.

Francisco Largo Caballero, 1869–1946. Toulouse: Ediciones El Socialista, 1947.

Frutos, Victor de. *Los que NO perdieron la guerra.* Buenos Aires: Oberon, 1967.

Führing, Hellmut H. *Wir funden für Franco.* Gütersloh: Verlag C. Bertelsmann, 1939.

Gabriel, José. *La vida y la muerte en Aragón.* Buenos Aires: Imán, 1938.

Galíndez, Jesús de. *Los vascos en el Madrid sitiado.* Buenos Aires: Vasca Ekin, 1945.

Galindo Herrero, Santiago. *Los partidos monárquicos bajo la segunda república.* Madrid: Rialp, 1956.

García, Regina. *Yo he sido marxista.* Madrid: Editora Nacional, 1946.

García, Victor. *El pensamiento anarquista.* Toulouse: "CENIT," 1963.

García Oliver, Juan. *El fascismo internacional y la guerra antifascista española.* Barcelona: Oficinas de Propaganda CNT-FAI, 1937.

García Pradas, José. *Antifascismo proletario.* Madrid: "Frente Libertario," n.d.

_____. *Rusia y España.* Paris: "Tierra y Libertad," 1948.

_____. *¡Teníamos que perder!* Madrid: Toro, 1974.

_____. *La traición de Stalin.* New York: Cultura Proletaria, 1939.

García-Valino y Marcen, Lieutenant General. *Guerra de liberación española.* Madrid: Bosca, 1949.

García Venero, Maximiano. *El General Fanjul: Madrid en el alzamiento nacional.* Madrid: Ediciones Cid, 1967.

_____. *Historia de las internacionales en España.* Vol. II, *1914–1936;* Vol. III, *1936–1939.* Madrid: Ediciones del Moviemiento, 1957.

_____. *Historia del nacionalismo catalán.* Colección "Tierra, Historia y Política." Vols. I, II. Madrid: Editora Nacional, 1967.

Garibaldini in Ispagna. Madrid: n.p., 1937.

Garrachón Cuesta, Antonio. *De Africa a Cádiz y de Cádiz a la España Imperial.* Cádiz: Establecimientos Cerón, 1938.

Gates, John. *The Story of an American Communist.* New York: Thomas Nelson, 1958.

Gaule, Jacques de. *La política española y la guerra civil.* Vols. I, II. Madrid: Círculo de Amigos de la Historia, 1973 and 1974.

_____. *Hacia el final.* Madrid: Círculo de Amigos de la Historia, 1973.

Generalnyi Shtab RKKA. *Upravlenie voiskami i rabota shtabov v ispanskoi respublikanskoi armii.* Moscow: Gosudarstvennoe Voennoe Izdatelstvo Narkomata Oborony Soiuza SSR, 1939.

Geraud, André (Pertinax), *The Gravediggers of France.* Garden City: Doubleday Doran, 1944.

Gibson, Ian. *La represión nacionalista de Granada en 1936 y la muerte de Federico García Lorca*. Paris: Ruedo Ibérico, 1971.

Gil Robles, José María. *No fué posible la paz*. Barcelona: Ariel, 1968.

_____. *Spain in Chains*. New York: America Press, 1937.

Gilabert, A.G. *Durruti, un anarquista íntegro*. Barcelona: Comité Nacional de la Confederación Nacional del Trabajo, n.d.

Gilbert, Martin, and Gott, Richard. *The Appeasers*. Boston: Houghton Mifflin, 1963.

Giral, o una historia de sangre. Spain: Ediciones Combate, n.d.

Goded, Manuel. *Un "faccioso" cien por cien*. Saragossa: Heraldo, 1939.

Gollonet, Angel, and Morales, José. *Sangre y fuego, Málaga*. Granada: Imperio, 1937.

Gomá y Tomás, Cardenal Isidro. *Pastorales de la guerra de España*. Madrid: Rialp, 1955.

Gómez, Sócrates. *Los jóvenes socialistas y la JSU*. Madrid: Rivadeneyra, n.d.

Gómez Bajuelo, Gil. *Malaga bajo el dominio rojo*. Cadiz: Establecimientos Cerón, 1937.

Gómez Casas, Juan. *Historia del anarcosindicalismo español*. Madrid: ZYX, 1969.

Gómez Málaga, Juan. *Estampas trágicas de Madrid*. Avila: Tip. y Enc. de Senén Martín, n.d.

Gómez Oliveros, Major Benito, in collaboration with Lieutenant General José Moscardó. *General Moscardó: Sin Novedad en el Alcázar*. Barcelona: AHR, 1956.

González, Valentín. *See* "El Campesino," General.

González Inestral, Miguel. *Cipriano Mera, revolucionario*. Havana: Atalaya, 1943.

Gorkin, Julián. *L'assassinat de Trotsky*. Paris: Julliard, 1970.

_____. *Caníbales políticos*. Mexico City: Quetzal, 1941.

_____. *España, Primer ensayo de democracia popular*. Buenos Aires: Asociación Argentina por la Libertad de la Cultura, 1961.

_____. *El proceso de Moscú en Barcelona*. Barcelona: Aymá, 1974.

_____. *El revolucionario profesional*. Barcelona: Aymá, 1975.

Gracia, Padre Vicente, S.J. *Aragón, baluarte de España*. Saragossa: "El Noticiero," 1938.

Graf Hoyos, Max. *Pedros y Pablos*. Munich: Verlag F. Bruckmann, 1939.

Guadalajara. Madrid: Comisariado General de Guerra (Inspección Centro) Comisión de Propaganda, 1937.

Guarner, Vicente. *Cataluña en la guerra de España, 1936–39*. Madrid: Toro, 1975.

Guérin, Daniel. *L'anarchisme: De la doctrine à l'action*. Paris: Editions Gallimard. 1965.

_____. *Front populaire: Révolution manquée, Témoignage militant*. Paris: François Maspero, 1970.

_____. *Ni dieu ni maître: Anthologie historique du mouvement anarchiste*. Paris: Delphes, [1967?].

Bibliography

La guerra de liberación nacional: Historia de la guerra. Vol. III. Zaragoza: Universidad de Zaragoza, 1961.

Guerra y revolución en España, 1936–1939. Vols. I, II, III. Moscow: Progreso, 1967, 1966, 1971.

Gutiérrez-Ravé, José. *Las cortes errantes del frente popular.* Madrid : Editora Nacional, 1953.

————. *José Gil Robles, caudillo frustrado.* Madrid: Luyve, 1967.

Guzmán, Eduardo de. *Madrid, rojo y negro.* Barcelona: Tierra y Libertad, 1938.

————. *La muerte de la esperanza.* Madrid: Toro, 1973.

Guzmán de Alfarache, J. *¡18 de julio! Historia del alzamiento glorioso de Sevilla.* Seville: F.E., 1937.

Hanighen, Frank, ed. *Nothing But Danger: Thrilling Adventures of Ten Newspaper Correspondents in the Civil War.* New York: McBride, 1939.

Held, Walter. *Die spanische Revolution.* Paris: Jean Mekhler, [1938?].

Hermet, Guy. *Los comunistas en España.* Paris: Ruedo Ibérico, 1972.

Hernández, Jesús. *A los intelectuales de España.* [Valencia?]: Partido Comunista de España, Comisión Nacional de Agit-Prop, 1937.

————. *¡Atras los invasores!* Barcelona: Partido Comunista de España, 1938.

————. *En el pais de la gran mentira.* Madrid: Toro, 1974.

————. *Negro y rojo: Los anarquistas en la revolución española.* Mexico City: La España Contemporánea, 1946.

————. *El orgullo de sentirnos españoles.* Barcelona: S.G. de Publicaciones, [1938?].

————. *El partido comunista antes, durante y después de la crisis del gobierno Largo Caballero.* Valencia: Partido Comunista de España, 1937.

————. *Todo dentro del frente popular.* [Valencia?]: Partido Comunista de España, Comisión Nacional de Agit-Prop, 1937.

————. *Yo fui un ministro de Stalin.* Mexico City: Editorial America, 1953.

*Hernández Zancajo, Carlos. *Tercera etapa de octubre.* Valencia: Meabe, 1937.

Hidalgo de Cisneros, Ignacio. *Memorias 2: La república y la guerra de España.* Paris: Société d'Éditions de la Librarie du Globe, 1964.

————. *Virage sur l'aile: Souvenirs.* Paris: Français Reunis, 1965.

Hispanicus. *Foreign Intervention in Spain.* London: United Editorial, 1938.

Historia de la revolución nacional española. 2 vols. Paris: La Sociedad Internacional de Ediciones y de Publicidad, 1940.

Historia del partido comunista de Espana. Paris: Ediciones Sociales, 1960.

Homenaje del comite peninsular de la FAI a Buenaventura Durruti, (1896–1936). En el segundo aniversario de su muerte. Barcelona: n.p., 1938.

How Mussolini Provoked the Spanish Civil War. London: United Editorial, [1938?].

Ibárruri, Dolores [La Pasionaria]. *Ejército popular unido, ejército de la victoria.* Madrid-Barcelona: Partido Comunista de España, 1938.

————. *Es hora ya de crear el gran partido único del proletariado.* Madrid: Stajanov. 1937.

Bibliography

———. *No hay mas posibilidad de gobernar que a través del frente popular.* Barcelona: Partido Comunista de España, 1938.

———. *Un pleno histórico.* [Valencia?]: Partido Comunista de España, Comisión Nacional de Agit-Prop, 1937.

———. *Speeches and Articles, 1936–38.* London: Lawrence and Wishart, 1938.

———. *El único camino.* Paris: Editions Sociales, 1962.

———. *Unión de todos los españoles: Por la independencia de España. Por la libertad. Por la república.* Madrid-Barcelona: Partido Communista de España, [1938?].

Iglesias, Ignacio. *La fase final de la guerra civil.* Barcelona: Planeta, 1977.

Iniesta, Juan de. *Escuchad, campesino.* Madrid: Comisión de Propaganda del Comité Regional del Centro, 1937.

Iribarren, José María. *Con el General Mola: Escenas y aspectos inéditos de la guerra civil.* Saragossa: Librería General, 1937.

———. *Mola.* Saragossa: Heraldo de Aragón, 1938.

Irujo, Manuel de. *See* Lizarza Iribarren, Antonio.

The Italian Air Force in Spain. London: United Editorial, n.d.

Iturburu, Cordova. *España bajo el comando del pueblo.* Buenos Aires: Acento, 1938.

Iturralde, Juan de (pseud. of Padre Juan Usabiaga). *El catolicismo y la cruzada de Franco.* Vienne, France: Egi-Indarra, 1960.

Jackson, Gabriel. *The Spanish Republic and the Civil War, 1931–1939.* Princeton, N.J.: Princeton University Press, 1965.

Jellinek, Frank. *The Civil War in Spain.* London: Victor Gollancz, 1938.

Jiménez de Asua, Luis. *La constitución política de la democracia española.* Santiago de Chile: Ediciones Ercilla, 1942.

Joaniquet, Aurelio. *Calvo Sotelo.* Santander: Espasa-Calpe, 1939.

Johnston, Verle B. *Legions of Babel: The International Brigades in the Spanish Civil War.* Hoover Institution Publications. University Park: The Pennsylvania State University Press, 1967.

Joll, James. *The Anarchists.* London: Eyre & Spottiswoode, 1964.

Kaminski, H.E. *Ceux de Barcelone.* Paris: Denoël, 1937.

Keding, Karl. *Feldgeistlicher bei Legion Condor.* Berlin: Ostwerk, [1938?].

Kerillis, Henri de. *Français, voici la guerre!* Paris: Bernard Grasset, 1936.

Khrushchev, Nikita. *Speech at a Session of the 20th Congress of the Communist Party of the Soviet Union on 25 February 1956.* Washington, D.C.: U.S. Department of State, 1956.

Kirkpatrick, Ivone. *Mussolini: A Study in Power.* New York: Hawthorn Books, 1964.

Kirkpatrick, Jeane J., ed. *The Strategy of Deception.* New York: Farrar Straus, 1963.

Koestler, Arthur. *The Invisible Writing.* London: Collins with Hamish Hamilton, 1956.

Koltzov, Mijail [Mikhail]. *Diario de la guerra de España.* Paris: Editions Ruedo Ibérico, 1963.

Bibliography

_____. *Izbrannye proizvedeniia.* Vol. III, *Ispanskii Dnevnik.* Moscow: Gos. Izd-vo Khudozh. Lit-ry, 1957.

Kirstanov, Tsvetan. *Za svobodu Ispanii: Memuary bolgarskogo kommunista.* Moscow: Progress, 1969.

Krivitsky, Walter G. *In Stalin's Secret Service.* New York: Harper, 1939.

Kropp, Major A. *So kämpfen deutsche Soldaten.* Berlin: Wilhelm Limpert, 1939.

Kuznetsov, Nikolai G. *Na dalekom meridiane.* Moscow: Nauka, 1966.

Lacruz, Francisco. *El alzamiento, la revolución y el terror en Barcelona.* Barcelona: Librería Arysel, 1943.

Lambda. *The Truth about the Barcelona Events.* New York: Independent Communist League of New York, 1937.

Landau, Katia. *Le stalinisme en Espagne.* Paris: Spartacus, 1938.

The Land of Socialism Today and Tomorrow: Reports and Speeches at the Eighteenth Congress of the Communist Party of the Soviet Union (Bolshevik), March 10–21, 1939. Moscow: Foreign Languages Publishing House, 1939.

Langdon-Davies, John. *Behind the Spanish Barricades.* New York: Robert M. McBride, 1937.

Lapeyre, Aristide. *Le problème espagnol.* Paris: Edition ''Ce qu'il faut dire,'' 1946.

Lapeyre, Paul. *Révolution et contre-révolution en Espagne.* Paris: Spartacus, 1938.

Largo Caballero, Francisco. *Discurso pronunciado en Valencia el día 1 de febrero de 1937.* Valencia: Comisarido General de Guerra, 1937.

_____. *Discursos a los trabajadores.* Madrid: Gráfica Socialista, 1934.

_____. *Mis recuerdos: Cartas a un amigo.* Mexico: ''Alianza,'' 1954.

*_____. *¿Qué se puede hacer?* Paris, 1940.

_____. *La UGT y la guerra.* Valencia: Meabe, 1937.

Last, Jef. *The Spanish Tragedy.* London: Routledge, 1939.

Lazareff, Pierre. *Deadline.* New York: Random House, 1942.

Lazarillo de Tormes (Benigno Bejarano). *España, cuña de la libertad.* Valencia: ''Ebro,'' [1937?].

_____. *España, tumba del fascismo.* Valencia: Ediciones del Comité Nacional de la CNT, Sección Propaganda y Prensa, [1938?].

Lazitch, Branko, and Drachkovitch, Milorad M. *Biographical Dictionary of the Comintern.* Stanford: Hoover Institution, 1973.

Lent, Alfred. *Wir kämpften für Spanien.* Berlin: Gerhard Stalling, 1939.

Lerroux, Alejandro. *Mis memorias.* Madrid: Afrodisio Aguado, S.A., 1963.

_____. *La pequeña historia.* Madrid: Afrodisio Aguado, [1963?].

Lettre collective des evêques espagnols à ceux du monde entier à propos de la guerre en Espagne. Paris: n.p., 1937.

Leval, Gaston. *Le communisme.* Paris: Les Editions du Libertaire, n.d.

_____. *Espagne libertaire, 1936–39: L'oeuvre constructive de la révolution espagnole.* Meuse: Editions du Cercle, 1971.

_____. *L'indispensable révolution.* Paris: Editions du Libertaire, 1948.

_____. *Né Franco né Stalin: Le collettività anarchische spagnole nella lotta contro*

Bibliography

Franco e la reazione staliniana. Milan: Istituto Editoriale Italiano, 1952.

———. *Nuestro program de reconstrucción.* Barcelona: Oficinas de Propaganda, CNT-FAI, [1937?].

———. *Social Reconstruction in Spain.* London: Spain and the World, 1938.

Levine, Isaac Don. *The Mind of an Assassin.* New York: Straus and Cudahy, 1959.

Lévy, Louis. *Vérités sur la France.* Harmsworth, Middlesex, England: Editions Pingouin, 1941.

Liébana, José Manuel, and Orizana, G. *El movimiento nacional.* Valladolid: Cat. Francisco G. Vicente, n.d.

Linz, Juan. *The Party System of Spain: Past and Future.* New York: Free Press, 1967.

Líster, Enrique. *¡Basta!* N.p., [1971?].

———. *Nuestra guerra: Aportaciones para una historia de la guerra nacional revolucionaria del pueblo español, 1936–1939.* Paris: Librarie du Globe, 1966.

Lizarra, A. de. *Los vascos y la república española.* Buenos Aires: Vasca Ekin, S.R.L., 1944.

Lizarza Iribarren, Antonio de. *Memorias de la conspiración 1931–1936.* Pamplona: Gómez, 1969.

Lladó i Figueres, J. *El 19 de julio a Barcelona.* [Barcelona?]: Biblioteca política de Catalunya, 1938.

Llarch, Joan. *La Batalla del Ebro.* Barcelona: Aura, 1972.

Llovera, Fernando. *La comumna Uribarry.* Valencia: Turia, [1937?].

Lloyd, Lord [George Ambrose]. *The British Case.* London: Eyre & Spottiswoode, 1939.

Lojendio, Luis María de. *Operaciones militares de la guerra de España.* Barcelona: Montaner y Simón, 1940.

London, Arthur G. *L'aveu.* Paris: Gallimard, 1968.

———. *Espagne.* Paris: Français Réunis, 1966.

Londonderry, Marquess of. *Wings of Destiny.* London: Macmillan, 1943.

Longo, Luigi (Gallo). *Un anno di guerra in Spagna.* Paris: Edizioni di Coltura Sociale, 1938.

———. *Las brigadas internacionales en España.* Mexico City: Ediciones Era, 1966.

López, Juan. *Concepto del federalismo en la guerra y en la revolución.* [Barcelona?]: Oficinas de Propaganda CNT-FAI, n.d.

López Fernández, Captain Antonio. *Defensa de Madrid:* Mexico City: A.P. Márquez, 1945.

López-Muñiz, Lieutenant Colonel de E. M. *La batalla de Madrid.* Madrid: Gloria, 1943.

Lorenzo, César M. *Les anarchistes espagnole et pouvoir, 1868–1969.* Paris: Du Seuil, 1969.

Louzon, R. *La contra revolución en España.* Buenos Aires: Imán, 1938.

Macleod, Iain. *Neville Chamberlain.* London: Muller, 1961.

MacMillan, Harold. *Winds of Change, 1914–1939.* New York: Harper & Row, 1966.

Bibliography

Madariaga, Salvador de. *España*. Buenos Aires: Editorial Sudamericana, 1942.
———. *Españoles de mi tiempo*. Barcelona: Planeta, 1974.
———. *Spain: A Modern History*. New York: Praeger, 1960. Second Printing.
Maeztu, Ramiro de. *En vísperas de la tragedia*. Preface by José M. de Areilza. Madrid: Cultura Española, 1941.
Maidanik, K. L. *Ispanskii proletariat v natsionalno-revolutsionnoi voine, 1936–1937*. Moscow: Akademiia Nauk, 1960.
Maisky, Ivan M. *Iz istorii osvoboditelnoi borby ispanskogo naroda*. Moscow: Akademiia Nauk SSSR, 1959.
———. *Memoirs of a Soviet Amabassador. The War: 1939–43*. New York: Charles Scribner's Sons, 1968.
———. *Spanish Notebooks*. London: Hutchinson, 1966.
Malefakis, Edward E. *Agrarian Reform and Peasant Revolution in Spain: Origins of the Civil War*. New Haven: Yale University Press, 1970.
Manuel, Frank E. *The Politics of Modern Spain*. New York: McGraw-Hill, 1938.
Mario de Coca, Gabriel. *Anti-Caballero: Critica Marxista de la bolchevización del partido socialista, 1930–1936*. Madrid: Engels, 1936.
Martín, J. *La transformation politique et social de la Catalogne durant la révolution: 19 juillet–31 décembre, 1936*. [Barcelona?]: Generalitat de Catalunya, n.d.
Martín Blázquez, José. *I Helped to Build an Army*. London: Secker & Warburg, 1939.
Martín Retortillo, Cirilo. *Huesca vencedora*. Huesca: Campo, 1938.
Martínez Abad, Julio. *¡17 de julio! La guarnición de Melilla inicia la salvación de España*. Melilla: Artes Gráficas Postal Exprés, 1937.
Martínez Bande, Colonel José Manuel. *La campaña de Andalucía*. Monografías de la guerra de liberación. Madrid: Servicio Histórico Militar, 1969.
———. *La guerra en el norte*. Monografías de la guerra de España. Madrid: Servicio Histórico Militar, 1969.
———. *La intervención comunista en la guerra de España, 1936–1939*. Madrid: Servicio Informativo Español, 1965.
———. *La invasión de Aragón y el desembarco en Mallorca*. Monografías de la guerra de España. Madrid: Servicio Histórico Militar, 1970.
———. *La marcha sobre Madrid*. Monografías de la guerra de liberación. Madrid: Servicio Histórico Militar, 1968.
Martínez Barrio, Diego. *Orígenes del frente popular español*. Buenos Aires: PHAC, 1943.
———. *Páginas para la historia del frente popular*. Madrid-Valencia: Ediciones Españolas, 1937.
Martínez de Campos, Carlos. *Ayer, 1931–1953*. Madrid: Instituto de Estudios Políticos, 1970.
Martínez Leal, Commandant. *El asedio del Alcázar de Toledo*. Toledo: Editorial Católica Toledana, 1937.
Martínez Lorenzo, César. *See* Lorenzo, César M.
Martínez Prieto, Horacio. *See* Prieto, Horacio M.

Bibliography

Marty, André. *En Espagne . . . où se joue le destin de l'Europe.* Paris: Bureau d'Editions, 1937.

Mateu, Julio. *La obra de la federación campesina.* Barcelona: Partido Comunista de España, 1937.

Matthews, Herbert L. *The Education of a Correspondent.* New York: Harcourt, Brace, 1946.

_____. *Half of Spain Died: A Reappraisal of the Spanish Civil War.* New York: Charles Scribner's Sons, 1973.

_____. *Two Wars and More to Come.* New York: Carrick & Evans, 1938.

_____. *The Yoke and the Arrows.* New York: Braziller, 1961.

Mattioli, Guido. *L'aviazione legionaria in Spagna.* Rome: Editrice "L'Aviazione," 1938.

Maura, Miguel. *Así cayó Alfonso XIII.* Mexico City: Mañez, 1962.

Maurín, Joaquín. *Revolución y contrarevolución en España.* Paris: Ruedo Ibérico, 1966.

McGovern, John. *Terror in Spain.* London: Independent Labour Party, [1937?].

McGraw-Hill Encyclopedia of Russia and the Soviet Union. New York: McGraw-Hill, [1961].

Meaker, Gerald H. *The Revolutionary Left in Spain.* Stanford: Stanford University Press, 1974.

Melchor, Federico. *Organicemos la producción.* Valencia: JSU de España, 1937.

Mera, Cipriano. *Guerra, exilio y cárcel de un anarcosindicalista.* Paris: Ruedo Ibérico, 1976.

Mercier Vega, Luis. *Anarquismo, ayer y hoy.* Caracas: Monte Avila Editores C.A., 1970.

Meretskov, Kirill A. *Na sluzhbe narodu: stranitsy vospominaniia.* Moscow: Politizdat, 1968.

Merin, Peter. *Spain between Death and Birth.* New York: Dodge, 1938.

Micaud, Charles A. *The French Right and Nazi Germany, 1933–1939.* Durham, N.C.: Duke University Press, 1943.

Mieli, Renato. *Togliatti 1937.* Milan: Rizzoli, 1964.

Mije, Antonio. *El papel de los sindicatos en los momentos actuales.* Madrid-Valencia: Partido Comunista de España, 1937.

_____. *Por una potente industria de guerra.* Barcelona: Partido Comunista de España, 1937.

Milicia Popular: Diario del 5° regimiento de milicias populares. Preface by Vittorio Vidali. Milan: La Pietra, 1973.

Mintz, Frank. *L'autogestion dans l'Espagne révolutionnaire.* Paris: Bélibaste, 1970.

Miralles, Rafael. *Hacia dónde va Rusia?* Mexico City: Miralles, 1946.

Miravitlles, Juame. *Episodis de la guerra civil espanyola.* Barcelona: Pòrtic, 1972.

Modesto, Juan. *Soy del quinto regimiento.* Paris: Librairie du Globe, 1969.

Mola Vidal, Emilio. *Obras completas.* Valladolid: Santarén, 1940.

Molodoi Leningrad. Leningrad: Molodaia Gvardiia, 1957.

Montero, Antonio. *Historia de la persecución religiosa en España, 1936–1939.* Madrid: Biblioteca de Autores Cristianos, 1961.

Bibliography

Montiel, Francisco Félix. *Por qué he ingresado en el partido comunista.* Barcelona: Partido Comunista de España, Comisión Nacional de Agit-Prop, 1937.

Montseny, Federica. *La commune de Paris y la revolucion española. Conferencia pronunciada en el Cine Coliseum de Valencia el dia 14 de marzo de 1937.* [Barcelona?]: Oficina de Información, Propaganda y Prensa del Comité Nacional CNT-FAI, [1937?].

―――. *María Silva: La libertaria.* Toulouse: "Universo," 1951.

Mora, Constancia de la. *In Place of Splendor.* New York: Harcourt Brace, 1939.

Moreno, Admiral Francisco. *La guerra en el mar.* Barcelona: AHR, 1959.

Morón, Gabriel. *Política de ayer y política de mañana.* Mexico City: Talleres Linotipográficos "Numancia," 1942.

Morrow, Felix. *The Civil War in Spain.* New York: Pioneer Publishers, 1938.

―――. *Revolution and Counter-Revolution in Spain.* New York: Pioneer Publishers, 1938.

Moscardó, General José. *Diario del Alcázar.* Preface by Joaquín Arrarás. Madrid: Ibiza, 1943.

Munis, G. *Jalones de derrota: Promesa de victoria.* [*España 1930–39.*] Mexico City: "Lucha Obrera," 1948.

Muñoz, Máximo. *Dos conductas: Indalecio Prieto y yo.* Mexico City: Agosto, 1952.

Muñoz Diez, Manuel. *Marianet.* Mexico City: Ediciones CNT, 1960.

Namier, L. B. *Diplomatic Prelude, 1938–1939.* London: Macmillan, 1948.

―――. *Europe in Decay, 1936–1940.* London: Macmillan, 1950.

Negre, Juan. *¿Qué es el colectivismo anarquista?* Barcelona: Agrupación Anarquista, Los de Ayer y Los de Hoy, 1937.

Nenni, Pietro. *La guerre d'Espagne.* Paris: Maspero, 1960.

Nicholson Helen (Zglinitzki). *Death in the Morning.* London: Lovat Dickson, 1937.

Nin, Andrés. *La revolución de octubre de 1934, la alianza obrera y el frente popular.* Preface by Juan Andrade. Paris: La Batalla, 1970.

―――. *Los problemas de la revolución española.* Preface and compilation by Juan Andrade. Paris: Ruedo Ibérico, 1971.

986 jours de lutte: La guerre nationale révolutionnaire du peuple espagnol. Preface by François Billoux. Paris: Editions Sociales, 1962.

Nuestra lucha por la unidad. Valencia: J.S.U., [1937?].

Nuestro programa y el de la CNT. Valencia: Partido Comunista de España, 1937.

Nuñez Morgado, Aurelio. *Los sucesos de España vistos por un diplomático.* Buenos Aires: Rosso, 1941.

Ollivier, Marcel. *Les journées sanglantes de Barcelone.* Paris: Spartacus, [1937?].

Olmedo Delgado, Antonio, and Cuesta Monereo, Lieutenant General José. *General Queipo de Llano.* Barcelona: AHR, 1958.

Orlov, Alexander. *Handbook of Intelligence and Guerrilla Warfare.* Ann Arbor: University of Michigan Press, 1963.

―――. *The Secret History of Stalin's Crimes.* New York: Random House, 1953.

Ormesson, Wladimir d'. *France.* London: Longmans, Green, 1939.

Bibliography

Orwell, George. *Homage to Catalonia*. London : Secker & Warburg, 1938.

Ossorio y Gallardo, Angel. *Discursos pronunciados los días 25 de agosto y 6 de septiembre de 1936 respectivamente*. Madrid: Socorro Rojo Internacional, 1936.

_____. *Mis memorias*. Buenos Aires: Losada, 1946.

_____. *Vida y sacrificio de Companys*. Buenos Aires: Losada, 1943.

Pacciardi, Randolfo. *Il battaglione garibaldi*. Lugano: Nuove Edizioni di Capolago, 1938.

Pagès, Pelai. *Andreu Nin: Su evolución política, 1911–1937*. Bilboa: Zero, 1975.

Palacio, Solano. *La tragedia del norte*. Barcelona: "Tierra y Libertad," 1938.

Palacio Atard, Vicente, ed. *Cuadernos bibliográficos de la guerra de España, 1936–1939: Memorias*. Madrid: Universidad de Madrid, 1967.

Pamies, Teresa. *Una española llamada Dolores Ibárruri*. Mexico City: Roca, 1975.

El partido comunista por la libertad y la independencia de España: Llamamientos y discursos. Valencia: Ediciones del P.C. de E. (S.E. de la I.C.), Comisión Nacional de Agitación y Propaganda, 1937.

El partido comunista y la unidad antifascista. Valencia: Sección de Prensa y Propaganda del Comité Peninsular de la FAI, 1937.

Payne, Robert. *The Civil War in Spain, 1936–1939*. New York: Putnam's, 1962.

Payne, Stanley G. *Falange*. Stanford: Stanford University Press, 1961.

_____. *Politics and the Military in Modern Spain*. Stanford: Stanford University Press, 1967.

_____. *The Spanish Revolution*. New York: Norton, 1970.

Paz, Abel. *Durruti*. Paris: Tête de Feuilles, 1972.

Peers, E. Allison. *Catalonia Infelix*. London: Methuen, 1937.

_____. *Spain, the Church and the Orders*. London: Eyre and Spottiswoode, 1939.

_____. *The Spanish Tragedy*. New York: Oxford University Press, 1937.

Peirats, José. *Los anarquistas en la crisis política española*. Buenos Aires: Alfa, 1964.

_____. *La CNT en la revolución española*. Vols. I, II, III. Toulouse: C.N.Y., 1951, 1952, and 1953.

Peiró, Juan. *Perill a la reraguarda*. Preface by Julià Gual. Mataró: Libertat, n.d.

_____. *Problemas del sindicalismo y del anarquismo*. Toulouse: E.M.L.E., 1945.

_____. *Problemas y cintarazos*. Preface by Domingo Torres. Rennes: Imprimeries Réunies, 1946.

Penchienati, Carlo. *Brigate internazionali in Spagna: Delitti della "Ceka" comunista*. Milan: Edizioni "Echi del Secolo," 1950.

Pérez-Baró, Albert. *30 mesos de col·lectivisme a Catalunya*. Barcelona: Ariel, 1970.

Pérez Madrigal, Joaquín. *Augurios, estallido y episodios de la guerra civil*. Avila: Sigirano Díaz, 1938.

Pérez Salas, Colonel Jesús. *Guerra en España, 1936–1939*. Preface by Colonel D. Mariano Salafranca. Mexico City: Imprenta Grafos, 1947.

Pérez Solis, Oscar. *Sitio y defensa de Oviedo*. Valladolid-Palencia: Afrodisio Aguado. 1938.

Bibliography

La persécution religieuse en Espagne. Paris: Plon, 1937.

Pike, David Wingeate. *Conjecture, Propaganda, and Deceit and the Spanish Civil War.* Stanford: California Institute of International Studies, 1968.

──────. *La crise espagnole de 1936: Vu par la presse française.* Toulouse: Université de Toulouse, 1966.

──────. *Les français et la guerre d'Espagne, 1936–1939.* Paris: Presses Universitaires de France. 1975.

Pi Sunyer, Carles. *La república y la guerra: Memorias de un político catalan.* Mexico City: Oasis, 1975.

Plá, José. *Historia de la segunda república española.* Vol. IV. Barcelona: Destino, 1941.

Pod znamenem ispanskoi respubliki, 1936–1939: Vospominaniia sovetskikh dobrovoltsev-uchastnikov. Moscow: Izdatelstvo Nauka, 1965.

Política del frente popular en agricultura. Madrid-Valencia: Españolas, 1937.

Ponce, Anibal. *Examen de la España actual.* Montevideo: Ediciones "Mundo," 1938.

Por la revolución agraria. Madrid: Federación Española de Trabajadores de la Tierra, UGT, 1937.

Pozharskaia, Svetlana Petrovna. *Sotsialisticheskaia rabochaia partiia Ispanii, 1931–1939.* Moscow: Nauka, 1966.

Prader, Jean. *Au secours de l'Espagne socialiste.* Paris: Spartacus, 1936.

Prats, Alardo. *Vanguardia y retaguardia de Aragón.* Buenos Aires: Perseo, 1938.

Prieto, Horacio M. *El anarquismo español en la lucha política.* Paris: N.p., 1946.

──────. *Marxismo y socialismo libertario.* Paris: Ediciones Madrid, n.d.

──────. *Posibilismo libertario.* Val-de-Marne, France: Gondoles, 1966.

Prieto, Indalecio. *Cómo y por qué salí del ministerio de defensa nacional.* Mexico City: Impresos y Papeles, 1940. Also French edition, Paris: Imprimerie Nouvelle, 1939.

──────. *Convulsiones de España.* Vols. I, II, III. Mexico City: Oasis, 1967.

──────. *De mi vida.* Mexico City: Ediciones "El Sitio," 1965.

──────. *Discursos fundamentales.* Preface by Edward Malefakis. Madrid: Turner, 1975.

──────. *Inauguración del círculo "Pablo Iglesias" de México.* Mexico City: n.p., 1940.

──────. *Palabras al viento.* Mexico City: Ediciones Minerva, 1942.

Primo de Rivera, José Antonio. *Discursos frente al parlamento.* Barcelona: F.E., 1939.

Programa de acción común para la creación del partido único del proletariado. Valencia: Partido Comunista de España, 1937.

Programa de unidad de acción entre UGT-CNT. Barcelona: Españolas, 1938.

Prominent Personalities in the USSR. Metuchen, N.J.: Scarecrow Press, 1968.

Propaganda y cultura en los frentes de guerra. Valencia: Ministerio de la Guerra, Comisariado General de Guerra, 1937.

Prudhommeaux, A., and Prudhommeaux, D. *Catalogne libertaire, 1936–1937: L'armement du peuple. Que sont la CNT et la FAI?* Paris: Spartacus, 1946.

Bibliography

Puente, Isaac. *Finalidad de la CNT: El comunismo libertario.* Barcelona: "Tierra y Libertad," 1936.

―――. *Propaganda.* Barcelona: "Tierra y Libertad," 1938.

Puig Mora, E. (El Ciudadano Desconocido.) *La tragedia roja en Barcelona.* Saragossa: Librería General, 1937.

Puzzo, Dante A. *Spain and the Great Powers, 1936–1941.* New York: Columbia University Press, 1962.

Queipo de Llano, Rosario. *De la cheka de Atadell a la prisión de Alacuas.* Valladolid: Santarén, 1939.

Quintanilla, Luis. *Los rehenes del Alcázar de Toledo: Testimonios 2.* Paris: Ruedo Ibérico, 1967.

Rabasseire, Henri [Henry M. Pachter]. *Espagne: creuset politique.* Paris: Fustier, 1938.

Rama, Carlos M. *La crisis española del siglo XX.* Mexico City: Fondo de Cultura Económica, 1960.

Ramos Oliveira, Antonio. *Politics, Economics and Men of Modern Spain, 1808–1946.* London: Gollancz, 1946.

Ravines, Eudocio. *La gran estafa.* Mexico City: Libros y Revistas, 1952.

Raymundo, Francisco J. de. *Cómo se inició el glorioso movimiento nacional en Valladolid y la gesta heroica del Alto del León.* Valladolid: Imprenta Católica, 1936.

La reforma agraria en España. Valencia: Instituto de Reforma Agraria, 1937.

La reforma agraria y los problemas del campo bajo la república española. Buenos Aires: Servicio Español de Información, "Prensa Hispánica," [1938?].

Regler, Gustav. *The Great Crusade.* New York: Longmans, Green, 1940.

―――. *The Owl of Minerva: The Autobiography of Gustav Regler.* London: Rupert Hart-Davis, 1959.

Renn, Ludwig. *Der spanische Krieg.* Berlin: Aufbau, 1956.

Reparaz y Tresgallo de Souza, Captain [Antonio]. *Desde el cuartel general de Miaja, al santuario de la Virgen de la Cabeza.* Valladolid: Afrodisio Aguado, 1937.

La révolution espagnole, 1936–1939. Supplément à "Etudes Marxistes" No. 7–8. Paris: Etudes Marxistes, 1969.

Reynaud, Paul. *La France a sauvé l'Europe.* Vol. I. Paris: Flammarion, 1947.

Richards, Vernon. *Lessons of the Spanish Revolution, 1936–1939.* London: Freedom Press, 1953. Also revised edition published in 1972.

Rieger, Max. *Espionnage en Espagne.* Preface by José Bergamin. Paris: Denoël, 1938.

Rivas-Xerif, Cipriano de. *Retrato de un desconocido: Vida de Manuel Azaña.* Mexico City: Oasis, 1961.

Robinson, Richard A. H. *The Origins of Franco's Spain: The Right, the Republic and Revolution, 1931–1936.* Newton Abbott: David & Charles, 1970.

Rocker, Rudolf. *Anarcho-Syndicalism.* London: Secker & Warburg, 1938.

―――. *Extranjeros en España.* Buenos Aires: Realidades Ibéricas, Imán, 1938.

Rodríguez de Cueto, José. *Epopeya del santuario de Santa María de la Cabeza.* San Sebastian: Editorial Española, 1939.

Bibliography

Rojas, Carlos. *Por qué perdimos la guerra: Antología de testimonios de los vencidos en la contienda civil.* Barcelona: Nauta, 1970.

Rojo, General Vicente. *¡Alerta los pueblos! Estudio político-militar del período final de la guerra española.* Buenos Aires: López, 1939.

――――. *Así fué la defensa de Madrid.* Mexico City: Era, 1967.

――――. *España heroica.* Buenos Aires: Editorial Americalee, 1942.

Rolfe, Edwin. *The Lincoln Battalion.* New York: Random House, 1939.

Romano, Julio. *Sanjurjo.* Madrid: Imprenta de la Viuda de Juan Pueyo, 1940.

Romero, Colonel Luis. *Impresiones de un militar republicano.* Barcelona: Oficinas de Propaganda CNT-FAI, [1937?].

Romero, Luis. *El final de la guerra.* Barcelona: Ariel, 1976.

――――. *Tres días de julio: 18, 19 y 20 de 1936.* Barcelona: Ariel, 1967.

Romero Solano, Luis. *Vísperas de la guerra de España.* Prologue by Indalecio Prieto. Mexico City: El Libro Perfecto, 1947.

Romilly, Esmond. *Boadilla.* London: Hamish Hamilton, 1937.

Rosal, Amaro del. *Historia de la U.G.T. de España, 1901–1939.* Vol. II. Barcelona: Grijalbo, 1977.

――――. *El oro del banco de España y la historia del Vita.* Barcelona: Grijalbo, 1977.

Rosselli, Carlo. *Oggi in Spagna, domani in Italia.* Paris: Edizioni di giustizia i libertà, 1938.

Roux, Georges. *La guerre civile d'Espagne.* Paris: Fayard, 1963.

Rubashkin, A. *Mikhail Koltsov.* Leningrad: Khudozhestvennaia Literatura, 1971.

Rubió i Tudurí, Mariano. *La justicia en Cataluña: 19 de julio de 1936–19 de febrero de 1937.* Paris: n.p., 1937.

Ruediger, Helmut. *Ensayo crítico sobre la revolución española.* Buenos Aires: Realidades Ibéricas, Imán, 1940.

Ruiz Vilaplana, Antonio. *Burgos Justice: A Year's Experience of Nationalist Spain.* London: Constable, 1938.

Russkie sovetskii pisateli-prozaiki. Vols. I, II, III, IV. Leningrad: Publichnaia Biblioteka, 1959–66.

Rust, William. *Britons in Spain.* London: Lawrence and Wishart, 1939.

Saborit, Andrés. *Asturias y sus hombres.* Toulouse: Imprimerie Dulaurier, 1964.

――――. *Julián Besteiro: Figuras del socialismo español.* Mexico City: Impresiones Modernas, S.A., 1961.

Sáenz, Vicente. *España en sus gloriosas jornadas de julio y agosto de 1936.* San José, Costa Rica: "La Tribuna," 1936.

――――. *España heroica.* New York: Iberoamericana, 1938.

Salas Larrazábal, Ramón. *Historia del ejército popular de la república.* Vols. I, II, III, IV. Madrid: Editora Nacional, 1973.

Sánchez del Arco, Manuel. *El sur de España en la reconquista de Madrid.* Seville: Sevillana, 1937.

Sanz, Ricardo. *Buenaventura Durruti.* Toulouse: "El Frente," 1945.

――――. *Los que fuimos a Madrid: Columna Durruti 26 Division.* Toulouse: Dulaurier, 1969.

Bibliography

_____. El sindicalismo y la política: Los "solidarios" y "nosotros." Toulouse: Dulaurier, 1966.

Schapiro, Leonard B. *The Communist Party of the Soviet Union.* London: Eyre & Spottiswoode, 1960.

Schempp, Otto. *Das autoritäre Spanien.* Leipzig: Wilhelm Goldmann, 1939.

Schlayer, Felix. *Diplomat im roten Madrid.* Berlin: Herbig, 1938.

Seco Serrano, Carlos. *Historia de España: Gran historia general de los pueblos hispanos.* Vol. VI. Barcelona: Instituto Gallach de Librería y Ediciones, 1962.

Sedwick, Frank. *The Tragedy of Manuel Azaña and the Fate of the Spanish Republic.* Columbus: Ohio State University Press, 1963.

Segundo congreso del partido socialista obrero español en el exilio. Toulouse: P.S.O.E., 1946.

Semprun-Maura, Carlos. *Revolution et contre-revolution en Catalogne.* Tours: Mame, 1974.

Serge, Victor. *Mémoires d'un révolutionnaire.* Paris: Seuil, 1951.

Serrano Poncela, Segundo. *La conferencia nacional de juventudes.* Valencia: JSU de España, 1937.

Serrano Suñer, Ramón. *Entre Hendaya y Gibraltar: Frente a una leyenda.* Madrid: Ediciones y Publicaciones Españolas, S.A., 1947.

Sevilla Andrés, Diego. *Historia política de la zona roja.* Madrid: Rialp, 1963.

Siete de octubre: Una nueva era en el campo. Madrid: Ministerio de Agricultura, 1936.

Silva, José. *La revolución popular en el campo.* [Valencia?]: Partido Comunista de España, [1937?].

Solano, Wilebaldo. *The Spanish Revolution: The Life of Andrés Nin.* London: Independent Labour Party, [1972?].

Sommerfield, John. *Volunteer in Spain.* New York: Knopf, 1937.

Somoza Silva, Lázaro. *El General Miaja: Biografía de un heroe.* Mexico City: Tyris, 1944.

Soria, Georges. *Trotskyism in the Service of Franco.* London: Lawrence and Wishart, [1937?].

Souchère, Eléna de la. *An Explanation of Spain.* New York: Random House, 1964.

Souchy, Agustín. *Entre los campesinos de Aragón.* Barcelona: Tierra y Libertad, [1937?].

_____. *El socialismo libertario.* Havana: Editorial Estudios, 1950.

_____. *The Tragic Week in May.* Barcelona: Oficina de Información Exterior de la CNT-FAI, 1937.

_____. *La verdad sobre los sucesos en la retaguardia leal.* Buenos Aires: F.A.C.A., 1937.

Southworth, Herbert Rutledge. *El mito de la cruzada de Franco.* Paris: Ruedo Ibérico, 1963.

_____. *Le mythe de la croisade de Franco.* Paris: Ruedo Ibérico, 1964. Revised edition of Spanish text.

Sovetskie pisateli. Vol. I. Moscow: Gos. Izd-vo Khudozh. Lit-ry, 1959.

Bibliography

The Soviet Diplomatic Corps, 1917–1967. Compiled by the Institute for the Study of the USSR, Munich. Metuchen, N.J.: Scarecrow Press, 1970.

Los Soviets en España: La lucha por el poder, por la república obrera y campesina en España. Paris: Sudam, 1935.

Stache, Rud. *Armee mit geheimen Auftrag.* Bremen: Henry Burmester, n.d.

Stackelberg, Karl-George von. *Legion Condor: Deutsche Freiwillige in Spanien.* Berlin: Die Heimbücherei, 1939.

Stalin, J. V. *Sochineniia*, VII. Moscow: Institut Marksa-Engelsa-Lenina pri TSK VKP (b), 1947.

Steer, G. L. *The Tree of Gernika.* London: Hodder and Stoughton, 1938.

Strong, Anna Louise. *Spain in Arms, 1937.* New York: Henry Holt, 1937.

Suárez, Andrés. *El proceso contra el POUM.* Paris. Ruedo Ibérico, 1974.

Los sucesos de Barcelona. Valencia: Ebro, 1937.

Los sucesos de mayo en Barcelona. New York: Federación Local de Grupos Libertarios, n.d.

Symons, Julian. *The Thirties: A Dream Revolved.* London: Cresset, 1960.

Tabouis, Geneviève. *Blackmail or War.* England: Penguin Books, Ltd., 1938.

————. *Ils l'ont appelée Cassandre.* New York: Editions de la Maison Française, 1942.

Tagüeña Lacorte, Manuel. *Testimonio de dos guerras.* Mexico City: Oasis, 1974.

Tasis i Marca, Rafael. *La revolución en los ayuntamientos.* Paris: "Associación Hispanophile de France," 1937.

Taylor, A. J. P. *The Origins of the Second World War.* London: Hamilton, 1961.

Tedeschi, Paolo. *Guadalajara.* Paris: Edizioni di Coltura Sociale, 1937.

Téry, Simone. *Front de la liberté.* Paris: Editions Sociales Internationales, 1938.

Thalmann, Clara, and Thalmann, Paul. *Revolution für die Freiheit.* Hamburg: Verlag Association GMBH, 1976.

Thomas, Hugh. *The Spanish Civil War.* London: Eyre & Spottiswoode, 1961.

————. *The Spanish Civil War.* Revised edition. Harmondsworth, England: Penguin Books, 1965.

Three Years of Struggle in Spain. London: Freedom Press, 1939.

Togliatti, Palmiro. *Escritos políticos.* Prologue by Adolfo Sánchez Vázquez. Mexico City: Era, 1971.

Torriente Brau, Pablo de la. *Peleando con los milicianos.* Mexico City: "México Nuevo," 1938.

Toryho, Jacinto. *La independencia de España.* Barcelona: Tierra y Libertad, 1938.

————. *La traición del Señor Azaña.* New York: Federación Libertaria, 1939.

Trautloft, Hannes. *Als Jagdflieger in Spanien.* Berlin: Nauch, n.d.

Trotsky, Léon. *Escritos sobre España.* Paris: Ruedo Ibérico, 1971.

————. *Leçon d'Espagne.* Paris: Pionniers, 1946.

————. *La révolution espagnole 1930–36.* Texts assembled, presented, and annotated by Pierre Broué. Paris: Editions de Minuit, 1975.

Tschapaiew: Das Bataillon der 21 Nationen. Madrid: Torrent, 1938.

Uhse, Bodo. *Die erste Schlacht.* Strasbourg: Editions Prométhée, 1938.

Umeste s patriotami ispanii. Kiev: Politicheskaia Literatura, 1976.

Bibliography

Urales, Federico. *La anarquía al alcance de todos*. Barcelona: Revista Blanca, 1932.

Uribarry Barutell, Manuel. *Sin contestar*. Valencia: Ruig, 1937.

Uribe, Vicente. *Los campesinos y la república*. Valencia: Partido Comunista de España, n.d.

————. *Nuestra labor en el campo*. Barcelona: Partido Comunista de España, 1937.

————. *Nuestros hermanos los campesinos*. Valencia: Partido Comunista de España, 1937.

————. *La política agraria del partido comunista*. Valencia: Partido Comunista de España, 1937.

U.S. Senate Internal Security Subcommittee. *The Legacy of Alexander Orlov*. Washington, D.C.: U.S. Government Printing Office, 1973.

Valdés, Miguel. *Informe presentado en la primera conferencia nacional del partido socialista unificado de cataluña, (I.C.) por el secretario de organizacion del c.c.* Barcelona: Secretariado de Agitación y Propaganda del PSUC, [1937?].

Valdesoto, Fernando de. *Francisco Franco*. Madrid: Afrodisio Aguado, 1943.

Válgoma, Carlos de la. *Mola*. Madrid: Pace, n.d.

Vallescà, Luhi. *Lluis Companys Jover*. Mexico City: n.p., 1944.

Vanni, Ettore. *Yo, comunista en Rusia*. Barcelona: Destino, 1950.

Varga, Evgenii S. *Ispaniia v revoluitsii*. Moscow: Gos. Sots.-Ekon. Izd-vo, 1936.

La victoria exije el partido único del proletariado. Valencia: Partido Comunista de España. 1937.

Vidali, Vittorio. *Spagna lunga battaglia*. Milan: Vangelista, 1975.

Vidarte, Juan-Simeón. *Todos fuimos culpables*. Mexico City: Fondo de Cultura Económica, 1973.

Vigón, General Jorge. *General Mola: El conspirador*. Barcelona: AHR, 1957.

————. *Milicia y política*. Madrid: Instituto de Estudios Políticos, 1957.

Villanueva, Francisco. *Azaña, el gobierno*. Mexico City: Moderna, 1941.

Villar, Manuel. *España en la ruta de la libertad*. Buenos Aires: Reconstruir, 1962.

Viñas Martín, Angel. *La alemania nazi y el 18 de julio*. Madrid: Alianza, 1977.

————. Manuscript on Spanish gold to be published by Ediciones Grijalbo in the fall of 1978. Title, as yet, undecided. (See chapter 9, no. 30.)

————. *El oro español en la guerra civil*. Madrid: Instituto de Estudios Fiscales. Ministerio de Hacienda, 1976.

Vita, A. de. *Battaglione garibaldi, Ottobre 1936–Aprile 1937*. Paris: Edizione di Coltura Sociale, 1937.

Weintraub, Stanley. *The Last Great Cause: The Intellectuals and the Spanish Civil War*. New York: Weybright and Talley, 1968.

Weizsäcker, Ernst von. *Memoirs of Ernst von Weizsäcker*. Chicago: Regnery, 1951.

Welles, Sumner. *The Time for Decision*. New York: Harper, 1944.

Werth, Alexander. *Which Way France?* New York and London: Harper, 1937.

Who Was Who in the USSR. Metuchen, N.J.: Scarecrow Press, 1972.

Bibliography

Wintringham, Tom. *English Captain*. London: Faber and Faber, 1939.
Wolfe, Bertram D. *Civil War in Spain*. New York: Workers' Age, 1937.
_____. *Khrushchev and Stalin's Ghost*. New York: Praeger, 1957.
Woodcock, George. *Anarchism: A History of Libertarian Ideas and Movements*. Cleveland: World Publishing Company, 1962.
Yakovlev, Alexander. *The Aim of a Lifetime*. Moscow: Progress, 1972.
Ypsilon. (pseud. Julian Gumperz and Robert Rindl.) *Pattern for World Revolution*. Chicago-New York: Ziff Davis, 1947.
Zilmanovich, Dmitrii Iakovlevich. *Na orbite bolshoi zhizni: Dokumentalnomemuarnoe povestvovanie o Dvazhdy Geroe Sovetskogo Soiuza Ia. V. Smushkeviche*. Vilnius: Mintis, 1971.
Zugazagoitia, Julián. *Historia de la guerra en España*. Buenos Aires: La Vanguardia, 1940.

II. Documents, Microfilm, and Miscellaneous Materials

This list includes documents and miscellaneous items referred to in the text or in the notes or used in the construction of this volume. Unless otherwise stated they can be found in the Bolloten Spanish Civil War Collection housed in the library or archives of the Hoover Institution on War, Revolution and Peace, Stanford University.

Actas de la junta de defensa de Madrid. (The Library of Congress.)
Actas del congreso regional de sindicatos de Levante celebrado en Alicante, en el Teatro Verano, los días 15, 16, 17, 18 y 19 de julio de 1937. Valencia: Publicaciones de la Confederación Regional del Trabajo de Levante, 1937. Photographic reproduction.
Actas del pleno regional de grupos celebrado los días 1, 2 y 3 mes de julio de 1937. *Federación regional de grupos anarquistas de Cataluña*. [Barcelona?]: Federación Anarquista Ibérica, Comité Peninsular Prensa y Propaganda, 1937.
La agresión italiana: Documentos ocupados a las unidades italianas en la acción de Guadalajara. Valencia: Ministerio de Estado, 1937.
Aguirre y Lecube, José Antonio de. Report to the central government by José Antonio Aguirre, premier of the autonomous Basque government. Microfilm copy of the first ninety-five pages of this report loaned to Burnett Bolloten by Manuel de Irujo.
Aiguadé, Jaime Anton. "Actuació del Govern de la Generalitat i del seu President Lluis Companys durant les Jornades de Maig de 1937." Copy of document loaned to Burnett Bolloten by Jordi Arquer.
"Los Amigos de Durruti." File containing three letters to Burnett Bolloten from Jaime Balius, vice-secretary of the Friends of Durruti, and a photostatic copy of typewritten data compiled by Jordi Arquer on this dissident anarchist organization.
Amsden, Jon. "Krivitsky." Typescript.

Bibliography

Les archives secrètes de la Wilhelmstrasse. Vol. I, *De Neurath a Ribbentrop. Septembre 1937–Septembre 1938*. Documents translated from German by Michel Tournier. Paris: Plon, 1950.

Azaña-Prieto teletyped messages. Tapes of messages exchanged between Prieto and Azaña during the May events in Barcelona, 3–7 May 1937. Microfilm copy.

Barcelona Traction, Light, and Power Company, Limited. Statements issued on 3 September and 16 November 1936. (Public Library of Toronto.)

Bolloten, Burnett. Dispatch from Valencia to the United Press. Excerpts from Largo Caballero's unpublished statement to British Members of Parliament on 4 December 1936.

Causa general: La dominación roja en Espana. Madrid: Dirección General de Información. Publicaciones Españolas, 1961. (The mass lawsuit brought by the nationalist government.)

Cierva y de Hoces, Ricardo de la. *Los documentos de la primavera trágica: Análisis documental de los antecedentes immediatos del 18 de julio de 1936*. Madrid: Ministerio de Información y Turismo, Secretaría General Técnica, 1967.

Clippings from newspapers, periodicals, and government publications listed in the Bibliography, III, and cited in Bolloten, *The Grand Camouflage*, and present volume.

Collectivisations: L'oeuvre constructive de la révolution espagnole, 1936–1939. Recueil de documents. Foreword by A. Souchy. Place of publication not indicated, n.d.

Communist International Executive Committee. *XIII Plenum IKKI. Stenograficheskii Otchet*. Moscow: Communist International, 1934.

Companys, Luis. "Notes and Documents on the Fighting in Barcelona, 3–7 May 1937." Carbon copy of original material given to the author by Ricardo del Río, director of the Febus news agency. It came into the possession of Ricardo del Río through Francisco Aguirre, director of *El Día Gráfico*, Barcelona, who received it from Companys.

Congress of the Valencia CNT, November 1936. Bound collection of clippings taken from *Fragua Social*, organ of the CNT, Valencia.

Deutschland und der Spanische Bürgerkrieg, 1936–1939. Akten zur Deutschen Auswärtigen Politik, 1918–1945. Serie D., 1937–1945. Vol. III. Baden-Baden: Imprimerie Nationale, 1951.

Díaz-Plaja, Fernando. *La historia de España en sus documentos. El Siglo XX. Dictadura . . . República, 1923–1936*. Madrid: Instituto de Estudios Políticos, 1964.

———. *La historia de España en sus documentos: La guerra, 1936–1939*. Madrid: Gráficas Faro, 1963.

Documents and Materials Relating to the Eve of the Second World War. Vols. I, II. *Dirksen Papers, 1938–1939*. Moscow: Ministry of Foreign Affairs of the U.S.S.R. Foreign Languages Publishing House, 1948.

Documents on German Foreign Policy, 1918–1945. Series D. Vol. III. See U.S. Department of State. (Stanford University Library.)

Bibliography

Duque, José. "La situación de Aragón al comienzo de la guerra." Unpublished manuscript given to the author by José Duque.

Les événements survenus en France de 1933 à 1945: Temoignages et documents recueillis par la commission d'enquête parlementaire. Vol. I. Paris: Presses Universitaires de France, n.d.

Fernández Ballesteros, Alberto. Reports to the General Commissariat of War, dated 18 Feb. and 12 Mar. 1937. Typewritten copies of original documents loaned to the author by Gabriel García Maroto, subcommissar general of propaganda.

Gates, John. Twelve pages of unpublished commentary on Verle B. Johnston's manuscript, "The International Brigades in the Spanish Civil War, 1936–1939."

International Military Tribunal. *The Trial of German Major War Criminals.* Parts IX and X. London: His Majesty's Stationery Office, 1947.

Interviews. Transcripts of shorthand notes taken during Burnett Bolloten's interviews with some of the leading Civil War participants, 1936–45. (Sealed until released by author.)

Irujo, Manuel de. "La guerra civil en Euzkadi antes del estatuto." Microfilm copy of this unpublished work loaned to Burnett Bolloten by Manuel de Irujo.

Johnston, Verle B. "The International Brigades in the Spanish Civil War." Xerox copy of original manuscript published by Pennsylvania State University Press in conjunction with the Hoover Institution under the title of *Legions of Babel.* The manuscript contains a considerable amount of amplifying and qualifying material, which was eliminated from the published version.

Lamoneda, Ramón, secretary of the Spanish Socialist party. Carbon copy of letter to a member of the party.

Lazarillo de Tormes (Benigno Bejarano). "Les morts ne vous pardonnent pas." Photographic reproduction of some of the pages of this unpublished work loaned to the author by José Peirats.

The Legacy of Alexander Orlov. See U.S. Congress.

Letters exchanged between Burnett Bolloten and participants in the conflict. (Sealed until released by author.)

Le livre blanc de l'intervention italienne en Espagne. Paris: Comite Franco-Espagnol, 1937.

Memoria del congreso extraordinario celebrado en Madrid los días 11 al 16 de junio de 1931: Confederación Nacional del Trabajo. Barcelona: Cosmos, n.d. Photographic reproduction.

Memoria del congreso extraordinario de la confederación regional del trabajo de Cataluña celebrado en Barcelona los días 25 de febrero al 3 de marzo de 1937. Barcelona: Talleres Gráficos Juan, 1937. Photographic reproduction.

Memoria del Peninsular de Regionales. FAI. Celebrado en Valencia los días 4, 5, 6 y 7 de julio, 1937. Valencia: n.p., 1937.

Memoria del pleno regional de grupos anarquistas de Levante celebrado en Alicante, durante los días 11, 12, 13, 14 y 15 del mes de abril de 1937: Federación Anarquista Ibérica. Valencia: Editorial "Nosotros," [1937?]. Photographic reproduction.

Miaja, General José. Communication sent to Largo Caballero, dated 1 May 1937. A copy of this document, signed by Miaja and by the political and military chiefs of the Army of the Center, is in the Library of Congress.

Microfilm collection of newspapers, periodicals, government publications, books, pamphlets, and documents comprising 7,250 items.

Milton, Harry. Copies of his correspondence with Léon Trotsky and George Kopp.

"Ministry of the National Defense: Documents on Battle for Teruel." Confidential reports on the progress of the republican offensive against Teruel, 31 December 1937–8 January 1938, by defense minister Indalecio Prieto. These copies were given to Burnett Bolloten by Francisco Giner de los Ríos, son of the minister of communications.

Miscellaneous Documents. Vols. I, II, III, IV. These consist of typewritten copies of directives and reports by political commissars and military leaders, manifestos and articles, as well as original passes by revolutionary organizations. The original directives and reports were loaned to Burnett Bolloten by Vittorio Vidali (Carlos Contreras).

Nazi-Soviet Relations, 1939–1941. See U.S. Department of State. (Stanford University Library.)

Negrín, Juan, and Prieto, Indalecio. Carbon copies of unpublished letters exchanged between the two Socialist leaders in June 1939.

Orlov, Alexander. "Answers to the questionnaire of Professor Stanley G. Payne," 1 April 1968.

Padelford, Norman J. *International Law and Diplomacy in the Spanish Civil Strife.* New York: Macmillan, 1939.

Río, Ricardo del, director of the Febus news agency. Unpublished report on the political and military situation in Catalonia during the last few months of the war.

Rio Tinto Company Limited: Report of the Transactions at the Sixty-Third Ordinary General Meeting. London: Rio Tinto Company Limited, 24 April 1936.

Ruediger, Helmut. *Informe para el congreso extraordinario de la AIT, el día 6 de diciembre de 1937.* Paris, 1937. (University of Michigan Library, Labadie Collection.)

———. Report to the AIT dated 8 May 1937.

Salas Larrazábal, Ramón. *Historia del ejército popular de la república.* Vols. I, II, III, IV. Madrid: Editora Nacional, 1973. This work is based on a large number of hitherto unpublished documents, which Salas Larrazábal was able to consult in the Archivo Histórico Militar, Archivo de la Dirección de Servicios Documentales, Archivo del Estado Mayor del Aire, and Archivos Generales Militar y del Aire.

Schwartzmann, Manuel. "La Naissance et l'Activité de la D.E.C.A. en Espagne." Three unpublished manuscripts, given to the author by

Bibliography

Schwartzmann, who worked under Russian direction in the antiaircraft defense and war industries in the republican zone.

Scope of Soviet Activity in the United States. See U.S. Congress.

Solano, Wilebaldo. "Notas sobre el POUM en la Revolución de 1936: El Período de Clandestinidad." Copy of typescript.

U.S. Congress. Senate. Committee on the Judiciary. *The Legacy of Alexander Orlov.* Prepared by the Subcommittee to Investigate the Administration of the Internal Security Act. 93d Cong., 1st sess., 1973. Washington D.C.: U.S. Government Printing Office, 1973.

――――. *Scope of Soviet Activity in the United States.* Hearings before the Subcommittee to Investigate the Administration of the Internal Security Act. 85th Cong., 1st sess., 1957, 14 and 15 February 1957. Part 51. Washington, D.C.: U.S. Government Printing Office, 1957. (Stanford University Library.)

U.S. Department of State. *Documents on German Foreign Policy, 1918–1945.* Series D. Vol. III, *Germany and the Spanish Civil War, 1936–1939.* Washington D.C.: U.S. Government Printing Office, 1950. (Stanford University Library.)

――――. *Foreign Relations of the United States: Diplomatic Papers, 1936 and 1937.* Vols. I, II. Washington, D.C.: U.S. Government Printing Office, 1954. (Stanford University Library.)

――――. *Nazi-Soviet Relations, 1939–1941: Documents from the Archives of the German Foreign Office,* ed. Ramond James Sontag and James Stuart Biddie. Washington D.C.: U.S. Government Printing Office, 1948. (Stanford University Library.)

"Unpublished Article by a Regular Army Corporal." Photostatic copy of original document loaned to the author by Jordi Arquer.

Verbatim report of a meeting of political and military leaders on the Aragon front in September 1936.

Villalba, Colonel José. Report on the fall of Malaga to the Higher War Council, dated 12 February 1937. Typewritten copy of original document loaned to Burnett Bolloten by Colonel Villalba.

III. Newspapers, Periodicals, and Government Publications

This list includes only those newspapers and periodicals that have been referred to in the text or notes. The material cited can be found in that section of the Bolloten Spanish Civil War Collection comprising bound newspapers, clippings, typewritten copies, photocopies, and microfilm housed in the library and archives of the Hoover Institution.

ABC, Madrid.

ABC, Seville.

Acción Libertaria: Boletín Informativo sobre España, Buenos Aires.

Acción Socialista, Paris.

Acracia, Lérida.

L'Action Française, Paris.

Adelante, Alicante.

Bibliography

Adelante, Marseilles.
Adelante, Mexico City.
Adelante, Valencia.
El Adelanto, Salamanca.
L'Adunata dei Refrattari, New York.
Anarquía, Barcelona.
Atlantic Monthly, Boston.
Avant, Barcelona.
La Batalla, Barcelona.
La Batalla, Paris.
Boletín de Información (CNT National Committee), Valencia.
Boletín de Información, CNT-FAI, Barcelona.
Boletín de Información y Orientación Orgánica del Comité Peninsular de la Federación Anarquista Ibérica, Barcelona.
Butlletí Oficial de la Generalitat de Catalunya, Barcelona.
Butlletí del Partit Socialista Catalá, Mexico City.
Cambio 16, Madrid.
Canadian Forum, Toronto (Public Library of Toronto).
Candide, Paris.
Castilla Libre, Madrid.
Catalunya, Barcelona.
Claridad, Madrid.
CNT, Madrid.
CNT, Paris.
CNT, Toulouse.
CNT-FAI-AIT Informationsdienst, Barcelona.
Colectivismo, Valencia.
Combat, Paris.
Commonweal, New York.
Communist International, London.
La Continental Obrera, Santiago, Chile.
Correo de Asturias, Buenos Aires.
La Correspondance Internationale, Paris.
La Correspondencia de Valencia, Valencia.
La Correspondencia Internacional, Paris.

Cuadernos para el Diálogo, Madrid.
IV Internacional, Mexico City.
Cultura Proletaria, New York.
Cultura y Acción, Alcaniz.
Daily Herald, London.
Daily Mail, London.
Daily Telegraph, London.
Daily Worker, London.
El Debate, Madrid.
Democracia, Madrid.
La Dépêche de Toulouse, Toulouse.
El Día Gráfico, Barcelona.
Dialéctica, Havana.
Diari de Barcelona, Barcelona.
Diario de Burgos, Burgos.
Diario de las Sesiones de Cortes, Madrid.
Diari Oficial de la Generalitat de Catalunya, Barcelona.
Diario Oficial del Ministerio de la Guerra, Madrid. [Published in Valencia after 7 November 1936.]
Documentos Históricos de España, Buenos Aires.
Enllà, Mexico City.
L'Ere Nouvelle, Paris.
Espagne Antifasciste, Paris.
Espagne Nouvelle, Montpellier.
España Libre, New York.
España Libre, Toulouse.
España Nueva, Mexico City.
España Popular, Mexico City.
España Republicana, Buenos Aires.
Espoir, Toulouse.
Le Forze Armate, Rome.
IV International, Mexico City.
Fragua Social, Valencia.
Frente Libertario, Madrid.
Frente Rojo, Valencia. [Published in Barcelona in November 1937.]
Frente y Retaguardia. [Place of publication not indicated.]
Full Catalá, Mexico City.
Gaceta de la República, Valencia.
Gaceta de Madrid, Madrid.

Bibliography

Guión, Madrid.
Heraldo de Aragón, Saragossa.
Historia 16, Madrid.
Hoja Oficial del Lunes, Barcelona.
Hoy, Mexico City.
La Humanitat, Barcelona.
L'Humanité, Paris.
Ideas, Hospitalet.
Independent News, Paris.
Informaciones, Madrid.
Inquietudes, Bordeaux.
Internacional, Paris.
International Press Correspondence,
    London.
L'Intransigeant, Paris.
Izvestiia, Moscow.
Le Jour, Paris.
Journal des Débats, Paris.
Juventud Libre, Madrid.
Komsomolskaya Pravda, Moscow.
Labour Monthly, London.
Left News, London.
La Libertad, Madrid.
Le Libertaire, Paris.
Life, Chicago.
Listener, London.
Llibertat, Mataró.
Luz y Fuerza, Barcelona.
Manchester Guardian, Manchester.
Mar y Tierra, Altea.
El Mercantil Valenciano, Valencia.
*Milicia Popular, Madrid.
Modern Monthly, New York.
Mujeres Libres, Barcelona.
Mundo, Mexico City.
Mundo Obrero, Madrid.

Mundo Obrero, Paris.
Nation, New York.
National Review, London.
New International, New York.
New Leader, London.
New Masses, New York.
New Militant, New York.
New Republic, New York.
News Chronicle, London.
New York Herald Tribune, New York.
New York Post, New York.
New York Times, New York.
La Noche, Barcelona.
El Norte de Castilla, Valladolid.
Nosotros, Valencia.
Las Noticias, Barcelona.
El Noticiero, Saragossa.
El Noticiero Universal, Barcelona.
La Nouvelle Espagne Antifasciste, Paris.
Novyi Mir, Moscow.
Nuestra Bandera, Barcelona.
Nuestra España, Havana.
El Obrero de la Tierra, Madrid.
Observer, London.
Orientaciones Nuevas, Granollers.
Pasaremos, Madrid.
El Pensamiento Navarro, Pamplona.
El Poble Català, Mexico City.
Política, Madrid.
Pravda, Moscow.
La Publicitat, Barcelona.
El Pueblo, Valencia.
Reader's Digest, Pleasantville.
Reconstruir, Buenos Aires.
Regeneración, Mexico City.
La République, Paris.

*This daily, published by the Fifth Regiment, is not available in any of the libraries listed at the beginning of this volume, but typewritten copies of the principal items, which were made from a collection loaned to the author by Vittorio Vidali (Carlos Contreras), the regiment's chief political commissar, are in the archives of the Hoover Institution. In addition, a facsimile of Vidali's collection was published in Italy in 1973 (see Bibliography), and, in 1974, many of the articles that appeared under his name were published in Vittorio Vidali, *Spagna lunga battaglia*.

Le Revista Blanca, Barcelona.
La Révolution Prolétarienne, Paris.
Il Risveglio Anarchico, Geneva.
Ruta, Barcelona.
Saturday Evening Post, Philadelphia.
Screen, London.
Service d'Information et de Presse por la Quatrième Internationale, Paris.
El Socialista, Algiers.
El Socialista, Madrid.
El Socialista, Paris.
El Socialista Español, Paris.
Socialist Review, New York.
El Sol, Madrid.
Solidaridad Obrera, Barcelona.
Solidaridad Obrera, Mexico City.
Solidaridad Obrera, Paris.
Sotsialisticheskii Vestnik, Berlin, Paris, New York.
Die Soziale Revolution, Barcelona.
Spanish Labor Bulletin, Chicago.
Spanish Revolution, Barcelona.
Spanish Revolution, New York.
Spartacus, Alicante.
Sunday Times, London.
Le Temps, Paris.
Tiempo, Mexico City.
Tiempos Nuevos, Barcelona.
Tierra y Libertad, Barcelona.

Tierra y Libertad, Mexico City.
Times, London.
Timón, Barcelona.
Timón, Buenos Aires.
Treball, Barcelona.
Tribuna, Mexico City.
Ultima Hora, Barcelona.
Umanità Nova, Rome.
Umbral, Barcelona.
Unión, Seville.
El Universal, Mexico City.
Universo, Toulouse.
Unser Wort, Brussels.
Vanguard, New York.
La Vanguardia, Barcelona.
Verdad, Valencia.
La Veu de Catalunya, Barcelona.
Vía Libre, New York.
Voenno-Istoricheskii Zhurnal, Moscow.
Volunteer for Liberty, Madrid.
La Voz Valenciana, Valencia.
Vu, Paris.
Washington Post, Washington, D.C.
Die Wehrmacht, Berlin.
Workers' Age, New York.
World Affairs Report, Stanford.
Ya, Madrid.

Acknowledgments

Diego Abad de Santillán.
Francisco Aguilera
  (Library of Congress).
Marcos Alcón.
José Almudí.
Jon Amsden.
Luis Araquistáin.
Jordi Arquer
  (see preface and chapter 28, n. 42).
General José Asensio.
Aymá S. A. Editora.
Marjorie Bailey.
Jaime Balius.
Arturo Barea.
Ralph Bates.
Nicolás Bernal.
Biblioteca Nacional, Madrid
  (Photographic Service).
Biblioteca Universitaria de Barcelona
  (Photographic Service).
Bibliothèque Nationale de Paris
  (Photographic Service).
Betty F. Bolloten.
Gladys Bolloten
  (see preface).
Georges Borchardt, Inc.
  (agents for Editions du Seuil).
Anna Bourguina
  (curator of the Nicolaevesky
  Collection, Hoover Institution,
  Stanford).
Gerald Brenan.
The British Museum
  (Newspaper Library and
  Photographic Service).
Ronald Bulatoff
  (Hoover Institution).

José Bullejos.
Cambridge University Press.
Severino Campos.
Captain Aniceto Carbajal.
F. P. Carbajal.
Mariano Cardona Rosell.
Raymond Carr
  (see preface).
Wenceslao Carrillo.
Ralph H. Carruthers
  (New York Public Library).
José Caruana y Gómez de Barreda
  (Servicio Histórico Militar,
  Madrid).
Enrique Castro.
Ricardo de la Cierva y de Hoces.
José Clavería Prenafeta
  (Servicio Histórico Militar,
  Madrid).
James Crafts
  (Hoover Institution).
Luis G. Cubero
  (Biblioteca Nacional, Madrid).
Curtis Brown Ltd.
David and Charles (Holdings) Ltd.
  (Agents for Richard A. H.
  Robinson).
Nadia Davies.
Peter Davies Ltd.
Midge Decter
  (see preface).
Moshe Decter.
Bernard Denham
  (Stanford University Library).
Milorad M. Drachkovitch
  (see preface).
Duell, Sloan & Pearce, Inc.

Acknowledgments

José Duque.
Ediciones Oasis.
Les Editions Denoël.
Editorial Juventud.
Editorial La Vanguardia.
Editorial Losada, S.A.
Editorial Sudamericana, S.A.
Sylvia England.
John Erickson.
Luis Escobar de la Serna.
Antonio Escribano.
Xenia J. Eudin.
Faber and Faber Ltd.
Febus news agency
  (members of the Civil War staff,
  Valencia).
Ramón Fernández-Pouza Gil
  (Hemeroteca Nacional, Madrid).
F. Ferrándiz Alborz.
Gerritt E. Fielstra
  (New York Public Library).
H. H. Fisher
  (Hoover Institution).
Manuel Fraga Iribarne.
Jesús de Galíndez.
Gabriel García Maroto.
Juan García Oliver.
J. García Pradas.
Alejandro García Val.
Antonio Garrigues Diaz-Cañabate.
Antoni Gilabert.
José Giral.
Naida Glick.
Victor Gollancz Ltd.
Colonel Juan Gomez.
F. González.
Efraín González Luna.
Julián Gorkin.
Charles L. Grace
  (Harvard College Library).
Jorge Gracia.
Granada Publishing Limited.
Howard Green.
Rachel and Robert Green.
Harcourt, Brace and Company, Inc.

Harper & Row.
Harvard College Library
  (Photographic Reference
  Department).
A. M. Heath & Co. Ltd.
William Heinemann Ltd.
Hemeroteca Municipal de Madrid
  (Microfilm Service).
Ignacio Hidalgo de Cisneros.
Ronald Hilton
  (see preface).
Donald C. Holmes
  (Library of Congress).
Henry Holt and Company, Inc.
Editoral Hoy.
Hoover Institution on War,
  Revolution, and Peace, Stanford
  (Library and archives staff).
Agnes Inglis
  (University of Michigan Library).
Instituto Municipal de Historia,
  Barcelona.
Andrés María de Irujo.
Manuel de Irujo.
David Jaffe.
Miguel Jiménez.
Verle B. Johnston.
Santos Juliá.
Charles F. Keyser
  (Library of Congress).
Kiepenheuer & Witsch.
Alfred A. Knopf, Inc.
Hilja Kukk
  (see preface and chapter 21,
  n. 111).
Rosemary Kurpuis.
Gaston Leval.
Lena Lever.
Ramón Liarte.
Le Libertaire.
Librairie Plon.
The Library of Congress
  (Division of Manuscripts and
  Serial Division).
Francisca Linares de Vidarte.

Acknowledgments

Rodolfo Llopis.
El Marqués Juan Ignacio Luca
de Tena.
The Macmillan Press, Ltd.,
London and Basingstoke.
Salvador de Madariaga.
Edward E. Malefakis
(see preface).
Herbert Marshall.
J. Martín Blázquez.
Pedro Martínez Carton.
S. Martínez Dasi.
Robert M. McBride and Company.
McGraw-Hill Book Company.
Philip T. McLean
(Hoover Institution).
José Miaja.
Harry Milton.
Frank Mintz.
Federica Montseny.
Constancia de la Mora.
Felix Morrow.
William Morrow and Company.
G. Munis (Manuel Grandizo Munis).
José Muñoz López.
Luciano J. Navas.
Margarita Nelken.
New York Public Library
(Photographic Service).
Jack Norpel
(Director of Research, U.S. Senate
Security Subcommittee).
Paul North Rice
(New York Public Library).
W. W. Norton and Company.
Ohio State University Press.
Eduardo Orozco y G. ("El Pintor").
Sonia Brownell Orwell.
Oxford University Press.
Randolfo Pacciardi.
H. S. Parsons
(Library of Congress).
Concha Patiño.
Arline B. Paul
(Hoover Institution).

Stanley G. Payne
(see preface).
José Peirats.
Pennsylvania State University Press.
Agnes F. Peterson
(Hoover Institution).
Jesús Pérez Salas.
A. D. Peters and Company.
Melody Phillips
(see preface).
D. Wingeate Pike
(see preface).
Librairie Plon.
Porrua Hermanos y Cia.
Eugene B. Power.
General Sebastián Pozas.
Jacobo Prince.
Putnam & Co., Ltd.
Alfonso Quintana y Pena.
A. Ramos Oliveira.
Reader's Digest.
Gustav Regler.
Ludwig Renn.
Reynal & Hitchcock, Inc.
Warner Rice
(University of Michigan).
Ricardo del Río
(Febus news agency).
Miguel Robledo.
Helmut Ruediger.
Felipe Sánchez Román.
Editorial San Martín.
William T. Sayre-Smith.
Manuel Schwartzmann.
Charles Scribner's Sons.
Martin Secker and Warburg, Ltd.
Miguel Serra Pamies.
Servicio Histórico Militar, Madrid.
Mark Sharron.
Simon and Schuster.
David Alfaro Siqueiros.
Wilebaldo Solano.
Agustín Souchy.
Stanford University Press.
Luis Suárez.

Acknowledgments

Leopoldo Suárez del Real.
Alma Tapia.
José Tarradellas.
Toronto Public Library.
Mathilda de la Torre.
Hugh Trevor-Roper
  (see preface).
Felipe Ubach.
University of California Library,
  San Diego.
University of Michigan Library
  (Photographic Service).
University of Michigan Press.
University of North Carolina Press
  (editorial and administrative staff).
Manuel Vidal.

Vittorio Vidali (Carlos Contreras).
The Viking Press, Inc.
José Villalba.
Antonio Villanueva.
Angel Viñas
  (see chapter 9, n. 30).
Pedro Voltes Bou
  (Instituto Municipal de Historia de
  Barcelona).
Bertram D. Wolfe
  (see preface).
Ella Wolfe
  (see preface).
Yale University Press.
Victor Zaragoza.

Index*

A

Abad de Santillán, Diego, CNT-FAI leader: on advantages of collective farming, 68; on lack of planning in urban collectives, 211; on anarchists meeting with Companys in July 1936, 369; on CNT-FAI opposition to dictatorship, 372; on CNT-FAI retaining Companys at head of Generalitat, 372; on functions of Central Antifascist Militia Committee, 374; on dissolution of Central Antifascist Militia Committee, 379; becomes councillor of economy in Generalitat cabinet, Dec. 1936, 387; on CNT not interested taking power in May 1937, 406; on "plot" against CNT and FAI, 408; on rage of militants against leaders during May events, 415; on faith of CNT in Companys until May events, 421; on conflict between CNT and FAI, 466; proposes return to anarchist orthodoxy, 469

ABC, monarchist newspaper: on 1931 revolution continuing its violent course until it encountered "an effective reaction," 13

Abeytua, Isaac, Left Republican director of *Política*: opposes Martínez Barrio's government, 50 (n. 235)

Adelante, Socialist organ: Caballero loses control of, 465

Adroher, Enrique, POUM leader: denounces Valencia's military policy toward Catalonia, 393; criticizes CNT councillors, 393

Agencia Española: Alvarez del Vayo and, 138

Agrarian crisis: pre-Civil War, 4–5 and n. 8, 6–7, 11–12

Agrarian Reform Law: attitude of Liberal Republicans toward, 25–26

*See Author's Note (Proper Names), p. xx.

Agricultural decree of 7 Oct. 1936: description of, 223; Communist praise of, 223; Communist misrepresentation of, 223; National Federation of Land Workers' criticism of, 223–25; criticism of by Morayta Nuñez, 224; CNT criticizes limitations of, 224; left-wing Socialists criticize limitations of, 225; used by Communists to support return of land, 225; Libertarian Youth against Communist use of, 225

Agricultural decree of June 1937, 229–31

Agriculture. *See* Agrarian crisis; Agrarian Reform Law; Agricultural decrees; Institute of Agrarian Reform

Aguirre, José Antonio, Basque premier: on Communist flattery of, 123

Aiguadé, Artemio: becomes councillor of internal security (Esquerra) in Generalitat cabinet, Sept. 1936, 380; councillor of internal security in Generalitat cabinet, Dec. 1936, 387; appoints PSUC member Rodríguez Salas as police commissioner, 390; requests additional forces from central government, 396; councillor of internal security in Generalitat governments, 3 and 16 Apr. 1937, 395–97; Libertarian Youth demands removal of, 399; and raid on central telephone exchange, 403–4 and n. 77; requests dispatch of 1,500 assault guards to Barcelona, 406–7; tribute to by Communists, 410 (n. 42); demands reinforcements from Valencia, 414

Aiguadé, Jaime, Esquerra leader: minister of labor and social welfare in Negrín government, 451; inconsequential role of in second Negrín government, 469; resigns from government, 469

AIT, International Workingmen's Association: on direct action, 184

Alba, Victor, left-wing historian: on Comorera's removal after war from PSUC leadership and denunciation to

[615]

Index

Spanish police by his own "friends," 379 (n. 64); on differences within POUM regarding its entering Catalan government, 387 (n. 76); on CNT, Socialists, and republicans not understanding Moscow trials, 383
Albalate de Cinca: libertarian communism in, 75
Alberri, Major, republican officer: on militia defects, 246–48
Alberti, Rafael, Communist poet, 278
Alcalá-Zamora, President Niceto, 8; yields to CEDA, 10; recoils from declaring martial law, 13; dislodged from presidency, 30
Alcora: libertarian communism in, 72
Alcoy: collectivization in, 64
Alfredo: alias of Togliatti, 133
Alianza de la Democracia Socialista, 77
Alliluyeva, Paul: congratulates Orlov on receiving Order of Lenin, 153
Almudí, Manuel, Communist leader in Aragon: criticizes Líster's repression in Aragon, 233
Alonso, Bruno, moderate Socialist and navy commissar general: on assassination of 70 percent of the naval officers, 54 and n. 31; on military leaders joining Communist party, 299
Alfonso, Elfidio: becomes member of executive of Board of Electricity, 210
Alvarez Coque, Colonel, republican officer: replaces Martínez Cabrera as chief of war ministry general staff, 348 (n. 78)
Alvarez del Vayo, Julio, left Socialist leader, pro-Communist: Zugazagoitia on, 24; on number of regular army officers in Popular Army, 52; on collapse of republican state, 53; on international law and nonintervention, 118 (n. 7); on Giral government crisis, 121–22; becomes foreign minister, 122; on importance of unity with Catholic Basque Nationalist party, 123; transfers allegiance to Communists, 131; and JSU, 131; and JSU leaders' decision to join Communist party, 132; visits Caballero in jail in 1934 accompanied by Comintern delegates, 132 (n. 68); supporter of Communist policy before and during war, 137–38; suspended from Madrid Socialist party in March 1939, 137; Communist opinion of, 137; and

Foreign Press Bureau, 137–38; and Agencia Española, 138; member editorial staff *Nation*, 137; on Stashevsky and Negrín, 140; on the Ley de Ordenación Bancaria, 143; on gold shipment to Russia, 146; on Prieto's participation in gold shipment, 151; on Negrín insisting Azaña be told of gold shipment, 151; note to Britain and France proposing transfer Spanish Morocco, 164–67; on hopes that Western democracies would change policy, 170–71; on anarchists entering government, 190; stopped by Rosal column at Tarancón, 192; and Koltzov's interview with Caballero, 243–44; promotes Communist influence in general commissariat of war, 262; approves Fischer's letter to Caballero questioning Asensio's loyalty, 268; votes for Asensio's dismissal, 268, 335; praises Asensio, 268; writes letter of encouragement to Asensio, 268; praises Rojo, 275; rebuked by Caballero for playing Communist game, 329, 353; called agent of Communists by Caballero, 334; on ceasing to be Caballero's most trusted minister, 335; appointed government representative on war ministry general staff, 348; Baráibar on 349–50, 360; accused by Caballero of appointing 200 political commissars without his knowledge, 353; defends his appointment of Communist political commissars, 353–54; denies betraying Caballero, 353; affirms love of Caballero, 353; retains post as head of commissariat of war under Prieto, 453; Vidarte on Caballero's detestation of, 453; replaced by Giral in foreign ministry, 453; leaves legacy of Communist functionaries in foreign ministry, 453; removal of by Prieto from commissariat of war, 463; role of in Thirteen-Point program, 472; appeals to Azaña to go to central zone, 474
Alvarez Buylla, Plácido, Republican Union leader: becomes minister of industry and commerce, 51; decree by on sequestration of plants abandoned by owners or managers, 210
Anarchism: and puritanism, 74; on God and religion, 77; and government, 177–81. See also CNT; FAI; Libertarian communism

Index

Index

Barea, Arturo, Socialist: on each group having own police, prison, and place of execution, 55; loses confidence in Socialist party's power of assuming responsibility and authority, 129; on rivalry between militia units, 246; on Koltzov, 266

Barnés, Francisco J., Left Republican leader: and closure of religious schools, 16; becomes minister of education in Giral cabinet, 52

Barrero, Hernando, left Socialist: appointed by Caballero to scrutinize work of officers and commissars, 337 (n. 19)

Basque autonomy, 123

Basque Nationalist party: enters Caballero government, 122; Communists exploit presence Catholic party in government, 123; Communists claim this first time Catholics and Communists form part of same government, 124. *See also* Aguirre, José Antonio

Bates, Ralph, assistant commissar Fifteenth International Brigade: criticizes Communist drive against rural collectivization, 229; on Fifth Regiment, 256–57 and n. 11, 258

Batov, P., Soviet officer: "Fritz," pseudonym of, 260 (n. 8); joins Líster's First Brigade before helping International Brigades, 260 (n. 8); succeeded by Meretskov, 260 (n. 8); survives purges, 293

Bebb, Captain Cecil: pilots Franco's plane to Morocco, 48

Belayev, Soviet NKVD agent: Hernández confuses with Orlov, 344; Bolloten on, 344–45; Fischer on, 345; Gorkin on, 345

Beloff, Max, 100–101

Benedito, José: commander of CNT Torres-Benedito column, appointed to organizational section general staff, 318

Benito, General Gregorio de, rebel general: declares martial law in Huesca, 47

Bergamin, José, Catholic writer, proCommunist: describes POUM as "very efficient tool of fascists," 461 (n. 59)

Berzin, General Ian K., Soviet officer: Krivitsky reveals presence of in Spain, 110; confused with Gorev, 287; known as Grishin, 287; true identity established, 287; perishes in Stalin's purges, 287–88, 290–91; liquidation of confirmed by Ehrenburg, *Komsomolskaya Pravda* and *Bortsy Latvii v Ispanii*,

290; Krivitsky on, 290–91; Orlov on execution of, 292

Besteiro, Julián, right-wing Socialist leader: opposed to revolution, 24; declares against dictatorship of proletariat, 27; looks to mediation to end conflict, 463; joins national council of defense, 476

Bielov. *See* Belayev

Bienio negro or black biennium, 3

Bilbao, Crescenciano, moderate Socialist: occupies subcommissariat of war, 262 (n. 28)

Blackstone: alias given to Orlov by Negrín, 146, 345

Blanco, Segundo, member of CNT: named minister of education in second Negrín government, 469

Blasco Garzón, Manuel, leader Republican Union: becomes minister of justice, 51

Blum, Léon, French Socialist premier: and neutral stand, 162

Bolín, Luis: London correspondent of *ABC*, 48; charters Havilland Dragon Rapide to fly Franco to Morocco, 48, 106; flies to Rome for help, 106–7

Bolívar, Cándido (Azaña's secretary): instructed by Azaña to urge Caballero to send reinforcements to Barcelona during May events, 406

Bolívar, Cayetano, Communist chief political commissar of Malaga sector: appoints excessive number of Communist political commissars, 323

Bolloten, Gladys Evie, xvii

Bolshevik Leninists (Trotskyists): organize Spanish section of Trotsky's Fourth International, 381; expelled by POUM, 381 and n. 73; some members allegedly executed by POUM, 381 (n. 73); polemic with POUM over entering Generalitat government, 382; Grandizo Munis, leader of, 394; relations of with Friends of Durruti, 394; activity of during May events, 408, 415; and discussions with Balius of Friends of Durruti to abandon his "innate anarchist mistrust of the Marxists," 415 (n. 61); arrest of leaders of, 461 (n. 57)

Borrás, Tomás, right-wing author, 105

Bourgeois democratic revolution: Communist party defines social revolution as, 94; Ibárruri on, 94; Marty on, 113–14; José Díaz on, 117; Carrillo on, 216,

[620]

Index

claims that Trotskyists by calling for social revolution play Franco's game, 385. *See also* JSU

Carrillo, Wenceslao, left Socialist leader: on lack of unity in Socialist party, 129–30; on hope of victory through world war, 170; replaced by Communist Ortega as director general security, 452; joins national council of defense against Negrín, 476

Casado, Segismundo, republican officer: on Soviet influence in war ministry, air force, and tank corps, 153; on favoritism shown to Fifth Regiment in distribution arms, 257, 268; helps to organize mixed brigades, 260 (n. 7); on Soviet aid and conduct of Soviet officers, 265; on Communist tactics regarding military commanders, 267; dismissal and reinstatement of by Caballero as chief of operations, 268; on Miaja intoxicated by popularity, 277; on Soviet advisers acting independently of war and air ministries, 296; forms national council of defense against Negrín with Socialist, republican, and CNT leaders, 476

Casares Quiroga, Santiago, Left Republican leader: succeeds Azaña in premiership, 23–24 and n. 99, 33–34; tries to maintain balancing position, 35; passivity of, 35–37; refuses to arm workers, 42

Castelló, General Luis, liberal republican officer: becomes war minister, 51

Castillo, Lieutenant José, left-wing member Assault Guard: murder of, 39

Castro: libertarian communism in, 73

Castro, Enrique, ex-Communist central committee member: on Codovila, 133; first commander in chief of Fifth Regiment, 256; on political composition of Fifth Regiment, 258; on first commanders Popular Army, 260; on Miaja and María Teresa Léon, 278; on Rojo's religious faith, 282; on Rojo's utility to Communists, 282; calls Communist demand for army purge step toward Communist hegemony, 327; on Communist campaign to destroy Socialist party and Caballero, 332–34; on political "stupidity" of Communists' allies, 334; on Uribe advised by Soviet technicians, 348; alleges Orlov selected Con-

treras as "immediate collaborator" in Nin case, 457

Catalonia: collectivization in, 59–61; Lorenzo on, 178; events from July 1936 to May 1937, 368–429; defeat of rebel garrison in Barcelona, 368; Miravitlles declares capitalism no longer exists in, 368; Madrid lacks strength to exert authority over, 368–69, 410 and n. 40; statute of autonomy of, 368–69; CNT controls Barcelona's economic life, 368; *Solidaridad Obrera* on "irresponsible elements" frightening small peasants and urban middle classes in, 375; Esquerra and middle classes in, 375; division of police power in, 380. *See also* CNT (Catalonia): Comorera, Juan; Companys, Luis; Esquerra Republicana de Catalunya; FAI; Police (Catalonia); POUM; PSUC

Catholics: Communist use of, 123

Cazorla, José, JSU leader: joins Communist party, 132 (n. 74)

CEDA, right-wing party federation, 4; Robinson on goal of, 9; on education, 16; disintegration of, 22; and discussions to form government national concentration, 34. *See also* Gil Robles, José María

Censorship: of prewar strike news, 11; of news about economic revolution, 138; allows foreign correspondents to publicize restitution private property, 470

Center-right governments 1933–35: undo work of Republic, 3

Central Antifascist Militia Committee: Companys and establishment of, 373–74; becomes de facto executive body in Catalonia, 59 (n. 63), 374; Abad de Santillán on work of, 374; needs of met by Catalan council of finance, 374; PSUC presses for dissolution of and concentration of power in hands Catalan government, 379; Abad de Santillán on reasons for dissolution of, 379

Chamberlain, Neville: on Russia wanting capitalist powers to destroy each other, 161–62; seeks political settlement with Germany at Poland's expense, 171–73

Checa, Pedro, politburo member: on Alvarez del Vayo serving Communist party, 137

Chomsky, Noam, xvi

Index

entering government, 197–98; defends committees, 200; ministers of yield to pressure to end power committees, 200–201; CNT minister Peiró on victory depending on Britain and France, 201; and dissolution committtees, 201; effect of dissolution committees upon, 201; fears *carabineros*, 205; opposes dissolution police squads and patrols, 206; plans of to remedy defects of collectivization, 212; and libertarian conception of socialization, 212; privileged enterprises refuse to help the less successful, 212; differences with UGT on industrial reorganization, 213; Soviet diplomatic representatives' advice to regarding establishment of "controlled democracy," 217; opposition to Communist slogan of democratic and parliamentary republic, 218–21; characterizes Communist party as representing "extreme right wing of Loyalist Spain," 221; criticizes agricultural decree of 7 Oct. 1936, 224; accuses Communists of encouraging break-up of collectives, 228–29; and National Service of Agricultural Credit assistance to collectives, 229–30; views Giral's attempt to recreate army with alarm, 240, 303; and military discipline and hierarchy, 251–54, 303; and structure of militia units, 251; on militia, 302; proposes creation of "war militia" under joint CNT-UGT control, 304; Villar on antimilitarist principles being inimical to, 304; Peiró on CNT ministers having no rights or responsibilities regarding direction of war, 305; proposes creation of Higher War Council, 305; efforts of to maintain control of its militia, 305–6; militia units of adopt military names, 306; Montseny and Mera on defects of militia system, 307; urges militarization and creation of cadres, 307–8; rank and file of resist enrolling in officers training schools, 309; about-face of on militarization, 309–10; opposition of members of to militarization, to saluting, and differential pay rates, 310; determined to maintain integrity and homogeneous character of its militia units, 311–12; opposes mixed brigades, 311; secretary Vázquez on militarization and mixed brigades, 312; and Iron Column, 315; on members of to be drafted only into CNT units, 326–27; demands Asensio's

removal, 335–36; secretary of opposes motion to protest suspension of *Nosotros*, 340; Ruediger on provincial newspapers unaware that Caballero opponent of Communists, 340; accuses Communist officers of using prerogatives to weaken other organizations, 351; supports Caballero on curbing powers of commissariat of war, 357; Caballero attempts to avoid antagonism of during May events, 408; and dissensions in libertarian movement on question of taking power, 413–14; national committee of describes renewed fighting on 6 May 1937 in Barcelona, 425; calls Caballero the "most capable and honorable person" for premiership, 442; criticizes Caballero for offering it only two cabinet seats, 442; Communists seek temporary accommodation with, 464; Hernández on breach in created by Communists, 464–65; accepts conciliatory gesture by Communists, 465; defies FAI and starts negotiations with new UGT executive, 466; FAI in conflict with leadership of, 466; and divisions in libertarian movement, 469–70; Horacio M. Prieto advocates creation libertarian Socialist party, 469–70; on holding only one cabinet seat to "placate the bourgeois democracies," 470; *Solidaridad Obrera* criticizes restitution of private property as "pernicious error," 471–72. *See also* Anarchism; CNT (Catalonia); FAI; Libertarian communism; Libertarian Youth

CNT, Catalonia: on Companys's suppression of in 1934, 370; opposes idea of CNT dictatorship and opts for collaboration, 372; has no program for taking power, 372; Escofet on lack of plans of, 372; Ruediger criticizes foreign anarchist opponents of for asserting CNT should have established own dictatorship, 372–73; sets up Central Antifascist Militia Committee, 373–74; regards Moscow trials as "family quarrel," 383; opposes PSUC demands for exclusion POUM from cabinet, then acquiesces, 386; hails preponderant trade-union character of new Catalan government, 387; criticizes both PSUC and POUM for crisis, 387; praises Companys as more sincere than some of his coreligionists, 389; Companys and Tarradellas anticipate eventual collapse of, 389; Comorera and Rodríguez Salas principal objects of execration of, 390; rejects PSUC proposal for creation of internal security corps, 391; holds that its militia should be drafted only into libertarian units, 392; demands legislation on public order undergo fundamental change, 394–95; demands ban on military parades, 395; refuses sign pledge to enforce military and public order decrees, 395; declares it has made too many concessions, 396; criticized by POUM for not seizing power, 397–98; accepts solution Catalan crisis, 398; urges workers not to allow themselves to be disarmed, 402; demands removal of Rodríguez Salas and Aiguadé, 404; appeals for cease-fire during May events, 408; exhorts workers to lay down arms, 411–12; some members of regard appeal for cease-fire as treachery, 413; Ruediger on dissensions in on question of taking power, 413–14; suggests that new government be formed, 414; regional committee of meets with POUM and regional committees of FAI and Libertarian Youth during May events, 407; Caballero attempts to avoid antagonism of, 408; on decision of central government to take over public order and defense, 420; on alleged attempts by Companys and Tarradellas to delay peace negotiations, 420; regional committee of denounces Friends of Durruti as *agents provocateurs*, 424; refuses to participate in new Catalan cabinet because of alleged "maneuver" by Companys, 454 and n. 23; dissolution of revolutionary committees of, 455

Cockburn, Claud: on personality and disappearance of Koltzov, 289–90; made London correspondent *Pravda* by Koltzov, 289–90

Codovila, Vittorio, Comintern delegate, alias Medina: Rosal on Caballero visited by in jail in 1934 accompanied by Araquistáin and Alvárez del Vayo, 132 (n. 68); role in creating JSU, 132, 134; called "eye of Moscow," 132; described as "real head of [Communist] party," 133; liquidates former leadership of Communist party, 133; presses Caballero for fusion Socialist and Commu-

nist parties, 332; attends politburo meeting to oust Caballero, 342–44

Collectivization, rural: CNT and FAI on, 67–84; UGT on parcelation of land, 68–69; Socialists on forced collectivization, 226; left Socialists distinguish between "loyal small proprietors" and "brazen enemies of the working class," 226; Carrillo restrains collectivist tendencies in JSU, 226; Carrillo on collectivization in USSR, 226–27; Zabalza and Vázquez accuse Communists of encouraging break-up collectives, 228; Bates on forced and voluntary collectives, 229; in Toledo province, 229; Communist campaign against causes dismay in countryside, 229; decree of June 1937 revises Communist policy toward, 229–30; assistance by Institute of Agrarian Reform and National Service of Agricultural Credit to collectives, 229–30; Communists destroy collectives in Aragon, 233–34; Communists restore some collectives, 234–35; dissolution Aragon collectives affects morale, 235; assault on, 455; Communists halt attacks on, 464. *See also* Appendixes II and III, 481–83

Collectivization, urban, 59–66; defects of, 211–12; Abad de Santillán on lack of planning, 211; Negrín takes advantage of financial plight of urban collectives, 212; and financial difficulties, 213–14; Communists attack "premature experiments in collectivization and socialization," 214. *See also* Appendix I, 479–81

Colodny, Robert: on role of Eleventh International Brigade in defense Madrid, 273

Colomer, Victor, agrarian secretary of PSUC: on *rabassaires* joining the PSUC, 378

Comintern: Seventh World Congress adopts Popular Front policy, 95, 100–101; tries to conceal or minimize revolution, 113–14; authority of delegates of over Spanish politburo, 133–34; and raising of arms embargo, 365. *See also* Codovila, Vittorio; Gerö, Ernö; Marty, André; Manuilski, Dmitri; Stefanov, Boris; Togliatti, Palmiro

Commissariat of War. *See* General Commissariat of War

Commission of War Industries: Tarra-

Index

dellas, president of, sides with CNT against PSUC criticism of, 389
Committee for the Popular Army: set up by PSUC, 392–93; Tarradellas urges suspension of activities of, 393; officially constituted as auxiliary body of defense council, 393
Committees, revolutionary: control by, 54–55; supplanting power of, 177, 199–203, 210–14; dissolution of in Catalonia, 455
Commune de Paris Battalion, 273
Communist International. *See* Comintern
Communist party: on agrarian crisis before Civil War, 5–7; attacks on church, 16 (n. 59); relations with Caballero and Prieto, 28–30, 116; hostility of to Caballero's policy before war, 29 and n. 131; demands purge of state apparatus, 37; on Martínez Barrio's government, 49; on destruction of state apparatus, 53; on plants, banks, and land in workers' hands, 59–60; middle classes focus hopes on, 89 and n. 8; size and composition of, 89, 124; on protecting small tradesmen and manufacturers, 89–90 and n. 15; attacks committees and defends small and medium proprietors in countryside, 91–94; sets up Peasant Federation in Valencia province, 93; defines social overturn as bourgeois democratic revolution, 94; alleged conspiracy before Civil War to set up Soviet regime, 104–5; policy before Civil War, 105, 199; on Madrid construction strike, 105; tries to conceal or minimize revolution, 113–15; opposes proposal to set up Socialist republic in July 1936, 117–18; praises Giral government, 119, 211; on Giral government crisis, 121–22; opposes, then accepts, participation in Caballero government, 122; receives directives from Moscow to join government, 122; exploits participation of Catholic Basque Nationalist party in government, 122–24; Giral on coincidence of views of Left Republicans and, 126–27; Vanni on discipline of, 127; Brenan on totalitarian spirit and appetite for power of, 127; reasons for growth of, 124–36; Lorenzo on superior militia and defense of Madrid by, 128; dynamic quality of attracts Socialists, 129; Morón on "the most zealous and unscrupulous" imposing

their views, 130; Hernández on Socialist infighting exploited by, 130; and Soviet aid, 154; relies for support in major issues on republican and moderate Socialists, 154; legal origins of government stressed by, 156; urges continued resistance February 1939, 170; calls for revolutionary committees in 1934, 199; against revolutionary committees in 1936, 199–200, 202–3; on democratic structure of the state conforming to present period, 203; infiltrates official police corps, 206–7; secures pivotal positions in police corps, 207; attacks premature experiments in collectivization and socialization, 214–15; on democratic revolution and "ideological deformation of broad section of working-class movement," 216; defends democratic republic at time of "greatest revolutionary effervescence," 216; defends democratic and parliamentary republic, 216, 219–20; modifies language regarding democratic republic, 219; on democratic republic of "a new type," 219–20; opposes libertarian communism and socialization, 220; libertarian criticism of, 220–21; on agricultural decree of 7 Oct. 1936, 223; uses agricultural decree to support demands for restitution land, 225, 227–28; organizes Valencia Peasant Federation to protect individual farmers, 225; strife with left-wing Socialists, 226; on collectivization, 226; uses decree of 7 Oct. 1936 to urge farmers to reclaim or divide up land, 227–28; and agricultural decree of June 1937, 230; agriculture minister Uribe, member of, does not grant permanent legal status to collectives, 230–31; destroys collective farms in Aragon, 233–34; restores some collectives, 234–35; repression by in Aragon, 233–35; Silva, Communist secretary Institute Agrarian Reform, criticizes dissolution Aragon collectives, 233–34; modifies policy regarding collectives, 235, 464; aids Giral cabinet in creating volunteer army, 241; motives for supporting government-controlled army, 241; on military discipline, 255, 257; on militia, 259; on creation of regular army, 259–60, welds battalions of Fifth Regiment into Popular Army, 260; secures control

Index

trolled by enemy, 412; launches synchronized campaign in Spain and abroad denouncing POUM, 418; ministers of demand dissolution of POUM, 433; ministers of resign, 434; and secret agreement with Prieto to oust Caballero, 439; Azaña on opposition of to Caballero, 440; demands that Caballero relinquish war ministry, 440; demands autonomy for commissariat of war, 440–41; and Negrín, 446–47; and support of Prieto, 447; on undersecretaryship of defense as important as defense ministry, 447; on rise of within ten months to position where it virtually controlled the destinies of anti-Franco camp, 448; "El Campesino" on rise to power of, 448; improves its positions in police administration, 452; tacit understanding of with Negrín on liquidation POUM, 459; Prieto provoked by proselytism and growing power of, 463; halts attacks on collective farms, 464; launches offensive against Prieto, 464; seeks temporary accommodation with CNT, 464; creates enemies with every step up ladder of power, 465; secretary of makes conciliatory gesture to CNT, 465; ousts Caballero from UGT executive, 465; organizes demonstration against "treacherous ministers," 467; Moscow instructs two ministers of to withdraw from cabinet to impress Anglo-French opinion, 468; Hernández on withdrawal from cabinet of two ministers of, 468; Hernández on Negrín relying on political and military power of, 468; holds more levers of command after Prieto's ouster, 468–69; retains all key positions in police apparatus, 469; "El Campesino" on hatred of by mass of people, 470; assassination of Socialists by, 470; politburo of calls for continued resistance in Feb. 1939, 473–74; leaders of arrive in central zone with Negrín, Togliatti, and Stefanov, 475; Zugazagoitia on resistance policy of, 475. *See also* Comintern; PSUC
Communists, Catalonia. *See* PSUC
Comorera, Juan, president of Socialist Union, later PSUC secretary: on seeking collaboration of European democracies, 163; on winning benevolent neutrality of England, 163; opposes any

connection of PSUC wth Comintern, 377; withdraws objections to adherence to Comintern, 377; becomes PSUC secretary, 377; made central committee member of Spanish Communist party, 378, 387; Spanish Communist party on loyalty of, 379; removed from leadership and denounced to Spanish police after war by his own "friends," 379 (n. 64); becomes councillor of public services in Generalitat government, Sept. 1936, 380; demands POUM ouster from cabinet, 386; demands suppression of Secretariado de Defensa and the Junta de Seguridad, 386; attacks committees, 386; decrees dissolution committees controlling wholesale food trades, 390; libertarians' principal object of execration, 390; councillor of public works, labor, and justice in Generalitat government, 3 Apr. 1937, 395; councillor of justice (UGT-PSUC) in Generalitat government, 16 Apr. 1937, 397; Libertarian Youth demands removal of, 399; on central telephone exchange, Barcelona, 403; Jamie Antón Aiguadé on his influence over Companys, 410
Compañía Telefónica Nacional de España, 61
Companys, Luis, Esquerra leader, president of Catalonia: conciliatory statement of to anarchist leaders in July 1936, 369; conciliatory statement of challenged by Escofet, but accepted by Ossorio and Pi Sunyer, 369; García Oliver and Abad de Santillán on meeting of with CNT leaders, 369–70; background of, 370; *Solidaridad Obrera* on, 370; adapts to Revolution, 370–71; Abad de Santillán in praise of, 371; urges restraint and censures violence in name of Revolution, 371; intervention of saves lives endangered persons, 371; proposes establishment Central Antifascist Militia Committee, 373–74; on real power in hands of CNT, 373; supports PSUC's demand for dissolution of Central Antifascist Militia Committee, 379; aims to end division of power in Catalonia, 380–81; wishes to domesticate the CNT, 381; demands government with plenary powers, 385; criticizes network of committees and juntas, 389; urges centralization authority in hands of government, 389; offers

[628]

Index

Derecha Regional Valenciana: prepares for violence, 19

Deutscher, Isaac, historian, 95–96

Díaz Tendero, Captain Eleuterio, left Socialist, pro-Communist: becomes head of information and control department, 261; principal organizer of UMRA before Civil War, 261; Caballero takes action against, 336; Pérez Salas on pro-Communist activities of, 336 (n. 16); importance of to Communists, 337; Nelken on, 337; Payne on role of, 337; Communists propose Asensio be replaced by, 337; used by Communists against Asensio, 337–38; uses *Nosotros* against Caballero, 337–38; *Nosotros* article in defense of, 338; arrest of, 339; reinstated in information and control department by Negrín, 453; removal of by Prieto, 463; appointed by Negrín to head personnel section of defense ministry, 468

Díaz Sandino, Felipe: councillor of defense (liberal republican) in Generalitat government, 28 Sept. 1936; militia of moderate parties under loose authority of, 380

Díaz, José, secretary Communist party: on land distribution and expropriation, 5–6; on plants and landed estates in hands of workers, 59–60; against setting up Socialist republic in July 1936, 117–18; advocates democratic republic, 117; Togliatti writes speeches of, 133; hopes democracies will resist fascist aggressors, 167; attacks premature experiments in collectivization and socialization, 214; on democratic and parliamentary republic of new type, 220; opposes libertarian communism and socialization, 220; Hernández on opposition of to overthrow of Caballero, 342; attacks Marty, 343; praises line of Caballero before Civil War, 363; declares "Trotskyists" of POUM inspired "criminal putsch" in Catalonia, 418; demands suppression of "Trotskyists," 431–32; makes conciliatory gesture to CNT, 465. *See also* Communist party

Díaz Alor, José, left Socialist: appointed by Caballero to scrutinize work of officers and commissars, 337 (n. 19)

Díaz de Ceballos, José María: appointed

general commissioner of security, 429 (n. 123)

Dictatorship of proletariat: Bakunin on, 82–83; Lenin on, 83; Bertram D. Wolfe on, 83

Dirkson, Herbert von, German ambassador to London: on Britain seeking political settlement with Germany at expense of Poland, 171–73

Discipline, military: and CNT, 251–54, 302; and Communists, 255–57

Dodd, William, U.S. ambassador to Berlin: on letter from Lord Lothian, 98

Dombrowski Battalion, 273

Domenech, Juan J.: councillor of supplies (CNT) in Generalitat government, Sept. 1936, 380; criticizes PSUC regarding GEPCI, 376; councillor of public services in Generalitat government, Dec. 1936, 387; councillor of economy, public services, and health in Generalitat government, 3 Apr. 1937, 395; councillor of public services in Generalitat goverrment, 16 Apr. 1937, 397

Domingo, Marcelino, Left Republican party president: criticized for joining Martínez Barrio's cabinet, 50

Domínguez, Edmundo, left Socialist Secretary of the National Federation of Building Workers (UGT): transfers allegiance to Communists, 131; becomes inspector-commissar of central front, 278 (n. 115); becomes vice-president of the UGT, 465

Douglas, General. *See* Smushkevich, Yakov

Drachkovitch, Milorad M., xvii

Draft (Catalonia): call-up of 1934–35 classes remains unheeded, 392; Isgleas sets firm dates for call-up of 1932–36 classes, 393

Duglas, General. *See* Smushkevich, Yakov

Duque, José, member of Communist central committee: on secret hostility of Communist leaders before war to Caballero's policy, 29 and n. 131; criticizes repression by Líster in Aragon, 233

Durán, Major Gustavo, pro-Communist head of Madrid section of SIM: removed by Prieto, 464

Durruti, Buenaventura, anarchist leader: on discipline, 253; death of, 253 (n. 14)

Index

anxious to provoke war in Western
Europe, 162; aims to avoid general
European war, 162–63; Spanish government communiqué to regarding
transfer of Spanish Morocco, 164–67;
opposition to Franco-Soviet Pact in,
162–63; purview of foreign policy of
goes beyond Spain, 171–73, 474; unaffected by attempts to roll back Revolution, 474; recognizes Franco regime,
474. *See also* Franco-Soviet Pact; French
Communist party; French right
Franco, General Francisco, rebel military
leader, later generalissimo and head
of state of Nationalist Spain: urges
Premier Portela Valladares to declare
martial law, 13; named generalissimo
and head of state, 13 (n. 42), 48; named
military commander in Canary Islands,
14; sends warning letter to Casares
Quiroga, 38; attitude toward conspiracy, 38; given command of Moorish
troops and Foreign Legionaries in
Morocco, 47–48; flies from Canary
Islands to Morocco, 48 and n. 227;
proclamation of, 48–49; declares end
Civil War on 1 Apr. 1939, 477
Franco-Soviet Pact of Mutual Assistance:
and German threat to USSR, 96; not
supplemented by positive military
agreement, 96; coolness of French
Foreign Affairs Ministry to, 96–97;
French Communist party on, 97;
Anglo-French opposition to, 163. *See
also* France
French Communist party: and opposition
to national defense program, 96; on
Franco-Soviet treaty, 97; André Marty
on Spain's bourgeois democratic revolution, 113–14
French right: on danger to West if Germany defeated, 98, 103
Friends of Durruti: formed to combat
"counterrevolutionary" policy of
CNT-FAI leadership, 394; Martínez becomes secretary, Balius vice-secretary
of, 394; Jellinek on, 394; plaster Barcelona with slogans, 401; activity of
during May events, 408; attempts to
keep tempers aflame, 415; and Bolshevik Leninists' attempts to persuade
Balius to abandon "innate mistrust of
the Marxists," 415 (n. 61); leaflet of
published by *La Batalla*, 415; circulates
leaflet announcing creation of "revolu-

tionary junta," 424; denounced as
agents provocateurs by CNT and FAI
regional committees, 424
"Fritz": pseudonym of P. Batov, 260 (n. 8)
Frontiers: Negrín on control of by
workers' committees, 54; Negrín dispatches carabineers to seize control of,
400; Companys urges Valencia to disarm,
454

G
Galán Francisco, Communist party member: promoted to colonel by Negrín, 475
Galán, José María, Communist party
member: becomes commander of Third
Brigade of Popular Army, 260
Galán, Juan, Communist party member:
made subchief of intelligence department, 207; made inspector of the armed
forces, 207 (n. 24)
Galarza, Angel, left Socialist: director
general of security under Maura, 47;
becomes minister interior under Caballero, 122; on growth of Assault Guard,
205; Koltzov on departure of from
Madrid, 269; suspends *Nosotros*, 339;
informs Caballero that Aiguadé had
requested dispatch of 1,500 assault
guards to Barcelona, 406; secret teletyped discussion with Montseny and
Vázquez to allow assault guards to
enter Catalonia and to arrange truce,
427–29
Gallo. *See* Longo, Luigi
Gallo, Miguel, Communist party
member: becomes commander of Sixth
Brigade of Popular Army, 260
Ganga, Ginés, left Socialist Cortes
deputy: on Rosenberg's military demands, 299; on expulsion of Rosenberg
from Caballero's office, 328–29
García Val, Alejandro, Communist commander of Fifth Regiment: on Communists stealing vehicles from CNT,
249; appointed to operations section
general staff by Caballero, 260–61;
Communist party membership of
confirmed, 261 (n. 14); made Estrada's
adjutant, 261 (n. 17); letter of to Asensio
making him honorary commander of
Fifth Regiment, 266 (n. 52); made chief
of transport section of general staff, 296
(n. 228)
García Birlan, Antonio, CNT leader:
councillor of health (CNT) in Generali-

Index

tat government, 28 Sept. 1936, 380
García Maroto, Gabriel, left-wing
Socialist, later Communist: replaces
Pestaña in general commissariat of war,
262; on Socialist complaints about appointment Communist political commissars, 262–63
García Pradas, José, director of *CNT,
Madrid*: on international bourgeoisie,
221; attacks Communist policy, 221;
member of CNT defense committee
Madrid, 311–12; on homogeneous
character of CNT military units, 311–12;
on CNT military commanders' support
of collective farms, 312
García Oliver, Juan, CNT-FAI leader: on
revolutionary justice, 55; becomes
minister of justice, 189; on reason for
CNT's entering government, 197; on
enemy's resistance, 250; becomes head
of officers training schools, 308; advocates military hierarchy, 308; urges CNT
to recruit members for officers training
schools, 309; ability of earns admiration
of ideological opponents, 309; on
CNT-FAI meeting with Companys at
outbreak Revolution, 360–70; on
CNT-FAI decision in favor of collaboration and democracy, 372; designated by
CNT national committee to go to Barcelona during May events, 409; appeals
for cease-fire, 412–13; secret teletyped
discussion with Montseny and Vázquez to allow assault guards to enter
Catalonia and arrange truce, 427–29;
warns Vázquez against POUM and
Estat Catalá, 428
García, Justiniano, Communist: made
chief of intelligence department, 207
Garvin, J. L., editor of Conservative
Observer: on overthrow of Germany
contrary to British interests, 162;
against Franco-Soviet Pact, 163
Gassol, Ventura: councillor of culture
(Esquerra) in Generalitat government
28 Sept. 1936, 380
Gates, John, ex-Communist, head com-
missar of the Fifteenth International
Brigade: on Togliatti "the most power-
ful Communist figure in Spain," 133
Gaykis, Leon, Soviet chargé, later ambas-
sador: recall to Moscow of ignored by
Orlov, 300; Azaña on disappearance of,
300; attends politburo meeting to oust
Caballero, 342–44; insists that Prieto

support fusion of Socialist and Communist parties, 365, 463; informs Prieto
that war material will not be shipped,
365
"Gaziel": pen name of Agustín Calvet, 22
Geddes, Sir Auckland, chairman
British-owned Rio Tinto mines:
criticizes Section I of Popular Front
program, 8
General Commissariat of War: Communists become embedded in, 261;
Mije, Pretel, Alvarez del Vayo promote
interests Communist party in, 262;
Communist control of, 263; Caballero
and, 263; Communists protest Caballero's order curbing powers of, 355–56;
Communists demand autonomy for,
440–41; Alvarez del Vayo retains post as
head of under Prieto, 453; Alvarez del
Vayo removed from by Prieto, 463. *See
also* Political commissars
Generalitat: government and parliament
of, 369; government of, a rubber stamp
for Revolution, 59 (n. 63), 374–75; police
and military power of, 380; government
of agrees to submit to Valencia's military decrees, 393. *See also* Governments
(Catalan)
GEPCI, created by PSUC: protects urban
middle classes in Catalonia, 90, 376;
criticized by CNT, 376
German-Soviet Non-Aggression Pact,
168. *See also* Kandelaki, David
Germany: Stalin's fear of, 95–96; deterioration of relations with USSR, 95–96;
on Franco-Soviet pact, 96–97; Anglo-
French policy toward, 97–100, 162–67,
171–73; French right on danger to West
if Germany defeated, 98, 103; British
policy favors expansion of eastward,
97–98; British support for rearmament
of, 100–101; views with alarm success
of Popular Front line, 102; aid of to
military rebellion, 102–3 and n. 2; objectives of in aiding Franco, 102–3; on
defeating Popular Front, 103; Stalin's
trade envoy Kandelaki seeks secret deal
with, 110; on motives Italian intervention, 107–8; on Soviet military intervention, 111; on Stalin's speech hinting
desire better relations with, 168; Stalin
opens formal negotiations for non-
aggression pact with, 168; Britain seeks
political settlement with at expense of
Poland, 171–73

Index

Caballero on reasons for shipment of, 152; Stalin's delight over safe arrival of, 152–53; Orlov receives Order of Lenin for his part in shipment of, 153

Gómez, Paulino, moderate Socialist, pro-Negrín: heads ministry of the interior, 469

Gómez, Trifón, moderate Socialist and head of quartermaster corps: on general hostility to Negrín and Communists on arrival in central zone, 475

Gónzalez Marín, CNT leader: joins national council of defense against Negrín, 476

González Inestal, Miguel: on libertarian fears that army would become "devourer of the Revolution," 310

González, Valentín, alias "El Campesino," Communist militia leader: on Kremlin using international working class as pawn, 174; embraces anarchist Mera, 465; describes Negrín as Communist party's "ambitious and docile tool," 468

González Peña, Ramón, president of Socialist party: Prieto supporter, 366; becomes president new UGT executive and Negrinista, 465

Gordón Ordás, Félix, leader Unión Republicana: on gold shipments and delays of British banks in releasing funds, 142

Gorev, Vladimir, Soviet officer: arrival in Madrid, 265; and Rojo, 280; proposes Kléber's removal, 284; supports Rojo on Kléber's removal, 284; described by Fischer as savior of Madrid, 286; Rojo on, 286 and n. 168; no mention of by Koltzov, 286 (n. 165); rank of, 286 (n. 168); identity of established, 287; Ehrenburg on, 286; partial credit for Madrid's defense belongs to, 286–87; confusion of with Berzin, 287; assisted by group of high-ranking Soviet officers, 287; death of, 290; Ehrenburg on fate of, 292; Kuznetsov on suppression of, 292; Orlov on death of, 292

Gorkin (Red Army engineer): Regler on Soviet officers' party for, 294

Gorkin, Julián, member of executive committee POUM, director of *La Batalla*: on Spain as testing ground for popular democracies, 295; on historical and universal significance of Civil War,

295; on Bielov (Belayev), 345; on Togliatti's presence in Spain, 346; on Ferrara biography of Togliatti, 347; attacked by PSUC as Trotskyist, 384; on choice between revolution and counter-revolution during May events, 407; on Communist press not publishing POUM sentence, 461 (n. 57)

Governments (Catalan), composition of: Sept. 1936, 379–80; Dec. 1936, 387; 3 Apr. 1937, 395; 16 Apr. 1937, 397; May 1937, 421

Governments (central), composition of: Martínez Barrio, July 1936, 45 (n. 207); Giral, July 1936, 51–52; Caballero, Sept. 1936, 122–23; Caballero, Nov. 1936, 189–90; Negrín, May 1937, 451; Negrín, Apr. 1938, 468–69

GPU. *See* NKVD

Gracia, Anastasio de, moderate Socialist: becomes minister of industry and commerce, 122; informs Caballero of resignation moderate Socialist ministers, 438–39

Grandizo Munis, Manuel: founded Spanish section of Fourth International (Bolshevik Leninists), 381 (n. 73); on expulsion by POUM of members sympathetic to Bolshevik Leninists, 381 (n. 73); on relations with Friends of Durruti, 394

Granollers: collectivization in, 62, 64

Graus: libertarian communism in, 74

Great Britain: favors German expansion eastwards, 97–98; encourages German rearmament, 100–101; aims to avoid general European war, 162–63; opposition to Franco-Soviet Pact, 162–63; Juan Comorera on winning "benevolent neutrality" of, 163; Spanish government note to regarding transfer Spanish Morocco, 164–67; seeks political settlement with Germany at expense of Poland, 171–72 and n. 54, 173; purview of foreign policy of goes beyond Spain, 171–73, 474; aims to purchase immunity for West at expense of eastern Europe, 173 and n. 56; indifferent to attempts to roll back Revolution, 474; recognizes Franco regime, 474. *See also* Chamberlain, Neville

Great Soviet Encyclopedia: on Koltzov, 288–89

Grigorovich, General. *See* Shtern, Gregoriy M.

Index

Huesca: military rising in, 46
Humanitat, Esquerra organ: cautious criticism of Revolution by, 371

I

Iakushin, M., Soviet officer: survives purges, 293
Ibárruri, Dolores (La Pasionaria), politburo member: defines social overturn as bourgeois democratic revolution, 94; calls for Soviets in 1933, 95; Togliatti writes speeches of, 123; memoirs of ignore Kléber, 285; escapes from central zone, 476; blames Negrín for decrees promoting Communist officers, 477; alleges Negrín hoping for catastrophe to free himself from government responsibility, 477
Institute of Agrarian Reform: deprived of funds by center-right coalition, 3; land seizures registered with, 60; Malefakis on land seizures retroactively legalized by, 67; controlled by Communist minister of agriculture, 229; aid of to collective farms, 229–330; and CNT, 229–30
Intellectuals: and Communist party, 125, 131
Internal security corps (Catalonia): PSUC proposes creation of, 390–91; government approves decrees on, 391; agitation against decrees on, 391–92; Catalan government agrees to postpone appointments to key positions in, 393
International Telephone and Telegraph Corp., 61; central telephone exchange, Barcelona, property of, 403
International Brigades: arrival and deployment of, 111–12; Communist control of, 112; differing opinions as to whether Madrid saved by, 273 (n. 84); as model for Spanish units, 296–97 and n. 231; efficiency of recognized by *Claridad*, 297; CNT on good example of in organization and efficiency, 308. *See also* Eleventh International Brigade; Twelfth International Brigade
Iron Column, 314–22; releases convicts from penitentiary, 314; convicts enrolled in bring opprobrium upon CNT, 314; friction with Valencia CNT, 315; critical of CNT's entry into government, 315; war ministry decides to withhold arms and pay from, 315–16; Martín Blázquez on, 316; war committee of urges militarization, 316–17; and

enforcement of paymaster decree, 318; part of column revolts, 318–19; member of urges militarization to save column, 319–22; column becomes Eighty-Third Brigade of regular army, 322
Irujo, Manuel de, Basque Nationalist leader: becomes minister without portfolio in Caballero cabinet, 123; minister of justice in Negrín government, 451; defends POUM leaders at trial, 460; role of in second Negrín government inconsequential, 469; resigns from government, 469
Isgleas, Francisco: councillor of defense (CNT) in Generalitat cabinet, Dec. 1936, 387; defended by Tarradellas against PSUC, 389; Committee of the Popular Army usurps authority of, 393; under pressure to subordinate Catalan militia to central government, 393; negotiates financial and military accords with Valencia, 393; sets firm dates for call-up of 1932–36 classes, 393; walks out of Generalitat government, 394; councillor of defense in Generalitat governments, 3 and 16 Apr. 1937, 395, 397
Italy: Goicoechea visits 1934, 12; no promise of aid by prior to conflict, 106; intervention of, 106 and n. 22, 105–8, 164 (n. 19); Goicoechea requests help from, 107; Gil Robles on military aid by, 106–7; German ambassador in Rome on motives intervention of, 107–8; Lizarza Iribarren on aid by, 106; Bolín flies for help to, 106–7; Count Ciano on Franco's request for help from, 106–7; Pierre Cot on aid by, 107; Yvonne Delbos on aid by, 107
Izquierda Republicana. *See* Left Republicans; Liberal republicans
Izvestiia: says USSR only state that has "no hostile sentiments toward Germany," 96

J

Jackson, Gabriel, 59
Jellinek, Frank, *Manchester Guardian* correspondent, on Friends of Durruti, 394
Jiménez de Asua, Luis, moderate Socialist deputy: attempted assassination of, 11
Johnson, Reverend Hewlett: claims no churches desecrated, 56–57
Johnston, Verle: mutilation of manuscript of, 273 (n. 84); on Kléber's removal, 284

Index

Krivitsky, Walter, former NKVD agent: on Soviet military intervention, 108–9; on Stalin's desire for pact with Germany, 109 and n. 35, 108–10; denounced as impostor, 109–10; Nicolaevsky on, 109; Hugh Thomas on, 110; accurate knowledge of regarding Soviet foreign policy aims and intervention, 110; on Kléber's true name, 110, 252; first to reveal Berzin's presence in Spain, 110; on Kandelaki's efforts to make deal with Hitler, 110 and n. 44; on Stashevsky and Negrín, 140–41; on gold shipment to Russia, 147; on Stalin's secret negotiations with Nazi government, 168; on establishment of NKVD in Spain by Orlov, 207; Orlov on, 207–8; on NKVD activity in Republican Spain, 209; on highest officers Caballero government tremble before NKVD, 209; and extraordinary knowledge of Soviet secret police, 290; on Berzin's and Stashevsky's recall to Moscow, 290–91; on Yezhov and Sloutski, 290–91

Krivoshein, Colonel S., Soviet officer: Melé, alias of, 146; assigns Orlov Soviet tank drivers to transport gold, 146; survives purges, 293

Kukk, Hilja, xvii, 278 (n. 111)

Kulik, General G., Soviet officer: adviser to Pozas, 287; Thomas on purge of, 293; Hernández and Castro on, 297; opposes Estremadura offensive, 437

Kuper or Kupper, General. *See* Kulik, General G.

Kurpuis, Rosemary, xvii

Kuznetsov, Nicolai G., Soviet officer: charged with protection of Spanish gold on high seas, 151; claims Spanish naval escort was provided, 151; on Gorev's suppression, 292; Kolya, pseudonym of, 292, escapes purges and becomes deputy minister of Soviet Navy, 292

L

Labonne, E., French ambassador: offers sanctuary to Negrín cabinet, 466

Labor courts: Madariaga on, 3; Robinson on, 4 (n. 4); CNT and, 183; Brenan on, 183

Laín, José, JSU leader: joins Communist party, 132 (n. 74); appointed director of school of commissars, 262

Lamoneda, Ramón, secretary of Socialist party: influenced by Prieto, 366; informs Caballero of resignation of moderate Socialist ministers, 438–39; states Socialist executive will not accept representation in Caballero's proposed government, 443

Land seizures: pre-Civil War, 6–7

Langdon-Davies, John, London *News Chronicle* correspondent: on May events, 418

La Pasionaria. *See* Ibárruri, Dolores

Lara, Antonio, member Martínez Barrio's government: *Claridad* on, 49–50

Largo Caballero, Francisco, left Socialist leader and secretary of UGT executive: on bourgeois democracy and revolutionary conquest of power, 10; Zugazagoitia on, 24; on Marxism, 25; fired by revolutionary ideas 1933, 25; Brenan on, 26, 182–83; fear of anarchosyndicalists, 26; promotes "Bolshevization" Socialist party, 26–27 and n. 107; on working-class dictatorship, 27; on Prieto, 27; strength of in Socialist movement, 27; advocates fusion with Communists, 28, 116; prewar official Communist support of, 28; prewar private Communist opposition to revolutionary posture of, 29; opposed to Prieto becoming premier, 32–33; demands distribution of arms to workers, 43; Communists disturbed by his revolutionary tendencies, 116; tempers revolutionary language, 118; reservations of respecting Communists' moderate policy, 118; discord with Communists over Giral government, 119–20, 242–43; Indalecio Prieto contemptuous of, 119–20; demands war ministry and premiership, 121; Communists oppose his heading government, 121–22; insists on Communist participation in government, 122; becomes prime minister, 122; irked by Communist drive to engulf Socialist movement, 130–32; trusted aides of transfer allegiance to Communists, 131; Rosal ascribes anti-Communist position to Araquistáin, 131 (n. 61); visited by Comintern delegates in jail in 1934 accompanied by Alvarez del Vayo and Araquistáin, 132 (n. 68); on Spanish gold reserves, 141; on shipment gold reserves to Russia, 152; attempts im-

Index

on the draft and purging military posts, 341; veiled attack on Communists as serpents of treason, disloyalty, and espionage, 342; Communists describe statement of as "toads and snakes manifesto," 342; politburo discusses ousting of, 342–44; forced by Communists to remove Martínez Cabrera, 348; on reasons for Communist attack on Martínez Cabrera and Asensio, 348; on preference shown Communists at front in clothing and food, 351; assails Communist positions in armed forces, 352; angered by practices political commissars, 352; learns of secret defection Alvarez del Vayo and Pretel, 352; accuses Alvarez del Vayo of being in service of Communist party, 353; accuses Alvarez del Vayo of appointing 200 political commissars without his knowledge, 353; Alvarez del Vayo denies his betrayal of and affirms love of, 353–54; informs Azaña of Alvarez del Vayo's disloyal conduct, 354; authorized by Azaña to remove Alvarez del Vayo, 354; accused by Prieto of weakness regarding Alvarez del Vayo, 354; inconsistency of regarding Alvarez del Vayo, 354–55; Communists, moderate Socialists, and liberal republicans united against, 355; issues executive order curbing powers general commissariat of war, 355; answers Communist protest against order curbing powers general commissariat war, 356–57; Communist press attacks on, 355–60; limits promotion of civilian militia leaders, 357; denies admission to officers training schools to anyone not recommended by CNT and UGT, 357; strained relations of with Prieto, 365; secret compact against by moderate Socialists and Communists, 367–68; hopes that fighting in Barcelona will subside without need for government intervention, 408; against antagonizing CNT and FAI, 408; sends UGT and CNT representatives to Barcelona, 409; on taking over of public order by central government, 410–12; Azaña on "glacial indifference" of, 422; overthrow of, 431–48; visits Azaña, 432; calls Communist ministers "liars and slanderers," 433; refuses to dissolve POUM, 433–34; tenders resignation,

435; informs Azaña of proposed Estremadura offensive, 435; and Estremadura offensive, 435–37; claims Prieto remained behind the scenes during cabinet crisis, 438; visits Azaña regarding resignation of moderate Socialist ministers, 439; Communists demand he relinquish war ministry, 440; demands portfolios of war, navy and air, 440–41; on duty to remain in war ministry to "fight it out" with Communists, 441–42; condemns other parties for not seeing Communist danger, 442; offers CNT only two cabinet seats, 442; defies Communist demands, 442–43; abandons attempt to form government, 443; Caballero nullified politically, 447–48; assailed as enemy number one of working class, 448; Communists' changed attitude towards, 448; Vidarte on Caballero's detestation of Alvarez del Vayo, 453; defends POUM leaders at trial, 460; negotiates provisional alliance with CNT, 465; denounces Communist party at mass meeting, 465–66; loses control of *Adelante* and *La Correspondence de Valencia*, 466. *See also* Socialist party; Socialists (left); Socialists (moderate)

Larraz, José, president of Editorial Católica, 34

League of Nations: USSR joins, 96

Left Republicans (Izquierda Republicana): Azaña, leader of, 23; on Agrarian Reform Law, 25–26; Caballero on, 33; divided over Martínez Barrio's government, 50; silence in face of Revolution, 88–89, 91, 126; favorable publicity to Communist party by, 126; Giral on coincidence of views of Communists and, 126–27; Indalecio Prieto on some members serving ambitions of Soviet Union, 126–27; affirm Spain waging struggle for republican and democratic consolidation, 156–57; demand Asensio's removal, 335; Caballero protests attack by on Baráibar, 339; privy to secret agreement to oust Caballero, 368; Azaña on decision of to change Caballero government, 432–33; echo Communist demand that premier should concern himself solely with his own office, 443; Hernández on Communists taking advantage of good faith of, 465. *See also* Giral, José; Liberal republicans

Index

Index

capitulate to rebels, 276; believes victory of insurrection inevitable, 276; career of, 276–77; becomes through Communist propaganda most glorified figure in defense of Madrid, 277; Regler on, 277; Martínez Cartón on, 277; intoxicated by popularity, 277; Zugazagoitia on, 277; Casado on, 277; Spanish Communists and Soviet participants explode myth of after Civil War, 277–78; Mije on, 277–78; Ehrenburg on, 278; Malinovsky on, 278; and María Teresa León, 278; Matthews and Fischer on myth of, 278; requires Communist party as protective shield, 278; Caballero on, 278; enters Communist party, 278; influenced by Antón, 278; Azaña on conversion to communism of, 278–79; warned against Kléber by Rojo, 284–85; Meretskov, adviser to, 293; and friction with Caballero, 296; asks to be relieved, 296; joins national council of defense against Negrín, 476

Middle classes. See Small bourgeoisie

Mije, Antonio, politburo member: on proletarian revolution and democratic republic, 117; defends democratic republic at time of "greatest revolutionary effervescence," 216; on role of political commissars, 262; promotes Communist influence in general commissariat of war, 262; describes Miaja as "dull-witted general," 278; on "overstepping of powers" by commissars, 352 (n. 96)

Militarization. See CNT; Communist party; Draft; Iron Column; Militia; Popular Army; PSUC

Militarization, Catalonia: measures in favor of remain unheeded, 392; anarchosyndicalists leave front in protest against, 394. See also CNT; Draft; Militia (Catalonia); PSUC

Militia: Left Republicans on vital role of, 204; Azaña on, 239; weight of struggle falls upon, 239; professional officers assigned to, 240; professional officers suspected by, 240; defects of, 244–50; indiscipline of, 251–54; and Communists, 259; Communist party and fusion of into regular army (Popular Army), 259; militarization of, 259; Caballero on, 260; CNT and, 302–13 passim; defects of, 306–7; CNT determined to maintain integrity and homogeneous

character of, 311–12; and mixed brigades, 311–13; Iron Column and, 314–22 passim; inflated payrolls of, 316; Caballero indulgent toward, 325; CNT on drafting of, 326–27; Asensio's stern measures against, 335; Communists attack Caballero's decree limiting promotion civilian leaders of, 357 and n. 117. See also Militia (Catalonia)

Militia, Catalonia: CNT militia under authority of Secretariado de Defensa, 380; militia of moderates under authority of Díaz Sandino, 380; PSUC agitates for fusion of into regular army, 392; CNT against fusion of into regular army, 392; POUM favors fusion of into regular army controlled by revolutionary organizations, 392; subordination of to central government under military accords, 393 and n. 139

Milton, Harry: on expulsion from POUM of Trotskyist Moulin, 381 (n. 73)

Miravitlles, Jaime, Esquerra member: affirms capitalism no longer exists in Catalonia, 368; describes Azaña during May events as "a man physically and morally destroyed," 406 (n. 22)

Miret, José: councillor of supplies (UGT-PSUC) in Generalitat government, 16 Apr. 1937, 397

Mirova: Tass news agency representative in Valencia, 265; disappearance of, 288

Mixed brigades: CNT opposition to, 311; aim of, 311; Mariano Vázquez on, 313

Modesto, Juan, Communist militia leader. later Popular Army officer: on arrival Soviet arms, 111; promoted to general by Negrín, 475

Mola, General Emilio, Nationalist officer: posted to Pamplona, 14; in charge of rebel plans on peninsula, 21; on efforts to provoke violent situation, 38–39; Cierva on leading role of in conspiracy, 39; refuses Martínez Barrio's offer of war ministry, 44

Molina, Juan, CNT member, undersecretary of defense council: defended by Tarradellas against PSUC, 389

Molotov, Vyacheslav, chairman of the Council of People's Commissars: on Nazi threat to USSR, 96; letter of to Caballero, 295

Montagu, Ivor, British Communist: inspires Negrín's Thirteen Points, 472

Montiel, Francisco: transfers allegiance to

Index

party, 138; regarded as Prieto's own man, 138; frees himself from Prieto, 138; Claude Bowers on, 138–39; Herbert Matthews in praise of, 139; Stanley Payne on, 139; influence of over Pablo de Azcárate, 140 (n. 23); and Stashevsky, 140; Fischer on close relations of with Stashevsky, 140; and shipment of gold reserves to Russia, 140–53; death of, 144; Orlov on "political naivety" of, 145; gives Orlov alias of Blackstone, 146, 345; directs loading of gold, 150; Pascua on close friendship with Prieto, 152; on Soviet aid offering hope that Paris and London would awaken to risks of Italo-German victory, 167; opposes CNT participation in government, 178 (n. 11); takes advantage of plight of urban collectives, 212; rescinds Peiró's decree collectivizing all industries, 213–14; assigns carabineers to seize frontier posts, 400; informs Caballero of resignation moderate Socialist ministers, 438–39; Prieto's view of, 444–45; Sedwick and others on, 445 (n. 73); selected by Stashevsky as Caballero's successor, 445; Krivitsky on, 445; "Pedro" on, 445; and Soviet aid, 445–46; promoted by Communists, 446–47; visited by Hernández, 446–47; becomes premier and finance minister, 451; government of condemned by opponents as counterrevolutionary, 451; appoints Vidarte undersecretaryship of interior, 452; on Zugazagoitia, 452; Vidarte on, 453; government of moves to Barcelona, 454; indignation of over disappearance Nin, 459–60; Vidarte on tacit understanding of with Communists regarding liquidation POUM, 459; subscribes to Communist version that Gestapo abducted Nin, 460 and n. 56; years later tells Vidarte he believes Communists killed Nin, 460 (n. 56); cabinet of offered sanctuary by French ambassador, 466; rejects offer of French ambassador to initiate peace negotiations, 466; on Prieto demoralizing his colleagues, 467; removes Prieto, 467; described by "El Campesino" as Communist party's "ambitious and docile tool," 468; described by Hernández as "Moscow's man of confidence," 468; takes over defense ministry from Prieto, 468; pursues "insensate policy

of assuring the predominance of one party," 468; elevates Communists Cordón, Nuñez Masas, Pedro Pradas, 468; appoints pro-Communist Díaz Tendero to head personnel section of defense ministry, 468; appoints pro-Communist Fernández Ossorio y Taffall as general commissar of war, 468; appoints Communist Hernández chief political commissar of Army of the Center, 468; assures Communist Cordón that Zugazagoitia's post is "honorary" one, 469; appoints PSUC member Marcelino Fernández head of carabineers, 469; becomes symbol of resistance, 470; government of tries to conciliate foreign capital, 470; government of returns plants to former owners, 470–71; enunciates Thirteen-Point program, 472; arrives in central zone, 475; at behest politburo promotes Communists Cordón and Modesto to rank of general, and Líster and Galán to colonel, 475; orders dismissal of various officers suspected of hostility to Communists, 475; government of described by Hernández as "mute, paralytic phantom," 475 (n. 132); escapes from central zone, 476; becomes scapegoat for Communists, 476–77

Negrín, Rómulo: turns over Spanish gold documents to Franco, 144

Nelken, Margarita, left Socialist deputy: transfers allegiance to Communists, 131

Nenni, Pietro: praises Prieto, 120

New York Post: on Negrín government's attempts to conciliate foreign capital, 470–71; on restoration to former owners of hundreds of industrial properties, 471; on Negrín government demonstrating to Britain, France, and USA that it is not Red, 471

New York Times. See Matthews, Herbert

Nicolaevsky, Boris: on Krivitsky, 109

Nin, Andrés: leader of Communist Left, later POUM secretary, 381; councillor of justice in Generalitat government, 28 Sept. 1936, 380; onetime disciple of Trotsky, 381; Bertram D. Wolfe on, 392; on reasons FOUS entered UGT instead of CNT, 383; welcomes stand of CNT against concessions to PSUC, 396; arrest, torture, and disappearance of, 456–59. *See also* POUM

NKVD: explanation of, 207 (n. 26); estab-

Index

Ciudad Real, 456; Zugazagoitia demands resignation of, 459–60; defended by Communist ministers, 459; removal of, 459–60

Orwell, George: on construction barricades Barcelona during May events, 405; on fighting in Barcelona, 408; on pessimism of POUM leaders, 408–9; foresees responsibility for May events laid upon POUM, 424

Ossorio y Gallardo, Angel, republican jurist: on flight of outstanding republicans, 57; on Central Antifascist Militia Committee, 59 (n. 63); on social revolution, 87; on Azaña's pessimism, 88; dissuades Azaña from renouncing presidency, 159; on Companys's conciliatory statement to CNT-FAI leaders, 369, 373

P

Pablo, General. *See* Pavlov, General D. G.

Pabón, Benito, leader of Syndicalist party: seeks legalization of the Defense Council of Aragon, 232

Padelford, Norman J.: on number of refugees in embassies and legations in Madrid, 57; on Non-Intervention Agreement, 103 (n. 7)

Palacio Atard, Vicente: on far-reaching military measures taken by Azaña to ward off rebellion, 14; on Azaña and Casares overlooking "the ability of the young officers to assure the success of the rebellion," 37

Partit Català Proletaria, 376

Partit Comunista de Catalunya, 376

Pascua, Marcelino, Socialist deputy, Spanish ambassador to Moscow: publishes letters of Caballero on Spanish gold, 141; on reason impractical to send gold to England, France, Switzerland, U.S.A., or Mexico, 143 (n. 52); on Russia's extraordinary care listing gold coins, 147; on Negrín claiming that Prieto's presence in Cartagena due to prior agreement, 150 (n. 79); claim by that four Soviet vessels carrying gold were unescorted contradicted by Kuznetsov, 151 and n. 87; on close friendship between Prieto and Negrín, 152; asks Caballero on behalf Stalin to carry out fusion of Socialist and Communist parties, 332

Pasionaria (La Pasionaria). *See* Ibárruri, Dolores

Patrols: under authority of CNT-dominated Junta de Seguridad, 380; under Communist attack, 454; offer services to Torres, 454; dissolution of by decree of Esquerra Councillor Martí Feced, 454 and n. 22; rebuffed by Companys, 454

Patrullas de control. *See* Patrols

Pavlov, General D. G., Soviet officer: referred to by Koltzov as "Del Pablo," 286 (n. 165); commands Soviet tank corps in Spain, 287; Líster on, 287; perishes in Stalin's purges, 287–88; Ehrenburg on execution of, 293

Payne, Stanley G., xvi; on transfer of Army leaders before Civil War, 14, 37–38; on naive and uncritical notions of left-wing Socialists, 28; on Miguel Maura and creation of Assault Guard, 46–47; on Popular Front government anticipating "People's Democracies," 124; on Negrín, 139; criticized by Herbert Matthews, 139; Orlov's reply to questionnaire by, 207–8, 291, 346, 456 (n. 32), 458, 464 (n. 73)

Peasant Federation: set up by Communists to protect small and medium proprietors, 93, 225; Socialist criticism of, 93; antagonizes large segment of rural population, 225; causes strife between Communists and left Socialists, 226

Pedro. *See* Gerö, Ernö

Peirats, José, anarchosyndicalist historian: on CNT and FAI, 178; criticizes Companys for not removing Rodríguez Salas and Aiguadé, 404

Peiró, Juan, CNT leader: attacks forced collectivization, 81–82; becomes minister of industry, 189; leaves Madrid, 192; on victory depending on Britain and France, 201; on "discreet" control of factories, 201; crticizes committees, 202; Caballero opposes decree of collectivizing all industries, 213–14; on CNT ministers having no rights or responsibilities regarding direction of the war, 305

Penchienati, Carlo: on Communist control of International Brigades, 112

Penitentiaries and jails: inmates liberated, 56, 314

motes Communist influence in general commissariat of war, 262; becomes treasurer of new executive UGT, 465

Prieto, Horacio M.: demands CNT enter government, 186; assails CNT proposal for national council defense, 188; on necessity for government collaboration, 189; criticized by Mera for abandoning Madrid, 193; criticized by militants, 194; resigns secretaryship CNT, 194; Montseny on, 196; on reasons for CNT entering government, 197–98; advocates creation libertarian Socialist party, 469–70

Prieto, Indalecio, 24; Zugazagoitia on, 24; on dislike of Caballero, 27, 120–21; pre-Civil War hostility to Communists, 29–30; instrumental in dislodging President Alcalá-Zamora and raising Azaña to presidency, 30; May Day 1936 speech attacking public disorders, 30–31; Maura attempts to place him in premiership, 31; refuses premiership, 32; opposition by Caballero before Civil War to his becoming premier, 32–33; secret negotiations of with Gil Robles, 34; sounds warning to rightists, 40; remains silent on distribution of arms to workers, 44; tries to dissuade Martínez Barrio from resigning premiership, 50 and n. 237; on Salazar's execution, 55–56; scorns impotence of Giral government, 120; behind-the-scenes role of, 120; on willingness join Caballero government, 121; becomes navy and air minister, 122; denies exhaustion Spanish gold deposit in Moscow, 149–50; on use of Spanish gold by French Communist party, 149; denies prior knowledge of gold shipment to Russia, 150–51; on Negrín's "uneasiness" in Cartagena, 150; approves permit to use Spanish sailors to load gold on Soviet ships, 150; dismisses as "lie" Alvarez del Vayo's assertion Negrín insisted Azaña be informed of gold shipment, 151; Pascua on close friendship of with Negrín, 152; Araquistáin's description of as "weak and cynical," 153; on Soviet intervention and coercion, 154; urges Azaña not to resign, 158; on note to Britain and France regarding transfer Spanish Morocco, 165; on government's abandoning Madrid, 192; instructs Líster to dissolve Council of

Aragon, 232; on Communist assassination of Socialists at the front, 264; on government's departure from Madrid, 270; believes Madrid lost, 271; on Caballero's "tumultuous discussions" with Rosenberg, 301; on "unbelievable tension" with Communist ministers, 301; on Alvarez del Vayo's disloyalty, 354; accuses Alvarez del Vayo of being Communist puppet, 354; accuses Caballero of weakness regarding Alvarez del Vayo, 354; more in common with republicans than left Socialists, 363; criticized by Communists before Civil War for repudiating "violent struggle for power," 364; Communists secretly more in sympathy with than with Caballero, 364; friendliness toward Rosenberg and Smushkevich, 364; inner reservations of regarding fusion with Communists, 364–65; refuses to support fusion of two parties, 365; needs Communists to compass ruin of Caballero, 365; strained relations of with Caballero, 365; hostility of to left wing of Revolution, 365; hopes moderate course will alter Anglo-French neutrality, 365; on popular sympathy for Russia because of aid, 365; misgivings of regarding growth and methods of Communist party do not interfere with close association, 366; demands reinforcements be sent to Barcelona during May events, 410; believes government should recover reins of power, 411; instructs Hidalgo de Cisneros to proceed to Catalonia with bomber and fighter squadrons, 411; orders two destroyers to evacuate Azaña, 411; does all he can to help Azaña in Barcelona, 423; denies acting in secret agreement with Communists to overthrow Caballero, 434; Uribe and Morón claim participation of in plan to remove Caballero, 434–35; and secret agreement with Communists to oust Caballero, 439; appointed minister of defense by mutual agreement with Communists, 441; assures Communist Uribe he will do nothing prejudicial to unity of Socialists and Communists, 441; and reasons why not appointed premier, 443–44; on Negrín's greater suitability for premiership, 444; hopes to control government through Negrín, 444; on

Index

Negrín, 444–45; on subservience of Negrín to Communists, 444; Madariaga on, 446; Hernández and Togliatti on, 446–47; becomes defense minister in Negrín government, 451; appoints Cordón, Díaz Tendero, Rojo in agreement with Communists, 453; and Nin's disappearance, 459–60; supports Zugazagoitia's demand for resignation Ortega, 460; dispatches Líster to Aragon, 462; rejects politburo offer to provide him with "suggestions, ideas, and views on military matters," 463; informs Gaykis he will not support fusion of Socialist and Communist parties, 463; hopes that Anglo-French aid will counteract mounting Soviet influence, 463; looks to mediation to end Civil War, 463; provoked by Communist proselytism and growing power, 463; removes Alvarez del Vayo from commissariat of war, 463; removes inspector-commissar Antón, 463; ousts Communist and pro-Communist political commissars and high officers, 463–64; Communist offensive against, 464; forms SIM on advice of Russians, 464; removes Durán from Madrid section SIM, 464; on French ambassador's offer of sanctuary to Negrín government, 466; removal of by Negrín, 467; on Negrín yielding to Communist demands, 467; on Negrín pursuing an "insensate policy of assuring the predominance of one party," 468
Primo de Rivera, José Antonio, leader of Falange: on pre-Civil War conditions in countryside, 3
Prisons, private, 55. *See also* Terror, revolutionary
Prokofiev, Major General G., Soviet officer: on Smushkevich, 287; survives purges, 293
PSUC: defends middle classes, 89–90, 375–76; organizes GEPCI to protect urban middle class, 90, 376; denies existence of Revolution, 114–15; formation of, 130; attacks revolutionary committees, 376; opposes CNT and FAI, 376; defends rabassaires, 376; criticized by CNT for forming GEPCI, 376; creation and composition of, 376–78; size of component parties of, 376; Comorera becomes secretary of, 376; size of initial membership of, 377;

Comorera claims 50,000 membership of in March 1937, 377; Communists become ruling nucleus of, 378; Joaquín Olaso heads control commission of, 378; directed behind scenes by "Pedro," 378; Communist party on friction within, 379; presses for dissolution of Central Antifascist Militia Committee and concentration of power in hands of Catalan government, 379; aims to end division of power in Catalonia, 380–81; asserts Catalan masses flee from Trotskyism as from plague, 384; attacks Gorkin as Trotskyist, 384; demands exclusion POUM from cabinet, 385; drops demand for suppression of Junta de Seguridad and Secretariado de Defensa, 386; helps CNT rationalize its sacrifice of POUM by withdrawing officially from cabinet, 386–87; PSUC reappears in new cabinet with UGT label, 387; attacks Tarradellas after war for collaborating with "counter-revolutionary policy of anarchism," 389; Esquerra leaders dismayed by loss to of members of Unió de Rabassaires and CADCI, 389–90; Comorera, as councillor of supplies in Catalan government, decrees dissolution revolutionary committees controlling wholesale food trades, 390; proposes that patrols, assault, and national republican guards form single internal security corps, 390–91; agitates for compulsory military service, 392; presses for fusion of militia into regular army, 392; sets up Committee for the Popular Army, 392–93; FAI denounces campaign by for regular army as policy of aggression against anarchism, 393; demands a government that will implement its decrees, 395; insists that CNT pledge itself to honor military and public order decrees, 395; launches "Victory Plan" for Catalonia, 395; demands war against *agents provocateurs*, 399; urges antifascist masses to unite against "uncontrollables," 400; and tribute to Aiguadé, 410 (n. 42); insists that fighting in Barcelona cease before new government is formed, 414
Ptukhin, E. S., Soviet officer: succeeds Smushkevich and perishes in Stalin's purges, 287–88, 292
Puente, Isaac, prominent anarchist: on

Index

next to Comorera becomes libertarians' principal object execration, 390; background of, 390; Libertarian Youth demands removal of, 399; attempt on life of, 399; raids central telephone exchange, 403; initiates new offensive actions during May events, 408; dismissal of, 427

Rodríguez Vega, José, former Caballero adherent, later Communist supporter: becomes secretary of new executive UGT, 465

Rojo, Major Vicente (later lieutenant colonel, then general): claims charges against Soviet officers "absolutely false," 265; on mixup of sealed orders to Miaja and Pozas, 270; on nonexistence battlefront Madrid, 271; appointed Miaja's chief of staff by Caballero, 273; puts together general staff to defend Madrid, 274; López Fernández on makeup of staff of, 274; ability of widely recognized, 274; respected by former comrades, 274; Koltzov praises knowledge and capacity for work of, 274–75; *El Socialista* on role of in Madrid's defense, 275; Alvarez del Vayo on, 275; joins UME before Civil War, 275; offers services to government, 276; on Bolloten, 279–80; Communists assured of active support of, 280–81; constant and intimate association of with Gorev and Communist military leaders, 280; no evidence enrollment of in Communist party, 280; establishes himself in Russian favor, 280; praised by Soviet participants, 280; praised by official Communist history, 280; brings terms of surrender to Alcázar, Toledo, 280; ambiguous position of, 280; returns to Spain, 281; death of in 1966, 281; promotion of from major to lieutenant colonel, then general, 281, 453; becomes chief of central general staff, 281, 453; promotes Communist predominance in army, 281; convinced war lost in February 1939; refuses to accompany Negrín to central zone after fall Catalonia in 1939, 281, 474; Catholic faith of, 281–82; Martín Blázquez on, 281–82; Castro on usefulness of to Communist party, 282; initiates attack on Kléber, 284; ignores Kléber in *España heroica* in 1942, 284; letter by to Miaja condemning Kléber, 284–85; removes

Kléber from Aragon front, 285; Ehrenburg on, 286; on Gorev, 286; partial credit for organization Madrid's defense belongs to, 286–87; supports Asensio, 340; Communists propose replacing Martínez Cabrera by, 348

Rome agreement 1934, 12

Romerales, General Manuel, republican general, 41–42

Rosal, Amaro del, left-wing Socialist, later pro-Communist: transfers allegiance to Communists, 131; ascribes Caballero's anti-Communist position to Araquistáin, 131 (n. 61); on Caballero being visited by Comintern delegates in jail accompanied by Araquistáin and Alvarez del Vayo, 138 (n. 68); controls National Federation of Employees of Credit and Finance, 213; describes Asensio as "great military man," 267 (n. 58); on unfair campaign against Asensio, 329; describes Araquistáin as "spiritual director" of Caballero group, 330 (n. 34)

Rosal Column: composition of, 192; detains ministers in Tarancón, 192–93

Rosell, Cardona: member of CNT national committee, 229; on aid to CNT collectives by Institute of Agrarian Reform and National Service of Agricultural Credit, 229–30; on homogeneous character of CNT military units, 311

Rosenberg, Marcel, Soviet ambassador: argues in favor of democratic republic, 119; Caballero letters to on Spanish gold, 141; described by Araquistáin as ambassador of straw, 153; Araquistáin on importunity of, 299; recall to Moscow of ignored by Orlov, 300; Ehrenburg on "fate" of, 300; Bolloten on, 300 and n. 254; violent clashes of with Caballero, 301; Caballero's expulsion of from office, 328–29; Stalin's letter to Caballero on, 329; Caballero's reply to Stalin on, 329

Rothermere, Viscount, British press lord: on turning Germany's territorial ambitions eastwards, 98

Rovira, Lieutenant Colonel Esteban, chief of Forty-Second Brigade: on role of political commissars, 261

Rubiera, Carlos, left Socialist: on preference shown to Communists in military hospitals, 351

Ruediger, Helmut, representative of AIT:

Index

Index

Viana, Marqués de, former King Alfonso's equerry: accompanies Bolín to Rome, 106
Vich: collectivization in, 64
Vidali, Vittorio (alias Carlos Contreras): chief political commissar Fifth Regiment, 255; interviewed by Ana Louisa Strong on Fifth Regiment, 255–56 and n. 3; on first commanders of Popular Army, 260; on political commissars, 261; on Communists uncertain of Rojo's true allegiance, 281; on Kléber's popularity, 283; on his removal, 283–84; on Gorev as savior of Madrid, 286; Castro on involvement of in Nin's assassination, 457
Vidarte, Juan-Simeón, moderate Socialist: Araquistáin on, 439; on Estremadura offensive, 439; becomes undersecretary of interior, 452; on Negrín's appointment of Ortega as director general of security, 452; on Alvarez del Vayo and Negrín, 453; on tacit understanding between Negrín and Communists on liquidation of POUM, 459; on Negrín telling him years later he believed Communists killed Nin, 460 (n. 56)
Vidiella, Rafael: abandons Caballero to form PSUC, 130; made central committee member of Communist party, 378, 387; councillor of justice in Generalitat cabinet, Dec. 1936, 387; councillor of labor and public works (UGT-PSUC) in Generalitat government, 16 Apr. 1937, 397; demands reinforcements from Valencia, 414
Vielayev. See Belayev
Vigilance Militia: incorporation of revolutionary police squads and patrols into, 205–6
Villalba, Colonel José: report of to Higher War Council on loss of Malaga, 323; selected by war ministry as scapegoat, 324; Cordón holds Asensio responsible for appointment of, 324 (n. 4); exculpation of, 324; accused by Mola of demanding 100,000 pesetas to bring his troops into conspiracy, 324 (n. 6)
Villar, Manuel, CNT member and director of *Fragua Social*: on reason for CNT entering government, 197; on antimilitarist principles being inimical to CNT, 304

Viñas, Angel: on German intervention, 102 (n. 7); on Spanish gold reserves, 140–50 passim and nn. 31–79 passim; books of on Spanish gold, 140 (n. 30); on Stashevsky, 140; on Negrín being "driving force" in decision to send gold to Russia, 141 (n. 34); on letter from Arturo Candela, 148; on departure from Russia of Spanish bank employees, 148; on virtual exhaustion of gold deposited in Russia, 148; on Soviet credits, 149
Volter. See Voronov
Volunteer Army: creation of by Giral, 240; opposed by CNT and left Socialists, 240; supported by Communists, 241–42; Martínez Barrio appointed head commission charged with organization of, 242
Voronov, N., Soviet officer: in charge of Soviet artillery in Spain, 287; escapes purges and becomes president of Soviet Artillery Academy, 292
Voroshilov, Kliment Y., Soviet commissar for defense: letter to Caballero, 295

W

Welles, Sumner, U.S. undersecretary of state: on war between Germany and USSR, 97–98
Wilson, Sir Horace, Chamberlain's chief collaborator and adviser: secret negotiations of for political settlement with Germany at expense of Poland, 171–72
Wolfe, Bertram D., xvii; on Lenin's definition of dictatorship of the proletariat, 83; confirms description of Orlov, 345 (n. 50); on POUM and Trotskyists, 382; on Orlov, 458
Wolfe, Ella, xvii; confirms description of Orlov, 345 (n. 50)

Y

Yakovlev, Alexander: on inferiority of Soviet aircraft, 292; on Stalin and Soviet reverses in Spain, 293; on Smushkevich, 293
Yezhov: Krivitsky on, 290–91

Z

Zabalza, Ricardo, left Socialist secretary of National Federation of Land Workers (UGT): on voluntary collectivization, 69; criticizes agricultural decree of 7 Oct. 1936, 227; accuses Communists of

The Author
A United States correspondent in Spain during the Civil War, Burnett Bolloten was also a lecturer and director of research on the Spanish Revolution and Civil War at Stanford University from 1962 to 1965. *The Spanish Revolution* is a revised and vastly expanded version of Bolloten's *The Grand Camouflage* (1961), one of the half dozen most important books written in any language on the Spanish Civil War.

The Book
Typeface: Mergenthaler VIP Palatino
Design and composition: The University of North Carolina Press
Paper: 50 pound text white opaque by Hammermill Paper Company
Binding cloth: Roxite Vellum B 51502 by The Holliston Mills, Incorporated
Printer and binder: Vail-Ballou Press, Incorporated
Published by The University of North Carolina Press